Psychophysiology:
Human Behavior
and
Physiological Response

Second Edition

Psychophysiology:
Human Behavior
and
Physiological Response

Second Edition

John L. Andreassi
Baruch College,
City University of New York

LAWRENCE ERLBAUM ASSOCIATES, PUBLISHERS
1989   Hillsdale, New Jersey   Hove and London

Lawrence Erlbaum Associates, Inc., Publishers
365 Broadway
Hillsdale, New Jersey 07642

Library of Congress Cataloging-in-Publication Data
Andreassi, John L.
    Psychophysiology : human behavior and physiological response/ by
John L. Andreassi. — 2nd ed.
        p.   cm.
    Bibliography: p.
    Includes index.
    ISBN 0-89859-801-X **ISBN 0-8058-0180-4** (pbk.)
    1. Psychophysiology.   2. Human behavior.   I. Title.
    [DNLM: 1. Behavior—physiology.   2. Psychophysiology.   WL 103
A557p]
QP360.A53   1989
152—dc19
DNLM/DLC
for Library of Congress   89-1616
                                                                                           CIP

Printed in the United States of America
10 9 8 7 6 5 4 3 2 1

To the Memory of my Parents,
Agnes and Croce

Contents

Preface to Second Edition

This second edition represents a systematic update of my 1980 text incorporating important new developments in psychophysiology. Even with careful selection from the recent literature, more than 450 new references have been cited, most of these published in the last 10 years.

Since the publication of the first edition, there have been a number of new handbooks and edited collections of writings in psychophysiology. These handbooks and edited texts are important for advanced students and professionals, but they do not, in most instances, meet the needs of the beginning student. This text, I feel, provides a comprehensive introduction to psychophysiology for neophytes whether they be upper level undergraduates, graduate students, or professionals new to the area.

This book is factual in nature and contains a minimum of speculation. The concepts described herein are based on empirical findings and are not far removed from data. Instructors wishing to introduce new students to salient issues could assign the chapter on psychophysiological concepts (chapter 15) early in the semester. The chapter organization is by response systems—brain, muscle, cardiac, and so forth. Within each chapter, issues that have led to a line of research are briefly outlined to give the student an appreciation of the rationale for the studies conducted. Although much of the material contained within these pages is considered basic research, three sections, chapters 13, 14, and Appendix I, deal with applications of psychophysiology. Chapter 13 covers a wide variety of applications ranging from lie detection to psychopathology. Chapter 14 presents applications of biofeedback to clinical problems, and Appendix I provides information concerning environmental effects on physiological responses.

The psychophysiological approach continues to offer the potential for greater understanding of the interactions between mental and bodily functions. This knowledge, while of great academic importance in understanding how "normal" people function, is also crucial in comprehending disequilibriums that may occur in bodily functions as a consequence of continued physical or mental "stress." It offers promise for learning more about the etiology of psychophysiologic disorders and other related malfunctioning. Although this book is primarily concerned with normal psychophysiological functioning, it is only through knowing the normal baseline conditions that we may learn more about and appreciate the effects of psychophysiological dysfunction.

Psychophysiology is an extremely vibrant and dynamic field. There are now more graduate students and new professionals entering this area than ever before. Improved electronic equipment and ways of processing data are continually being developed with the result that new phenomena can be studied and evaluated. For instance, the technique known as magnetoencephalography allows the recording of brain activity through the use of sensing devices that do not have to be attached to the scalp of a person. The growth of psychophysiology continues to be reflected in the growth of the number of organizations composed of scientists who work in the area. In the United States there are the Society for Psychophysiological Research and the Association for Applied Psychophysiology and Biofeedback, which publish the journals *Psychophysiology* and *Biofeedback and Self-Regulation,* respectively. In Great Britain there is the Psychophysiology Society, and on a worldwide scale, and associated with the United Nations, is the International Organization of Psychophysiology, whose Board of Directors includes scientists from six continents and whose editorial board is responsible for publishing the *International Journal of Psychophysiology.* There are other groups with less formal organizations than the ones mentioned, which are, nevertheless, still important to psychophysiology as a whole.

A number of people have helped in some way in the preparation of this revised edition. Encouragement and research support for "Physiological Responses and Information Processing" were provided by the Air Force Office of Scientific Research with Dr. Alfred R. Fregly as scientific officer. In addition, Dr. John J. Furedy, Department of Psychology, University of Toronto, made many insightful comments on the first draft of the book. Dr. Joseph J. Tecce, Department of Psychology, Boston College, reviewed chapters 5, 6, and 7. Dr. Robert G. Eason, Department of Psychology, University of North Carolina at Greensboro, kindly provided comments on chapter 8, and Dr. Mindy Engel-Friedman, Department of Psychology, Baruch College, City University of New York, read and commented on chapters 3 and 4. Dr. Susan J. Middaugh, Department of Physical Medicine and Rehabilitation, Medical University of South Carolina reviewed chapter 14. A greater appreciation of event-related potentials resulted from a sabbatical leave spent in the laboratory of a gracious host, Dr. Charles S. Rebert, Program Director of the Neurosciences Department, at SRI International in Menlo Park, California. Words of encouragement and advice were given by Dr. Constantine A. Mangina, president of the International Organization of Psychophysiology, in the early stages of preparing this new edition. Dr. Herbert G. Vaughan, Jr. and Dr. Diane Kurtzberg, both in the Department of Neuroscience, Albert Einstein College of Medicine, New York, and Dr. Emanual Donchin, Department of Psychology, University of Illinois, at Champaign were all very generous in providing many references to the event-related brain potential literature. In addition, the late Dr. Samuel Sutton helped through his opinions and provision of references regarding important new work on the P300 brain response. Dr. John T. Cacioppo, Department of Psychology, Ohio State University, Columbus, Ohio, provided a large number of references in the area of social psychophysiology. Ms. Carol Lachman and Mr. John Eagleson of Lawrence Erlbaum Associates assisted in many practical ways.

Others who deserve special thanks are my wife Gina and my children, John, Jeanine, and Cristina. The help of my wife and children cannot really be estimated. They provided unlimited emotional support and enthusiasm for the project, and many delightful work breaks from the beginning of this work through its final stages.

I have spent a great deal of time talking to myself during the preparation of this book. I gave myself numerous words of advice on how best to explain this concept or describe that study. Now I would like to hear from you, the reader of this book. Let me know what is clear or unclear in the text, and about weaknesses and strengths of the book, from your point of view. I can get direct feedback from students in my own classes, but I must depend on written communications for information from others regarding ways in which this book can be improved. Write and communicate your opinions and ideas to me at the Department of Psychology, Baruch College, Box 512, City University of New York, 17 Lexington Avenue, New York, N.Y. 10017.

New York   J. L. A.
March, 1989

Preface

The material for this book was originally gathered and organized for a course which I introduced at New York University's School of Engineering and Science. Since that time, the material has been presented several times to psychology majors on an undergraduate level and to students on both undergraduate and graduate levels at NYU and Baruch College of the City University of New York. The objectives of the course were to provide students with elementary information regarding the anatomy and physiology of various body systems, methods of recording electrical activity of these systems, and ways in which these measures have been correlated with various aspects of human behavior and performance. These are also the objectives of this book.

Concepts in the field and applications of physiological measures in practical situations are presented to provide a conceptual framework for this research area and to illustrate the use of these measures in real life. A separate chapter is devoted to the rapidly developing area of biofeedback applications. Psychology students, students in other life sciences, and biomedical engineering students should find useful basic information in this presentation. The beginning researcher and interested professional were also kept in mind as the text was being written.

This book reflects my own research interests in the form of relatively extensive coverage of event-related brain potentials and behavior. Very helpful encouragement and research support for studies under the general heading of "Evoked Cortical Potentials and Information Processing" have been provided to me by the Physiology branch, Office of Naval Research, over the past several years. Dr. Donald P. Woodward, project officer for ONR, has patiently read and made valuable comments on a preliminary draft of the entire manuscript. Mr.

Joseph A. Gallichio and Ms. Nancy E. Young also read and commented upon the entire first draft from the student's point of view. In addition, Ms. Young assisted in organizing the bibliographic materials and Ms. Janice Coburn helped in preparing the subject index.

A number of individuals graciously agreed to read and comment upon the first draft of one or more chapters. To these persons I am greatly indebted because they provided important insights into areas with which I was not thoroughly familiar, suggested additional references, and in general helped to improve the presentation of material. These individuals are: Dr. Joseph Arezzo, Albert Einstein College of Medicine; Dr. Jackson Beatty, University of California at Los Angeles; Dr. Robert H. Browner, New York Medical College; Dr. Robert G. Eason, University of North Carolina at Greensboro; Dr. Arthur Gaynor, Montefiore Hospital and Albert Einstein College of Medicine; Dr. James H. Geer, State University of New York at Stony Brook; Dr. John D. Gould, IBM, Thomas J. Watson Research Center; Dr. Rafael Klorman, University of Rochester; Dr. Susan J. Middaugh, Medical University of South Carolina; Dr. Walter Ritter, Lehman College, City University of New York and Albert Einstein College of Medicine; Dr. Stover H. Snook, Liberty Mutual Insurance Co.; Dr. Walter W. Surwillo, University of Louisville School of Medicine; Dr. Joseph J. Tecce, Tuffts University School of Medicine and Boston State Hospital; Professor Bernard Tursky, State University of New York at Stony Brook; and Dr. Robert C. Wilcott, Case Western Reserve University. I am also indebted to Bob Wilcott for introducing me to psychophysiology. Any conclusions in this book, and any shortcomings that remain, are solely my responsibility and cannot be attributed to any organization or person.

Others who deserve special thanks are my parents, Agnes and Croce, and siblings George, Eugene, and Matilda for their faith in me, Mr. William Halpin and Mr. Marcus Boggs of Oxford University Press for their faith in the project, Ms. Nancy Amy of Oxford for her editorial assistance, Ms. Joyce Hyman for her typing of the entire manuscript from initial to final draft, and my wife Gina and children John, Jeanine, and Cristina who provided emotional support and numerous refreshing moments during the many hours devoted to working on this book.

New York   J. L. A.
September, 1979

1

Introduction to Psychophysiology

DEFINITIONS OF PSYCHOPHYSIOLOGY

In the first edition of this book, I wrote that "The field of psychophysiology is concerned with the measurement of physiological responses as they relate to behavior." The word "behavior" is used now, as then, in the broadest sense to include such diverse activities as sleep, problem solving, and simple motor acts. This characterization of the field requires some clarification. The reader may ask how psychophysiology differs from the discipline known traditionally as physiological psychology, and the answer is that it is mainly in the approach and subject matter of these areas. Stern (1964) and Lykken (1984) have made a distinction in terms of how dependent and independent variables are used. The dependent variable refers to what is actually being measured in an experiment, and the independent variable is the aspect being manipulated. Stern and Lykken have said that in psychophysiology, the dependent variables are physiological (for instance, heart rate) and the independent variables are psychological (for example, problem difficulty). However, in physiological psychology the dependent variables are mainly psychological (perceptual accuracy, as an example), whereas independent variables are physiological (for instance, brain stimulation). This distinction in terms of dependent and independent variables is useful, but not entirely satisfactory to Furedy (1983), who argued that this approach does not cover the example of a physiological psychologist who records and studies changes in a single neuron while psychological stimuli are manipulated. Furedy's own definition is this: "psychophysiology is the study of psychological processes in the intact organism as a whole by means of unobtrusively measured physiological processes'' (p. 13). He emphasized that a measurement made unobtrusively, as with surface electrodes, results in a more accurate picture of the behaving organism. Mangina (1983) has objected to Furedy's use of the term ''intact organism'' because this would exclude the study of brain damaged, mentally retarded, or drug influenced persons, and patients suffering from various psychophysiological disorders. Mangina defined psychophysiology as ''the science which studies the physiology of the psychic functions through the brain–body–behavior interrelationships of the living organism in conjunction with the environment'' (p. 22).

At this point, I propose a definition that attempts to integrate those previously offered: *Psychophysiology is the study of relations between psychological manipulations and resulting physiological responses, measured in the living organism, to promote understanding of the relation between mental and bodily processes.*

ACTIVITIES AND SUBJECT MATTER

There are a number of activities that are as important to the field of psychophysiology as they are to other life sciences. These include the conduct of animal research to allow fuller understanding of basic physiological mechanisms, the development of electronic instrumentation to enable increasingly sophisticated measurements, and the testing of hypotheses that allow researchers to ask questions and obtain answers in their pursuit of knowledge.

Psychological processes studied in psychophysiology range from emotional responses, as in fear and anger, to cognitive activities, such as decision making. The reader will find that, in this text, the word ''behavior'' is used broadly to encompass a variety of human activities such as learning, problem solving, sensing, perceiving, attending, and emotional response. The physiological responses include brain, heart, and muscle activity, among others. Thus, in psychophysiology, we are interested in heart rate changes that occur in response to unexpected stimuli or in brain activity patterns recorded while, for example, an individual listens to music. Speed of response and related muscle activity are also topics of study, as well as eye movement patterns when a person searches for a specific target among other visual stimuli.

An underlying premise in the conduct of these studies is that the information obtained will enable us to better understand the relations and interactions between physiology and behavior. Ultimately, this understanding will allow the development of conceptualizations regarding physiology–behavior relationships, an endeavor that is examined in chapter 15 of this book. At this point, it would be instructive to take a brief look at the historical development of psychophysiology.

HISTORICAL DEVELOPMENT
OF PSYCHOPHYSIOLOGY

The rationale for the psychophysiological approach stems from a desire to know more about the behaving organism; and this is possible only through very careful observation or the use of specialized instruments. Just as a blood sample tells a physician something about the physical condition of an apparently healthy patient, a sampling of heart rate tells the psychophysiologist something about the emotional state of an outwardly calm individual. It is the point of view here that behavior is the result of ongoing mental processes. Thus, observed behavior is not the equivalent of mental activities, because these activities are not always translated into motor acts. However, these mental activities themselves, although not directly observable, are behaviors.

How did a desire to know more about physiological correlates of behavior develop? Records of when humans first asked about psychophysiological relationships do not exist. It is reasonable to assume, however, that very early humans must have wondered about the source of our thoughts and other mental activities. There is evidence that Stone Age cavepeople associated distressing thoughts or evil spirits with the inside of the head, because trephined skulls have been found among the remains of cave dwellers (Coleman, Butcher, & Carson 1984). One might imagine a scene, taking place some 250,000 years ago, inside a cave illuminated by light from a fire: Some unfortunate caveperson, probably one who had continuous head pain or heard strange voices, is being held down by several others while an early ''neurosurgeon'' carefully removes bits of bone with a stone hammer and chisel to form an opening at the top of the skull. That this trephining did take place many thousands of years ago is surmised from some skulls of stone age cave dwellers because the holes observed were, from their neat appearance, obviously made with care. In addition, the areas of healed bone around the edges of the opening suggest that the individual survived the procedure for some time after it was performed. Historical records show that trephining was sometimes performed in medieval times to allow evil spirits to escape from inside the heads of tormented or deranged individuals.

One of the earliest recorded expressions of a relationship between a body organ (brain) and mental events is found in Egyptian papyri dating from the 16th Century B.C. These written records indicate clearly that the brain was recognized as the locus of mental activities (Coleman et al., 1984). About 500 B.C., Hippocrates, the father of medicine, wrote that the brain is the organ by which we experience sights, sounds, thoughts, joy, laughter, sorrow, and pain (Penfield & Roberts, 1959). He wrote further that the brain is our interpreter of conscious experience. Plato, who lived four centuries B.C., also believed that mental activities were localized in the brain. He and other Greek philosophers of his time were concerned with the body–mind problem, or the relationship between physiological activities and mental events. Aristotle, who lived three centuries B.C., taught that the seat of mental functions was in the heart. The Roman physician Galen, who lived in the second century A.D., supported the idea that the mind is located in the brain. Galen's position was widely accepted through the Middle Ages without much refinement. It was not until the 19th century that the experimental investigations of Flourens clearly related different brain areas with various animal behaviors, such as visual perception and voluntary movement (Boring, 1950).

Thus, early philosophers and later physiologists devoted thought and experimentation to understanding the physiological correlates of behavior. French physiologists of the 19th century held that the brain is the center for perception, intelligence, and judgment, but that emotions are generated by the internal organs (Boring, 1950). In the late 19th century, this idea influenced what is now known as the James-Lange concept of emotional behavior. This concept holds that an emotional state is experienced because of the internal events, such as increased heart rate and muscle activity, produced by a provocative stimulus. Thus, according to the James-Lange theory, if we encounter a frightening event, we feel afraid because we run; we do not run because we are afraid! The perception of danger occurs first, then escape behavior, and finally the feeling of fear. This concept was opposed by the Cannon-Bard theory of the 1930s, which proposed that an emotional state resulted from the influence of lower brain centers (hypothalamus and thalamus) on higher ones (cortex), rather than from impulses produced by internal organs. Thus, danger is perceived, fear is experienced, and we flee the threatening situation.

Up to this point, our brief historical excursion has emphasized the relationship between the brain and behavior. Early observers and investigators were also interested in the relationship between physiological changes and psychological processes. In an interesting account of early psychophysiological approaches, Mesulam and Perry (1972) described observations in the practices of Erasistratos, Galen, and Ibn Sina (Avicenna), physicians who lived in a time ranging from the third century B.C. to the 11th century A.D. Erasistratos noticed in the third century B.C. that a teen-age prince named Antiochas had certain symptoms including sweating, pounding heart, and palid skin coloring. The young man was confined to bed and Erasistratos determined to see whether any of the boy's visitors would bring on the symptoms. Erasistratos concluded correctly that the boy was secretly in love with his stepmother, because he showed all of the symptoms only when she visited his sickroom. The diagnosis made by Erasistratos depended on three important assumptions: (a) there was an interaction between psychological and physiological events; (b) there was a type of conditioning in which a particular stimulus brought forth a variety of autonomic responses; and (c) Antiochas might be able to conceal his love for the woman in terms of overt motor behavior, but could not hide his covert physiological responses. Also illustrated is an early diagnosis of a psychosomatic illness.

Four centuries later, at the beginning of the second century A.D., the physician Galen related a case history from his clinical experience. The patient was a woman who suffered from insomnia, was very restless, and was hesitant to answer questions about her condition. The following quote is from Galen's observation (Mesulam & Perry, 1972):

> While I was convinced the woman was afflicted by not bodily disease, but rather that some emotional trouble grieved her, it happened that at the very moment I was examining her this was confirmed. Someone returning from the theatre mentioned he had seen Pylades dancing. Indeed, at that instant, her expression and the color of her face were greatly altered. Attentive, my hand laid on the woman's wrist and I observed her pulse was irregular, suddenly, violently agitated, which points to a troubled mind. The same thing occurred to people engaged in an argument over a given subject. (p. 549)

Galen later surmised that the woman was in love with Pylades and was able to confirm this conclusion a few days later. Galen criticized the other physicians who had attended the woman for not noticing the ways in which the body could be influenced by the state of the mind.

In his *Canon Medicinae*, the physician Avicenna (10th century A.D.) included a chapter on "Love Sickness." Avicenna observed that the pulse of a patient suffering ". . . love sickness is a fluctuating pulse without any regularity whatever, as is the pulse of the fatigued. Moreover, the patient's pulse and disposition are altered when mention is made of the person he loves, and especially when this occurs suddenly. It is possible in this way to ascertain whom he loves, even when he will not reveal it himself." (Mesulam & Perry, 1972, p. 550). The observations and writings of these early physicians show that they clearly understood the relationship between a psychological stimulus and physiological effects. Their interests were similar to those of contemporary psychophysiologists in that they differentiated between psychological processes through physiological changes. They were able to observe outward changes in skin color or to determine the pulse rate by feeling the patient's wrist without instruments. The modern development of psychophysiological research has depended on the development of sophisticated instrumentation for measuring electrical changes that take place in body tissues, and that reflect a variety of physiological responses. These developments in instrumentation took place for the most part in the latter part of the 19th century and the early part of the 20th century.

Concepts that have implications for understanding the physiological correlates of emotional behavior and for integrating data in the field of psychophysiology are presented in a later chapter. It is clear that throughout recorded history, the brain and the heart have been focal points in attempts by physicians, philosophers, physiologists, and psychologists to understand behavior. These focal points have taken a new twist since contemporary psychophysiologists have discovered interactions between heart and brain activity that have behavioral implications (see chapter 15).

CONTEMPORARY PSYCHOPHYSIOLOGY

In the last 25 years, there has been a tremendous growth in the number of research studies in which physiological measures, as well as behavioral ones, have been taken in the course of studying human activities and performance. That this particular field has been growing rapidly is evidenced by the increasing number of publications in the area, as well as by the increasing number of universities that offer courses and training in psychophysiology (see Feuerstein & Schwartz, 1977; Johnson & May, 1973).

Applications of Psychophysiology

There is currently a growing trend toward applying psychophysiological techniques and information to practical problems. No single area illustrates this widespread interest in applications of psychophysiology as does the discipline known as *biofeedback*. In recent years, biofeedback training has been applied to a wide variety of human ailments ranging from tension headaches to asthma and high blood pressure. There is, in fact, suggestive evidence that the provision of feedback (information) about muscle activity in the throat and facial areas may help in treating the common speech disorder known as stuttering. Because of the large number of biofeedback studies completed in recent years, as well as the potential importance of this field, a separate chapter is devoted to this area (see chapter 14).

Chapter 13 presents examples of psychophysiological applications ranging from the controversial procedure of lie detection to the study of behavioral disorders. An important and very recent psychophysiological application involves the use of event-related brain potentials to study sensory capacities. For example, in chapter 13, vision and hearing tests of young infants, accomplished with this physiological measure, are described.

Importance of Brain Measures

In this text, psychophysiological studies that relate brain activity (the electroencephalogram and event-related brain potentials) to behavior play a prominent role in the overall presentation. This is partly because the brain is the central organ of behavior. Without it we would not be able to think, move, create, or perform any of the complex functions that we associate with human endeavors. However, other physiological measures such as heart, muscle, electrodermal, eye movements and pupil size, blood pressure, and blood volume changes all provide important insights into behavior that may not be directly available through the study of brain activity. For example, regular increments in muscle potentials have been associated with increased rewards for efficient performance in a motor task. Feedback from muscle to brain and back to motor units is a crucial aspect of this observed relationship.

Another reason for the prominent position given to brain measures in this text is the surge in brain psychophysiology over the past 25 years. Much of this has been the result of the application of computer technology to the study of brain processes, enabling scientists to obtain a number of new measures, particularly event-related brain potentials (ERPs) and magneto-evoked potentials. These latter measures enable the noninvasive study of cortical and subcortical brain responses to specific stimuli. Various brain measures and related research are presented in chapters 3 through 7.

Physiological Measures in Relation to the Nervous System

The measures taken by psychophysiologists may include one or more of the following: the electroencephalogram (EEG), the event-related brain potential (ERP), the electromyogram (EMG, a measure of muscle activity), pupillometry (measures of changes in pupil size), electroculography (EOG, a measure of eye movement), electrodermal activity (EDA, changes in electrical activity at the skin surface), heart responses, blood volume, and blood pressure. Some other measures obtained by psychophysiologists include respiration, oxygen consumption, salivation, skin temperature, and gastric motility.

The average scientist in this field normally focuses on one or several of these physiological measures, but usually not all of them, at any one time. An example of multiple physiological measurements and how some people may view the scientist in this field is illustrated in Fig. 1.1.

The physiological measures just outlined are all under the control of the nervous system. The nervous system is highly integrated, but for the sake of convenience, we can list the various measures as being primarily controlled by one or another subdivision of this system. First, a brief diagrammatic summary of the nervous system is in order. As can be seen in Fig. 1.2, it may be divided into two main branches, the central nervous system (CNS) and the peripheral nervous system. The CNS includes the brain and spinal cord. The peripheral nervous system refers to nervous tissue outside the brain and spinal cord, including the cranial and spinal nerves. The peripheral nervous system is further divided into the somatic system, concerned with muscular activities, and the autonomic nervous system (ANS), which controls visceral structures (glands and organs of the body). Finally, the ANS is subdivided into the parasympathetic

FIG. 1.1.   How some people view the psychophysiologist at work.

nervous system (PNS), the innervation mechanisms of which are dominant when the individual is at rest, and the sympathetic nervous system (SNS), which is dominant in situations requiring mobilization of energy. The PNS can be thought of as a system of rest and repair, whereas the SNS is a system of energy mobilization and work. The schematic drawing in Fig. 1.2 is imperfect, because there are parts of the ANS that are in and under the control of the CNS; for example, the hypothalamus and medulla of the brain are important in the control of ANS functions.

The assignment of physiological measures to the nervous system and its subdivisions from the point of view of general control of function would lead to the organization shown in Table 1.1. Many of the physiological responses of interest are controlled by the ANS, and, accordingly, this is a very important system for the field of psychophysiology. The student interested in obtaining more detailed information about the anatomy and physiology of the ANS can consult such texts as those of Pick (1970) and Gardner (1975). A brief treatment of the autonomic and somatic systems is presented in chapter 2.

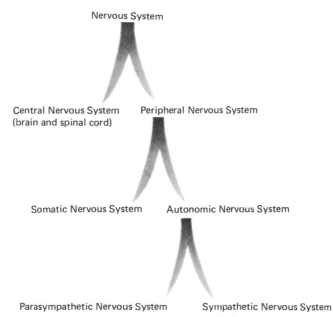

FIG. 1.2. Schematic drawing of nervous system showing its major divisions.

AIMS AND ORGANIZATION OF THIS BOOK

One important aim of this text is to illustrate the kinds of questions being asked by researchers, the studies they are conducting, and the conclusions that are being drawn or that seem justified at this time. Conclusions are provided at the end of each major section of each chapter. In some cases, specific conclusions

TABLE 1.1
Nervous System Mechanisms in the Control
of Physiological Responses

Central Nervous System	Somatic System	Autonomic Nervous System
EEG (ongoing activity)	EMG	Heart rate (PNS, SNS)
Event-related potentials	EOG	Blood pressure (PNS, SNS)
		Electrodermal activity (SNS only)
		Pupil response (PNS, SNS)
		Blood volume (PNS, SNS)

are reached, whereas in others, no definite conclusions are formulated, indicating either that more work is required to clear up an issue or that a stalemate exists. The existence of a stalemate may mean that satisfactory conclusions may never be reached with the approaches that are currently being used.

Other aims of this book are to provide elementary information regarding the anatomy and physiology of the various body systems under discussion and examples of how the activity is measured. The purpose of this coverage is to provide basic information about how to obtain physiological measures. The student who requires more detailed information about anatomy and physiology and recording techniques can refer to specialized texts on these subjects. For example, *Gray's Anatomy* (Gray, 1977), *Basic Human Physiology* (Guyton, 1977), *Techniques in Psychophysiological Methods* (Martin & Venables, 1980), and *Psychophysiological Recording* (Stern, Ray, & Davis, 1980) may be consulted. Chapters 2 through 7 focus mainly on the central nervous system and the relations between measures of its activity and psychological processes. Chapters 8 through 12 treat the psychophysiology of body systems peripheral to the brain. They include, in order, the muscles, sweat glands, eyes, heart, and blood vessels. Chapters 13 and 14 are concerned with applications of psychophysiology, and chapter 15 covers concepts in the field. The organization of this book emphasizes the brain as the central organ of behavior, with activity in the peripheral systems reflecting the outflow of brain influence. This is not to minimize the role played by these peripheral systems in psychophysiology, because it is known that (a) feedback of their activity can influence brain activity, and (b) peripheral measures often contribute information about body–behavior relationships that measures of brain activity do not.

Once the student has obtained some knowledge of body systems, measuring techniques, and representative studies in the field, he or she will be ready to appreciate the theoretical issues that characterize the field of psychophysiology. Although the organization of the text reflects the view that concepts should follow empirical data, individual instructors may prefer to cover the conceptual material at some earlier point. This could have the advantage of alerting the student to issues in the field and how one or another study either supports or refutes a particular view. Other instructors may prefer to present the material dealing with peripheral body systems prior to that which covers brain activity. A feature of this text is that the coverage of the various body systems is such that each is self-contained. Hence, the individual instructor may choose any particular chapter sequence he or she wishes without losing the flavor of the book.

Information regarding environmental influences on various physiological responses appears in Appendix I. These factors include external (e.g., temperature, air) and internal (e.g., drugs and hormones) influences. Although some of the environmental studies may not be strictly psychophysiological, in that they fail to manipulate psychological variables, environmental factors must be considered because of their possible interaction with both behavioral and physiological measures. It should be noted that research with humans is emphasized in this book. Animal research has been, and continues to be, crucial to the development of psychophysiology. However, a comprehensive treatment of animal studies requires a separate book. Appendix II provides detailed information regarding equipment requirements for recording the electroencephalogram, and Appendix III outlines laboratory safety precautions.

REFERENCES

Boring, E. G. (1950). *A history of experimental psychology* (2nd ed.). New York: Appleton-Century-Crofts.

Coleman, J. C., Butcher, J. N. & Carson, R. C. (1984). *Abnormal psychology and modern life.* Dallas: Scott, Foresman.

Feuerstein, M., & Schwartz, G. E. (1977). Training in clinical psychophysiology: Present trends and future goals. *American Psychologist, 32,* 560–567.

Furedy, J. J. (1983). Operational, analogical and genuine definitions of psychophysiology. *International Journal of Psychophysiology, 1,* 13–19.

Gardner, E. (1975). *Fundamentals of neurology* (6th ed.). Philadelphia: Saunders.

Gray, H. (1977). *Anatomy—descriptive and surgical.* (T. P. Pick & R. Howden, Eds.). New York: Bounty Books.

Guyton, A. C. (1977). *Basic human physiology: Normal function and mechanisms of disease.* Philadelphia: Saunders.

Johnson, H. J. & May, J. R. (1973). The educational process in psychophysiology. *Psychophysiology, 10,* 215–217.

Lykken, D. T. (1984). Psychophysiology. In R.J. Corsini (Ed.), *Encyclopedia of psychology* (pp. 934–937). New York: Wiley.

Mangina, C. A. (1983). Towards an international consensus in defining psychophysiology. *International Journal of Psychophysiology, 1,* 21–23.

Martin, I., & Venables, P. H. (1980). *Techniques in psychophysiology.* New York: Wiley.

Mesulam, M. & Perry, J. (1972). The diagnosis of love-sickness: Experimental psychology without the polygraph. *Psychophysiology, 9,* 13–19.

Penfield, W., & Roberts, L. (1959). *Speech and brain mechanisms.* Princeton: Princeton University Press.

Pick, J. (1970). *The autonomic nervous system.* Philadelphia: Lippincott.

Stern, J. A. (1964). Towards a definition of psychophysiology. *Psychophysiology, 1,* 90–91.

Stern, R. M., Ray, W. J., & Davis, C. M. (1980). *Psychophysiological recording.* New York: Oxford University Press.

2

The Nervous System and Measurement of Its Activity

This chapter focuses primarily on the source and nature of the electrical activity of the nervous system and how it is measured. Included is a brief presentation of some neuroanatomy and neurophysiology necessary to understand the activity being measured. The material presented here forms the background for understanding some of the physiological bases of the EEG and the evoked cortical potentials that are discussed in subsequent chapters. As outlined in chapter 1, the nervous system, for the sake of convenience, may be divided into central (brain and spinal cord) and peripheral (nerves outside CNS) systems. These two systems are briefly discussed in separate sections of this chapter.

SOURCE OF THE BRAIN'S ELECTRICAL ACTIVITY

Electrical activity of the brain is produced by billions of brain cells, called neurons. Activity is never absent in the healthy living brain. Neurons are always active: when we are asleep or awake, active or passive, during meditation or hypnosis. The entire nervous system is dependent on neurons for its activity. These cells are the functional units of the brain and spinal cord.

Although there is general agreement among scientists that neurons are the source of brain electrical activity, the exact nature of their contribution is an area of contention. For example, Noback and Demarest (1975) proposed that the EEG is produced by electrical activity at synapses (where brain cells transmit information) and by electrical activity within brain cells. They suggested further that recordings made from the scalp reflect the algebraic summation of excitatory and inhibitory activities that occur in underlying brain tissue. That is, some brain cells produce excitation and some reduce the level of activity; the resultant is the record called the EEG.

Elul (1972) made a strong argument for the position that the EEG is a resultant of activity within nerve cells in the cerebral cortex. He indicated that analyses of correlations between gross EEGs (recorded from many cells) and the activity of individual nerve cells suggest that gross activity is due to the synchronized firing of a relatively small number of cerebral neurons. Thus, according to Elul, the EEG is produced through the intermittent synchronization of cortical neurons, with different neurons becoming synchronized in successive instants. This implies that the EEG represents a series of bursts of aggregate neuronal activity, with each burst being the synchronized activity of different groups of cortical neurons. According to Elul, these bursts of activity are what we see in the EEG recording. He also pointed out that subcortical areas, such as the thalamus, have an influence over the EEG, because it is known that the thalamus plays a role in the production of at least one type of spontaneous brain activity called "sleep spindles." He suggested, however, that other subcortical centers may also contribute to EEG rhythms. Let us now briefly examine the structures that produce the brain's electrical activity.

The Neuron

Neurons consist of a cell body, dendrites, and a single axon. There are an estimated 50–100 billion neurons in the nervous system. The cell body contains the nucleus, which controls cellular activity. The dendrites are extensions that come off the cell body and transmit impulses to the cell. As many as 75 to 80 dendrites may be present on a motor cell, whereas sensory neurons may only have a single dendrite. Dendrites are short, relative to axons. The single axon comes off the cell body and transmits information away from the cell body to other neurons. Axons sometimes reach a length of several feet. Diagrams of a neuron within the CNS and a motor neuron located in both the CNS and peripheral nervous system are shown in Fig. 2.1. In addition to neurons, there are billions of support cells in the nervous system, called *glia*. The most common type of glial cell is the "astrocyte," named for its star-shaped configuration. Some scientists believe that astrocytes provide nourishment to neurons in the form of glucose and play a role in forming the "blood–brain" barrier that protects neurons from effects of potentially toxic substances. The fact that blood vessels of the CNS cannot transport large molecules across their walls and have astrocytes attached to their outer surfaces severely limits materials that can enter the brain. Thus, only oxygen, carbon dioxide, glucose, and certain amino acids required by the brain can pass the blood–brain barrier.

Neurons can be multipolar, bipolar, or unipolar. Multipolar neurons have many dendrites coming off the cell body. The motor neuron illustrated in Fig.

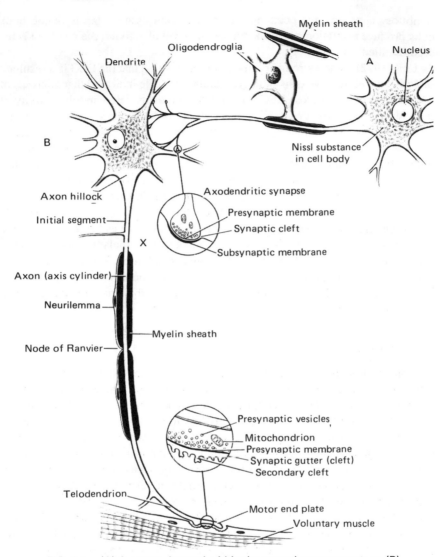

FIG. 2.1. (A) A neuron located within the central nervous system. (B) A lower motor neuron located in both the central and peripheral nervous systems. This synapses with a voluntary muscle cell to form a motor end plate. The hiatus in the nerve at X represents the border between the central nervous system above and the peripheral nervous system below.

2.1 is an example of a multipolar neuron. Also shown is the neurilemma covering, which exists only in neurons outside of the brain and spinal cord—that is, in the peripheral nervous system. A concept of nervous system function holds that the neurilemma is the substance that allows a neuron outside the CNS to regenerate by providing a pathway and protection for the regenerating neuron. Once neurons inside the CNS are destroyed, through accident or disease, they do not regenerate functionally; that is, they may show some anatomical signs of regeneration, but their function does not return.

Bipolar neurons consist of a single dendrite conducting impulses to the cell body and a single axon conducting information away from it. The neurilemma never appears on bipolar neurons. The function of the bipolar neuron is sensory. They are found, for example, in the visual system (retina) and in the auditory system (cochlea).

The unipolar neuron is composed of a single process coming off the cell body and splitting into a dendrite and an axon. Therefore, the dendrite and axon are anatomically the same. The neurilemma appears only on unipolar neurons located outside the CNS. Their functions are sensory only, and they are found in the dorsal roots of spinal nerves and sensory portions of the cranial nerves.

Excitation of Neurons

Neurons are effectively stimulated by natural stimuli from receptor organs (e.g., in the eyes or ears) or by neural impulses coming from other nerves. They may also respond to appropriate chemical, electrical, thermal, or mechanical stimuli. Their responsiveness to artificial stimuli has enabled investigators to study electrical activity of single neurons or small groups of neurons through tiny recording microelectrodes. Because neurons are rather small, their size ranging from 4 to 100 μm (microns, or millionths of a meter), the electrodes for recording from single cells must be only a few micrometers in diameter to enable insertion into these cells. In experimental work, electric current has often been used because of its convenience, accuracy of quantification, and the fact that it does not damage the neuron at appropriate levels of stimulation. To produce an impulse from a neuron, a stimulus must be of a certain strength and duration. The stimulus strength just capable of producing a neuron response is termed *the threshold intensity* and is usually given in terms of voltage. A stimulus must be applied for a certain period of time before it will produce a neuronal impulse. Thus, a strong stimulus will not have to be applied as long as a weak one to elicit a neuronal response. The strength of this minimal level stimulus required to produce a response is called the *threshold* or *rheobase*. The excitability of neurons can be determined by ascertaining the chronaxy or the minimum length of time it takes an electric current two times the rheobase value to create an impulse (Gardner, 1975).

A neuron must receive a certain minimal level of stimulation, or it will not fire

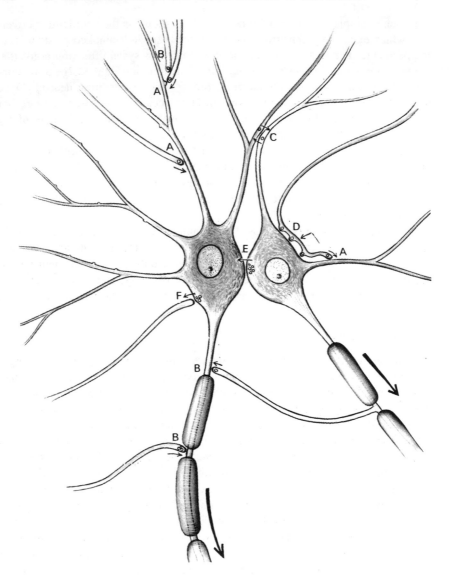

FIG. 2.2. Several types of synapses: (A) axodendritic synapses; (B) axonaxonic synapse; (C) reciprocal dendrodentritic synapses; (D) enpassant axosomatic synapses; (E) somatosomatic synapse; (F) somatoaxonic synapse.

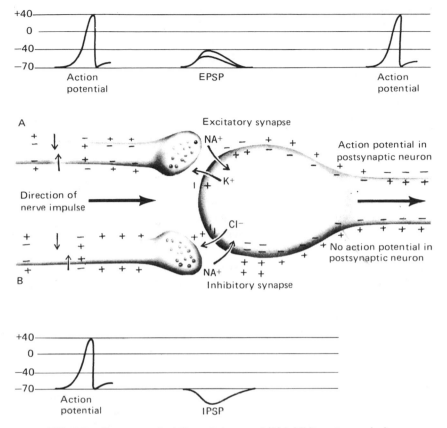

FIG. 2.3.   Sequences in (A) excitatory and (B) inhibitory transmission
from presynaptic neurons (left) and across synapses to postsynaptic
neuron (right). (A) the action potential conducted along the presynaptic axon to an excitatory synapse produces an EPSP, which in turn can
contribute to the generation of an action potential in the postsynaptic
neuron. (B) The action potential conducted along the presynaptic axon
to an inhibitory synapse produces an IPSP, which in turn suppresses
the generation of an action potential in the postsynaptic neuron.

at all. Upon adequate stimulation, it will fire with its maximum strength. This
has been termed the "all-or-none principle" of neuronal firing. Once the stimulus triggers the firing of a neuron, the electrical impulse continues along the
entire length of the axon and possibly to the dendrites of another neuron. Transmission to another neuron takes place across a small juncture called a *synapse*.
The terminal portion of an axon and the dendrites of another neuron do not touch.
Transmission across the synapse is accomplished by chemical mediators. Figure
2.2 shows a schematic drawing of several types of synapses, and Fig. 2.3
illustrates both excitatory and inhibitory activity at a synapse.

The speed of electrical impulse conduction along a neuron depends on axon diameter. Large-diameter axons transmit impulses at higher speeds. A rough estimate of transmission speed can be made for mammalian neurons that contain myelin. The diameter is multiplied by a constant of 6 to give approximate conduction speed in meters per second or ($V = KD$), where V = velocity, K = 6 and D = diameter. Thus, for an axon 20 μm in diameter, conduction velocity is about 120 m/sec (Gardner, 1975). Myelin is a whitish material composed of protein and fat that appears on some axons in the nervous system. It is the myelin that causes masses of axons to appear as "white matter" of the brain, as compared to the masses of cell bodies that comprise the "gray matter."

Neuron Potentials

Although the neuronal impulse can be measured in terms of changes in electrical activity, it is actually produced by physiochemical activity that occurs when the neuron is stimulated. To understand how this physiochemical activity occurs, a brief explanation of the chemicals existing inside and outside the neuron and their relation to various potential states of the neuron are given.

There is usually what is termed a resting potential difference on the two sides of the cell membrane, so that the inside of the cell is negative relative to the outside. This occurs because the inside of the cell has higher concentrations of potassium ions and the outside of the cell has more sodium ions. When a stimulus of sufficient strength and duration comes along, it causes physiochemical changes to take place in which the cell membrane becomes permeable, allowing the sodium to enter at a high rate and the potassium to move outside the cell, thus causing a reversal of the resting potential along the entire length of the axon. This reversal of resting potential is called a wave of depolarization. When depolarization occurs, the inside of the membrane registers a potential of about +30 mV, a change of 100 mV from the resing potential of approximately −70 mV. After depolarization has occurred along the axon, the neuron returns to its original resting state. The exchange of positive and negative ions produces a potential difference between the active and inactive areas of the neuron, and a current flows between the two regions. The mechanism by which sodium is returned to the outside of the cell and potassium to the inside has been termed the "sodium–potassium pump." The precise nature of how this pump works is not known (Gardner, 1975).

The Action Potential of the Neuron

The action potential of the neuron is made up of three components: the spike potential, the negative afterpotential, and the positive afterpotential. The spike potential is the large, sharply rising part of the action potential represented in Fig. 2.3. Note that the action potential may excite or inhibit activity in the postsynaptic neuron. The spike potential represents the period during which depolarization takes place. The spike potential lasts only .5 to 1 msec (thousandths of a second). The excitability of the neuron, in terms of its ability to respond to another stimulus, is greatly reduced during the spike period. In fact, during the absolute refractory period, lasting about .5 msec, no stimulus will produce another neuron response. The relative refractory period of the spike is the period during which only a stimulus of much greater intensity than normal will produce another firing of the neuron. The relative refractory period lasts about .5 msec. An absolute refractory period of .5 to 1 msec would limit the response of an individual neuron to about 1,000 or 2,000 a second.

The next phase of the action potential is the negative afterpotential, which lasts from 5 to 15 msec and is lower in magnitude than the spike potential. The excitability of the neuron is "supernormal" during the negative afterpotential. This means that a stimulus of lower intensity than normal will be sufficient to cause another neuron response. Some scientists have hypothesized that this occurs because more than the usual number of sodium ions are still inside the neuron, causing it to be more excitable than normal.

The last portion of the action potential is the positive afterpotential, which lasts for about 50 to 80 msec. However, the neuron is in a "subnormal" phase during the positive afterpotential, meaning that it will take a stronger than normal stimulus to produce another spike potential during this period. One notion is that the sodium pump has pushed too much sodium outside, resulting in a lower than usual number of sodium ions inside the cell and, therefore, a lower excitability. After about 80 to 100 msec, the normal excitability of the neuron returns.

The action potential is an example of neuronal activity that occurs in response to specific adequate stimulation. Another, more common neural activity is the graded potential, which occurs primarily in the cell bodies and dendrites of the neurons. These are continuous potentials, and they also occur in neurons in situations when stimuli are subthreshold or not intense enough to produce a spike potential.

Now that we have reviewed some aspects of electrical activity changes in neurons, it would be instructive to examine the organization of large masses of neurons in the human brain. This description of brain areas will prove useful in understanding the brain measure studies discussed in chapters 3 through 7. For example, when the patterning of EEG responses occurs during the performance of a task, a proper interpretation requires knowledge about the brain areas contributing to this patterning.

GROSS BRAIN ANATOMY

The average weight of the adult human brain is about 1,400 g (3 lb.). The brain may be divided into three main portions for convenience of description: the

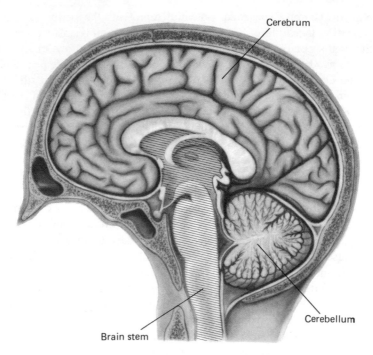

FIG. 2.4. Diagram showing three divisions of the brain: brain stem, cerebellum, and cerebrum. The brain stem is illustrated as the shaded portion of the diagram.

cerebrum, the cerebellum, and the brain stem. The cerebrum, or cerebral hemispheres, occupies much of the external surface of the brain. The two hemispheres, right and left, contain virtually identical structures. The cerebellum overlies the posterior aspect of the brain stem. The brain stem is the portion that remains after removal of the cerebral hemispheres and the cerebellum and is the structure upon which the cerebellum rests (see Fig. 2.4).

The surface of the cerebrum has many convolutions. The raised portions of these convolutions are called gyri (gyrus) and the grooved portions are termed sulci (sulcus) or fissures. The cerebellum is also convoluted, and the raised portions are called folia. There are slight differences in the shape and location of the gyri and sulci in the cerebrum of individual brains, but they are still useful in localizing various brain areas. For example, the fissure of Rolando (also called the central sulcus) travels down from the top of the brain toward the sides in both hemispheres to the lateral sulcus. It conveniently serves as a dividing line between what is termed the precentral cortex (motor functions) and the postcentral cortex (body sensory functions), as shown in the lateral view of the cortex in Fig. 2.5. The numbers in Fig. 2.5 are from the system of functional localization of

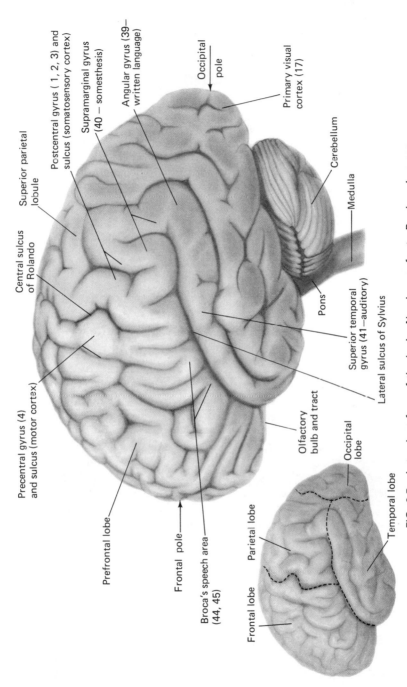

Precentral gyrus (4)
and sulcus (motor cortex)

Central sulcus
of Rolando

Superior parietal
lobule

Postcentral gyrus (1, 2, 3) and
sulcus (somatosensory cortex)

Supramarginal gyrus
(40 — somesthesis)

Angular gyrus (39—
written language)

Occipital
pole

Primary visual
cortex (17)

Cerebellum

Medulla

Pons

Superior temporal
gyrus (41—auditory)

Lateral sulcus of Sylvius

Prefrontal lobe

Frontal pole

Broca's speech area
(44, 45)

Olfactory
bulb and tract

Occipital
lobe

Parietal lobe

Temporal lobe

Frontal lobe

FIG. 2.5.   Lateral surface of the brain. Numbers refer to Brodman's areas.

21

Brodmann. The other drawing in Fig. 2.5 illustrates the division of the cerebral cortex into four lobes: the frontal, parietal, occipital, and temporal. Note that the fissure of Sylvius (also called the lateral sulcus) separates the temporal lobe from the frontal and parietal lobes.

The medial aspect is what would be seen if the brain were cut in half, from front to back (called a midsagittal section). The medial aspect is presented in Fig. 2.6. Note that if we examine the head area from outside to inside, we first see the scalp and then the skull bone. Immediately below the skull is the dura mater, which is a tough, elastic membrane covering the brain. Below the dura is the arachnoid tissue. The pia mater is a very thin, soft membrane below the arachnoid that covers the brain and follows the gyri and sulci very closely. In the subarachnoid space is located the cerebrospinal fluid, which is believed to supply nourishment to the brain as well as providing a protective envelope of liquid for the brain and spinal cord. The subarachnoid space communicates with the ventricular system of the brain.

There are four ventricles in the brain: two lateral ventricles (one in each cerebral hemisphere), a third ventricle located between each thalamus, and a fourth ventricle connected to the third by a narrow channel (cerebral aqueduct).

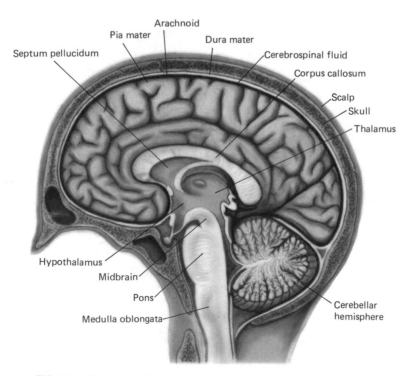

FIG. 2.6.   Median sagittal section of the brain and part of the head.

The ventricles are spaces through which the cerebrospinal fluid circulates in and around the brain. One subcortical area, the thalamus (brain stem; see Fig. 2.6), is singled out here for a brief elaboration, because it has important functions as a relay station for sensory and motor input to the cortex. The thalamus contains many important nuclei, such as the ventral nuclei, posteroventral nucleus, lateroventral nucleus, medial and lateral geniculate bodies, pulvinar, and reticular nucleus. The reticular nucleus (reticular formation) has a role in influencing both general and specific cortical activity and functions. This reticular formation has been referred to as the ascending reticular activating system (ARAS) and has important implications for behavior.

Another structure of special interest is the corpus callosum, a thick band of fibers that connects the left and right hemispheres of the brain. The corpus callosum allows the transfer of sensory and other information between the cerebral hemispheres.

This basic information about neuron and brain structures will allow you to better understand the material that follows in chapters on the EEG and event-related brain potentials.

THE ELECTROENCEPHALOGRAM (EEG)

The electroencephalogram (EEG) or "brain wave" was described in rabbits and monkeys by Richard Caton in 1875. Caton was interested in studying localization of sensory function in the brain. He presented visual stimuli while recording from electrodes placed directly on the exposed brains of rabbits and monkeys (Brazier, 1957). He showed that when a flash of light was presented to the animal's eyes, a change in electrical activity occurred at the occipital area. This response may have been the first sensory-evoked potential. Caton also noticed that when his electrodes were resting on the surface of a rabbit's cortex, with no sensory stimulation being presented, feeble oscillations occurred in his recording. He concluded that his recordings represented the electrical activity of the resting brain, and presented his findings to the British Medical Society in 1875. The work caught little attention, even though Caton later presented his findings in both the United States and Russia.

In 1902, Hans Berger began his work on brain waves with dogs, and in 1920, he started to study human EEGs. His goal from the beginning was to detect, from the scalp surface in humans, the same waves that could be obtained from the brain surface of animals. Finally, in 1929, after a great deal of work in which EEGs were recorded from many individuals, including himself and his teen-age son, Berger published his findings. In his paper, entitled "On the Electroencephalogram of Man" (see Porges & Coles, 1976), Berger identified two basic brain wave patterns; one that was relatively large and occurred 10–11 times per second, and a smaller one at a frequency of 20–30 per second. Berger termed the

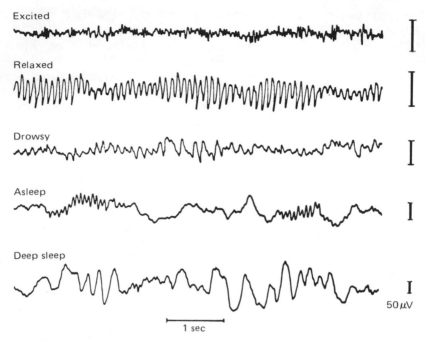

FIG. 2.7. Electroencephalographic records during excitement, relaxation, and varying degrees of sleep. In the fourth strip, runs of 14/sec rhythm, superimposed on slow waves, are termed "sleep spindles." Notice that excitement is characterized by a rapid frequency and small amplitude and that varying degrees of sleep are marked by increasing irregularity and by the appearance of slow waves.

larger and slower waves "alpha" and the smaller, faster activity "beta." Later, investigators identified other types of brain waves and continued using the Greek alphabet labels, calling them delta, theta, kappa, lambda, and mu waves. The most reliable of these later-identified waves, in terms of consistency of occurrence, has been the delta wave, although it has been found possible to condition theta waves (Beatty, Greenberg, Deibler, & O'Hanlon, 1974; Brown, 1974). The characteristics of some of these waves are described hereafter and depicted in Fig. 2.7. In addition to these waves, there are the "K complexes" and "sleep spindles" of the sleeping EEG (see Fig. 4.2 and Table 4.2). The sleeping EEG is discussed in chapter 4.

Alpha Waves

The alpha is a rhythmic wave that occurs at a rate of 8 to 13 times a second (cycles per second [cps] or hertz [Hz]) at a magnitude of about 20 to 60 μV (millionths of a volt). Alpha waves can be produced by almost anyone sitting quietly in a relaxed position and with eyes closed. (There is a small percentage of persons who have difficulty in producing alpha waves.) As soon as the individual becomes involved in any mental or physical activity, the alpha waves generally become reduced in amplitude or disappear. For example, a person may be sitting in a chair, relaxed or not thinking of anything in particular, and at least some alpha waves will be in evidence. If the person is asked to spell a word, the alpha will change to a higher frequency and lower amplitude wave called beta. Alpha is illustrated by the second wave from the top in Fig. 2.7, labeled "relaxed."

Beta Waves

The beta is an irregular wave that occurs at a frequency of 14 to 30 cps at an amplitude of approximately 2 to 20 μV. Beta waves are common when a person is involved in mental or physical activity and is illustrated by the topmost tracing in Fig. 2.7 (labeled "excited").

Delta Waves

The delta wave is a large-amplitude, low-frequency wave. It is typically between .5 and 3.5 cps in frequency, in the range of 20 to 200 μV. The delta wave appears only during deep sleep in normal individuals. If it occurs in a waking person, it could indicate some kind of brain abnormality, such as a tumor. See the bottom tracing in Fig. 2.7 for an example of delta activity.

Theta Waves

The theta is a relatively less common type of brain rhythm that occurs at about 4 to 7 Hz, at an amplitude ranging anywhere from 20 to 100 μV. It has been reported to occur more frequently in the spontaneous EEG recordings of children than in adults. Walter (1953) found it to occur during states of displeasure, pleasure, and drowsiness in young adults, and Maulsby (1971) reported amplitudes of 100 μV in babies experiencing "pleasurable" events (e.g., drinking from a bottle or being fondled by their mother).

Kappa Waves

Kennedy, Gottsdanker, Armington, and Gray (1948) discovered waves of about 10 Hz that appear to be associated with thinking. They reported that it occurred in about 30% of their subjects.

Lambda Waves

Lambda waves were discovered in humans by Evans (1952) and Y. Gastaut (1951). They have been recorded from over the visual cortex and are considered to be a type of visual response resulting from a shifting image of some object in a person's visual field. They are triangular in shape, range from 20 to 50 μV, and last about 150 to 250 msec in response to stimulation.

Mu Waves

The mu rhythm (described by H. Gastaut, 1952) has sharp peaks and rounded negative portions. It appears in the normal EEG of about 7% of the population and can be recorded from over the fissure of Rolando. The frequency is usually 9 to 11 Hz. A recent study of Koshino and Niedermeyer (1976) found that it was enhanced by scanning a patterned stimulus and not suppressed, as has usually been reported. These latter researchers found that 182 of 2,284 persons sampled (8.1%) showed evidence of the mu rhythm.

MEASUREMENT OF THE EEG

The various kinds of brain waves can be measured by means of electrodes attached to the scalp. This is the most common technique used by researchers studying brain activity. It must be pointed out that the amplitude of the EEG as measured from the scalp is much lower than if it were measured from the surface of the cortex (the electrocorticogram), because the electrical activity must pass through the dura mater, the cerebrospinal fluid, the skull bone, and the skin of the scalp before it reaches the scalp electrode. This greatly reduces its amplitude. The electrocorticogram is measured in millivolts, whereas the EEG is in microvolts, showing the great disparity in magnitudes. Because the difficulty and hazards of penetrating the skull are great, the electrocorticogram is rarely recorded, even in clinical cases. Because the EEG signal is so small at the scalp, the electronic circuitry for measuring it must be very sensitive.

Electrode Location (Monopolar)

To measure EEG, one may use either a monopolar or bipolar recording technique. The monopolar method is described in this section, and the bipolar is discussed in a later section. A monopolar technique involves placing one so-called active electrode in good contact with the skin over an area of interest, for example, the occipital (visual) cortex. Another electrode, termed the reference lead is placed on a relatively inactive area, such as the earlobe or tip of the nose. Because any reference electrode on the head is not completely inactive, some investigators prefer to place them on other parts of the body, for example, the back or chest. These may be difficult to use, because they could pick up muscle activity if the subject is not completely relaxed.

The diagram shown in Fig. 2.8 illustrates some commonly used scalp loca-

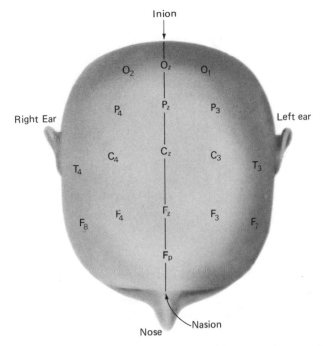

FIG. 2.8. Top view of scalp locations used by researchers studying relations between brain activity and performance. The locations are the active, or EEG-producing, areas. The reference area may be the earlobes, singly or in combination as "linked ears," or the tip of the nose. The numbering system is a portion of that used in the International EEG 10-20 system. The nasion refers to the bridge of the nose, whereas the inion is the occipital protuberance.

tions in EEG research. The locations are based on a portion of the International EEG nomenclature (Jasper, 1958). It is called the "10-20 System" because the various locations are either 10% or 20% of the distance between standard points for measurement. For example, in obtaining the location designated Oz, a centimeter measurement is taken between the nasion (bridge of nose) and inion (a projection of bone at the back of the head found over the occipital area, also known as the occipital protuberance). Then 10% of this distance is measured (toward the nasion), and the electrode is placed at this spot. The tape measure must pass straight along the midline between nasion and inion, through those points labeled with a "z" (indicating midline). This area is designated Oz and is over the occipital cortex. Those labeled P, F, and T are over parietal, frontal, and temporal areas, respectively. The C locations are central areas, with Cz as the center of both the anterior–posterior (front–back) and coronal (side to side) planes. The location labeled Fp is the frontal pole and is 10% of the nasion–inion

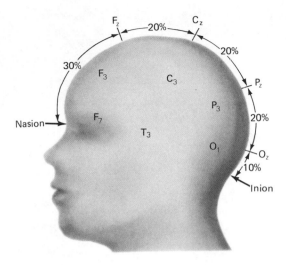

FIG. 2.9.   In this diagram the 10-20 system locations are shown for the left side of the scalp. Note that left side locations have odd-numbered designations, whereas the right side locations are indicated by even numbers. (F, frontal; C, central; P, parietal; O, occipital; T, temporal.)

distance. The Fz, Cz, and Pz locations are each 20% of the nasion–inion distance back, starting from Fp. The locations along the coronal plane are based on the distance measured between the midpoints of the two ears taken through Cz. The other locations along this anterior–posterior line are 20% of the distance apart from each other, except for the nasion-F_2 distance of 30%. This side view is illustrated in Fig. 2.9. Note that the locations on the left side of the head are indicated by odd numbers. This system of electrode location has enabled different investigators to communicate the sites in their EEG studies in a standard way. The method also has the advantage of being based on each subject's own head size. Anatomical studies carried out when the numbering system was first presented (Jasper, 1958) indicated that the locations do approximate the areas that they are claimed to be over, for example, occipital, parietal, frontal, or temporal lobes.

Electrode Attachment

The electronics of the recording equipment enable a comparison of the activity measured from over the cortical area of interest with that at the reference electrode, and the difference is the written EEG record. The electrodes should be small (6 to 8 mm in diameter) and easy to attach. The scalp area should be prepared by rubbing it with a cleansing material (alcohol on a cotton ball works well) until the skin shows a slight pink tinge. Then a standard electrode paste (a conducting agent) is carefully rubbed into the skin of the scalp until it permeates the pores. The electrode can be held firmly in place with an elastic headband or a variety of other devices available commercially. The reference lead can be a convenient clip electrode, which merely is attached to the earlobe or tip of the nose after the area has been cleansed of any oils or dead skin by rubbing with alcohol. Many researchers use "linked ears" as a reference—that is, electrodes are attached to both earlobes and then connected together to serve as a reference for all scalp leads. This bilateral reference technique is especially important if one wishes to investigate hemispheric asymmetries. Electrode paste is also used when attaching the reference. The resistance between the active and reference leads can be measured by impedance meters either conveniently built into the recording device or used as a separate measuring unit. It should read less than 5000 Ohms (units of impedance). If it does, you know that your electrodes are making good contact. A ground electrode may be placed on the other earlobe, on the mastoid area behind the ear, or on the wrist. Even with a good contact through careful electrode attachments, artifacts can be seen in the EEG record if subjects move about excessively or tense up the muscles of their forehead or jaw or blink their eyes. Subjects must be cautioned against producing this type of EEG artifact. Other unwanted signals, such as heart activity or skin potential responses, would be considered artifacts if they appeared in the EEG.

Silver cup electrodes are commonly used for active leads, whereas flat silver electrodes held in a clip are convenient reference electrodes. Some investigators use gold electrodes or a cellulose sponge permeated with the conducting material and held in place by an elastic headband.

Electrode Placement (Bipolar)

When using a bipolar recording technique, two active electrodes are placed over cortical areas of interest. Bipolar leads record the difference or algebraic sum of the electrical potentials beneath the two regions at every instant. Some researchers prefer bipolar recording because it avoids some of the problems of selecting an inactive reference area inherent in monopolar recording. However, bipolar recordings have the disadvantage of producing a record of combined activity at two locations. For clinical purposes (i.e., the recording of EEG to detect brain abnormalities), the interpretation of EEG records usually requires the comparison of data obtained from symmetrically placed electrodes (e.g., from two electrodes on the right frontal area compared with two on the left frontal area). The presence or absence of symmetry in the two tracings may be of clinical significance. Bipolar leads may also be used in research applications other than clinical. The monopolar technique is convenient in situations where activity produced at a specific area is monitored, for example, the left occipital area, or in recording event-related potentials (see chapter 5). The characteristics of a good EEG recording system are outlined in Appendix II. Laboratory safety procedures are presented in Appendix III.

BIOMAGNETISM AND THE
MAGNETOENCEPHALOGRAM (MEG)

Biomagnetism refers to the study of magnetic fields whose origin is in specific biological systems (Williamson & Kaufman, 1981). The weak magnetic fields of many body organs could not be practically studied until the application of the superconducting quantum interfering device (SQUID) to this type of measurement. The SQUID has been used to measure magnetic fields produced by the heart, lungs, and brain. The magnetic brain fields, called neuromagnetism, are among the weakest produced by biological systems. Thus, spontaneous brain activity is of extremely low magnitude when measured in terms of magnetic variations, and brain changes that occur in response to specific events, called evoked fields, are smaller still.

The strength of a magnetic field is indicated by the value of its magnetic induction for which the tesla (T) is the unit of measurement. Spontaneous brain activity produces such low levels of magnetic activity that it is measured in picoteslas (10^{-12} tesla). Brain activity changes produced in response to specific stimuli (evoked fields) have strengths as low as 10^{-15} tesla (femoteslas). Hence, in making biomagnetic measurements, the scientist must be able to measure extremely weak signals and must screen out possible interference from the much stronger magnetic field fluctuations in the surrounding environment (approximately 10^{-4} tesla). This requires rather elaborate procedures and instrumentation. Figure 2.10 illustrates the placement of the SQUID apparatus over the temporal area of the brain to measure magnetic brain fields in response to sound stimuli.

Neuromagnetism: The Magnetoencephalogram (MEG)
and Magneto Evoked Field (MEF)

Similar to the EEG, the observed MEG represents the combined activity of millions of neurons. The advantages of being able to measure neuromagnetic fields of the brain are the following: (a) Use of the SQUID eliminates the use of reference electrodes, thus allowing the MEG to compare activity in two different brains more directly; (b) the MEG measured outside the head may be better in determining subcortical sources of neural activity, because the magnetic signals are less influenced by tissue lying between the source and the sensing device; (c) some currents may be detected magnetically and cannot be observed through recordings of electrical changes; and (d) the magnetic detector can conveniently scan field patterns of the brain, because the detector is not attached to the scalp

FIG. 2.10. Arrangement of magnetic sensors within a magnetically shielded room at the Neuromagnetism Laboratory at the Departments of Physics and Psychology at New York University. A 5-sensor array is supported within the dewar held over the subject's head, and two single-person units are directed inward from the sides. The latter are cooled by refrigerators and need no liquid helium to keep the sensors superconducting. (Photo by courtesy of Drs. Williamson and Kaufman of New York University.)

surface, as in the case of fixed electrodes used to measure the EEG. The MEG may be obtained simultaneously with the EEG. Simultaneous alpha and beta activity will be observed with both kinds of records in the awake person. However, the MEG recording will not be as clear, because the very tiny signal is more susceptible to noise fields than the EEG.

THE PERIPHERAL NERVOUS SYSTEM

The peripheral nervous system allows communication between the brain and spinal cord and the rest of the body. This communication link is made possible by 31 pairs of spinal nerves, which branch off from the spinal cord (See Fig. 2.11), and 12 pairs of cranial nerves that emerge directly from the surface of the brain stem. The spinal and cranial nerves make possible the activities of the somatic and autonomic nervous systems. Most of the peripheral nerves (with the exception of a few cranial nerves) have both sensory and motor functions.

The Somatic System

This system consists of motor nerves that control voluntary muscles. The nerves, along with their dendrites and cell bodies, are found at different levels of the spinal cord, and form the motor portion of the spinal nerves (ventral root) at the point where spinal nerves and spinal cord meet. The ventral (motor) roots and dorsal (sensory) roots merge to form the complete spinal nerve. The spinal nerves connect to sympathetic ganglia by way of rami communicantes. More is said about these sympathetic ganglia when the autonomic nervous system is discussed.

The Autonomic Nervous System (ANS)

Many of the responses of interest to psychophysiologists are controlled by the ANS, thus making this a very important system for the field of psychophysiology. The ANS is the regulator and coordinator of important bodily activities, including digestion, body temperature, blood pressure, and many aspects of emotional behavior. Its activities have traditionally been regarded to be automatic or taking place without conscious control. However, research in the area of self-regulation of physiological responses through operant conditioning techniques suggests that it might be possible to alter one's own level of ANS activity, for example, heart rate (see chapters 11 and 14).

The main function of the ANS is to keep a constant internal body environment in the face of internal or external changes that could upset the balance. The term for the concept that describes the maintenance of a stable internal environment is homeostasis, coined by the physiologist Claude Bernard. The ANS involves innervation of three types of cell: smooth muscle cells, cardiac muscle cells, and glandular (secretory) cells. The main neurotransmitters of the autonomic nervous system are acetylcholine and norepinephrine. Acetylcholine is the neurotransmitter of the parasympathetic nervous system (cholinergic system), whereas norepinephrine is released at the junctions between sympathetic nerves and some effector cell (adrenergic system). As mentioned previously, the ANS is divided into two distinct anatomical parts, the sympathetic and parasympathetic systems.

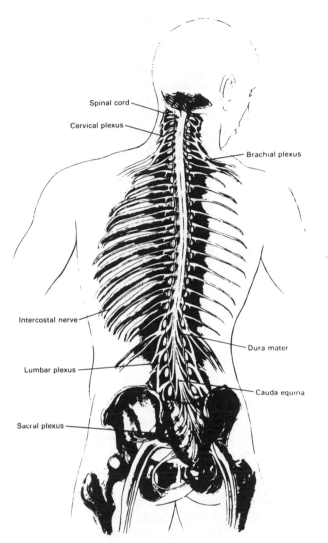

FIG. 2.11.   A dorsal view of the human body, showing the routes traveled by the principal spinal nerves. Redrawn with permission from Neil R. Carlson, *Physiology of Behavior,* 2nd ed. (Boston: Allyn & Bacon, Inc., 1980) p. 128.

The sympathetic system controls those activities which are mobilized during emergency and stress situations, sometimes referred to as "flight or fight" reactions. The sympathetic reactions include expenditure of energy, the acceleration of heart rate, increased blood pressure, increased blood sugar, increased blood flow to the voluntary muscles, and decreased blood flow to the internal organs and skin of the extremities. On the other hand, the parasympathetic system is involved with activities concerned with rest and repair of the body and restoration of energy stores. The reactions include decreases in heart rate and blood pressure, stimulation of the digestive system, and resting activities. Although the two systems have different functions, the activities are integrated and not antagonistic. The systems tend to act in a complementary fashion with a great deal of reciprocity that usually enables a smooth flow of bodily activities and behavior.

The Sympathetic Nervous System (SNS)

The sympathetic nervous system is also called the thoracico-lumbar system, because all of the motor neurons of this system emerge from the spinal cord via the spinal nerves of the thoracic and lumbar regions. After emerging from the spinal cord, they make linkages to a series of 22 ganglia in the so-called "sympathetic chain." The diagram in Fig. 2.12 shows a schematic of the brain and spinal cord, the chain of SNS ganglia, the PNS ganglia and the organs that are innervated by both systems. The organization of the chain of sympathetic ganglia enables the SNS to act as an integrated whole. This is why sympathetic reactions tend to occur simultaneously. For example, during stress, possibly caused by fear, anger, pain, exercise, or asphyxia, the SNS activities that occur together might include increased pulse rate, blood pressure, sweating, cardiac output, and respiration responses that will enhance a "flight or fight" reaction. Note in Fig. 2.12 that, whereas pre-ganglionic fibers from cord to sympathetic chain are short, the post-ganglionic fibers from chain to organ of innervation are long. This is the exact opposite of the PNS, in which ganglia are located near the organ to be innervated, thus resulting in long pre-ganglionic fibers and short post-ganglionic connections.

The Parasympathetic Nervous System (PNS)

This system is termed the craniosacral division of the ANS because its activities are controlled by motor cells whose nuclei are found in certain cranial nerves and in the sacral part of the spinal cord (See Fig. 2.12). PNS activity is more specific than that of the SNS, because the PNS ganglia are located near the target organ. For example, the oculomotor (third cranial nerve) regulates the iris of the eye, thus producing pupillary constriction without producing other reactions.

The PNS is the system of rest, repair, and enjoyment. It is dominant during

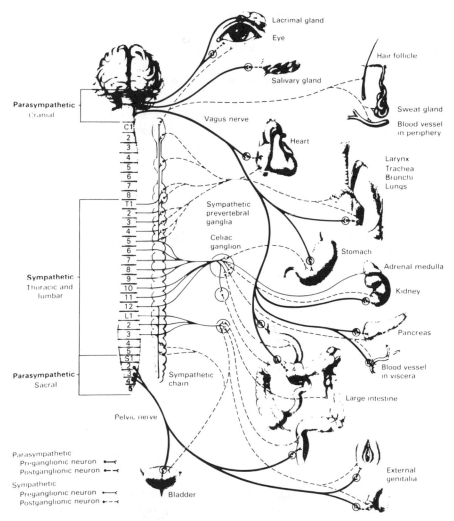

FIG. 2.12. A schematic representation of the autonomic nervous system and the target organs it serves. Redrawn with permission from Neil R. Carlson, *Physiology of Behavior,* 2nd ed. (Boston: Allyn & Bacon, Inc., 1980) p. 132.

eating, sleeping, and sexual activity. Some of its activities would include the stimulation of salivary secretions, digestive secretions in the stomach, peristalsis in the intestines, decreases in heart rate, and increased blood flow to the genitalia (erection) during sexual excitement.

The PNS influence from the sacral portion of the spinal cord is directed at the genitalia, sphincters (anal, urethral), bladder, and colon. The cranial nerves (c.n.) subserving PNS functions are the oculomotor (third c.n.), facial (seventh c.n.), glossopharyngeal (ninth c.n.), and vagus (tenth c.n.). The 12 cranial nerves and a sample of their functions are as follows:

1. Olfactory nerve (sensory)—connects olfactory cells of nose to olfactory bulb of brain (smell).
2. Optic nerve (sensory)—a CNS tract from the retina of the eye to visual structures in the brain. Actually, this is a portion of brain tissue (vision).
3. Oculomotor nerve (motor)—controls turning of eyes and pupillary opening.
4. Trochlear nerve (motor)—controls oblique eye movements.
5. Trigeminal (sensory and motor)—carries sensations of touch from face, scalp and teeth, and sends motor fibers to chewing muscles.
6. Abducens nerve (motor)—controls horizontal eye movements.
7. Facial nerve (sensory and motor)—conveys taste from front two-thirds of tongue. This nerve also controls face and scalp muscles.
8. Auditory-Vestibular nerve (sensory)—controls organs of hearing and balance.
9. Glossopharyngeal (sensory and motor)—conveys taste from back one-third of tongue. It also provides motor control to vocal organs and salivary glands (parotid).
10. Vagus nerve (sensory and motor)—sensory stimuli from thoracic and abdominal viscera, it sends motor fibers to tongue, heart, smooth muscle of lungs, and most abdominal organs.
11. Spinal-Accessory nerve (motor)—innervates vocal organs and back muscles.
12. Hypoglossal nerve (motor)—controls muscles of the tongue.

Thus, we conclude a brief presentation of the Peripheral Nervous System, including the somatic and ANS branches and the peripheral nerves, both spinal and cranial. Now that we have considered briefly the anatomy and physiology of the nervous system, and ways of recording brain activity, we are ready for a description of experimental studies. Chapter 3 introduces you to studies of EEG and behavior.

REFERENCES

Beatty, J., Greenberg, A., Deibler, W. P., & O'Hanlon, J. F. (1974). Operant control of theta rhythm affects performance in a radar monitoring task. *Science, 183,* 871–873.
Brazier, M. A. B. (1957). Rise of neurophysiology in the 19th century. *Journal of Neurophysiology, 20,* 212–226.

Brown, B. (1974). *New mind, new body, biofeedback: New directions for the mind*. New York: Harper & Row.

Callaway, E. (1975). *Brain electrical potentials and individual psychological differences*. New York: Grune & Stratton.

Carlson, N. R. (1980). *Physiology of behavior* (2nd ed.). Boston: Allyn & Bacon.

Elul, R. (1972). Randomness and synchrony in the generation of the electroencephalogram. In H. Petsche & M. A. B. Brazier (Eds.), *Synchronization of EEG activity in epilepsies* (pp. 59–77). New York: Springer-Verlag.

Evans, C. C. (1952). Comments on: "Occipital sharp waves responsive to visual stimuli." *Electroencephalography and Clinical Neurophysiology, 4*, 111.

Gardner, E. (1975). *Fundamentals of neurology*. Philadelphia: Saunders.

Gastaut, H. (1952). Etude electrocorticographique de la reactivite des rhthmes rolandiques. *Revue Neurologique, 87*, 176–182.

Gastaut, Y. (1951). Un signe electroencephalographique peu conne: Les pointes occipitales survenant pendant 1 ouverture des yeux. *Revue neurologique, 84*, 640–643.

Grossman, S. P. (1973). *Essentials of physiological psychology*. New York: Wiley.

Jasper, H. H. (1958). Report of the committee on methods of clinical examination in electroencephalography. *Electroencephalography and Clinical Neurophysiology, 10*, 370–375.

Kennedy, J. L., Gottsdanker, R. M., Armington, J. C., & Gray, F. E. (1948). A new electroencephalogram associated with thinking. *Science, 108*, 527–529.

Koshino, Y., & Neidermeyer, E. (1976). Enhancement of rolandic mu rhythm by pattern vision. *Electroencephalography and Clinical Neurophysiology, 38*, 535–538.

Maulsby, R. L. (1971). An illustration of emotionally evoked theta rhythm in infancy: Hedonic hypersynchrony. *Electroencephalography and Clinical Neurophysiology, 31*,157–165.

Noback, D. R., & Demarest, R. J. (1975). *The human nervous system*. New York: McGraw-Hill.

Porges, S. W., & Coles, G. H. (1976). *Psychophysiology*. Stroudsberg, PA: Dowden, Hutchinson & Ross.

Walter, W. G. (1953). *The living brain*. New York: Norton.

Williamson, S. J., & Kaufman, L. (1981). Biomagnetism. *Journal of Magnetism & Magnetic Materials, 22*, 129–202.

3

The EEG and Behavior: Motor and Mental Activities

Many long-time EEG researchers still experience a degree of fascination and awe as they watch the pens of their physiological recorders trace out the patterns of electrical activity occurring at that instant of time in the human brain. It is very difficult to convey to an audience or a reader the sense of wonderment experienced as the pens vibrate and quiver to the changing frequencies and amplitudes of the various kinds of brain waves. From the very beginning, the fascinating nature of EEG activity made it very tempting for scientists to study relationships of this measure to behavior. Some kinds of relationships, which seemed very logical at first, have proved very elusive to establish. One example is the effort expended in attempts to relate intelligence to EEG activity. No doubt this has been due, at least in part, to the tremendous complexity of the brain itself, and to difficulties in the interpretation of large masses of EEG data. Nevertheless, researchers have pursued questions of brainwave–behavior relationships, and a great deal of effort has been expended on this topic.

This chapter explores the effect that cognitive and physical activities have on EEG waveforms. Variations in EEG that occur with the movements involved in reaction time and other motor activities are discussed first, and then the question of whether intelligence can be determined from EEG patterns is considered. Spatial abilities and right–left hemispheric asymmetries as related to EEG measures are discussed in later sections of this chapter. A consideration of environmental factors affecting EEG activity is presented in Appendix I.

MOTOR PERFORMANCE AND THE EEG

This section first examines the relationships between EEG recordings and simple motor reaction time. Then, under the subheading of Visuomotor Performance, we consider EEGs measured simultaneously with more complex motor performance, requiring continuous eye and hand coordination.

Reaction Time

In their classic book *Experimental Psychology,* Woodworth and Schlosberg (1954) noted that reaction time (RT) includes the time it takes for a sense organ to react to some stimulus, brain processing time, nerve time (to carry impulses to and from the brain), and muscle time (the time for muscles to contract and move some external object). One of the most common RT experiments involves one stimulus and one response (simple RT). For example, a light comes on and a subject is requested to press a response key as soon as the light is seen. The interval between the onset of the light and the response is timed to the nearest thousandth of a second and constitutes the RT in milliseconds (msec).

Some investigators have related speed of reaction to EEG activation (Lansing, Schwartz, & Lindsley, 1959). Because alpha activity is associated with relaxed wakefulness, typically with eyes closed, the desynchronization, or blocking, of alpha with stimulation is called EEG activation. When EEG activation occurs, alpha is replaced by low amplitude, high frequency beta activity. Lansing and his colleagues recorded RTs to a visual stimulus and found that RTs were significantly faster when alpha block occurred before the visual stimulus was presented. The alpha block was produced by warning signals presented shortly before the stimulus. They interpreted both the faster RT and the alpha block in terms of an alerted state produced through action of the ascending reticular activation system (ARAS). More recent studies have indicated that the alpha blocking and faster RTs may not be related to each other, but instead may be independently related to the warning signal that produces a preparatory set to react (Leavitt, 1968; Thompson & Botwinick, 1966). Leavitt (1968) has rejected the concept that faster reactions were caused by a unitary arousal system such as the ARAS and suggested instead that several neural processes underlie the relation between the point in time at which the warning signal occurs and the speed of reaction. He found that when a warning signal appeared 500 msec before the stimulus, the quickest RTs occurred, along with maximal desynchronization of the EEG. At different foreperiods of 200, 1500, and 4000 msec, however, the degree of alpha desynchronization was not related to speed of reaction. There were times, in fact, when RT was similar whether the percentage of alpha desynchronization was 0% or 56%.

Thompson and Botwinick (1968) measured the RTs and EEGs of people between the ages of 19 and 35 and compared these to those of a group between 62 and 87 years old. They found that the younger group responded more quickly than the older group, but the groups did not differ in EEG desynchronization.

In a series of developmental studies, Surwillo (1968, 1971a, 1971b, 1974) has found relationships between speed of response and period of the EEG. Period of the EEG is defined by the total number of waves recorded in the interval of time between the stimulus and the response. The average duration (period) of these waves is obtained by dividing the number of waves into the length of the interval. Thus, if the stimulus–response interval is 1.0 sec and EEG frequency is 10 cps, the EEG period is 0.1. Therefore, EEG period becomes smaller as EEG frequency increases. Surwillo (1968) reasoned that, because behavior and CNS activity occur at the same time, they should be examined at identical moments. He reported that RTs became slower and more variable in old age, and he interpreted this as being due to slower brain processes that can be measured by period of the EEG. Slowing of EEG as a function of old age was reported by Hubbard, Sunde, and Goldensohn (1976). In his 1971 study, Surwillo (1971a) measured EEG period and correlated this with RT of 110 boys ranging in age from approximately 4 to 17 years. One task used was disjunctive RT, in which the subject had to decide whether or not to respond to two auditory stimuli, according to a predetermined criterion. The other task used was simple RT to an auditory stimulus. Increases in the EEG period were associated with slower RTs.

The time it took to make a movement to a sound, as well as simple auditory RT, was measured along with EEG period by Surwillo (1974). The movement time (MT) was the time it took the subject to leave a contact and touch a target 28 cm away. The subjects were boys between the ages of 9 and 17. Both RT and MT decreased with age. The RT was found to be faster when EEG period was shorter, thus confirming the results of Surwillo's earlier studies. MT was not related to EEG period, however, suggesting that frequency of the EEG could not account for more gross motor response time. In addition, there was no relation between MT and RT, a finding that also indicates different types of motor processes for a few small muscles as compared to a larger group of bigger muscles. Another laboratory (Sersen, Clausen, & Lidsky, 1982) has reported a significant relationship between EEG frequency and RT in the interval between stimulus and response, in agreement with Surwillo's findings. Surwillo (1975) has hypothesized that speed of information processing is a function of a "cortical gating signal" that can be measured by EEG period. It is assumed that the frequency of the EEG determines the frequency of the gating signal. This concept would predict a strong relationship between speed of RT and EEG frequency at the moment of stimulation, a very testable hypothesis.

The positive relationship between RT and EEG observed by Surwillo has been obtained when the EEG period was used as the measure of CNS activity. Studies reporting no relation between EEG and RT (Leavitt, 1968; Thompson & Botwinick, 1966, 1968) used degree of alpha desynchronization; for example, a 50% decrease in the amplitude of the alpha rhythm for more than 200 msec (Leavitt, 1968). In fact, when Surwillo (1972) used a measure similar to alpha desynchronization, namely, blocking latency of the EEG (the time it took EEG to drop in amplitude when stimulation occurred), he found no relationship between the EEG and RT. Thus, while degree of alpha desynchronization may not be related to RT, other measures such as EEG period, EEG half waves (Surwillo, 1975), and average alpha frequency (Creutzfeldt et al., 1976) are related.

The following illustrates EEG Period:

$$\frac{\text{Stimulus-Response Interval}}{\text{\# of EEG waves}} = \frac{.4 \text{ sec}}{4 \text{ waves}} = .10$$

$$\text{or} = \frac{.4 \text{ sec}}{8 \text{ waves}} = .05$$

shorter period = faster RT

Visuomotor Performance

The study of RT concerns a simple abrupt type of motion. Most movements involve more complex and continuous kinds of motor adjustments also involving the visual system. A study of EEG during motor activity was conducted by Khrizman (1973), in 2- and 3-year-olds. The tasks involved continuous finger tapping and arranging checkers in rows according to color. The EEG was recorded from frontal, motor, parietal, temporal, and occipital placements. In the tapping task, the motor cortex showed the highest frequency and amplitude correlations with the lower parietal regions, whereas the checker arrangement task produced the highest correlations between the motor and frontal areas. The high motor–frontal correlations might be interpreted in terms of coordination of motor and cognitive (checker arrangement) activities believed to be a frontal lobe function. The high parietal–motor correlation (tapping task) suggests cooperation between two brain areas for a task involving a low level of eye–hand coordination.

The use of computer analyses has enabled investigators to derive a measure of relationship between two areas of EEG recording. One such derivation is the coherence function (COH). Thus, when measuring EEG from a number of sites, a high COH from two of the locations suggests that they are functionally and/or structurally connected. In one study using COH, Busk and Galbraith (1975) analyzed EEGs from over four areas of the brain while 15 male subjects performed three motor tasks (eye tracking, hand tracking, and eye–hand tracking). The EEG was recorded from over the visual cortex (Oz), left and right motor areas (C_3 and C_4), and premotor cortex (Fz). Sites that showed the highest COH scores corresponded to areas with greatest anatomical connections, whereas electrode combinations with low COH were areas with fewest anatomical connections. In addition, the more difficult the task, the greater the increase in COH measures. This is an interesting finding, because it indicates an increase in required cooperation between two cortical motor areas when the task is more complicated. Possible criticisms of this study are that the EEG was contaminated by eye movement and muscle artifact. In a follow-up study to further investigate COH as a measure of functional connectivity and to examine reference and artifact effects, Ford, Goethe, and Dekker (1986) measured COH during a continuous movement task. These investigators reasoned that if a person moves the right hand, for example, increased COH should be observed over the contralateral motor areas (left hemisphere) compared to the motor areas not controlling the movement (right hemisphere). This is what they found at motor and premotor sites, especially for the 9–12 Hz EEG band. Increased COH values were most apparent for the cortical areas known to be involved (frontal, premotor, and motor). The use of a right earlobe reference for right hemisphere sites and left earlobe for left hemisphere placements did not seem to effect the results. However, it would have been more convincing if Ford et al. had used linked ears as an additional reference. The purposeful production of eye and muscle artifact by subjects led to lowered COH values. Thus, if anything, the Busk and Galbraith results would have been stronger if these had been more carefully controlled.

It has been demonstrated that COH measures can differentiate the mu rhythm from coexisting alpha activity. Mu can be masked by alpha because it is of low amplitude and in a similar frequency band.

The EEG patterns from bilateral temporal and occipital placements were obtained for skilled rifle marksmen in the period just before the trigger was pulled (Hatfield, Landers, & Ray, 1984). The task consisted of firing 40 shots at a target 50 feet away using the standing position. Analyses of three consecutive 2.5 sec EEG samples just prior to pulling the trigger revealed a significant shift toward right hemisphere activity as the time to fire approached. The authors suggested that the shift to right hemisphere dominance may be indicative of the subject's ability to suppress left hemisphere processes. They pointed out that many coaches and sports theorists believe that covert verbal self-instruction (left-hemisphere process) can disrupt athletic performance at higher levels of skilled performance. Further, they stressed, a visual image of the desired performance is preferable to verbal instruction. In another study of EEGs in skilled motor performance, Sterman (1984) measured EEGs during a flight simulation task. The experiment was carried out in a mock-up of an F-16 fighter cockpit in which subjects used a joystick to achieve a series of flight paths in a video-simulated flight. The subjects were tested over a 6-hour period with six 45-minute "flights" being alternated with six 15-minute rest periods. Sterman found that task engagement was associated with greater activity in central cortical areas, with a decrease in parietal–occipital activity. Conversely, greater parietal–occipital activity was observed during rest periods. Increased central activity in the 8–11 Hz range was associated with better performance. The author believes that such EEG information could be used to track both alertness and competency of pilots during flight.

In summary, demonstrations of relationships between EEG and RT seem to depend on the method of measuring EEG. In particular, Surwillo's technique of measuring EEG period during the stimulus–response interval has been successful, whereas the use of alpha desynchronization as a measure has produced equivocal results. EEG coherence measures offer another way of examining possible functional and anatomical relationships between different brain areas.

Increases in COH scores seem to be greatest from cortical areas most likely to be involved in a given task. Measures of EEG during skilled visuo-motor performance have yielded interesting results that have possible implications for training in those skills or in monitoring proficiency.

EEG AND MENTAL ACTIVITY

In this section, we consider research bearing on the controversial question regarding the relationship between EEG and intelligence, the intriguing findings with respect to EEG correlates of verbal and spatial performance, and some reports of EEG, hypnosis, and imagery.

EEG and Intelligence (The Search for a Culture-Free Test)

The Binet-Simon intelligence scale appeared in 1905 as an instrument to classify mentally retarded children for the purpose of educating them in the school system of Paris. This test included items related to judgment, comprehension, and reasoning, because Binet considered these as essential components of intelligence. The test also included some sensory and perceptual items, but was heavily weighted with verbal content. The Binet-Simon test and its two revisions served as a model for many tests that followed, including the well-known American version, the Stanford-Binet. One criticism that has been leveled at tests of the Binet-Simon mold is that they are not "culture free." Living in some subcultures rather than others affects scores on these traditional intelligence tests because of at least some dependence on information learned in educational or urban settings that might be unavailable to less educated or rural populations. Attempts to develop culture-free tests have included using items that not only make very little use of language, but that are not dependent on symbols and information of a given culture. However, psychologists have found it difficult to construct tests that are completely culture-free. At first blush, the EEG might appear to be a completely culture-free technique for assessing intelligence in a manner that would not discriminate against culturally deprived persons. The reasoning might go something like this: The brain is the seat of biological intelligence, the EEG represents brain activity, therefore one should be able to predict intelligence from EEG patterns, including amplitude and frequency. Regardless of how logical (or illogical) this argument might seem, the correlation of EEG and intelligence has proven to be a very elusive endeavor, to say the least.

After many years of research, the question of the relationship between EEG and intelligence (usually measured by intelligence test scores) is still controversial. The literature on this question was reviewed by Lindsley (1944), and it covered studies conducted in the 1930s and early 1940s. At the time of his review, Lindsley concluded that most of the studies indicated no relationship between EEG and intelligence. A review of the literature by Ellingson (1956) covered the years between 1944 and 1956. In it, he also concluded that the available evidence did not establish a relation between EEG and intellectual performance. Vogel and Broverman (1964) argued that although no significant relationships had been found between EEG and intelligence for normal adults, such a relationship had been shown for children, mentally retarded persons, geriatric patients, and brain-damaged patients. Ellingson (1966) reviewed the Vogel and Broverman conclusions and reported that the evidence for children and mentally retarded individuals was contradictory and inconclusive; in addition, with regard to geriatric and brain-injured patients, he noted that EEG abnormality and decreased intellectual capacity are both effects of organic brain disorder. That is, the EEG does not reflect intelligence but instead reflects decreased CNS functioning in brain-damaged and geriatric patients. Vogel and Broverman (1966) made an effective reply to Ellingson's critique and accused him of inhibiting EEG research in this area. They pointed out that there are competent and well-designed replications that support an EEG–intelligence relationship, and they accused Ellingson of minimizing the positive results.

Thus, it appears that the bulk of evidence amassed up to the late 1960s indicated a stalemate regarding the relation between EEG and intelligence. Let us examine a few of the more recent research efforts to see whether there have been any changes in this situation.

Surwillo (1971a) has criticized some of the positive findings with respect to EEG and intelligence on the basis that studies either did not control for age of the subjects or that the EEG was, in most instances, recorded when the subject was "resting" and not engaged in the task that was the measure of intelligence. One such task is the digit span of the Wechsler Intelligence Scale for Children (WISC), which tests ability to hold information in short-term mental storage. In digit span, lists of digits are presented, and the subject is asked to repeat them exactly or in a reverse order. Seventy-nine normal boys ranging in age from $4\frac{1}{2}$ years to 17 years were the subjects. The EEG period was based on recordings from occipital and parietal leads during the interval when digits were presented. Correlations between digit span length and EEG frequency were in the expected direction. The greater the digit span, or capacity for short-term storage of information, the higher the EEG frequencies. When age was held constant, through a technique known as partial correlation, the relationship disappeared. Surwillo concluded that there was no evidence that digit span and EEG frequency were related in normal children.

In another approach, Surwillo (1971b) recorded EEGs from over the parietal and occipital cortex while subjects performed the digit span (backwards) test. The EEG period was examined from O_1-P_3 (left hemisphere) and O_2-P_4 (right hemisphere) and compared. When longer lists were processed, the EEG periods from right and left hemispheres were more alike than when shorter lists were processed. In addition, subjects who were capable of processing longer lists of digits showed more synchrony between EEG of the two hemispheres than subjects who did not do as well. Thus, Surwillo seems to have support for the hypothesis that when increased EEG synchrony between the hemispheres occurs, a greater amount of information is being processed.

In one of the better-conceived studies, Giannitrapani (1969) reported that a frequency asymmetry score correlated significantly with verbal, performance, and total IQ scores in the Wechsler Adult Intelligence Scale (WAIS). He measured average EEG frequencies from frontal, parietal, occipital, and temporal sites during mental multiplication and correlated these with intelligence test performance (WAIS). A relationship was found between EEG frequency and full-scale IQ scores, because higher frequencies went with higher IQ. This was especially true for EEG frequency from left hemisphere (parietal) derivations. Griesel (1973) investigated the relationship between EEG frequency and period and several tests of intellectual ability. The tests measured mental alertness (numerical, verbal, and reasoning ability), information processing, and ability to think analytically (Gottschaldt Figures Test). The results indicated no relationship between the intelligence test scores and the EEG frequency or period measures.

Maxwell, Fenwick, Fenton, and Dollimore (1974) evaluated the EEG spectra (analysis based on amplitudes of the EEG at various frequencies) of 150 children (mean age of 7 years) for whom they had intelligence test scores. The children were divided into two groups, below average and above average in reading. The EEG analysis resulted in the conclusion that the poor readers used larger portions of their brain than the good readers; that is, they exerted more physiological effort to less effect. To test the hypothesis that EEG spectrum analysis would differ for poor and good readers, two new groups of subjects were tested. The subjects were 52 good readers and 52 poor readers, all of whom were 14 years of age. EEG spectrum analysis for the two groups confirmed that power generated by the poor readers was greater for all EEG frequencies measured than that of the good readers. They suggested that more neurons are used by the less proficient individual in a cognitive task, resulting in the larger EEG amplitudes observed. One might ask whether this finding can be related to that of Busk and Galbraith (1975), namely that greater amounts of EEG synchrony occurred between cortical areas in the performance of a difficult tracking task as compared to an easy one (reading could be regarded as a difficult task for the poor readers). Also, Surwillo (1971b) noted more EEG synchrony between the two hemispheres when subjects were processing longer, more difficult lists of numbers.

Positive correlations between EEG parameters and intelligence test scores were reported for separate groups of 25 mildly retarded (IQ 50–70) and 31 normal children by Gasser, Von Lucadov-Muller, Verleger, and Bacher (1983). The EEG was recorded via 8 unipolar leads overlying frontal, central, parietal, and occipital areas. The tests used were the Columbia Mental Maturity scale and the Wechsler Intelligence Scale for Children (WISC-verbal subscale). One of their findings was that children with more mature EEG (e.g., less delta and more theta) had higher test scores. Further, the correlations were higher for the mildly retarded than for normal subjects. They suggest that a certain proportion of mildly retarded children have deviant brain function that is causally related to intellectual subnormality.

In summary, it seems that the several recent studies reviewed do not completely resolve the impasse regarding the relationship between EEG and intelligence, but they offer some hope for refining future approaches. One promising approach may involve the comparison of EEG activity from both right and left hemispheres and noting the relationship of the two hemispheres to intellectual performance. This approach resulted in two of the positive findings reported (Giannitrapani, 1969; Surwillo, 1971b). Perhaps new or more complete methods of analysis will lead to more positive results in the future. The positive results obtained by Gasser et al. (1983) were partly attributed to computer analyses of multiple scalp sites that enabled detailed examination of EEG in frequency bands ranging from delta to beta. Gale and Edwards (1983b) made a number of suggestions for improving methodology of brain activity–intelligence studies. They recommended the use of more than one IQ test, multiple EEG recording sites, heterogeneous subject populations representing the full ability range, controlling for age and gender as variables, and blind scoring techniques so that experimenters are not aware of the IQ scores of those whose brain records are under examination until completion of data analyses. They suggested these and several other procedures to avoid errors in method and interpretation. These are the kinds of steps that would be necessary to give the EEG–intelligence work a firmer basis for either acceptance or rejection. It should be noted that the amount of EEG research in this area seems to be decreasing, perhaps because of the interest generated in the late 1960s and the 1970s in relating the averaged evoked cortical potential to intelligence, a development that is discussed in a subsequent chapter.

A final note concerns a caution advanced by Satterfield, Cantwell, Saul, and Usin (1974) that EEG abnormalities may not be a good criterion for the placement of children in special education programs. When they compared the WISC scores of 22 hyperactive young boys, considered to have abnormal EEGs, with those of 63 hyperactive boys with normal EEGs, they found that those with abnormal patterns scored significantly higher (WISC full-scale scores of 106 compared to a mean of 98). This finding would seem to justify their cautionary note.

Hemispheric Asymmetries in the EEG

The past two decades have witnessed increased interest in possible functional differences between the left and right hemispheres of the brain. This interest, among both the general population and scientists alike, was stimulated by work in the late 1960s of Sperry and his associates with patients who had their two hemispheres disconnected by surgery to alleviate epileptic seizures (e.g., see Sperry 1982). The work dramatically showed that the left hemisphere was specialized for language functions, whereas the right hemisphere processed spatial information more efficiently. Non-invasive techniques were required to extend these findings to normal populations, and so measures such as EEG and event-related potentials were increasingly used to determine whether various stimuli and tasks would result in differential hemisphere activity and performance differences. The abundance of research on EEG hemispheric asymmetries reflects the fascination of scientists with this topic. Some reliable findings have emerged while others have been fleeting. This EEG section reviews representative studies in the area and presents conclusions that seem to be warranted at this time. However, before beginning the discussion of EEG studies, it is important to note that purely behavioral studies have paralleled those using brain activity. These studies have emphasized performance differences based on type of stimuli presented to the left or right hemisphere. For example, it has been reported that people can better identify words presented to the left hemisphere as compared to the right hemisphere. The method of selective stimulation of either hemisphere makes use of the fact that the visual system is organized in a "crossed" manner, such that stimuli presented to the right of a central fixation point (right visual field) project initially to the left hemisphere. This type of stimulation of left or right visual field has led to an advantage in terms of shorter brain response in the hemisphere contralateral to the field of stimulation (see Andreassi, Stern, & Okamura, 1975). Similarly, auditory verbal stimuli have been found to be more effectively processed when presented to the right ear, a finding due to the fact that each ear has dominant projections to the contralateral hemisphere. Thus, behavioral studies in normal individuals have indicated hemispheric specialization. Studies that can show both EEG and performance differences can make even a stronger argument for lateralization of function.

It has long been known that EEG activity becomes desynchronized, that is, higher in frequency and lower in amplitude, with the onset of mental activity (Ellingson, 1956). This activation of the EEG has been used as an indicant of cerebral involvement in processing information. In a study by Robbins and McAdam (1974), asymmetry was studied for identical stimuli presented in ways expected to activate one or the other of the hemispheres. Subjects were asked to respond to identical pictures in three different ways: (a) to generate visual images of scenes shown; (b) to compose a letter about the pictures; (c) to generate images and write a letter about the pictures. It was reported that when visual images alone were generated, the right hemisphere showed more activity. This reversed for letter composition, with the left hemisphere registering greater involvement. The combination of the imagery and verbal tasks produced similar activity in the two hemispheres. Hemispheric asymmetry of EEG patterns was studied while subjects performed either verbal or spatial tasks (Galin & Ornstein,

1972). The results showed that right hemispheric involvement was greater in the spatial task, and left hemispheric participation was dominant during verbal activities. This finding of Galin and Ornstein was confirmed and extended by McKee, Humphrey, and McAdam (1973). They found that lower amplitude EEG activity was present (more involvement) in recordings from the right hemisphere when persons performed a musical task (detecting a theme in an unfamiliar Bach concerto). When a linguistic task was used, lower amplitude EEGs were observed from left-hemisphere recordings.

Research findings have indicated that musical activities are a function of the right hemisphere. However, it has been suggested that musically trained individuals process music more analytically (left hemisphere) than nontrained persons. To examine this possibility further, Davidson and Schwartz (1977) measured EEGs of musically trained persons and those who had never received music instruction in an experiment that required all subjects to whistle, sing, and talk each of three songs. They found that nonmusically trained subjects showed a significantly greater activation of the right hemisphere while whistling the melody of a song versus speaking the lyrics of the song, as compared to musically trained persons. The musicians had similar patterns of hemispheric activation for the whistle and talk conditions. They showed EEG in the form of a ratio: R-L/R+L, in which R and L refer to amounts of alpha activity produced in right and left hemispheres. Higher numbers in this score indicate greater relative left-hemisphere activity. The results indicate that individuals show different patterns of brain activity, to an identical task, depending on their training. Musically trained subjects listened to the melody analytically, thus making it a left-hemisphere task rather than a right-hemisphere function. The authors suggest that long-term training in a cognitive skill, such as reading and playing music, may be accompanied by permanent changes in brain activity.

Instead of assuming in advance that a particular task would produce verbal or visuospatial processes in subjects, Ehrlichman and Wiener (1980) had their subjects make ratings of mental processes actually used while doing a variety of tasks. They found that EEG asymmetry was related to verbal processes, but not to visual imagery. Because recordings were made from over temporal and parietal areas, the authors suggest that verbal processes may be a more important influence on EEG asymmetry at these brain areas than are visual imagery processes. They also made the point that the asymmetry was observed in the absence of external stimuli or motor responses. This was in response to a criticism of Gevins et al. (1979) that the major factor in task-dependent changes in EEG asymmetry are uncontrolled perceptual and motor differences between the tasks employed to engage the two hemispheres. In support of the contention by Gevins and colleagues, Rugg and Dickens (1982) observed no asymmetries in alpha activity for visuospatial or verbal tasks in the absence of motor responses. However, theta activity was greater in the right hemisphere during the visuospatial as opposed to the verbal task. Further, this difference between tasks in right-hemisphere theta correlated significantly with level of visuospatial performance.

There is some evidence that the two hemispheres show asymmetries to stimuli associated with emotional reactions. In one study, subjects rated degree of positive or negative feelings produced by a film as EEG was measured from over frontal and parietal areas of both hemispheres (Davidson, Schwartz, Saron, Bennett, & Goleman, 1979). Stimuli rated as producing positive feelings produced more left hemisphere activity from the frontal lobes. Asymmetries over parietal lobes did not discriminate between positive and negative feelings. The authors attributed their findings to the extensive anatomical connections that exist between frontal lobes and subcortical limbic system structures important in emotional expression. A follow-up study by Davidson and Fox (1982) led to observations of similar patterns of brain response in 10-month-old infants watching a video tape of an actress portraying sad and happy facial expressions. Tucker and Dawson (1984) designed an experiment to examine differential hemispheric involvement in two emotional states, sexual arousal and depression. The EEG was obtained from left and right frontal, central, occipital, and parietal locations as "method" actors recalled personal experiences to create states of depression or sexual arousal. The results showed greater right-hemisphere activity for sexual arousal than for depression. In addition, COH measures showed higher theta coherence in right central and posterior regions during sexual arousal. This increased theta COH during arousal may be consistent with a reported increase in right hemispheric theta activity during orgasm (Cohen, Rosen, & Goldstein, 1976).

In summary, recent evidence strongly supports the contention that the type of mental activity differentially affects the two hemispheres of the brain, as indicated by EEG measures. The consensus is that the right hemisphere is involved to a greater extent than the left in the performance of spatial and musical tasks, while semantic, verbal, and mathematical tasks primarily involve the left hemisphere. Exceptions may arise, as in the case of musically trained individuals in whom the analytic information processing of music may transform music related activities into a left-hemisphere function. Available data indicate that the two hemispheres are specialized for different emotional reactions. Davidson (1983) drew on the speculation of Kinsbourne in his suggestion that the basis for hemispheric specialization for emotional response is approach/avoidance. That is, approach (positive reaction) is associated with relatively greater left frontal lobe activation, whereas avoidance (negative reaction) produces relatively greater right frontal activity.

In an interesting approach, Gevins et al. (1983) have reported the use of multi-scalp locations, single trial analyses, and extensive intercorrelation techniques in experiments that show rapid changes in the side and site of localized brain processes during task performance. Their subjects performed in a visuospatial task that required that they make a movement to complete it. The results showed that during the early part of the response (100 to 200 msec after initiation), brain activity is similar in both hemispheres; shortly after (around 300 msec), a right-hemisphere focus occurs as subjects perform the spatial task.

Finally (approximately 400–600 msec), there is a left hemisphere focus as the right-handed subjects make the required motor response. What Gevins and associates are saying is that lateralization occurs, but that it is sometimes fleeting. Furthermore, extremely rapid sampling and sophisticated analytic techniques may be required to observe these quick shifts between hemispheres and the changes in hemispheric activities that reflect the task changes. Thus, it appears safe to conclude that hemispheric specialization does exist. This is shown in differential brain activity and performance when appropriate material is processed by the appropriate hemisphere. The relationship is not always as predicted, due to individual differences in skill, degree of laterality, and interpretation of the task by subjects. In the final analysis, even though each hemisphere has its special functions, the entire brain must work as a unit in the processing of stimuli and the preparation of an optimal response.

EEG, Hypnosis, Imagery, and Meditation

Hypnosis.   The phenomenon of hypnosis holds a strange fascination for most people. Mention of the word "hypnosis" might conjur up images of the stage hypnotist who causes a subject to go into a trance and do strange things, such as regression to an early stage of childhood or supporting someone's weight while lying stretched across two chairs! For many years it had been thought that hypnosis was some type of sleep during which a person could carry out suggestions. Most contemporary evidence, however, favors the view that hypnosis is actually a modification of the waking state, with all the EEG characteristics that are indicative of such a state. The question of the relationship between EEG and hypnotic susceptibility has been investigated by a number of researchers. For example, London, Hart, and Leibovitz (1968) reported greater amounts of alpha activity among subjects who scored high on a test of hypnotic susceptibility. Galbraith, London, Leibovitz, Cooper, and Hart (1970) examined this question further in a study of 59 volunteer subjects. Scores on the Harvard Group Hypnotic Susceptibility Scale (HGS) and EEG from frontal, parietal, occipital, and temporal leads were recorded. The findings supported the previous ones regarding a relationship between EEG and hypnotic susceptibility, because subjects with high HGS scores produced more alpha activity than those with low scores, especially under an "eyes open" condition. Galbraith and his collaborators suggested that the common factor between hypnotic susceptibility and the high alpha amplitude with eyes open is "attention." Subjects with high HGS scores may be better able to attend to hypnotic suggestions among competing stimuli, thereby shutting out distracting stimuli of various kinds. Morgan, MacDonald, and Hilgard (1974) also found that persons who were highly susceptible to hypnosis produced more alpha activity during task performance and hypnosis than those who were less susceptible. MacLeod-Morgan (1982) measured EEGs of persons scoring high and low on hypnotizability while they rested, when under hypnosis, and when given a right-hemisphere task during hypnosis. The 41 highly hypnotizable persons shifted from greater left hemisphere activity during rest to a right hemisphere bias during hypnosis, a change that was even stronger with the dream task. The low hypnotizables did not show this significant shift from left to right hemisphere activity. Thus, it appears that hypnosis involves the right hemisphere more than the left. In another study, MacLeod-Morgan and Lack (1982) provided evidence that highly hypnotizable persons also show greater shifts in EEG when performing verbal or spatial tasks; and this is especially true for tasks that are continuous rather than discontinuous. The authors suggest that low and high hypnotizables show different EEGs in focused attention and tasks involving hemispheric specialties. In these tasks, high hypnotizables seem to show greater degrees of focused cortical activation.

Imagery. The word "imagery" is often used in reference to visual scenes pictured in "the mind's eye." However, imagery can also refer to other sensory experiences such as sounds, tastes, touches, and smells. In an EEG study involving imagery, a "vividness" scale was given to 71 undergraduates to assess degree of visual, auditory, and kinesthetic imagery (Gale, Morris, Lucas, & Richardson, 1972). Then, while EEG was recorded from the occipital area, subjects responded to instructions designed to produce minimal imagery, passive elicited imagery, voluntary elicited imagery, and autonomous voluntary imagery. The minimal imagery condition involved relaxing with eyes open or closed. In the passive elicited imagery task, 10 high-imagery words (e.g., acrobat) and 10 low-imagery words (e.g., answer) were presented and subjects were instructed to "see if the words suggest mental pictures." The elicited imagery task required subjects to move a circle and a triangle around in their minds. Imagining the activities of a family (father, mother, and two small children) on a beach over a 2-minute period constituted the autonomous imagery task. The most clear-cut result was the decrease in alpha activity during all of the imagery tasks except the minimal imagery one. The EEG of weak and vivid imagers was differentiated by alpha frequency under the eyes-open condition; that is, it was significantly higher for the vivid imagers as compared to weak imagers. Experimental studies of imagery and EEG have been few in number. One problem is that it is difficult to quantify the type of imagery generated in different people by the same instructions. Other problems have included an insufficient number of EEG recording sites and the lack of a systematic research approach (Gale & Edwards, 1983a). It is unfortunate that this is the current state of EEG–imagery affairs, because basic information is needed concerning imaginal processes and brain activity, for both practical and theoretical reasons.

Meditation. In a study of physiological changes during meditation, Elson, Hauri, and Cunis (1977) matched a group of regular meditators with nonmeditating control subjects. The EEGs of both groups were measured over a 40-minute period, during which the controls were instructed to remain "wakefully relaxed" for 40 minutes, while the others meditated for the same amount of time. The meditators remained in a relatively stable state of alpha and theta EEG activity, and none fell asleep. However, six of the controls fell asleep during the experiment as indicated by K-complexes and spindles in their EEG records. The results indicate that meditation produces a physiological effect different from that produced in nonmeditating controls who try to relax with eyes closed for the same length of time. On the other hand, no difference in EEG responses to tone stimuli were found for a group of 17 meditators and a group of 17 control subjects (Heide, 1986). In Heide's study, experimental subjects were asked to meditate for 20 minutes while controls were asked to sit quietly for 20 minutes without falling asleep. The 1,000 Hz tones were at a sound level of 80dB and were presented on the average of once a minute. The two groups did not differ in duration of alpha desynchronization to stimuli or in time to habituate to the tones. Clearly, the lack of differences between the two groups in the Heide study was due to the auditory stimulation, which obviously intruded to an equal degree for meditators and nonmeditators.

The recording of EEG during hypnosis, meditation, and imagery is a potentially rich source of information because it can give us information that will enable us to differentiate among these states. One interesting finding concerns the greater amount of alpha activity produced by highly hypnotizable persons compared to low hypnotizables under a variety of conditions. This high degree of alpha has been related to attentive ability by at least one investigative team (Galbraith et al., 1970). The greater shift to right hemisphere activity for highly hypnotizable persons suggests a degree of hemispheric specialization for hypnosis. The evidence reviewed with respect to imagery is less clear, but it suggests that EEG does change according to type of mental activity, regardless of whether these are produced by imposed or naturally occurring mental events. Gale and Edwards (1983a) noted a decline in EEG studies of imagery in recent years and suggested that the reason for this is that researchers have not progressed much beyond observing effects that occur with different kinds of imagery. There have been few attempts to predict and theorize. They also pointed out that most studies of EEG and imagery have not used multiple recording sites on the head, nor have they studied a wide range of variables in a systematic fashion. These criticisms can be leveled at EEG studies in general, not only those of imagery. On the positive side, EEG evidence seems to establish meditation as a state that is different from hypnosis, autosuggestion, or sleep.

The next chapter covers EEG measures taken under different conditions of sensory stimulation, attention, and perception. Conditioning of the EEG and patterns of EEG in a variety of sleep studies are also presented in chapter 4.

REFERENCES

Busk, J., & Galbraith, G. C. (1975). Electroencephalography of visual–motor practice in man. *Electroencephalography and Clinical Neurophysiology, 38,* 415–422.

Cohen, H. D., Rosen, R. C., & Goldstein, I. (1976). Electroencephalographic laterality changes during human sexual orgasm. *Archives of Sexual Behavior, 5,* 189.

Creutzfeldt, O. D., Arnold, P. M., Becker, D., Langenstein, S., Tirsch, W., Wilhelm, H., & Wuttke, W. (1976). EEG changes during spontaneous and controlled menstrual cycles and their correlations with psychological performance. *Electroencephalography and Clinical Neurophysiology, 40,* 113–131.

Davidson, R. J. (1983). Hemispheric specialization for cognition and affect. In A. Gale & J. Edwards (Eds.), *Physiological correlates of behavior: Vol. 2: Attention and performance* (pp. 203–216). New York: Academic Press.

Davidson, R. J., & Fox, N. A. (1982). Asymmetrical brain activity discriminates between positive and negative stimuli in human infants. *Science, 218,* 1235–1237.

Davidson, R. J., & Schwartz, G. E. (1977). The influence of musical training on patterns of EEG asymmetry during musical and non-musical self-regeneration tasks. *Psychophysiology, 14,* 58–63.

Davidson, R. J., Schwartz, G. E., Saron, C., Bennett, J., & Goleman, D. J. (1979). Frontal versus parietal EEG asymmetry during positive and negative affect. (abstract). *Psychophysiology, 16,* 202–203.

Ellingson, R. J. (1956). Brain waves and problems of psychology. *Psychological Bulletin, 53,* 1–34.

Ellingson, R. J. (1966). Relationship between EEG and test intelligence: A commentary. *Psychological Bulletin, 65,* 91–98.

Ehrlichman, H., & Wiener, M. S. (1980). EEG asymmetry during covert mental activity. *Psychophysiology, 17,* 228–235.

Elson, B. D., Hauri, P., & Cunis, D. (1977). Physiological changes in yoga meditation. *Psychophysiology, 14,* 52–57.

Ford, M. R., Goethe, J. W., & Dekker, D. K. (1986). EEG coherence and power changes during a continuous movement task. *International Journal of Psychophysiology, 4,* 99–110.

Galbraith, G. C., London, P., Leibovitz, M. P., Cooper, L. M., & Hart, J. T. (1970) Electroencephalography and hypnotic susceptibility. *Journal of Comparative and Physiological Psychology, 72,* 125–131.

Gale, A., & Edwards, J. (1983a). The EEG and Human Behavior: In A. Gale & J. Edwards (Eds.), *Physiological correlates of human behavior: Vol. 2: Attention and performance* (pp. 99–127). New York: Academic Press.

Gale, A., & Edwards, J. (1983b). Cortical correlates of intelligence: In A. Gale & J. Edwards (Eds.), *Physiological correlates of behavior: Vol. 3: Individual differences and psychopathology* (pp. 79–97). New York: Academic Press.

Gale, A., Morris, P., Lucas, B., & Richardson, A. (1972). Types of imagery and imagery types: An EEG study. *British Journal of Psychology, 63,* 523–531.

Galin, D., & Ornstein, R. (1972). Lateral specialization of cognitive mode: An EEG study. *Psychophysiology, 9,* 412–418.

Gasser, Th., Von Lucadou-Muller, I., Verleger, R., & Bacher, P. (1983). Correlating EEG and IQ: A new look at an old problem using computerized EEG parameters. *Electroencephalography and Clinical Neurophysiology, 55,* 493–504.

Gevins, A. S., Schaffer, R. E., Doyle, J. C., Cutillo, B. A., Tannehill, R. S., & Bressler, S. L. (1983). Shadows of thought: Shifting lateralization of human brain electrical patterns during brief visuomotor task. *Science, 220,* 97–99.

Gevins, A. S., Zeitlin, G. M., Doyle, J. C., Yingling, C. D., Schaffer, R. E., Callaway, E., & Yeager, C. L. (1979). Electroencephalogram correlates of higher cortical functions. *Science, 203,* 665–668.

Giannitrapani, D. (1969). EEG average frequency and intelligence. *Electroencephalography and Clinical Neurophysiology, 27,* 480–486.

Griesel, R. D. (1973). A study of cognitive test performance in relation to measures of speed in the electroencephalogram. *Psychologia Africana, 15,* 41–52.

Hatfield, B. D., Landers, D. M., & Ray, W. J. (1984). Cognitive processes during self-paced motor performance: An electroencephalographic profile of skilled marksmen. *Journal of Sport Psychology, 6,* 42–59.

Heide, F. J. (1986). Psychophysiological responsiveness to auditory stimulation during transcendental meditation. *Psychophysiology, 23,* 71–75.

Hubbard, O., Sunde, D., & Goldensohn, E. S. (1976). The EEG in Centenarians. *Electroencephalography and Clinical Neurophysiology, 40,* 407–417.

Khrizman, T. P. (1973). Characteristics of interventral relationships in electrical processes of the brain in 2 to 3 year old children during voluntary motor acts. *Voprosy Psikhologii, 19,* 107–117.

Lansing, R. W., Schwartz, E., & Lindsley, D. B. (1959). Reaction time and EEG activation under alerted and nonalerted conditions. *Journal of Experimental Psychology, 58,* 1–7.

Leavitt, F. (1968). EEG activation and reaction time. *Journal of Experimental Psychology, 77,* 194–199.

Lindsley, D. B. (1944). Electroencephalography. In J. McV Hunt (Ed.), *Personality and the behavior disorders* (pp. 1033–1106). New York: Ronald Press.

London, P., Hart, J. T., & Leibovitz, M. P. (1968). EEG alpha rhythms and susceptibility to hypnosis. *Nature, 219,* 71–72.

Macleod-Morgan, C. (1982). EEG lateralization in hypnosis: A preliminary report. *Australian Journal of Clinical and Experimental Hypnosis, 10,* 99–102.

Macleod-Morgan, C., & Lack, L. (1982). Hemispheric specificity: A physiological concomitant of hypnotizability. *Psychophysiology, 23,* 71–75.

Maxwell, A. E., Fenwick, P. B., Fenton, G. W., & Dollimore, J. (1974). Reading ability and brain function: A simple statistical model. *Psychological Medicine, 4,* 274–280.

McKee, G., Humphrey, B., & McAdam, D. W. (1973). Scaled lateralization of alpha activity during linguistic and musical tasks. *Psychophysiology, 10,* 441–443.

Morgan, A. H., MacDonald, H., & Hilgard, E. R. (1974). EEG alpha: Lateral asymmetry related to task, and hypnotizability. *Psychophysiology, 11,* 275–282.

Robbins, K. I., & McAdam, D. (1974). Interhemispheric alpha asymmetry and imagery mode. *Brain and Language, 1,*189–193.

Rugg, M. D., & Dickens, A. M. J. (1982). Dissociation of alpha and theta activity as a function of verbal and visuospatial tasks. *Electroencephalography and Clinical Neurophysiology, 53,*201–207.

Satterfield, J. H., Cantwell, D. P., Saul, R. E., & Usin, A. (1974). Intelligence, academic achievement and electroencephalography abnormalities in hyperactive children. *American Journal of Psychiatry, 131,* 391–395.

Sersen, E. A., Clausen, J., & Lidsky, A. (1982). Reaction time and psychophysiological activity. *Perceptual and Motor Skills, 54,* 379–390.

Sperry, R. W. (1982). Some effects of disconnecting the cerebral hemispheres. *Science, 217,* 1223–1226.

Sterman, M. B. (1984). *Measurement and modification of sensory system EEG characteristics during visual–motor performance* (AFOSR Report No. 82-0335). Washington, D.C.: Air Force Office of Scientific Research.

Surwillo, W. W. (1968). Timing of behavior in senescence and the role of the central nervous system. In G. A. Talland (Ed.), *Human aging and behavior* (pp. 117–130). New York: Academic Press.

Surwillo, W. W. (1971a). Human reaction time and period of the EEG in relation to development. *Psychophysiology, 8,* 468–482.

Surwillo, W. W. (1971b). Interhemispheric EEG differences in relation to short-term memory. *Cortex, 7,* 246–253.

Surwillo, W. W. (1972). Latency of EEG attenuation ("blocking") in relation to age and reaction time in normal children. *Developmental Psychobiology, 5,* 223–230.

Surwillo, W. W. (1974). Speed of movement in relation to period of the EEG in normal children. *Psychophysiology, 11*, 491–496.

Surwillo, W. W. (1975). The EEG in the prediction of human reaction time during growth and development. *Biological Psychology, 3*, 79–90.

Thompson L., & Botwinick, J. (1966). The role of the preparatory interval in the relationship between EEG, alpha-blocking and reaction time. *Psychophysiology, 3*, 131–142.

Thompson, L., & Botwinick, J. (1968). Age differences in the relationship between EEG arousal and reaction time. *Journal of Psychology, 68*, 167–172.

Tucker, D. M., & Dawson, S. L. (1984). Asymmetric EEG changes as method actors generated emotions. *Biological Psychology, 19*, 63–75.

Vogel, W., & Broverman, D. M., (1964). Relationship between EEG and test intelligence: A critical review. *Psychological Bulletin, 62*, 132–144.

Vogel, W., & Broverman, D. M. (1966). A reply to "Relationship between EEG and test intelligence: a commentary." *Psychological Bulletin, 65*, 99–109.

Woodworth, R. S., & Schlosberg, H. (1954). *Experimental psychology*. New York: Holt.

4
The EEG and Behavior: Sensation, Attention, Perception, Conditioning, and Sleep

In an influential chapter, Donald B. Lindsley (1960) described patterns of EEG activity produced across behavioral states ranging from deep sleep to high alertness. Table 4.1 is adapted from Lindsley and shows his conception of a behavioral continuum, its characteristic EEG waves, associated states of awareness, and corresponding behavioral efficiency. Lindsley attributed an important role to the ascending reticular activating system (ARAS) in regulating states of attention, consciousness, sleep, and wakefulness. The functions of the ARAS also play a part in activation theory that describes the relation between levels of physiological activity and performance (see chapter 15). In 1960, Lindsley wrote:

> Attention is closely allied to arousal and wakefulness and, like wakefulness and consciousness, appears to be a graded phenomenon extending from general alerting, as in the orienting reflex, to specific alerting, as when attention is focused upon a given sense mode and dominates sensory input to the point of exclusion of other sense modes. Still higher or more finely focused attention may be restricted to a limited aspect of a given sense mode. (p. 1589)

This description of attention in general and specific form can serve as a general model for contemporary psychophysiologists.

This chapter discusses various human processes and their relation to EEG activity. The sections concerned with sensory, attentional, and perceptual mechanisms are followed by a brief treatment of EEG during different kinds of conditioning. The EEG and its relation to sleep includes discussions on dreaming, depth of sleep, effects of presleep work on sleeping EEG, sleep learning, and sleep deprivation.

TABLE 4.1
Psychological States and Their EEG,
Conscious and Behavioral Correlates*

Behavioral Continuum	Electroencephalogram Characteristics	State of Awareness	Efficiency
Strong, excited emotion; fear, range, anxiety	Desynchronized: low to moderate amplitude; fast mixed frequencies	Restricted awareness; divided attention; diffuse, hazy; 'confusion'	Poor: lack of control, freezing up, disorganized
Alert attentiveness	Partially synchronized: mainly fast low-amplitude waves	Selective attention, but may vary of shift; 'concentration' anticipation, 'set'	Good: efficient, selective, quick reactions; organized for serial responses
Relaxed wakefulness	Synchronized: optimal alpha rhythm	Attention wanders—not forced; favors free association	Good: routine reactions and creative thought
Drowsiness	Reduced alpha and occasional low-amplitude slow waves	Borderline partial awareness; imagery and reverie; 'dreamlike' states	Poor: uncoordinated, sporadic, lacking sequential timing
Light sleep	Spindle bursts and slow waves (larger); loss of alphas	Markedly reduced consciousness (loss of consciousness); dream state	Absent
Deep sleep	Large and very slow waves (synchrony but on slow time bases); random irregular patterns	Complete loss of awareness (no memory for stimulation or for dreams)	Absent
Coma	Isoelectric to irregular large slow waves	Complete loss of consciousness; little or no response to stimulation; amnesia	Absent
Death	Isoelectric: gradual and permanent disappearance of all electrical activity	Complete loss of awareness as death ensues	Absent

Note. From Lindsley, D. B. (1960). Attention, consciousness, sleep & wakefulness. In J. Field, H. W. Magoun, & V. E. Hall (Eds.), *Handbook of physiology, Section I, Neurophysiology* (Vol. III, pp. 1553–1593). Washington, DC: American Physiological Society. (p. 1554)

SENSATION, ATTENTION, PERCEPTION, AND THE EEG

In the context of this chapter, perception is considered to involve the active processing (making meaning) of sensory data. Thus, it is proposed that the detection of a stimulus and attending to it precede perceptual integration by the individual. In this interpretation, the processes of sensation, attention, and perception are viewed as being functionally linked. The purpose of the resulting integration is to allow the perceived material to be used in some cognitive activity (e.g., decision making, problem solving, or thinking). In this section, the assignment of EEG research into one of these categories is based on whether a given study is primarily concerned with stimuli, attentional processes, or perceptual-integrative functions. The separation is artificial, and the close interactive influence among sensation, attention, and perception must be emphasized.

Sensation and the EEG

Stimulus Complexity.   The effects of stimulus complexity on desynchronization of the EEG alpha wave was the topic of an investigation by Berlyne and McDonnell (1965). They hypothesized that more complex and incongruous visual stimulus patterns would produce longer lasting desynchronization of alpha activity; for example, that more complex stimuli, presented while subjects were in alpha, would result in a longer-lasting disappearance of alpha than less complex stimuli. Based on EEG recordings of 88 male subjects, their hypothesis was confirmed. The more complex or incongruous patterns produced, on the average, 500 msec longer desynchronizations than the simple patterns. The result was consistent with those indicating that aspects of the external environment, such as novelty and surprise, can induce heightened levels of arousal.

This intriguing notion that stimulus complexity can affect arousal level of an observer (as measured by duration of EEG desynchronization) was examined by Christie, Delafield, Lucas, Winwood, and Gale (1972). They criticized the Berlyne and McDonnell experiment on the basis that no measure of the subject's reaction to the stimuli was taken, that is, the experimenters themselves judged whether a stimulus was complex or simple. Another criticism was that EEG desynchronization was a relatively crude measure. Christie et al. (1972) set out to correct these shortcomings by obtaining subjective ratings of complexity and by measuring EEG amplitude in detail over a frequency range of 2 to 20 Hz. Displays presented to the subjects had differing numbers of items (2, 4, 8, 16, or 32) that corresponded to subjective complexity. The alpha activity decreased as the number of items increased. Thus, the level of complexity (as judged by subjects) did affect the amount of EEG alpha, confirming the earlier results of Berlyne and McDonnell.

Stimulus Aftereffects.   The effects of fixating a rotating spiral on alpha activity and the time required for alpha to return after eye closure were measured by Claridge and Harrington (1963). They found a relationship between the reported duration of this visual aftereffect and the time it took alpha to return (longer duration, longer time to return). This result is related to those of Ali (1972), who found differential effects of red and blue lights on the amplitude and amount of EEG alpha recovery in the post-stimulation period. That is, blue light favored earlier alpha recovery than did red light. On the basis of this result, he predicted that the longer duration and greater alpha attenuation associated with the red stimulus would lead to a longer estimate of its duration by subjects than would a blue light. This prediction was tested in another experiment (Ali, 1973). The stimuli, either red or blue lights, were presented to 40 subjects while EEG was measured from the occipital area. The subject was asked to look at the light as soon as it appeared and to keep looking until it was turned off. The prediction regarding time estimation was confirmed, as subjects made a mean estimate of 58.52 seconds for the red light and 47.50 seconds for the blue light. As for the differential effect of the red and blue lights, Ali suggested several possibilities: (a) Red light is more effective in central (foveal) vision, whereas blue is more effective in peripheral vision; (b) red may elicit greater attention; (c) red has autonomic arousal effects, but blue light has soothing effects. The differential effects of red and blue light could cause the variation in alpha EEG, which in turn might affect time estimation. Thus, the brief review suggests that stimuli have aftereffects with respect to EEG activity. The possibility that red light has greater effects on foveal receptors than blue light remains to be investigated.

Stimulus Thresholds.   The relationship between EEG alpha and detection of auditory stimuli was studied in a novel paradigm by Bohdanecky, Bozkov, and Radil (1984). Their experimental set-up enabled EEG criteria (alpha or non-alpha) to determine the automatic presentation of different intensity auditory stimuli at unexpected times for subjects. They found that the threshold for detection was higher during alpha periods than nonalpha ones. This means that the auditory system was less sensitive during periods of alpha as compared to alpha desynchronization, as would be expected because alpha is associated with lower attention levels than desynchronized EEG.

Attention and the EEG

A good working definition of attention is one offered by Tecce (1972). Attention is defined as a hypothetical process of an organism that facilitates the selection of relevant stimuli from the environment (internal or external) to the exclusion of other stimuli and results in a response to the relevant stimuli. Tecce emphasized that the process of attention has steering functions, a point previously made in definitions proposed by Berlyne (1970) and Hebb (1958). Thus, attention is seen as an active, directional process that continues up until, and perhaps after, a response to the stimulus is made.

Attention was a lively topic of psychology in the early 1900s, but research and interest in the area declined with the rise of behaviorism, because this school of psychology tended to reject the study of attention on the grounds that it was "mentalistic." It was not until relatively recently (1960s and 1970s) that interest in problems of attention has been revived, partly because of attempts to find neurophysiological bases of attention and related phenomena, such as the orienting response.

Vigilance and Signal Detection.   A bridge between early studies of attention and modern investigations was constructed by studies of vigilance in the 1940s and 1950s. The term "vigilance" was used by Mackworth (1950) and others to describe the situation in which an individual had to respond to randomly occurring and infrequent signals over an extended period of time. The original reason for studying vigilance performance was a very practical one, because it was noted that detection efficiency of World War II radar operators dropped off drastically in a short period of time. In fact, the Mackworth studies indicated a serious drop within the first 15 to 30 minutes of performance. The study of vigilance decrement has implications for other practical situations. For example, monitoring of relatively monotonous stimuli for long durations occurs in assembly line inspection, as well as in the long-term vehicular control of truck drivers, airline pilots, and train operators. Some of the more recent studies relating brain activity to signal detection and fluctuations of attention with monotonous stimulation are presented in this chapter and in chapter 6 on cortical evoked potentials.

Beatty, Greenberg, Deibler, and O'Hanlon (1974) hypothesized that learned regulation of theta activity (3 to 7 Hz) would affect detection performance in a prolonged monitoring task. They proposed that learned suppression of the occipital theta rhythm would maintain efficient detection, whereas increased theta activity would lead to a greater than normal decrement in performance of a monitoring task. The EEGs of 19 undergraduates were recorded from over the left occipital and parietal cortex. Twelve of the individuals were trained to suppress theta and seven to increase the amount of EEG activity in the theta band. The poorest detection performance was that of the group that produced theta during monitoring a radar simulator, in whom vigilance performance dropped continuously over the 2-hour period. Conversely, the best monitoring performance was shown by the group that was taught to suppress theta activity. In fact, an improvement in detection was observed for the theta-suppressed group in the last segment of the experiment, a period during which the theta-augmented group showed its worst performance. The results suggest that, because theta is associated with lowered arousal, greater activation of EEG is associated with better vigilance performance. This result would have implications for improving the performance of persons who are involved in long-term monitoring activities, such as the inspectors, drivers, and radar operators mentioned previously. If one could teach these kinds of operators to suppress theta, then monitoring performance might be improved for certain monotonous, but critical, tasks.

In a paper submitted to a NATO Symposium on Vigilance, Gale (1977) made a strong argument for the use of EEG in the study and prediction of signal detection performance. One of his own findings was that greater amounts of theta activity occurred in persons performing more poorly. More recently, Beatty and O'Hanlon (1980) reported on an experiment in which they repeated and expanded the original 1974 study. They showed that the relationship between regulated theta activity and performance was stable over repeated sessions with three groups of subjects: a theta-suppress group, a theta-enhance group, and a control group (not given training in enhancement or suppression of theta). In addition, the two trained groups were able to transfer control of EEG activity from the condition where they were given feedback about EEG to one where no feedback was given. The results on EEG theta obtained under the various conditions of their experiment are shown in Fig. 4.1. Note that in the beginning there

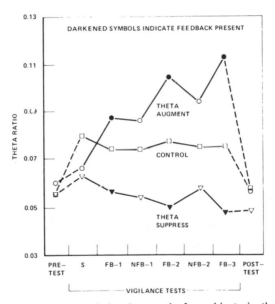

FIG.. 4.1. Mean values of the theta ratio for subjects in the theta-augment, theta suppress, and control groups in the pretest, posttest, and six 1-hour vigilance tests. Darkened symbols indicate the presence of EEG-contingent feedback. The six vigilance tests are designed as follows: S-spontaneous or unregulated EEG; FB-EEG contingent feedback present for the experimental groups; NFB-EEG contingent feedback absent for the experimental groups but regulation attempted.

was no difference among the groups in amount of theta produced (pre-test). As training progressed, theta became differentiated and so did performance; that is, the theta-suppress group did best, followed by the control subjects and then the augment group.

The findings regarding EEG and attention are not numerous, but those that exist are interesting. The question of how and why theta production influences signal detection requires more study.

Perception and the EEG

Perceptual Structuring.   In an interesting approach to studying the role of perceptual processes as reflected in the EEG, Giannitrapani (1971) measured EEGs of 32 males, aged 11 to 13, under eight conditions. Measurements were made from 16 areas over frontal, parietal, occipital, and temporal locations during (a) awake resting, (b) listening to white noise, (c) listening to a portion of Tchaikovsky's "Marche Miniature," (d) listening to a segment of Mark Twain's Tom Sawyer, (e) silently performing mental arithmetic, (f) looking at a poster, (g) looking through diffusing goggles, and (h) awake resting. The amount of high beta activity (21 to 33 Hz) increased when subjects were required to structure the stimuli. For example, listening to a portion of Tom Sawyer required structuring in that the verbal material is perceived by organizing sounds into words and words into a context; therefore, high beta activity increased under this condition. Conversely, the music condition showed a minimal beta effect, because it was probably already structured for the subjects used. Beta activity disappeared when the stimulus acquired the necessary structure.

Object Recognition and Discrimination.   The EEG was analyzed during the preparatory stages and during recognition of objects, by Zhirmunskaya, Beyn, Volkov, Voitenko, and Konyukhova (1975). They presented 174 objects to 15 subjects by means of a tachistoscope. The exposure time was gradually increased from subthreshold values until the subject could name the object. The EEG was recorded from leads within each hemisphere (longitudinal placement) and from leads at similar areas of the two hemispheres (transverse placement). They reported greater degrees of EEG desynchronization (low voltage, fast activity) during recognition of objects than during simple mobilization of the subject's attention. The authors expressed the view that the EEG desynchronization is caused by the influence of subcortical brain structures on cortical neurons.

The difficulty of an auditory discrimination task was varied as occipital EEG of 19 college students was measured (Wang, Marple, & Carlson, 1975). As difficulty of discrimination increased, the subjects made more errors and produced less alpha activity. This result supports the notion that more difficult discriminations demand greater mental effort with a resulting increase in the amount of alpha desynchronization. Performance in a music recognition task was correlated with EEG alpha in an experiment by Walker (1980). The subjects were required to recognize melodies from Beethoven's piano sonatas. At the end of each 5 sec excerpt, they were asked whether it had been presented earlier in the session. If it had and the subjects said "yes," it was a true positive (TP); if it had not and they said "no," this was a true negative (TN). An interesting result was that there was more alpha activity during the TN trials compared to TP, suggesting that cortical activation was higher when a stimulus was judged to match a previously presented one.

In summary, complexity of stimuli, visual aftereffects, and stimulus color appear to be factors in producing changes in EEG activity. Modern studies of attention often come under the heading of vigilance or signal detection. The utilization of such approaches along with EEG measurements seems to be a fruitful one. For example, the production of theta activity has been related to inferior vigilance performance, whereas theta suppression is associated with the prevention of vigilance decrement. Perhaps it may someday be possible to predict and control levels of attention and alertness by providing EEG-related feedback measures, as suggested by Mulholland (1974). Other studies have indicated that perceptual structuring and recognition and discrimination of stimuli appear to be accompanied by EEG changes in the direction of faster activity.

CONDITIONING OF THE EEG

Classical Conditioning of the EEG

Shagass (1972) reviewed a number of studies that indicated that classical conditioning of EEG responses could be produced; that is, after pairing of conditioned and unconditioned stimuli, changes in EEG patterns were observed at various recording sites on the scalp with presentations of the conditioned stimulus (CS) alone. A common EEG change that occurs with conditioning is alpha blocking to the CS (the formerly neutral stimulus). In a typical experiment, the CS might be a tone and the unconditioned stimulus (US) a light. The unconditioned response (UR) is the natural alpha blocking that occurs with light stimulation, to be replaced by the conditioned response (CR) after sufficient pairings of CS and US produce alpha blocking to CS alone. Braggio and Putney (1980) examined the influence of US intensity, perceived US intensity, UR magnitude, and awareness of the CS–US relationship on conditioned alpha blocking. They found that UR magnitude (amount of alpha blocking to the US) was a better predictor of conditioning than either US intensity or perceived US intensity. Also, conditioned alpha blocking was apparently unrelated to a subject's awareness of the conditioning process. Shagass believes that conditioning may play an important role in determining an individual's EEG pattern, and might indicate that certain more or less permanent EEG characteristics, for example, the alpha index, may be affected by conditioning.

Operant Conditioning of the EEG

There do not appear to be many recent reports in the area of classical conditioning of the EEG with awake humans. On the other hand, there are many reports of attempts to operantly condition EEG, where the presentation of a stimulus or a reward is contingent on the production of a particular EEG pattern by the subject. The operant conditioning of certain physiological activities is considered to be helpful in alleviating a variety of symptoms. For instance, beneficial effects with epileptics have been observed when specific EEG frequencies were conditioned. A more detailed discussion of studies aimed at alleviating certain symptoms through operant conditioning (commonly called biofeedback) is presented in chapter 14. Some EEG operant conditioning studies, not expressly done in a clinical context, are reviewed in this section. Thus, in this section, the question dealt with is whether EEG can be conditioned through operant techniques. A second, more general question is whether the operant conditioning of any physiological activity has beneficial effects in alleviating certain symptoms, for example, migraine headache. This second question is addressed in chapter 14.

Dr. J. Kamiya has been one of the pioneers in attempts to demonstrate that human subjects can exert operant control over their EEG activity (Kamiya, 1969). The control of EEG alpha activity and the mental state associated with such production was investigated by Nowlis and Kamiya (1970). A tone was presented whenever the individual produced rhythmic activity in the 8 to 13 Hz range that measured at least 20 μV. The subjects were given some trials in which they were asked to produce as much alpha as possible and others in which they tried to suppress alpha. The results showed that they were able to exert differential control over alpha production. Postsession questioning regarding how they exerted the control led to such responses as "relaxation," "letting go," and "floating" being associated with alpha production. The alpha-suppressed condition was associated with "being alert and vigilant." Brown (1970) was able to demonstrate similar effects in a situation where subjects enhanced the amount of alpha activity signaled by a blue light. They were also asked to describe the feeling states associated with keeping the blue light on. Persons who "lost all awareness" or "drifted" or "floated" tended to have greater amounts of alpha activity. The techniques used included "relaxation" or concentration on mental imagery.

A question arises as to whether the achievement of the feeling states alone can be sufficient to produce alpha activity without the use of some external signaling device (sounds or lights). Beatty (1972) showed that it was possible for individuals to control alpha activity equally well if they were given feedback when it occurred (a tone) or if they were instructed about the nature of alpha and beta activity and the feeling states associated with them, thus indicating that feedback was not critical. If given neither type of information, alpha regulation did not occur. Beatty and Kornfeld trained subjects to operantly control alpha and beta frequency while heart rate and respiration were measured. No significant changes were found in heart or breathing activity during conditioning of the EEG, ruling them out as possible contributing factors. In another study, training of theta activity was demonstrated by the ability of subjects to suppress the 3 to 7 Hz band of EEG activity when being given reinforcement to do so, and by the ability of others to increase the amount of such activity (Beatty, et al., 1974). The ability of subjects to recognize alpha and nonalpha states was questioned by Cott, Pavloski, and Black (1980). They reported that subjects acquired control of alpha activity during feedback through the use of specific strategies and were then able to use those strategies to control alpha when feedback was not provided, again indicating that feedback is not crucial to obtaining increased alpha. In another study, Cott, Pavloski, and Goldman (1981) determined that increases or decreases in alpha could alter mood. The factor of major influence was the instruction designed to set subjects for positive or negative alterations in feelings as a result of alpha changes. Instructional set also influenced success at controlling and changing EEG during operant conditioning trials.

Is operant conditioning of EEG possible? A qualified ''yes'' must be given because, although some control has been demonstrated, there are also results to indicate that the feedback itself may not be crucial to the EEG changes observed. In addition, there are other factors in the conduct of operant EEG conditioning procedures, as indicated in the next section.

Expectancies and Noncontingent Stimuli

At least two studies indicate that researchers must be careful in their experimental design to eliminate or reduce the possibility of expectancy effects in the operant control of EEG (Clarke, Michie, Andreassen, Viney, & Rosenthal, 1976; Valle & Levine, 1975). In the Valle and Levine study, subjects who were led to believe that they enhanced alpha were actually able to control alpha better than those who believed that they suppressed alpha. In the Clarke study, both ''experimenters'' and subjects were naive, and the biasing effects of the experimenters' expectations were found to influence EEG alpha measures in the direction of the expectation.

A study by Fath, Wallace, & Worsham (1976) shows the importance of using proper controls before claiming that operant conditioning has been demonstrated. They monitored alpha EEG activity of 17 subjects who were divided into three groups: (a) feedback (auditory clicks) contingent on production of alpha; (b) noncontingent clicks; and (c) no clicks. The noncontingent group produced the greatest amount of alpha, with the contingent group second and the control group third with respect to amount of alpha activity. Noncontingent control groups should be used in operant conditioning of alpha because alpha increases could otherwise be attributed to randomly occurring or noncontingent stimuli.

Eberlin and Mulholland (1976) performed an interesting experiment, in which they controlled for intermittent, noncontingent stimulation in a novel way. They recorded EEG from left and right parietal-occipital locations. Presentation of a visual stimulus was contingent on the production of alpha in one hemisphere only; if the other hemisphere produced alpha, no control over the stimulus occurred. Thus, in this second hemisphere, when stimulation occurred, it would be noncontingent; that is, it had nothing to do with the type of brain activity being produced. The results showed that EEG changes were due to the contingency between EEG and stimulation, not to the effects of noncontingent intermittent visual stimulation.

Thus, it appears from the several studies reviewed here that control of alpha activity does occur. However, Johnson (1977) argued that unmediated operant control of alpha activity has not been demonstrated. In other words, the person may not be learning to produce alpha per se, but may be influencing the amount of alpha through learning something else, such as the ability to ignore distracting stimuli, or controlling moods or feelings. The study of Eberlin and Mulholland (1976) strengthens the possibility of operant control, because it would be difficult to explain why mediators would affect one brain hemisphere and not the other.

SLEEP AND THE EEG

There has been a substantial amount of effort devoted to the study of EEG patterns during sleep, despite the fact that sleep studies are not at all easy to carry out. They may require that subjects sleep in a laboratory at least several nights while EEG is recorded, and they require a considerable amount of effort and patience on the part of experimenters. The justification for this continued effort is that sleep is such an important biological activity and has implications for human performance, behavior, and well-being.

The Nature of Sleep EEG

Why should researchers be interested in a state that appears to occur at such a low behavioral level? The answer is that there is actually much "behavior" going on during sleep, and investigators have been tackling such problems as levels of mental activity during sleep, depth of sleep and capacity to respond, dreaming behavior, sleep learning, effects of work schedule and exercise on sleep EEG, and effects of sleep deprivation on EEG and performance. Behavioral studies on the depth of sleep were carried out in the 1800s, and often involved the question of how loud or strong a stimulus had to be in order to wake a person from sleep. It was not until the 1930s, however, when EEG-measuring devices became widely available, that researchers were able to examine brain activity during sleep.

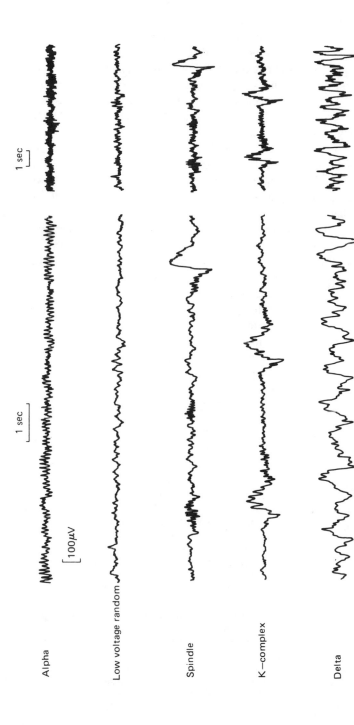

Alpha

Low voltage random

Spindle

K—complex

Delta

1 sec

100μV

1 sec

FIG. 4.2. EEG wave forms distinguishing sleep from waking. The same patterns are shown at two recording speeds: on the left, a conventional rate of 25 mm/sec; and on the right, a rate of 10 mm/sec, widely used in sleep research.

Contemporary sleep laboratories are equipped with physiological recorders that measure a variety of responses such as EEG, electromyogram (EMG), electro-occulogram (EOG), respiration, and rectal temperature. Sleep researchers call these recordings "polysomnograms" to refer to the many physiological measures obtained during sleep. Figure 4.2 presents EEG wave forms that distinguish sleep from waking. Sleep has been classified into four stages by Dement and Kleitman (1957a). The top tracing in Fig. 4.2 illustrates the regular, cyclical alpha activity of the waking state. The second line from the top illustrates Stage 1 sleep, characterized by low-voltage random EEG activity. Stage 2 is shown in the third tracing and indicates an irregular EEG pattern with 12 to 14 Hz spindles and the K-complex, a 75 μV burst. Some people have sleep spindles every few seconds, whereas others have them only infrequently. Stage 3 sleep is depicted in the fourth line, and is characterized by alternate fast activity, low-voltage waves and large, slow waves (delta). The large wave with faster frequencies superimposed on it (line 4) was first described by Loomis, Harvey, and Hobart (1938) as the "K-complex." The K-complex is not associated with Stage 3 sleep per se but instead appears to occur spontaneously during Stages 2 and 3 of sleep. It is considered to indicate arousal similar to the orienting response of the waking state (Snyder & Scott, 1972). The term "orienting response" was introduced by Pavlov (1927) to describe reactions of animals to novel stimuli, a response that interfered with the conditioning process. One component of the orienting response is a change in EEG activity toward increased arousal, that is, faster and lower amplitude activity (Sokolov, 1963). The orienting response, as a concept, is discussed more fully in the final chapter of this book.

TABLE 4.2
Classification of Sleep EEG

Stage W (waking)	Alpha activity and/or low-voltage, mixed frequency EEG
Stage 1	Low-voltage, mixed-frequency EEG with much 2–7 Hz activity (no rapid eye movements, REM)
Stage 2	Presence of sleep spindles (12–14 Hz) and/or K-complexes (high-voltage, negative-positive spikes) on background of low-voltage, mixed-frequency EEG
Stage 3	20% to 50% of epoch with high-amplitude delta waves (2 Hz or less)
Stage 4	Delta waves in more than 50% of epoch[a]
Stage REM	Low-voltage, mixed-frequency EEG activity and episodic rapid eye movements
Stage NREM	Stages 1, 2, 3, and 4 combined, i.e., those stages with no rapid eye movements

Note. From *A Manual of Standardized Terminology, Techniques and Scoring Systems for Sleep Stages of Human Subjects* by A. Rechtschaffen and A. Kales (Eds.). Washington, D.C.: U.S. Public Health Service, U.S. Government Printing Office, 1968.
[a]Measurement epochs are 20–30 seconds.

Dement and Kleitman quantified Stage 3 sleep as containing 10% to 50% delta activity (delta being defined as those waves of at least 100 μV amplitude, with a frequency of less than 2 Hz). The last line shows Stage 4 sleep, defined as containing more than 50% delta waves. The method of sleep classification used today is that developed by Rechtschaffen and Kales (1968), shown in Table 4.2.

Differences in the amount of Stages 3 and 4 sleep in normal, healthy, young adult males was investigated by Bliwise and Bergman (1987). The percent of delta time occurring in consecutive 30-second periods (0.5 to 2.0 Hz, at 75 μV) was scored to determine the 20% (Stage 3) or 50% (Stage 4) criteria. Interestingly, the authors reported large ranges in amounts of Stage 3 (9.0 to 34.0%) and 4 (7.9 to 50.0%) during the first 3 hours of sleep, where slow waves are most likely to occur. Persons high in one of these stages had relatively little of the other. The reasons for these wide individual differences in slow-wave sleep are unknown, but the result supports the combining of Stages 3 and 4 sleep activity, if differences regarding the relative amounts of each is not of interest.

EEG and Dreaming

The discovery that rapid eye movements (REM) were associated with dreaming was made by Aserinsky and Kleitman (1953). The eye movements they noticed varied in direction and amplitude and were 1 second or less in duration. They reported that persons awakened during REM periods could remember their dreams 75% of the time, whereas they could remember dreams in only 7% of the non-REM (NREM) awakenings. Later estimates of the percentage of times that dreams could be vividly recalled after awakening from REM sleep vary from about 60% to 90% (Snyder & Scott, 1972). Dreaming occurs fairly commonly in NREM sleep, but the contents are not as vivid or detailed as those associated with REM awakenings (Rechtschaffen, 1973). Foulkes (1962) reported that 74% of NREM awakenings produced recall of mental activity, and 54% resulted in accounts that could be classified as dreams. Thus, dreams cannot be said to occur exclusively in REM sleep, although there are qualitative and quantitative differences between REM and NREM dreams. The study by Aserinsky and Kleitman was classic in that it initiated the scientific study of dreaming. Researchers interested in the psychophysiology of dreaming now knew fairly precisely when dreaming occurred and could obtain reports of dreams and correlate these with various experimental manipulations and physiological responses. Some areas explored with the REM technique include: (a) changes in dream content over the night, (b) dream content among patients with differential psychiatric diagnoses, (c) effects of drugs on dream content, and (d) effects of presleep stimulation on dreaming.

Since 1953, many investigators have tried to find physiological correlates of dream content. One aspect of dream content is "lucidity," or the realization that one is dreaming in the midst of the dream without awakening. It has been found that lucidity occurs most frequently within the REM stage and is not related to awakening from sleep. Tyson, Ogilvie, and Hunt (1984) tested the suggestion of an association between lucid dreams and high amplitude EEG alpha during REM sleep. They reported that lucid dreams had high alpha early in the REM period followed by a distinct lowering of REM alpha. In contrast, consistently high REM alpha was associated with "prelucid" dreams having bizarre, emotional dream content. They hypothesized that lucid content sometimes emerges from prelucid experiences, a suggestion that calls for further investigation of the REM alpha and lucidity relationship.

Depth of Sleep and Capacity To Respond

Cyclical variations in EEG patterns occurring throughout the night were noted by Dement and Kleitman (1957a) and indicated a progression from light (Stage 1) to deep (Stage 4) sleep and back to light sleep again. The cycle from Stage 1 back to Stage 1 again takes approximately 90 to 100 minutes. After the first and second cycles, the deeper stages of sleep (3 and 4) rarely occur, that is, sleep becomes progressively lighter as the end of the sleep period approaches. This cyclical pattern of EEG activity throughout a night's sleep has been observed in many subjects. Figure 4.3 shows the relationship between different EEG patterns and stages of sleep. Also shown is the relative depth of sleep at various hours after a typical person has gone to sleep.

Studies have shown that the capacity of a sleeping individual to respond to stimuli depends on a number of factors, including the stage of EEG sleep, stimulus intensity, and significance of stimuli (Snyder & Scott, 1972). For example, Dement and Kleitman (1957a) found that louder sounds were required to wake subjects when they were in REM sleep as compared to onset of Stage 1 sleep. Williams, Hammack, Daly, Dement, and Lubin (1964) suggested that this might stem from the person's involvement in the content of some dream being experienced during REM Sleep. Current findings indicate that wakenings by sounds is similar for REM and Stage 2 sleep.

The effect of meaningfulness of stimuli on arousal from sleep has been demonstrated by a number of researchers. For example, Oswald, Taylor, and Treisman (1960) reported that a subject's name produced more EEG and behavioral responses during sleep than did the name presented backwards, that is, keeping the stimuli the same but the meaning different. The EEG response was the K-complex. Williams, Morlock, and Morlock (1966) reported that the probability of responding during sleep to an auditory stimulus was increased when failure to respond resulted in punishment. The required response was closing a switch within 4 seconds, and the aversive stimulus was a fire alarm about 100 dB above threshold. They suggested that these findings indicate the operation of "higher" nervous functions during some stages of sleep. Correct responses were greatest in Stage 1 sleep, and decreased progressively to Stage 4 sleep. Mean-

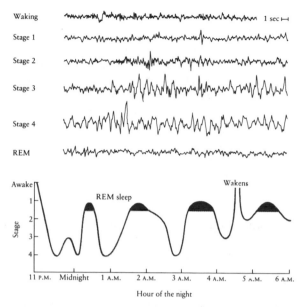

FIG. 4.3. EEG patterns during REM sleep resemble those of waking EEGs (top). Sleep increases and decreases in depth, and periods of REM sleep get longer as the night progresses. From *Brain, Mind, and Behavior*, 2/E by Floyd E. Bloom and Arlyne Lazerson. Copyright 1985, 1988 Educational Broadcasting Corporation. Reprinted with the permission of W. H. Freeman and Company.

ingful stimuli produced quicker awakening from sleep than nonmeaningful stimuli in an investigation by Langford, Meddis, and Pearson (1974). Criteria for awakening were both behavioral (sleeper's acknowledgment of waking) and physiological (onset of alpha rhythm).

Dreaming and REM Sleep

In general, findings suggest that in REM periods, as well as in other stages of sleep, the individual is psychologically active. Apparently, the sleeper is occupied with inner mental events, and responses to external events may depend on whether they are significant compared to ongoing events (Snyder & Scott, 1972). This theory was reinforced by findings such as those of Levere, Davis, Mills, and Berger (1976) regarding the hypothesized intrusion into sleep of stimuli related to reward consistency. Variations in REM duration have been related to estimates of dream duration by Dement and Kleitman (1957b). Subjects were awakened after 5 or 15 minutes of REM sleep and were able to estimate dream duration in 92 of 111 cases.

Examination of Fig. 4.3 shows that REM sleep is more like a waking state than a sleeping one. Other physiological measures also indicate waking characteristics during REM sleep. Some of these measures include an increase in heart rate, respiration, blood pressure, and blood volume of the penis (erection). However, muscle activity decreases, and most body muscles become very limp. No one can really say why this divergence between the muscles and other body systems occurs. As far as the frequency and duration of REM sleep is concerned, the bottom portion of Fig. 4.3 indicates that the first REM period is the shortest (about 10 minutes) with later periods becoming slightly longer. One hypothesis about the utility of REM sleep or dreaming is that of Crick and Mitchison (1983). They said that unsynchronized, almost random brain activity during REM sleep might represent the eliminating of some connections by sets of brain neurons. The purpose of this elimination, or loosening of connections, would be to allow the brain to "unlearn" certain unnecessary information. Bloom, Lazerson, and Hofstadter (1985) suggested that such an hypothesis might explain why infants spend so much time in REM sleep (50% versus about 20% in adults). Because babies' brains have much to learn, they also have to loosen or eliminate many no longer needed connections.

Another hypothesis about the function of REM sleep or dreaming stems from the writings of Sigmund Freud, who suggested that one function of dreams is to allow the release of anxieties and pent-up emotions that build up during everyday life. This hypothesis would seem to gain some support, at least for adults, from a study described by Dement (1972). It was noted that a decided increase in hostility, irritability, and unwillingness to continue in a sleep experiment occurred in subjects whose REM sleep was disturbed through awakenings. A control group consisted of subjects who were awakened an equal number of times, but during NREM periods, over the several-night laboratory sessions. This latter group did not show the same symptoms as the REM-disturbed group. When the procedure was reversed for the two groups, the symptoms emerged in the first group and disappeared in the second group.

Learning During Sleep

The practical implications of being able to learn during sleep are considerable; but the question of whether sleep-learning really occurs is a controversial one, as indicated in a review of sleep-learning research by Aarons (1976). A very basic question is whether people are really asleep when materials are being presented. In a study that used EEG criteria for sleep, Simon and Emmons (1956) tested subjects before and after sleep with 96 information items. The answers were given during sleep. Sleep was defined as the absence of alpha activity for at least 30 seconds before and for 10 seconds after answers were given to ensure that the act of giving the answer did not awaken the individual. The number of correct answers before and after sleep showed no evidence of learning.

More recent studies, however, suggest that the EEG criteria set up by Simon may have been too restrictive. Studies by Williams et al. (1966), Langford et al. (1974), and Levere et al. (1976) indicated that an operant response can be performed during sleep, and that meaningful materials were successful in arousing persons from sleep. These indicated at least some rudimentary information processing during sleep.

A study by Firth (1973) suggests that habituation of the EEG response, a very simple form of learning, can take place during sleep. Firth used auditory stimuli presented at either three regular intervals (10 to 30 seconds) or three irregular intervals (8 to 36 seconds). The number of K-complexes (sleeping analog of the orienting response) decreased with the number of repetitive, irrelevant stimuli. The greatest habituation occurred for the 10-second, regular interstimulus interval. Firth suggested that earlier attempts to find habituation in sleep may have failed because stimulus intervals were too long. However, in a carefully conducted study by Johnson, Townsend, and Wilson (1975), which, in one part, duplicated the 10-second, regular interstimulus interval used by Firth, no evidence of the EEG K-complex was found. They analyzed the K-complex during Stage 2 sleep and found that, in fact, the percentage of subjects giving K-complexes increased over trials, probably reflecting arousal within Stage 2 sleep with repeated tone presentations. On the other hand, more encouraging results were presented for the EEG K-complex by McDonald, Schicht, Frazier, Shallenberger, and Edwards (1975). They reported that a conditioned discrimination, learned during a waking condition, was carried over into Stage 2 sleep as indicated by K-complex responses to the conditioned stimulus (tones of either 200 or 2000 Hz). The authors proposed that these results may indicate that information stored in long-term memory (processed during waking) remains available for processing during sleep, and that information from long-term memory is most available in Stage 2 and less so in Stage 4 sleep. This is somewhat similar to results showing EEG responses to meaningful stimuli, because in McDonald's study, the conditioned stimuli attained meaning during the waking state. The studies reviewed thus far indicate that a response to a simple, meaningful stimulus may take place during sleep, but none show learning of verbal materials.

In a detailed review of sleep-learning studies, Aarons (1976) analyzed 11 studies that monitored EEG and sleep in procedures designed to estimate learning of verbal materials during sleep. Aarons concluded that some learning was evident in all but one study. Learning of small amounts of material was shown more often for the less rigorous recognition tests than for recall tests. The consistently small amount of learning led Aarons to agree with the conclusion that sleep learning of verbal materials is possible but not practical. An examination of Aaron's data indicates that in 7 of the 10 studies showing some learning, the learning was associated with fast-wave sleep or alpha activity. It would appear that the minimal amount of sleep-learning observed occurred in lighter stages of sleep. Another possibility is that the act of presenting the verbal materials may have served to keep subjects in lighter stages of sleep. For example, Lehmann and Koukkou (1974) found that presentations of verbal materials during sleep caused EEG activation of varying duration. Successful learning was related to higher and longer EEG activations after the presentation of the material.

In summary, it seems that some simple learning can take place during the lightest stages of sleep such as Stages 1 and 2, especially with respect to meaningful materials. The information processed appears to extend to verbal materials. Whether the amount of verbal material retained would ever justify the extensive use of sleep-learning procedures and devices would have to be decided on the basis of practicality and possible detrimental effects stemming from the loss of restful sleep over long periods of time.

Effects of Work Schedule and Exercise on Sleep EEG

The daytime sleep EEGs of hospital corpsmen, working an 11:00 pm to 7:00 am shift, were recorded by Kripke, Cook, and Lewis (1970). The daytime EEG sleep patterns were similar to those previously reported for young adults: Waking (W) = 2%, Stage 1 = 7%, Stage 2 = 46%, Stage 3 = 12%, Stage 4 = 13%, and REM sleep = 20%. However, REM sleep tended to occur early and was frequently interrupted, and Stages 1 and 3 occurred later than usually recorded in nighttime sleep. The authors interpreted these changes in terms of biological effects produced by inversion of the sleep–wakefulness cycle.

The day and night sleep of 12 nursing students was found to differ with respect to both duration and pattern (Bryden & Holdstock, 1973). They fell asleep sooner during day sleep periods, but slept shorter amounts of time (6.6 hours vs. 7.2 hours). In addition, they showed an increased amount of Stage 1 sleep and a decrease in slow-wave sleep during daytime as compared to nighttime sleep. As in Kripke's study, REM sleep of the student nurses occurred sooner during day sleep periods. A reduction in daytime REM sleep was also found in permanent night-shift workers and those on a weekly rotating day–night shift (Dahlgren, 1981). Dahlgren also reported that, compared to rotating shiftworkers, the permanent nightworkers showed better adjustment of body temperature rhythm to night work and day sleep and also had fewer disturbances in sleep functions during day sleep. The results suggest that both physiological and sleep adjustment to night work is facilitated by permanent night work schedules. In general, studies indicate that sleep onset is slower in daytime, and that total sleep may be shorter. Some reduction of REM sleep occurs, with an increase in Stage 1 sleep.

The effects of exercise on sleep EEGs of eight healthy males were examined by Horne and Porter (1975). Afternoon exercise (85 minutes on a bicycle ergometer with a 15-minute break at the halfway mark) resulted in increased slow-wave sleep during the first half of the night. The same amounts of morning exercise produced no changes in sleep EEGs. The authors interpreted the results as reflecting the role of slow-wave sleep in recovery from work done later in the day. Recovery from work done earlier presumably takes place during the rest of the day. Browman and Tepas (1976) had nine young males engage in either progressive relaxation, light exercise, or a monotonous task (vigilance) on three separate nights, immediately prior to measurement of sleep EEGs. The three different pre-sleep activities (approximately 45 minutes each) did not differentially affect sleep EEG patterns during the 7.5-hour sleep period. The subjects fell asleep faster after the relaxation condition, whereas the exercise condition kept them awake the longest period of time. It has been suggested that slow-wave sleep (SWS or Stages 3 and 4) is a time when the body repairs and restores itself. If this is the case, then it might be expected that SWS would increase after exercise because of a depletion of bodily energy reserves. This expectation has not been confirmed, because of conflicting findings. Bunnell, Bevier, and Horvath (1983) wondered whether having subjects exercise to a point of exhaustion during the afternoon, and quantifying the exhaustion with measures of oxygen consumption, would clarify the relationship between exercise and SWS. They recorded physiological variables on four consecutive nights: adaptation, baseline, exercise, and recovery. On the exercise day, subjects walked on a treadmill until they could go no longer, an average time of 138 min. for men and 160 min. for women. On the night after exercise, there was a significant increase in SWS (both Stage 3 and 4), and a decrease in REM. Thus it seems that daytime exercise can affect sleep brain activity if it is sufficient in duration and intensity.

The studies reviewed in this section indicate that daytime sleep differs from nighttime sleep, and that the effects of exercise and pre-sleep activities may depend on the time of day and amount of work involved. Adjustment to night work, in terms of EEG and sleep quality, is facilitated by permanent night work schedules. It is apparent in all of these studies that adaptation to the sleep laboratory conditions and continuing the investigation over a number of nights is critical for obtaining meaningful results.

Effects of Sleep Deprivation on EEG and Performance

Naitoh (1975) distinguished between three types of sleep deprivation studies using human subjects: (a) total sleep deprivation, in which the person is kept awake throughout one or more entire sleep periods; (b) partial sleep deprivation, which involves loss of a portion of the regular sleep period; and (c) differential sleep stage deprivation, where certain sleep stages are selectively prevented from occurring, usually by arousing the person when the EEG records show signs of the particular stage to be deprived.

A systematic review of sleep loss effects on performance was conducted by Woodward and Nelson (1974). They noted that the types of activities most likely to suffer impairment were those that involved quick reactions, short-term memory, reasoning, decision making, and attention. The amount of total sleep deprivation required to produce deficits in performance ranged from 24 hours for monotonous, routine tasks to 48 hours for cognitive tasks, such as decision making. Williams and Williams (1966) studied the recovery period sleep EEGs of army men after total sleep deprivation. The sleep loss took place over a period of 64 hours (loss of two complete sleep periods). The EEGs during recovery from sleep loss showed an increase in slow-wave sleep during the first night. The subjects showed impaired short-term memory as a result of sleep deprivation. Lubin, Moses, Johnson, and Naitoh (1974) also found impaired short-term memory during total sleep deprivation. Other sleep deprivation effects are slowing of RT, decrease in vigilance performance, increased irritability, and microsleeps (short lapses in attention). Engle-Friedman (personal communication, 1988) is of the opinion that observed deficits in short-term memory result from lapses in attention and motivational decrements caused by sleep deprivation.

A long-term study of partial sleep deprivation was conducted by Webb and Agnew (1974). The subjects had sleep EEGs measured one night a week, over a 60-day period, while on a schedule of 5½ hours of sleep per night. Performance on a variety of tests (vigilance, addition, word memory, grip strength, and psychological mood) was also measured once a week. Initially, the amount of Stage 4 sleep increased, but this returned to normal levels by the fifth week. The amount of REM stage seep decreased by 25% during the course of the experiment. Performance on only one test (vigilance) decreased with continued sleep restriction. The authors concluded that a chronic loss of sleep of about 2½ hours a night is not likely to result in major behavioral consequences. Similar results were obtained by Horne and Wilkinson (1985), although their approach was different. They paired two groups of 8-hour sleepers, and one of the groups had sleep time systematically reduced to 6 hours per night over a 6-week period. The EEG records showed that sleep deprivation resulted in decreased REM and Stage 2 sleep. Sleep onset time was much quicker for the deprived group. Overall daytime sleepiness did not increase for the deprived group and vigilance performance was maintained. The fact that subjects in the Webb and Agnew study showed a vigilance decrement with a 5½ hours sleep may mean that 6 hours sleep is the minimum necessary to maintain successful vigilance performance in young adults.

Moses, Johnson, Naitoh, and Lubin (1975) selectively deprived subjects of either Stage 4 or REM sleep in two separate experiments. In the first experiment, they examined effects of REM deprivation or Stage 4 sleep deprivation after two nights of total sleep loss, whereas in the second experiment, effects of total sleep loss were examined after three nights of REM or Stage 4 deprivation. The number of arousals required to keep subjects from entering Stage 4 was significantly greater after sleep loss (Experiment 1) than it was in Experiment 2. The number and patterns of arousals indicate that the two nights of wakefulness increased the tendency to obtain Stage 4 sleep but not REM sleep. They interpreted the results as supporting the hypothesis from previous studies that Stage

4 has priority over REM sleep in terms of recovery from sleep loss. The effects of graded amounts of sleep deprivation, without regard to stage, were studied by Akerstedt and Gillberg (1986). Subjects had 0, 2, 4, or 8 hours total sleep on four experimental nights separated by one week, and then were allowed to sleep as long as they wanted, starting at 11:00 am the next day. They found that during day sleep, SWS showed dramatic increases that were dependent on the amount of sleep loss. One fascinating finding was that subjects did not awaken until at least the baseline amount of SWS was obtained. This tendency of SWS to reach some quota before sleep ends, as well as its sensitivity to loss, suggests that it plays an important role in sleep regulation. Total sleep time, Stage 2, and REM showed only limited amounts of recovery compared to the loss.

Insomnia is a problem for both elderly women and men. However, it seems that although elderly women have superior patterns in terms of amount of SWS and sleep maintenance, they also complain more about poor sleep than elderly men. A possible reason for the greater complaining emerges from an investigation by Hoch et al. (1987), in which EEG patterns and self-reports about sleep were more closely related for the women, suggesting that they report sleep loss more accurately than men. With regard to insomnia in general, it has been suggested that it may represent a chronic SWS deficiency. Sewitch (1987) has argued that a rapid drop in rectal, body-core temperature upon sleep onset is a necessary prerequisite for sustained SWS, defined as Stage 4 sleep. In a well-reasoned review article, she presented a theory suggesting that chronic insomnia results from a failure of the thermoregulatory system to show a rapid decrease in body temperature at sleep onset, that persists for at least 1 to 2 hours into the sleep period. This theory is certainly testable and calls for studies that examine EEG and thermoregulatory patterns in both insomniacs and normal sleepers.

In an interesting study entitled "An Extreme Case of Healthy Insomnia," Meddis, Pearson, and Langford (1973) described the case of a 70-year-old woman (Miss M.) who slept less than 1 hour each night. She rarely experienced fatigue, and this had been her sleep schedule since childhood days. In one experiment, she remained awake for 56 consecutive hours and then only slept for 99 minutes while her EEGs were recorded. This sleep period was divided into the following stages: 37 minutes of REM sleep, 13 minutes of Stage 2, 31 minutes of Stage 3, and 18 minutes of Stage 4 sleep. In a second investigation, she slept in the laboratory on five consecutive nights, during which she averaged 67 minutes of sleep per night, without any behavioral signs of sleep deprivation. During the five nights, she spent 51% of the time in Stage 2 sleep, 23% in Stage 3, 9% in Stage 4, and 17% in REM sleep. With the exception of the absence of Stage 1 sleep, this pattern is not much different from that reported for healthy young adults (Kripke et al., 1970). This unusual woman spent much of her waking time engaged in activities that she enjoyed, such as writing and painting. She could not understand why other people slept for such long periods and wasted so much time!

In summary, it has been shown that sleep loss can affect short-term memory in normal persons. Slower RT, poor vigilance performance, and irritability also result from sleep deprivation. The amount of slow-wave sleep increases immediately after sleep deprivation. Results from studies of long-term partial sleep deprivation do not indicate serious consequences for performance, even though amount of REM sleep is reduced. Selective deprivation of various sleep stages indicates the apparently greater importance of Stage 4 versus REM sleep. In fact, after sleep deprivation, SWS is the stage most compensated for in the recovery period. It has been suggested that insomnia may be associated with chronic SWS deficiency. One theory says that SWS deficiency may be due to a failure of the body to show a rapid decrease in core temperature upon sleep onset. Rare individuals show no detrimental effects of very little sleep on either performance or sleeping EEG pattern. Perhaps in "healthy insomnia" the restorative functions attributed to sleep occur more quickly. Individuals such as Miss M. may be at some extreme point of a normal distribution of sleep time requirements. There are individuals at the other extreme who require 12 or more hours of sleep for normal functioning, thus attesting to the wide range of individual differences in the amount of sleep needed.

Research in the area of brain psychophysiology has been given impetus by electronic developments that enable the measurement of evoked brain potentials from the scalp. This development and associated studies of brain psychophysiology are discussed in the next three chapters.

REFERENCES

Aarons, L. (1976). Sleep-assisted instruction. *Psychological Bulletin, 83,* 1–40.

Akerstedt, T., & Gillberg, M. (1986). A dose–response study of sleep loss and spontaneous sleep termination. *Psychophysiology, 23,* 293–297.

Ali, M. R. (1972). Pattern of EEG recovery under photic stimulation by light of different colors. *Electroencephalography & Clinical Neurophysiology, 33,* 332–335.

Ali, M. R. (1973). Cortical habituation response to coloured lights and its relation to perception of stimulus duration, *Electroencephalography & Clinical Neurophysiology, 35,* 550–552.

Aserinsky, E., & Kleitman, N. (1953). Regularly occurring periods of eye motility, and concomitant phenomena, during sleep. *Science, 118,* 273–274.

Beatty, J. (1972). Similar effects of feedback signals and instructional information on EEG activity. *Physiology and Behavior, 9,* 151–154.

Beatty, J., Greenberg, A., Deibler, W. P., & O'Hanlon, J. F. (1974). Operant control of occipital theta rhythm affects performance in a radar monitoring task. *Science, 183,* 871–873.

Beatty, J., & O'Hanlon, J. (1980). Operant control of posterior theta rhythm and vigilance performance: Repeated treatments and transfer of training. In: N. Birbaumer & H. Kimmel (Eds.), *Biofeedback and self-regulation* (pp. 247–258). Hillsdale, NJ: Lawrence Erlbaum Associates.

Berlyne, D. E. (1970). Attention as a problem in behavior therapy. In D. I. Mostofsky (Ed.), *Attention: Contemporary theory and analysis* (pp. 25–29). New York: Appleton-Century-Crofts.

Berlyne, D. E., & McDonnell, P. (1965). Effects of stimulus complexity and incongruity on duration of EEG desynchronization. *Electroencephalography & Clinical Neurophysiology, 18,* 156–161.

Bliwise, D., & Bergman, B. M. (1987). Individual differences in Stages 3 and 4 sleep. *Psychophysiology, 24,* 35–40.

Bloom, F. E., Lazerson, A., & Hofstadter, L. (1985). *Brain, mind, and behavior.* New York: W. H. Freeman.

Bohdanecky, Z., Bozkov, V., & Radil, T. (1984). Acoustic stimulus threshold related to EEG alpha and non-alpha epochs. *International Journal of Psychophysiology, 2,* 63–66.

Braggio. J. T., & Putney, R. T. (1980). UR magnitude as predictor of conditioned alpha blocking. *Psychophysiology, 18,* 417–420.

Brown, B. (1970). Recognition of aspects of consciousness through association with EEG alpha activity represented by a light signal. *Psychophysiology, 6,* 442–452.

Brownman, C. P., & Tepas, D. I. (1976). The effects of pre-sleep activity on all-night sleep. *Psychophysiology, 13,* 536–540.

Bryden, G., & Holdstock, T. L. (1973). Effects of night duty on sleep patterns of nurses. *Psychophysiology, 10,* 36–42.

Bunnell, D. E., Bevier, W., & Horvath, S. M. (1983). Effects of exhaustive exercise on the sleep of men and women. *Psychophysiology, 20,* 50–58.

Christie, B., Delafield, G., Lucas, B., Winwood, M., & Gale, A. (1972). Stimulus complexity and the electroencephalogram: Differential effects of the number and the variety of display elements. *Canadian Journal of Psychology, 26,* 155–170.

Claridge, G. S., & Harrington, R. N. (1963). An EEG correlate of the Archimedes spiral aftereffect and its relationship with personality. *Behavior Research and Therapy, 1,* 217–229.

Clarke, A. M., Michie, P. T., Andreassen, A. G., Viney, L. L., & Rosenthal, R. (1976). Expectancy effects in a psychophysical experiment. *Physiological Psychology, 4,* 137–144.

Cott, A., Pavloski, R. P., & Black, A. H. (1980). Operant conditioning and discrimination of alpha: Some methodological limitations inherent in response-discrimination experiments. *Journal of Experimental Psychology: General, 110,* 398–414.

Cott, A., Pavloski, R. P., & Goldman, J. A. (1981). Cortical alpha rhythm, biofeedback, and the determinants of subjective state. *Journal of Experimental Psychology: General, 110,* 381–397.

Crick, F., & Mitchison, G. (1983). The function of dream sleep. *Nature, 304,* 111–114.

Dahlgren, D. (1981). Adjustment of circadian rhylythms and EEG sleep functions to day and night sleep among permanent night-workers and rotating shiftworkers. *Psychophysiology, 18,* 381–391.

Dement, W. C. (1972). *Some must watch while some must sleep.* New York: W. H. Freeman.

Dement, W. C., & Kleitman, N. (1957a). Cyclic variations in EEG during sleep and their relation to eye movements, body motility, and dreaming. *Electroencephalography & Clinical Neurophysiology, 9,* 673–690.

Dement, W. C., & Kleitman, N. (1957b). The relation of eye movements during sleep to dream activity: An objective method for the study of dreaming. *Journal of Experimental Psychology, 53,* 339–346.

Eberlin, P., & Mulholland, T. (1976). Bilateral differences in parietal–occipital EEG induced by contingent visual feedback. *Psychobiology, 13,* 212–218.

Fath, S. J., Wallace, L. A., & Worsham, R. W. (1976). The effect of intermittent auditory stimulation on the occipital alpha rhythm. *Physiological Psychology, 4,* 185–188.

Firth, H. (1973). Habituation during sleep. *Psychophysiology, 10,* 43–51.

Foulkes, W. D. (1962). Dream reports from different stages of sleep. *Journal of Abnormal and Social Psychology, 65,* 14–25.

Gale, A., (1977). Some EEG correlates of sustained attention. In R. R. Mackie (Ed.), *Vigilance* (pp. 263–283). New York: Plenum Press.

Giannitrapani, D. (1971). Scanning mechanisms and the EEG. *Electroencephalography & Clinical Neurophysiology, 30,* 139–146.

Hebb, D. O. (1958). *A textbook of psychology.* Philadelphia: Saunders.

Hoch, C. C., Reynolds, C. F. III., Kupfer, D. J., Berman, S., Houck, P. R., & Stack, J. (1987). Empirical note: Self-report versus recorded sleep in healthy seniors. *Psychophysiology, 24*, 293–297.

Horne, J. A., & Porter, J. M. (1975). Exercise and human sleep. *Nature, 256*, 573–575.

Horne, J. A., & Wilkinson, S. (1985). Chronic sleep reduction: Daytime vigilance performance and EEG measures of sleepiness, with particular reference to "practice" effects. *Psychophysiology, 22*, 69–78.

Johnson, L. C. (1977). Learned control of brain wave activity. In J. Beatty & H. Legewie (Eds.), *Biofeedback and behavior* (pp. 73–93). New York: Plenum.

Johnson, L. C., Townsend, R. E., & Wilson, M. R. (1975). Habituation during sleeping and waking. *Psychophysiology, 12*, 574–584.

Kamiya, J. (1969). Operant control of the EEG alpha rhythm and some of its reported effects on consciousness. In C. T. Tart (Ed.), *Altered states of consciousness* (pp. 507–515). New York: Wiley.

Kripke, D. F., Cook, B., & Lewis, O. F. (1976). Sleep of night workers: Electroencephalography recordings. *Psychophysiology, 7*, 377–384.

Langford, G. W., Meddis, R., & Pearson, A. J. D. (1974). Awakening latency from sleep for meaningful and non-meaningful stimuli. *Psychophysiology, 11*, 1–5.

Lehmann, D., & Koukkou, M. (1974). Computer analysis of EEG wakefulness–sleep patterns during learning of novel and familiar sentences. *Electroencephalography & Clinical Neurophysiology, 37*, 73–84.

Levere, T. E., Davis, N., Mills, J., & Berger, E. H. (1976). Arousal from sleep: The effects of cognitive value of auditory stimuli. *Physiological Psychology, 4*, 376–382.

Lindsley, D. B. (1960). Attention, consciousness, sleep and wakefulness. In: J. Field, H. W. Magoun, & V. E. Hall (Eds.), *Handbook of physiology* (vol. 3, pp. 1553–1593). Washington, DC: American Physiological Society.

Loomis, A. L., Harvey, E. N., & Hobart, G. (1938). Distribution of disturbance patterns in the human electroencephalogram, with special reference to sleep. *Journal of Neurophysiology, 1*, 413–430.

Lubin, A., Moses, J. M., Johnson, L. D., & Naitoh, P. (1974). The recuperative effects of REM sleep and Stage 4 sleep on human performance after complete sleep loss: Experiment 1. *Psychophysiology, 11*, 133–146.

Mackworth, N. H. (1950). *Researches on the measurement of human performance* (Medical Research Council Special Report No. 268). London: H. M. Stationary Office.

McDonald, D. G., Schicht, W. W., Frazier, R. E., Shallenberger, H. D., & Edwards, D. J. (1975). Studies of information processing in sleep. *Psychophysiology, 12*, 624–629.

Meddis, R., Pearson, A. J., & Langford, G. (1973). An extreme case of healthy insomnia. *Electroencephalography & Clinical Neurophysiology, 3*, 181–186.

Moses, J. M., Johnson, L. C., Naitoh, P., & Lubin, A. (1975). Sleep stage deprivation and total sleep loss: Effects on sleep behavior. *Psychophysiology, 12*, 141–146.

Mulholland, T. (1974). Training visual attention. *Academic Therapy, Fall*, 10.

Naitoh, P. (1975). Sleep deprivation in humans. In P. H. Venables & M. J. Christie (Eds.), *Research in psychophysiology* (pp. 153–180). New York: Wiley.

Nowlis, D. P., & Kamiya, J. (1970). The control of electroencephalographic alpha rhythms through auditory feedback and the associated mental activity. *Psychophysiology, 6*, 476–484.

Oswald, I., Taylor, A. M., & Treisman, M. (1960). Discriminative responses to stimulation during human sleep. *Brain, 83*, 440–453.

Pavlov, I. P. (1927). *Conditioned reflexes*. Oxford: Clarendon Press.

Rechtschaffen, A. (1973). The psychophysiology of mental activity during sleep. In F. J. McGuigan & R. A. Schoonover (Eds.), *The psychophysiology of thinking* (pp. 153–205). New York: Academic Press.

Sewitch, D. E. (1987). Slow wave sleep deficiency insomnia: A problem in thermo-downregulation at sleep onset. *Psychophysiology, 24,* 200–215.

Shagass, C. (1972). Electrical activity of the brain. In N. S. Greenfield & R. A. Sternbach (Eds.), *Handbook of psychophysiology* (pp. 263–328). New York: Holt, Rinehart & Winston.

Simon, C. W., & Emmons, W. H. (1956). Responses to material presented during various levels of sleep. *Journal of Experimental Psychology, 51,* 89–97.

Snyder, F., & Scott, J. (1972). The psychophysiology of sleep. In N. S. Greenfield & R. A. Sternbach. *Handbook of psychophysiology* (pp. 645–708). New York: Holt, Rinehart & Winston.

Sokolov, E. N. (1963). *Perception and the conditioned reflex.* Oxford: Pergamon Press.

Tecce, J. J. (1972). Contingent negative variation (CNV) and psychological processes in man. *Psychological Bulletin, 77,* 73–108.

Tyson, P. D., Ogilvie, R. D., & Hunt, H. T. (1984). Lucid, prelucid, and nonlucid dreams related to the amount of EEG alpha activity during REM sleep. *Psychophysiology, 21,* 442–451.

Valle, R. S., & Levine, J. M. (1975). Expectation effects in alpha wave control. *Psychophysiology, 12,* 306–309.

Walker, J. L. (1980). Alpha EEG correlates of performance on a music recognition test. *Physiological Psychology, 8,* 417–420.

Wang, C. C., Marple, H. D., & Carlson, H. (1975). EEG desynchronization during pitch discrimination. *Journal of Auditory Research, 15,* 140–145.

Webb, W. B., & Agnew, H. W. (1974). The effects of a chronic limitation of sleep length. *Psychophysiology, 11,* 265–274.

Williams, H. L., Hammack, J. T., Daly, R. L., Dement, W. C., & Lubin, A. (1964). Responses to auditory stimulation, sleep loss and the EEG stages of sleep. *Electroencephalography & Clinical Neurophysiology, 16,* 269–279.

Williams, H. L., Morlock, H. C., & Morlock, J. V. (1966). Instrumental behavior during sleep. *Psychophysiology, 2,* 208–216.

Williams, H. L., & Williams, C. L. (1966). Nocturnal EEG profiles and performance. *Psychophysiology, 3,* 164–175.

Woodward, D. P., & Nelson, P. D. (1974). *A user oriented review of the literature on the effects of sleep loss, work–rest schedules, and recovery on performance* (Tech. Rep. No. ARC-206). Arlington, VA: Office of Naval Research.

Zhirmunskaya, E. A., Beyn, E. S., Volkov, V. N., Voitenko, G. A., & Konyukhova, G. R. (1975). Correlation analysis of EEG changes during recognition of images of objects. *Electroencephalography & Clinical Neurophysiology, 39,* 255–259.

5

Event-Related Brain
Potentials and Behavior:
Measurement, Motor Activity,
Hemispheric Asymmetries,
and Sleep

Another measure of brain activity, derived from EEG recordings, is the event-related brain potential, or ERP. Unlike the EEG, which represents spontaneous brain activity, the ERP is generated as a response to specific stimuli. These ERPs are time-locked to stimulus events and have proven valuable to the psychophysiologist interested in a record of brain responses to stimuli, even when no other noticeable response occurs. A great deal of research effort has been devoted to studying the relationship between ERPs and human psychological activities. Most of the work has been conducted over the past 25 years and is continuing at a high rate. What makes the ERP so appealing is the possibility of relating specific, ongoing changes in brain activity to discrete psychological states and events. The voluminous research on ERPs suggests that it equals heart activity as the most popular physiological variable studied by psychophysiologists.

The ERP has been found to be dependent on both physical and psychological characteristics of stimuli, although in some instances, ERPs are independent of specific stimuli. For example, brain responses have been found to occur at the precise time that stimuli were expected but not actually presented (Sutton, Teuting, Zubin, & John, 1967).

Vaughan (1969) proposed the term "event-related potentials" to refer to a variety of brain responses that show stable time relationships to actual or anticipated stimuli. Those ERPs were classified by Vaughan as (a) sensory ERPs, (b) motor potentials, (c) long-latency potentials, and (d) steady potential shifts (SPS).

The sensory ERPs include those produced by visual, auditory, somatosensory, and olfactory stimuli. Examples of sensory ERPs are shown in Fig. 5.1. They

82

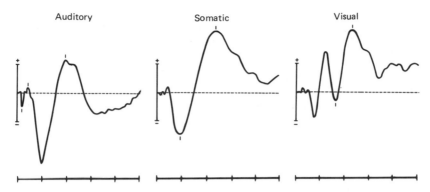

FIG. 5.1. Averaged evoked responses obtained from eight adult subjects. Each tracing is the computer average of 4800 individual responses. Calibration 10 μV, 100 msec/division (negative down).

are based on the composite averaged potentials of eight individuals. The various negative and positive waves (components) of these ERPs can be seen in the illustration. Motor potentials (MP) refer to potentials that precede and accompany voluntary movement. Vaughan observed that the amplitude of the MP varies with the strength and speed of muscle contraction.

The long-latency potentials refer to those positive or negative components of the ERP that occur at 250 to 750 msec. They reflect subjective responses to expected or unexpected stimuli, including the orienting response (see Ritter, Vaughan, & Costa, 1968). This is especially true for a positive component occurring at about 300 msec after stimulus onset, originally termed P300, but now referred to as P3 (discovered by Sutton, Braren, & Zubin, 1965).

One example of a steady potential shift is the contingent negative variation (CNV) first described by Walter, Cooper, Aldridge, McCallum, and Winter (1964). The CNV may be observed when a subject is told that he or she must respond to an event some time after a warning signal is given. For example, a warning light flash (S1) may be given, and approximately 1 second later a tone (S2) beeps, at which time the subject must press a button. The CNV occurs between S1 and S2. Another SPS is the readiness potential (RP) of Kornhuber and Deecke (1965), which builds up just before the onset of voluntary movement. This RP was originally called "Bereitschaftspotential" by Kornhuber and Deecke, a term still used by many European scientists. Examples of the CNV, motor potential, and readiness potential are given in Fig. 5.2. The long-latency potentials and SPS are discussed further in chapter 7.

At the other extreme of long-latency potentials are the very early "far field" potentials. These were originally discovered in humans by Jewett, Romano, and Williston (1970), who demonstrated that several auditory ERPs of very short latencies (2 to 7 msec) could be recorded from the vertex after presentations of

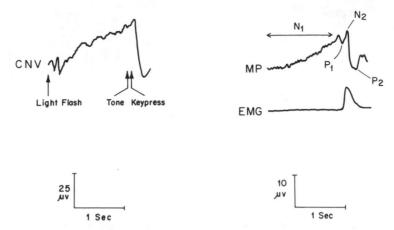

FIG. 5.2.   Examples of CNV, motor potential, and Bereitschaftspotential (readiness potential). On the left is CNV ($n=6$ trials) recorded from
vertex (Cz) to right mastoid. Relative negativity at the vertex is upward.
On the right (upper trace) is a motor potential ($n=400$ responses) associated with dorsiflection of the right wrist and recorded from the left
Rolandic area 4 cm from midline to a linked ear reference. The lower
trace on the right is the summation of the rectified EMG resulting from
muscle contraction. The slow negative component "N1" is the readiness potential.

stimuli. These low-amplitude responses (0.5 to 1.5 μV) were attributed to electrical activity in various brain stem structures. Their existence has subsequently
been confirmed by many other investigators. They are termed "far field" because they can be recorded from scalp electrodes (e.g., Cz) that are some distance from the source of the activity (brain stem). These brain stem potentials are
discussed again in chapter 13.

ORIGIN OF ERPS

The specific brain areas involved in the generation of various kinds and components of ERPs are currently being sought by a number of researchers. Knowledge
of these sources is important to the understanding of how brain areas participate
in certain mental processes and in the application of ERP findings to practical
clinical situations (Arezzo, Vaughan, Kraut, Steinschneider, & Legatt, 1986;
Beck, 1975). The methods by which these sources are determined involve recording activity from subcortical and cortical areas of animal and human subjects. Information about the subcortical brain areas that generate ERPs in humans
and animals is very fragmentary and will require much more time and effort
before a more complete picture is obtained (Vaughan & Arezzo, 1988).

Other techniques involve the use of multiple electrode placements on the scalp surface to provide information about possible cortical sources for various ERPs and the use of event-related magnetic fields to suggest possible subcortical and cortical generators. The use of multi-scalp locations involves the mapping out of widely distributed ERPs under various stimulus conditions, and is termed *topographical analysis*. Despite the problems, which include possible summation at a particular scalp area of activity from more than one underlying brain structure, investigators have been able to suggest the sources of a number of ERP components. For example, there is evidence that early auditory-evoked potential components (0 to 8 msec) recorded from the scalp in humans are produced at the brain stem (Jewett & Williston, 1971). Further, components of this response appear to be generated by specific structures in the auditory system. For example, a positive component occurring at about 2 msec after stimulation has been related to activity at the auditory nerve (Vaughan & Arezzo, 1988; also see wave I of Fig. 13.1). Wave II of this brain stem response reflects activity in the trapezoid body and neurons ascending towards the superior olive. Wave III in man has been localized to a structure called the pons, and waves IV and V have generators near the inferior colliculus, an area concerned with auditory system reflexes. The wave components labeled VI and VII reflect activity of neurons that transmit auditory impulses from the thalamus to auditory cortex, the so-called "thalamocortical radiations."

The largest amplitude auditory ERP components to a brief click or tone are a negative peak occurring at 80–90 msec, and a positive one at around 170 msec. This negative–positive sequence is referred to as the "N1–P2 complex", and it appears to be generated at the auditory cortex in the temporal lobe (Vaughan & Arezzo, 1988).

Components of the somatosensory-evoked potential have been related to specific brain areas. For example, a negative wave occurring at 55 msec appears to be generated in the postcenteral gyrus (Goff, Allison, & Vaughan, 1978). A later SEP, peaking around 200 msec, has been localized to primary somatosensory cortex through electrical and magnetic field recordings. With regard to visual stimulation, transient visual-evoked potentials to low intensity flashes are largest at the occipital pole (area 17 or striate cortex) and fall off rapidly with distance from this area. This is consistent with a principal generator located in primary visual cortex (Vaughan & Arezzo, 1988). In accord with scalp-recorded data, recordings made from the cortical surface of humans indicate that most sensory ERP components (auditory, visual, and somatosensory) seem to originate in or near the primary cortical sensory areas (Goff et al., 1978).

Motor potentials recorded in humans with the onset of voluntary movements indicate origins in the precentral (motor) cortex at the hemisphere opposite to the moving limb (Vaughan, Costa, & Ritter, 1968). The MP has been found maximal from the precentral cortex of monkeys trained to make wrist extension movements (Arezzo & Vaughan, 1975). The relative contribution of premotor and supplementary motor cortex to scalp-recorded MPs remains to be more fully explored.

As implied earlier, the long-latency potentials are strongly influenced by subjective factors (e.g., task-relevant information). Scalp recordings of late potentials indicate maximal response from over frontal cortical areas, with a secondary focus at the parietal areas (Courchesne, Hillyard, & Galambos, 1975; Squires, Squires, & Hillyard, 1975). Studies of scalp distributions of the late positive components (LPCs) by Simson, Vaughan, and Ritter (1977) also suggest generators within frontal and parietal association cortex. Subcortical recordings have obtained LPCs at widespread areas of the cerebral hemispheres (Yingling & Hosobuchi, 1984). Recordings from implanted electrodes in human patients have suggested the hippocampus (a subcortical region) as a possible generator of the LPC (Halgren et al., 1980). However, there is lack of agreement about this hippocampal generator. As one example, Johnson and Fedio (1986) were still able to record the LPC in patients whose hippocampus had been removed on the same side as the recording. It is likely that LPCs are derived from activity in a number of areas, including parietal and frontal association cortex and structures within the limbic region, such as hippocampus and amygdala. The relative contributions of these areas has yet to be determined.

One type of SPS, the CNV, has been found maximal over the central cortex and less pronounced at frontal and parietal areas (Cohen, 1969). This finding has been confirmed by Simson et al. (1977), who found the later segment of the CNV to be localized primarily over the central cortex. McCallum, Papakostopoulos, and Griffith (1976) recorded CNVs from areas of the human brain stem and midbrain. Delineation of CNV generators, however, is a complicated business, because, as pointed out by Vaughan and Arezzo (1988), these slow negative potentials have contributions from sensory, motor, and association cortex that vary in relative magnitude according to the nature of the stimuli, the task, and motor response requirements.

Another type of SPS, the readiness potential, has been recorded from areas of brain stem and midbrain in human patients by McCallum et al. (1976). These investigators reported that the RPs had distributions throughout the brain stem and midbrain. Deecke (1976) observed that the scalp-recorded RP is pronounced over parietal areas and nonexistent at frontal sites.

In summary, there are data that link certain sensory-evoked potentials and motor potentials to activity in or near subcortical and coritcal sensory and motor areas. Results from human and animal studies have implicated contralateral precentral cortical areas in the production of MPs associated with voluntary movements. Scalp recordings of late positive components, CNVs, and RPs indicated maximal response at frontal, central, and parietal areas, respectively. The continued use of topographical approaches and the development of appropriate research using animal models and data from human clinical patients are essential to further progress in identifying the brain areas responsible for generating various ERPs.

METHOD FOR OBTAINING ERPS

As was pointed out previously, ERPs are derived from the EEG. Therefore, before one can obtain these potentials, the EEG must be recorded, as discussed in chapter 2. That is, the system of placing electrodes is the same, as well as the location designations, according to the "10–20 International System." If a researcher is interested in obtaining visual ERPs, he or she might place recording electrodes at 0_1 and 0_2 corresponding to locations over the left and right occipital areas. The researcher may also wish to place electrodes over other brain areas, such as parietal, temporal, and frontal, to determine how responses from these areas may vary with the kind of visual stimulus (its shape or color or its meaning, e.g., pure sounds or words).

Normally, when the EEG is recorded in a relaxed person and a visual stimulus is presented, some gross activity change, such as alpha desynchronization, may be seen. The ERP will not usually be discernible in the EEG recording, because it is much smaller than background EEG activity. Therefore, the evoked potential must be extracted from the EEG by using an averaging technique in which EEG samples are taken at the instant each successive visual stimulus is presented. The EEG samples are fed into a digital computer, which sums the individual evoked potentials to successive flashes of light, for example. Thus, the system is set up so that the presentation of a stimulus will produce sampling by a computer over a preset period of time, perhaps 500 or 1000 msec. It should be emphasized, therefore, that ERPs are usually averages of a number of brain responses. There are instances where an ERP may be produced by one or a few presentations of a stimulus. For example, in a study by Cooper et al. (1977), ERPs were obtained to a single stimulus; and it is common to obtain the CNV with as few as 6 to 12 stimuli.

A basic premise in obtaining averaged ERPs is that the changes in brain activity are time-locked to some event, whereas the background EEG activity stays approximately the same during stimulus presentation periods. For example, suppose a single ERP is 5 μV and the background EEG activity is 20 μV. It is assumed that the evoked potential will increase as a function of N samples (e.g., $N=100$), while the background EEG will increase as a function of $\sqrt{N}$. This can be expressed mathematically as:

$$\frac{\text{Evoked potential amplitude (N)}}{\text{EEG amplitude } (\sqrt{N})} = \frac{5 \ \mu V \ (100)}{20 \ \mu V \ (10)} = \frac{500}{200} = 2.50$$

Thus, the 2.50 figure represents an ERP that will be larger than the background activity. Usually, an averaged ERP that is twice the background EEG

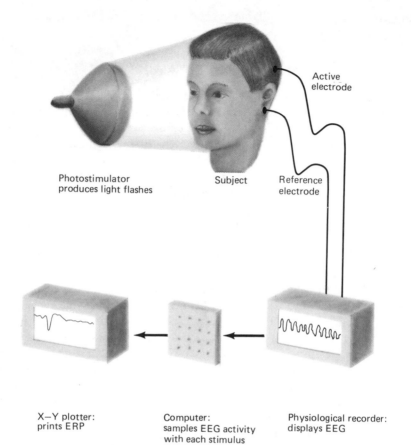

Photostimulator
produces light flashes

Subject

Reference
electrode

Active
electrode

X—Y plotter:
prints ERP

Computer:
samples EEG activity
with each stimulus

Physiological recorder:
displays EEG

FIG. 5.3.   Schematic drawing of recording situation to obtain a visual
ERP. A stimulus source (light flashes), electrodes, physiological recorder, digital computer, and X-Y plotter are shown in the sequence
from initiation of the stimulus to the printout of the ERP. Additional
equipment might be a tape system to store brain activity and an oscilloscope for additional on-line monitoring of the EEG.

amplitude will be easily recognized. This ratio may be increased by increasing
the number of samples.

Figure 5.3 shows a schematic drawing of the basic elements required to obtain
a visual ERP (VEP). Depicted are a light source, a subject with appropriate
electrode attachments, a physiological recorder, a computer of average transients, and an X—Y plotter. If the light intensity is high, the visual ERP may be
obtained with the eyes closed. Note that the left ear is shown as the location of a
reference electrode. In actual practice, researchers prefer to place electrodes in a
"linked ear" configuration, in which leads from the two earlobes are joined to

form a single reference. Another popular reference is "linked mastoids," where leads from behind the lower portions of both ears are connected to form a common reference representing both sides of the head. Some prefer to use a nose reference to equate for possible spatial effects of locating a reference on one side of the head only.

Equipment manufacturers have simplified the task of the ERP researcher by developing convenient equipment packages that have a number of excellent features to allow much greater flexibility than the early-used computer of average transients. These devices allow for easy acquisition of ERP data by providing programmable parameters through an interactive keyboard. For example, the researcher may enter the number of trials to be taken, the amplification for the signal, required time constants, and appropriate filtering. There can be an automatic reject feature that allows omission of eye movement or muscle artifact from the ERP because any values beyond a preset criterion are not added to the average. Sampling can continue until the programmed number of uncontaminated responses are obtained. In most systems of data acquisition, the resulting ERPs are stored onto disk for later analysis, including evaluation of amplitudes and latencies of the various ERP components through the use of a cursor. ERPs are typically printed out for a hardcopy record, which includes latency and amplitude measurements for selected components. There is usually enough flexibility to obtain a variety of ERPs, from the very short latency brainstem responses to the slowly developing CNVs. Although "pre-packaged" systems are convenient, they are very expensive, and many different computer systems are used to obtain ERPs in the various research laboratories in the United States and abroad. Researchers with appropriate engineering support often design their own systems, making use of commercially available equipment components from different manufacturers in meeting their own needs.

QUANTIFICATION OF ERPS

There are a number of ways to designate and measure amplitudes and latencies of the various positive and negative waves of the ERP. The two visual ERPs shown in Fig. 5.4 were each produced by 100 flashes of light presented to the same person. Negative components are labeled N and positive components, P. (It should be noted that some investigators designate the downward-going component as positive, or P, and the upward one as negative, or N. This usage was originated in European laboratories). There are two positive and two negative waves, or components, clearly visible in Fig. 5.4. The N1 component was considered to be the first negative dip in the tracing that occurred 50 msec after presentation of the stimulus. The amplitude of the N1 component was measured as the vertical distance from "baseline" (initial horizontal portion of the X–Y plot) to the trough of this first depression. The P1 component was measured as

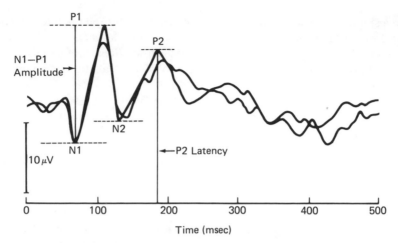

FIG. 5.4.   Method for measuring amplitudes and latencies of ERP components. The amplitude of the N1-P1 component (larger of the two traces) is 17.2 μV, based on the calibrated 10 μV signal. The P2 latency is 190 msec. Each of these two ERPs was based on averaged responses to 100 light flashes, on two different occasions. Negativity is downward. (From author's unpublished data.)

the vertical distance from N1 to the peak of the first positive component, whereas N2 was measured as the vertical distance from the peak of P1 to the trough of the second major depression, and so on for P2. The latencies (or time after stimulus presentation) were measured to the midpoints of each positive and negative peak. If the "peak" is flat and appears more as a plateau, the midpoint of the plateau is taken as the latency measurement. The amplitude (in microvolts) and latencies (in milliseconds) of the larger of the two visual ERPs in Fig. 5.4 (Condition A) were obtained according to these criteria. The amplitude measurements of each component are not strictly independent, that is, the amplitude of P1 will depend on the degree of negativity of N1, and so on. Therefore, it is more accurate to refer to N1–P1 amplitude or N2–P2 amplitude when giving magnitudes of response.

Vaughan (1969) suggested a flexible system for indicating polarity and latency of various ERP components. For example, a negative component at 150 msec would be labeled N150, and a positive wave at 200 msec would be designated P200. This suggestion has been adopted by most ERP workers and is used to this day.

The equipment for obtaining a P300 is identical to that used for sensory ERPs. However, the sample time after stimulus presentation is extended to about 1000 to 1500 msec. To demonstrate P300, a subject might be requested to detect an occasional different stimulus (e.g., a soft tone) interspersed in a series of relatively loud tones. This task is called an "odd-ball" paradigm. When ERPs to soft and loud tones are summed, odd (infrequent) stimuli will produce a larger positive wave in the ERP than will frequent stimuli at approximately 300 msec after presentation.

The typical method for obtaining CNV involves the presentation of a warning stimulus (S1), followed within a fixed time period by a second stimulus (S2) to which the subject responds. The S1 may be a light, S2 may be a tone, and the response might be a key press. The interval between S1–S2 might be 1.5 seconds (see Fig. 5.2). The CNV is maximally recorded with a scalp lead at Cz (vertex) with an appropriate reference site. An important consideration in the measurement of CNV is the time constant (TC) used. (The TC is the time for the amplitude of a wave to fall from 100% to 37% of its input value; Geddes, 1967.) The TC should be long with respect to the physiological event being recorded. Cooper (1976) has recommended, as a rule of thumb, that the TC should be at least three times the S1–S2 interval. Cooper has mentioned that use of too short a time constant results in a CNV that falls below baseline after resolution of CNV. Tecce (in personal communication) has recommended a TC of 8 seconds for S1–S2 intervals varying from 1 to 2 sec. The concensus among investigators is that time constants between 1 and 10 sec be used with all endogenous components including P300. The CNV may be obtained by averaging responses to between 6 and 12 combinations (trials) of S1 and S2 (Tecce, 1972). Electrical potentials produced by eye movements and blinks are possible sources of contamination in ERPs, especially the CNV. The measurement of these eye potentials and exclusion of contaminated trials produces satisfactory results.

The readiness potential can be produced in situations that require subjects to make voluntary movements at regular intervals. The recording electrode may be placed at Cz, and brain activity is sampled for several seconds prior to the movement until shortly after the motion is completed. A typical RP between 10 and 15 μV in amplitude may be obtained by taking 32 to 64 samples of brain activity with a time constant of 5 seconds (e.g., see Becker, Iwase, Jurgens, & Kornhuber, 1976). Now that a variety of ERPs have been described, we shall see how they are related to human activities.

ERPS AND BEHAVIOR

As mentioned previously, studies using the ERP have multiplied at an increasing rate over the years. The review presented here must of necessity be very restricted because of space limitations. However, an attempt is made to convey to the beginning student a flavor of the past and present work in this area. The advanced student is referred to Rebert, Tecce, Marczynski, Pirch, and Thompson (1986) for an interesting account of underlying ERP physiology and theory that uses both animal and human models.

The discussion concerning ERPs and behavior has been divided into three chapters. This chapter covers ERP correlates of motor performance, hemispheric asymmetries, and ERPs during sleep. Chapter 6 is devoted to a treatment of mental activities and ERPs and sensory, attentional, and perceptual functions. Chapter 7 considers the long-latency potentials and steady potential shifts and their relation to behavior and performance.

ERPs and Motor Performance

Reaction Time. The time it takes to respond to an external stimulus is a function of many factors, including stimulus intensity. Studies have shown that response time of the visual system decreases as stimulus intensity increases, whether the measure of time is purely physiological or behavioral. For example, Vaughan and Hull (1965) found that latencies of VEP components decreased with stimulus intensity. Further, Vaughan, Costa, and Gilden (1966) reported that RT, as well as VEP component latencies, decreased as a function of increasing stimulus intensity. Thus, quick reactions were related to shorter VEP latencies.

Donchin and Lindsley (1966) measured RT to a flash of light, using a warning click and a variable foreperiod (from 1.0 to 2.5 sec). They found that VEP amplitude and RT were definitely related, with faster RTs associated with larger VEP amplitudes. Telling the subjects how quickly they responded tended to shorten RT and increase VEP amplitude. Morrell and Morrell (1966) also measured visual RT and VEP, the latter being recorded at occipital and central locations. Their results agree with those of Donchin and Lindsley in that increased amplitudes of both positive and negative VEP components were associated with faster RTs. They suggested that factors such as selective attention and fluctuations in alertness are possible determinants of the relationship between RT and VEP amplitude.

Karlin, Martz, Brauth, and Mordkoff (1971) extended the relationship found between ERP amplitude and RT to auditory stimuli. They measured ERPs during simple and choice RT tasks and found larger auditory ERP amplitudes to be associated with faster RTs. In one choice RT condition, stimuli that did not require a motor response resulted in a higher late positive component (P300) than stimuli that did require a response. Thus, it could not be said that the enhancement of late positive components was due to movement potentials. The studies reviewed thus far seem to indicate that there is a relationship between the CNS response to a stimulus and speed of reaction. The relationship has variously been explained in terms of increased reactivity of the nervous system, arousal, or attentiveness. Karlin et al. (1971) suggested that the enhancement of the P300 component found in their study might be related to ''effort, or the degree of a subject's self mobilization'' (p. 135), and they proposed that holding back a response, in a context where responses are required to be made quickly, may require effort.

Ritter, Simson, and Vaughan (1972) measured ERPs to auditory stimuli while subjects engaged in simple RT and an auditory discrimination task (responding to changes in pitch). They found that the P200 component did not vary much in latency under the different conditions. However, P300 latencies were longer (100 to 200 msec) when subjects were required to make auditory (pitch) discriminations. Reaction times were also longer when discriminations were required. Further, P300 latencies and RT were longer with difficult discriminations than with relatively easy ones. The P300 component was largest at Pz, smaller at Cz, and smallest at Oz. Thus, the P300 component was related to both discrimination difficulty and response speed.

The effects of bisensory stimulation on RT and the ERP were investigated by Andreassi and Greco (1975). Bisensory stimulation refers to the simultaneous, or near simultaneous, stimulation of two sensory systems (e.g., visual and auditory). Because it has long been known that RT to auditory stimuli is faster than to visual presentations, these investigators presented the visual stimuli prior to auditory stimuli. The time difference was determined in two ways: The first, called ΔRT, used a temporal offset equal to the difference between each subject's RT to light and sound; the second, called ΔN2, set the offset to equal the average latency difference of the N2 component to light and sound. The ERPs were measured from Oz and Cz under conditions of light alone, sound alone, light–sound offset by ΔRT, and light–sound offset by ΔN2. All conditions of bisensory stimulation resulted in faster RTs than did unisensory stimulation. In addition, bisensory stimulation produced larger amplitude ERPs than did auditory or visual stimulation alone. Andreassi and Greco proposed that the results indicated the occurrence of facilitative sensory interaction in the nervous system, because bisensory stimulation resulted in faster RTs. They hypothesized that a possible site for this sensory interaction is the ascending reticular formation, because it is known that this subcortical structure has a role in coordinating sensory input and attentional mechanisms (Samuels, 1959; Scheibel & Scheibel, 1967) and has diffuse projections to the cortex.

In summary, some studies suggest that faster RTs are associated with higher amplitude ERPs. Others indicate the relation between latencies of certain ERP components and response speed. The ERP amplitude–RT relationship could be a reflection of greater attention and CNS arousal when RTs are fast. Additionally, the P300 response latencies and RT were longer when auditory discriminations were more difficult.

Motor Activity and the ERP

Movement-related brain potentials (MPs) have been detected both before and after the onset of voluntary hand movements. Kornhuber and Deecke (1965) first recorded a potential prior to voluntary movement. They found a slow negative wave beginning about 1 second before the movement, and a large positive

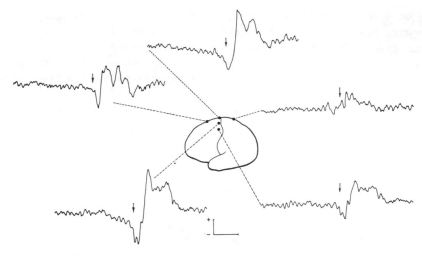

FIG. 5.5.   MPs associated with dorsiflexion of the right foot. Sum of
400 contractions. Calibration 500 msec, 2.5 µV.

complex following movement. The slow negative wave is now termed the
"readiness potential" and is discussed further in chapter 7. Vaughan, Costa,
Gilden, and Schimmel (1965) recorded a brain potential related to voluntary
movement in an RT experiment. In addition, Vaughan and colleagues (1968)
found that the MP accompanying voluntary movements was maximal over the
Rolandic cortex (see Fig. 5.5). Figure 5.5 shows data from Vaughan et al. (1968)
in which MPs recorded from different scalp locations of one subject are illustrated for movements of the right foot. The points of maximal MP amplitude for
foot, hand, and tongue movements are related to those brain areas known to
produce these movements.

   In a careful study of pre- and post-movement brain potentials, Shibasaki,
Barrett, Halliday, and Halliday (1980a) identified eight separate components;
four pre-motion and four post-motion. The experiment utilized brisk finger flexions and extensions while MPs were recorded from multiple locations over both
hemispheres. The pre-motion potentials were the readiness potential, beginning
500 msec prior to movement, a negative component 90 msec before, a positive
wave 50 msec before, and a negative component 10 msec prior to motion. The
post-motion components included a sharp negative component at 50 msec over
the contralateral frontal region, a positive wave at 90 msec, a negative component at 160 msec, and positive component at 300 msec. This last component was
maximal over the precentral brain, larger on the side opposite to the movement,
and widely distributed. These same scientists then compared the MPs accompanying both passive and voluntary movements in a follow-up study (Shibasaki
et al., 1980b). To produce passive movement, the middle finger was tied with a

string and pulled up by one of the experimenters. The voluntary movement was an extension of the same finger. There were no pre-motion components with passive movement, confirming that these components are related to preparation for voluntary movement. The post movement MPs also differed, and Shibasaki and co-workers suggested that the MPs from passive movements represent kinesthetic feedback from muscle activity.

The MPs preceding flexion of the index fingers and feet were compared for recording sites over frontal, central, and parietal areas of both hemispheres by Brunia and Van Den Bosch (1984). These researchers proposed that, prior to finger movements, amplitudes of MPs would be larger over the contralateral hemisphere, whereas prior to foot flexion, amplitudes would be larger on the same side (ipsilaterally). Their hypothesis was confirmed by the results, which, they said, point to different sources of MPs for finger and foot movements. They suggested that the ipsilateral MP prior to foot movement is due to a source in the depths of the longitudinal fissure (the deep furrow that separates the hemispheres) at the contralateral side. Because the preparation for foot movement results in activity so close to the midline, the neuronal response is projected to the opposite hemisphere, producing what appears to be an ipsilateral response.

The effects of muscular activity on the VEP have been studied by several investigators. Eason, Aiken, White, and Lichtenstein (1964) measured VEPs to flashes of light while subjects maintained a 25-lb. force on a hand grip. The muscular work increased the amplitude of VEPs to light flashes. Andreassi, Mayzner, Beyda, and Davidovics (1970) measured visual ERPs and motor ERPs from O_2 and C_3, respectively, while subjects maintained a right hand dynamometer grip equivalent to one-eighth of their maximal squeeze. The major findings were that VEP was greater in magnitude with muscle tension than with a visual stimulus alone, and that the MP was also enhanced uner condition of dual stimulation as compared to squeezing only. Landau and Buchsbaum (1973) used four light intensities and two tasks (relaxation and mental arithmetic) over several days to test effects of holding 10 lbs. of weight on visual ERPs. Their recordings were made from the vertex (Cz). They noted two effects (a) an overall decrease in ERP across days when subjects held the weights, and (b) an increase in ERP amplitude under the weight condition, as compared to relaxation, on the third day of testing. They concluded that both arousal and attentional factors interact with muscle activity to influence the visual ERP.

Investigations examining movement-related potentials indicate that brain responses occur both before and after voluntary movements. The lack of MPs with passively produced movements supports the conclusion that pre-motion MPs represent preparation for voluntary movements. Topographical analyses have provided insights regarding the cortical sources of MPs. The muscle tension studies, in general, indicate that impulses from two senses can interact to influence ERPs recorded at the cortex. For example, input from visual and proprioceptive (muscle) impulses may sum at some level and lead to enlargement of

ERPs under conditions of dual stimulation. Attentional and arousal factors may also be involved, as suggested by several investigators.

HEMISPHERIC ASYMMETRIES IN ERPS

In the context of ERP research, hemispheric asymmetry refers to the observation of a difference in the evoked potential recorded from left and right hemispheres as a function of different stimulus or task conditions. In chapter 3, it was concluded that there was evidence for EEG asymmetry with different tasks. For example, the left hemisphere EEG was activated with numerical and verbal tasks, whereas the right hemisphere EEG showed engagement with spatial and muscial activities. In this section, we consider evidence regarding ERP asymmetries under a variety of task and stimulus conditions.

Asymmetries with Visual Stimulation

If the eyes are fixated straight ahead, the locus of retinal stimulation varies with the position of a stimulus in the visual field. For example, if you look straight ahead while driving a car, the object you focus on will stimulate receptors in the foveal area of the retina, whereas objects off to the side will produce peripheral stimulation. A number of studies by Eason and his colleagues have indicated a relationship between locus of retinal stimulation and visual ERPs. For example, Eason, Oden and White (1967) recorded from over left and right hemispheres and found that the occipital area receiving primary projections from the retinal area stimulated produced larger amplitude VEPs than did the other lobe. The right lobe is primary when stimuli appear in the left visual field (LVF), and the left is primary for stimuli in the right visual field (RVF). This is because the temporal retina (outside half) of the right eye and nasal (toward nose) retina of the left eye are primarily stimulated by objects in the LVF. Both of these retinal areas project visual impulses to the right hemisphere. The opposite occurs for stimuli in the RVF.

Common strategies in neuropsychological and psychophysiological research involve the presentation of stimuli in left and right visual fields in order to study possible processing asymmetries of the left and right hemispheres of the brain. This strategy makes use of the visual system's organization, in which primary projection of information is to the contralateral hemisphere, for example, RVF stimulation results in primary excitation of neurons in the left hemisphere. The effects of stimulus location on the visual ERP were examined by Andreassi, Okamura, & Stern (1975). They found that stimuli presented in the LVF resulted in shorter VEP latencies at the right occipital area than at the left, whereas for stimuli presented in the RVF, the opposite occurred. The same .67 degree stimulus was presented in seven different locations, ranging from center to 4 degrees of visual angle in the left and right fields. In addition, amplitudes of these early VEP components (N2 peaking at about 170 msec and P2 at about 200 msec) were larger with contralateral stimulation. This field effect on visual ERP latency differentials from the two hemispheres has also been reported by Ledlow, Swanson, and Kinsbourne (1978), Andreassi, Rebert, and Larsen (1980), and Rugg, Lines, and Milner (1985). A likely explanation for the delay in VEP from the secondary hemisphere is that it represents the time it takes for the visual impulse to cross over from the primary projection area via the corpus callosum. The callosal transfer of VEP from contralateral to ipsilateral hemisphere is supported by results obtained with two individuals each born without a corpus callosum (Rugg, Milner, & Lines, 1985). It was found that the N160 VEP component was not observable as in normal individuals. In both patients, visual ERPs were obtained at hemispheres contralateral to the stimulus, but the N160 component was not observable ipsilaterally. Thus, the integrity of the corpus callosum is necessary for the interhemispheric transmission of the N160 component of the visual ERP. Transmission of other component activity to the ipsilateral hemisphere was possibly due to less prominent connections between the two hemispheres, such as the anterior commissure.

Some controversy has arisen over whether estimates of the time it takes to transfer impulses from one side of the brain to the other (interhemispheric transmission time, or IHTT) are more accurate with ERPs or RT. The model of RT as a measure of IHTT says that if a stimulus is projected to the contralateral hemisphere the RT will be shorter if that hemisphere also controls the hand that makes the response. Thus, a stimulus in the RVF results in quicker RT if the right hand is used, because the left hemisphere controls motor activity on the right side. The difference between a right hand and left hand response with RVF stimulation would be the estimate of IHTT (eg., see Berlucchi, Crea, DiStefano, & Tassinari, 1977). Estimates of IHTT using RT have reached a concensus of 2.5 msec in a number of studies (Rugg, Milner, & Lines, 1985). Ledlow et al. (1978) used both RT and ERP measures of IHTT and concluded that RT was not as good an estimate because slight changes in hand position could result in different measures. Kinsbourne, Swanson, and Ledlow (1977) suggested that RT measure are confounded by attentional variables that produce RT variations greater than the IHTT being measured. Estimates of IHTT using ERPs range from 10 msec (Andreassi & Juszczak, 1983) to 20 msec (Ledlow et al., 1978).

The Importance of Central Fixation in VEP Asymmetry Research.   The finding of contralateral ERP latency advantages has been very consistent (Andreassi & Juszczak, 1983). An exception to this contralateral advantage has been observed in strabismic subjects (Andreassi & Juszczak, 1984). Strabismus is a condition of unequal muscle balance of the two eyes. Persons with this problem have difficulty in focusing the two eyes on an object. When compared to those with normal eye balance, strabismic individuals do not show the expected latency advantage at the hemisphere contralateral to stimulation. Therefore, in using the strategy of differential visual field stimulation to study hemisphere asymmetries in function, subjects should be screened for strabismus because stimuli do not arrive at the contralateral hemisphere in the expected manner for these persons.

There is evidence that the visual presentation of verbal materials results in hemispheric asymmetries. For example, Buchsbaum and Fedio (1969) reported greater VEP differences to words and nonsense patterns for the left occipital hemisphere than for the right hemisphere. Similar findings were obtained by Buchsbaum and Fedio (1970) when they compared VEPs to very common three-letter words and nonsense stimuli composed of random dot patterns. Both experiments by Buchsbaum and Fedio were conducted with right-handed subjects (i.e., persons who had a very high probability of left hemisphere dominance with respect to speech functions).

The logic behind examining ERP hemispheric differences is that varied amplitudes or latencies to various kinds of stimuli suggest differential processing of these stimuli. Small (1983) conducted a study to see if visual ERPs would show hemispheric asymmetry to slides of familiar and unfamiliar faces. An early component (P100) was of similar amplitude from both hemispheres, whereas the later P300 was larger over the right hemisphere for known faces. This interesting finding suggests greater right-hemisphere participation in the perception of faces, but definite conclusions should await confirmation by other ERP researchers, although there is evidence from clinical work that patients with right-hemisphere damage show greater loss in facial recognition than those with lesions in the left hemisphere. Aine and Harter (1984) reported larger left-hemisphere responses in processing relevant words as compared to irrelevant ones. This was not observed at right-hemisphere sites.

Davis and Wada (1974) measured visual and auditory ERPs in 12 normal (left-sided speech-dominant) persons and in 10 epileptics (5 right and 5 left speech-dominant). The visual stimuli (light flashes) produced ERPs of similar form in the non-speech-dominant hemisphere, while auditory stimuli (clicks) produced similar ERPs in the speech-dominant hemisphere. Davis and Wada hypothesized that the speech-dominant hemisphere possesses superior auditory perception capabilities, whereas visual perception is more of a nondominant hemisphere function. Although these asymmetries are related to speech dominance, they may be more fundamental than speech processing, because they do not require verbal stimuli. These are provocative suggestions, and they certainly deserve continued research effort.

Asymmetries with Auditory Stimulation

Right hemispheric auditory ERPs were recorded under conditions of monaural and binaural stimulation by Butler, Keidel, and Spreng (1969). A 1000 Hz tone was presented at intensities ranging from 20 to 100 dB. They found that when the monaural stimulus was delivered to the left ear, the right-hemisphere-derived

ERP components showed consistently shorter latencies than when the monaural stimulus was presented to the right ear (when the tone was in the range of 50 to 100 dB). That is, auditory ERP latencies were shorter for contralateral (opposite side) than for ipsilateral (same side) stimulation. They explained this finding in terms of the more direct route to the cortex offered by contralateral auditory pathways as compared to ipsilateral projections. But this explanation is unlikely, because ipsilateral and contralateral pathways are equally complex. They also noted that contralateral stimulation produced larger ERP amplitudes than did stimulation of the ear on the same side of the head.

Andreassi, DiSimone, Friend, & Grota (1975) examined auditory ERPs recorded from over both left (C_3) and right (C_4) hemispheres during monaural and binaural stimulation. The stimulus used was white noise at a level of 80 dB. They found that auditory stimulation produced larger amplitude ERPs in the contralateral hemispheres as compared to the ipsilateral. This agrees with one of the findings of Butler et al. (1969). However, Andreassi et al. found no difference in ERP latencies from contralateral and ipsilateral hemispheres. The amplitude results were interpreted as providing further evidence for the predominance of the contralateral pathways of the auditory system. It is known that each ear has more neuronal connections leading to the hemisphere on the opposite side than to the auditory cortex on the same side as the ear that is stimulated.

The reliability of auditory ERP measures of contralateral dominance was demonstrated in a careful experiment by Connolly (1985). He tested people on six different occasions, using recordings from T_3 and T_4, and reported consistently larger responses in the hemisphere contralateral to the ear of stimulation. Thus, the stability of the contralateral effect is strongly supported, and Connolly has suggested its potential importance in assessing effects of drugs or psychopathology on brain activity.

One might expect that simultaneous stimulation of left and right ears with verbal stimuli would lead to superior detection performance by the right ear, because dominant pathways from the right ear lead to the left hemisphere, which controls language function in most people. This has been found to be the case in a number of studies in which the two ears were presented with different stimuli at the same time (Kimura, 1961, 1967). The superiority of contralateral presentations has been consistently reported by Kimura and her colleagues in this so-called "dichotic listening" paradigm.

Peters and Mendel (1974) determined effects of monaural and binaural stimulation (40 dB clicks) on the early components of the ERP, that is, components with latencies of less than 50 msec. No contralateral–ipsilateral differences were found. Possible reasons for this given by the authors included a suggestion of different underlying neural mechanisms for early versus late ERP components and the use of a low level of stimulation (40 dB). It can be recalled that Butler et al. (1969) found evidence for laterality in late ERP components only with stimuli of 50 dB or greater in intensity.

The effects of more complex stimuli on the ERP, such as speech stimuli and word meaning, are discussed in chapter 6. With regard to asymmetry, however, it may be noted that Morrell and Salamy (1971) found ERP amplitudes recorded from over the left hemisphere to be larger than those from the right in response to speech stimuli. Asymmetries have also been reported for linguistic information (Wood, Goff, & Day, 1971), speech versus mechanical sound-effect stimuli (Matsumiya, Tagliasco, & Lombroso, 1972), contextual meaning of words (Brown, Marsh, & Smith, 1973), and verb and noun meanings of ambiguous words (Teyler, Roemer, & Harrison, 1973). However, Grabow and Elliott (1974), who required their 14 subjects to make either simple speech sounds (e.g., ba) or words (e.g., kangaroo) found no evidence for hemispheric asymmetries during verbalization. A similar negative finding has been reported by Galambos, Benson, Smith, Schulman-Galambos, and Osier (1975). More recent attempts to find greater activity in the left hemisphere with speech stimuli have not met with success. For example, Grabow, Aronson, Offord, Rose, and Greene (1980) and Grabow, Aronson, Rose, and Greene (1980) failed to repeat the findings of Morrell and Salamy (1971) and Wood et al (1971). Further, Woods and Elmasian (1986) found that the hemispheres had similar responses to speech or tone stimuli. Thus, functional asymmetries of the hemispheres has yet to be convincingly demonstrated through the use of ERPs.

Asymmetries and Cognitive Functions

Rhodes, Dustman, and Beck (1969) reported that bright children produced right hemisphere visual ERPs that were larger than their left-sided ERPs. This contrasted with dull children, who had no hemispheric amplitude asymmetries. A similar finding was obtained by Richlin, Weisinger, Weinstein, Giannini, and Morganstern (1971), who found larger right-hemisphere visual ERPs in children of normal intelligence but the reverse effect with retarded children. Galin and Ellis (1975) recorded visual ERPs to probe stimuli from over left and right hemispheres while subjects performed verbal and spatial tasks. It was concluded that The ERP asymmetry obtained reflected hemispheric specialization for these tasks. However, Mayes and Beaumont (1977) failed to repeat these results. They suggested that the original study of Galin and Ellis was flawed because of differences in hand–arm use and direction of gaze required in the two tasks. Papanicolaou, Schmidt, Moore, and Eisenberg (1983) avoided the difficulties of the Galin and Ellis study by using a procedure involving the recording of ERPs to a probe stimulus while different cognitive operations were performed on the same materials. Auditory ERPs to a probe tone stimulus were recorded while subjects engaged in either an arithmetic or a visuospatial task that used the same irregular geometric shapes. The probe ERP was smaller at left-hemisphere sites during arithmetic computations and at right-hemisphere areas with the spatial task. The researchers interpreted the decreases in ERP amplitudes as indicants of greater hemispheric engagement in a given task. In another study, Papanicolaou,

Levin, Eisenberg, and Moore (1983) recorded ERPs to a probe click stimulus while subjects listened only to the click (control), detected a given syllable (phonetic processing), or judged the emotions communicated by different speakers (affective processing). The two experimental conditions involved listening to the same taped conversation. The probe ERPs were much larger in both hemispheres under the control condition than with either phonetic (left hemisphere) or emotional (right hemisphere) processing. The results indicated dominance of the left hemisphere during phonetic processing and greater right hemisphere involvement in reacting to verbal emotional content.

In summary, a number of studies have indicated a relationship between location of stimuli in the visual field and hemispheric asymmetries in the VEP. The observed latency and amplitude differences have been explained in terms of the primary projection of stimuli to the contralateral hemisphere. That a response occurs at the ipsilateral cortex at all is due to crossing of neural impulses via the corpus callosum and other commissures that connect the left and right hemispheres. Visual ERP asymmetries have also been reported for verbal versus nonsense visual stimuli (i.e., the speech-dominant hemisphere produces larger responses to verbal material), and for consonant-vowel syllables (left hemisphere response).

Hemispheric asymmetries occur with auditory stimulation as a function of the ear stimulated. The higher amplitude responses from the contralateral hemispheres have been interpreted as consistent with the known contralateral predominance in the pathways of the auditory system—that is, the contralateral pathways contain a larger number of neurons. Auditory ERP asymmetries for speech and language materials have been reported by some investigators and not by others. This area is still unsettled, and perhaps we will not see any firm conclusions until more sensitive recording techniques have been developed.

There is some evidence to indicate that ERP asymmetries may be related to intelligence and cognitive functioning. The evidence concerning intelligence is rather tenuous, whereas that regarding cognitive functioning seems to be gaining, for example, findings regarding differential hemispheric engagement in phonetic and affective processing.

THE ERP AND SLEEP

The classification of sleep into distinct stages on the basis of brain wave activity was discussed in chapter 4 (see Table 4.2). These distinctions have enabled investigators to present sensory stimuli to persons in different sleep stages in order to study ERPs as a function of sleep stage. Shagass (1972b) summarized findings regarding the somatosensory ERP (SEP) obtained during sleep as follows: (a) latencies of SEPs become longer as sleep progresses from Stage 1 to 4; (b) the SEP during REM sleep is similar to that obtained during light sleep stages; (c) amplitude changes are not as consistent as those observed for latency, but early components are generally enlarged during slow-wave sleep; and (d) the SEP gradually (taking as long as 30 minutes) returns to the pre-sleep level after awakening.

Shagass and Trusty (1966) found a systematic relationship between visual ERP latencies and sleep stage, that is, progressive lengthening of latencies from Stage 1 to Stage 4. Weitzman and Kremen (1965) reported similar relationships between auditory ERP latencies and sleep stage.

Very early auditory ERPs, occurring between 1 and 10 msec after stimulation, have been found by Jewett and Williston (1971) and related to activity evoked from brainstem auditory structures. These early responses have been termed brainstem auditory evoked potentials (BAEPs). Amadeo and Shagass (1973) experimented to determine whether the BAEP would differ in awake and sleeping individuals. Their results showed little difference in amplitude and latency of these brain stem potentials either between waking and sleep or between sleep stages. They interpreted this finding as indicating that changes in later AEP components that occur during sleep are mediated by brain areas above the level of the brain stem, either at the thalamus or the cerebral cortex. However, this finding of no change in the BAEP is now questionable because of more recent research. Marshall and Donchin (1981) observed delays in several components of the BAEP with decreases in body temperature, and the temperature decreases occurred when the subjects slept. Other investigators have examined effects of light sleep on the BAEP in a detailed study, (Hughes, Fino, & Hart, 1984). They also found significant delays in several BAEP components when comparing waking to light sleep conditions. Thus, the assumption that BAEPs do not change from the waking state to sleep needs to be reexamined.

Early components (latencies less than 40 msec) of the AEP were studied during REM and Stages 2, 3, and 4, sleep by Mendel and Kupperman (1974). These early components, obtained during REM sleep, had the same latency, amplitude, and wave form as AEPs elicited during other sleep stages. ERP waveforms with latencies of about 150 to 170 msec have been shown to decrease in amplitude with sleep (Naatanen & Picton, 1987). These latter researchers reported on some recent work that confirms decreases in the 150–170 latency wave, but shows an additional later wave to auditory stimuli during NREM sleep, especially early in the night (see Naatanen & Picton, 1987, p. 407). Buchsbaum, Ginnin, and Pfefferbaum (1975) studied the effects of sleep stage and stimulus intensity on AEPs. Clicks ranging from 50 to 80 dB were used as stimuli. They found that AEP amplitudes increased more with increasing stimulus intensity during Stages 2, 3, and 4 sleep than during REM sleep or when subjects were awake. Townsend, House, and Johnson (1976) exposed 10 subjects to tone pulses 24 hours a day for 30 days. The intensity levels were at 80 and 90 dB for 10 days each, in that order. The AEPs were examined in Stage 2 and REM sleep on every fifth night of the 30-day period. One finding was that the AEP in Stage 2 sleep was consistently larger than in REM sleep. The main finding was that during sleep there was little habituation of the AEP, even with long-term, daily exposure to the same stimulus. Thus, they concluded that the AEP during sleep is similar to the K-complex (see chapter 4) in terms of resistance to habituation. (Recall that the K-complex is considered to be the sleeping EEG analog of the orienting response.) Thus, the authors pointed out that during sleep, the AEP behaves as though each succeeding stimulus is a "first" presentation.

In summary, the overall findings regarding ERPs during sleep indicate that they definitely occur, and that the later components differ from waking ERPs in latency and amplitude. Sleep is an example, therefore, of a situation where a brain response occurs to a stimulus that is probably not consciously perceived.

Event-related brain potentials and various mental functions, including intelligence, meaning of stimuli, linguistic processing, learning, and hypnosis are covered in the next chapter. Sensory, attentional, and perceptual processes and their relations to ERPs are also presented in chapter 6.

REFERENCES

Aine, C. J., & Harter, M. R. (1984). Hemispheric differences in event-related potentials to stroop stimuli. In R. Karrer, J. Cohen, & P. Teuting (Eds.), *Brain & information: Event-related potentials* (pp. 154–156). New York: Annals of the N.Y. Academy of Sciences.

Amadeo, M., & Shagass, C. (1973). Brief latency click-evoked potentials during waking and sleep in man. *Psychophysiology, 10,* 244–250.

Andreassi, J. L., DeSimone, J. J., Friend, M. A., & Grota, P. A. (1975). Hemispheric amplitude asymmetries in the auditory evoked potential with monaural and binaural stimulation. *Physiological Psychology, 3,* 169–171.

Andreassi, J. L., & Greco, J. R. (1975). Effects of bisensory stimulation on reaction time and the evoked cortical potential. *Physiological Psychology, 3,* 189–194.

Andreassi, J. L., & Juszczak, N. M. (1983). *Brain responses and information processing IV: Investigations of hemispheric asymmetry in event-related potentials and performance during discrimination of line orientation, color, shape, and under visual masking.* Fourth Annual Report, Baruch College, CUNY, AFOSR Contract F49620-80-C-0013.

Andreassi, J. L., & Juszczak, N. M. (1984). To fixate or not to fixate: The problem of undetected strabismic subjects in visual evoked potential research: In R. Karrer, J. Cohen, & P. Teuting (Eds.), *Brain & information: Event-related potentials* (pp. 157–161). New York: Annals of the N.Y. Academy of Sciences.

Andreassi, J. L., Mayzner, M. S., Beyda, D. R., & Davidovics, S. (1970). Effects of induced muscle tension upon the visual evoked potential and motor potential. *Psychonomic Science, 20,* 245–247.

Andreassi, J. L., Okamura, H., & Stern, M. S. (1975). Hemispheric asymmetries in the visual evoked cortical potential as a function of stimulus location. *Psychophysiology, 12,* 541–546.

Andreassi, J. L., Rebert, C. S., & Larsen, F. F. (1980). *Brain responses and information processing I: Hemispheric asymmetries in event-related potentials during signal detection.* First Annual Report, Baruch College, CUNY, AFOSR Contract F49620-80-C-0013.

Arezzo, J. C., & Vaughan, H. G., Jr. (1975). Cortical potentials associated with voluntary movements in the monkey. *Brain Research, 88,* 99–104.

Arezzo, J. C., Vaughan, H. G., Jr., Kraut, M. A., Steinschneider, M., & Legatt, A. D. (1986). Intracranial generators of event-related potentials in the monkey. In R. Q. Cracco & I. Bodis-Wollner (Eds.), *Evoked potentials* (pp. 174–189). New York: Liss.

Beck, E. C. (1975). Electrophysiology and behavior. *Annual Review of Psychology, 26,* 233–262.

Becker, W., Iwase, R., Jurgens, R., & Kornhuber, H. H. (1976). Bercitschaftspotential preceding voluntary slow and rapid hand movements. In W. C. McCallum & J. R. Knott (Eds.), *The responsive brain* (pp. 99–102). Bristol: John Wright & Sons.

Berlucchi, G., Crea, T., DiStefano, M., & Tassinari, G. (1977). Influence of spatial stimulus–response compatibility on reaction time of ipsilateral and contralateral hand to lateralized light stimuli. *Journal of Experimental Psychology: Human Perception and Performance, 3,* 505–517.

Brown, W. S., Marsh, J. T., & Smith, J. C. (1973). Contextual meaning effects on speech-evoked potentials. *Behavioral Biology, 9,* 755–761.

Brunia, C. H. M., & Van Den Bosch, W. E. J. (1984). Movement-related slow potentials. I. A contrast between finger and foot movements in right-handed subjects. *Electroencephalography & Clinical Neurophysiology, 57,* 515–527.

Buchsbaum, M., & Fedio, P. (1969). Visual information and evoked responses from the left and right hemispheres. *Electroencephalography and Clinical Neurophysiology,26,* 266–272.

Buchsbaum, M., & Fedio, P. (1970). Visual information and evoked potentials to verbal and nonverbal stimuli in the left and right visual fields. *Physiology and Behavior, 5,* 207–210.

Buchsbaum, M., Ginnin, J. C., & Pfefferbaum, A. (1975). Effect of sleep stage and stimulus intensity on auditory average evoked responses. *Psychophysiology, 12,* 707–712.

Butler, R. A., Keidel, W. D., & Spreng, M. (1969). An investigation of the human cortical evoked potential under conditions of monaural and binaural stimulation. *Acta Otolaryngologica, 68,* 317–326.

Cohen, J. (1969). Very slow brain potentials relating to expectancy: The CNV. In E. Donchin & D. B. Lindsley (Eds.), *Average evoked potentials: Methods, results, evaluations* NASA, Washington, DC: U.S. Government Printing Office.

Connolly, J. F. (1985). Stability of pathway-hemisphere differences in the auditory event-related potential (ERP) to monaural stimulation. *Psychophysiology, 22,* 87–95.

Cooper, R. Methodology of slow potential changes. In W. C. McCallum & J. R. Knott (Eds.), *The responsive brain* (pp. 1–4). Bristol: John Wright & Sons.

Cooper, R., McCallum, W. C., Newton, P., Papakostopoulos, D., Pocock, P. V., & Warren, W. J. (1977). Cortical potentials associated with the detection of visual events. *Science, 196,* 74–77.

Courchesne, E., Hillyard, S. A., & Galambos, R. (1975). Stimulus novelty, task relevance and the visual evoked potential in man. *Electroencephalography and Clinical Neurophysiology, 39,* 131–143.

Davis, A. E., & Wada, J. A. (1974). Hemispheric asymmetry: Frequency analysis of visual and auditory evoked responses to non-verbal stimuli. *Electroencephalography and Clinical Neurophysiology, 37,* 1–9.

Deecke, L. (1976). Potential changes associated with motor action, reflex responses and readiness (Chairman's opening remarks). In W. C. McCallum & J. R. Knott (Eds.), *The responsive brain* (pp. 91–93). Bristol: John Wright & Sons.

Donchin, E., & Lindsley, D. B. (1966). Average evoked potentials and reaction times to visual stimuli. *Electroencephalography and Clinical Neurophysiology, 20,* 217–223.

Eason, R. G., Aiken, L. R., White, C. T., & Lichtenstein, M. (1964). Activation and behavior: II. Visually evoked cortical potentials in man as indicants of activation level. *Perceptual and Motor Skills, 19,* 875–895.

Eason, R. G., Oden, D., & White, C. T. (1967). Visually evoked cortical potentials and reaction time in relation to site of retinal stimulation. *Electroencephalography & Clinical Neurophysiology, 22,* 313–324.

Galambos, R., Benson, P., Smith, T. S., Schulman-Galambos, C., & Osier, H. (1975). On hemispheric differences in evoked potentials to speech stimuli. *Electroencephalography and Clinical Neurophysiology, 39,* 279–283.

Galin, D., & Ellis, R. (1975). Asymmetry in evoked potentials as an index of lateralized cognitive processes: Relation to EEG alpha asymmetry. *Neuropsychologia, 13,* 45–50.

Geddes, L. A. (1967). The measurement of physiological phenomena. In C. C. Brown (Ed.), *Methods in psychophysiology* (pp. 369–452). Baltimore: Williams & Wilkins.

Goff, W. R., Allison, T., & Vaughan, H. G. Jr. (1978). The functional neuroanatomy of event-related potentials. In E. Callaway, P. Teuting, & S. H. Koslow (Eds.), *Event-related potentials in man* (pp. 1–80). New York: Academic Press.

Grabow, J. D., Aronson, A. E., Offord, K. P., Rose, D. E., & Greene, K. L. (1980). Hemispheric potentials evoked by speech sounds during discrimination tasks. *Electroencephalography and Clinical Neurophysiology, 49,* 48–58.

Grabow, J. D., Aronson, A. E., Rose, D. E., & Greene, K. L. (1980). Summated potentials evoked by speech sounds for determining cerebral dominance for language. *Electroencephalography and Clinical Neurophysiology, 49* 38–47.

Grabow, J., & Elliott, F. W. (1974). The electrophysiologic assessment of hemispheric asymmetries during speech. *Journal of Speech and Hearing Research, 17,* 64–72.

Halgren, E., Squires, N. K., Wilson, C. S., Rohrbaugh, J. W., Babb, T. L., & Crandall, P. H. (1980). Endogenous potentials generated in the human hippocampal formation and the amygdala by infrequent events. *Science, 210,* 803–805.

Hughes, J. R., Fino, J. J., & Hart, L. A. (1984). The effect of light sleep on the brainstem auditory evoked potential (BAEP). *International Journal of Neuroscience, 24,* 267–274.

Jewett, D. L., Romano, M. N., & Williston, J. S. (1970). Human auditory evoked potentials: Possible brain stem components detected on the scalp. *Science, 167,* 1517–1518.

Jewett, D. L., & Williston, J. S. (1971). Auditory evoked far fields averaged for the scalp of humans. *Brain, 94,* 681–696.

Johnson, R., Jr., & Fedio, P. (1986). P300 activity in patients following unilateral temporal lobectomy: A preliminary report. In W. C. McCallum, R. Zappoli, & F. Denoth (Eds.), *Cerebral psychophysiology: Studies in event-related potentials* (pp. 552–554). Amsterdam: Elsevier.

Karlin, L., Martz, M. J., Brauth, S. E., & Mordkoff, A. M. (1971). Auditory evoked potentials, motor potentials and reaction time. *Electroencephalography and Clinical Neurophysiology, 31,* 129–136.

Kimura, D. (1961). Cerebral dominance and the perception of verbal stimuli. *Canadian Journal of Psychology, 15,* 166–171.

Kimura, D. (1967). Functional asymmetry of the brain in dichotic listening. *Cortex, 3,* 163–178.

Kinsbourne, M., Swanson, J. M., & Ledlow, A. (1977). Measuring interhemispheric transfer time in man. *Transactions of the American Neurological Association, 102,* 1–4.

Kornhuber, H. H., & Deecke, L. (1965). Cerebral potential changes in voluntary and passive movements in man: Readiness potential and reafferent potential. *Pflugers Archives gesamte Physiologi, 284,* 1–17.

Landau, S. G., & Buchsbaum, M. (1973). Average evoked response and muscle tension. *Phsyiological Psychology, 1,* 56–60.

Ledlow, A., Swanson, J. M., & Kinsbourne, M. (1978). Reaction times and evoked potentials as indicators of hemispheric differences for laterally presented name and physical matches. *Journal of Experimental Psychology: Human Perception and Performance, 4,*440–454.

Marshall, N., & Donchin, E. (1981). Circadian variation in the latency of brainstem responses and its relation to body temperature. *Science, 212,* 356–358.

Matsumiya, Y., Tagliasco, V., & Lombroso, C. T. (1972). Auditory evoked response: Meaningfulness of stimuli and interhemispheric asymmetry. *Science, 175,* 790–792.

Mayes, A., & Beaumont, G. (1977). Does visual evoked potential asymmetry index cognitive activity? *Neuropsychologia, 15,* 249–256.

McCallum, W. C., Papakostopoulos, D., & Griffith, H. B. (1976). Distribution of CNV and other slow potential changes in human brainstem structures. In W. C. McCallum & J. R. Knott (Eds.), *The responsive brain*, (pp. 205–210). Bristol: John Wright & Sons.

Mendel, M. I., & Kupperman, G. L. (1974). Early component of the averaged electroencephalic response to constant level clicks during rapid eye movement sleep. *Audiology, 13,* 23–32.

Morrell, L. K., & Morrell, F. (1966). Evoked potentials and reaction times: A study of intraindividual variability. *Electroencephalography and Clinical Neurophysiology, 20,* 567–575.

Morrell, L. K., & Salamy, J. G. (1971). Hemispheric asymmetry of electrocortical responses to speech stimuli. *Science, 23,* 193–195.

Naatanen, R., & Picton, T. W. (1987). The N1 wave of the human electric and magnetic response to sound: A review and an analysis of the component structure. *Psychophysiology, 24,* 375–425.

Papanicolaou, A. C., Levin, H. S., Eisenberg, H. M., & Moore, B. D. (1983). Evoked potential indices of selective hemispheric engagement in affective and phonetic tasks. *Neuropsychologia, 21,* 401–405.

Papanicolaou, A. C., Schmidt, A. L., Moore, B. D., & Eisenberg, H. M. (1983). Cerebral activation patterns in an arithmetic and a visuaospatial processing task. *International Journal of Neuroscience, 20,* 283–288.

Peters, J. F., & Mendel, M. I. (1974). Early components of the averaged electroencephalic response to monaural and binaural stimulation. *Audiology, 13,* 195–204.

Rebert, C. S., Tecce, J. J., Marczynski, T. J., Pirch, J. H., & Thompson, J. W. (1986). Neural anatomy, chemistry, and event-related brain potentials: An approach to understanding the substrates of mind. In W. C. McCallum, R. Zappoli & F. Denoth (Eds.), *Cerebral psychophysiology: Studies in event-related potentials* (pp. 343–393). Amsterdam: Elsevier.

Rhodes, L. E., Dustman, R. E., & Beck, E. C. (1969). The visual evoked response: A comparison of bright and dull children. *Electroencephalography and Clinical Neurophysiology, 27,* 364–372.

Richlin, M., Weisinger, M., Weinstein, S., Giannini, M., & Morganstern, M. (1971). Interhemispheric asymmetries of evoked cortical responses in retarded and normal children. *Cortex, 7,* 98–105.

Ritter, W., Simson, R., & Vaughan, H. G. (1982). Association cortex potentials and reaction time in auditory discrimination. *Electroencephalography and Clinical Neurophysiology, 33,* 547–555.

Ritter, W., Vaughan, H. G., Jr., & Costa, L. D. (1968). Orienting and habituation to auditory stimuli: A study of short term changes in average evoked responses. *Electroencephalography and Clinical Neurophysiology, 25,* 550–556.

Rugg, M. D., Lines, C. R., & Milner, A. D. (1985). Further investigation of visual evoked potentials elicited by lateralized stimuli: Effects of stimulus eccentricity and reference site. *Electroencephalography and Clinical Neurophysiology, 62,* 81–87.

Rugg, M. D., Milner, A. D., & Lines C. R. (1985). Visual evoked potentials to lateralized stimuli in two cases of callosal agensis. *Journal of Neurology, Neurosurgery & Psychiatry, 48,* 367–373.

Samuels, I. (1959). Reticular mechanisms and behavior. *Psychological Bulletin, 56,* 1–25.

Scheibel, M. E., & Scheibel, A. B. (1967). Anatomical basis of attention mechanisms in vertebrate brains. In G. L. Quarton, T. Melnechuk, & F. O. Schmitt (Eds.), *The neurosciences: A study program* (pp. 420–437). New York: The Rockefeller University Press.

Shagass, C. (1972b). *Evoked brain potentials in psychiatry*. New York: Plenum.

Shagass, C., & Trusty, D. (1966). Somatosensory and visual cerebral evoked response changes during sleep. In J. Wortis (Ed.), *Recent advances in biological psychiatry*, (vol. VIII, pp. 213–334). New York: Plenum Press.

Shibasaki, H., Barrett, G., Halliday, E., & Halliday, A. M. (1980a). Components of the movement-related cortical potential and their scalp topography. *Electroencephalography and Clinical Neurophysiology, 49,* 213–226.

Shibasaki, H., Barrett, G., Halliday, E., & Halliday, A. M. (1980b). Cortical potentials following voluntary and passive finger movements. *Electroencephalography and Clinical Neurophysiology, 50,* 201–213.

Simson, R. C., Vaughan, H. G., Jr., & Ritter, W. (1977). The scalp topography of potentials in auditory and visual go–no go tasks. *Electroencephalography and Clinical Neurophysiology, 43,* 864–875.

Small, M. (1983). Asymmetrical evoked potentials in response to face stimuli. *Cortex, 19,* 441–450.

Squires, N. K., Squires, K. C., & Hillyard, S. A. (1975). Two varieties of long-latency positive waves evoked by unpredictable auditory stimuli in man. *Electroencephalography and Clinical Neurophysiology, 38,* 387–401.

Sutton, S., Braren, M., & Zubin, J. (1965). Evoked-potential correlates of stimulus uncertainty, *Science, 150,* 1187–1188.

Sutton, S., Teuting, P., Zubin, J., & John, E. R. (1967). Information delivery and the sensory evoked potential. *Science, 155,* 1436–1439.

Tcccc, J. J. (1972). Contingent negative variation (CNV) and psychological processes in man. *Psychological Bulletin, 77,* 73–108.

Teyler, T. J., Roemer, R. A., & Harrison, T. F. (1973). Human scalp-recorded evoked potential correlates of linguistic stimuli. *Bulletin of the Psychonomic Society, 1,* 333–334.

Townsend, R. E., House, J. F., & Johnson, L. C. (1976). Auditory evoked potential in Stage 2 and REM sleep during a 30-day exposure to tone pulses. *Psychophysiology, 13,* 54–57.

Vaughan, H. G., Jr. (1969). The relationship of brain activity to scalp recordings of event-related potentials. In E. Donchin & D. B. Lindsley (Eds.), *Average evoked potentials* (pp. 45–94) Washington, DC: NASA.

Vaughan, H. G., Jr., & Arezzo, J. C. (1988). The neural basis of event related potentials: In T. W. Picton (Ed.), *Human event related potentials: Handbook of electroencephalography and clinical neurophysiology, Vol. III.* Amsterdam: Elsevier.

Vaughan, H. G., Costa, L. D., & Gilden, L. (1966). The functional relation of visual evoked response and reaction time to stimulus intensity. *Vision Research, 6,* 645–656.

Vaughan, H. G., Jr., Costa, L. D., Gilden, L., & Schimmel,H. (1965). Identification of sensory and motor components of cerebral activity in simple reaction time tasks. *Proceedings of the 73rd Annual Convention of the American Psychological Association, 1,* 179–180.

Vaughan, H. G., Costa, L. D. & Ritter, W. (1968). Topography of the human motor potential. *Electroencephalography and Clinical Neurophysiology, 25,* 1–10.

Vaughan, H. G., & Hull, R. C. (1965). Functional relation between stimulus intensity and photically evoked cerebral responses in man. *Nature, 206,* 720–722.

Walter, W. G., Cooper, R., Aldridge, V. J., McCallum, W. C., & Winter, A. L. (1964). Contingent negative variation: An electrical sign of sensory motor association and expectancy in the human brain. *Nature, 203,* 380–384.

Weitzman, E. D., & Kremen, H. (1965). Auditory evoked responses during different stages of sleep in man. *Electroencephalography and Clinical Neurophysiology, 18,* 65–70.

Wood, C., Goff, W. R., & Day, R. S. (1971). Auditory evoked potentials during speech perception. *Science, 173,* 1248–1251.

Woods, D. L., & Elmasian, R. (1986). The habituation of event-related potentials to speech sounds and tones. *Electroencephalography and Clinical Neurophysiology, 65,* 447–459.

Yingling, C. D., & Hosobuchi, Y. A. (1984). Subcortical correlate of P300 in man. *Electroencephalography and Clinical Neurophysiology, 59,* 72–76.

6

Event-Related Brain Potentials and Behavior: Mental Activities and Sensory, Attentional, and Perceptual Functions

An interesting picture of brain function begins to emerge as we consider data obtained from ERP studies. The brain can be considered as a highly integrated organ in which the many areas, both cortical and subcortical, cooperate in carrying out its many functions. We see this in the ERPs that develop over many areas of the brain simultaneously in response to a given stimulus. Thus, for example, topographical studies show that although occipital cortex may respond maximally to a word flashed on a screen, there is sufficient response from parietal and frontal areas to suggest that they are also involved in processing the stimulus. This chapter considers, in general, the study of ERPs as they relate to more complex behavior than that discussed in chapter 5. Thus, in this chapter we discuss some of the findings concerning the ERP and mental activities, including measures of intellectual functioning, meaning, linguistic processes, learning, and hypnotic suggestion. We also examine some ERP correlates of sensation, attention, and perception. The long-latency ERPs and steady potential shifts (e.g., P300 and CNV) are discussed in chapter 7 with regard to their observed relationships to higher cognitive activities such as attention, preparation for events, and information processing.

EVENT-RELATED POTENTIALS AND MENTAL ACTIVITY

In this section, we consider a number of human mental processes as they have been related to ERPs. Among these are intelligence, linguistic processes, learning, meaning, imagery, and ERPs produced during hypnotic suggestion.

ERPs and Intelligence

Similar to EEG, the ERP has been viewed by some as a possible culture-free technique to assess intelligence. Also, like EEG, attempts to relate ERPs to intelligence have met with mixed results. The approach in this area has been to attempt to relate some characteristic of ERPs (e.g., latency, amplitude, variability) to some measure of intellectual performance, most commonly, performance on an intelligence test. An early experiment was performed by Chalke and Ertl (1965), who postulated that latencies of ERP components may be an index of information-processing efficiency; that is, biologically efficient organisms process data more quickly than less efficient ones, and thus their ERP latencies should be shorter. This proposal is known as the neural efficiency hypothesis. In their study, Chalke and Ertl obtained ERPs to light flashes, using bipolar, F_4-P_4, electrodes. The measure of IQ was performance on a paper-and-pencil intelligence test (Otis Higher Form A). The subjects were 33 graduate students with high Otis scores, 11 army cadets with average scores, and 4 mentally retarded individuals with very low scores. The results indicated that latencies of later ERP components (those occurring after 100 msec, were related to intelligence test scores (i.e., the higher the score the shorter the latency). Methodologically, this study is flawed because it used such a lopsided sample with scores that clustered at the high end (33 graduate students at one extreme and only 4 mentally retarded at the other). The use of a group paper-and-pencil test of intelligence is poor procedure with the mentally retarded who need individual testing, such as the Stanford-Binet or the Wechsler Intelligence Scale for Children (WISC). However, a much larger-scale study by Ertl and Schafer (1969), based on a sample of 566 school children, indicated significant correlations between test scores and ERP latencies.

Investigators subsequent to Ertl have reported both negative and positive findings. On the negative side, Davis (1971) reported no relation in a large-scale study in which visual ERP latencies were measured in more than 1,000 school children and compared to test scores and school performance. This 1971 study by Davis was carried out in association with Ertl. In another study with negative findings, the auditory ERP was measured using a bipolar placement with 84 persons in a first experiment and with 212 subjects in a second one (Rust, 1975). The measure of intelligence was the Mill Hill Vocabulary Scale in the first experiment and the Ravens Progressive Matrices in the second experiment. Neither study found a relation between intelligence and latency measures. Rust noted that more evidence has been produced for the visual ERP than the auditory in the intelligence context, but saw no reason for a restriction of neural efficiency to any particular sensory modality, a comment similar to that made by Callaway (1975). In his 1975 book Callaway described studies of his own in which he found that auditory ERPs correlated positively with IQ but negatively with age. This represents a serious difficulty for the neural efficiency hypothesis of Ertl, because it is hard to explain why neural efficiency would be higher for brighter children, but not for older ones.

Some investigators who have reported positive findings are Blinkhorn and Hendrickson (1982), Gucker (1973), Hendrickson and Hendrickson (1980), Perry, McCoy, Cunningham, Falgout, and Street (1976), and Shucard and Horn (1972). Shucard and Horn (1972) measured visual ERPs and intelligence scores of 108 persons under conditions of high, medium and low arousal. They found the greatest degree of correspondence between fast latency and high scores under the low-arousal condition. One suggested possibility was that brighter subjects were better able to maintain alertness in the boring low-arousal condition in which subjects merely watched light flashes. Shucard and Horn argued that arousal levels of subjects must be low in order to successfully use ERP latencies to predict intelligence. Gucker (1973) measured the VEPs of 17 children ranging in age from 8 to 13. Their WISC scores were correlated with measures of VEP latency and a high negative relationship was found, indicating that higher test scores were related to faster latencies.

A number of visual ERP and intelligence measures were studied by Perry et al. (1976). They administered a battery of abilities tests to 98 5-year-old children. Visual ERPs were recorded from left and right hemispheres (monopolar) and occipital midline (bipolar) under three stimulus conditions. The measures used were amplitude, latency, and complexity (number of peaks) of ERPs. They reported significant multiple correlations between these VEP measures and Wechsler Preschool and Primary Scale of Intelligence (WPPSI). An interesting aspect of this study is that the subjects were not selected on the basis of extreme IQ scores; in fact, the mean WPPSI scores was 119, with a range of from 94 to 141. Thus, Perry and his colleagues seem to have found a relationship between intelligence test scores and a complex of ERP measures, not amplitude alone.

A testable hypothesis relating IQ to ERP was developed by Hendrickson and Hendrickson (1980). According to their model, IQ is positively related to complexity of the ERP trace, and complexity decreases with higher error rates in the brain. If the ERP trace is stretched out into a straight line (what the Hendricksons call a "string" measure), they predict that longer strings will be related to higher IQs. This hypothesis was confirmed in two studies. In the first study (Hendrickson & Hendrickson, 1980), full scale Wechsler scores correlated highly with string length for 254 children aged 14 to 16. In the second, by Blinkhorn and Hendrickson (1982), high correlations between string length and Advanced Progressive Matrices were obtained for 33 subjects. In both studies, the auditory ERP was obtained to simple tones. Note that in the Hendrickson's theory, ERP traces with more components and larger amplitudes result in longer strings, and these longer strings are related to higher test scores.

The available evidence appears to indicate some relation between the ERP and intellectual functioning. Ertl and his colleagues were the first to stimulate research in this area, but their neural efficiency hypothesis has been criticized. For example, Callaway (1975) has argued that it is unlikely that a single neurophysiological factor, such as shorter ERP latencies, can be identified as the biological substrate of intelligence. Callaway rejected the Ertl hypothesis on other grounds, all of which suggest that the approach is oversimplified. The Hendrickson's theory is also appealingly simple, and, like Ertl's theory, it is testable. A major difficulty with the Hendrickson's construct is that it relies too heavily on ERP amplitude in determining string length. Studies suggest the possibility that skull thickness can affect magnitude of response—that is, a thicker skull leads to greater attenuation of brain response than a thin skull area, and this would result in lower ERP amplitude. Vetterli and Furedy (1985) have also criticized two versions of the string measure. They tested one of the string measures as a predictor of IQ, and compared it to one using latency. The pure latency measure was superior, because the string measure gave inconsistent results and ones in an opposite direction to the predicted relationship. Additional empirical studies are required to determine if the string length–IQ relationship will hold.

Some valuable suggestions for future research in this area were made by Gale and Edwards (1983). Their ideal approach for future studies includes repeated measurements of both EEG and ERPs in a group of subjects, obtaining both auditory and visual ERPs, multichannel topographical recordings, and a range of tasks ranging from listening to simple tones to solving complex problems. Gale and Edwards have also made a reasonable appeal for the development of a general model of brain function to help interpret present and future findings in this area.

ERPs and Stimulus Meaning

A number of studies have been conducted to determine whether significance or meaning of a stimulus, either natural or experimentally contrived, would affect the ERP. One early investigation in this area was that of Begleiter, Gross, and Kissin (1967), who manipulated visual stimuli by giving them positive, negative, or neutral meaning through a conditioning procedure. Visual ERPs were recorded from over the right occipital hemispheres of 31 male college students. They found significantly lower ERP amplitudes to objects that had acquired negative and positive meanings, as compared to neutral stimuli. The authors suggested that the lower amplitudes for negative and positive stimuli, as compared to the neutral stimulus, indicate some sort of inhibitory brain activity for these affective stimuli.

However, Begleiter and Platz (1969a) used taboo words (e.g., fuck) and neutral words (e.g, tile), which were printed in capital letters and equal in area, to obtain visual ERPs. Blank flashes of light were also used. They reported that VEP components appearing shortly after 100 msec were larger in amplitude for taboo words than for neutral words or flashes. A later component was larger for both types of words than the blank flash. Thus, meaning seemed to alter the late VEP components, but not in a manner consistent with the results of Begleiter et al. (1967). Perhaps the taboo words produced more of a response in subjects than previously used stimuli because of the stronger inherent affective value of these stimuli as compared to those that attain such meaning through conditioning.

An interesting demonstration of how internal factors such as expectancy might affect ERP amplitude was performed by Begleiter, Porjesz, Yerre, and Kissin (1973). In their experiment, moderate-intensity light flashes elicited either large or small amplitude ERPs, depending on whether a warning tone signaled that a bright or dim flash would follow. Thus the importance of subjective factors, independent of objective stimulus characteristics, in generating the ERP was again shown. Further, there have been reports of changes in the ERP that appeared at about the time that an expected, but absent, stimulus should have been presented. For example, Sutton, Teuting, Zubin, and John (1967) found that an ERP would occur in the absence of an expected click. Weinberg, Walter, and Crow (1970) referred to this as an "emitted" potential, in contrast to potentials that are "evoked" by a specific stimulus. Ruchkin and Sutton (1973) reported the same result for visual stimuli, that is, a P300 response appeared with a peak latency of 400 msec at Cz and 480 msec at Oz, following the time of the missing flash. The lower amplitude and longer duration of the emitted P300 (compared to the evoked P300) was hypothesized to be due to the lack of a precisely timed external stimulus. In other words, the P300 associated with an expected, but missing, stimulus is an internally produced potential influenced by the variability inherent in subjective time estimates.

Auditory ERPs were recorded from scalp locations over left and right hemispheres in response to words and nonsense syllables (groupings of letters that do not make words) by Molfese (1979). Brain responses that occurred between 240 and 280 msec after stimulation distinguished between meaningful and nonsense words. Both hemispheres showed differentiation between the words and nonwords, thus failing to show a processing distinction for the two hemispheres. In a study by Vanderploeg, Brown, and Marsh (1987), later ERP components (240 to 616 msec) were found to differ for positive, neutral, and negative facial expressions. They noted that processing of facial expression appeared in two stages: (a) discrimination of neutral faces involved the left hemisphere earlier (240–448 msec), and (b) continued processing of the emotional faces (positive or negative expressions) was indexed by a later right-hemisphere response (448–616 msec). The results suggest a complex interhemispheric processing of emotional facial expressions, with lateralization shifting as indexed by latency of ERP components.

In summary, the studies reviewed in this section indicate that meaningfulness of stimuli appears to alter the ERP. Factors such as stimulus content, affective value, and expectancies exert an influence on the recorded brain response. The two hemispheres appear to cooperate in a complicated way in processing emotional connotations in facial expressions.

ERPs and Linguistic Processes

This section is primarily concerned with ERPs to language and nonlanguage stimuli. The recording of ERPs from the scalp makes it possible to study linguistic processes and hemispheric specialization with greater precision than can be accomplished with performance measures alone. A number of investigators have reported differences in ERPs recorded over right and left hemispheres, depending on whether stimuli were language-related or not. For example, Wood, Goff, and Day (1971) recorded ERPs during two auditory identification tasks: One task provided linguistic information, and the other did not. Auditory ERPs from the left hemisphere differed for the two tasks, but were identical over the right hemisphere. The authors concluded that different neural events occur in the left hemisphere during analysis of language versus nonlanguage stimuli.

Another approach was taken by Brown, Marsh, and Smith, (1973), who observed that wave forms of ERPs differed according to the meaning of a word. For example, ERPs to the word "fire" differed when it was presented in the phrase "sit by the fire," as compared to "ready, aim, fire." The wave-form differences were significantly greater from over the left hemisphere than for right hemispheric locations (see Fig. 6.1). In another part of this study, no hemispheric differences occurred when the meaning of the word "fire" was ambiguous. This was accomplished by using phrases such as "fire is hot" and "fire the gun."

To dispel possible criticisms that the words accompanying the critical stimuli were different and therefore could have produced the asymmetries found, Brown, Marsh, and Smith (1976) conducted another experiment. They tested 15 young adults in a situation in which meaning was assigned immediately before the critical stimulus was delivered along with other words. That is, meaning was established for the ambiguous phrase "it was led" by telling subjects that the last word would be a noun, as in "the metal was lead," or a verb, as "the horse was led." The ERPs were recorded from two leads each over the left and right hemispheres. The leads were over F7 (approximately Broca's area related to speech articulation); F8, 3 cm from T3 (Wernicke's area related to speech comprehension); and 3 cm from T4. Again, as in the 1973 study, Brown et al. reported that ERPs from over Broca's area were dissimilar for the two meanings, whereas they were similar at the other locations.

Friedman, Simson, Ritter, and Rapin (1975a) reported an experiment in which auditory ERPs were produced by real speech words and human sounds. An example of a real word was "kick" and a sound example was "pssst,"

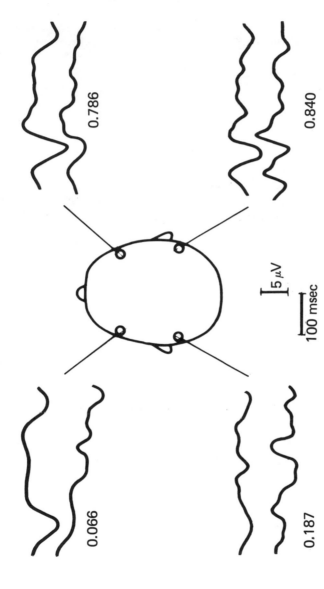

FIG. 6.1. Averaged evoked potentials (N=100) from one subject to the word "fire." For each pair of traces, the upper is the average response to the word "fire" presented in the phrase "sit by the fire." The lower is the response to "fire" in the phrase "ready, aim, fire!" The coefficients of correlation below each pair are a measure of degree of similarity between the wave forms of the two traces. Upward deflections are positive with respect to the reference leads. The coefficients show lower relationships in the left hemisphere, indicating that greater discrimination is made there to the different forms of the word "fire."

uttered by the same person. The ERPs were measured under conditions in which the sounds and words were merely listened to and where one of them served as a signal for a finger movement. They found the P300 component amplitude to be largest to signal stimuli and smallest under passive listening. Sounds produced larger P300s than words at all electrode locations (left and right hemispheres, midline). The authors suggested that this might be due to the novelty of the sounds, because they occur less frequently in everyday speech. Analyses of left–right hemispheric differences yielded only two greater left than right differences. The authors concluded that earlier studies of ERP correlates of differential hemispheric processing had design and statistical flaws and that reflection of hemispheric functioning by ERPs may not be as strong as indicated in the past.

In still another experiment, Friedman, Simson, Ritter, and Rapin (1975b) recorded visual ERPs from over right and left hemispheres and vertex. The stimuli consisted of sequentially presented words that comprised a sentence. In one condition, an ingenious technique prevented the subject from knowing the meaning of the second word in the sequence until the last was shown. For example, subjects were told the form of the three sentences that were used throughout the experiment: The _eel is on the axle; The _eel in on the shoe; The _eel is on the orange. Thus, by omitting the wh, h, or p, the subject could not know the meaning of the second word until the last word in the sequence was presented. In other conditions, the meaning of the second word was known immediately. The latency of P300 to words that delivered information (last word or second word) was consistently longer than to other words in the sentence. No hemispheric differences were noted. The authors interpreted the finding that all words produced P300 components as indicating that the P300 system is engaged whenever task-related language stimuli are used.

The ERPs occurring when an inappropriate word appeared unexpectedly at the end of a sentence were studied by Kutas and Hillyard (1980). In 25% of sentences read by their subjects, the ending was moderately or strongly inappropriate. An example of moderate was, "He took a sip from a waterfall" and strong, "He took a sip from the transmitter." They found that the inappropriate words were followed by a negative component (N400) beginning at about 250 msec and peaking at 400 msec after stimulus onset. This N400 was much larger after a strong semantic mismatch compared to a moderate one. The authors proposed that the N400 might be an ERP sign of the interruption of sentence processing by inappropriate words and an attempt to reinterpret the information (Hillyard & Kutas, 1983). There is also suggestive evidence that ERPs to "open class" or content words differ from those to "closed class" or function words. Examples of open class words are verbs and nouns, whereas prepositions and articles are in the closed-class category. The ERPs associated with open-class words resulted in larger positive ERP components between 200–700 msec post-stimulus, and by a greater left–right asymmetry in the 400–700 period than ERPs to closed-class words (Hillyard & Kutas, 1983). In summary, although early studies of hemispheric ERP differences to language and nonlanguage stimuli produced promising results, recent investigations, using stringent criteria for differences, have resulted in more conservative statements regarding ERP changes. However, studies that have related hemispheric differences to linguistic meaning have yielded more positive results. Neville (1980) suggested that when subjects perform demanding tasks designed to produce behavioral asymmetries (e.g., dichotic listening), the concurrently recorded ERPs show hemispheric asymmetries. Studies of semantically inappropriate words and different word categories indicate that ERPs can add important information not observable with strictly behavioral approaches.

Learning and ERPs

In relation to the number of ERP investigations in general, only a few have used the ERP in studies of human learning or conditioning. Begleiter and Platz (1969b) used a classical conditioning paradigm to study VEPs (occipital) to conditioned stimuli during acquisition, extinction, and reacquisition. The reinforcement consisted of a series of auditory clicks delivered over a loudspeaker. A positive-conditioned stimulus (CS+) was reinforced on 50% of the trials, whereas a negative-conditioned stimulus (CS−) was never reinforced. The CS+ consisted of an arrow (↑); the CS− was a downward arrow (↓). Prior to conditioning, VEP amplitude (negative peak at 155 to 160 msec) to CS+ and CS− did not differ. After conditioning, however, VEP amplitudes were significantly higher to CS+. During extinction (no reinforcement), amplitudes returned to preconditioning levels, whereas after acquisition, CS+ again resulted in higher VEP amplitudes than CS−. The authors hypothesized that their result was consistent with the notion of increased rate of neuronal firing to the CS+ after conditioning. In addition, stimulus generalization was shown, in that when arrows were rotated 10 degrees from the original CS+ or CS−, the same difference in VEP was found. That is, the "up" arrow at a 10-degree angle produced larger amplitude VEPs than the "down" arrow at a 10-degree angle from the original.

Lelord, Laffont, and Jusseaume (1976) classically conditioned ERPs in children of three different intelligence levels. The three groups were (I) normal (nonretarded children), (II) mildly retarded (IQ between 50 and 60), and (III) severely retarded (IQ between 20 and 50). Sound was used as the conditioned stimulus (CS) and light as the unconditioned stimulus (UCS). After pairing of CS and UCS, the Group I children showed increased amplitude of ERPs to the sound (CS), but the two retarded groups did not. That is, conditioning of ERPs occurred in normal children but not in retarded subjects. The ERPs of normal and autistic children were compared in a sensory conditioning study by Martineau, Garreau, Barthelemy, and Lelord (1984). The autistic child is characterized by extreme social withdrawal and impairment of verbal and nonverbal communication, among other symptoms. These investigators found marked ERP differences in normal and autistic children during conditioning trials. Namely, the autistic subjects showed smaller responses to stimulus pairs (sound–light) than they did to the CS (sound) alone, a finding attributed to attentional deficits usually found in these patients.

There have been some reports of operant conditioning of ERPs. For example, Rosenfeld, Dowman, Silvia, and Heinricher (1984) found evidence of operant control over a P200 component at a vertex location in four of eight subjects. Correct modification of P200 was reinforced by a tone signal. Operant conditioning of slow brain potential shifts was described by Rockstroh, Birbaumer, Elbert, and Lutzenberger (1984). In their paradigm, feedback was provided by the outline of a rocket ship that moved across a TV screen. Subjects directed the ship into one of two goals, depending on instructions. One of the goals required a shift towards SP negativity, whereas reaching the other goal required a positive shift. Subjects received a monetary reward for reaching the correct goal. These investigators reported that human subjects demonstrate operant control over their own slow brain potentials within 100 to 160 trials (usually two experimental sessions).

The several studies reviewed here indicate that changes in ERPs occur under different learning paradigms. Namely, ERPs were larger in amplitude to a positively conditioned stimulus. The ERPs also indicated differences in acquisition of the conditioned response of retarded and autistic children, most likely reflecting impaired intellectual and attentional functioning, respectively. There is also evidence that operant control over a positive vertex component of the ERP and slow brain potential shifts may be possible.

The ERP and Hypnosis (Suggestion)

Is there evidence that hypnotic or other forms of suggestion can influence the ERP? Some early evidence with patients undergoing brain surgery indicated that suggestion of higher or lower light intensities could influence visual ERPs in the expected direction (Guerrero-Figueroa & Heath, 1964; Hernandez-Peon & Donoso, 1959). Clynes, Kohn, & Lifschitz (1964) were able to alter visual ERPs of one person through hypnotic suggestion of selective blindness for peripheral aspects of her visual field, but they were unable to duplicate the effects with a second subject.

Studies conducted with larger numbers of subjects indicate that hypnotic suggestion does not alter ERPs to somatosensory stimuli even though subjects reported no perception of the stimulus under hypnotic anesthesia (Halliday & Mason, 1964: Shagass & Schwartz, 1964). Beck (1963) reported no enhancement of visual ERPs for 12 individuals under hypnotic suggestion of brightness, nor was there a decrease in ERP amplitude when dimness was suggested. Beck noted that the light appeared either brighter or dimmer to subjects, depending on the hypnotic suggestion, even though the light intensity remained the same throughout the experimental session. Beck, Dustman, and Beier (1966) matched 10 hypnotically suggestible persons with 10 control subjects. Whereas the controls showed increases and decreases in the VEP with intensity changes, the hypnotized subjects showed no changes with suggested brightness and dimness. The authors noted that the findings did not support the concept that hypnotic suggestion may selectively inhibit or enhance sensory transmission.

Galbraith, Cooper, and London (1972) found that persons scoring high on a scale of hypnotic susceptibility had higher visual and auditory ERPs when instructed to selectively attend to these stimuli than did persons who had low susceptibility scores. No attempt was made to hypnotize any of the subjects. The authors suggested that hypnotically susceptible persons may be better able to comply with an externally imposed task, whereas unsusceptible persons appear to do just the opposite. That is, larger ERPs of unsusceptible subjects to irrelevant stimuli indicate that they pay attention to the distractors, not to the critical stimuli.

Andreassi, Balinsky, Gallichio, DeSimone, and Mellers (1976) measured VEPs of 12 subjects under hypnotic suggestions that equally intense light flashes were ''very bright'' or ''very dim'' and under no suggestion at all. No changes in VEP amplitudes or latencies were produced by the suggestions. In a second experiment, the VEPs of six subjects were obtained during hypnotic suggestion and no suggestion on two separate days. Again, no changes in the VEP were observed. Both experiments revealed remarkable stability of the VEP obtained during the hypnotic state, suggesting a heightened attentional state.

Thus, although mental states have been demonstrated to affect ERPs in other situations, hypnotic suggestion does not appear to do so. The conclusion here is the same as that of Tecce (1970), who noted that the evidence for ERP changes with hypnosis or suggestion has been negative whenever more than two subjects were studied. Experiments on the ERP correlates of hypnosis seem to emphasize the importance of attentional factors in this state, and weaken the notion that hypnotic suggestion may selectively inhibit or enhance sensory transmission in the nervous system.

The lack of ERP change with hypnotic suggestion may be related to the fact that it is external to the person—that is, the suggestion comes from another individual. When stimulus characteristics are influenced by internal factors, the ERP may show appropriate changes. Some evidence for this stems from an experiment by Porjesz and Begleiter (1975), in which subjects set up their own internal expectancy by choosing to see a bright or dim flash. In that situation, the ERP amplitudes corresponded to the expectation, even though the stimuli were identical.

SENSATION, ATTENTION, PERCEPTION, AND ERPS

As in chapter 4, the studies in this section are categorized according to whether the research is primarily concerned with stimulus variations, attentional aspects, or integrative perceptual functions.

Sensation and ERPs

Intensity of Stimulation.   In general, more intense stimuli produce larger ERP amplitudes. For example, this has been found for visual stimuli by Vaughan and Hull (1965), for auditory tones by Bull and Lang (1972), and for somatosensory stimulation by Shagass and Schwartz (1963).

Vaughan, Costa, and Gilden (1966) reported a decrease in visual ERP latencies with increases in light flash intensity. The latency of the somatosensory ERP depends on the part of the body stimulated (e.g., latency is about 10 msec longer with stimulation of the knee as compared to the wrist; Shagass, 1972). The amplitude of the auditory ERP was found to increase with increasing stimulus intensities (Picton, Goodman, & Bryce, 1970). However, at intensities above 70 dB, the relation was not as clear-cut. Bull and Lang (1972) varied the intensity levels while the ERP was measured from the vertex. The intensity levels were 50, 62.5, 75, 87.5, and 100 dB. They reported that ERP amplitudes increased directly with increments in physical intensity. Schweitzer and Tepas (1974) used pure tone (1,000 Hz) at 10 intensities of stimulation, and reported amplitude changes linearly related to intensity. Walsh and Tepas (1975) found that a temporary loss in hearing sensitivity after exposure to high-intensity sounds was reflected by decreased ERP amplitudes. These investigators measured ERPs to a 1,000-Hz tone at 80-dB intensity level following 5 minutes of exposure to a 720-Hz tone at either 45 dB or 110 dB. The ERPs immediately following the 100-dB tone were smaller, thus correlating with temporary subjective loss of hearing sensitivity.

Frequency of Stimulation.   The effects of stimulus repetition on ERPs have been studied by a number of investigators. For example, the rate of click presentation was varied between one per second and three per second while auditory ERP was measured by Fruhstorfer, Soveri, and Jarvilehto (1970). Although continued stimulation at both rates produced some habituation, the higher presentation rate resulted in greater decreases in ERP amplitudes than the lower rate. Ritter, Vaughan, and Costa (1968) noted a drop in amplitude of the positive ERP component occurring between 150 and 200 msec with a stimulus presentation rate of one per 2 seconds, but not with an interval of 10 seconds. Butler (1973) reported interesting results that indicated a decrease in ERP amplitudes with increased stimulation frequency up to 10 per second. Further increases in repetition rate reversed this trend. Thus, sounds presented at a rate of 25 per second showed a revived N1-P2 amplitude as though they were now perceived as a continuous 1-second duration sound instead of a series of separate sounds.

The finding of short-term or fast habituation of the N1-P2 component of the auditory ERP recorded from the vertex (Cz) is well established. This decline in ERP amplitude that results from a train of repetitive stimuli also occurs at the vertex for visual stimulation, but slightly less so at the occipital area (Wastell & Kleinman, 1980). These investigators used flash rates of .5, 1.0, 2.0, and 3.0 per sec, and found that the visual ERP showed greater decreases with higher rates. They used an "artificial pupil," placed over the eye, to rule out pupillary mechanisms in the ERP habituation.

Smell, Taste, Touch, Pain, and Acceleration.   Although the auditory, visual, and somatosensory stimuli have been the most frequently investigated in ERP studies, it is possible to examine other forms of sensory stimulation, such as olfactory, gustatory, pain, and vestibular. For example, Smith, Allison, Goff, and Principato (1971) studied smell-generated ERPs of three patients with surgically produced smell deficits and of three normal persons. Streams of compressed air containing odorous and nonodorous substances were directed into the nostrils for 200 msec at 5-second intervals to produce the ERP. The results indicated that the ERP (recorded from Cz) was elicited by stimulation of olfactory receptors. No ERP was obtained when jets of air, passed over distilled water flasks, were directed into the nostrils. Substantial ERPs—that is, components of 10 μV or more—could be obtained by averaging 30 responses to the olfactory stimuli. The stimuli used apparently stimulated both the olfactory and trigeminal systems, a possibility that would pose problems for studying responses of the olfactory system alone. Another problem in work on smell, taste, and pain ERPs is that of synchronizing the stimulus presentations with the trigger pulse that initiates the averaging of brain responses.

The gustatory (taste) ERPs of humans were analyzed in detail by Funakoshi and Kawamura (1971). Demineralized water, sucrose, sodium chloride, tartaric acid, and quinine hydrochloride provided control, sweet, salty, sour, and bitter solutions, respectively. The subjects rinsed their mouths between each application of a solution to the tongue. The researchers reported the onset of an "early" wave at 150 msec after the stimulus was applied (10 μV in amplitude) and a "late" wave at about 500 msec, which was approximately 20 μV in amplitude. The early wave occurred with all solutions and with tactile stimulation of the tongue; but the later wave only appeared with the salt and tartaric acid (sour) applications. Therefore, the early component was due to the mechanical stimulation of pouring the solution on the tongue surface, and the late wave was the taste ERP. The authors suggested that the lack of ERPs to sweet and bitter may be related to the relatively small tongue areas sensitive to sweet and bitter tastes.

This, in turn, could result in smaller cortical responses to sweet and bitter, perhaps not visible within the limitations imposed by 40 samples.

The somatosensory ERP to stimulation of the skin was studied by Soininen and Jarvilehto (1983). The left hand was stimulated by a tactile probe that delivered stimuli ranging from ones that could not be detected (below threshold) to those that were clearly felt. Tactile stimuli just above detection threshold were capable of producing a distinct somatosensory ERP. This shows that a minimal peripheral sensation (at the hand) is sufficient to activate a large number of neural elements in the brain, as indicated by the sizable ERP from over central cortex. On the other hand, no ERP was produced to the subthreshold touch stimuli.

Chatrian, Canfield, Knauss, and Lettich (1975) produced pain in 17 persons by electrically stimulating the pulp of individual teeth. All subjects described the electrical stimulus to the tooth pulp as producing sharp pain of a very brief duration. The pain ERP was recorded from many scalp areas, including that over the postcentral cortex. The ERP was prominent over the somatosensory cortex, a finding that was interpreted as indicating the existence of a representation of tooth pulp sensation in the somatosensory area of the postcentral gyrus. Buchsbaum, Davis, Coppola, and Naber (1981) found that both aspirin and morphine led to a reduction in somatosensory ERP to painful electrical shock stimulation. The ERP was derived from over central and somatosensory cortex.

The vestibular sense provides information about body position. The receptors for linear and angular acceleration lie in the semicircular canals and utricles of the inner ear. The study of vestibular ERPs is more difficult than the study of visual or auditory ERPs, because it is difficult to produce a suitable means of stimulating the vestibular receptors. Salamy, Potvin, Jones, and Landreth (1975) studied ERPs to semicircular canal stimulation by using whole-body rotation (angular acceleration) as the stimulus. The ERP was summed for a 2-second period simultaneous with about 84 degrees of body rotation in a swing chair. The ERP was recorded from over both hemispheres (central, parietal, temporal, and frontal leads). The investigators obtained a consistent negative–positive ERP with peaks at about 193 and 345 msec, respectively. The negative peak seemed to be the most prominent feature related to angular acceleration. The negative–positive complex amplitude was greatest at the vertex (mean of 13.7 μV). This complex was not influenced by auditory and visual stimuli, because these were ruled out by experimental procedures. Salamy et al. also pointed out that somatosensory ERPs have negative–positive latencies peaking at about 135 and 220 msec, much earlier than ERPs obtained with acceleration, thus distinguishing somatosensory from vestibular components.

In general, greater intensity stimuli result in higher amplitude ERPs. Higher rates of stimulus presentation result in greater ERP amplitude decreases than do lower rates. This seems to follow up to a certain point, beyond which further rate increases may reverse the trend.

It is possible, although more difficult, to generate ERPs to smell, taste, pain, and body acceleration. One difficulty, for example, is that of synchronizing stimuli with the trigger pulse used to start computer sampling in obtaining ERPs. Another problem is that stimulation of the appropriate receptors is not as readily accomplished as with the visual and auditory systems. Somatosensory ERPs to touch and pain stimuli have indicated no response to subthreshold stimuli and a decrease in ERP amplitude to painful electric shock when analgesics are administered.

Attention and ERPs

The definition of attention offered in chapter 4 is also used here. Performance effects of attended and unattended stimuli were nicely summarized by Hillyard and Hansen (1986) in their review of ERP correlates of attention. They pointed out that attended stimuli have more control over motor responses, are detected more accurately, and are better remembered than unattended stimuli. Attempts to find neurophysiological bases of this complex mental phenomenon in humans have involved ERPs to a greater extent than the measurement of changes in ongoing EEG activity. It appears that the demonstration of a physiological correlate of attention could be established if some change in ERPs occurred when subjects attended to a stimulus and if no alteration could be observed when they did not attend. In fact, there were a number of studies conducted during the 1960s that indicated that the amplitude of ERP components to attended stimuli was increased, whereas the ignored stimulus produced low-amplitude responses.

For example, Haider, Spong, and Lindsley (1964) measured visual ERPs to signal and nonsignal stimuli during a prolonged vigilance task. They noted that lower amplitude ERPs were associated with lapses of attention, that is, failure to detect signals. Satterfield (1965) asked subjects to attend alternately to auditory clicks and electric shocks. The ERPs were greatly enhanced when subjects were attending to either the shock or click stimuli. A late positive peak (about 150 msec, recorded from Cz) was enhanced by the attended stimulus, whether it was a shock or a click.

Although a number of other investigations produced similar positive results, Naatanen (1967) argued that the increased ERP amplitude did not reflect attention or cognitive activity per se, but rather that it was due to nonspecific arousal effects produced in response to expected, task-relevant, stimuli. That is, because stimuli were presented in a regular manner, subjects could anticipate, and be prepared for, the critical stimulus, and therefore, ERP amplitude increases could be due to general cortical activation, not selective attention. In his own research, Naatanen (1967) randomly mixed relevant and irrelevant stimuli so that their occurrence could not be predicted. He found no ERP differences to relevant and irrelevant stimuli, suggesting that when differential prepartion for these stimuli was precluded, ERP changes did not occur.

Karlin (1970) supported Naatanen's view regarding the importance of differential preparation in producing ERP changes in the attention experimental paradigm. Karlin (1970) and Naatanen (1967) pointed out possible uncontrolled variables in selective attention experiments, including stimulus intensity, duration, sensory modality stimulated, and peripheral orienting responses (e.g., pupil dilation).

However, a number of studies, which appear to avoid the criticisms of Naatanen and Karlin, do indicate the role of selective attention in enhancing ERP amplitude. For example, Eason, Harter, and White (1969) presented unpredictable relevant stimuli to one visual field and irrelevant stimuli to the other field. The ERP component occurring between 120 and 220 msec increased in amplitude with presentations of relevant stimuli, those to which subjects paid more attention. Harter and Salmon (1972) presented equal numbers of relevant and irrelevant stimuli in an unpredictable manner and found enhancement of an ERP negative component peaking between 220 and 250 msec and a positive component at 290 to 340 msec when the stimuli were attended, as compared to when they were not attended. As later discussed for contingent negative variation, attention–arousal dissociations can also be demonstrated within a divided attention paradigm (Tecce, 1972).

Selectivity in Attention.   Examination of ERP latencies have provided information regarding the point at which brain responses indicate differences to attended and unattended stimuli. A review by Hillyard and Kutas (1983) suggests that there is little evidence to support the notion that early ERP components (20–40 msec) are sensitive to attention shifts for different stimuli. However, under high load conditions where auditory stimuli were delivered rapidly over at least two different channels (e.g., left and right ears) a negative component 60–80 msec in onset) was increased in size. At first, it was thought that this ERP to attended tones was an enhancement of a peak called N1. But because the wave also outlasted N1, the term "negative difference" (Nd) is now used to describe this attentional effect. Hillyard and Hansen (1986) pointed out that the later portions of Nd appear to be endogenous (stimulus independent), whereas the earlier portions overlap N1. An example of the difference between the N1 and Nd waves is shown in Fig. 6.2. The result illustrated in the figure represents auditory ERPs to tones alternately attended to by left and right ears. Naatanen and his colleagues (e.g., Naatanen, Gaillard & Mantysalo, 1978) referred to the Nd wave as "processing negativity," and Naatanen (1982) emphasized that this component is not just a simple increase in the exogeneous (stimulus dependent) N1. Because of its short onset time, Nd was initially interpreted by Hillyard, Hink, Schwent, & Picton (1973) as indicating a tonic "stimulus set" by which relevant stimuli from the attended ear were automatically processed. Naatanen criticized this idea on the grounds that even discriminating the ear of entry required active processing that could take place as early as 60 to 70 msec. Naatanen suggested that Nd reflects decisions about whether a stimulus on the attended channel is a target or

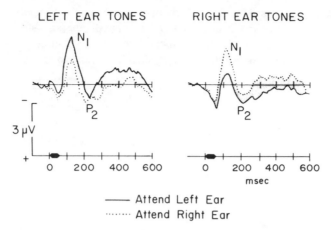

FIG. 6.2.   Auditory ERPs to standard tones in a selective listening task, in which attention was switched between tones in the two ears. Left-ear tones were 1800 Hz and right-ear tones were 2800 Hz, all at 45 dB SL and 75 msec durations. Shaded differences between attended and unattended ERPs for each ear represent the Nd component. (Grand average data over 10 subjects.)

not. There is general agreement that Nd is a neural sign of stimulus processing that follows stimulus set selection (Hillyard & Kutas, 1983).

If a series of auditory stimuli suddenly changes, a negative wave at about 200 msec will occur. This N2 component is said to indicate "mismatch negativity," and has been clearly described by Loveless (1983). Loveless explained that the N2 may occur with a change in physical characteristics of a repetitive stimulus, or even its omission when expected. This processing negativity seems related to a mismatch between the current stimulus and a "neuronal model" established by previous stimuli. Further, the N2 most likely reflects an automatic discrimination of stimulus change and might play a role in the initiation of the orienting response (Naatanen & Michie, 1979). A theory of selective attention based on processing negativity has been proposed by Naatanen (1982). He suggested that selective attention involves the rehearsal of certain stimulus traces. This produces an automatic bias in the sensory system toward processing certain stimuli. The result of this selective processing is an attentional trace that lasts only as long as it is rehearsed and the sensory input is recent. The attentional trace allows rapid identification of stimulus differences when they are large enough. The Nd represents the comparison of the incoming stimulus with an internal representation and is larger and longer with increasing similarity. The N2 is related to a mismatch between the expected stimulus and its internal representation.

There is evidence that an attention-related negativity to tactile stimuli occurs in the somatosensory ERP (Desmedt & Robertson, 1977). The negativity occurred at about 75 msec and lasted long enough to enhance an N140 component, suggesting a similarity to the extended effect of the auditory Nd wave. The visual ERPs with selective attention are more complex than for other modalities. The earliest changes take place when subjects attend to flashing lights in one visual field while ignoring lights in the other field (Eason & Ritchie, 1976). Hillyard and Kutas (1983) noted that in this situation, attended-field ERPs are enlarged in parietal–occipital areas and involve multiple components: P1 (80–110 msec); N1 (160–180 msec); and P2 (200–250 msec).

Resource Allocation.   In a concept advanced by Kahneman (1973) and Norman and Bobrow (1975), attention is limited in certain situations because we have only a certain amount of mental resources to spend on a task. If several tasks demand part of the same limited resources, then attention must be divided among the competing tasks. Allocation of resources among competing stimuli can be demonstrated by changes in ERP amplitudes. In one study, the Nd component of the ERP was found to be decreased during divided attention as compared to when attention was focused (Hink, Van Voorhis, Hillyard, & Smith, 1977). In a study by Wickens, Kramer, Vanesse, and Donchin (1983), subjects performed a manual tracking task while responding to probe stimuli of a secondary task. As the primary tracking task became more difficult, the ERPs elicited by the secondary task became smaller. Thus, as more resources were required for the main task, fewer were available for secondary tasks.

The ERP has contributed to understanding attentional processes in a number of ways. The preceding section has briefly discussed ERP contributions to the study of early and later processes in selective attention, processing negativity, mismatch negativity, and resource allocation. The ERP studies have also enabled psychophysiologists to make contributions to attentional theories. A discussion of attention as related to longer latency potentials is presented in the next chapter.

Perception and ERPs

In this section, we examine the existing evidence to determine whether reliable relationships have been shown between the ERP and such perceptual activities as form and pattern perception, perceptual masking, color perception, and motion perception.

Shape.   The basic question here is whether stimulus shape and pattern will influence ERPs as well as perception. Spehlmann (1965) reported differences between VEPs produced by an unpatterned visual field versus a patterned one. A positive ERP component, which peaked at 180 to 250 msec, was much larger to patterned stimuli. John, Harrington, and Sutton (1967) found that different geometric shapes (e.g., square, diamond) produced different VEP wave forms. Little change in wave form of the VEP occurred with variation in the size of the figure (i.e., a small or large square evoked similar ERPs). They also reported that VEPs for a blank flash were different from those produced by geometric shapes.

Honda (1973) employed a pattern discrimination task that was designed to focus the subject's attention on either the size or shape of geometric figures (circles and squares). When subjects were required to make size discriminations and ignore form, the VEPs were affected by stimulus size. When shape discriminations were required, however, it was form and not size that resulted in VEP changes. These results were repeated by Honda (1974) with square and diamond stimuli. He concluded that the results showed the effects of selective attention on VEP wave forms and reflect electrical brain activities related to perceptual processing of patterns.

Pattern Size. White (1969), using four stimulus patterns (a checkerboard, a horizontal grating, a set of concentric circles, and a set of radial lines), found striking differences in VEP wave forms with the different stimulus patterns. He described an additional experiment in which VEPs were recorded to checkerboard patterns composed of different check sizes. It was observed that larger checks produced smaller amplitude VEPs (e.g., a check size that subtended 10 minutes of visual angle produced a response approximately twice the amplitude of that produced by a check that was four times larger). Visual angle depends on the size of an object and its distance from the eye. At a given distance, smaller size objects produce smaller visual angles at the eye. It is measured in seconds, minutes, and degrees of arc (60 seconds of visual angle equal 1 minute, and 60 minutes equal 1 degree).

Harter (1970) and Siegfried (1975) confirmed White's result with respect to the inverse relationship between VEP amplitude and check size. Harter (1970) also reported that this relationship depends on the portion of the retina stimulated. That is, when the foveal area (central 2 to 2.5 degrees of vision) was stimulated, relatively small checks (15 to 30 minutes of visual angle) evoked the greatest amplitude responses. However, when progressively more peripheral areas of the retina were stimulated (7.5 degrees out from the fovea), larger check sizes (up to 60 minutes of visual angle) produced the greatest amplitude ERPs. Check size had little effect on VEP when the retina was stimulated 12.5 to 27.5 degrees from the fovea. Hypotheses regarding the factors that may be operating here include: (a) the greater number of edges separating light and dark areas, so that patterns with many edges may produce larger responses, and (b) the angles, or total number of pattern elements, may affect VEP amplitude (Armington, Corwin, & Marsetta 1971).

Defocusing a checkerboard pattern, resulting in blurred images, resulted in decreased amplitude VEPs (Harter & White, 1968). Conversely, with sharper checkerboard pattern images, the VEP was larger. This has led to suggestions by White (1969) that VEP amplitude differences may be used as a basis for testing vision, especially refractive errors in persons who cannot verbalize well enough for adequate testing by many of the currently used testing methods (e.g., retarded individuals or young children). This possible application is discussed further in chapter 13.

Eason, White, and Bartlett (1970) stimulated the upper and lower halves of the visual field and reported that VEP amplitude varied with visual field and check size. Checks subtending 10 minutes of angle produced larger VEPs in the upper field, whereas checks subtending 40 minutes of visual angle were optimal for lower field stimulation. The overall ERP amplitudes suggested to Eason and his colleagues that the cortical visual system is more responsive to patterned stimuli appearing in the lower visual field than in the upper. However, it also seemed that the system may be relatively more sensitive to smaller objects in the upper field. They speculated that the differential sensitivity of the upper and lower visual fields may have survival value for humans as ground-dwelling animals. That is, the upper field may be more attuned to "specks in the sky" that move rapidly and must be detected at a distance if the organism is to respond appropriately. However, ground objects that are close enough to pose a threat produce a larger visual angle. Thus, the part of the visual system responding to them (lower field) may have greater sensitivity to objects subtending angles of 30 minutes or more.

Discriminations of line length were studied by Andreassi and Juszczak (1984). A single vertical 1.0 cm line (standard) was displayed for 40 msec and was followed 2 sec later by 0.9 cm, 1.0 cm, or 1.1 cm (comparison) lines. Subjects were asked to judge whether the second of the lines (comparison) was "shorter" or "longer" than the first. Latencies of a P3 component (positive wave between 300 and 400 msec) were longer with the 1.0 cm line compared to the other lengths. It was proposed that the difficulty experienced by subjects in judging whether the same length was longer or shorter required more time, and this was reflected in the longer P3 latencies. Earlier papers had also suggested that P3 latency is sensitive to stimulus evaluation processes (Donchin, Ritter, & McCallum, 1978; McCarthy & Donchin, 1981). In another experiment, Juszczak & Andreassi (1985) examined areal size and semantic discriminations in an ERP study of hemispheric asymmetries. In this study, subjects were required to discriminate between three sizes of rectangle whose widths were 14, 15, and 16 min. of arc, respectively, and the meanings of three words. The size discrimination was much more difficult (58% correct) than word meanings (70% correct). Latencies of the P3 component were again longer with the more difficult task. This is further evidence indicating that stimulus evaluation must be completed before P3 occurs. This is useful information, because it suggests that P3 latency is an objective indicator of stimulus discriminability or task difficulty.

Ritter, Simson, Vaughan, and Macht (1982) have identified a negative component (designated NA) that seems to be associated with pattern recognition. This component occurs about 200 msec post-stimulus, or about 100 msec prior to an N2 component thought to reflect classification of stimuli. Ritter and colleagues found support for the interpretation that NA and N2 reflect two sequential stages of information processing because the timing of NA was affected by the difficulty of a perceptual task whereas N2 was influenced by the nature of the classification task. It should be noted that the NA component is derived via a subtraction procedure to delineate it from other, possibly overlapping components.

Corners.   Patterns that include corners have been found to produce larger amplitude visual ERPs than those containing stripes (MacKay, 1969; Rietveld, Tordoir, Hagenouw, Lubbers, & Spoor, 1967). Moskowitz, Armington, and Timberlake (1974) measured ERPs to rounded and sharply cornered stimuli, which varied in angularity, in 45-degree steps, from 180 to 45 degrees. The visual ERP was greatest in amplitude for the 90-degree sharply cornered pattern. This can be seen in Fig. 6.3. Cornered and rounded-corner patterns produced larger ERPs than straight lines (180 degrees). The peak latency of responses to cornered patterns was shorter than that of responses to rounded and straight patterns. Moskowitz et al. postulated a "center-surrounded receptive field" model of the visual cortex to explain the major portion of their findings. The argument presented was that interactions between excitatory and inhibitory areas of the visual cortex allowed maximal neuronal response to occur with 90-degree cornered stimuli.

Orientation of Figures.   Maffei and Campbell (1970) presented vertical, horizontal, and oblique sets of lines (moving gratings) to subjects while visual ERPs were measured. They found VEPs to vertical and horizontal arrays to be similar, but the amplitude in response to the oblique array was considerably smaller than to the others. The authors concluded that the resolving power of the visual system is greater in the vertical and horizontal orientation than in the oblique. Yoshida, Iwahara, and Nagamura (1975) postulated that human visual cortical cells may be more responsive to horizontally and vertically oriented stimuli because our visual world is oriented mostly in horizontal or vertical planes. Leaning towers, such as the one in Pisa, are relatively rare in our visual environment!

   To summarize, we conclude that perceptions of different forms, patterns, and orientations are paralleled by changes in visual ERPs. The various experiments with checkerboard patterns indicate that effects such as check size, sharpness of image, and location in the visual field can influence the ERP. Visual ERPs are larger with small check sizes, with sharp images, and with stimuli in the lower visual field. Results in size discrimination studies indicate that more difficult judgments are accompanied by delayed P3 latencies. It has been suggested that stimulus evaluation must be complete before P3 occurs. Other findings implicate a pair of negative components, NA and N2, in pattern recognition and classifica-

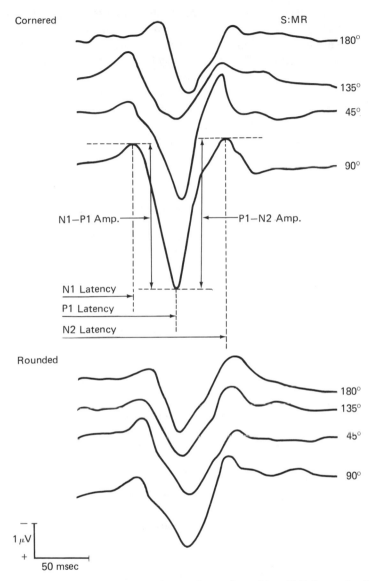

FIG. 6.3.   Typical summated wave forms for subject M.F. for each of the eight experimental stimulus patterns. Positivity at the occipital electrode produced downward deflections in the recordings. Also shown is the method of amplitude and latency measurement. Note that in this figure positivity is downward.

tion, respectively. Patterns containing sharply angled corners appear to result in larger VEPs than those with corners that are rounded or not angled as sharply. A possible conclusion is that the greater responsivity of the visual cortical system to stimuli oriented vertically and horizontally may be due to experiential factors that determine sensitivity of visual cortical cells.

Visual Masking.   There are instances in which stimuli may be presented to the visual system and yet not be perceived by the individual. For example, backward visual masking refers to a situation where presentation of a later stimulus (mask) interferes with the perception of an earlier presented stimulus (target). The question that concerns us here is the nature of the VEP to the stimulus that is not perceived.

Metacontrast, a type of backward visual masking, was studied in detail by Werner (1935), who showed that when two equally intense visual stimuli, having adjacent contours, were presented in rapid sequence, the first stimulus was not seen at all, and only the second was reported. For example, a filled-in square was presented for 20 msec and was followed 150 msec later by an outlined square, also presented for 20 msec. The interpretation of this was that the outlined square appropriated the contour of the solid square before it could establish itself in the visual system of the perceiver.

The question of whether or not the perceptual changes observed under metacontrast would be correlated with changes in the visual ERP was investigated by Schiller and Chorover (1966). They reported no changes in the VEP with metacontrast and concluded that the VEP does not necessarily reflect changes in subjective perception. However, Vaughan and Silverstein (1968) reported attenuation of VEPs to foveal stimulation but not parafoveal during metacontrast suppression. They concluded that the failure of VEPs to reflect metacontrast suppression in the Schiller and Chorover study was because of the parafoveal conditions used.

Schiller (1969) has referred to metacontrast as visual masking involving contour interaction as distinguished from a situation where no contour interaction occurs, as when a large, intense patch of light follows a small, relatively dim light flash. Studies of this latter type were carried out by Donchin, Wicke, and Lindsley (1963), who measured the visual ERP under conditions in which a second (brighter) flash masked perception of the initial flash. At 20 msec ISI (intersignal interval), when visual masking occurred, the VEPs were similar to those elicited by the second flash presented alone, that is, the VEP to the first stimulus was completely suppressed. A similar result obtained by Donchin and Lindsley (1965) led them to conclude that the interference with the first flash by the second took place at or preceding the point at which VEPs were recorded (occipital cortex). They expressed the opinion that the same processes that are involved in perceptual suppression seem to be involved in the VEP change. It must be noted that in these two studies by Donchin and others, the second flash was many times more intense than the first one (from 100 to 10,000 times), and this is probably the reason why the VEP to the first stimulus was completely obliterated rather than merely attenuated as in the metacontrast study of Vaughan and Silverstein (1968).

Andreassi, Mayzner, Beyda, and Davidovics (1971) studied the VEP under separate conditions designed to produce backward visual masking and no masking. Masking occurred when five equally intense Xs were displayed on a screen in an order that produced a disappearance of the first two in the sequence, namely, when presented in the order 3, 1, 4, 2, 5, the Xs in locations 1 and 2 were not perceived by the subjects. The two masked Xs were the only ones spatially bounded by later appearing stimuli (e.g., 1 was bounded by 3 and 4). The main finding was that although the subjects did not perceive the first two Xs, they did produce a VEP in response to these stimuli that was similar to the VEP obtained under conditions in which no masking occurred, for example, presentation of Xs in the order: 1, 2, 3, 4, 5, resulting in the perceptions of all five Xs. Further experimentation (Andreassi et al., 1971), using the presentation order: 3, 1, 4, 2, 5, revealed that if the third, fourth, and fifth stimuli were three times more intense than the first two, then not only did perceptual suppression occur but there was also partial suppression of the VEP in the form of significant VEP latency delays in response to the perceptually masked Xs. The authors concluded that the excitation produced in the visual cortex by the early stimuli in the series was decreased in activity by the inhibitory activity of the later, more intense stimuli.

In another experiment, Andreassi, Stern, and Okamura (1974) varied the intensity ratios of the masking (later) and masked (earlier) stimuli in a systematic manner while measuring VEPs. The intensity ratios used were 3:1, 5.8:1, and 10.8:1. It was found that the amount of delay in the occurrence of the VEP to the masked stimulus depended on the ratio of the intensity differences between the first two stimuli and the next three; that is, the greater the difference, the longer the delay in the appearance of the VEP to the first stimulus in the string. The results were the same from right and left occipital areas. Thus, it was concluded that as the ratio of the intensity difference between the earlier (masked) and later (masking) stimuli increased, the greater was the effect of cortical inhibitory fields on excitatory receptive fields, and the greater was the VEP temporal displacement produced.

In backward masking, using single sequential stimuli, the earlier stimuli were never spatially bounded on more than one side, simultaneously, by later stimuli. To answer questions regarding changes in amount of contour interaction between sequential sets of multiple stimuli, Andreassi, DeSimone, and Mellers (1976) conducted three experiments. In the first, sequential sets of like stimuli (i.e., two grids, followed by three grids, followed by six grids) were presented, while VEPs were measured from Oz. The time between grid sets was 40 msec. The total light energy was equated for the three grid sets. The schematic of the spatial

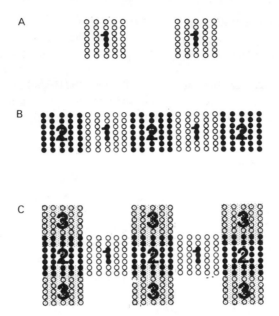

FIG. 6.4.   Schematic drawing of spatial and temporal arrangement of stimuli as they appeared in the Andreassi et al. (1976) study. Numbers merely indicate order of presentation and were not part of the actual display.

and temporal arrangement of stimuli as they appeared on a CRT screen in the first experiment is shown in Fig. 6.4. In Condition A, all subjects reported two grids, in B they reported seeing only the second set of three grids, while in C they saw only the last set of six grids. The VEP component, which occurred at about 200 msec (P2), was significantly reduced in amplitude in Conditions B and C as compared to A. In Experiment 2, sets of the letter B were used to determine the reliability of the findings from Experiment 1 with a new stimulus configuration. The same results were obtained; that is, backward masking was accompanied by decreased P2 amplitudes. In Experiment 3, however, unlike sets of stimuli (two Bs, two Bs followed by three grids, and two Bs followed by three grids, followed by six grids) backward masking of the first set of two Bs did not occur, and neither did changes in VEP amplitude. Thus, when the amount of contour interaction between target and mask stimuli was increased to 50% (as compared to 25% in the single sequential blanking situation), VEP amplitudes decreased with backward masking. When sets of unlike stimuli were used, the change in configuration reduced contour interaction between target and mask stimuli, thus preventing backward masking and the occurrence of VEP changes.

Andreassi, DeSimone, Gallichio, and Young (1976) investigated the effects of increasing amounts of target–mask contour interaction on perception of the

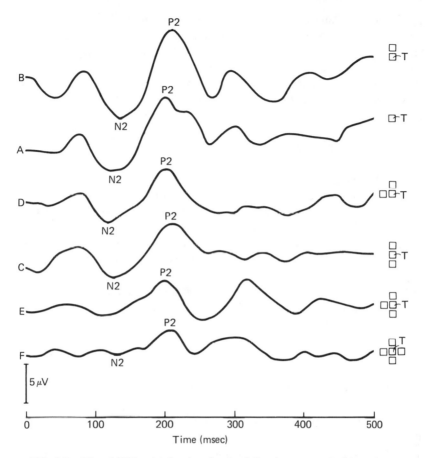

FIG. 6.5.   Visual ERPs obtained under the following amount of target-mask contour interaction: Condition B = 25%, A = 0%, D = 50%, C = 50%, E = 75%, and F = 100%. In the inset, the labeled squares (T) represent the earlier presented targets, whereas the unlabeled elements represent masking stimuli. The ERP traces show, in general, a decrease in N2-P2 amplitude with increased amounts of contour interaction. All subjects experienced apparent motion under Condition B in which the target appeared to jump upward to a new location. This could be the reason for a lack of amplitude difference between conditions B and A; that is, contour interaction effects may be lost in apparent motion. Each trace is based on 100 responses to a target square (grid). Negativity is downward.

target and the visual ERP. An experiment was designed in which a single grid stimulus (target) was followed by either one, two, three, or four grid stimuli. A final condition was presentation of the target alone. In all instances, the stimulus energy of target and mask was equated. Thus, the amount of target–mask contour interaction was 0%, 25%, 50%, 75%, and 100%. Greater amounts of backward masking occurred with increases in contour interaction, and this was accompanied by increasing degrees of attenuation of the P2 component of the VEP. Samples of VEP recordings from one subject under the conditions of this experiment are presented in Fig. 6.5.

The effects of varying the time interval between target and mask was examined by Andreassi (1984). The target grid was followed by four "masking" grids at intervals of 10 msec, 40 msec, and 100 msec. The 40 msec interval produced visual masking and attenuation of the P200 component of the visual ERP. However, the 10 and 100 msec intervals did not produce masking and neither did ERP reduction occur. This result shows that the timing and the spatial relationships are critical in masking. If the mask is presented too close in time, the effect is lost because target and mask are perceived as one unit. And if the interval is too long, target and mask are perceived sequentially. Another result observed in this study was that the ERP reduction was specific to the occipital site, because recordings from Cz differed little with masking or no masking.

In summary, a number of studies have indicated that backward visual masking was accompanied by changes in VEP amplitude or latency. An excitatory–inhibitory model has been proposed to explain the visual ERP reductions observed with visual masking: When a stimulus is presented to the visual system, it results in excitation being produced at a given location in the visual cortex. When similar stimuli follow the initial one closely in time and space, approximately adjacent areas of the visual cortex are stimulated, resulting in a reduction in response to the first stimulus. This inhibitory activity may not be sufficient to eliminate the VEP entirely, but it is enough to reduce it significantly, and the degree of VEP reduction is related to the degree of spatial bounding of the first stimulus by later ones. The excitatory–inhibitory model draws support from studies that have tested the feasibility of visual cortical prostheses with blind patients (e.g., Dobelle & Mladejovsky, 1974). In work of this type, direct electrical stimulation of discrete portions of visual cortex has been used to produce "electrical phosphenes" or sensations of light, in patients with peripherally caused blindness (eye damage). These electrically produced phosphenes interacted when two adjacent areas of visual cortex were stimulated (Dobelle, Mladejovsky, & Girvin, 1974). Simultaneous or sequential stimulation of two adjacent areas resulted in reports by patients of "seeing" one phosphene instead of two. The possibility that inhibitory effects can take place at the level of the visual cortex is directly suggested by these observations.

Color. Pulses of electromagnetic energy (light) produce perceptions of color if they are within the visible spectrum for human subjects. The visible wavelength spectrum ranges from about 380 to 700 nm, or billionths of a meter. The question that concerns us here is whether changes in wavelength (color) will be reflected in visual ERPs.

A number of investigators have reported that the wave form of the VEP was changed with different colors. For example, Clynes and Kohn (1967) indicated that VEPs to lines and dots were color-sensitive with respect to color of the surrounding field. Different VEP wave forms were obtained to stimulation with red, green, yellow, and orange stimuli. White and Eason (1966) also found that components of the VEP varied as a function of stimulus color. Differences in VEP pattern were observed with stimulation by red, green, and blue and by the three colors simultaneously. Shipley, Jones, and Fry (1966) found that VEP wave form changed with wavelength over a range of 380 to 680 nm. For example, in the red range (640 to 680 nm), a larger positive component appeared at about 200 msec, whereas smaller, biphasic responses appeared with wavelengths in the violet range (380 to 420 nm). Regan (1972) criticized the use of large stimulus fields because they resulted in stimulation of both receptors in the fovea (cones) and receptors outside the fovea (rods and cones), which have different wavelength sensitivities. Another problem pointed out by Regan is that of equating the light intensity of different wavelengths, thus making it difficult to separate color and brightness effects.

Perry, Childers, and Falgout (1972) used a technique that maintained intensity of red and green stimuli constant and their size small enough to be presented entirely within the fovea (i.e., they produced a size of .5 degrees of visual angle). Most estimates of foveal extent place it at 2 to 2.5 degrees of visual angle (e.g., see Ruch, Patton, Woodbury, & Towe, 1965). The differences found in ERPs with red and green stimuli led Perry and associates to conclude that there appear to be fundamental differences in cortical processing of red and green.

Significantly different VEPs to patterned red, green, and blue stimuli in persons with normal color vision were reported by Kinney, McKay, Mensch, and Luria (1972). Their results for one color-blind subject, who confused reds and greens but could distinguish them from blue (deuteranopia), showed VEPs that differed from normals. The VEPs for this deuteranope showed no differences in response to red and green but did show a different response to blue. Using six normal subjects and one deuteranope, Regan and Spekreijse (1974) compared their VEPs to two-colored visual patterns. They found that the appearance of a pattern of equal intensity red and green checks produced normal VEPs in persons with normal vision, but smaller VEPs in the color-blind individual. When the brightness of the red and green checks were made equal, the amplitude of the color-blind subject's VEPs dropped sharply. Based on studies of normal color vision, these researchers concluded that the human visual system processes color information differently when the color is presented as patterned rather than as spatially unpatterned stimulation.

The experiments of Kinney et al. (1972) and Regan and Spekreijse (1974) suggest possible methods for the objective detection of color blindness. This possibility was emphasized in a study by Kinney and McKay (1974), in which VEPs of persons with normal color vision and of others with different types of color defects were measured. The color defects were deuteranopia (red–green confusion), protanopia (insensitivity to deep red light), and tritanopia (red–blue–green confusion). Patterned stimuli varying in luminance (brightness) and color were used. The normals gave pattern responses (large positive wave at about 100 msec) for both color and luminance, whereas color defectives produced VEPs only to luminance and not to any of the colors to which they were insensitive. Andreassi and Juszczak (1983) found no differences in right- and left-hemisphere-derived VEPs to red and blue stimuli in color normals. They did find that with central visual field stimulation, P200 amplitudes to blue were larger than to red stimuli.

Thus, it appears that studies that have used appropriate methodological controls result in findings indicating that different VEPs occur to stimuli varying in color. Some results suggest the use of visual ERPs as objective indicators of color vision, which may be especially useful in cases where verbal responses are either not possible or are purposely misleading.

Motion.   Barlow (1964) found that sudden changes in the vertical position of a spot on an oscilloscope screen resulted in a definable visual ERP. Measurements of eye movements ruled out the contribution of this possible artifact in the production of the ERP. Mackay and Rietveld (1968) reported that a visual ERP occurred in response to movement of a single horizontal line, 7 cm in length. The line moved from rest at a velocity of 2 cm/sec. The presence of a reference line enhanced the VEP. Their finding is related to the fact that perceived velocity of a moving figure is increased in the vicinity of a stationary reference point.

The VEPs produced by two conditions of apparent motion and one of no motion were studied by Andreassi, Mayzner, Stern, and Okamura (1973). In all conditions, 20 Xs of identical stimulus energy and constant "on" and "off" times of 5 msec were presented sequentially on a CRT screen. Three different display orders resulted in three strongly different subjective perceptual experiences as follows: (a) an impression that "Xs converged toward the center from right and left," (b) "Xs diverged from the center with a small gap in the middle," and (c) the perception of "about 10 Xs with spaces in between." The VEPs, measured from O_1 and O_2, did not differ under the three conditions, indicating that, at least in this case, the cortical mechanisms that produced the VEPs were similar even though the subject's perceptual experiences were very different.

Reversals in the horizontal motion of a visual noise pattern (random dots) were used to produce VEPs in an experiment by Clarke (1974). The velocity of motion was 10 degrees of visual angle per second, and motion reversal took 5 msec to occur. Clarke obtained suggestive evidence that motion-reversal VEPs were produced largely by direction-sensitive mechanisms within the human brain. He tentatively proposed that the mechanisms might be similar to the directionally sensitive neurons reported to exist in the visual cortex of the monkey.

In another study, Cooper et al. (1977) measured visual ERPs when stimuli such as cars, vans, and trucks moved at unpredictable and infrequent times in a televised landscape. Measurements were made from frontal, central, parietal, and occipital areas in nine subjects. They reported that the main cortical sign of detecting the moving target was the occurrence of a large (30 μV) positive potential at the vertex and parietal locations shortly after the eyes fixated in the area of the vehicle (300 msec). This response occurred when the subject saw the event that he or she was told to detect. These investigators suggest that the potential they observed has origins in common with the P300, a response reported to occur during discrimination and decision-making tasks.

If you present the same object at two different points in space at the right time intervals, a person will see the object as moving from the first to the second position. This experience of motion is called the Phi phenomenon and often cannot be distinguished from real motion. Gallichio and Andreassi (1982) examined this type of apparent motion (calling it "discrete") and another type in which a vertical line appeared to move smoothly from left to right, rather than making a discrete jump ("continuous motion"). The visual ERPs were recorded from Oz and Cz for the two apparent motion conditions under three different velocities (8.00 deg/sec; 13.08 deg/sec; and 19.18 deg/sec). A seventh condition was a stationary presentation of two vertical lines at the beginning and end points. The main finding was that at the Oz site, the two higher velocity continuous motion conditions resulted in longer latency P200 components than the discrete motion condition. In addition, the highest velocity discrete motion condition resulted in longer P200 latencies compared to other discrete conditions. The results indicate a greater amount of brain processing time for continuous and higher velocities of motion in the human visual system, suggesting differential processing for the two types of motion and for higher velocity movement. Because these differences were not observed at the central site (Cz), the role of the occipital area as the primary processor of differential motion and velocity is also suggested. In summary, investigations into the role of movement in producing ERPs have yielded positive results. Researchers have presented suggestive evidence for direction-sensitive mechanisms in the human brain and large amplitude responses accompanying the detection of a moving target. In addition, there is suggestive evidence that different types of apparent motion and velocity of motion may be processed differently in the visual system.

In the next chapter, long-latency ERPs and steady potential shifts in recorded brain activity are discussed. These ERPs have been associated with the performance of various cognitive and information-processing activities and have intriguing implications with respect to understanding brain-behavior relationships.

REFERENCES

Andreassi, J. L. (1984). Interactions between target and masking stimuli: Perceptual and event-related potential effects. *International Journal of Psychophysiology, 1,* 153–162.

Andreassi, J. L., Balinsky, B., Gallichio, J. A., DeSimone, J. J., & Mellers, B. W. (1976). Hypnotic suggestion of stimulus change and visual cortical evoked potential. *Perceptual and Motor Skills, 42,* 371–378.

Andreassi, J. L., DeSimone, J. J., Gallichio, J. A., & Young, N. E. (1976, December). *Evoked cortical potentials and information processing.* Fourth Annual Report, contract N00014-72-A-0406-0006. Office of Naval Research. Washington, D.C.

Andreassi, J. L., DeSimone, J. J., & Mellers, B. W. (1976). Amplitude changes in the visual evoked cortical potential with backward masking. *Electroencephalography and Clinical Neurophysiology, 41,* 387–398.

Andreassi, J. L., & Juszczak N. M. (1983). Brain responses and information processing. Annual Report, Contract F49620-80-C-0013. Air Force Office of Scientific Research, Washington, D.C.

Andreassi, J. L., & Juszczak, N. M. (1984). An investigation of hemispheric specialization and visual event-related potentials in discriminations of line length. *International Journal of Psychophysiology, 2,* 87–95.

Andreassi, J. L., Mayzner, M. S., Beyda, D. R., & Davidovics, S. (1971). Visual cortical evoked potentials under conditions of sequential blanking. *Perception & Psychophysics, 10,*164–168.

Andreassi, J. L., Mayzner, M. S., Stern, M., & Okamura, H. (1973). Visual cortical evoked potentials under conditions of apparent motion. *Physiological Psychology, 1,* 118–120.

Andreassi, J. L., Stern, M., & Okamura, H. (1974). Visual cortical evoked potentials as a function of intensity variations in sequential blanking. *Psychophysiology, 11,* 336–345.

Armington, J. C., Corwin, T. R., & Marsetta, R. (1971). Simultaneously recorded retinal and cortical responses to patterned stimuli. *Journal of the Optical Society of America, 61,* 1514–1521.

Barlow, J. S. (1964). Evoked responses in relation to visual perception and oculomotor reaction times in man. *Annals of the New York Academy of Sciences, 112,* 432–467.

Beck, E. C. (1963). The variability of potentials evoked by light in man; the effect of hypnotic suggestion. *Proceedings of the 3rd Annual Convention of the Utah Academy of Sciences, Arts, and Letters, 40,* 202–204.

Beck, E. C., Dustman, R. E., & Beier, E. G. (1966). Hypnotic suggestions and visually evoked potentials. *Electroencephalography and Clinical Neurophysiology, 20,* 397–400.

Begleiter, H., & Platz, A. (1969a). Cortical evoked potentials to semantic stimuli. *Psychophysiology, 6,* 91–100.

Begleiter, H., & Platz, A. (1969b). Evoked potentials: Modifications by classical conditioning. *Science, 166,* 769–771.

Begleiter, H., Porjesz, B., Yerre, C., & Kissin, B. (1973). Evoked potential correlates of expected stimulus intensity. *Science, 179,* 814–816.

Begleiter, H., Gross, M. M., & Kissin, B. (1967). Evoked cortical responses to affective visual stimuli. *Psychophysiology, 3,* 336–344.

Blinkhorn, S. F., & Hendrickson, D. E. (1982). Averaged evoked responses and psychometric intelligence. *Nature, 295,* 596–597.

Brown, W. S., Marsh, J. T., & Smith, J. C. (1973). Contextual meaning effects on speech-evoked potentials. *Behavioral Biology, 9,* 755–761.

Brown, W. S., Marsh, J. T., & Smith, J. C. (1976). Evoked potential waveform differences produced by the perception of different meanings of an ambiguous phrase. *Electroencephalography & Clinical Neurophysiology, 41,* 113–123.

Buchsbaum, M. S., Davis, G. C., Coppola, R., & Naber, D. (1981). Opiate pharmacology and individual differences: II somatosensory evoked potentials. *Pain, 6,* 121–130.

Bull, K., & Lang, P. J. (1972). Intensity judgments and physiological response amplitude. *Psychophysiology, 9,* 428–436.

Butler, R. A. (1973). The cumulative effects of different stimulus repetition rates on the auditory evoked response in man. *Electroencephalography & Clinical Neurophysiology, 35,* 337–345.

Callaway, E. (1975). *Brain electrical potentials and individual psychological differences.* New York: Grune & Statton.

Chalke, F. C. R., & Ertl, J. (1965). Evoked potentials and intelligence. *Life Sciences, 4,* 1319–1322.

Chatrian, G. E., Canfield, R. C., Knauss, T. A., & Lettich, E. (1975). Cerebral responses to electrical tooth pulp stimulation in man: An objective correlate of acute experimental pain. *Neurology, 25,* 745–757.

Clarke, P. G. (1974). Are visual evoked potentials to motion-reversal produced by direction-sensitive brain mechanisms? *Vision Research, 14,* 1281–1284.

Clynes, M., Kohn, M., & Lifschitz, K. (1964). Dynamics and spatial behavior of light evoked potentials, their modification under hypnosis, and on-line correlation in relation to rhythmic components. In H. Whipple & R. Katzman (Eds.), *Sensory evoked responses* (Vol. 112, pp. 468–509). New York: Annals of the New York Academy of Sciences.

Cooper, R., McCallum, W. C., Newton, P., Papakostopoulos, D., Pocock, P. V., & Warren, W. J. (1977). Cortical potentials associated with the detection of visual events. *Science, 196,* 74–77.

Davis, F. B. (1971). *The measurement of mental capability through evoked potential recordings.* (Educational Records Research Bulletin No. 1), Greenwich, CT: Educational Records Bureau.

Desmedt, J. E., & Robertson, D. (1977). Differential enhancement of early and late components of the cerebral somatosensory evoked potentials during forced-pace cognitive tasks in man. *Journal of Physiology, 271,* 761–782.

Dobelle, W., & Mladejovsky, M. G. (1974). Phosphenes produced by electrical stimulation of human occipital cortex and their application to the development of a prosthesis for the blind. *Journal of Physiology, 243,* 553–576.

Dobelle, W., Mladejovsky, M. G., & Girvin, J. P. (1974). Artificial vision for the blind: Electrical stimulation of visual cortex offers hope for a functional prosthesis. *Science, 183,* 440–443.

Donchin, E., & Lindsley, D. B. (1965). Visually evoked response correlates of perceptual masking and enhancement. *Electroencephalography & Clinical Neurophysiology, 19,* 325–335.

Donchin, E., Ritter, W., & McCallum, C. (1978). Cognitive psychophysiology: The endogenous components of the ERP. In E. Callaway, P. Teuting, & S. Koslow (Eds.), *Event-related potentials in man* (pp. 349–411). New York: Academic Press.

Donchin, E., Wicke, J., & Lindsley, D. B. (1963). Cortical evoked potentials and perception of paired flashes. *Science, 141,* 1285–1286.

Eason, R. G., Harter, M. R., & White, C. T. (1969). Effects of attention and arousal on visually evoked cortical potentials and reaction time in man. *Physiology and Behavior, 4,* 283–289.

Eason, R. G., & Ritchie, G. (1976). *Effects of stimulus set on early and late components of visually evoked potentials.* Paper presented at the meeting of the Psychonomic Society, St. Louis, MO.

Eason, R. G., White, C. T., & Bartlett, N. (1970). Effects of checkerboard pattern stimulation on evoked cortical responses in relation to check size and visual field. *Psychonomic Science, 21,* 113–115.

Ertl, J. P., & Schafer, W. W. P. (1969). Brain response correlates of psychometric intelligence. *Nature, 223,* 421–422.

Friedman, D., Simson, R., Ritter, W., & Rapin, I. (1975a). Cortical evoked potentials elicited by real speech words and human sounds. *Electroencephalography & Clinical Neurophysiology, 38,* 13–19.

Friedman, D., Simson, R., Ritter, W., & Rapin, I. (1975b). The late positive component (P 300) and information processing in sentences. *Electroencephalography & Clinical Neurophysiology, 38,* 255–262.

Fruhstorfer, H., Soveri, P., & Jarvilehto, T. (1970). Short-term habituation of the auditory evoked response in man. *Electroencephalography & Clinical Neurophysiology, 28,* 153–161.

Funakoshi, M., & Kawamura, Y. (1971). Summated cerebral evoked responses to taste stimuli in man. *Electroencephalography & Clinical Neurophysiology, 30,* 205–209.

Galbraith, G. C., Cooper, L. M., & London, P. (1972). Hypnotic susceptibility and the sensory evoked response. *Journal of Comparative & Physiological Psychology, 80,* 509–514.

Gale, A., & Edwards, J. (1983). Cortical correlates of intelligence: In A. Gale & J. Edwards (Eds.), *Physiological correlates of human behavior,* (Vol 3, pp. 79–97). New York: Academic Press.

Gallichio, J. A., & Andreassi, J. L. (1982). Visual evoked potentials under varied velocities of continuous and discrete apparent motion. *International Journal of Neuroscience, 17,* 169–177.

Gucker, D. K. (1973). Correlating visual evoked potentials with psychometric intelligence variation in technique. *Perceptual and Motor Skills, 37,* 189–190.

Guerrero-Figueroa, R., & Heath, R. G. (1964). Evoked responses and changes during attentive factors in man. *Archives of Neurology, 10,* 74–84.

Haider, M., Spong, P., & Lindsley, D. B. (1964). Attention, vigilance, and cortical evoked potentials in humans. *Science, 145,* 180–182.

Halliday, A. M., & Mason, A. A. (1964). The effect of hypnotic anaesthesia on cortical responses. *Journal of Neurology, Neurosurgery & Psychiatry, 27,* 300–312.

Harter, M. R. (1970). Evoked cortical responses to checkerboard patterns: Effect of check-size as a function of retinal eccentricity. *Vision Research, 10,* 1365–1376.

Harter, M. R., & Salmon, L. E. (1972). Intra-modality selective attention and evoked cortical potentials to randomly presented patterns. *Electroencephalography & Clinical Neurophysiology, 32,* 605–613.

Harter, M. R., & White, C. T. (1968). Effects of contour sharpness and checksize on visually evoked cortical potentials. *Vision Research, 8,* 701–711.

Hernandez-Peon, R., & Donoso, M. (1959). Influence of attention and suggestion upon subcortical evoked electrical activity in the human brain. In L. vanBogaert & J. Radermacker (Eds.), *First international on neurological sciences* (Vol. 3, pp. 385–396). New York: Pergamon Press.

Hendrickson, E. E., & Hendrickson, A. E. (1980). The biological basis of individual differences in intelligence. *Personality & Individual Differences, 1,* 3–33.

Hillyard, S. A., & Hansen, J. C. (1986). Attention: Electrophysiological approaches: In M. G. H. Coles, E. Donchin, & S. W. Porges (Eds.), *Psychophysiology: Systems, processes & applications* (pp. 227–267). New York: The Guilford Press.

Hillyard, S. A., Hink, R. F., Schwent, V. L., & Picton, T. W. (1973). Electrical signs of selective attention in the human brain. *Science, 182,* 177–180.

Hillyard, S. A., & Kutas, M. (1983). Electrophysiology of cognitive processing. *Annual Review of Psychology, 34,* 33–61.

Hink, R. F., Van Voorhis, S. T., Hillyard, S. A., & Smith, T. (1977). The division of attention and the human auditory evoked potentials. *Neuropsychologia, 15,* 597–605.

Honda, H. (1973). Visually evoked potentials during pattern discrimination tasks. *Tohoku Psychologica Folia, 32,* 45–54.

Honda, H. (1974). Visually evoked potentials during pattern discrimination tasks (II): Further evidence. *Tohoku Psychologica Folia, 33,* 119–133.

John, E. R., Harrington, R. N., & Sutton, S. (1967). Effects of visual form on the evoked response. *Science, 155,* 1439–1442.

Juszczak, N. M., & Andreassi, J. L. (1985). An investigation of hemispheric asymmetry in size and semantic discriminations and related visual ERPs. *International Journal of Neuroscience, 27,* 283–297.

Kahneman, D. (1973). *Attention and effort.* Englewood Cliffs, NJ: Prentice-Hall.

Karlin, L. (1970). Cognition, preparation and sensory-evoked potentials. *Psychological Bulletin, 73,* 122–136.

Kinney, J. A. S., McKay, C. L. (1974). Test of color-defective vision using the visual evoked response. *Journal of the Optical Society of America, 64,* 1244–1250.

Kinney, J. A. S., McKay, C. L., Mensch, A. J., & Luria, S. M. (1972). Techniques for analysing differences in VERs: Colored and patterned stimuli. *Vision Research, 12,* 1733–1747.

Kutas, M., & Hillyard, S. A. (1980). Reading senseless sentences: Brain potentials reflect semantic incongruity. *Science, 207,* 203–205.

Lelord, G., Laffont, F., & Jusseaume, P. H. (1976). Conditioning of evoked potentials in children of differing intelligence. *Psychophysiology, 13,* 81–85.

Loveless, N. E. (1983). Event-related brain potentials and human performance: In A. Gale & J. Edwards (Eds.), *Physiological correlates of human behavior* (Vol. 2, pp. 79–97). New York: Academic Press.

Mackay, D. M. (1969). Evoked brain potentials as indicatory of sensory information processing. *Neurosciences Research Program Bulletin, 7,* 3.

Mackay, D. M., & Rietveld, W. J. (1968). Electroencephalogram potentials evoked by accelerated visual motion. *Nature, 217,* 677–678.

Maffei, L., & Campbell, F. W. (1970). Neurophysiological localization of the vertical and horizontal visual coordinates in man. *Science, 167,* 386–387.

Martineau, J., Garreau, B., Barthelemy, C., & Lelord, G. (1984). Evoked potentials and P300 during sensory conditioning in autistic children. In R. Karrer, J. Cohen, & P. Tetuing (Eds.), *Brain & information,* (Vol. 425, pp. 362–369). New York: Annals of the New York Academy of Sciences.

McCarthy, G., & Donchin, E. (1981). A metric for thought: A comparison of P300 latency and reaction time. *Science, 211,* 77–79.

Molfese, D. L. (1979). Cortical involvement in the semantic processing of coarticulated speech cues. *Brain & Language, 7,* 86–100.

Moskowitz, A. F., Armington, J. C., & Timberlake, G. (1974). Corners, receptive fields, and visually evoked potentials. *Perception and Psychophysics, 15,* 325–330.

Naatanen, R. (1967). Selective attention and evoked potentials. *Annales Academie Scientiarum Fennica, 151,* 1–226.

Naatanen, R. (1982). Processing negativity: An evoked-potential reflection of selective attention. *Psychological Bulletin, 92,* 605–640.

Naatanen, R., Gailard, A. W. K., & Mantysalo, S. (1978). The N1 effect of selective attention reinterpreted. *Acta Psychologica, 42,* 313–329.

Naatanen, R., & Michie, P. T. (1979). Early selective-attention effects on the evoked potential: A critical review and reinterpretation. *Biological Psychology, 8,* 81–136.

Neville, H. J. (1980). Event-related potentials in neuropsychological studies of language. *Brain & Language, 11,* 300–318.

Norman, D. A., & Bobrow, D. G. (1975). On data-limited and resource-limited processes. *Cognitive Psychology, 7,* 44–64.

Perry, N. W., Childers, D. G., & Falgout, J. C. (1972). Chromatic specificity of the visual evoked response. *Science, 177,* 813–815.

Perry, N. W., McCoy, J. G., Cunningham, W. R., Falgout, J. C., & Street, W. J. (1976). Multivariate visual evoked response correlates of intelligence. *Psychophysiology, 13,* 323–329.

Picton, T. W., Goodman, W. S., & Bryce, D. P. (1970). Amplitude of evoked responses to tones of high intensity. *Acta Oto-Laryngologica, 70,* 77–82.

Porjesz, B., & Begleiter, H. (1975). The effects of stimulus expectancy on evoked brain potentials. *Psychophysiology, 12,* 152–157.

Regan, D. (1972). *Evoked potentials in psychology, sensory physiology and clinical medicine,* New York: Wiley.

Regan, D., & Spekreijse, H. (1974). Evoked potential indications of color blindness. *Vision Research, 14,* 89–95.

Rietveld, W. J., Tordoir, W. E. M., Hagenouw, J. R. B., Lubbers, J. A., & Spoor, Th. (1967). Visual evoked responses to blank and to checkerboard patterned flashes. *Acta Physiologica Pharmacologia Neerlandia, 14,* 259–285.

Ritter, W., Simson, R., Vaughan, H. G. Jr., & Macht, M. (1982). Manipulation of event-related potential manifestations of information processing stages. *Science, 218,* 909–911.

Ritter, W., Vaughan, H. G., Jr., & Costa, L. D. (1968). Orienting and habituation to auditory stimuli: A study of short term changes in average evoked responses. *Electroencephalography & Clinical Neurophysiology, 25,* 550–556.

Rockstroh, B., Birbaumer, N., Elbert, T., & Lutzenberger, W. (1984). Operant control of EEG and event-related slow brain potentials. *Biofeedback & Self-Regulation, 9,* 139–157.

Rosenfeld, J. P., Dowman, R., Silvia, R., & Heinricher, M. (1984). Operantly controlled somatosensory brain potentials: Specific effects on pain processes: In T. Elbert, B. Rockstroh, W. Lutzenberger, & N. Birbaumer (Eds.), *Self-regulation of the brain and behavior,* (pp. 139–153). Heidelberg: Springer.

Ruch, T. C., Patton, H. D., Woodbury, J. W., & Towe, D. L. (Eds.). (1965). *Neurophysiology.* Philadelphia: Saunders.

Ruchkin, D. S., & Sutton, S. (1973). Visual evoked and emitted potentials and stimulus significance. *Bulletin of the Psychonomic Society, 2,* 144–146.

Rust, J. (1975). Cortical evoked potential, personality and intelligence. *Journal of Comparative and Physiological Psychology, 89,* 1220–1226.

Salamy, J., Potvin, A., Jones, K., & Landreth, J. (1975). Cortical evoked responses to labyrinthine stimulation in man. *Psychophysiology, 12,* 55–61.

Satterfield, J. H. (1965). Evoked cortical response enhancement and attention in man: A study of responses to auditory and shock stimuli. *Electroencephalography & Clinical Neurophysiology, 19,*470–475.

Schiller, P. H. (1969). Behavioral and electrophysiological studies of visual masking. In K. N. Leibovic (Ed.), *Information processing in the nervous system* (pp. 141–165.). New York: Springer-Verlag.

Schiller, P. H., & Chorover, S. L. (1966). Metacontrast: Its relation to evoked potentials. *Science, 153,* 1398–1400.

Schweitzer, P. K., & Tepas, D. I. (1974). Intensity effects of the auditory evoked brain response to stimulus onset and cessation. *Perception and Psychophysics, 16,* 396–400.

Shagass, C. (1972). *Evoked brain potentials in psychiatry.* New York: Plenum Press.

Shagass, C., & Schwartz, M. (1963). Cerebral responsiveness in psychiatric patients. *Archives of General Psychiatry, 8,* 177–189.

Shagass, C., & Schwartz, M. (1964). Recovery functions of somato-sensory peripheral nerve and cerebral evoked responses in man. *Electroencephalography & Clinical Neurophysiology, 17,* 126–135.

Shipley, T., Jones, R. W., & Fry, A. (1966). Intensity and the evoked occipitogram in man. *Vision Research, 6,* 657–667.

Shucard, D. W., & Horn, J. L. (1972). Evoked cortical potentials and measurement of human abilities. *Journal of Comparative & Physiological Psychology, 78,* 59–68.

Siegfried, J. B. (1975). The effects of checkerboard pattern check size on the VECP. *Bulletin of the Psychonomic Society, 6,* 306–308.

Simson, R., Ritter, W., & Vaughan, H. G. Jr. (1985). Effects of expectation on negative potentials during visual processing. *Electroencephalography & Clinical Neurophysiology, 62,* 25–31.

Smith, D. B., Allison, T., Goff, W. R., & Principato, J. J. (1971). Human odorant evoked responses: Effects of trigeminal or olfactory deficit. *Electroencephalography & Clinical Neurophysiology, 30,* 313–317.

Soininen, K., & Jarvilehto, T. (1983). Somatosensory evoked potentials associated with tactile stimulation at detection threshold in man. *Electroencephalography & Clinical Neurophysiology, 56,* 494–500.

Spehlmann, R. (1965). The averaged electrical responses to diffuse and patterned light in the human. *Electroencephalography & Clinical Neurophysiology, 19,* 560–569.

Sutton, S., Teuting, P., Zubin, J., & John E. R. (1967). Information delivery and the sensory evoked potential. *Science, 155,* 1436–1439.

Tecce, J. J. (1970). Attention and evoked potentials in man. In D. I. Mostofsky (Ed.), *Attention:Contemporary theory and analysis* (pp. 331–365). New York: Appleton-Century-Crofts.

Tecce, J. J. (1972). Contingent negative variation (CNV) and psychological processes in man. *Psychological Bulletin, 77,* 73–108.

Vanderploeg, R. D., Brown, W. S., & Marsh, J. T. (1987). Judgments of emotion in words and faces: ERP correlates. *International Journal of Psychophysiology, 5,* 193–205.

Vaughan, H. G., Jr., Costa, L. D., & Gilden, L. (1966). The functional relation of visual evoked response and reaction time to stimulus intensity. *Vision Research, 6,* 645–656.

Vaughan, H. G., & Hull, R. C. (1965). Functional relation between stimulus intensity and photically evoked cerebral responses in man. *Nature, 206,* 720–722.

Vaughan, H. G., & Silverstein, L. (1968). Metacontrast and evoked potentials: A reappraisal. *Science, 160,* 207–208.

Vetterli, C. F., & Furedy, J. J. (1985). Evoked potential correlates of intelligence: Some problems with Hendrickson's string measure of evoked potential complexity and error theory of intelligence. *International Journal of Psychophysiology, 3,* 1–3.

Walsh, J. K., & Tepas, D. I. (1975). Human evoked brain responses following loud pure tones. *Bulletin of the Psychonomic Society, 5,* 375–377.

Wastell, D. G., & Kleinman, D. (1980). Fast habituation of the late components of the visual evoked potential in man. *Physiology & Behavior, 25,* 93–97.

Weinberg, H., Walter, W. G., & Crow, H. J. (1970). Intra-cerebral events in humans related to real and imaginary stimuli. *Electroencephalography & Clinical Neurophysiology, 29,* 1–9.

Werner, H. (1935). Studies on countour. I. Quantitative analyses. *American Journal of Psychology, 47,* 40–64.

White, C. T. (1969). Evoked cortical responses and patterned stimuli, *American Psychologist, 24,* 211–214.

White, C. T., & Eason, R. G. (1966). Evoked cortical potentials in relation to certain aspects of visual perception. *Psychological Monographs: General & Applied, 80,* 1–14.

Wickens, C., Kramer, A., Vanasse, L. & Donchin, E. (1983). Performance of concurrent tasks: A psychophysiological analysis of reciprocity of information-processing resources. *Science, 221,* 1080–1082.

Wood, C. C., Goff, W. R., & Day. R. S. (1971). Auditory evoked potentials during speech perception. *Science, 173,* 1248–1251.

Yoshida, S., Iwahara, S., & Nagamura, N. (1975). The effect of stimulus orientation on the visual evoked potential in human subjects. *Electroencephalography & Clinical Neurophysiology, 39,* 53–57.

7

Event-Related Slow Brain Potentials and Behavior

Among the more interesting brain responses are the "slow potentials" or "slow waves." They are "slow" in the sense that they take longer to develop than do the sensory-evoked potentials and motor potentials discussed earlier. Two of these slow potentials are the contingent negative variation (CNV) and the readiness potential (RP), categorized by Vaughan (1969) as steady potential shifts. A third type of slow wave includes the components of the ERP that occur between 250 to 900 msec after the stimulus and are commonly referred to as "P300." Some researchers prefer to call these later positive components P3 without imposing a particular latency on the responses. The term P300 is still commonly used because the original studies by Sutton and his associates found that the response occurred about 300 msec after some initiating stimulus. All of the slow waves mentioned thus far are endogenous in nature. This means that they are produced by internal (endogenous) processes. These internal processes are among the more fascinating ones that can be studied by psychologists and include, among other attributes, intentions to move (readiness potential), expectancies regarding the occurrence of some stimulus (CNV), and decisions (P300). Because of their relation to cognitive events, many cognitive scientists have become interested in these slow waves, especially the P300.

THE CONTINGENT NEGATIVE VARIATION

In the now classic paper by Walter, Cooper, Aldridge, McCallum, and Winter (1964), CNV was described as a steady, relatively long-lasting, negative shift in brain activity, which developed between the time of a warning signal (S1) and a second stimulus (S2) that demanded a response. Grey Walter called this slow shift in EEG baseline, in the S1–S2 interval, CNV because its occurrence depends on the contingency between two events and because it shows a negative drift. It was later found that CNV can occur without motor responses to S2. For example, Cohen and Walter (1966) obtained CNV in anticipation of pictorial stimuli that were used as S2. No motor response was made by the subjects. On the basis of this kind of result, Cohen and Walter suggested that the CNV reflects a state of "expectancy" and have used the term "E wave" as a substitute for CNV. Other investigators proposed that CNV indicates an intention to act (Low, Borda, Frost, & Kellaway, 1966), subject motivation (Irwin, Knott, McAdam, & Rebert, 1966) or attention (McCallum, 1969; Tecce & Scheff, 1969). Whatever the terminology used, it is clear that CNV is related to psychological and performance factors, and some of these are reviewed shortly hereafter.

The amplitude of CNV measured at vertex is about 15 uV, on the average, in young adults. It begins within 200 to 400 msec after S1 and reaches its peak within 400 to 900 msec if the S1–S2 interval is 1000 msec. The CNV amplitude drops abruptly with S2. The time needed to reach peak amplitude is related to CNV shape. Two basic shapes have been identified (see Fig. 7.1) and are referred to as Type A (fast rise time) and Type B (slow rise time) by Tecce (1971). Type A CNVs have been found to occur when subjects were uncertain about when S2 would occur, and Type B occurred when they were more certain about its time of appearance (see Tecce, 1972). This CNV typology also accounts for individual differences in response to psychoactive drugs such as amphetamines and barbiturates (Tecce, Savignano-Bowman, & Cole, 1978). The magnitude of CNV appears related to stimulus intensity. When S2 intensity is very low (e.g., a barely audible tone) or very high (loud tone or intense electric shock), CNV magnitude is increased, perhaps because of enhanced attentiveness and alertness with regard to S2. When the S1–S2 interval is 4 seconds or more, the CNV recordings appear to show early and late portions. The early wave is maximal at about 700 msec after S1, and the late wave peaks just before S2.

The CNV has been related to a number of performance parameters. We examine several of these here, including CNV and speed of reaction, distraction–attention, effort, and stimulus modality.

CNV and Reaction Time

There have been a number of reports in which an association between CNV amplitude and RT was noted, and several that indicate no relation between CNV and speed of response. For example, Cant and Bickford (1967) found that avoidable shock increased CNV amplitude and quickened RT. Also, Tecce and Scheff (1969) observed that distraction decreased CNV amplitude and slowed RT. They found, too, that reward increased CNV and led to faster RTs. On the other hand, Naitoh, Johnson, and Lubin (1971) reported that sleep loss produced decreased

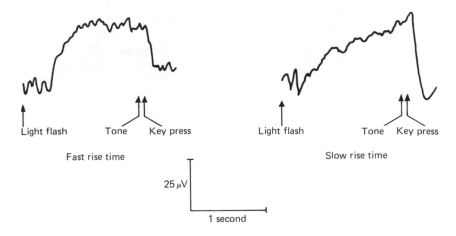

FIG. 7.1. Two types of CNV morphology based on fast (type A) and slow (type B) rise time to maximum voltage.

CNV amplitudes but did not affect RT. Further, Rebert (1972) observed that feedback about speed of RT led to faster responses by subjects, but resulted in no CNV changes. Hillyard (1969) found that larger amplitude CNVs were associated with faster RTs for 5 of 10 subjects tested, indicating that individual differences may occur.

Rebert and Tecce (1973) performed a careful review of the literature available at the time and noted that the CNV and RT relationships that had been reported resulted from experimental manipulations and did not reflect any strong causal relationship between the two processes. They concluded that CNV and RT are relatively independent factors. Haagh and Brunia (1985) found no relation between RT and response-relevant muscle activity with its increased CNV amplitude. Muscle activity was recorded from the leg muscles as subjects waited to give a response to S2.

In summary, it appears that in a number of studies, CNV has been linked to speed of reaction only under experimental manipulations that are likely to affect both of them (e.g., distraction). Otherwise, CNV and RT seem to be relatively independent processes.

CNV and Distraction—Attention

An informative review of processes and concepts related to CNV was presented by Tecce and Cattanach (1987), who wrote that distraction is among the most powerful disruptors of CNV development. This is true whether extraneous stimuli are presented in the S1–S2 interval or just prior to the interval. CNV amplitude has been found to be higher when subjects reported concentration on a task, as compared to when distracting stimuli were introduced (McCallum & Walter, 1968; Tecce & Scheff, 1969). For example, Tecce and Scheff presented four letters or numbers during the S1–S2 interval, and required subjects to recall them after their response to S2; this led to a reduction in CNV amplitude. This reduction was interpreted as being due to an interference with attention. Tecce and Hamilton (1973) introduced distraction into intertrial (S1–S2) intervals by requiring that subjects do mental arithmetic (add 7s continuously). This resulted in reduced CNV amplitude and longer RTs to S2. The finding illustrates, incidentally, that slow RTs are not necessarily related to low-amplitude CNVs, but rather to the experimental manipulation that affected both processes.

The holding of a key during the S1–S2 interval has led to decreased CNV (Otto, Benignus, Ryan, & Leifer, 1977). Also, Tecce, Savignano-Bowman, and Dessonville (1984) reported that muscle tension induced in the forearm and upper torso at the time of response to S2 led to decreased CNV amplitude. It is possible that this motor activity in both studies was disruptive to the primary task of responding to S2. In addition, sleep deprivation, anxiety, and fear of failure also reduce CNV magnitude (Tecce & Cattanach, 1987).

Tecce (1972) made two hypotheses: (a) that CNV amplitude is monotonically related to attention; that is, as attention increases, CNV increases; and (b) that the relationship between CNV amplitude and arousal can be described by an inverted-U function; that is, at low or high levels of arousal, CNV magnitude is low, and at moderate arousal levels, CNV is at its highest amplitude. Tecce, Savignano-Bowman, and Meinbresse (1976) found some evidence in support of these arousal hypotheses. Subjects were required to respond to S2, after an S1–S2 interval in which letters were presented. In one condition, they were asked to recall the letters and in another, to ignore the letters. The letter recall task caused a lowered CNV amplitude, lengthened RT, increased heart rate, and elevated eye blink rate. The reduction of CNV and RT slowing was interpreted as a distraction effect. The increased heart rate and eye blinking was attributed to increased arousal produced by distraction, an important factor in the disruption of CNV development. Thus, attention increased CNV amplitude, whereas distraction causes CNV attenuation. Other support for the arousal hypotheses are the increased CNV observed with high task interest (Fenelon, 1984) in humans, and with positive reinforcement in the monkey (Boyd, Boyd, & Brown, 1980). On the other hand, CNV reduction has been associated with lowered attention (distraction) in sleep deprivation, and in clinical populations showing impaired attention such as neurotics, depressives, and psychosurgery patients (Tecce & Cattanach, 1987).

The pattern of findings outlined here has led to formulation of a distraction–arousal model by Tecce and his associates (see Tecce & Cattanach, 1987). In this model, CNV is reduced at the highest arousal levels because of distraction, is optimal at some moderate level, and falls off again under the low attentive states of minimal arousal levels.

CNV and Effort

The amplitude of CNV increases when greater amounts of energy expenditure are anticipated to allow performance of a task (Low & McSherry, 1968). These investigators found that the anticipation of greater energy expenditure was related to higher CNV amplitudes. Further, Low, Coats, Rettig, and McSherry (1967) reported that CNV amplitude increased as S2 level decreased to a barely audible level. This was interpreted as indicating that greater effort was required to detect the low intensity imperative stimulus and that motivation has an effect. However, motor activity during the S1–S2 interval does not enhance CNV. In fact, Otto et al. (1977) reported that key-holding during the interval decreased CNV. Further, other studies indicate that increased muscular activity (fist clench) during S1–S2 reduces CNV amplitude (Tecce, Cattanach, Boehner-Davis, & Clifford, 1984). Briefly, then, CNV tends to be associated with anticipated degree of physical and psychological effort, and some investigators have related it to degree of motivation. Imposed muscular activity during the S1–S2 interval may decrease CNV or have no effect, results that argue against the position that CNV is purely due to motor activity.

Stimulus Modality and the CNV

Although early studies indicated that modality of the stimulus did not appear to influence the CNV, there is some later evidence that it may. Gaillard (1976) investigated the differential effects of auditory and visual warning signals on the CNV. Two S1–S2 intervals were used, 1 and 3 seconds. The CNV was composed of two waves, one following S1 at about 650 msec and a second that peaked at the end of the inter-stimulus-interval (ISI). The first wave was called an orientation (O) wave and the second an expectancy (E) wave. A modality effect was shown, because the O wave was enhanced after an auditory S1, as compared to a visual S1. The finding that the CNV may not be a unitary potential had been previously reported in experiments by Borda (1970) based on his work with monkeys. Further, Loveless and Sanford (1974) and Weerts and Lang (1973) interpreted the O wave as a cortical component of the orienting response to S1, and the E wave as the traditional CNV. A brief discussion of the relationship between the CNV and P300 is presented in a later section of this chapter.

Other CNV Phenomena

In the course of studying the effects of stimulus presentations during the S1–S2 interval, Tecce and colleagues discovered a "rebound" effect in the CNV (e.g., see Tecce, Yrchik, Meinbresse, Dessonville, & Cole, 1980). When short-term memory items were presented within the S1–S2 interval, distraction effects were indicated by reduced CNV. However, when the items were then unpredictably omitted, CNV rebounded to higher than normal amplitudes. They viewed CNV rebound as a brain correlate of stimulus processing, especially attentional processes. The absence of CNV rebound in Alzheimer and psychosurgery patients suggests that it may be a useful way of assessing abnormal brain functioning associated with pathophysiology (Tecce & Cattanach, 1987).

The term *postimperative negative variation* (PINV) is a delay in CNV resolution that occurs in normals with sustained distraction (Tecce & Cattanach, 1987). What happens is that return to baseline levels is delayed long after the occurrence of S2. The PINV has also been observed in schizophrenic, depressive, and dementia patients.

The effects of stimulus uncertainty on the CNV, auditory ERP, and pupillary diameter was studied by Friedman, Hakerem, Sutton, and Fleiss (1973). The subject had to guess which of two auditory stimuli would be presented after a warning signal. The degree of certainty was manipulated by information about the second stimulus given prior to each trial. The CNV amplitude was higher in the uncertain as compared to the certain condition. In addition, P300 and pupillary diameter were also larger with uncertainty. The results indicated a higher arousal level associated with greater task involvement on the part of subjects during the uncertain conditions.

The CNV was found useful as an index of sexual preference in groups of 12 male and 12 female college-age students (Costell, Lunde, Kopell, & Wittner, 1972). The subjects were shown paired visual exposures of male nudes, female nudes, and sexually neutral silhouettes. The first presentation, serving as S1, lasted 500 msec. The second presentation (S2) was the same slide that appeared after a delay of 1,500 msec and remained on for 2,000 msec. Both males and females responded with larger CNVs to stimuli of the opposite sex than to either the same sex or neutral stimuli.

Weinberg, Walter, Cooper, and Aldridge (1974) set up an experimental situation in which possible CNVs and ERPs would be produced to an expected, but absent, stimulus. Previous research had shown that a brain potential could occur to an absent stimulus (Sutton, Teuting, Zubin, & Hohn, 1967; Weinberg, Walter, & Crow, 1970). They also wanted to determine whether an emitted potential would be preceded by a CNV and whether the CNV would occur before or after feedback about correctness of the response. They found that emitted potentials occurred on occasions when the imperative stimulus (S2) was absent. A CNV was found to precede the emitted potential, which suggested that the expectancy of occurrence of a stimulus is important for the appearance of an emitted potential. This showed that CNV reflects the expectation to receive information.

The conclusion by Weinberg et al. (1974) that CNV represents expectation of information reception, and not necessarily expectation to respond, could also be used to interpret the results of Friedman et al. (1973), because more information was yielded by the uncertain as compared to the certain event because subjects already knew what was coming in the certain situation. The phenomena of CNV rebound, PINV and CNV as an indicator of sexual preference and task involvement are interesting possibilities for continued research.

The CNV is a fascinating phenomenon, from both a psychological and a physiological point of view. As Tecce (1972) has pointed out, the main hypotheses regarding the psychological performance correlates of the CNV have been expectancy, motivation, conation (intention to act), and attention. An arousal–distraction hypothesis of CNV production advanced by Tecce et al. (1976) is related to attention concepts. Demonstrations that distraction disrupts CNV illustrates its relation to arousal and attentional mechanisms. Changes in CNV observed in schizophrenic, depressive, and Alzheimer patients, and its sensitivity to drug effects, point to possible applications for CNV research, a point that is taken up again in chapter 13.

THE READINESS POTENTIAL, OR BEREITSCHAFTSPOTENTIAL

Readiness potential, or Bereitschaftspotential, was the term used by Kornhuber and Deecke (1965) to describe a slow-rising negative wave with amplitudes between 10 to 15 μV. It begins about 500 to 1,000 msec before a voluntary movement and peaks at the time of response (see Fig. 7.2). It has been pointed out that this potential has a slow rise time and resembles a Type B CNV (see Tecce, 1972, and Fig. 7.1). Tecce (1972) has observed that when a motor response (e.g., a key press) is required to S2 in a CNV paradigm, both CNV and RP occur, resulting in a hybrid wave, or "CNV complex." However, when only attention to S2 is required, without an immediate motor response, only CNV occurs.

McCallum, Papakostopoulos, and Griffith (1976) recorded CNVs and RPs from areas of the human brain stem and midbrain. They reported that these slow potentials appeared to have similar, but not identical distributions throughout the brain stem. They caution that the results should be interpreted conservatively, because recording electrode placement was not confirmed. Deecke (1976) observed that CNV and RP have different scalp distributions. For example, CNV can be recorded from frontal areas, whereas RP cannot. Whereas RP shows a distinct lateral asymmetry, CNV has only slight laterality, except where the two hemispheres are differentially activated by verbal and nonverbal stimulation (Rebert & Low, 1978). Thus, evidence derived from different experimental paradigms and as a result of recording over different brain areas indicates that the CNV and RP are separate phenomena.

McAdam and Seales (1969) reported that the amplitude of the RP was influenced by monetary reward. They recorded the RP under reward and no-reward conditions and found that the amplitude of the RP could be approximately doubled in size with monetary reinforcement. Thus RP, like CNV, may be influ-

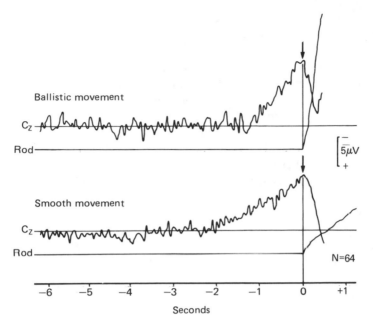

FIG. 7.2.   Brain potentials preceding rapid ballistic movements (upper plot) and slow smooth movements (lower plot) in the same subject. Upper trace of pair shows average potentials at the vertex (TC = 5 sec, 64 sweeps), lower shows rod positions. In both cases, there is a clear Bereitschaftspotential.

enced by subject motivational level. More research is required to determine the extent to which RP and CNV will vary together as a function of experimental (psychological) manipulations.

The RP in Simple and Complex Movements

The RP has a wider scalp distribution for complex as compared to simple movements. For simple movements it may be absent at frontal areas (Deecke, 1976); whereas for complex movements an early frontal RP may indicate the planning of a skilled motor act (Kristeva, 1984). Becker, Iwase, Jurgens, and Kornhuber (1976) measured RPs from 10 subjects who were instructed to vary the speed at which they pushed a 10-cm rod into a 10-cm tube. They were asked to produce fast movements as well as slow ones. The investigators reported that the RP started 800 msec prior to fast movements and 1300 msec before the slow, smooth movements (see Fig. 7.2). These results led them to conclude that it takes more time to prepare for voluntary, slow, smooth, movements than for quick movements. The latency results, plus the finding that the RP was greater in amplitude for smooth movements, also led them to suggest that different neural organization is involved in the production of quick movements versus slow, smooth ones. The RP was maximal at the vertex, as typically found for simple hand and finger movements. This result differs from findings obtained by Deecke, Bernd, Kornhuber, Lang, and Lang (1984), in which RP was recorded during a complex visual and tactile tracking task. In this task, the subjects had to duplicate the movements of either a visually or tactually presented target. The RP preceding this task had a much wider scalp distribution than seen with simple movements. It was task-dependent, because the RP was observed in occipital areas during visual tracking, but not at parietal areas. Conversely, tactual tracking produced the RP at parietal but not at occipital sites. Kristeva (1984) examined the RP during the well-learned complex movements of skilled pianists. All the pianists had more than 20 years of experience, and RPs were recorded when playing a single note and playing a melody. Kristeva found that the RP was earlier in onset and higher in amplitude before playing a melody. In addition, both tasks produced earlier onset RPs in frontal as compared to central areas. These results "suggest that the motor plan and readiness for a complex motor sequence begins in the frontal cortex prior to its initiation in motor cortex" (Kristeva, 1984, p. 482).

RP and Site of Body Response

The portion of the body involved in a particular movement influences the scalp-recorded RP. Brunia and Van Den Bosch (1984) found that prior to finger movements, RP amplitudes were larger over the contralateral hemisphere. In contrast, prior to plantar flexion of the foot (toes pointed away from the face), RP amplitudes were larger at the same-sided hemisphere. This ipsilateral advantage prior to foot movements is due to the fact that the neurons controlling this movement arc actually located at the contralateral side at the depths of the fissure that separates the left and right hemispheres. Thus, because the source is so close, the electrical activity is projected across to the ipsilateral hemisphere, according to these researchers. The same ipsilateral distribution for RPs was found for dorsiflexion (toes pointed towards the face) and planter flexion of the right and left feet (Brunia & Dautzenberg, 1986).

Spontaneous and Planned Movements

The RP was recorded under three different instructional conditions, in which subjects were required to squeeze a hand grip as follows: (a) under self-paced conditions; (b) in response to tones; and (c) to the second of two tones, separated by 1000 msec (Kutas & Donchin, 1980). The self-paced and warned conditions (1 and 3) produced clear RPs at the central recording site, whereas unwarned movements did not. A difference in RPs under spontaneous and planned movement conditions was also observed by Libet, Wright, and Gleason (1982). Subjects performed finger flexions at a time of their own choosing or according to a preset signal. The spontaneous RPs were of two types: Type I had an early onset (about 1050 msec before the movement), and a Type II RP had an onset, beginning about 575 msec prior to movement. On the basis of these results, Libet and associates proposed that voluntary acts involve more than one process. Process I is associated with an intention to act at some time in the near future, and Process II is associated with a more specific intention to act and immediately precedes the act. The Process I and II outlined here reflect the Type I and II RPs described in the study. They also concluded that all RPs, whether self-initiated or pre-planned, are specifically related to preparation for motor activity.

Maturational Influences on the RP

The RPs of children age 8 to 13 were studied during skilled performance by Chiarenza, Papakostopoulos, Giordana, and Guareschi-Cazzullo (1983). The skilled performance consisted of initiating a target sweep on a screen by a button held in one hand, and stopping the sweep in a defined central area of the screen by pressing a button in the other hand. Consistent RPs were recorded in children 10 years of age and older and had a scalp distribution similar to adults, with a maximum at the vertex. From the age of 11, RP preceded muscle activity by 600 to 800 msec. Karrer and associates have found positive components preceding movement in children and preadolescents (see Chisholm, Karrer, & Cone, 1984). This positivity has been attributed to inhibitory processes that are needed to increase the accuracy of the motor act, and might be related to development of motor control. In a study by Chisholm et al. (1984), the RPs of children 8 to 19 were measured during self-paced hand squeezes. They found that RP positivity decreased with age, consistent with their own earlier results and those of Chiarenza et al. (1983).

In summary, the RP is a brain potential that precedes both voluntary and spontaneous movements. Experimental evidence indicates that it is related to psychological and performance variables such as motivation, speed of movement, task complexity, site of body response, and maturational factors.

THE P300, OR P3, POTENTIAL

Sutton and colleagues (Sutton, Braren, & Zubin, 1965; Sutton et al., 1967) discovered that a late positive going ERP occurred to task-relevant stimuli that delivered significant information. Because this component had a latency of about 300 msec after stimulus presentation, and it was positive, it was referred to as P300. Donchin, McCarthy, Kutas, and Ritter (1983) pointed out that the term P300 is now a misnomer, because many reports since the original work by Sutton and colleagues have found the ''classical P300'' at anywhere from 300 to 900 msec. These positive peaks share the classical features in that they are largest at parietal scalp areas and occur in situations known to produce P300. Further, an economy in usage is achieved by referring to all of them by a common term.

The P300 response has been associated with a variety of cognitive activities, including decision making, signal probability, attention, discrimination, uncertainty resolution, stimulus relevance, and information delivery. In fact, so many cognitive events have been related to P300 and other late waves that Beck (1975) wryly commented, "One would not be greatly surprised to encounter a slow rising late wave of 'brotherly love' " (p.243). The proliferation of terms is due not to ambiguity of P300 as a physical occurrence, but to the variety of interpretations by different investigators who prefer to use their own labels to describe relationships found in a wide variety of experimental situations. If one were to look for a common factor to which the various cognitive activities associated with P300 were related, it would be "information processing." Donchin et al. (1983) emphasized that when researchers carefully consider the circumstances under which they observe P300, the data fall into a coherent pattern.

In this section, we examine the association of P300 with various processes that could be described as decision making, stimulus probability, attention, signal detection, discrimination, and so on; but it should be emphasized that any differences in the observed P300 brain response are due to the variety of psychological circumstances orchestrated by the researchers.

Decision Making, Decision Confidence, and P300

Some investigators have related P300 to decision making (e.g., Smith, Donchin, Cohen, & Starr, 1970; Rohrbaugh, Donchin, & Ericksen, 1974). Rohrbaugh and associates devised an experimental situation in which only the second of two rapidly successive and relevant visual stimuli permitted subjects to make a decision. Analyses of the ERPs indicated that only this second stimulus produced a prominent and enhanced P300. Because P300 was not reliably enhanced in response to the first stimulus, the researchers concluded that neither relevance nor information delivery, per se, determines the amplitude of P300. Rohrbaugh et al. emphasized that the subject's activity as an information processor determined the amplitude of P300, and they believe that the term "decision" is appropriate to describe its psychological correlate.

In an experiment by Woods, Hillyard, Courchesne, and Galambos (1980), young adults were required to detect auditory stimuli at split-second intervals. They found that the P300 component was fully recovered in less than 1.0 second, while earlier N1–P2 components (latencies 100 to 180 msec) were reduced in amplitude with stimulus repetition. They proposed that the rapid recovery of P300 suggests that it is generated at the same high rates as the decision processes with which it is associated. Also, the differences in habituation to stimuli of P300 (endogeneous) and earlier (exogeneous) components suggest that they are generated in different brain areas.

Hillyard, Squires, Bauer, and Lindsay (1971) reported that confidence in a decision regarding detection was related to P300 amplitude; that is, higher amplitudes were associated with greater degrees of confidence. Squires, Hillyard, and Lindsay (1973) used a signal detection task in which subjects had to decide whether or not a very low level auditory signal was heard during a specified time interval. Based on their results, they made the suggestion that an early negative component of the ERP (N1, peaking between 140 and 190 msec) and P300 (354 and 450 msec) represented aspects of decision making. They also reported a relationship between P300 amplitude and decision confidence. In a later study, K. Squires, N. Squires, and Hillyard (1975) expanded this experimental design and were able to conclude that when the decision is difficult, P300 is mainly a function of decision confidence. When decision making is made easy, however, P300 varies with the probability of occurrence of a second stimulus such that higher amplitude P300 is associated with lower probability signals.

In summary, the general result is that P300 amplitude is enhanced when persons are required to make decisions about stimuli. Furthermore, greater amplitude increases appear to be related to increased confidence in the decision. There is also some evidence that P300 is generated at the same rate as the decision processes with which it is related.

The P300 and Probability

The studies reviewed in this section consider the relation between P300 and relative certainty–uncertainty that a stimulus will occur. Sutton et al. (1965) discovered that P300 was greater in amplitude when subjects were uncertain about whether a second stimulus would be a sound or a light. This pioneering effort underscored the importance of a subjective (endogenous) reaction in the production of late ERP components, as compared to stimulus (exogenous) factors that influenced the earlier ERP components. Figure 7.3 shows auditory ERPs to certain and uncertain stimuli. Note the large dips in the ERP at around 300 msec; this is the "P300." Also note that, in this figure, positivity is indicated by a downward deflection.

Tueting, Sutton, and Zubin (1970) found that P300 amplitude was high when the probability of a guessed outcome was low, and small when the probability of an event occurring was high. Thus, P300 was larger, the more unexpected the outcome of the guess.

In an interesting experiment, Ruchkin, Sutton, and Tueting (1975) provided evidence that both evoked and emitted P300s were affected by stimulus probability. They devised a situation in which either the presence or absence of an auditory click provided information. The probability of stimulus presence or absence was varied between 25% and 75%. Both the emitted and evoked P300s were larger for the less frequent event and smaller for the event that had a higher probability of occurrence. The authors concluded, therefore, that evoked and emitted P300s are manifestations of the same brain processes.

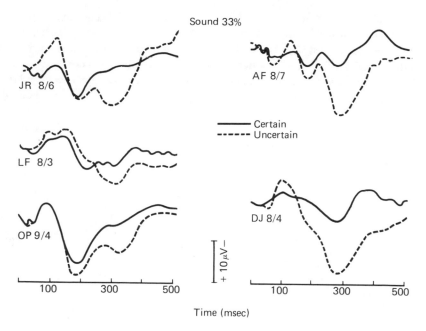

FIG. 7.3. Average wave forms for certain and uncertain (P = .33) sounds for five subjects.

A study conducted by Squires, Donchin, Herning, and McCarthy (1977) required subjects to ignore or count loud or soft tones whose probability was either high (.90) or low (.10). These researchers reported three prominent ERP components: a large negativity occurring at about 210 msec (N210), a large positive component at abut 350 msec (P350), and a slow wave (SW) that appeared over the last 200 msec of the 768-msec period. They noted that the P350 component was enhanced whenever the stimulus was rare and relevant to the task. The same was true for the SW component, except that its scalp distribution was different from P350. The 210 wave was most pronounced following rare stimuli. Hence, they concluded that the P350 and SW components are related to active processing of stimulus information, whereas N210 reflects stimulus probability, independent of the task.

In summary, a number of studies have consistently associated P300 with stimulus probability; that is, higher P300 amplitudes were related to lower probabilities of stimulus events. More detailed analyses reveal that there is more than one component of the ERP, within the latency range of the classical P300, related to stimulus probability and information processing (e.g., P3a and P3b of N. Squires, K. Squires, & Hillyard, 1975, and P350 and SW of K. Squires et al., 1977). As the research findings mount, it is becoming increasingly clear that a critical factor in the elicitation of P300 is subjective probability, or the subject's perception of the likelihood that a certain stimulus will be delivered. The importance of subjective factors in determining P300 amplitude was demonstrated by Horst, Johnson, and Donchin (1980). In that study, the largest P300s were produced when subjects were ''surprised'' that they were correct when they thought they were wrong, and vice versa.

Selective Attention and P300

Auditory ERPs were recorded in persons who listened to a series of tones in one ear and ignored simultaneous tones in the other (Hillyard, Hink, Schwent, & Picton, 1973). The negative component (N1) of the ERP (peaking at 80 to 100 msec) was enlarged for the attended tones. A later, positive component, peaking at 250 to 400 msec (P300), also occurred to infrequent stimulus changes in the attended ear. These researchers interpreted the early ERP component as representing stimulus set and the later one as indicating response set in the selective attention situation. They proposed that stimulus set preferentially admits all sensory input to an attended channel, whereas response set facilitates recognition of these specific, task-related stimuli. To illustrate this, they give an example using the familiar cocktail party situation (with many competing stimuli) in which there is a stimulus set for a particular speaker's voice and a response set to recognize the contents of his speech.

A very detailed review of the selective attention-ERP literature was compiled by Naatanen (1975). In it, he concluded that the ERP correlates of selective attention are by no means established, especially the functional significance of the early N1 component. He suggested that one reason for its apparent involvement in selective attention was that subjects were able to predict the occurrence of relevant stimuli, at least to some extent, from the pattern of stimuli in the sequence. Later, Naatanen and Michie (1979) suggested that N1 in this situation was really a part of a more complex wave that combined an endogenous negative shift with the N1 component. Hillyard and Hansen (1986) concluded that this negativity is not simply an enlargement of the exogenous N1, but is an attention effect beginning at 60 to 80 msec that is superimposed on the N1. Because this attention-sensitive component is defined as an ERP difference between inattention and attention, Hillyard and associates referred to it as the Nd, or ''negative difference'' wave. Naatanen's criticisms were taken seriously by ERP researchers who utilized them to sharpen their experimental procedures in elucidating the relation between ERPs and selective attention.

In 1975, Callaway outlined some possible relationships between ERPs and attentional mechanisms in the following statement:

> The earlier AEP components (before 200 msec) seem to be affected by the simpler functions of attention (i.e., recognizing the stimuli as being in the relevant modality). Later components (200 to 400 msec) are most affected when more

complex cognitive processes are involved. When very complex discriminations are called for there may be effects on very late (400 to 500 msec) components of the AEP. (p. 16)

Some would disagree with the hypotheses regarding the late and early ERP components and their relation to attentional mechanisms. However, they are testable and have suggested interesting research approaches.

Several investigations have helped to clarify some relations between attentional mechanisms and ERPs. For example, N. Squires et al. (1975) found evidence for two types of P300 waves. One of these they labeled P3a (latency about 240 msec), which was produced by unpredictable shifts in tone frequency and amplitude, regardless of whether instructions were to attend to or ignore the tones. The second, labeled P3b, with a latency of about 350 msec, occurred to tone changes only when subjects were actively attending to them. The P3a was distributed frontally–centrally, whereas P3b had a parietal–central distribution (see Fig. 7.4). An experiment by Ford, Roth, and Kopell (1976) supported the notion of more than one type of P300 wave. They used a task designed to produce three levels of attention, and found that P300 to the infrequent event became larger with increased attention. The P300 recorded from parietal leads was larger than that recorded from frontal areas during active attention. However, frontally recorded P300 was larger than parietal P300 during the ignore condition.

The effects of tone presentation rate on selective attention was examined by Schwent, Hillyard, and Galambos (1976). The measures of attention were the auditory ERP and detection efficiency. The ISIs averaged 350 msec, 960 msec, and 1,920 msec in the fast, medium, and slow rate conditions. Interestingly, the early N1 component (latency 80 to 130 msec) was enhanced by attention only with the fast presentation rate, whereas P3 (300 to 450 msec) was enlarged to attended stimuli at all ISIs. Thus, the enhancement of the early component was produced by imposing a high "information load" upon the subject. The authors commented that the fast stimulus presentation condition may have caused the subject to focus his or her attention more intently, an observation supported by performance data, because signal detection was more efficient with the faster rates. The authors interpreted their results as further evidence that the N1 and P300 components reflect different selective attention processes.

In his review of P300 research, Pritchard (1981) pointed out that selective attention appears to be a necessary condition for producing P300. Even low-probability stimuli will not produce P300 if they are not task-relevant and are ignored while a subject engages in another task.

In summary, attentional mechanisms have been found to produce changes in both early and late components of the ERP. Most of the studies conducted after 1970 have attempted to eliminate extraneous factors such as generalized arousal or preparation as the reason for ERP enhancement in selective attention. Some

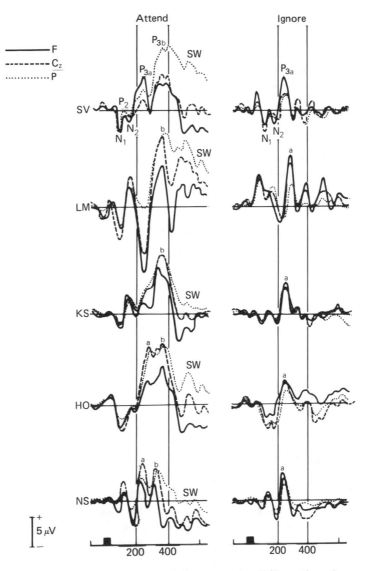

FIG. 7.4. Evoked responses to infrequent stimuli (P = .1) at three electrode locations for five subjects in the attend (left) and ignore (right) conditions. The infrequent stimulus was soft for subjects SV, LM, KS, and NS, and loud for HO. For each subject the wave forms from the three electrode sites, frontal (F), vertex (Cz), and parietal (P) are superimposed.

investigators have postulated that enhancement of early ERP components with selective attention results from stimulus set, whereas a response set is responsible for enhancement of later components. Research reveals the complexity of the situation, because ERP components may differ according to stimulus rate used, the brain area sampled, and the level of attention required by the task.

P300 and the Orienting Response

The orienting response (OR) to novel stimuli includes a whole complex of physiological changes that occur when the organism shifts its attention to the unexpected event (see chapter 15 for a more detailed discussion of the orienting response). The suggestion that P300 accompanied the OR was first made by Ritter and colleagues (Ritter, & Vaughan, 1969; Ritter, Vaughan, & Costa, 1968). Ritter et al. (1968) found that when the first of a series of tones was presented unexpectedly, it produced a P300 response. This also occurred when a change in pitch of the tone was unexpectedly introduced. Predictable changes in pitch did not produce a P300 response. They therefore concluded that the P300 reflected a shift of attention associated with the OR. Ritter and Vaughan (1969) reported P300 responses when signals were detected but not with undetected signals or nonsignal stimuli. They concluded that P300 could be associated with the OR or stimulus discrimination and that it reflected brain processes concerned with the evaluation of stimulus significance. Roth and Kopell (1973) expanded on the work of Ritter and colleagues by increasing the number of subjects and ERP analyses. They obtained an ERP associated with infrequent, unpredictable stimuli, which had a positive component with a latency of about 300 msec and interpreted this P300 as reflecting the OR to unexpected stimuli.

One problem with relating P300 to the orienting response is that the P300 does not show substantial decrement across large numbers of trials (Courchesne, Courchesne, & Hillyard, 1978). Because the orienting response usually habituates with continued presentation, one would expect the P300 to decrease in amplitude over time. Pritchard (1981) wrote that the P300 seen in orienting situations may be a different brain response than that observed with attended, task-relevant stimuli. Moreover, Donchin et al. (1983) have suggested that the P300 represents neural activity that occurs whenever a neuronal model of a stimulus must be updated. This concept of a neuronal model is central to Sokolov's (1969) formulation, which says that the orienting response occurs whenever there is a discrepancy between a stimulus and the person's internal model of the stimulus. Donchin and colleagues further suggested that whether the model will be updated, and the extent of this revision, depends on the surprise value and relevance of the events.

P300 and the Detection and Discrimination of Stimuli

Stimulus Detection.   Psychophysiologists have designed clever experiments to determine the nature of P300 in "detection" and "guess" tasks. In the detection situation, the subject tells after a trial whether a stimulus was presented or not, whereas in a guess task, the subject predicts prior to the trial whether or not the stimulus will be presented. Hillyard et al. (1971) used a signal detection procedure in which the subject's task was to decide on each trial whether or not an auditory signal (at threshold) had been added to continuous background noise. They found that P300 was several times larger when signals were detected than when they were not detected. It was concluded that P300 was enlarged only when stimulus information was being actively processed and that it was associated with the occurrence of a signal and its correct detection. However, the situation is more complex than originally thought because Ruchkin, Sutton, Kietzman, and Silver (1980) reported that P300 is enlarged not only for correct detections but for correct rejections. In addition to the P300, they reported a slow wave (SW) that showed the opposite relationship, because it decreased with increased accuracy. (The SW occurs at a latency of 400 to 800 msec and is positive over parietal and negative over frontal scalp areas; see Fig. 7.4). Ruchkin et al. proposed that because P300 is involved in the initial cognitive evaluation of the stimulus, it becomes larger as the amount of information provided by an event increases. On the other hand, the SW increases in amplitude as accuracy decreases, because more prolonged processing is required when the decision is more difficult.

Sutton et al. (1967) and Ruchkin and Sutton (1973) found that a P300 appeared in the absence of a stimulus when the omitted signal was expected and provided information. For example, Sutton and associates asked subjects to guess, before each trial, whether the stimulus would consist of one or two clicks. The presence or absence of a second click told subjects whether their guess was correct or incorrect. A large P300 occurred at about the time of the second click, whether or not it had actually been presented. Sutton and colleagues interpreted the P300 as reflecting the delivery of information to the subject. Ruchkin and Sutton (1978a) have noted that the emitted P300 was of lower amplitude and broader duration than the evoked P300. They suggest that this may be due to the more imprecise internal timing that occurs when a subject is estimating the time of stimulus occurrence. Ruchkin, Sutton, and Stega (1980) believe that P300s "evoked" by a stimulus and P300s that are "emitted" in response to the absence of a stimulus are essentially identical phenomena. These investigators examined emitted P300s and slow waves in detection and guessing tasks in which the same stimuli were used. A significant difference was found in the slow wave for the two tasks, but not for P300. For the guessing task, the slow wave was large and positive at the vertex, whereas in the detection task, it was almost zero in amplitude at the same site. The researchers suggested that the P300s reflect an intermediate stage of event evaluation that is common to more than one type of task, whereas the SW may represent a final evaluation that differs for detect and guess trials, perhaps being more complex for the guess trials. The interested reader is referred to a thoughtful article by Sutton and Ruchkin (1984), which discusses possible relationships and differences among a variety of late positive components including P300, P3b, P3a, and SW. (Most researchers in this area agree that P300 and P3b represent the "classic" P300 in that the latency is about 300 msec and the maximal response is recorded at Pz.) Sutton and Ruchkin presented evidence that the SW may include a tonic variety, with slow return to baseline, and a phasic type with a relatively quick return.

Discrimination of Stimuli. The general finding has been that P300 latency increases and amplitude decreases with increased difficulty in discriminating stimuli. The latency increases have been related to the longer time for stimulus evaluation required when discriminations are difficult or ambiguous (Andreassi & Jusczcak, 1984; McCarthy & Donchin, 1981). The reduced P300 amplitude has been ascribed to "equivocation" by Ruchkin & Sutton (1978b). They used the term in reference to the reduced information resulting from the subject's uncertainty about the perceived event when discriminations are difficult. Ford, Roth, Dirks, and Kopell (1973) required their subjects to make discriminations between stimuli in the same sensory modality (e.g., flashes of lights) and between modalities (e.g., clicks and flashes). Stimuli were either made relevant or irrelevant through instructions. They found that the P300 was of high amplitude to relevant stimuli, medium-sized if the stimulus was irrelevant but in the relevant modality, and nonexistent if in the irrelevant modality. The P300, therefore, seemed to reflect discriminations between and within modalities, and the effects of stimulus importance on amplitude of the response.

The effects of varying the difficulty of target discrimination on the P300 was examined by Fitzgerald and Picton (1983) in a series of three experiments. Both easy and difficult discriminations occurred within the same condition, and RT was recorded to determine actual difficulty of the discriminations. In all experiments, the latencies of P300 were later and the amplitudes were smaller as a function of increasing discrimination difficulty.

The occurrence of P300 and a negative N400 wave in a variety of visual discrimination tasks was noted by Stuss, Picton, and Cerri (1986). In their experiment, subjects were required to name pictures presented on a screen 1 second after a brief warning tone. A P300 occurred when a stimulus from a low-probability category was detected. The N400 (large negativity in 300–500 msec range) was observed when target stimuli came from a more extensive set of possibilities. These researchers proposed that the N400 represents a search of memory to name the object. A larger range of possibilities might result in larger amplitude N400 because of the greater effort involved in searching among stimuli stored in long-term memory. The general finding seems to be that tasks requiring discrimination of stimuli result in P300 responses, with larger responses being related to relevant stimuli and easier discriminations. This finding fits in with those that show larger P300s with correct detections and guesses. Recent investigations have related a late negative component (N400) to cognitive activities involving discriminations.

P300 and Memory

A convenient paradigm to study the P300 correlates of short term memory is a task developed by Sternberg (1966). In a typical study, a "memory set" of up to six items is presented on a screen (e.g., the numbers: 9, 7, 4, 3, 1, 6). About 2 seconds later, a "probe" stimulus (e.g., the number 3) is flashed, and the subject must decide whether it was a member or the original memory set (probability is usually set at 50%). The ERP and RT are recorded as the probe is presented. Reaction time has been found to increase linearly as a function of memory set size, the larger the set the more items the subject must scan in short-term memory. Sternberg's original purpose was to study the retrieval of information from short-term memory, reasoning that RT can provide clues to retrieval processes. His model proposes four stages of information processing to perform the task: stimulus encoding, serial comparison, binary decision, and response execution. Donchin, Karis, Bashore, Coles, and Gratton (1986) have described the utility of P300 in helping to refine models of cognitive processes such as Sternberg's. For example, it has been argued that P300 latency is better than RT as an estimate of memory scanning rate, because P300 latency slope is constant when RT slope varies (e.g., for young and old subjects, Ford, Roth, Mohs, Hipkins, & Kopell, 1979).

Gomer, Spicuzza, and O'Donnell (1976) found that RT and P300 latency increased linearly as memory set size increased. They related delayed P300 to the greater time needed to do the more difficult task. Further, they reported that P300 amplitude was larger to items identified as members of the original memory set, compared to P300s to nonset members, a result observed previously for target and nontarget stimuli. In a study by Ford et al. (1979), P300 latency and RT were evaluated in a Sternberg paradigm to compare short-term memory processes in young (mean age of 23) and elderly (mean age of 81) individuals. The elderly were slower in RT to probe stimuli, and evidenced a steeper increasing RT slope as a function of memory set size than did young subjects. Their P300 latencies, however, were only slightly longer than younger persons and showed similar slopes, indicating that the two age groups compared the probe with memory items at the same rate. Ford and colleagues concluded from these and other data that although older subjects encoded stimuli more slowly, they scanned memory at the same speed as younger persons.

In 1983, Polich, Howard, and Starr conducted a study to determine the relationship between P300 latency and the digits forward and backward tasks of the Wechsler Adult Intelligence Scale. They used a total of 93 neurologically normal subjects, aged 5 to 87, with approximately equal numbers in each decade. The P300 complex appeared reliably to rare tones, but not to frequent ones. Correlations between P300 latencies and short-term memory scores (digit span) suggest the possibility that P300 latency is related to memory capacity. The researchers suggested that P300 latency reflects an individual's capacity to retain recently encoded information for comparison with the new incoming information, the greater the capacity the shorter the latency. The authors pointed out that the implications of human depth electrode recordings, animal studies, and clinical observation suggest that P300 may be initiated in brain sites related to memory operations, that is, the subcortical hippocampus and amygdala. Of particular interest is the work of Halgren et al. (1980) at UCLA and Wood, Allison, Goff, Williamson, and Spencer (1980) and Wood et al. (1984) at Yale, in which P300 paradigms resulted in P300-like responses from hippocampus and amygdala. The subcortical recordings were made from patients undergoing treatment for epilepsy, and shared many functional characteristics of the scalp-recorded P300.

If some words in a list are made different in some respect, for example, having larger or smaller letters than other words, then these items are better remembered in a later test of recall. The better recall of these ''isolated'' words is called the von Restorff effect. Karis, Fabiani, and Donchin (1984) predicted that such isolates would result in larger P300 amplitudes and would be better remembered. The prediction was partially correct, because there were individual differences in subjects' results. Those that showed a strong von Restorff effect also had large P300s to the isolates and remembered them better. These individuals used rote memorization (e.g., repeating the words) to do the task. Those that used other memory strategies (e.g., combining the words in sentences or short stories) showed little von Restorff effect, and the P300 did not differentiate between the recalled and nonrecalled words. In a follow-up study, Fabiani, Karis, and Donchin (1986) confirmed that P300 amplitude is related to subsequent recall. This time, subjects engaged in one task and then were asked unexpectedly to recall as many male and female names that had been previously presented. The names that were recalled originally elicited larger P300s than names not recalled. The results supported their hypothesis that a relationship between P300 amplitude and memory emerges when elaborate rehearsal strategies are minimized. Fabiani et al. also interpreted the data as being consistent with the theory that P300 manifests processes invoked when events occur and create a need to revise representations of these events in memory.

In summary, rather consistent relationships have been reported by various investigators regarding P300 and decision making and P300 and stimulus probability; that is, enhancement occurs with the decision process and with less probable stimuli. Studies of selective attention and the orienting response have indicated that the P300 is not a unitary process and may reflect variations in stimulus and response sets, in stimulus relevance, and in novelty of stimuli. Signal detection and discrimination processes have also been associated with P300 in a manner that indicates larger responses for correct detections and rejections, and decreased amplitude with increased difficulty in discriminating stimuli. Further, increased P300 latency occurs with more difficult discriminations. Experimental findings also indicate that P300 latency increases in a way showing that it depends on time to evaluate stimuli. Memory processes can also be indexed by P300 latency. For example, the greater the number of items that must be scanned in short-term memory, the longer is P300 latency. Further, verbal materials that elicit larger P300s are recalled better by subjects.

We have noted in this section that the classic P300 has been separated into P3a and P3b components. Moreover, the picture of the P300 is complicated by the identification of SW and N400 components that overlap in time the appearance of the classic P300. However, now that investigators are aware of these additional components, they will be able to relate them to various aspects of behavior.

Is there any common psychological process to which the P300 and its related components can be attached? A number of writers have suggested that P300 is related to active processing of stimulus information (Beck, 1975; Hillyard, Squires, Bauer, & Lindsay, 1971). In fact, many of the processes reviewed in this section, including signal detection and discrimination, selective attention and the OR, decision making and memory scanning are aspects of active information processing. However, Sutton and Ruchkin (1984) have proposed that P300 reflects "value" of a stimulus to subjects. Value in the sense that task-relevant events have more value than task-irrelevant events, targets have more value than nontargets, and pictures that are recognized have greater value than those that are not, and so on. Johnson (1986) pointed out that many constructs have been proposed to influence the occurrence of P300 and its amplitude variations, including: attention, the OR, decision making, uncertainty reduction, processing demand, task relevance, and value. Johnson noted the similarities among the constructs and presented a model that reduces explanations of variations in P300 to three dimensions, thereby rejecting the notion that a single behavioral process accounts for P300. The three dimensions proposed are: (a) subjective probability, (b) stimulus meaning, and (c) information transmission. He contended that the subjective probability and stimulus meaning dimensions have independent and additive effects on P300 amplitude, and that the amplitude contributions of these two factors are dependent on the proportion of stimulus information they transmit. In a careful exposition, Johnson presented the most systematic model to date of psychological processes, and their interactions, that affect P300 amplitude.

THE RELATIONSHIP BETWEEN CNV AND P300

Some investigators have suggested that P300 and CNV are related phenomena (Karlin, 1970; Naatanen, 1970). That is, P300 is merely the return to the baseline of the CNV. However, a number of studies have produced evidence that the two are separate phenomena. For example, Donald and Goff (1971) showed that P300 was enhanced by certain relevant stimuli, but that enhancement was unrelated to CNV amplitude. Friedman et al. (1973) found that P300 changed systematically with changes in stimulus probability, but CNV did not. Donchin, Tueting, Ritter, Kutas, and Heffley (1975) reported that P300 amplitude was not affected by the presence or absence of a warning stimulus, whereas CNV was elicited only for warned trials. In addition, scalp distributions of CNV and P300 differed, indicating that they are generated by different neuronal populations in the brain. Poon, Thompson, and Marsh (1976) observed smaller CNV amplitudes and enhanced P300 with more difficult discriminations. Peters, Billinger, and Knott (1977) measured CNV and P300 during verbal learning (paired-associates) and discrimination RT. They found that CNV amplitude showed an inverse relation to learning, whereas P300 increased with learning. Both wave forms were larger at central and parietal areas than at the frontal location during learning. During discrimination RT, however, the CNV was maximal at the frontal area and P300 was greatest at the parietal location. The CNV data were interpreted as reflecting early arousal and attentional processes, whereas P300 was related to the subject's decision about stimulus relevance. Peters and colleagues concluded that CNV and P300 could be regarded, on the basis of their data, as indices of learning activity taking place in the brain. The findings also indicated that they are separate processes.

The consensus at this writing seems to be that P300 and CNV are independent phenomena. No doubt, their association with interesting psychological processes will lead to continued fruitful research on the nature of these and other slow potentials.

In the last few chapters, we have seen how brain measures are correlated with different behaviors. In the next chapter, we examine how changes in muscle activity are related to various human activities. This is the first of the peripheral measures to be presented. Like many of the peripheral measures that are discussed, brain and muscle activity influence each other in a mutually interactive manner.

REFERENCES

Andreassi, J. L., & Juszczak, N. M. (1984). An investigation of hemispheric specialization and visual event-related potentials in discriminations of line length. *International Journal of Psychophysiology, 2,* 87–95.

Beck, E. C. (1975). Electrophysiology and behavior. *Annual Review of Psychology, 26,* 233–262.

Becker, W., Iwase, R., Jurgens, R., & Kornhuber, H. H. (1976). Bereitschaftspotential preceding voluntary slow and rapid hand movements. In W. C. McCallum & J. R. Knott (Eds.), *The responsive brain* (pp. 99–102). Bristol: John Wright and Sons.

Borda, R. P. (1970). Drive and performance related aspects of the CNV in rhesus monkeys. *Electroencephalography & Clinical Neurophysiology, 29,* 173–180.

Boyd, E. S., Boyd, E. H., & Brown, L. E. (1980). The M-wave and CNV in the squirrel monkey: Generality of cue modality and of reward. *Electroencephalography & Clinical Neurophysiology, 49,* 66–80.

Brunia, C. H. M., & Dautzenberg, J. E. M. W. (1986). In W. C. McCallum, R. Zappoli, & F. Denoth (Eds.), *Cerebral psychophysiology: Studies in event-related potentials* (EEG Suppl. 38, pp. 238–241). Amsterdam: Elsevier.

Brunia, C. H. M., & Van Den Bosch, W. E. J. (1984). Movement-related slow potentials. I: A contrast between finger and foot movements in right-handed subjects. *Electroencephalography & Clinical Neurophysiology, 57,* 515–527.

Callaway, E. (1975). *Brain electrical potentials and individual differences.* New York: Grune & Stratton.

Cant, B. R., & Bickford, R. G. (1967). The effects of motivation on the contingent negative variation (CNV). *Electroencephalography & Clinical Neurophysiology* (abstract), *23,* 594.

Chiarenza, G. A., Papakostopoulos, D., Giordana, F., & Guareschi-Cazzullo, A. (1983). Movement-related brain macropotentials during skilled performances: A developmental study. *Electroencephalography & Clinical Neurophysiology, 56,* 373–383.

Chisholm, R., Karrer, R., & Cone, R. (1984). Movement-related ERPs during right vs. left hand squeeze: Effects of age, motor control, and independence of components. In R. Karrer, J. Cohen, & P. Teuting (Eds.), *Brain and information: Event-related potentials* (Vol. 425, pp. 445–449). New York: New York Academy of Sciences.

Cohen, J., & Walter, W. G. (1966). The interaction of responses in the brain to semantic stimuli. *Psychophysiology, 2,* 287–296.

Costell, R. M., Lunde, D. T., Kopell, B. S., & Wittner, W. K. (1972). Contingent negative variation as an indicator of sexual object preference. *Science, 177,* 718–720.

Courchesne, E., Courchesne, Y., & Hillyard, S. A. (1978). The effect of stimulus deviation on P3 waves to easily recognized stimuli. *Neuropsychologia, 16,* 189–199.

Deecke, K. (1976). Potential changes associated with motor action, reflex responses and readiness (Chairman's opening remarks). In W. C. McCallum & J. R. Knott (Eds.), *The responsive brain* (pp. 91–93). Bristol: John Wright & Sons.

Deecke, L., Bernd, H., Kornhuber, H. H., Lang, M., & Lang, W. (1984). Brain potentials associated with voluntary manual tracking: Bereitschaftspotential, conditioned premotion positivity, directed attention potential, and relaxation potential. In R. Karrer, J. Cohen, & P. Teuting (Eds.), *Brain and information: Event-related potentials* (Vol. 425, pp. 450–464). New York: New York Academy of Sciences.

Donald, M. W., & Goff, W. R. (1971). Attention related increases in cortical responsivity dissociated from the contingent negative variation. *Science, 172,* 1163–1166.

Donchin, E., Karis, D., Bashore, T. R., Coles, M. G. H., & Gratton, G. (1986). Cognitive psychophysiology and human information processing. In M. G. H. Coles, E. Donchin, & S. W. Porges (Eds.), *Psychophysiology: Systems, processes & applications* (pp. 244–267). New York: Guilford.

Donchin, E., McCarthy, G., Kutas, M., & Ritter, W. (1983). Event-related brain potentials in the study of conciousness. In R. J. Davidson, G. E. Schwartz, & D. Shapiro (Eds.), *Conciousness and self-regulation* (Vol. 3, pp. 81–121). New York: Plenum.

Donchin, E., Teuting, P., Ritter, W., Kutas, M., & Heffley, E. (1975). On the independence of the CNV and P300 components of the human averaged evoked potential. *Electroencephalography & Clinical Neurophysiology, 38,* 449–461.

Fabiani, M., Karis, D., & Donchin, E. (1986). P300 and recall in an incidental memory paradigm. *Psychophysiology, 23,* 298–308.

Fenelon, B. (1984). Effects of stimulus coding on the contingent negative variation recorded in an information processing task. In R. Karrer, J. Cohen, & P. Teuting (Eds.), *Brain and information: Event-related potentials* (Vol. 425, pp. 194–198). New York: New York Academy of Sciences.

Fitzgerald, P. G., & Picton, T. W. (1983). Event-related potentials recorded during the discrimination of improbable stimuli. *Biological Psychology, 17,* 241–276.

Ford, J. M., Roth, W. T., Dirks, S. J., & Kopell, B. S. (1973). Evoked potential correlates of signal recognition between and within modalities. *Science, 181,* 465–466.

Ford, J. M., Roth, W. T., & Kopell, B. S. (1976). Attention effects on auditory evoked potentials to infrequent events. *Biological Psychology, 4,* 65–77.

Ford, J. M., Roth, W. T., Mohs, R. C., Hipkins, W. F., III, & Kopell, B. S. (1979). Event-related potentials recorded from young and old adults during a memory retrieval task. *Electroencephalography & Clinical Neurophysiology, 47,* 450–459.

Friedman, D., Hakerem, G., Sutton, S., & Fleiss, J. L. (1973). Effect of stimulus uncertainty on the pupillary dilation response and the vertex evoked potential. *Electroencephalography & Clinical Neurophysiology, 34,* 475–484.

Gaillard, A. W. (1976). Effects of warning signal modality on the contingent negative variation (CNV). *Biological Psychology, 4,* 139–154.

Gomer, F. E., Spicuzza, R. J., & O'Donnell, R. D. (1976). Evoked potential correlates of visual item recognition during memory-scanning tasks. *Physiological Psychology, 4,* 61–65.

Haagh, S. A. V. M., & Brunia, C. H. M. (1985). Anticipatory response-relevant muscle activity, CNV amplitude and simple reaction time. *Electroencephalography & Clinical Neurophysiology, 61,* 30–39.

Halgren, E., Squires, N. K., Wilson, J. W., Rohrbaugh, J. W., Babb, T. L., & Crandall, P. H. (1980). Endogenous potentials generated in the human hippocampal formation aand amygdala by infrequent events. *Science, 210,* 803–805.

Hillyard, S. A. (1969). Relationships between the contingent negative variation (CNV) and reaction time. *Physiology & Behavior, 4,* 351–357.

Hillyard, S. A., & Hansen, J. C. (91186). Attention: Electrophysiological approaches. In M. G. H. Coles, E. Donchin, & S. W. Porges (Eds.), *Psychophysiology: Systems, processes & applications* (pp. 227–243). New York: Guilford.

Hillyard, S. A., Hink, R. F., Schwent, V. L., & Picton, T. W. (1973). Electrical signs of selective attention in the human brain. *Science, 182,* 177–180.

Hillyard, S. A., Squires, K. C., Bauer, J. W., & Lindsay, P. H. (1971). Evoked potential correlates of auditory signal detection. *Science, 172,* 1357–1360.

Horst, R. L., Johnson, R., & Donchin, E. (1980). Event-related brain Potentials and subjective probability in a learning task. *Memory and Cognition, 8,* 476–488.

Irwin, D. A., Knott, J. R., McAdam, D. W., & Rebert, C. S. (1966). Motivational determinants of the "contingent negative variation." *Electroencephalography & Clinical Neurophysiology, 21,* 538–543.

Johnson, R. (1986). A triarchic model of P300 amplitude. *Psychophysiology, 23,* 367–384.

Karis, D., Fabiani, M., & Donchin, E. (1984). "P300" and memory: Individual differences in the von Restorff effect. *Cognitive Psychology, 16,* 177–216.

Karlin, L. (1970). Cognition, preparation, and sensory-evoked potentials. *Psychological Bulletin, 73,* 122–136.

Kornhuber, H. H., & Deecke, L. (1965). Hirnpotentialanderungen bei Willkurbewegungen und passiven Berwegungen des Menschen: Bereitschaftspotential und reafferente Potentiale [Cerebral potential changes in voluntary and passive movements in man: Readiness potential and reaffervent potential]. *Pflugers Archives Gesamte Physiologie, 284,* 1–17.

Kristeva, R. (1984). Bereitschaftspotential of pianists. In R. Karrer, J. Cohen, & P. Teuting (Eds.), *Brain and information: Event-related potentials* (Vol. 425, pp. 477–482). New York: New York Academy of Sciences.

Kutas, M., & Donchin, E. (1980). Preparation to respond as manifested by movement-related brain potentials. *Brain Research, 202,* 95–115.

Libet, B., Wright, E. W., Jr., & Gleason, C. A. (1982). Readiness-potentials preceding unrestricted "spontaneous" vs. pre-planned voluntary acts. *Electroencephalography & Clinical Neurophysiology, 54,* 322–335.

Loveless, N. E., & Sanford, A. J. (1974). Slow potential correlates of preparatory set. *Biological Psychology, 1,* 308–314.

Low, M. D., Borda, R. P., Frost, J. D., Jr., & Kellaway, P. (1966). Surface negative slow potential shift associated with conditioning in man. *Neurology, 16,* 771–782.

Low, M. D., Coats, A. C., Rettig, G. M., & McSherry, J. W. (1967). Anxiety, attentiveness-alertness: A phenomenological study of the CNV. *Neuropsychologia, 5,* 379–384.

Low, M. D., & McSherry, J. W. (1968). Further observations of psychological factors involved in CNV genesis. *Electroencephalography & Clinical Neurophysiology, 25,* 203–207.

McAdam, D. W., & Seales, D. M. (1969). Bereitschaftspotential enhancement with increased level of motivation. *Electroencephalography & Clinical Neurophysiology, 27,* 73–75.

McCallum, C. (1969). The contingent negative variation as a cortical sign of attention in man. In C. R. Evans & T. B. Mulholland (Eds.), *Attention in neurophysiology* (pp. 40–63). London: Butterworths.

McCallum, W. C., Papakostopoulos, D., & Griffith, H. B. (1976). Distribution of CNV and other slow potential changes in human brainstem structures. In W. C. McCallum & J. R. Knott (Eds.), *The responsive brain* (pp. 205–210). Bristol: John Wright & Sons.

McCallum, W. C., & Walter, W. G. (1968). The effects of attention and distraction on the contingent negative variation in normal and neurotic subjects. *Electroencephalography & Clinical Neurophysiology, 25,* 319–329.

McCarthy, G., & Donchin, E. (1981). A metric for thought: A comparison of P300 latency and reaction time. *Science, 211,* 77–79.

Naatanen, R. (1970). Evoked potential, EEG, and slow potential correlates of selective attention. *Acta Psychological Supplement, 33,* 178–192.

Naatanen, R. (1975). Selective attention and evoked potentials in humans: A critical rview. *Biological Psychology, 2,* 237–307.

Naatanen, R., & Michie, P. T. (1979). Early selective-attention effects on the evoked potential: A critical review and reinterpretation. *Biological Psychology, 8,* 81–136.

Naitoh, P., Johnson, L. C., & Lubin, A. (1971). Modification of surface negative slow potential (CNV) in the human brain after total sleep loss. *Electroencephalography & Clinical Neurophysiology, 36,* 191–200.

Otto, D. A., Benignus, V. A., Ryan, L. J., & Leifer, L. J. (1977). Slow potential components of stimulus, response and preparatory processes: A multiple linear regression model: In J. E. Desmedt (Ed.), *Progress in clinical neurophysiology: Vol. 1. Attention, voluntary contraction and event-related potentials* (pp. 211–230). Basel: Karger.

Peters, J., Billinger, T. W., & Knott, J. R. (1977). Event-related potentials of brain (CNV and P300) in a paired associate learning paradigm. *Psychophysiology, 14,* 579–585.

Polich, J., Howard, L., & Starr, A. (1983). P300 latency correlates with digit span. *Psychophysiology, 20,* 665–669.

Poon, T. W., Thompson, L. W., & Marsh, G. R. (1976). Average evoked potential changes as a function of processing complexity. *Psychophysiology, 13,* 43–49.

Pritchard, W. S. (1981). Psychophysiology of P300. *Psychological Bulletin, 89,* 506–540.

Rebert, C. S. (1972). The effect of reaction time feedback on reaction time and contingent negative variation. *Psychophysiology, 9,* 334–339.

Rebert, C. S., & Low, D. W. (1978). Differential hemispheric activation during complex visuomotor performance. *Electroencephalography & Clinical Neurophysiology, 44,* 724–734.

Rebert, C. S., & Tecce, J. J. (1973). A summary of CNV and reaction time. In: W. C. McCallum & J. R. Knott (Eds.), *Event-related slow potentials of the brain: Their relations to behavior* (pp. 173–178). Amsterdam: Elsevier.

Ritter, W., & Vaughan, H. G., Jr. (1969). Averaged evoked responses in vigilance and discrimination: A reassessment. *Science, 164,* 326–328.

Ritter, W., Vaughan, H. G., Jr., & Costa, L. D. (1968). Orienting and habituation to auditory stimuli: A study of short term changes in average evoked responses. *Electroencephalography & Clinical Neurophysioloyg, 25,* 550–556.

Rohrbaugh, J. W., Donchin, E., & Ericksen, C. W. (1974). Decision making and the P300 component of the cortical evoked response. *Perception and Psychophysics, 15,* 368–374.

Roth, W. T., & Kopell, B. S. (1973). P300: An orienting reaction in the human auditory evoked response. *Perceptual & Motor Skills, 36,* 219–225.

Ruchkin, D. S., & Sutton, S. (1973). Visual evoked and emitted potentials and stimulus significance. *Bulletin of the Psychonomic Society, 2,* 144–146.

Ruchkin, D. S., & Sutton, S. (1978a). Emitted P300 potentials and temporal uncertainty. *Electroencephalography & Clinical Neurophysiology, 45,* 268–277.

Ruchkin, D. S., & Sutton, S. (1978b). Equivocation and P300 amplitude. In D. Otto (Ed.), *Multidisciplinary perspectives in event-related potential research* (pp. 175–177). Washington, DC: EPA-600/9-97-043.

Ruchkin, D. S., & Sutton, S. (in press). Latency characteristics and trial by trial variation of emitted potentials. In J. E. Desmedt (Ed.), *Cerebral evoked potentials in man.*

Ruchkin, D. S., Sutton, S., Kietzman, M., & Silver, K. (1980). Slow wave and P300 in signal detection. *Electroencephalography & Clinical Neurophysiology, 50,* 35–47.

Ruchkin, D. S., Sutton, S., & Stega, M. (1980). Emitted P300 and slow wave event-related potentials in guessing and detection tasks. *Electroencephalography & Clinical Neurophysiology, 49,* 1–14.

Ruchkin, D. S., Sutton, S., & Tueting, P. (1975). Emitted and evoked P300 potentials and variation in stimulus probability. *Psychophysiology, 12,* 591–595.

Schwent, V. L., Hillyard, S. A., & Galambos, R. (1976). Selective attention and the auditory vertex potential: I. Effects of stimulus delivery rate. *Electroencephalography & Clinical Neurophysiology, 40,* 604–614.

Smith, D., Donchin, E., Cohen, L., & Starr, A. (1970). Auditory evoked potentials in man during selective binaural listening. *Electroencephalography & Clinical Neurophysiology, 78,* 146–152.

Sokolov, E. N. (1969). The modeling properties of the nervous system: In M. Cole & I. Maltzman (Eds.), *Handbook of Soviet Psychology* (pp. 671–704). New York: Basic Books.

Squires, K. C., Donchin, E., Herning, R. I., & McCarthy, G. (1977). On the influence of task relevance and stimulus probability on the event related potential components. *Electroencephalography & Clinical Neurophysiology, 42,* 1–14.

Squires, K. C., Hillyard, S., & Lindsay, P. (1973). Vertex potentials evoked during auditory signal detection: Relation to decision criteria. *Perception & Psychophysics, 14,* 265–272.

Squires, K. C., Squires, N. K., & Hillyard, S. A. (1975). Decision related cortical potentials during an auditory signal detection task with cued observation intervals. *Journal of Experimental Psychology: Human Perception & Performance, 104,* 268–279.

Squires, N. K., Squires, K. C., & Hillyard, S. A. (1975). Two varieties of long-latency positive waves evoked by unpredictable auditory stimuli in man. *Electroencephalography & Clinical Neurophysiology, 38,* 387–401.

Sternberg, S. (1966). High-speed scanning in human memory. *Science, 153,* 652–654.

Stuss, D. T., Picton, T. W., & Cerri, A. M. (1986). Searching for the names of pictures: An event-related study. *Psychophysiology, 23,* 215–223.

Sutton, S., Braren, M., & Zubin, J. (1965). Evoked potential correlates of stimulus uncertainty. *Science, 150,* 1187–1188.

Sutton, S., & Ruchkin, D. S. (1984). The late positive complex: Advances and new problems. In R. Karrer, J. Cohen, & P. Teuting (Eds.), *Brain and information: Event-related potentials* (pp. 1–23). *Annals of the New York Academy of Sciences,* Vol. 425. New York: N.Y. Academy of Sciences.

Sutton, S., Teuting, P., Zubin, J., & Hohn, E. R. (1967). Evoked potential correlates of stimulus uncertainty. *Science, 155,* 1436–1439.

Tecce, J. J. (1971). Contingent negative variation and individual differences. *Archives of General Psychiatry, 24,* 1–16.

Tecce, J. J. (1972). Contingent negative variation (CNV) and psychological processes in man. *Psychological Bulletin, 77,* 73–108.

Tecce, J. J., & Cattanach, L. (1987). Contingent negative variation (CNV). In E. Niedermeyer & F. Lopes da Silva (Eds.), *Electroencephalography: Basic principles, clinical applications and related fields* (2nd ed., pp. 657–679). Baltimore: Urban & Schwarzenberg.

Tecce, J. J., Cattanach, L., Boehner-Davis, M. B., & Clifford, T. S. (1984). CNV and myogenic functions: II. Divided attention produces a double dissociation of CNV and EMG. In R. Karrer, J. Cohen, & P. Teuting (Eds.), *Brain and information: Event-related potentials* (Vol. 425, pp. 289–294). New York: New York Academy of Sciences.

Tecce, J. J., & Hamilton, B. T. (1973). CNV reduction by sustained cognitive activity (distraction). In W. C. McCallum & J. R. Knott (Eds.), *Event-related slow potentials of the brain: Their relations to behavior* (Suppl. 33, pp. 229–237). Amsterdam: Elsevier.

Tecce, J. J., Savignano-Bowman, J., & Cole, J. O. (1978). Drug effects on contingent negative variation and eyeblinks: The distraction-arousal hypothesis. In M. A. Lipton, A. DiMascio, & K. F. Killam (Eds.), *Psychopharmacology: A generation of progress* (pp. 745–758). New York: Raven Press.

Tecce, J. J., Savignano-Bowman, J., & Dessonville, C. L. (1984). CNV and myogenic functions: I. Muscle tension produces a dissociation of CNV and EMG. In R. Karrer, J. Cohen, & P. Teuting (Eds.), *Brain and information: Event-related potentials* (Vol. 425, pp. 283–288). New York: New York Academy of Sciences.

Tecce, J. J., Savignano-Bowman, J., & Meinbresse, D. (1976). Contingent negative variation and the distraction-arousal hypothesis. *Electroencephalography & Clinical Neurophysiology, 41,* 227–286.

Tecce, J. J., & Scheff, N. M. (1969). Attention reduction and suppressed direct-current potentials in the human brain. *Science, 164,* 331–333.

Tecce, J. J., Yrchik, D. A., Meinbresse, D., Dessonville, C. L., & Cole, J. O. (1980). CNV rebound and aging. I. Attention functions. In H. H. Kornhuber & L. Deecke (Eds.), *Motor and sensory processes of the brain. Electrical potentials, behaviour and clinical use. Progress in brain research* (Vol. 54, pp. 553–561). Amsterdam: Elsevier.

Tueting, P., Sutton, S., & Zubin, J. (1970). Quantitative evoked potential correlates of the probability of events. *Psychophysiology, 7,* 385–394.

Vaughan, H. G., Jr. (1969). The relationship of brain activity to scalp recordings of event-related potentials. In E. Donchin & D. B. Lindsley (Eds.), *Average evoked potentials* (pp. 45–94). Washington, DC: NASA.

Walter, W. G., Cooper, R., Aldrige, V. J., McCallum, W. C., & Winter, A. L. (1964). Contingent negative variation: An electrical sign of sensory-motor association and expectancy in the human brain. *Nature, 203,* 380–384.

Weerts, T. C., & Lang, P. J. (1973). The effects of eye fixation and stimulus and response location on the contingent negative variation (CNV). *Biological Psychology, 1,* 1–19.

Weinberg, H., Walter, W. G., Cooper, R., & Aldridge, V. J. (1974). Emitted cerebral events. *Electroencephalography & Clinical Neurophysiology, 36,* 449–456.

Weinberg, H., Walter, W. G., & Crow, H. J. (1970). Intracerebral events in humans related to real and imaginary stimuli. *Electroencephalography & Clinical Neurophysiology, 29,* 1–9.

Wood, C. C., Allison, T., Goff, W. R., Williamson, P. D., & Spencer, D. (1980). On the neural origin of P300 in man. In H. H. Kornhuber & L. Deecke (Eds.), *Progress in brain research. Motivation, motor and sensory processes of the brain* (Vol. 54, pp. 51–56). Amsterdam: Elsevier.

Wood, C. C., McCarthy, G., Squires, N. K., Vaughan, H. G., Jr., Woods, D. L., & McCallum, C. (1984). In R. Karrer, J. Cohen, & P. Teuting (Eds.), *Brain and information: Event-related potentials* (Vol. 425, pp. 681–721). New York: New York Academy of Sciences.

Woods, D. L., Hillyard, S. A., Courchesne, E., & Galambos, R. (1980). Electrophysiological signs of split-second decision-making. *Science, 207,* 655–657.

8

Muscle Activity and Behavior

The muscles are critical factors in almost every form of human behavior. In fact, without muscle activity there would be no observable behavior. Studies of electromyograms (EMGs) and behavior have yielded interesting findings. Examples are the patterning of facial muscle activity during the expression of emotions, and the EMG "gradients" that have been observed in motivated behavior.

The most common way in which psychophysiologists measure muscular activity in their behavioral studies is through the surface electromyogram (EMG). This is obtained through the placement of recording electrodes over a muscle group of interest and amplifying the tiny electrical signals that muscles produce when they are active or at rest. The EMGs may also be obtained by inserting needle electrodes directly into the target muscle. However, this somewhat painful procedure is used mainly in clinical diagnosis and in some forms of muscle rehabilitation to measure activity of small portions of a larger muscle, known as motor units. In this chapter, we briefly discuss the anatomy and physiology of muscle and the measurement of muscular activity in the form of the surface EMG. Psychological studies of the relationship between the EMG and various behaviors, including speed of reaction, tracking, conditioning, cognition, speech, emotional expression, sleep, and conditions of motivation are topics of this chapter.

THE CONTROL OF MOTOR BEHAVIOR

All of the outward behavior that we observe is the result of muscular activity. For example, an individual may have a notion to write a letter, but this is not possible without the fine motor coordination involved in moving a pen across a piece of paper to form the necessary words. The origin of the thoughts placed on the paper is in the brain of the person, and the initiation of these skilled movements is controlled by the motor cortex of the brain. When writing starts, complex, rapid brain-to-muscle feedback circuits interact, and changes in both brain and muscle activity can be recorded at these times. One of the motor systems of the central nervous system (CNS) is termed the pyramidal system, and its origins are primarily in the precentral gyrus of the cortex (motor area). It descends through various subcortical structures to the medulla, where an estimated 70% to 90% of the fibers originating in each hemisphere cross to the opposite side and descend within the spinal cord (Gardner, 1975). The area of the medulla at which the fibers cross over forms the shape of a pyramid, hence the term "pyramidal system." The pyramidal system is concerned with the initiation and control of fine muscle movements and is excitatory only; that is, it is involved only in the initiation of movements.

The extrapyramidal system, on the other hand, is a system that controls gross motor activities, such as those required to roll over in bed or make postural adjustments, and it has both excitatory and inhibitory components. This complex system has its primary origin in the prefrontal cortex, but it also has origins in the precentral, postcentral, and temporal cortex. It descends to the spinal cord in a very complicated manner, but it does not pass through the medullary pyramids, hence the name "extrapyramidal." The cerebellum is considered to be part of the extrapyramidal motor system, and it plays a role in the regulation and modification of motor activities, receiving input and having output to the rest of the brain and the spinal cord. This brief reminder of CNS mechanisms is presented here to emphasize the fact that there are complex brain and muscle interactions that occur in carrying out behavior; interactions whose effects can be measured electrophysiologically at central (brain) or peripheral (muscle) locations. It should also be emphasized that brain–muscle interactions are not merely one-way, because varying levels of muscle involvement influence brain activity through feedback mechanisms from peripheral to central areas.

Anatomy and Physiology of Muscles

Muscles are named according to action (e.g., extensor and flexor); according to shape (e.g., quadratus); according to origin and insertion (sternocleidomastoid); number of divisions (e.g., triceps); location (e.g., radialis); and direction of fibers (e.g., transversus). The origin of a muscle is a more fixed attachment that serves as a basis for action. The moveable attachment is called the insertion. Most voluntary muscles are not inserted directly into bone, but are connected by strong fibrous cords called tendons. Tendons can vary in length from a fraction of an inch to longer than 12 inches. Muscles that bend a limb at a joint are called flexors (also agonists). Those that straighten limbs at a joint are referred to as

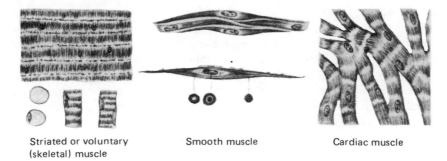

Striated or voluntary   Smooth muscle   Cardiac muscle
(skeletal) muscle

FIG. 8.1.   Types of muscle cells.

extensors (and antagonists). The flexor muscle must relax for the extensor to perform. If a limb is moved away from the midline of the body, an abductor is responsible, while adductors move limbs toward the midline. Levators are muscles that raise parts of the body, and depressors lower them.

There are three types of muscle tissue in the body: skeletal, smooth, and cardiac muscle. The skeletal muscles make up the voluntary motor system and are exemplified by such familiar structures as the biceps of the upper arm and the flexor digitorum of the forearm. Individual skeletal muscle fibers have striations and many nuclei, as shown in Fig. 8.1. Smooth, or unstriated, muscles are considered to be part of the involuntary motor system, because we ordinarily do not exert control over them. There is some evidence that control of smooth muscle may be learned if appropriate feedback is provided (see chapter 14). The smooth muscles of the blood vessels are good examples. These muscle fibers travel in a circular path and can change the diameter of the blood vessel by constriction or dilation. Individual smooth muscle fibers have a single nucleus and no striations. Cardiac muscle is also classified as involuntary muscle. It is striated, similar to skeletal muscle, but is considered to be a separate variety. Skeletal muscles make up approximately 40% of total body weight, and smooth and cardiac muscle account for another 5% to 10%. The primary focus of this chapter is on the activity of skeletal (voluntary) muscle.

Skeletal Muscle.   Most voluntary muscles are attached to a bone through strong, nonelastic fibrous cords known as tendons. A muscle consists of groups of muscle fibers that form a primary bundle (fasciculus). A muscle is composed of a group of these fasciculi (see Fig. 8.2). The fasciculus, in turn, contains many muscle fibers, and muscle fibers are composed of even smaller diameter myofibrils. Each muscle fiber contains several hundred to several thousand myfibrils. Each myofibril has about 1,500 myosin filaments and 3,000 actin filaments, which are protein molecules responsible for muscle contraction. Viewed under a microscope, the myosin filaments are thick and dark in appearance, whereas the

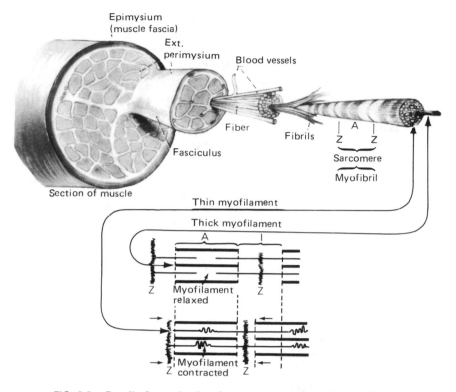

FIG. 8.2.   Detail of muscle showing structure and mechanics of muscular contraction.

actin filaments are thin and light colored. It is the myosin and actin filaments that cause the myofibrils to have alternate light and dark bands, imparting the striated appearance to skeletal muscle. The dark striations are also known as A-bands and the light ones as I-bands. Striated muscle fibers may vary in length from 1 to 40 mm (often extending the entire length of the muscle) and range in diameter between 10 and 80 μm. The sarcolemma is an electrically polarized membrane that surrounds each muscle cell. It is the cell membrane of the muscle fiber.

Mechanisms of Muscle Contraction.   Action potentials in muscle fibers are responsible for the initiation of muscle contractions. We briefly examine muscular contraction at the relatively gross level of the motor unit and at the molecular level, describing the interaction between actin and myosin filaments.

The Motor Unit.   The basic mechanism of muscle contraction is the motor unit, which consists of a nerve cell, its axon, and the muscle fibers supplied by it. The motor neuron–muscle fiber link represents the last stage in the transmission of motor impulses from the cortex, down through the subcortical areas of the brain, over descending tracts of the spinal cord, and out over the motor neuron. The "final common pathway" was the name given by the noted neurophysiologist Sherrington to the motor pathway from the CNS to a muscle. The innervation ratio, or number of muscle fibers innervated by a single neuron, may range from 1 : 3 for those muscle fibers that control fine motor adjustments (e.g., the laryngeal muscles) to 1 : 1,000 for fibers involved in gross movements (e.g., gastrocnemius muscle of the leg).

Motor units obey the all-or-none principle discussed in chapter 2 in connection with neuronal action potentials. That is, the neurons and muscle fibers that comprise the motor unit either do not fire at all or fire with their full capacity. The information regarding action potentials in neurons applies to skeletal muscle fibers, except for some quantitative differences. For example, the resting potential is approximately -85 mV in skeletal muscle fibers, slightly higher than for neurons. The duration of the muscle fiber action potential ranges from 1 to 5 msec, which is longer than that of the large myelinated neuron. The biggest difference is in the velocity of conduction along a muscle fiber, because it is about 3 to 5 meters per second, or about $\frac{1}{18}$th the velocity of conduction in large myelinated neurons. The skeletal muscles are normally innervated by large myelinated neurons at the neuromuscular junction (also known as the motor end plate). The neuromuscular junction is located near the middle of the muscle fiber. Thus, the action potential spreads from the middle toward the ends, allowing all sarcomeres of the muscle to contract simultaneously. The strength of muscle contraction depends on the number of motor units contracting and the rate of contraction. The action potential of the fiber is brief, but the duration of muscle contraction may last up to 100 msec or more. Muscles are in a constant state of tonus to allow quick responses to external stimuli. The tonus is maintained by a steady flow of impulses from the spinal cord to each motor unit and varies with level of activity of the person and the nervous system. It should also be noted that feedback of activity from motor units can also affect spinal cord neurons. For example, flow of impulses from spinal cord to muscle fibers can be reduced by purposely lowering level of muscle activity through techniques such as progressive muscle relaxation. Reduction of muscle tonus may also occur if the neuron supplying the muscle is damaged, thus preventing the constant flow of impulses. Additionally, in the case of immobilized limbs, such as when placed in a cast, the flow of impulses is reduced, and some atrophy may occur.

Muscular Contraction at the Molecular Level.   When a neuronal impulse reaches the neuromuscular junction, acetylcholine is released. The muscle fiber membrane thus becomes permeable to sodium ions, and depolarization of the membrane occurs, resulting in the action potential. The presence of acetylcholinesterase at the neuromuscular junction causes the breakdown of acetylcholine, and the muscle fiber is ready to be stimulated again.

When an action potential travels down the muscle fiber, it causes the release of calcium ions into the sarcoplasm surrounding the myofibrils. This sets up attractive forces that cause the actin filaments to slide into spaces between the myosin fibrils. Thus, the positive calcium ions produce an energy-releasing reaction, which brings on the sliding of the myofibril filaments said to underly muscle contraction. It is believed that the energy for this contraction is derived from the enzyme adenosine triphosphate (ATP) which is broken down into adenosine diphosphate (ADP) when the motor neuron impulse reaches the muscle fiber. The ATP is broken down to form ADP, and the hypothesis is that large amounts of energy are thereby released. A relaxing factor has been discovered in muscle and has been postulated to react with the energizing substance of muscle to halt contraction until the next stimulus reaches the fiber (Jacob & Francone, 1970).

Muscle Fatigue.   Prolonged and strong contraction of a muscle leads to muscle fatigue. This results from the inability of the muscle fibers to maintain work output because of ATP depletion. The nerves, as well as their action potentials, continue to function properly, but contractions become weaker and weaker with time (Guyton, 1977). Continuous muscle contraction contributes to interruption of the blood supply to muscle tissue and causes fatigue in about 1 minute because of nutrient loss.

Muscular Hypertrophy.   Forceful exercise, in which muscles contract to at least 75% of their maximum tension, produces an increased number of myofibrils. Thus, the diameters of the individual muscle fibers increase. In addition, the nutrients and metabolic substances, such as ATP and glycogen, are increased. Hypertrophy results from very forceful muscle activity, even though it might only occur for a few minutes each day.

THE MEASUREMENT OF MUSCLE ACTIVITY

Now that we have briefly reviewed the sources of electrical activity produced by muscles, methods for measuring this activity are presented. We then briefly review the literature to determine the kinds of changes in muscle activity that accompany the performance of various tasks.

Electromyography

Electromyography is the technique for measuring and recording electrical potentials that are associated with contractions of muscle fibers. The EMG is often used in the clinic to study muscular disorders. Very thin needle electrodes can be inserted into muscle tissue, and recordings can be made from limited muscle regions or even from single motor units. The EMG can also be recorded from the skin surface, because some portion of the action potentials produced in muscle fibers is transmitted to the skin. The closer the muscle tissue is to the skin surface, and the stronger the contractions, the greater will be the amount of electrical activity recorded at the surface. Most studies relating EMG to human performance deal with the activity occurring in large muscle groups. Therefore, the information in this chapter is derived mainly from surface EMG recordings.

General Properties of the EMG

The surface EMG records the electrical activity of motor units, which occurs prior to contraction of a muscle (Thompson, Lindsley, & Eason, 1966). Electrodes placed on the skin over an active muscle record the algebraic sum of a large number of depolarizations that occur when a group of motor units are activated (Lippold, 1967).

Muscular Effort and the EMG

Studies that have examined the relation between EMG level and degree of muscle tension indicate that the EMG is a fairly good indicator of tension in skeletal muscles. For example, in a study by Malmo (cited by J. F. Davis, 1959), EMG was recorded from the flexor muscles of the forearm while subjects varied the amount of squeeze on a hand dynamometer. (A hand dynamometer is a device to produce and measure variations in hand grip strength.) The recordings showed regular increases in EMG amplitude (in microvolts) as grip strength increased. The data for the 9 females and 11 males indicated that, on the average, a higher EMG level was produced by females than males to maintain a given grip level. Essentially similar results were obtained by Wilcott and Beenken (1957) for their female and male subjects. Their results are shown in Fig. 8.3. The male–female differences indicate that females must bring more motor units into action to accomplish the same amount of work as males. One might wonder if such striking differences would be found in contemporary times, which see weight training and body building becoming more popular among women!

The EMG Wave Form

The surface EMG that accompanies muscle contraction consists of a series of spiked discharges from motor units underlying the electrode. The frequency of the components may range from 20 to 1,000 Hz, with an amplitude of about 100 to 1,000 μV, depending on the mass of muscle tissue beneath the recording electrodes and the degree to which they are contracting. However, amplitudes as low as 1 to 2 μV may be recorded when a relatively small muscle is in a relaxed state. The recorded EMG wave form is not as regular as some of the other

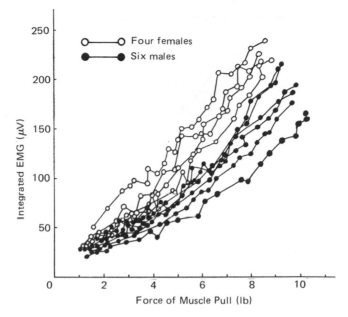

FIG. 8.3.   The relation between the force of muscle pull in pounds and integrated EMG in microvolts for the bicep muscle.

physiological measures, for example, the alpha wave of the EEG. This is why, in studies that attempt to quantify EMG and relate it to behavior, the integrated surface EMG is often derived. This is accomplished by feeding the EMG into an integrator circuit, which will show the total amount of activity over a certain period of time (e.g., 10 seconds). An example of an integrated EMG record is presented in Fig. 8.4. The EMG is shown at two stages in Fig. 8.4: (a) a first level of integration produces the EMG (first line) with no activity shown below baseline; and (b) a second line shows the summed EMG and its calibration in microvolts, and provides a measure of total muscle activity in a given time period. The investigator in this experiment was studying the amount of forearm EMG produced during a 30-second verbal learning trial. The other measures depicted are skin resistance and heart rate.

Electrode Placement for EMG Recording

The general principles for electrode application are the same as for other physiological measures. That is, the skin must be cleansed with alcohol or some mildly abrasive material to remove dead skin and oils. Then, after electrode paste is rubbed into the area and the excess is removed, the recording electrode containing a new supply of paste is placed into the desired position. The EMG is best

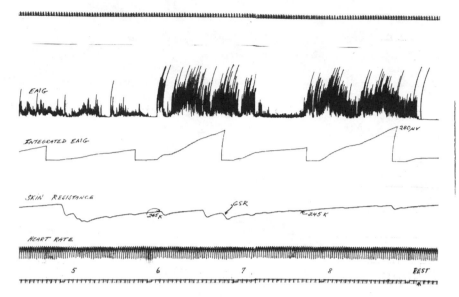

FIG. 8.4. Right forearm EMG measured during trial 5-8 in a verbal learning experiment. Partially integrated EMG is shown in the top trace, and the integrated EMG (second line) shows that total EMG activity over a 30-second trial (trial 8) was 280 uV. Note the sharp cessation of EMG activity at the end of trial 8 (rest). Also shown are records of skin resistance, changes in skin resistance (GSR) and heart rate. The vertical marks in the bottom line indicate serial presentation of items to be learned in trials 5 through 8. (From author's unpublished data.)

recorded with a bipolar electrode arrangement, with both electrodes located over the muscle of interest. The resistance between the electrodes should not exceed 10,000 Ohms and should be lower if possible (e.g., 5,000 Ohms). Too low a resistance, say, less than 1,000 Ohms, should be regarded with suspicion, because it could mean that there is a conducting bridge of paste between the electrodes or that they are too close. This situation could result in a short-circuiting of the EMG potentials. The subject, the EMG recorder, and the electrical equipment close to it should all be grounded to protect the subject and to prevent 60-cycle interference in the recording. Once exposed to electrode paste or jelly, the electrodes will start to deteriorate. They must be washed in warm water and soap after each use and then rinsed thoroughly in clear water to remove all traces of electrolyte.

Specific Electrode Placements

In order to place electrodes over the muscle of interest, some standardization is necessary. The electrode array usually consists of two active and one inactive

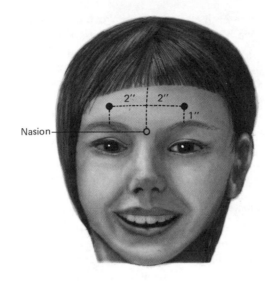

Standard Forehead Lead (frontalis muscle)

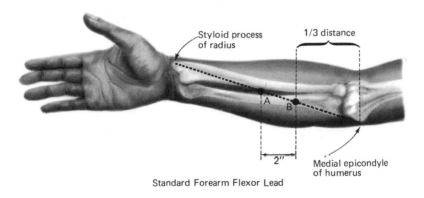

Standard Forearm Flexor Lead

FIG. 8.5.   Standard forehead and forearm leads for measurement of EMG.

electrode (ground). The active electrodes are placed in a bipolar pattern along the long axis of the muscle. The amount of EMG recorded is the algebraic sum of all action potentials of the contracting fibers located between the electrodes. The exact specifications for placement of electrodes over different muscle areas have been outlined by J. F. Davis (1959) and Basmajian and Blumenstein (1983). Examples of two common placements are given in Fig. 8.5, adapted from J. F. Davis (1959). The examples are for the frontalis muscle of the forehead and the flexor muscles of the forearm. The placements for the frontalis muscle are obtained by measuring 2 in. to the left and right of midline (nasion as the midline reference point) and placing each electrode 1 in. above the eyebrow. One must be careful to watch for eye-blink and EEG artifact with this placement.

For purposes of EMG research, there is a problem with this placement for frontalis measurement, although the specifications for other muscle groups as outlined by J. F. Davis (1959) and Lippold (1967) are satisfactory. The problem, as pointed out by C. Davis, Brickett, Stern, and Kimball (1978) is this: The frontales on the forehead, over each eye, are two separate muscles. Because only the potential difference between the two electrodes is amplified, activity occurring simultaneously in both muscles would not be recorded. C. Davis and colleagues recommended a placement in which both electrodes of a pair are placed vertically on the forehead along the longitudinal axis of a single frontalis muscle (see Fig. 8.7). The placement of an active lead over each frontalis muscle, as shown in Fig. 8.5 (horizontal array), is suitable for use in clinical biofeedback applications, because it provides information about within-session changes in muscle tension and allows more reliable differential EMG control than the vertical placement (Williamson, Epstein, & Lombardo, 1980).

The forearm flexor (flexor carpi radialis and flexor digitorum sublimis) leads involve measuring the distance from the medial epicondyle of the humerus to the styloid process of the radius, while the subject has his or her forearm on a table with his or her palm up. Next, a point that is one third of the distance from epicondyle to styloid is taken. The center of electrode A is placed over this point. Electcode B is placed 2 in. distally from the center of A. This placement should show visible movement with flexor movement of the middle finger of this hand. The ground may be placed at the elbow or wrist of the same arm to reduce ECG artifact. Because the EMG is susceptible to movement artifact, it is best to use relatively small electrode surfaces and an attachment that is flexible as opposed to rigid. Placement over a pulsating artery should be avoided.

Recording the EMG

Because the EMG is a relatively small signal, a similar level of amplification as that required in the recording of EEG is required. Although the EMG produces a wide range of frequencies, some experts agree that the maximal activity occurs at the lower end of the spectrum (Goldstein, 1972). The frequencies of interest range from approximately 20 to 400 Hz. This means that the filtering system must allow at least this frequency range of EMG to be recorded. Because ink-writer pen systems cannot follow the signal very well after 150 Hz, one approach has been to record the EMG on magnetic tape for later playback into a computer or to record at a slowed rate that the ink-writer can follow. Still another method utilizes a cathode-ray oscilloscope to display the EMG recording during experimental trials, because it has no difficulty in following and displaying even very high frequencies. As mentioned previously, the technique of integration helps considerably in the analysis of EMG activity. Essentially, the integrator provides a measure of total EMG output over a given period of time. Or, alternately, it may be designed to automatically reset when a certain level of activity has occurred, for example, reset occurs after every 300 μV of accumulated EMG activity. The total integrated activity is proportional to both the positive and negative components of the EMG wave form. Goldstein (1972) pointed out a possible problem inherent in the use of integrators. That is, because they do not discriminate between artifacts and real muscle action potentials (MAPs), the artifacts may be integrated along with MAPs. An encouraging note concerns the reliability or consistency of the EMG measures in the same individual, performing some standard task, over a period of time. Goldstein (1972) cited several studies that indicate that the EMG yields good test–retest reliability, suggesting that it is a consistent measure.

THE EMG AND BEHAVIOR

Many studies relating EMG to various kinds of human behavior and performance have been reviewed by Duffy (1962, 1972) and by Goldstein (1972). An examination of the EMG literature for the period from 1970 on indicates that there were quite a few studies of EMG in a biofeedback context. Several EMG biofeedback studies that relate to basic learning and conditioning processes are presented in this chapter, whereas representative EMG studies aimed at using biofeedback to treat some specific disorder are examined in chapter 14.

Motor Performance and the EMG

The EMG has been recorded by investigators during the performance of various kinds of motor activities, including time to react, tracking, speech production, and fatigue-producing muscular activities. Some of these studies are briefly reviewed in this section.

EMG and Reaction Time

In a study by R. C. Davis (1940), the electromyogram was recorded from the forearm extensor muscles while a subject waited to obtain a signal for his response. Muscle tension began about 200 to 400 msec after the ready signal and increased up to the moment of reaction. Two other findings were of interest: (a) the higher the muscle tension at the end of the foreperiod, the faster the RT; and (b) muscle tension was higher and RT was quicker at the end of regular foreperiods as compared to irregular ones. The finding that RT is faster with regular foreperiods is not surprising, because other investigators before and since have obtained this result. It is interesting, however, that muscle tension should be higher with regular foreperiods. Davis attributed this to a form of set or an increased readiness to respond.

It is also of interest to relate these findings to those of other studies using different physiological measures. For example, the alpha-blocking response begins about 300 msec after the stimulus (Lansing, Schwartz, & Lindsley, 1959) or at a similar interval for the start of muscle tension buildup. Also, skin conductance has been found to be higher and RT faster during experimental conditions under which there were regular intervals between stimuli as compared to irregular intervals (Andreassi, Rapisardi, & Whalen, 1969).

Kennedy and Travis (1948) investigated the relationship between EMG, RT, and level of performance in a continuous (2-hour) tracking task. Thirty-two subjects performed a pursuit tracking task while EMG was recorded from the frontalis muscle. A warning light was placed 24 degrees peripherally from the main task and flashed on when muscle tension fell below predetermined levels. The subject was required to lift his foot from a pedal when the light flashed, and this RT was measured. Thus, RT and tracking performance were measured at various tension levels. Kennedy and Travis reported that RTs became progressively slower with low levels of tension and faster when tension level was high. The number of failures to respond greatly increased at the low tension levels, indicating that the subjects were probably drowsy at those times. On the basis of this and other studies (Kennedy & Travis, 1947; Travis & Kennedy, 1949), they proposed that frontalis muscle tension might serve as an indicator of alertness in situations where persons were involved in monotonous tasks over prolonged periods of time.

In the Davis (1940) study, the muscle group actually involved in the response showed an increase in tension during the foreperiod, whereas in the Kennedy and Travis investigation, the frontalis muscle was not involved in the response, but the task was a visuomotor one in which subjects had to follow changes in a visual display by making hand and arm movements. Goldstein (1972) noted that with increased practice, activity in muscle not involved in the reaction tends to decrease. For example, Obrist, Webb, and Sutterer (1969) reported decreased activity in chin and neck muscles just before and during the time that subjects depressed a telegraph key with their hand. This was correlated with decreased heart rate. They interpreted this to indicate a decrease in irrelevant muscular activity that might otherwise interfere with the task that the subject was to perform. Further study led them to suggest that EMG measured from chin muscles may be a good index of irrelevant motor activity. Obrist, Webb, Sutterer, & Howard (1970) obtained additional evidence that the decreased chin EMG was related to cardiac deceleration. Again, they found inhibition of task-irrelevant somatic activities during the foreperiod, just as the response was made in a simple RT task. It was this kind of result that led Obrist to formulate his cardiac–somatic concept in which heart rate and activity in muscles irrelevant to performance of a task covary (see chapter 15). The cardiac–somatic coupling hypothesis was investigated by Haagh and Brunia (1984), who had 31 subjects participate in a simple auditory RT task with a constant 4-sec foreperiod. In addition to HR, the EMG of 9 striate muscle groups varying in relevance to response execution were recorded. Only one muscle group was coupled to the decrease in HR noted at the end of the foreperiod, hence the results do not support the cardiac–somatic hypothesis.

EMG was measured from the masseter muscles (jaw) while 19 subjects performed in an RT experiment (Holloway & Parsons, 1972). The warning signal preceded the execution stimulus by a variable interval, and subjects were instructed to terminate the buzzer as quickly as possible by pressing a foot switch. Their results were similar to those of Obrist and associates, in that fast RTs were associated with less EMG activity during the preparatory foreperiod of the task. Notice that in this experiment, as with previous ones showing decreased EMG in the period just preceding the response, the muscle tension was measured from muscles other than those involved in the task and the response. It would have been informative if these investigators had also provided information on EMGs from responding muscle groups to enable some statement regarding the relative activity of task-involved and noninvolved muscle groups. The implication is that only activity in muscles not concerned with task execution would be reduced during the time just before and during the response.

To briefly summarize, it appears that when a muscle group is involved in the execution of a RT task, progressively increasing activity during the foreperiod is related to faster responses. However, noninvolved muscles show a decrease in activity, presumably lessening the possibility of interference with the relevant motor response. The relationship between muscle and heart activity in these kinds of tasks forms part of the basis for Obrist's cardiac–somatic hypothesis.

EMG and Tracking

Tracking involves the movement of some control (wheel or stick) to keep an indicator on a moving target. Continuous motor adjustments must be made to perform the task correctly. A pilot maintaining a correct altitude and heading and a driver keeping a car in his or her own lane are performing tracking tasks. Many of the video games that occupy the time of today's youngsters (and some oldsters) provide good examples of tracking tasks.

Kennedy and Travis (1948) obtained results that indicated that low frontalis EMG was related to poor tracking performance. A number of tracking studies have indicated a relation between subjective effort and EMG. For example, experiments by Eason and his colleagues have shown, in general, that conditions that required increased effort led to increased EMG levels and improved performance (Eason, 1963; Eason & White, 1960, 1961). Eason and White (1960) observed that EMG level increased and tracking performance improved as a function of practice trials, up to a certain point. After this point, performance dropped, even though EMG increased, suggesting that fatigue was occurring. When subjects were given either 0, 10, 20, or 40 seconds between trials, performance improved with intertrial interval, but the EMG level was lower. This inverse relationship between EMG and performance was interpreted as evidence that muscular fatigue is partly responsible for the commonly observed superiority of distributed over massed practice in pursuit rotor tracking and other perceptual-motor tasks. Eason and White advanced a two-factor hypothesis of muscular tension. They proposed that muscular tension is positively related to both motivation and fatigue. Because motivation facilitates performance and fatigue hinders it, the tension level at any given time is a summation of the motivation and fatigue components. Results similar to those of White and Eason were reported by Mulder and Hulston (1984). They found that fatigue caused integrated EMG activity to increase, but actual muscle efficiency decreased. On the other hand, simple repetition of the task without allowing fatigue to occur led to increased efficiency. These results suggest that learning a motor skill partially involves the dropping out of irrelevant muscle activity. This idea receives support from a study by French (1980), in which a group of subjects given feedback of muscle activity while learning a pursuit tracking task had lower EMG levels and better performance than a group not receiving feedback. This kind of effect is not limited to those learning a novel motor task, as is shown in a study of skilled violin and viola players (LeVine & Irvine, 1984). The musicians were provided EMG feedback as a method for removing unwanted left hand muscle tension. Electrodes attached to the left hand during the playing of a difficult piece sounded an alarm whenever EMG exceeded a level observed during the playing of an easy scale. Irrelevant muscle activity dropped out quickly (average of 5 sessions) an effect that persisted at a 6-month follow-up check.

To briefly summarize, it seems that efficient tracking performance is related to some moderate to high EMG level. Very low muscular tension (possibly indicative of drowsiness) and very high tension (perhaps associated with over exertion or fatigue) seem to be associated with less efficient performance. The drop in efficiency with fatigue shows up in muscle output as well. Feedback from irrelevant muscles, promoting a decrease in EMG in those muscles, seems to benefit both skilled and unskilled performers.

EMG and Speech Activity

The notion that thinking is nothing more than subvocal speech has commonly been attributed to behaviorists such as J. B. Watson. This position suggests that the muscles of speech operate separately from the brain. McGuigan (1981) contended that early behaviorists, including Watson, did not believe this to be the case, but thought instead in terms of many channels running back and forth between the brain and speech muscles. Goldstein (1972) reviewed a number of studies that indicated that EMGs occurred during thinking, but they were not confined to the vocal mechanism (laryngeal muscle activity), because EMG changes were observed in many different muscle groups. McGuigan (1981) argued that the available data justify the generalization that muscle activity is present in all cognitive phenomena, even though it may be of small amplitude. There are studies that have examined subvocal speech as it occurs during reading in some individuals. Such occurrences are said to limit the rate of reading for these persons to about 150 words per minute, or approximately the maximum attainable while reading aloud. In one study, Hardyck, Petrinovich, and Ellsworth (1966) recorded EMG activity from the surface of the throat, over the laryngeal muscle, of 50 subjects. The presence of subvocalization was determined by noting EMG changes that occurred when the subjects were asked to read silently and then to stop reading. The presence of EMG activity during reading indicated subvocalization. Out of the 50 subjects tested, 17 were found to be subvocalizers. These 17 persons were tested further in the following manner: First, they were allowed to hear their own amplified EMG activity over headphones, then they were shown how it could be controlled, and finally they began to read under instructions to keep the EMG level at a minimum, that is, to maintain silence in the headphones. Most of the subjects showed a reduction in speech muscle EMG level within 5 minutes. After 30 minutes, all 17 subjects were able to read at an EMG level that was comparable to their resting level. Follow-up tests after 1 and 3 months revealed no subvocalization during reading, using the EMG as the criterion. The authors attributed this rapid, and apparently long-term, disappearance of subvocalization to the ability of subjects to make fine motor adjustments of the speech musculature on the basis of auditory cues. This is in contrast to the situation in which attempts to reduce speech muscle activity by instructions alone were not successful. The authors cited the work of Basmajian (1963), who reported that subjects can learn to control the contractions of single motor units, with auditory and visual cues, within 15 to 30 minutes.

In a later study, Hardyck and Petrinovich (1969) identified 50 college and 13 high school students who were habitual subvocalizers during silent reading. Forty-eight of the college students learned to eliminate the subvocal activity within 1 hour. The 13 high school students required from one to three sessions to eliminate the subvocal speech. The researchers noted that speed of eliminating the subvocal pattern was quicker for those persons who scored higher on intelligence tests. The immediate effect of eliminating subvocalization was that subjects reported a reduction of fatigue previously associated with reading for periods of 1 to 3 hours. Hardyck and Petrinovich suggested that elimination of subvocal speech and reading improvement instruction should enable a high speed of reading, with good comprehension, for those with sufficient ability to benefit from the techniques.

McGuigan and his associates have found increases in chin, lip, and tongue EMGs during silent reading as compared to resting levels (McGuigan, Keller, & Stanton, 1964; McGuigan & Bailey, 1969; McGuigan & Rodier, 1968). In addition, McGuigan and Rodier (1968) observed increased amplitude of chin and tongue EMG for college students during the memorization of prose materials.

They also found that EMG levels were higher during silent reading when they presented auditory "noise" in the form of prose different from that being read. They interpreted this latter finding as indicating that subjects changed the amplitude of their covert oral behavior to facilitate the reading process. McGuigan (1973) suggested that the higher level of oral EMG activity during silent reading in children and less proficient adults indicates that these individuals exaggerate their covert oral behavior to bring their comprehension up to a proper level. Likewise, under demanding conditions (e.g., noisy environment) the average individual enhances reading proficiency by exaggerating the amplitude of covert oral activity, sometimes reading aloud to do this, perhaps to overcome a distracting conversation in the vicinity. Contrary to the view of others who would eliminate subvocal activity related to silent reading, McGuigan believed that the covert oral response is beneficial to this and other types of linguistic tasks. McGuigan (1981) also claimed, in contrast to Hardyck, that the more rapidly a person reads, the greater the amplitude of covert speech muscle activity.

In summary, EMG studies have reliably detected subvocal speech during silent reading. Feedback of EMG may have practical applications in terms of eliminating this habit in adults if they are hindered by it. However, children appear to subvocalize naturally while reading silently, and perhaps teachers should not try to eliminate this activity if it helps in comprehending the material at an early learning stage.

EMG and Muscular Fatigue

Investigations have indicated that persons can maintain maximum muscular effort (i.e., 100%) for less than 1 minute (McCormick, 1976). However, a level of about 25% of their own maximum can be maintained for 10 minutes or more. The implications of these findings are that muscular efficiency decreases when a high level of exertion is required over a continuous period, and that this is due to muscle fatigue. With respect to performance in tracking, Eason and White (1960) have argued that muscular fatigue is partly responsible for the superiority of distributed practice over massed practice. They also suggest that a fatigued subject would have to increase muscular tension in order to continue making rotary pursuit movements. Thus, additional motor units would be recruited to compensate for the reduced activity of fatigued units.

Some support for this notion is derived from a study by Wilkinson (1962), although a completely different type of task was used. Twelve persons were required to perform a 20-minute pencil-and-paper addition test under the following conditions: (a) after a normal night of sleep, and (b) after 32 to 56 hours of sleep deprivation. The EMG recorded from the inactive forearm indicated that subjects who maintained performance best after deprivation had the greatest increases in EMG over normal levels. Thus, the maintenance of performance level under somewhat stressful conditions seems to be at the cost of extra energy expenditure.

Ortengren, Anderson, Broman, Magnusson, and Petersen (1975) conducted studies of localized muscle fatigue in both laboratory and factory assembly-line conditions. Two assembly-line stations, considered to be heavy work, were examined, and results were found to be comparable for both the laboratory simulation and the actual assembly line. At one station, the muscles were under heavy static load for periods of 60 seconds at a time. The other station required that individuals perform much of their work above their shoulders. The EMGs were recorded from biceps, triceps, forearm, deltoid, and trapezius muscles of five experienced male workers. Subjective incidents of localized fatigue corresponded highly with increased EMG level of various muscles. The technique enabled comparison of muscle strain for different work tasks and may be used to provide information about how jobs can be designed to make them less strenuous.

The effect of desk slant on EMG and fatigue ratings was tested by Eastman and Kamon (1976). They photographed back posture and recorded EMG from deltoid, trapezius, and spinae erector (lower back) muscles while six subjects performed reading and writing tasks at either a flat desk, a 12-degree tilt desk, or a 24-degree tilt desk. The subjects participated in $2\frac{1}{2}$-hour sessions on each of 3 days. The major finding was that EMG activity from the lower back muscles was significantly lessened with the 24-degree desk slant. Fatigue ratings were also least for the desk slanted at 24 degrees of angle.

The several studies reviewed in this section indicate that feelings of localized fatigue are associated with increased local EMG activity. Studies of EMG activity may be useful in reducing fatigue produced by different types of work tasks and work places.

EMG AND MENTAL ACTIVITY

In this section, we briefly consider EMG in conditioning, cognitive activities, sleep, motivated performance, and emotional expression.

Conditioning of the EMG

The control of single motor units through conditioning procedures is well established, and much of the relevant work has been summarized by Basmajian (1977, 1986). The emphasis in this section is on EMG changes during conditioning as revealed by surface recordings.

Operant conditioning of the EMG was demonstrated by Cohen (1973). Two groups of subjects were reinforced for producing either 40 to 60 μV of activity or 90 to 110 μV of chin EMG, for a minimum duration of .5 second. Both experimental groups learned to emit the correct EMG level to obtain reinforcement. A comparison of EMG feedback with more commonly used verbal relaxation instructions in reducing frontalis muscle tension was made by Haynes, Mosely, and McGowan (1975). During EMG feedback conditions, 22 subjects heard a tone that decreased in pitch as they became more relaxed and increased in pitch as muscular tension increased. Four other subjects received verbal instructions to relax according to either the techniques of Wolpe (passive relaxation) or Jacobson (active relaxation). A control group of 17 subjects were told to become as relaxed as possible but received no other assistance. A final group received noncontingent feedback in the form of a tone that was presented at random intervals and was not related to low or high EMG levels. The EMG biofeedback group achieved greater degrees of muscle relaxation than either of the other two relaxation groups and much greater than that achieved by persons in the two control conditions.

Alexander (1975) questioned two basic assumptions implicit in the use of EMG feedback to achieve lowered muscular tension. These were (a) that tension reduction in one muscle (e.g., the frontalis) is generalized to other skeletal muscles, and (b) that the subjective feeling of being relaxed is related to EMG reduction. Alexander's experimental group achieved significant decreases in frontalis EMG with feedback, but this lowering of tension did not spread to two other skeletal muscles (forearm and leg). In addition, a comparison of the ratings of relaxation made by experimental and control groups (no feedback) indicated that "mild" relaxation was achieved by both groups over the 5-day period of the experiment. Thus, Alexander proposed that his data do not support a claim that frontalis EMG reduction is either related to or produces general feelings of relaxation. The generalization of muscle relaxation from frontalis to other muscles was studied by Fridlund, Fowler, and Pritchard (1980). Four subjects had frontalis EMG training on 5 separate days while muscle activity was measured at 7 other sites including the arms, legs, and neck. Frontalis EMG levels decreased significantly with feedback, but activity from the other muscles did not, thus supporting Alexander's position. A study by LeBoeuf (1980), in which 60 subjects were used, tested the degree to which frontalis relaxation would generalize to trapezius (shoulder) and masseter (jaw) muscles. He found evidence that frontalis feedback was effective in lowering EMG in the other facial area (masseter) but not in the trapezius. This last study suggests that generalization of relaxation from frontalis feedback may be limited to adjacent facial muscles. However, it must be emphasized that much of the research indicates that while biofeedback leads to reduced EMG in the targeted muscle, relaxation does not generalize to adjacent muscles (Fridlund, Cottam, & Fowler, 1982; Thompson, Haber, & Tearnan, 1981).

To summarize, it is clear that operant conditioning of the surface EMG, using appropriate feedback, has been obtained by a number of researchers. It seems that by providing accurate informtion about internal processes, EMG feedback can lead to instrumental control of muscle tension level. However, the contention that lowering level of EMG in one muscle (frontalis) will generalize to other muscles has not been experimentally supported. The studies mentioned here are general in nature, because they deal primarily with the learned control of EMG.

Investigations that have studied EMG biofeedback in the context of treating certain disorders, such as tension headache, are discussed in chapter 14.

The classical conditioning of EMG has been demonstrated in several studies. For example, Van Liere (1953) measured EMG from the masseter and forearm muscles in an experimental group, in which the CS (tone) was followed by the UCS (another tone), and in a control group, which received the CS only. As conditioning progressed, the experimental group showed a larger EMG increase to the CS than the control group, indicating conditioning of these muscles. Obrist (1968) also showed EMG activity of neck, chin, and forearm muscles during classical conditioning. In another study (Obrist et al., 1969), using a blue light as the CS and an electric shock as the UCS, it was found that chin EMG activity decreased in anticipation of the aversive UCS. The drop in EMG activity reflected a decrease in discrete movements, not in tension level.

EMG and Cognitive Activities

Included in this section are a number of studies that have related EMG to cognitive activities, including problem solving, verbal learning, and concept identification. Clites (1936) measured the forearm EMGs of subjects solving a verbal problem. He found that EMGs were greater when subjects were successful in problem solving than when they were unsuccessful. Perhaps success led to more interest and involvement in the task and was reflected in the higher EMG levels.

The question of probability of success and its effect on muscular effort expended in a task was investigated by Diggory, Klein, and Cohen (1964). These experimenters measured EMG from the forearms of three groups of subjects: (a) those who were led to believe that they had a high probability of success (Ps) in a task, (b) subjects who believed that Ps was very low, and (c) those who believed that Ps was 50-50. The investigators manipulated Ps by showing the subjects predetermined graphs of past performance and extrapolations to future performance after each trial. The results supported the conclusion that persons who expected to succeed exerted more effort, as measured by EMG level, than those who expected to fail. Thus, there would seem to be some support for the idea that the experience of success influences EMG in an upward direction.

The picture is slightly complicated, however, when one considers results of studies that have varied difficulty without considering success or failure. For example, R. C. Davis (1938) measured forearm and neck EMGs while subjects solved number problems that became progressively more difficult. He reported that with increased task difficulty, EMGs at both locations increased correspondingly. The difficulty of a problem was judged by the proportion of subjects who failed it. Pishkin and Shurley (1968) measured frontalis EMGs of psychiatric patients during a concept identification task. The EMG was higher with unsolvable than with solvable problems. The investigators concluded that the EMGs

represented tension associated with difficulty in processing complex information. In a later study, Pishkin (1973) reported that schizophrenics produced
higher EMGs than normal as complexity of problems to be solved increased.
Both groups, however, showed higher EMG activity with increased complexity.

Hence, some of the obtained results indicate heightened EMG activity when
subjects were "successful" in their tasks. However, other findings showed
increased EMG with increased task difficulty. In the latter instances, the increased EMG was related to less successful performance. The reason for this
discrepancy is not clear. Perhaps the common denominator is effort, and the
transfer of impulses from brain to muscle and back when a person is engaged in a
difficult cognitive task. Cacioppo and Petty (1981) have shown that depth of
covert processing was related to oral (lip) EMG but not to nonoral (forearm
EMG) or heart activity measures. The more abstract and difficult the mental
coding task, the greater was the activity of the speech-related muscles. One
possible explanation offered by Cacioppo and Petty is that the increased proprioceptive feedback from speech muscles to brain may help in the processing of
new information. They suggest that oral EMG activity may be useful in studying
central information processing operations.

EMG During Sleep

The question of EMG activity during sleep and dreaming was reviewed by
Goldstein (1972). The consensus of several studies that she examined was that
the onset of dreaming was marked by a reduction in neck and head EMG activity.
This general conclusion was supported in an investigation conducted by Bliwise
et al. (1974). These researchers measured chin and lip EMG during sleep on
three consecutive nights. They found that EMGs decreased toward their lowest
levels starting 5 minutes before the onset of REM sleep. The lowest EMG levels
of the night occurred throughout REM sleep. A sample of EEG, eye movements,
and integrated EMG obtained by Bliwise and colleagues is presented in Fig. 8.6.
The chin EMG was superior to lip recordings in identifying REM sleep.

The EMG from muscles in the throat and upper air passages of persons
suffering obstructive sleep apnea was studied by Guilleminault, Hill, Simmons,
and Dement (1978). Sleep apnea involves a cessation of breathing during sleep.
In comparison to normal controls, the apnea victims had a decrease or complete
disappearance of activity in the muscles measured during parts of the sleep cycle,
and this led to the obstructed airways.

EMG and Motivated Performance

Several studies have shown that the EMG increased progressively from the
beginning to the end of a task (e.g., Bartoshuk, 1955; Surwillo, 1956). These
increases have been termed *EMG gradients*. There is evidence that the slope of

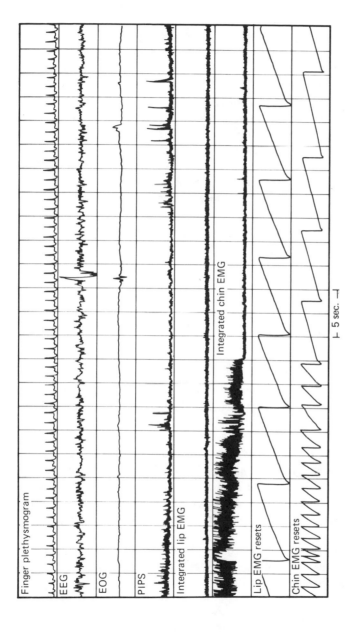

├ 5 sec. ┤

FIG. 8.6. Polygraph tracing. This example shows a marked decline in integrated chin EMG 10 seconds prior to the transition to REM sleep (which starts at the end of the K-complex in the middle of the EEG tracing). The decline is paralleled by a slowing of chin EMG reset rate. Integrated lip EMG and reset rate are already low pre-REM and do not decline further during REM sleep. Four single phasic spikes can be seen in the integrated chin EMG and one in the integrated lip EMG during REM sleep. Such spikes may appear simultaneously with, or independently of, spikes form the periorbital electrodes (PIPs). Note the simultaneous appearance of PIPs and phasic inhibition in the integrated chin EMG about 7 seconds prior to the chin EMG drop.

193

these gradients is related to level of motivation. Bartoshuk (1955) reported that EMG gradients were related to quality of performance in mirror tracing. With subjects equated for practice, the gradient slope (especially for right forearm EMGs) was found to be directly related to speed and accuracy of performance. Surwillo (1956) tested the hypothesis that the slope of the EMG gradient could be increased by raising the level of incentives in a tracking task. In his first experiment, two incentive levels were produced, and the higher one resulted in steeper EMG gradients as measured from the biceps, wrist, and frontalis muscles. In a second experiment, a new group of subjects was tested at three incentive levels. Again, incentive level was found to be a factor in raising the EMG gradient.

The effects of an experimenter's presence on EMG gradients were tested by Chapman (1974). Three groups of subjects listened to a recorded story under three conditions: (a) unobserved, (b) experimenter present in the same room, and (c) experimenter in an adjoining room. The story was Maugham's "The Dream," which took 11 minutes to present. Frontalis EMG showed a regular gradient from the beginning of the story to the end. The gradients were significantly higher under both conditions in which the experimenter was present, as compared to the completely unobserved condition. Chapman concluded that the mere presence of the experimenter was a source of arousal.

Malmo (1975), in his book *On Emotions, Needs, and Our Archaic Brain*, discussed EMG gradients and their significance at some length. He hypothesized that the appearance of an EMG gradient indicates the occurrence of an organized behavior sequence. According to Malmo, the stronger the person's involvement in the task, the steeper the somatic (muscle) and autonomic (e.g., heart activity) gradients. Svebak, Dalen, and Storfjell (1981) tested the hypotheses that somatic and autonomic gradients occur jointly, and that gradients are steeper with greater involvement and effort of subjects. In two experiments, they found that a difficult continuous RT task produced steeper EMG gradients than an easier version, but that autonomic measures (heart rate, skin conductance) did not show gradients. Thus, Malmo's hypothesis was only partially supported. In addition, Svebak and colleagues assert that the autonomic–somatic coupling hypothesis of Obrist (see chapter 15) does not explain the result. In another study, Svebak and Murgatroyd (1985) found that "serious-minded" subjects had steeper EMG gradients than "playful" persons while performing a video car-racing simulation.

To summarize briefly, EMG gradients have been reported for both mental (e.g., listening to a story) and physical activities (e.g., tracking). Thus, it appears that level of involvement and task difficulty can affect EMG activity, and could be confounding elements in studies that do not take them into account.

EMG and Emotional Facial Expression

One of the early students of facial expressions of emotion was Charles Darwin. In his 1872 book, *Expression of the Emotions in Man and Animals*, Darwin argued that man's expressive movements are remnants of earlier movements (Woodworth 1938). For example, the expression of grief in the adult is a toned down version of crying in the infant. The wide-open mouth of crying involves muscles of the corner of the mouth, and the slight movement of these remain as a sign of grief after vocal crying has disappeared as a response. Darwin introduced the procedure of having people judge expressions of emotions from facial photographs. The face is a logical choice, because the muscles and skin of the face are very mobile. In addition, the face is visible to others and is an important source of information in both verbal and nonverbal social communications. The procedure of using photos to study patterning in facial expressions and the question of whether they are inherited or learned has continued from the time of Darwin to the present, and has led to the interesting work of Ekman (1973), who compared cross-cultural judgments of emotion from posed facial expressions. Typically, reactions such as happiness, anger, fear, disgust, sadness, and contempt are posed in contemporary studies. In his cross-cultural work, Ekman showed that expressions such as happiness and anger are readily recognized in diverse cultures, a result that could be supportive of evolutionary origins. The study of facial expressions of emotion entered a new phase in the 1970s with the use of EMG measures in studies by Schwartz and his associates. The 19th century anatomist Sir Charles Bell believed that certain muscles peculiar to primates, such as the corrugators that knit the brows or the triangularis that depresses the mouth, have no other function than to express emotion (Woodworth, 1938). Schwartz and colleagues found that imagining pleasant thoughts (e.g., happy) increased muscle activity in the cheek area responsible for smiles (zygomatic), whereas unpleasant imagining (e. g., anger, sadness) produced an increase in corrugator muscle activity at the eyebrows (Schwartz, Ahern, & Brown, 1976; Schwartz, Brown, & Ahern, 1980; Schwartz, Fair, Salt, Mandel, & Klerman, 1976). Dimberg (1982) conducted a study to investigate whether individuals exposed to pictures of happy and angry facial expressions would be influenced by the facial pattern through a form of social interaction. He found that facial EMG activity was differentially affected by happy and angry faces because happy faces evoked increased zygomatic activity and angry faces evoked elevated corrugator response, the same pattern observed in the Schwartz studies for imagined emotional states. The patterning of response was of interest, but still to be determined was whether the pictures resulted in changed mood states or merely involved mimicking behavior on the part of subjects. This question was answered by Sirota and Schwartz (1982), who took measures of mood as well as EMG while subjects imagined scenes with elated, depressed, and neutral content. Feelings of elation and depression were elicited in approximately 70% of subjects, and among these persons, elation was accompanied by increases in zygomatic activity, and depression produced increases in corrugator activity. Thus, facial EMG patterning seems to be a good indicator of mood state. A detailed and sophisticated computer-based analysis of facial EMG patterns during imagery and posed facial expressions was carried out by Fridlund et al.

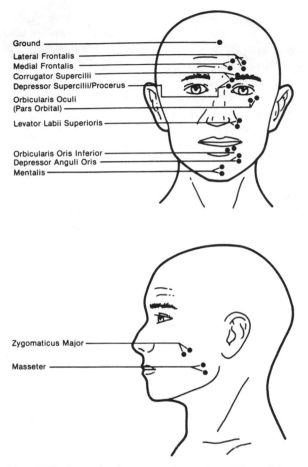

FIG. 8.7.   EMG electrode placements for surface differential recording over major facial mimetic muscles. (Diagram Courtesy of Drs. Fridlund, Cacioppo, and Tassinary.)

(1984). They showed the usefulness of measuring from multiple facial sites, and confirmed the importance of corrugator activity during the experience of "negative emotions." The student interested in research methodology and possible future directions in this area should read the article by Fridlund and colleagues. Fridlund and Cacioppo (1986) presented guidelines for electrode placements in facial EMG research. Figure 8.7 shows these placements and modifications based on empirical work and anatomical review by Tassinary, Cacioppo, Geen, and Vanman (1987) and Tassinary, Cacioppo, and Geen (in press). The use of facial EMG was explored in a study of pleasant and unpleasant sexual and nonsexual arousal in a study by Sullivan and Brender (1986). Female subjects listened to four different kinds of stories: pleasant-sexual, unpleasant-sexual, pleasant-nonsexual, and unpleasant-nonsexual, while EMG was measured. Greater corrugator activity was noted for both kinds of unpleasant stimuli, but especially the one with sexual content. Zygomatic muscle activity was greater in response to sexual as compared to nonsexual stories. These interesting results argue for the use of facial EMG in studies of sexual response, but with additional recording sites to provide more information regarding differential muscle activity with different kinds of arousing or nonarousing stimuli. The use of facial EMG patterning in the study of emotional reactions is an exciting approach. Some consistent trends have already been observed, and continued research in this area promises interesting results.

In the next chapter, we discuss electrodermal activity (EDA) and behavior. This measure, like the EMG, is another peripheral physiological response that is very sensitive to changes in CNS activity and psychological states.

REFERENCES

Alexander, A. B. (1975). An experimental test of assumptions relating to the use of electromyographic biofeedback as a general relaxation technique. *Psychophysiology, 12,* 656–662.

Andreassi, J. L., Rapisardi, S., & Whalen, P. M. (1969). Autonomic responsivity and reaction time under fixed and variable signal schedules. *Psychophysiology, 6,* 58–69.

Bartoshuk, A. K. (1955). Electromyographic gradients as indicants of motivation. *Canadian Journal of Psychology, 9,* 215–230.

Basmajian, J. V. (1963). Control and training of individual motor units. *Science, 30,* 662–664.

Basmajian, J. V. (1977). Motor learning and control: A working hypothesis. *Archives of Physical Medicine and Rehabilitation, 58,* 38–41.

Basmajian, J. V. (1986). The musculature. In: M. G. H. Coles, E. Donchin, & S. W. Porges (Eds.), *Psychophysiology: Systems, processes & applications* (pp. 97–106). New York: Guilford Press.

Basmajian, J. V., & Blumenstein, R. (1983). Electrode placement in electromyographic biofeedback. In: J. V. Basmajian (Ed.), *Biofeedback: Principles & practice for clinicians* (pp. 363–378). Baltimore: Williams & Wilkins.

Bliwise, D., Coleman, R., Bergmann, B., Wincor, M. S., Pivik, R. T., & Rechtschaffen, A. (1974). Facial muscle tonus during REM and NREM sleep. *Psychophysiology, 11,* 497–508.

Cacioppo, J. T., & Petty, R. E. (1981). Electromyographic specificity during covert information processing. *Psychophysiology, 18,* 518–523.

Chapman, A. J. (1974). An electromyographic study of social facilitation: A test of the "Mere Presence" hypothesis. *British Journal of Psychology, 65,* 123–128.

Clites, M. S. (1936). Certain somatic activities in relation to successful and unsuccessful problem solving: III. *Journal of Experimental Psychology, 19,* 172–192.

Cohen, M. J. (1973). The relation between heart rate and electromyographic activity in a discriminated escape–avoidance paradigm. *Psychophysiology, 10,* 8–20.

Davis, J. F. (1959). *Manual of surface electromyography* (WADC Technical Report 59-184). Dayton, OH: Wright Air Development Center.

Davis, C. M., Brickett, P., Stern, R. M., & Kimball, W. H. (1978). Tension in the two frontales: Electrode placement and artifact in the recording of forehead EMG. *Psychophysiology, 15,* 591–593.

Davis, R. C. (1938). The relation of muscle action potentials to difficulty and frustration. *Journal of Experimental Psychology, 23,* 141–158.

Davis, R. C. (1940). *Set and muscular tension.* Indiana University Publications, Science Series, No. 10.

Diggory, J. C., Klein, S. J., & Cohen, M. (1964). Muscle-action potentials and estimated probability of success. *Journal of Experimental Psychology, 68,* 449–455.

Dimberg, U. (1982). Facial reactions to facial expressions. *Psychophysiology, 19,* 643–647.

Duffy, E. (1962). *Activation and behavior.* New York: Wiley.

Duffy, E. (1972). Activation. In N. S. Greenfield & R. A. Sternbach (Eds.), *Handbook of psychophysiology* (pp. 577–622). New York: Holt, Rinehart & Winston.

Eason, R. G. (1963). Relation between effort, tension level, skill and performance efficiency in a perceptual-motor task. *Perceptual and Motor Skills, 16,* 297–317.

Eason, R. G., & White, C. T. (1960). Relationship between muscular tension and performance during rotary pursuit. *Perceptual & Motor Skills, 10,* 199–210.

Eason, R. G., & White, C. T. (1961). Muscular tension, effort and tracking difficulty: studies of parameters which affect tension level and performance efficiency. *Perceptual and Motor Skills, 12,* 331–372.

Eastman, M. C., & Kamon, E. (1976). Posture and subjective evaluation at flat and slanted desks. *Human Factors, 18,* 15–26.

Ekman, P. (1973). Cross-cultural studies of facial expression. In: P. Ekman (Ed.), *Darwin and facial expression: A century of research in review* (pp. 63–93). New York: Academic Press.

French, S. N. (1980). Electromyographic biofeedback for tension control during fine motor skill acquisition. *Biofeedback and Self Regulation, 5,* 221–228.

Fridlund, A. J., & Cacioppo, J. T. (1986). Guidelines for human electromyographic research. *Psychophysiology, 23,* 567–589.

Fridlund, A. J., Cottam, G. L., & Fowler, S. C. (1982). In search of the general tension factor: Tensional patterning during auditory stimulation. *Psychophysiology, 19,* 136–145.

Fridlund, A. J., Fowler, S. C., & Pritchard, D. A. (1980). Striate muscle tensional patterning in frontalis EMG biofeedback. *Psychophysiology, 17,* 47–55.

Fridlund, A. J., Schwartz, G. E., & Fowler, S. C. (1984). Pattern recognition of self-reported emotional state from multiple-site facial EMG activity during affective imagery. *Psychophysiology, 21,* 622–637.

Gardner, E. (1975). *Fundamentals of neurology.* Philadelphia: Saunders.

Goldstein, I. B. (1972). Electromyography: A measure of skeletal muscle response. In N. S. Greenfield & R. A. Sternbach (Eds.), *Handbook of psychophysiology* (pp. 329–365). New York: Holt, Rinehart & Winston.

Guilleminault, C., Hill, M. W., Simmons, F. B., & Dement, W. C. (1978). Obstructive sleep apnea: Electromyographic and fiberoptic studies. *Experimental Neurology, 62,* 48–67.

Guyton, A. C. (1977). *Basic human physiology.* Philadelphia: Saunders.

Haagh, S. A., & Brunia, C. H. (1984). Cardiac somatic coupling during the foreperiod in a simple reaction-time task. *Psychological Research, 46,* 3–13.

Hardyck, D. C., & Petrinovich, L. F. (1969). Treatment of subvocal speech during reading. *Journal of Reading, 12,* 1–11.

Hardyck, D. C., Petrinovich, L. F., & Ellsworth, D. W. (1966). Feedback of speech muscle activity during silent reading: Rapid extinction. *Science, 154,* 1467.

Haynes, J., Mosely, D., & McGowan, W. T. (1975). Relaxation training and biofeedback in the reduction of frontalis muscle tension. *Psychophysiology, 12,* 547–552.

Holloway, F. A., & Parsons, O. A. (1972). Physiological concomitants of reaction time performance in normal and brain-damaged subjects. *Psychophysiology, 9,* 189–198.

Jacob, S. W., & Francone, C. A. (1970). *Structure and function in man.* Philadelphia: Saunders.

Kennedy, J. L., & Travis, R. C. (1947). Prediction of speed of performance by muscle action potentials. *Science, 105,* 410–411.

Kennedy, J. L., & Travis, R. C. (1948). Prediction and control of alertness: II. Continuous tracking. *Journal of Comparative & Physiological Psychology, 41,* 203–210.

Lansing, R. W., Schwartz, E., & Lindsley, D. B. (1959). Reaction time and EEG activation under alerted and non-alerted conditions. *Journal of Experimental Psychology, 58,* 1–7.

LeBoeuf, A. (1980). An experiment to test generalization of feedback from frontalis EMG. *Perceptual & Motor Skills, 50,* 27–31.

Levine, W. R., & Irvine, J. K. (1984). In vivo EMG feedback in violin and viola pedagogy. *Biofeedback & Self Regulation, 9,* 161–168.

Lippold, O. C. J. (1967). Electromyography. In P. H. Venables & I. Martin (Eds.), *Manual of psycho-physiological methods* (pp. 245–297). Amsterdam: North-Holland.

Malmo, R. B. (1975). *On emotions, needs, and our archaic brain.* New York: Holt, Rinehart, & Winston.

McCormick, E. J. (1976). Human factors in engineering and design. New York: McGraw-Hill.

McGuigan, F. J. (1973). Electrical measurement of covert processes as an explication of "higher mental events." In F. J. McGuigan & R. A. Schoonover (Eds.), *The psychophysiology of thinking* (pp. 343–385). New York: Academic Press.

McGuigan, F. J. (1981). Review of Andreassi's "Psychophysiology: Human behavior and physiological response." *American Journal of Psychology, 94,* 359–362.

McGuigan, F. J., & Bailey, S. C. (1969). Covertresponse patterns during the processing of language stimuli *Interamerican Journal of Psychology, 3,* 289–299.

McGuigan, F. J., Keller, B., & Stanton, E. (1964). Covert language responses during silent reading. *Journal of Educational Psychology, 55,* 339–343.

McGuigan, F. J., & Rodier, W. I., III. (1968). Effects of auditory stimulation on covert oral behavior during silent reading. *Journal of Experimental Psychology, 76,* 649–655.

Mulder, T., & Hulston, W. (1984). The effects of fatigue and task repetition on the surface electromyographic signal. *Psychophysiology, 21,* 528–534.

Obrist, P. A. (1968). Heart rate and somatic-motor coupling during classical aversive conditioning in humans. *Journal of Experimental Psychology, 77,* 180–183.

Obrist, P. A., Webb, R. A., & Sutterer, J. R. (1969). Heart rate and somatic changes during aversive conditioning and a simple reaction time task. *Psychophysiology, 5,* 696–723.

Obrist, P. A., Webb, R. A., Sutterer, J. R., & Howard, J. L. (1970). Cardiac deceleration and reaction time: An evaluation of two hypotheses. *Psychophysiology, 6,* 695–706.

Ortengren, R., Anderson, G., Broman, M., Magnusson, R., & Petersen, I. (1975). Vocational electromyography: Studies of localized muscle fatigue at the assembly line. *Ergonomics, 18,* 157–174.

Pishkin, V. (1973). Electromyography in cognitive performance by schizophrenics and normals. *Perceptual & Motor Skills, 37,* 382.

Pishkin, V., & Shurley, J. T. (1968). Electrodermal and electromyographic parameters in concept identification. *Psychophysiology, 5,* 112–118.

Schwartz, G. E., Ahern, L., & Brown, S. L. (1979). Lateralized facial muscle response to positive and negative emotional stimuli. *Psychophysiology, 16,* 561–571.

Schwartz, G. E., Brown, S. L., & Ahern, G. L. (1980). Facial muscle patterning and subjective experience during affective imagery: Sex differences. *Psychophysiology, 17,* 75–82.

Schwartz, G. E., Fair, P. L., Salt, P., Mandel, M. R., & Klerman, G. L. (1976). Facial muscle patterning to affective imagery in depressed and nondepressed subjects. *Science, 192,* 489–491.

Sirota, A. D., & Schwartz, G. E. (1982). Facial muscle patterning and lateralization during elation and depression imagery. *Journal of Abnormal Psychology, 91,* 25–34.

Sullivan, M. J., & Brender, W. (1986). Facial electromyography: A measure of affective processes during sexual arousal. *Psychophysiology, 23,* 182–188.

Surwillo, W. W. (1956). Psychological factors in muscle-action potentials: EMG gradients. *Journal of Experimental Psychology, 52,* 263–272.

Svebak, S., Dalen, K., & Storfjell, O. (1981). The psychological significance of task-induced tonic changes in somatic and autonomic activity. *Psychophysiology, 18,* 403–409.

Svebak, S., & Murgatroyd, S. (1985). Metamotivational dominance: A multimethod validation of reversal theory constructs. *JournL of Personality & Social Psychology, 48,* 107–116.

Tassinary, L. G., Cacioppo, J. T., Geen, T. R., & Vanman, E. (1987). Optimizing surface electrode placements for facial EMG recordings: Guidelines for recording from the perioral muscle region. *Psychophysiology, 24,* 615–616.

Tassinary, L. G., Cacioppo, J. T., & Geen, T. R. (in press). A psychometric study of surface electrode placements for facial electromyographic recording: I. The brow and cheek muscle regions. *Psychophysiology.*

Thompson, J. K., Haber, J. D., & Tearnan, B. H. (1981). Generalization of frontalis electromyographic feedback to adjacent muscle groups: A critical review. *Psychosomatic Medicine, 43,* 19–24.

Thompson, R. F., Lindsley, D. B., & Eason, R. G. (1966). *Physiological psychology* New York: McGraw-Hill.

Travis, R. C., & Kennedy, J. L. (1949). Prediction and control of alertness. III. Calibration of the alertness indicator and further results. *Journal of Comparative & Physiological Psychology, 40,* 457–461.

Van Liere, D. W. (1953). Characteristics of the muscle tension response to paired tones. *Journal of Experimental Psychology, 46,* 319–324.

Wilcott, R. C., & Beenken, M. G. (1957). Relation of integrated surface electromyography and muscle tension. *Perceptual & Motor Skills, 7,* 295–298.

Wilkinson, R. T. (1962). Muscle tension during mental work under sleep deprivation. *Journal of Experimental Psychology, 64,* 565–571.

Williamson, D. A., Epstein, L. H., & Lombardo, T. W. (1980). EMG measurement as a function of electrode placement and level of EMG. *Psychophysiology, 17,* 279–282.

Woodworth, R. S. (1938). *Experimental psychology.* New York: Holt.

9

Electrodermal Activity and Behavior

The idea of studying electrical activity of the skin probably does not cause much excitement in the average person. However, as a measure in psychophysiology, it has had a long and interesting history; and it has been a very popular research area. The fact that changes in electrical activity of the skin can be produced by various physical and emotional stimuli was first reported by Charles Féré, a French neurologist, in 1888. He passed a small current between two electrodes on the skin surface and observed changes in electrodermal activity (EDA) when a person was presented with various stimuli (Woodworth & Schlosberg, 1954; Neumann & Blanton, 1970). A galvanometer was used to measure the increases in skin conductance that occurred when visual, auditory, or olfactory stimuli were introduced. This phenomenon was soon labeled the psychogalvanic reflex (PGR) or the galvanic skin response (GSR) by early investigators. Féré felt that his results with sensory and emotional stimuli showed that the responses were indicators of nervous system excitation, or "arousal," to put it in more modern terms. Measures of EDA were used in the early 1900s by Carl Jung, the noted Swiss psychiatrist, to study reactions of patients to word associations.

In 1890, a Russian scientist, Ivan Tarchanoff, reported that he could obtain similar galvanometer deflections without the use of externally applied current; that is, there were natural differences in electrical potential between two skin areas, and this potential changed when the subject was stimulated. Féré and Tarchanoff contributed what were to become two basic methods for the measurement of EDA: the recording of skin conductance (SC) and skin potential (SP). Figure 9.1 shows a typical change in SC and SP levels with stimulation. The physiological bases for these responses are still not fully understood, but changes in sweat gland activity have been strongly implicated in a variety of research

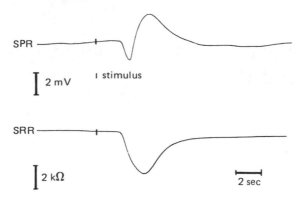

FIG. 9.1.   Characteristic skin resistance and skin potential responses.

studies (Edelberg, 1972a). Because sweat glands are located in the skin, we now briefly consider the anatomy and physiology of the skin in order to more fully understand the nature of the phenomena being examined in this chapter.

ANATOMY AND PHYSIOLOGY OF THE SKIN

The skin consists of two layers: an epidermis, or outer layer, which is about 1 mm or less in thickness, and a dermis, or inner layer, which ranges from about 0.5 mm over the eyelids to 6 mm over the upper back, palms of the hands, and soles of the feet. The epidermis consists of five separate cellular layers: stratum corneum (outermost layer, also known as the keratinous or "horny" layer), stratum lucidum, stratum granulosum, stratum spinosum, and stratum ger-minativum (see Fig. 9.2). The dermis contains blood vessels, nerves, lymph vessels, hair follicles, smooth muscle, sweat glands, and sebaceous glands. Just below the dermis is the hypodermis (subcutaneous connective tissue), which contains blood and lymph vessels, the roots of hair follicles, sensory nerves, and secretory portions of the sweat glands (Woodburne, 1978).

The eccrine sweat glands are the ones with which we are most concerned. They have a wide distribution over the body surface and are found everywhere in the skin except at the margins of the lips, the concha (outer ear), the glans penis, the prepuce, and the clitoris. They are most numerous in the palms of the hands and the soles of the feet, of intermediate density on the head, and least dense on the arms, legs, and trunk. One estimate is that a square inch on the palm contains 3000 sweat glands (Jacob & Francone, 1970). The total number of sweat glands on the body, based on studies of cadavers, ranges from 2 to 5 million (Fowles, 1986). The eccrine glands are simple, tubular structures with a rounded secretory portion and a duct that leads to the surface of the skin. The secretory portion is formed by several unequal coils rolled into a ball of about 0.3 to 0.4 mm in diameter. The secretory duct from the eccrine gland opens as a small pore at the

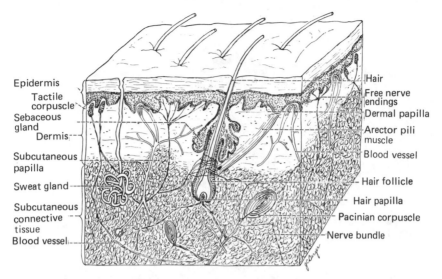

FIG. 9.2. The structure of the skin.

surface of the epidermis. An example of surface epidermal sweat pores is shown in Fig. 9.3. This is a photograph of a fingertip, which was prepared in order to count the number of active sweat glands present, as indicated by chemical reactions at the pores.

The secretory portion of the eccrine sweat gland has a profuse nerve supply via cholinergic fibers of the SNS. That is, although innervated by SNS fibers, the transmitting agent is acetylcholine, a chemical usually associated with PNS functions. Discussions by Edelberg (1972a) and Venables and Christie (1973) indicate that EDA is a complex reaction with a number of control centers in the CNS. The CNS mechanisms include the premotor cortex, limbic and hypothalamic areas (both concerned with motivational and emotional behavior), and the reticular formation. The reticular formation at the level of the medulla inhibits EDA, whereas the midbrain reticular area is excitatory. The EDA does, however, strongly reflect SNS activity, and behavioral researchers often interpret EDA as indicative of arousal level or emotional reactivity of an organism.

Although an important function of the skin is to protect the organism it covers, for example, by keeping bacteria, parasites, and noxious chemicals out and keeping vital fluids in, it also has a role in thermoregulatory activities. The thermoregulatory contribution is produced by dilation of blood vessels in the skin and increased sweating, both of which result in decreased skin and body temperature. Conversely, constriction of blood vessels in the skin (which reduces blood flow to the surface) and piloerection (''goose bumps'') help to maintain body heat. Piloerection produces its effect by increasing the area of the insulating air that surrounds the skin, thus preserving heat.

An interesting aspect of sweating is that it is not only thermoregulatory. This

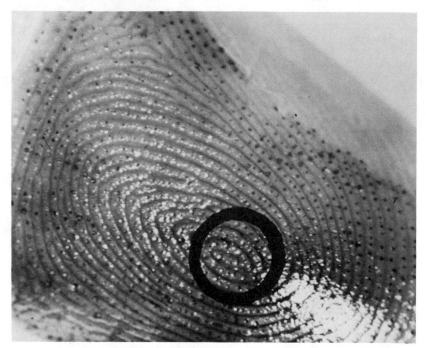

FIG. 9.3. A photograph of a fingertip prepared for a sweat gland count. The circle indicates the usual area of the ridge pattern used for counting. Active sweat glands produce black dots because of the starch-iodine reaction at the tips of the ducts.

fact forms the basis for the behavioral studies in this chapter. Sweating, or sweat gland activity, is reflected as changes in skin potential (SP) and skin conductance (SC) in a variety of situations, including ones that are emotionally arousing. For example, eccrine glands of the palms and fingers of the hand respond weakly at certain levels of heat and strongly to psychological and sensory stimuli. You may have noticed wet or "clammy" palms in situations that were fear- or anxiety-provoking but that were otherwise not very warm. The sweating to psychological stimuli has sometimes been termed "arousal" sweating, and some workers believe it has adaptive value (Darrow, 1933; Wilcott, 1967). Darrow suggested that the sweating of palms and soles may be an adaptive response that persisted over the course of evolution, because it aids in grasping objects. For example, the grasping of a weapon in a fight, or branches of trees during flight. Wilcott hypothesized that arousal sweating in any part of the body may toughen the skin and protect it from mechanical injury. He noted an observation by Edelberg and Wright (1962), who found that palmar skin was difficult to cut during profuse sweating. When sweating is blocked, the skin is more susceptible to mechanical injury. Thus, these interpretations of arousal sweating suggest that it has survival value for the organism, as do other SNS responses in emergency situations. In contrast to eccrine glands of the fingers and palms, those on the forehead, neck, back of the hands, and other areas respond quickly and strongly to thermal stimuli but weakly to psychological or sensory stimuli.

TYPES OF ELECTRODERMAL ACTIVITY

As already noted, changes in EDA will occur with a wide variety of sensory and psychological stimuli. The momentary fluctuations of EDA that occur with stimulation have been termed *phasic responses,* whereas the relatively stable EDA is referred to as the *tonic level.* A classificatory scheme for the various terms relating to EDA was suggested by Venables and Martin (1967). They proposed the following designations and abbreviations:

SRR = skin resistance response
SRL = skin resistance level
SCR = skin conductance response
SCL = skin conductance level
SPR = skin potential response
SPL = skin potential level

The first four of these are related to the Féré effect, because they rely on an external source of current for their observation (exosomatic), whereas the last two (Tarchanoff effect) do not require the application of current and may be thought of as endosomatic. Skin conductance and skin potential are considered separately, because, despite their apparent common origin, they are different phenomena.

Skin Conductance

The term *skin resistance response* (SRR) refers to momentary fluctuations in SR, as did the older GSR terminology. Skin resistance level (SRL) indicates the baseline SR at any given time. Skin conductance response (SCR) and skin conductance level (SRL) are conductance unit measures of SRR and SRL, respectively. Units of conductance are preferred by many investigators instead of resistance values. One reason for this is that conductance values are more suitable for averaging and other statistical manipulations; that is, because conductance is the reciprocal of resistance, it is more likely to conform to the normal distribution of measures required for many statistical analyses. Another reason is that conductance increases with higher levels of arousal or activity of the organism and decreases at low levels, a relationship that is more logical for most persons.

The unit of conductance is the mho (ohm spelled backward) to distinguish it from the ohm, which is the unit of resistance. To give an example of a reciprocal transformation, a micromho (μmho) of conductance is equal to 1,000,000 ohms of resistance, and 10 μmhos equals 100,000 ohms. Log conductance measures go one step further and take the log of micromho values. The log conductance measures also conform to assumptions required for parametric statistical analyses of SC measures, such as analysis of variance or t tests. Venables and Christie (1973) have recently proposed, because the case for the use of conductance units is strong, that the terms SCR and SCL be used to refer to exosomatic measures of EDA, and this is the usage in the remainder of the present chapter.

The amplitude of the SCR depends on electrode size and might vary from .01 μmho to 5 μmho. Appearance of the SCR ranges from 1.3 to 2.5 seconds after stimulus presentation.

Skin Potential

The skin potential response (SPR) refers to changes in SP, whereas skin potential level (SPL) is the level of SP at any point in time. The recordings depicted in Fig. 9.1 show the SPR to be a biphasic (negative then positive) response measured in millivolts. However, SPR can also have a uniphasic negative wave or a uniphasic positive wave. The amplitude of the negative wave of the SPR may typically be about 2 mV, and the positive portion about 4 mV. Measures of SPR amplitudes may be difficult, because SPL is not always easy to establish. The latency of the negative SPR component is similar to that of the SCR (Venables & Christie, 1973).

ORIGIN OF EDA

In research relating performance and psychological factors to EDA, measures of SC or SP can be interpreted as mainly reflecting changes in sweating activity. For a subject during a single recording period, the amplitude of palmar SCRs and SPRs and the amplitude of sweating responses are usually found to be highly correlated (Wilcott, 1967).

THE MEASUREMENT OF ELECTRODERMAL ACTIVITY (EDA)

Skin Conductance Level (SCL)

Fortunately, there are good commercial instruments available today that contain the appropriate amplification, filtering, and ink-writing characteristics to enable the recording of SCL. This includes the availability of appropriate input couplers that convert activity recorded at the skin surface into conductance units (μmhos). The circuits used to measure SCL are of two basic types: those that employ a constant voltage and those using a constant current. The constant-voltage system holds the voltage across the electrodes constant, and the current through the skin varies with conductance changes; this is what is measured on the ink writer. If, however, the current through the skin is held constant, then the voltage, or potential difference between the two electrodes placed on the skin surface, varies with resistance. This latter system is the constant-current technique. Edelberg (1972a) recommended a current density of 8 μA/cm2 (measured at either site) with the constant-current method. For the constant-voltage technique, he suggested a source of 0.75 to 1.0 V across the sites. Lykken and Venables (1971) recommended the use of a constant-voltage circuit limited to 0.50 V. Most commercially available instruments for the measurement of SC use the constant-current technique, and it has proven satisfactory for many researchers. For the student or researcher interested in more detail regarding the electronic circuitry involved in SC measurements, there are several excellent sources (see, e.g., Edelberg, 1967, 1972a; Venables & Christie, 1973; Venables & Martin, 1967).

Skin Potential

Whereas the bipolar placement of electrodes is preferred for SCL measures, a unipolar arrangement is essential to record SPL. The active electrode may be placed on the palm of the hand and referred to a relatively inactive site on the forearm. Edelberg (1972a) mentioned the inner portion of the earlobe as an inactive area. Alternatively, an experimenter may produce an inactive area by using a dental burr to remove a portion of the epidermis or by pricking the skin under the electrode with a needle (e.g., Shackel, 1959; Wilcott, 1959). Stimulation in the form of mental multiplication or having the individual participate in making word associations, will produce changes in SP. The SP may be measured with a sensitive dc amplifier.

A diagram illustrating the placement of electrodes to measure both SP and SC is presented in Fig. 9.4. The figure shows a bipolar placement on the medial phalanges of two fingers for the SCL recording. Venables and Christie (1973) recommended that the electrodes be placed on two adjacent fingers: either the second and third or the fourth and fifth fingers. For the SPL measure, the active electrode is placed on the palm of the hand, and the reference electrode is located on the forearm. The inactive electrode should be placed on an abraded site (accomplished by skin pricking, rubbing with sandpaper, or skin drilling). The fingers or soles of the feet may also be used as the site of the active electrode in SP recording. The researcher must be careful to avoid skin areas that have cuts or other kinds of blemishes, because this may interfere with the response obtained. Difficulty in preparing the reference site and the possibility of skin injury are factors that should be considered in the use of SP measures.

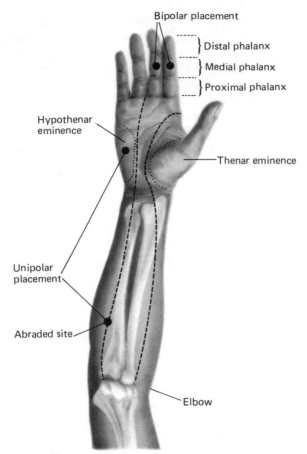

FIG. 9.4.   Recommended placements of electrodes for measuring SC and SP.

Electrodes for Recording EDA

Nonpolarizing electrodes should be used for both SC and SP measurements, and these are commercially available. An appropriate technique is to use a metal coated with the salt of that metal. For example, Ag/AgCl (silver/silver chloride) or Zn/ZnSo4 (zinc/zinc sulphate) electrodes. Venables and Martin (1967) recommended the use of Ag/AgCl electrodes with solutions of either KCL or NaCl as the electrolyte. Wilcott (personal communication) recommends the use of zinc electrodes, because they are easier to use than silver and are entirely adequate if kept clean and polished. Commercial electrode jellies and pastes are available.

Electrode size is significant in the recording of SCL, because resistance of the electrodes varies inversely with area. Therefore, the larger the area, the smaller the resistance. This fact argues for the use of as large an electrode as possible. The electrolyte used should not be allowed to spread beyond the electrode site, because it increases the effective area of the electrode. A typical electrode for use in palmar or plantar (sole of foot) placements may be 1.5 to 2.0 cm in diameter, whereas those used on the fingers may be 1.0 cm or less in diameter. Electrodes may be held in place by strips of surgical tape, plastic adhesive, or elastic bands. Commercial electrodes are of appropriate size and are conveniently attached with double-sided adhesive collars.

Ground Electrodes

A ground lead may not be necessary in SC or SP measurement if there is no interference present, for example, 60 Hz from room outlets. If artifact does occur, a ground electrode should be placed on an inactive site, on the same side of the body as active electrodes.

ANALYSIS OF EDA DATA

If one records directly in conductance units, three kinds of measures are possible: (a) the level of conductance (SCL) during a given period of time, (b) the number of conductance changes (SCR) during the same period, and (c) the magnitude of the SCR. The first and third measures will be micromhos, whereas the second will be based on the number of times a change of a given magnitude takes place. For example, if SCL is at 10 μmhos, a response may be defined as any change of 0.01 μmho or greater that occurs within a specified time, say, 1.3 to 2.5 seconds. The magnitude of the SCR can be treated as a percentage of SCL and thus be related to prestimulus baseline level.

When baseline changes occur, the pen may have to be reset by hand and the new SCL level recorded. If many SCRs occur, this constant resetting could be cumbersome. One way to solve this problem is to use automatic resetting or, alternatively, to feed the EDA data into two channels of the polygraph: one channel for baseline SCL and another for SCR. With this latter procedure, the gain for SCL is adjusted so that it is relatively insensitive to the SCRs regarded as significantly large. Some commercial devices provide automatic recentering when SCRs occur or when SCL extends beyond certain predetermined ranges. Contemporary devices that present SCL continuously in digital form are available. Although this is sufficient if information on SCL is desired, it is inadequate for SCR measures.

In the treatment of SP data, counts of the number of SPRs occurring in a given time period may be made. In addition, level of SP (mV) can be recorded directly on the ink-writer paper. The SPR measure is complicated by the fact that it has negative and positive components. Investigators commonly measure the degree of negativity and positivity of the waves (in mV) and the latencies of their occurrence. Edelberg (1972a) suggested that the magnitude of the positive response should be measured from the peak of the negative component to the peak of the positive wave (in mV) without regard to whether the baseline is crossed or not. Paper speeds of 15 mm/sec are suitable for observing baseline changes in SCL or SPL and the more rapid SCRs and and SPRs.

ELECTRODERMAL PHENOMENA AND BEHAVIOR

This section briefly reviews a number of areas in which EDA has been related to behavior and performance. Investigations in this area may be categorized in the following manner: reaction time, mental activity, positive and negative affect (emotional responses), motivation, signal detection, the orienting reaction, and conditoning of EDA. It will become obvious to the reader that SC is used much more frequently than SP by investigators seeking to relate EDA to behavior. Basically, this is because SC is easier to measure and offers fewer problems of interpretation than SP.

Reaction Time

One of the early studies of the relation between SCL and speed of reaction was conducted by Freeman (1940). He studied the RT of a single subject under various states of alertness, with the subject's condition ranging from half asleep to extremely tense. The results of 100 experimental sessions were recorded over a number of days, and Freeman found an inverted-U-shaped relation between SCL and RT, in which RT's were slower at high and low SCL levels and fastest at moderate levels. Freeman's result has often been mentioned in support of the activation concept, which describes the relation between level of physiological activity and performance as an inverted-U (e.g., Woodworth & Schlosberg, 1954). Schlosberg (1954) reported that Freeman's results had been duplicated with another subject, but a later study, using a greater number of subjects (Schlosberg & Kling, 1959), failed to replicate these findings. In a study by Andreassi (1966b), SCL was measured continuously as 16 persons reacted to a fixed number of "random" signals occurring over a 40-minute experimental period. Andreassi found evidence for the conclusion that at the highest SCL, RT is significantly faster than at moderate or low SCLs. Decreases in SCL over the course of the experimental session correlated significantly with a slowing of RT. The plotted results did not approach an inverted-U function; in fact, the relationship approached linearity, and it was suggested that this may have been due to a limited range of arousal in a situation where level of activity was not purposely manipulated.

Surwillo and Quilter (1965) measured RTs and SPRs of 132 healthy males, aged 22 to 85 years, in an hour-long vigilance situation. The subjects were required to monitor the movements of a clock pointer and to press a key as quickly as possible when it traveled through twice the usual distance. Those above the median in SPR production were termed "labiles" (mean of 2.27 SPRs), and those below were called "stabiles" (mean of .73 SPRs) in accordance with the terminology of Lacey and Lacey (1958). The RT for labiles (488 msec) was significantly shorter than that of stabiles (540 msec). This confirmed the hypothesis that autonomic labiles (those with a large number of spontaneous autonomic responses) would have faster RTs than stabiles.

Andreassi, Rapisardi, and Whalen (1969) measured SCL, SCRs, and heart rate while subjects detected critical signals that occurred at either fixed or variable intervals. Individuals were required to make responses, which required some effort, in order to have the opportunity to detect the signals. The results showed that SCL and SCRs were significantly higher when signals came at fixed intervals (30 seconds) than when they were variable (between 11 and 66 seconds). Further, RTs were significantly faster with regularly appearing signals. Records of responses made to detect signals showed typical "scalloping" patterns with fixed intervals and high steady rates with the variable signal schedules. The elevated EDA observed with fixed intervals was attributed to an increased readiness to respond when subjects could anticipate the occurrence of a signal. There was evidence for "directional fractionation" in the results (see chapter 15), because HR was lower under fixed signal schedules than for variable ones, whereas SCL was higher for the fixed signals.

The number of spontaneous SCRs that occurred during a 40-minute vigilance task was measured by Baugher (1975). The 36 male subjects were divided into low-arousal and high-arousal groups on the basis of the SCL value at the time of signal occurrence. The RTs to critical signals were found to be significantly faster for the high-arousal as compared to the low-arousal group. The author concluded that the direct relationship between SCRs and RT was expected (i.e., instead of an inverted-U function) because of the limited range of arousal conditions used. This was similar to the conclusion reached by Andreassi (1966b).

To summarize, it seems that faster RTs are associated with higher SCL. In addition, the number of spontaneous SPRs and SCRs is also related to speed of reaction, that is, a greater number of these responses being associated with faster RTs. Whether there is an inverted-U-shaped relation between SCL and RT, performance has not been established. Perhaps the subject's level of arousal (as indicated by EDA) must be actively manipulated by the experimenter to show this relationship.

MENTAL ACTIVITY AND ELECTRODERMAL PHENOMENA

Changes in electrodermal responses have been observed to occur while persons were involved in a variety of mental activities, including adding numbers, learning, and producing word associations. This section examines electrodermal activity during verbal learning, conditions of positive and negative affect (feeling), motivation, and relaxation.

Verbal Learning and EDA

In a relatively early study, Brown (1937) found that quickly learned words were accompanied by larger magnitude SCRs than those not learned as readily. Andreassi (1966a) required Navy enlisted men to learn three lists of nonsense syllables, on three successive days while SCL and heart rate were recorded. The lists had 100%, 53%, and 0% association values, corresponding to easy, moderately difficult, and difficult learning materials, respectively. He found that SCL and HR were significantly higher during the learning of the easy list as compared to the other two. The findings were interpreted in terms of greater subject involvement in the learning task when their performance was more successful. This conclusion was given some support from the performance of the only subject whose physiological responses did not vary with list difficulty. This subject's learning was uniformly poor, regardless of list difficulty level, and, in addition, he was the only person to fall asleep during the 2-minute rest periods between lists!

Lists of eight high-arousal words (e.g., vomit) and eight low-arousal words (e.g., swim) were presented to 40 male and 40 female students (Maltzman, Kantor, & Langdon, 1966). They were asked to listen to these words while EDA was recorded, and were told that the physiological correlates of relaxation were being measured. The investigators reported that the high-arousal words produced significantly larger SCRs than the low-arousal words. Further, retention tests administered after all the items had been presented revealed that the subjects could remember more of the high-arousal words. Maltzman and his associates hypothesized that the SCRs were evidence that orienting responses (OR) occurred, and that the OR facilitated the reception of words and their retention.

A number of physiological measures including SCL, SCRs, and heart rate (HR) were obtained during verbal learning in a study by Andreassi and Whalen (1967). In a first experiment, after lists of materials were learned to perfection, the same material was presented for 20 overlearning trials. The overlearning phase was accompanied by significant decreases in all of the physiological measures. However, when a new list was presented subsequent to overlearning, there were increases in SCL, SCRs, and HR. In a second experiment, the initial learning phase was followed by two overlearning sessions with the same list. This time, all three measures showed progressive decreases during the first and then the second overlearning phase. The results indicated that new learning, perhaps because of the novelty of the situation and the materials to be learned, produced the highest levels of physiological activity. Overlearning, because of stimulus and situational habituation, led to significant decreases in activity.

The results of a number of studies have implicated SCL as a useful measure of arousal in short-term memory (STM) tasks. It is believed that EDA may reflect the registration of stimuli in central (brain) areas, just as it seems to indicate stimulus reception as part of the OR to novel stimuli. Yuille and Hare (1980) monitored SC and HR during a STM task. Subjects were required to recall words after 15 sec. of interference. When the best and poorest trials were compared, they found that optimal performance was associated with the largest increases in SC and HR. The researchers interpreted these results in terms of the roles of attention and effort (as indicated by physiological response) in short-term memory.

To briefly summarize, studies of EDA and verbal learning indicate that more successful learning, in general, tends to be associated with greater amounts of activity. The higher levels of EDA are associated with increased alertness and effort when individuals are involved in the acquisition of novel materials. This same process is implicated in respect to SCL in short-term memory tasks. Electrodermal activity has been identified as an important component of the orienting response to novel stimuli, an area that is covered later in this chapter.

Positive and Negative Affect and EDA

Affect refers to subjective feelings roughly related to like or dislike of objects, people, or events, that is, feelings that produce an emotional reaction. Music is an example of a type of stimulus that can produce an affective response. The effects of three types of music on the SCR and HR of 18 college students were investigated by Zimny and Weidenfeller (1963). These pieces had been previously judged to be exciting, neutral, and calming by 59 other students. Selected 6-minute portions of Dvorak's *New World Symphony,* Chopin's *Les Sylphides,* and Bach's *Air for the G String* were judged as exciting, neutral, and calming, respectively. Significant SCRs occurred in response to the exciting music but not to the calming or the neutral pieces. No HR changes were observed as a function of music played. The authors interpreted the SCR results as indicating that different kinds of music produce differential EDA, and that this reflects emotional responsivity.

The interpretation that a subject is encouraged to use with respect to observed violence appeared to influence SCRs in a study by Geen and Rakosky (1973). The subjects were 55 male undergraduates whose SCRs were measured while they viewed a prize fight sequence from the film *Champion.* The showing of the film was preceded by narratives that described events leading to the 6-minute fight scene. The narratives depicted the sequence as aggression, vengeance, or fictional vengeance. In the introductory remarks relating to fictional vengeance, subjects were reminded that the fight was not real and that the injuries were only makeup. The greatest number of SCRs were observed following the aggression narratives, whereas significantly fewer SCRs occurred after the remarks emphasizing the fictional (make-believe) aspects of the fight scene. The interpretations offered by Geen and Rakosky suggest that by emphasizing the fictional aspects of the fight scene, the subjects were able to dissociate the observed violence from their own lives.

The effects of erotic and neutral stimuli on SCR, HR, and subjective ratings of 52 females were studied by Hamrick (1974). The erotic stimuli (slides of nude males) resulted in significant increases in SCR and decreases in HR. The changes in SCR and HR to the nude males were accompanied by subjective ratings that indicated sexual arousal and positive affective reactions. The decreased HR is consistent with the work of Lacey, Kagan, Lacey, and Moss (1963), in which HR deceleration was found to accompany situations in which subjects "take in" perceptual materials.

Lanzetta, Cartwright-Smith, and Kleck (1976) tested Darwin's assertion that freely expressing an emotion will intensify the emotional experience, whereas suppressing it will lead to a reduction of experienced intensity. In a series of experiments, subjects were asked to either conceal or exaggerate facial expressions associated with the anticipated reception of electric shocks. It was found that suppression of expressive responses led to smaller SCRs and lower pain ratings than when exaggeration of the emotional response was required. They interpreted these results as supporting hypotheses regarding the role of nonverbal displays of emotion in regulating the emotional experience itself, as well as serving a social-communicative function. Darwin's hypothesis was also supported, suggesting that a "cool" response to an emotional situation could aid in preventing reactions from spiraling out of control. The fact that these results were contrary to the "discharge model of emotion" was explained as being due to the short-term, experimentally manipulated control of emotional expression. The discharge model predicts that active facial display of emotionality reduces physiological response to emotionally arousing situations. Support for this model was obtained by Notarius and Levenson (1979), who divided subjects into natural "expressers" or "inhibiters," based on unconstrained facial expressions to a stressful film. The more naturally expressive subjects were less physiologically reactive to an emotional stressor than nonexpressive persons, as shown by SC and HR measures. The researchers suggest that the differential physiological responding may be related to personality and cognitive style of expressive versus inhibited persons. In any event, it must be recognized that natural expressive tendencies cannot be equated with experimentally manipulated emotional displays in studies of this type.

Interactions between mothers and babies play an important role in the formation of attachment and in determining maternal response to the infant's signals. There is research evidence that breast-feeding mothers differ from bottle feeders in satisfaction with the feeding experience, in acceptance of the maternal role, and emotional investment in the infant. Wiesenfeld, Malatesta, Whitman, Granrose, and Uili (1985) carried this line of investigation one step further by examining the physiological responses of breast- and bottle-feeding mothers to their infants' signals. The mothers viewed videotapes of their own infants' emotional expressions (smiling, crying, and neutral) while SC and HR were measured. Also obtained were subjective ratings of desire to pick up the infant during the viewing episode. The bottle-feeders showed higher resting EDA and more extreme HR accelerations during viewing videotapes of their infant's emotional signals. Bottle-feeders reported less desire to pick up their infants than nursing mothers. The finding that nursing mothers were apparently more relaxed in the laboratory situation may be related to pre-existing differences in personality or attitudes. Another possibility is that maternal hormones associated with lactation may act to lower general arousal, as reflected in lower physiological responsivity, greater relaxation during feeding, and greater satisfaction during feeding reported by nursing mothers.

In summary, it appears that EDA can serve as an index of affective value of stimuli for a subject. This would seem to be true both for nonverbal stimuli (music, film sequence) and for emotionally tinged words. The findings of Lanzetta et al. (1976) may have important implications for the study and control of various types of emotional behavior, and should be pursued further. The work of Notarius and Levenson points up the importance of considering how the emotional expression is obtained (manipulated or naturally occurring) in predicting EDA effects. Physiological variables offer potential in differentiating responses of breast- and bottle-feeding mothers to infants' emotional signals.

Motivation and SCR Recovery Time

An additional measure of SC, called *SCR recovery rate,* was introduced by Edelberg (1970). It is used with exosomatic measures of EDA, and is based on the time it takes for SC to return to a level midway between the peak of the response and its initial level. Edelberg (1970, 1972b) has related this recovery rate, also called recovery half-time, to the degree to which a subject is goal-oriented. That is, the half-time recovery is faster under conditions of goal-oriented activity than under other conditions of arousal. For example, recovery times are faster when a subject is involved in a mirror-tracing task as compared to resting with eyes open. Edelberg (1972b) concluded that the measure is stable over time, and that it is related to relative quality of performance of an individual. Waid (1974) obtained results that supported those of Edelberg in that electrodermal recovery rate was faster during goal-oriented activity than during less directed behavior. The finding that recovery rate was slower during a timed arithmetic task, as compared to a verbal RT task was interpreted as being similar to previous findings in which recovery time was slower when electric shock was threatened. However, the independence of SCR recovery time from other measures was questioned by Bundy (1974). His data showed that when an SCR was preceded by a high degree of electrodermal activity, there was a tendency for

SCR recovery time to be faster than when preceded by less ongoing EDA. Edelberg and Muller (1981) obtained data that confirmed Bundy's result. They noted that although SCR recovery time may not provide unique information, it has been useful in differentiating responses to stimuli and levels of performance. However, some EDA researchers argue that it is still appropriate to treat SCR recovery time as an independent variable (e.g., see Venables & Fletcher, 1981; Janes, 1982).

These studies of SCR recovery rate and goal orientation provide another way of analyzing EDA and correlating it with performance, as well as providing information about EDA correlates of motivation. There is some debate about the independence of SCR recovery time as a measure, but it has been found useful in a variety of investigations. The finding that this measure of EDA is related to degree of task involvement corresponds to earlier findings of Andreassi (1966a), who suggested a similar relationship for SCL and performance.

Signal Detection and EDA

In a previous section, we discussed EDA associated with RT to detected signals. In this section, we examine some studies that have related EDA to efficiency or accuracy of signal detection in vigilance-type situations. In a study by Surwillo and Quilter (1965), the number of SPRs that occurred within the 18-second period before the critical signal was significantly greater for detected signals than for missed signals.

Various measures were studied (i.e., SCL, HR, and neck EMG) during a vigilance task that required subjects to attend to a flashing light and to report when it stayed on longer than usual (Eason, Beardshall, & Jaffee, 1965). The most consistent finding was that during the course of a vigil, performance and SCL decreased significantly. Eason and colleagues interpreted the decreased SCL as representing a drop in SNS activity, which in turn was due to the drowsiness-producing effects of the experimental situation.

Krupski, Raskin, and Bakan (1971) measured SCL while 31 persons performed a vigilance task. The investigators were interested in the number of commission errors, that is, responding in the absence of a signal, and its relation to EDA. They found that subjects who had large-amplitude SCRs when they detected a signal made fewer commission errors than those who had small detection-related SCRs. The larger SCRs were interpreted in terms of greater attention level, which resulted in superior vigilance performance. In addition, subjects who had large orienting responses (defined as the SCR amplitude to the first signal) also made fewer commission errors, a finding that would support the conclusion regarding attention level and vigilance performance.

If a signal is presented repeatedly, the SCR will decrease in amplitude, a result ascribed to habituation of response to the signal. Research has shown that persons whose SCRs habituate slowly are superior in auditory vigilance performance, because they detect more signals and show less decline in detection over time. Vossel and Rossmann (1984) extended these findings to a vigilance study that employed a complex visual monitoring task. Their slow habituators detected more signals than fast habituators. One explanation attributes the result to basic arousal differences between the groups, whereas another suggests differential sensitivity to stimuli. The question remains to be resolved through further work.

In an interesting approach, Nishimura and Nagumo (1985) used data concerning SPL and signal detection to influence vigilance performance. During their study, a bell sounded when SPLs decreased to preset levels. This procedure alerted their subjects and avoided performance decrements. Electrodermal activity was used in a different type of signal detection by Tranel, Fowles, and Damasio (1985). College students observed 50 slides that included 42 unfamiliar faces and 8 familiar ones (famous people). The SCRs to the familiar faces were reliably greater, indicating that significance of the "signal" had an impact on autonomic response even though no verbal report was required. The authors hope to use these basic procedures to study prosopagnosia, a neurological disorder in which humans lose the ability to recognize faces.

The studies briefly reviewed in this segment indicate that higher levels of skin conductance, greater numbers of SPRs, and slower habituation of SCRs are associated with superior signal detection. Krupski et al. (1971) interpreted this type of finding in terms of higher levels of attention (reflected in EDA), which led to more efficient detection. Other possible explanations involve greater arousal and sensitivity to stimuli indicated by EDA.

THE ORIENTING RESPONSE AND EDA

In his book *Attention, Arousal and the Orientation Reaction,* Lynn (1966) detailed a variety of physiological changes that occur when an organism is presented with a novel stimulus. Among these are pupil dilation, increased EMG activity, increased frequency, and lower amplitude EEG, increase in amplitude and decrease in frequency of respiration, a slowing of heart rate, and changes in EDA. Berlyne (1960) categorized stimuli that have the potential to elicit the OR as follows: novelty, intensity, color, meaning, surprise, complexity, incongruity, and conflict. Sokolov (1963) has presented a theory of the OR in which incoming stimuli are compared with representations of past stimuli that reside in the cortex of the brain. If a stimulus is novel, that is, if it does not match any of the existing "neuronal models," an orienting response occurs. If the incoming stimulus is familiar, it matches a model in the cortex, and the orienting reaction does not occur. Hence, in Sokolov's theory, the match or mismatch between stimulus properties (degree of novelty) is the critical factor in producing an OR. There are a large number of studies in which EDA correlates of the OR have been studied. Many of these have dealt with issues raised by Sokolov's theory. Some researchers have confirmed and refined aspects of Sokolov's approach, whereas others have proposed modifications. Only a few of these are presented here to give a flavor of the type of research in this area and the usefulness of EDA in OR research.

Bernstein (1969) habituated subjects to a given stimulus intensity and found that the OR (indicated by SCR frequency) was greater when the stimulus was changed to a greater intensity than when the change involved lowering the intensity. He concluded that the direction of stimulus change was an important variable in eliciting the OR, after the original OR had been habituated. Bernstein hypothesized that increased stimulus intensity might signify "something approaching the organism" (p. 128), and that this could lead to a more intense OR. This hypothesis was confirmed by Bernstein, Taylor, Austen, Nathanson, and Scarpelli (1971), who measured SCRs in a situation where patterned visual stimuli were stationary or appeared to move either toward or away from the individuals tested. Frequency and amplitude of SCRs were greater under apparent motion than with the stationary perceptual condition. Further, physiological changes were more prolonged when objects appeared to approach than when they appeared to recede. These results indicated to the authors that the onset of movement in the visual field is associated with a momentary increase in perceptual receptivity. In addition, stimuli that move toward a person are more significant that those that move away, as indicated by the respective ORs.

The hypothesis that an OR to stimulus change can attenuate a subsequent OR to a second stimulus change was examined by Maltzman, Harris, Ingram, and Wolff (1971). This hypothesis was confirmed with a group of 96 subjects who experienced the two stimulus changes at 5-, 10-, or 30-second intervals. In addition, Maltzman and colleagues noted that the magnitude of the SCR was greater when the stimulus change was an increase in illumination as opposed to a decrease, a similar finding to that of Bernstein (1969) for auditory stimuli. Yaremko, Blair, and Leckart (1970) examined the OR (magnitude of SCR) as a function of degree of deviation from an expected stimulus. The numbers 10 through 19 were presented serially to subjects. On the next trial (when 20 should have been presented), the numbers 31, 21, 19, or 9 were delivered. Therefore, the critical number was either 1 or 11 places out of sequence in either the positive or negative direction. The SCR magnitude was related to degree of discrepancy between the expected and the observed number, that is, the 11-unit discrepancies produced larger SCRs than the smaller ones, regardless of direction. The results were interpreted as supporting Sokolov's (1963) hypothesis that OR magnitude depends on the amount of stimulus change.

The effects of repeatedly imagining a stimulus on habituation of the OR was studied by Yaremko, Glanville, and Leckart (1972). Subjects who imagined hearing a tone showed greater habituation of the SCR component of the OR to a 500-Hz tone when compared to subjects who imagined seeing a light or those in a control group. The habituation rate did not differ from that of subjects who had previously received 10 trials with a 500-Hz tone. It was suggested that the imagery process aided in the formation of a "neuronal model" (Sokolov, 1963) and facilitated habituation. According to Sokolov's theory, the repeated imagery of a tone primed the formation of a neuronal model of the stimulus, and the partially formed model functioned to inhibit the OR. Similar results were found for the sense of touch; Yaremko and Butler (1975) reported that imagining electric shocks prior to receiving actual shocks resulted in decreased SCRs.

Siddle and Heron (1978) used SCR magnitude, HR, and finger pulse volume (FPV) to test OR to a change in tonal frequency. Following habituation to a 1000-Hz tone at 70 db intensity, new tones of either 670 Hz or 380 Hz (both 70 db) were presented to subjects. Significant changes in all measures occurred to changes in auditory stimulus frequency. The results were contrary to O'Gorman's (1973) contention that the OR is only sensitive to changes in stimulus intensity or modality. In addition, SCR magnitude was significantly larger to the greater degree of stimulus change (i.e., with 380 Hz as compared to 670 Hz). The HR and FPV measures did not vary as a function of degree of difference between training (habituated) and test (new) stimuli. Hence, EDA was the most sensitive OR component to changes in tonal frequency.

A. S. Bernstein and I. Maltzman, two of the researchers mentioned earlier, have sought to expand the OR theory advanced by Sokolov to include cognitive activity of the individual. Recall that Sokolov stressed the match–mismatch of stimuli to neuronal models as the critical factor in producing the OR. Bernstein (1979) and Maltzman (1979) have argued that stimulus significance, as well as novelty, is important in eliciting the OR. Bernstein emphasized that an interaction between stimulus uncertainty and significance triggers the OR. Maltzman believes that a "cortical set," present prior to the presentation of experimental events, influences the OR to stimuli. This set may be a relatively short-lived disposition due to task instructions, or it may be a long-standing disposition already important in determining significance and selective orienting to stimuli. As an example of a study examining the effects of pre-existing set on the OR, Wingard and Maltzman (1980) found that recreational interests influenced selective orienting. Participants were selected from among members of three university clubs: surfing, chess, and fishing. Students showed significantly larger SCRs to slides depicting their recreational interest as compared to other recreations and neutral slides. The findings were interpreted as support for the notion that prior experiences establish a dominant focus or cortical set for certain events and not others. Thus, in the case of recreational interests, it is familiar stimuli that lead to an OR, not unfamiliar ones as proposed by Sokolov.

In a critical article, O'Gorman (1979) questioned the need for a revision of OR theory in the first place, and, in the second place, he questioned the adequacy of the revisions proposed by Maltzman and Bernstein. Both Bernstein (1979) and Maltzman (1979) made very thoughtful replies to O'Gorman that highlight some of the important issues in contemporary OR theory. The interested reader would do well to consult these papers. In the meantime, experimental work continues on the issues. Maltzman, Gould, Pendery, and Wolff (1982) showed that task instructions (short-term set) resulted in different rates of OR habituation as indicated by magnitude of SCRs. Some earlier results obtained by Bernstein et al. (1971) were not repeated by Fredrikson, Berggren, Wanko, and von Scheele (1984). Perceptions of an auditory stimulus as moving toward or away from a subject did not influence habituation or dishabituation (return of responding) to the OR. Recall, however, that Bernstein and colleagues used visual stimuli. Fredrikson and coworkers also observed that changing, as compared to constant stimuli, elicited ORs that habituated more slowly, a finding that is generally supportive of Sokolov.

In another approach, Ohman (1979) has proposed an information-processing model of the OR that combines Sokolov's notions with constructs derived from contemporary work in attention and memory. Namely, Ohman proposed that an OR is produced when an incoming stimulus fails to find a match in short-term memory (memory function that holds items for a number of seconds). The mismatch results in a search in long-term memory (LTM), and this cognitive effort results in registration of the novel stimulus in LTM. The processing facilitates later retrieval of the stimulus, but results in inhibition of the OR, because a match between the stimulus and memory trace is made. In a study that bears on Ohman's theory, Plouffe and Stelmack (1984) studied the OR to picture stimuli during the study phase of a free-recall task. Young and elderly female subjects had larger SCRs to recalled pictures, especially to recall of uncommon ones. In habituation trials, pictures that were not recalled produced smaller SCRs than pictures not shown in the study phase. This was taken as evidence for "stimulus priming", that is, the inhibition of the OR that occurs when a match between a stimulus and its memory trace is made. The authors conclude that the results support Ohman's proposals about the role of cognitive effort in encoding incoming stimuli, and the dependence of novel stimulus recall on production of the OR. They also suggest that the age decrement in recall may be due to a reduction of cognitive effort on the part of elderly persons.

In a warning-stimulus, imperative-stimulus paradigm reminiscent of the paradigm used to elicit the CNV (see chapter 7), it was found that OR activity in the WS–IS interval is sensitive to task demands (Spinks, Blowers, & Shek, 1985). The largest SCRs that occurred 1 to 5 sec after the WS were in response to the most informative warning stimuli, whereas those that occurred 5 to 9 sec after were responsive to only partially informative WS. According to Spinks and colleagues, the nature of the SCRs occurring in different time frames supports those theorists who see the OR as part of a process that prepares the person to be receptive to future stimulation. They also suggested that the role of the OR is one that generally facilitates information processing.

In summary, EDA has proven to be a useful physiological indicator in experimentation on the nature of the OR. Frequency and amplitude of SCRs are affected by changes in stimulus direction. Perceived approach of visual stimuli produced larger magnitude ORs. Magnitude of conceptual deviation and imagery have been related to magnitude of SCRs and tendency of the OR to habituate, respectively, in support of Sokolov. The EDA measure of OR also indicates that it can vary with changes in stimulus quality as well as intensity. The influence of both long-term and short-term dispositions (set) on the OR have been demonstrated. Effects of cognitive effort and the role of the OR in preparing for future stimulation are promising areas for exploration. Attempts to expand Sokolov's OR theory have resulted in some controversy, but have also stimulated new work on some of the issues. On the whole, it is obvious that Sokolov's OR theory is useful, but it requires revision to accommodate findings regarding such influences as long- and short-term set and cognitive effort.

CONDITIONING AND ELECTRODERMAL ACTIVITY

In the well-known Pavlovian classical conditioning paradigm, a conditioned stimulus (CS) eventually leads to a conditioned response (CR) after it has been paired with an unconditioned stimulus (UCS) a sufficient number of times. Thus, in the final stages of conditioning, salivation (CR) occurs to the sound of a bell (CS). The classical conditioning of EDA and of other autonomic responses (e.g., HR) has been an extensively studied phenomenon with both animal and human subjects. Edelberg (1972a) pointed out that because of the well-defined nature of SCRs and SPRs, they serve well as the CR, because it is often possible to distinguish them from the orienting response to the CS. A wide variety of unconditioned stimuli have been used in the classical conditioning of EDA in humans. Some examples are white noise, electric shock, a puff of air, and sexually arousing stimuli (Prokasy & Kumpfer, 1973). A good UCS must produce effective ANS activation, and it should habituate slowly.

In the instrumental conditioning paradigm, the subject must emit some kind of response to obtain a reinforcement. The response is not defined for the subject, and in the case of EDA the required response might be an increase in the rate of SCRs. At one time, it was believed that ANS responses could not be instrumentally conditioned. However, there is now considerable evidence that some degree of instrumental conditioning can be demonstrated with EDA (Kimmel, 1973). Some reinforcers that have been used in the instrumental conditioning of EDA include pleasant odors, lights presented to subjects in a dark room, lights or sounds that indicated monetary rewards, pictures of nude women presented to male subjects, and cool air for persons in a hot and humid chamber (Kimmel & Gurucharri, 1975).

Classical Conditioning of EDA

A discussion of a variety of independent variables that have been manipulated in studies of electrodermal conditioning has been presented by Prokasy and

Kumpfer (1973). Some of these variables include the effects of interstimulus interval on the magnitude of the conditioned EDA, percentage of reinforced trials, and the modality of the CS (e.g., light or sound). Successful EDA conditioning has been observed to occur in a variety of experimental conditions. Complex variables in the classical conditioning situation were examined in a review by Grings and Dawson (1973). These included the effects of instructional variables, for example, regarding the CS–UCS relation, and individual differences, for example, the effects of age, sex, and intelligence on the classical conditioning of EDA. Because the classical conditioning of EDA has been presented in detail elsewhere (Prokasy & Kumpfer, 1973; Grings & Dawson, 1973), only a few sample experiments are presented here.

Prokasy, Williams, and Clark (1975) tested the hypothesis derived from Pavlov's (1927) work that if a CS is greater than or equal to the intensity of a UCS, then conditioning to that CS should not occur. The amplitude and probability of SCRs were used as the criteria of conditioning. The results indicated that conditioning was obtained even when the CS was greater in intensity than the UCS, thus refuting Pavlov's hypothesis. No difference in the amount of conditioning was associated with either CS or UCS intensity. Verbal conditioning of EDA is an established phenomenon. For example, if subjects are informed that a UCS (electric shock) will follow a tone CS, a large SCR is observed at the first presentation of the CS, before it has been paired with the UCS. This result was long thought to be due to anxiety produced by the expected unpleasant experience. However, Pendery and Maltzman (1979) showed that similar verbal conditioning could be produced by an innocuous CS (tone) serving as a warning signal in a RT situation. These types of results can be taken as indicating the important of cognitive factors in human conditioning.

In an interesting approach, Ohman and Dimberg (1978) used different facial expressions as the CS in an experiment where electric shock was the UCS. As they predicted, angry faces produced greater resistance to extinction than happy or neutral faces. Presumably, the angry faces produced a greater affective reaction in the subjects, and thereby the conditioned EDA did not extinguish as quickly. In a follow-up study, Dimberg and Ohman (1983) examined the effects of directing the angry faces towards or away from subjects. The recorded SCRs revealed that angry facial expressions gave conditioning effects that were resistant to extinction only if they were directed toward the observer. Perhaps the results indicate the importance of the eyes and head orientation in social communication.

It has been established that multiple SCRs occur in conditioning experiments where the time interval between CS and UCS is long, especially with an unpleasant UCS. The flurry of responses early in the interval has been related to the OR, whereas later ones are associated with preparation for the UCS. Backs and Grings (1985) varied UCS probability in studying EDAs during a long CS–UCS interval. The probabilities of the UCS (loud noise) occurring were .17, .50, or

.83, and the interval was 8 seconds. Both magnitude and frequency of early SCRs (first 4 seconds after the CS) increased as a function of UCS probability. The authors suggested that preparation for a more likely aversive event resulted in greater amounts of EDA early in the CS–UCS interval. If this is true, then both orienting and preparation would be attributed to the early part of the interval.

Instrumental Conditioning of EDA

Much of the experimental work on the instrumental conditioning of EDA has been reviewed by Kimmel (1973). Basically, the review indicates that EDA, for example, the frequency or magnitude of SCRs, will be increased or decreased when the delivery of some reinforcement is contingent upon this response. The reinforcement may involve either the presentation of some pleasant stimulus (e.g., monetary reward) or the avoidance of some unpleasant stimulus (e.g., electric shock). The review by Kimmel will serve the student who desires more detail about this topic.

An example of a study that explored the instrumental conditioning of EDA was one conducted by Kimmel and Gurucharri (1975). Two groups of 20 subjects each were placed in a hot (115 deg. F), humid (100% humidity) chamber while SCRs were measured. The first group of 20 experimental subjects received cool air whenever an SCR was emitted. As the experimental session progressed, the number of SCRs increased, indicating that the cool air was an effective reinforcer for producing the SCR. Twenty control subjects, who were individually matched with each experimental subject on the basis of pre-experimental level of spontaneously produced SCRs, were then tested under the same conditions. Each control subject then received cool air at the same time, based on the record of when his or her matched experimental subject received the SCR contingent reinforcement. Thus, both groups received the same number of cool air presentations, but the control group's rewards were not contingent on producing a SCR. Nevertheless, the control group showed an increase in unelicited SCRs, although not at the same accelerating rate as the experimental subjects. Detailed examination of the SCR records of the controls indicated that they coincidentally received cool air with 38% of their SCRs, and this accounted for their increased rate of SCR production. The researchers further noted that the SCR responses of the experimental subjects resembled results from traditional instrumental conditioning studies more closely than any previously conducted SCR investigation.

In summary, the classical conditioning of EDA has been achieved under a variety of experimental conditions. Similarly, there is evidence that instrumental conditioning of EDA is possible with a variety of reinforcers. However, the effects of subjective thoughts, or cognitive mediation, have not been clearly delineated in instrumental EDA conditioning paradigms. Some investigators (e.g., Shean, 1970; Stern, 1970; Stern & Kaplan, 1967) have suggested that cognitive mediation plays a role in EDA conditioning. For example, a subject might find that a certain type of thought (e.g., a favorite activity) is related to receiving cool air, whereas, in actuality, it was the SCR produced by the arousing thought that resulted in delivery of the reinforcement. Therefore, it may be that the number of SCR-producing thoughts are increased rather than a subject's ability to influence sweat gland activity. This possibility must be investigated.

The next chapter considers two different peripheral responses, both involving the eyes. The student may be surprised to learn that a wide variety of behavioral states and activities have been associated with changes in pupil diameter and eye movements.

REFERENCES

Andreassi, J. L. (1966a). Some physiological correlates of verbal learning task difficulty. *Psychonomic Science, 6,* 69–70.

Andreassi, J. L. (1966b). Skin-conductance and reaction-time in a continuous auditory monitoring task. *American Journal of Psychology, 79,* 470–474.

Andreassi, J. L., & Whalen, P. M. (1967). Some physiological correlates of learning and over-learning. *Psychophysiology, 3,* 406–413.

Andreassi, J. L., Rapisardi, S. C., & Whalen, P. M. (1969). Autonomic responsivity and reaction time under fixed and variable signal schedules. *Psychophysiology, 6,* 58–69.

Backs, R. W., & Grings, W. W. (1985). Effects of UCS probability on the contingent negative variation and electrodermal response during long ISI conditioning. *Psychophysiology, 22,* 269–275.

Baugher, D. M. (1975). An examination of the nonspecific skin resistance response. *Bulletin of the Psychonomic Society, 6,* 254–256.

Berlyne, D. E. (1960). *Conflict, arousal and curiosity.* New York: McGraw-Hill.

Bernstein, A. S. (1969). The orienting response and direction of stimulus change. *Psychonomic Science, 112,* 127–128.

Bernstein, A. S. (1979). The orienting reflex as novelty and significance detector. *Psychophysiology, 16,* 263–273.

Bernstein, A. S., Taylor, K., Austen, B. G., Nathanson, M., & Scarpelli, A. (1971). Orienting response and apparent movement toward or away from the observer. *Journal of Experimental Psychology, 84,* 37–45.

Brown, C. H. (1937). The relation of magnitude of galvanic skin responses and resistance levels to the rate of learning. *Journal of Experimental Psychology, 20,* 262–278.

Bundy, R. S. (1974). The influence of previous responses on the skin conductance recovery limb. (Abstract) *Psychophysiology, 11,* 221–222.

Darrow, C. W. (1933). The functional significance of the galvanic skin reflex and perspiration on the backs a.·d palms of the hands. *Psychological Bulletin, 30,* 712.

Dimberg, U., & Ohman, A. (1983). The effects of directional facial cues on electrodermal conditioning to facial stimuli. *Psychophysiology, 20,* 160–167.

Eason, R. G., Beardshall, A., & Jaffee, S. (1965). Performance and physiological indicants of activation in a vigilance situation. *Perceptual & Motor Skills, 20,* 3–13.

Edelberg, R. (1967). Electrical properties of the skin. In C. C. Brown (Ed.), *Methods in psychophysiology* (pp. 1–53). Baltimore: Williams & Wilkins.

Edelberg, R. (1970). The information content of the recovery limb of the electrodermal response. *Psychophysiology, 6,* 527–539.

Edelberg, R. (1972a). Electrical activity of the skin. In N. S. Greenfield & R. A. Sternbach (Eds.), *Handbook of psychophysiology* (pp. 367–418). New York: Holt, Rinehart & Winston.

Edelberg, R. (1972b). Electrodermal recovery rate, goal-orientation and aversion. *Psychophysiology, 9,* 512–520.

Edelberg, R., & Muller, M. (1981). Prior activity as a determinant of electrodermal recovery rate. *Psychophysiology, 18,* 17–25.

Edelberg, R., & Wright, D. J. (1962, October). *Two GSR effector organs and their stimulus specificity.* Paper presented at the meeting of the Society for Psychophysiological Research, Denver, CO.

Fowles, D. C. (1986). The eccrine system and electrodermal activity: In M. G. H. Coles, E. Donchin, & S. W. Porges (Eds.), *Psychophysiology: Systems, processes and applications* (pp. 51–96). New York: Guilford Press.

Fredrikson, M., Berggren, T., Wanko, G., & von Scheele, B. (1984). Habituation and dishabituation of the orienting reaction to between and within trial changes in pitch and loudness. *Psychophysiology, 21,* 219–227.

Freeman, G. L. (1940). The relationship between performance level and bodily activity level. *Journal of Experimental Psychology, 26,* 602–608.

Geen, R. G., & Rakosky, J. J. (1973). Interpretations of observed aggression and their effect on GSR. *Journal of Experimental Research in Personality, 6,* 280–292.

Grings, W. W., & Dawson, M. E. (1973). Complex variables in conditioning. In W. F. Prokasy & D. C. Raskin (Eds.), *Electrodermal activity in psychological research* (pp. 203–254). New York: Academic Press.

Hamrick, N. D. (1974). Physiological and verbal responses to erotic visual stimuli in a female population. *Behavioral Engineering, 2,* 9–16.

Jacob, S. W., & Francone, C. A. (1970). *Structure and function in man.* Philadelphia: Saunders.

Janes, C. L. (1982). Electrodermal recovery and stimulus significance. *Psychophysiology, 19,* 129–135.

Kimmel, H. D. (1973). Instrumental conditioning. In W. F. Prokasy & D. C. Raskin (Eds.), *Electrodermal activity in psychological research* (pp. 255–282). New York: Academic Press.

Kimmel, H. D., & Gurucharri, F. W. (1975). Operant GSR conditioning with cool air reinforcement. *Pavlovian Journal of Biological Science, 10,* 239–245.

Krupski, A., Raskin, D. C., & Bakan, P. (1971). Physiological and personality correlates of commission errors in an auditory vigilance task. *Psychophysiology, 8,* 304–311.

Lacey, J. I., Kagan, J., Lacey, B. C., & Moss, H. A. (1963). The visceral level: Situational determinants and behavioral correlates of autonomic response patterns. In P. H. Knapp (Ed.), *Expression of the emotions in man* (pp. 161–196). New York: International University Press.

Lacey, J. I., & Lacey, B. C. (1958). The relationship of resting autonomic activity to motor impulsivity. In J. I. Lacey & B. C. Lacey (Eds.), *The brain and human behavior* (pp. 144–209). Baltimore: Williams & Wilkins.

Lanzetta, J. T., Cartwright-Smith, J., & Kleck, R. E. (1976). Effects on non-verbal dissimulation on emotional experience and autonomic arousal. *Journal of Personality and Social Psychology, 33,* 354–370.

Lykken, D. T., & Venables, P. H. (1971). Direct measurement of skin conductance: A proposal for standardization. *Psychophysiology, 8,* 656–671.

Lynn, R. (1966). *Attention, arousal and the orientation reaction.* Oxford: Pergamon Press.

Maltzman, I. (1979). Orienting reflexes and significance: A reply to O'Gorman. *Psychophysiology, 16,* 274–282.

Maltzman, I., Gould, J., Pendery, M., & Wolff, C. (1982). Task instructions as a determiner of the GSR index of the orienting reflex. *Physiological Psychology, 10,* 235–238.

Maltzman, I., Harris, L., Ingram, E., & Wolff, C. (1971). A primacy effect in the orienting reflex to stimulus change. *Journal of Experimental Psychology, 87,* 202–206.

Maltzman, I., Kantor, W., & Langdon, B. (1966). Immediate and delayed retention, arousal, and the orienting and defensive reflexes. *Psychonomic Science, 6,* 445–446.

Neumann, E., & Blanton, R. (1970). The early history of electrodermal research. *Psychophysiology, 6,* 453–475.

Nishimura, C., & Nagumo, J. (1985). Feedback control of the level of arousal using skin potential level as an index. *Ergonomics, 28,* 905–913.

Notarius, C. I., & Levenson, R. W. (1979). Expressive tendencies and physiological response to stress. *Journal of Personality and Social Psychology, 37,* 1204–1210.

O'Gorman, J. G. (1973). Change in stimulus conditions and the orienting response. *Psychophysiology, 10,* 465–470.

O'Gorman, J. G. (1979). The orienting reflex: Novelty or significance detector? *Psychophysiology, 16,* 253–262.

Ohman, A. (1979). The orienting response, attention and learning: An information processing perspective. In H. D. Kimmel, E. H. Van Olst, & J. F. Orlebecke (Eds.), *The orienting reflex in humans* (pp. 443–471). Hillsdale, NJ: Lawrence Erlbaum Association.

Ohman, A., & Dimberg, U. (1978). Facial expressions as conditioned stimuli for electrodermal responses: A case of preparedness? *Journal of Personality & Social Psychology, 36,* 1251–1258.

Pavlov, I. P. (1927). *Conditioned reflexes* (G. V. Anrep, Trans.). London: Oxford University Press. (Original work published 1927).

Pendery, M., & Maltzman, I. (1979). Verbal conditioning and extinction of the GSR index of the orienting reflex. *Physiological Psychology, 7,* 185–192.

Plouffe, L., & Stelmack, R. M. (1984). The electrodermal orienting response and memory: An analysis of age differences in picture recall. *Psychophysiology, 21,* 191–198.

Prokasy, W. F., & Kumpfer, K. L. (1973). Classical conditioning. In W. F. Prokasy & D. C. Raskin (Eds.), *Electrodermal activity in psychological research* (pp. 157–202). New York: Academic Press.

Prokasy, W. F., Williams, W. C., & Clark, L. G. (1975). Skin conductance response conditioning with CS intensities equal to and greater than UCS intensity. *Memory & Cognition, 3,* 227–281.

Shlosberg, H. (1954). Three dimensions of emotion. *Psychological Review, 61,* 81–88.

Schlosberg, H., & Kling, J. W. (1959). The relationship between "tension" and efficiency. *Perceptual & Motor Skills, 9,* 395–397.

Shackel, B. (1959). Skin drilling: A method of diminishing galvanic skin potentials. *American Journal of Psychology, 72,* 114–121.

Shean, G. D. (1970). Instrumental modification of the galvanic skin response: Conditioning or control? *Journal of Psychosomatic Research, 1,* 155–160.

Siddle, D. A., & Heron, P. A. (1978). Effects of length of training and amount of tone frequency change on amplitude of autonomic components of the orienting response. *Psychophysiology, 13,* 281–287.

Sokolov, E. N. (1963). *Perception and the conditioned reflex.* New York: Pergamon Press.

Spinks, J. A., Blowers, G. H., & Shek, D. T. L. (1985). The role of the orienting response in the anticipation of information: A skin conductance response study. *Psychophysiology, 22,* 385–394.

Stern, R. M. (1970, October). *Operant modification of electrodermal responses and/or voluntary control of GSR.* Paper presented at the meeting of the Society for Psychophysiological Research, Washington, DC.

Stern, R. M., & Kaplan, B. E. (1967). Galvanic skin response: Voluntary control and externalization. *Journal of Psychosomatic Research, 10,* 349–353.

Surwillo, W. W., & Quilter, R. E. (1965). The relation of frequency of spontaneous skin potential responses to vigilance and age. *Psychophysiology, 1,* 272–276.

Tranel, D., Fowles, D. C., & Damasio, A. R. (1985). Electrodermal discrimination of familiar and unfamiliar faces: A methodology. *Psychophysiology, 22,* 403–408.

Venables, P. H., & Christie, M. J. (1973). Mechanism, instrumentation, recording techniques and quantification of responses. In W. F. Prokasy & D. C. Raskin (Eds.), *Electrodermal activity in psychological research* (pp. 1–124). New York: Academic Press.

Venables, P. H., & Fletcher, R. P. (1981). The status of skin conductance recovery time: An examination of the Bundy effect. *Psychophysiology, 18,* 10–16.

Venables, P. H., & Martin, I. (1967). Skin resistance and skin potential. In. P. H. Venables & I. Martin (Eds.), *Manual of psycho-physiological methods* (pp. 53–102). Amsterdam: North-Holland.

Vossel, G., & Rossmann, R. (1984). Electrodermal habituation speed and visual monitoring performance. *Psychophysiology, 21,* 97–100.

Waid, W. M. (1974). Degree of goal orientation, level of cognitive activity and electrodermal recovery rate. *Perceptual & Motor Skills, 38,* 103–109.

Wiesenfeld, A. R., Malatesta, C. Z., Whitman, P. B., Granrose, L., & Uili, R. (1985). Psychophysiological response of breast- and bottle-feeding mothers to their infants' signals. *Psychophysiology, 22,* 79–86.

Wilcott, R. C. (1959). On the role of the epidermis in the production of skin resistance and potential. *Journal of Comparative & Physiological Psychology, 52,* 642–649.

Wilcott, R. C. (1967). Arousal sweating and electrodermal phenomena. *Psychological Bulletin, 67,* 58–72.

Wingard, J. A., & Maltzman, I. (1980). Interest as a predeterminer of the GSR index of the orienting reflex. *Acta Psychologica, 40,* 153–160.

Woodburne, R. T. (1978). *Essentials of human anatomy.* New York: Oxford University Press.

Woodworth, R. S., & Schlosberg, H. (1954). *Experimental psychology.* New York: Holt.

Yaremko, R. M., Blair, M. W., & Leckart, B. T. (1970). The orienting reflex to changes in a conceptual stimulus dimension. *Psychonomic Science, 2,* 115–116.

Yaremko, R. M., & Butler, M. C. (1975). Imaginal experience and attenuation of the galvanic skin response to shock. *Bulletin of the Psychonomic Society, 5,* 317–318.

Yaremko, R. M., Glanville, B. B., & Leckart, B. T. (1972). Imagery-mediated habituation of the orienting reflex. *Psychonomic Science, 27,* 204, 206.

Yuille, J. C., & Hare, R. D. (1980). A psychophysiological investigation of short-term memory. *Psychophysiology, 17,* 423–430.

Zimny, G. H., & Weidenfeller, E. W. (1963). Effects of music upon GSR and heart-rate. *The American Journal of Psychology, 76,* 311–314.

10
Pupillary Response, Eye Movements, and Behavior

The pupils of the eyes have been referred to as "windows to the soul." Although this romantic notion is not strictly true, scientists have discovered some interesting things about pupillary size changes and behavior. Pupillometrics refers to the measurement of variations in the diameter of the pupillary aperture of the eye.

In his book on pupillometry, Pierre Janisse (1977) wrote that one of the earliest references to the pupil of the eye was made by Travisa (1495) in his translation of Bartholomaeus (Angelica Palli, 1398), in which is stated that "the blacke of theye . . . is callyd Pupilla in latyn for small ymages ben seen therin" (p. 1). The word "pupil" is derived from the Latin "pupilla," meaning "little girl," thus referring to the tiny reflections of objects that one can see when looking into the eyes of another person. At least two different writers of the past (Joshua Sylvester, 1591, and Guillaume de Salluste) have referred to the pupillary apertures as "windows to the soul," implying that they were observation points for a person's innermost thoughts. Scientific observation of pupils is much less romantic than implied by these early writers, because we now know that dilations and constrictions of the pupil are governed by the autonomic nervous system. As we shall see in this chapter, pupillometry has provided psychophysiologists with interesting information about pupil size changes in various situations.

The process of measuring eye movements in different environmental contexts is called electroculography (EOG). The EOG technique is concerned with measuring changes in electrical potential that occur when the eyes move. Eye movements enable the visual system to acquire information by scanning relevant aspects of the environment. Object recognition, discrimination, and other information intake by the visual system is accomplished mostly through unconscious scanning eye movements. The major part of processing the new information takes place when the eyes make brief pauses. The EOG has been useful in a wide range of applications from the rapid eye movements measured in sleep studies to the recording of visual fixations while consumers examine different advertising displays. Studies of reading, eye movements during real and simulated car driving, radar scanning, and reading instrument dials under vibrating conditions have been some of the practical tasks examined with eye movement recordings. Eye blinks are easily recorded with EOG procedures and are particularly useful in studies of eyelid conditioning and as a control for possible eyeblink contamination in EEG research. In the remainder of this chapter, a discussion of pupillary response and its use in psychology is presented first, followed by a section on eye movements and their relation to behavior.

ANATOMY AND PHYSIOLOGY OF THE PUPILLARY RESPONSE

The pupil is the opening at the center of the iris of the eye through which light passes. Thus, the pupil is merely a hole surrounded by the iris muscle. A major function of the iris is to increase pupillary diameter in dim light and to decrease it in bright light. This adjusts the amount of light allowed to enter the eye according to the environment of an individual. The pupil of the human eye can constrict to 1.5 mm in diameter, it dilates to about 8–9 mm or more, and can react to stimuli in .2 seconds (Guyton, 1977; Lowenstein & Loewenfeld, 1962). The constriction and dilation of the pupillary aperture is produced mainly through ANS control exerted on the muscles of the iris. More specifically, neurons of the PNS innervate circular fibers of the iris, causing pupillary constriction, whereas excitation by SNS neurons causes the radial fibers of the iris to produce dilation of the pupil. Both the circular and radial fibers are smooth muscle (see Fig. 10.1). The circular muscle fibers are also termed the *sphincter pupillae,* and their parasympathetic innervation begins at a group of brain cells located in the midbrain (Edinger-Westphal nucleus). The radial fibers, also termed the *dilator pupillae,* are under control of SNS processes originating in the hypothalamus and other brain areas close by.

The ANS is intimately involved in emotional behavior. Janisse (1977) pointed out that the relation of pupillary response to ANS activity appears to have been accepted as early as the 1850s by investigators such as Claude Bernard. Charles Darwin, that exquisite observer, related pupil dilation to fear and other "emotions" in animals in his 1872 book entitled *Expressions of Emotions in Man and Animals.* A strong emotional stimulus (e.g., an unexpected pistol firing) will cause the pupils to dilate. Thus, a dilated pupil will appear as part of a startle reaction, with a response occurring in as little as .2 second and peaking in .5 to 1.0 second. The dilation will persist even if a bright light is presented to the eye,

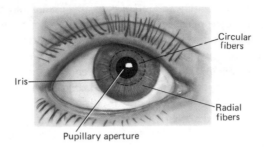

FIG. 10.1.   Diagram of the eye. The diameter of the pupillary aperture is the measure used in pupillometry. Pupillary constriction occurs with contraction of circular fibers, whereas dilation results from contraction of radial fibers.

indicating that the emotional response can override the usual pupillary constriction to intense light stimuli. Animal studies have shown that pupillary dilation occurs with stimulation of the hypothalamus, thalamus, and reticular formation. These are brain areas that have been implicated in emotional behavior and behavioral arousal.

THE MEASUREMENT OF PUPILLARY SIZE

Although many observations about changes in pupil size under different emotional or performance conditions have been reported over the years, it is only within the last 30 years that the development of practical and reliable instrumentation has enabled the precise measurement of pupillary aperture under different experimental conditions and psychological states. One problem in the measurement of pupil size is the constant fluctuation in pupil diameter that occurs during waking hours. These spontaneous changes occur simultaneously in the two eyes and are about 1 mm in amplitude. They are thought to be under control of brain centers that continuously regulate pupil size according to intensity of light stimulation. Measurements obtained under normal lighting conditions must take these fluctuations into account.

Early devices in the measurement of pupil size included the use of infrared photography, which made it possible to get pictures of pupil diameter in dim light. Photoelectric methods, which measured reflected light from the iris, were also used. Both were cumbersome and not very accurate. Hakerem (1967) considered the best available device at that time to be the "Lowenstein pupillograph," which used infrared scanning of the iris to determine the amount of reflected light. This device measured the diameters of both pupils and provided information about the rate of change in pupil size. However, Janisse (1977) has questioned the accuracy of the system. Hess (1972) described his own device in some detail, along with procedures for its use. Essentially, his device consists of a movie camera, a projector (movie or slide), a screen, and reflecting mirrors. The use of infrared film enables recordings of pupil diameter regardless of the subject's eye color. For any given visual stimulus, the averaged pupil diameter for 20 individual frames is used as the measure of pupil size for that presentation. Hess emphasized the importance of holding constant the factors of stimulus brightness and brightness contrast. Brightness contrast refers to the relative brightness of a stimulus and its background. The Hess technique is the most economical, but the frame-by-frame measurement of pupil size, and errors of hand measurement, make this technique time-consuming and of questionable reliability.

A widely used pupil-measuring technique in modern laboratories is the video-based pupillometer. These electronic devices use a closed-circuit TV system to observe the eye and a signal processor to measure and display pupil diameter. A low-intensity infrared light source illuminates the eye, and a low light level silicon matrix tube camera is used to record pupil size. Pupil diameter is presented as either a direct numerical readout or appears on a chart recorder showing continuous changes in size. The system also has automatic circuitry to maintain proper measurement over a wide range of recording conditions. Pupil diameter may be measured over a 0- to 10-mm range, with provisions for expanding subintervals of this range. A more recent development uses momentary estimates of pupillary diameter, which are then continuously available for on-line computer analysis. Using this approach, task-evoked pupillary responses (TEPR) can be obtained when changes in pupil size that occur with respect to certain events in a task are averaged (Beatty, 1986). With this type of averaging, changes in pupil size to significant events in the experimental trial can be specified, and background variations can be canceled out.

Fatigue and Pupil Size

Lowenstein and Loewenfeld (1964) have noted that pupil diameter is maximal in a well-rested individual, decreases with fatigue, and reaches a minimal diameter just before sleep. Kahneman and Peavler (1969) observed a continuous decrease in pupil size between the beginning and end of an experimental session. Hess (1972) cautioned experimenters to avoid presentation of an excessive number of stimuli in studies of pupil size, because fatigue causes the pupil to decrease in diameter.

Geacintov and Peavler (1974) measured pupil sizes of telephone operators to determine whether pupil constriction would reflect fatigue in a work environment. Each subject was measured before and after a full day's work of providing directory assistance with either the usual telephone book or an automated microfilm reader. The average pupil size for all subjects at the beginning of the day

TABLE 10.1
Factors That May Influence Changes in Pupil Size

Factor	Effect on Pupil Size
Darkness reflex	Momentary dilation due to interruption of a constant adapting light
Consensual reflex	Stimulation of one eye affects both eyes equally
Near reflex	Constriction due to decreasing the point of focus, i.e., the pupil constricts with convergence of the eyes on a near object
Lid-closure reflex	Momentary contraction followed by redilation
Psychosensory reflex	Restoration of diminished reflexes due to external stimulation
Age	Decreased diameter and increased variability with age
Habituation	Pupil diameter decreases, speed of contraction increases, and magnitude of reflex decreases with continued stimulus presentations
Binocular summation	Constriction greater when both eyes are stimulated simultaneously

Source: Adapted from W. W. Tryon, Pupillometry: A survey of sources of variation. Psychophysiology, 1975, 12, 90–93.

was 4.6 mm at the book position and 4.5 mm at the microfilm location. Pupil diameter decreased on the average between morning and evening measures. However, the data analyses indicated that a significant decrease (.43 mm) occurred only for the microfilm condition. Thus, a size difference between prework and postwork measurements was found with the microfilm readers but not with the book readers. Subjects reported more fatigue symptoms, such as backaches, headaches, and eyestrain, when using the microfilm device than when they used the telephone book. However, performance was superior with the microfilm reader because of the greater access speed of this automated device.

There are a number of environmental factors that can have an effect on pupil size. Some of these variables that are not otherwise mentioned in this chapter are listed in Table 10.1.

PUPILLOMETRY AND BEHAVIOR

The most influential person in the application of pupillometry to psychology was Eckhard Hess. His earliest publications in the area date back to about 1960, and stimulated a great deal of interest among psychologists, because Hess's work suggested ways in which mental activities, information processing, perception, attitudes, and interests could be understood in terms of pupillary changes. He was not the first to indicate the possibility of such relationships, but his provocative work led to increased activity in this area by contemporary psychologists. It is fitting that our account of psychophysiological investigations of pupillary changes associated with different behaviors begins with a study done by Hess.

Interest Value of Stimuli and Pupil Size

One of the most intriguing results of the original Hess study (Hess & Polt, 1960) was that pupil size appeared to be related to affect, or "feeling tone," generated by different pictures. For example, they reported that when viewing pictures of a male nude and of a baby, female subjects gave larger pupil dilation responses than did males. On the other hand, males reacted with larger pupillary dilation to a picture of a nude female. The researchers concluded that the gender differences indicated greater interest in nudes of the opposite sex. As a follow-up, Hess, Seltzer, and Shlien (1965) found that homosexual males had greater pupil dilations to photographs of male nudes compared to female nudes, whereas the results for heterosexual males showed the opposite pupillary response. Others have provided support for the relationship between sexual arousal and pupil size. For example, Simms (1967) reported that not only did opposite-sex pictures result in greater dilation, but that this was especially true when the photos were retouched to produce enlarged pupils. The implication of this finding is that pupil dilation in others may be subtly perceived as signifying interest on the part of that other person.

Chapman, Chapman, and Brelje (1969) demonstrated a possible source of bias in the pupil size–sexual interest relationship. They used "businesslike" and "carefree" experimenters to present nude male and female pinups to male subjects. Only the subjects tested by the carefree experimenter showed larger pupil dilation to the female nudes. If the two experimenters had been in different laboratories, conflicting findings would have been reported. In this same study, a large number of the male subjects showed some dilation to male nudes, leading Chapman et al. to conclude that dilation could reflect general interest and positive evaluation as well as sexual interest. Bernick, Kling, and Borowitz (1971) measured pupil responses of heterosexual male medical students to three movies: an erotic heterosexual movie, a suspense film, and an erotic homosexual movie. The erotic heterosexual and homosexual films produced the same degree of dilation, which was greater than that to the suspense film. In addition, the degree of self-reported penile erection related closely to increases in pupil diameter during the viewing of sexual films. This finding of Bernick et al. comes closest to supporting a pupillary dilation–sexual arousal hypothesis, but, unfortunately, amount of erection was not objectively measured.

Caution is recommended for those who would use extent of pupillary dilation as an indicator of sexual preference. Not only have some studies not shown pupillary differences as a function of opposite sex nudity, (e.g., Peavler & McLaughlin, 1967), but it is also true that pupil dilation occurs to novel stimuli, and naked people are certainly more novel in our culture than clothed individuals. In a study by Hamel (1974), pictures of females and males in varying degrees of nudity were shown to female undergraduates. He found that viewing opposite-sex pictures in order of increasing nudity produced increasingly greater dilation. The greatest dilation was recorded in response to totally nude males and the smallest to fully clothed female models. Rather than sexual arousal, one could easily use the alternate explanation of novelty or interest, because total male nudity could be so categorized for these subjects, whereas female models are common pictures for them. Pupillary dilation has also been reported in response to erotic and unpleasant passages from a book presented in a tape recording (White & Maltzman, 1977). Subjects listened to 2-minute passages from the same novel: one erotic, one describing mutilation, and one neutral. They found immediate dilation at the beginning of each passage, with erotic and mutilation segments maintaining this for about 60 seconds. Pupil size during the neutral passage began declining within 10 secs after the reading started. These results suggest an orienting response, which was then followed by habituation to the neutral passage.

Pupil Size and Nonverbal Communication

Hess (1975) has concluded that pupil size is important in nonverbal communication, because it seems to act as an unlearned mechanism in facilitating certain social behaviors such as "sexual interest." In his own work, Hess manipulated pupil size in two pictures of the same attractive young woman. Male subjects described the woman with large pupils as soft, more feminine, or pretty, whereas the smaller pupil photograph was described as hard, selfish, or cold. Subjects could not distinguish between the photographs, nor could they give reasons for their preference. Other studies by Hess showed that subjects associated large pupils with happy faces and small ones with angry faces. He concluded that larger pupils are associated with attractiveness, sexual interest, and happiness, whereas small ones are related to the opposite characteristics. However, some investigators, like Janisse (1977), are still not convinced about the reliability or adequacy of pupillary communications. He pointed out that although there is information about what information the dilated pupil communicates to an observer, the validity of the communication is still questionable. The main reason for this is that most of the data have been collected with visual stimuli where the light reflex could not be ruled out as a possible cause of pupillary change. Hess has developed another research technique in which subjects are allowed to draw in pupils on line drawings of faces. Subjects consistently drew in large pupils on happy faces and small pupils on the sad faces. This result has been obtained with both adults and children as subjects. Hicks and co-workers have conducted several studies to test Hess's hypotheses that females and light-eyed people are more sensitive to pupillary cues. In one study (Hicks, Williams, & Ferrante, 1979), 223 college students drew in pupils on angry and happy faces. In support of Hess, they did find that the students drew in significantly larger pupils on the happy face. However, male–female sensitivity did not differ. Williams and Hicks (1980) used the happy–angry faces task and reported that women and light-eyed persons were more sensitive to pupillary cues than men and dark-eyed persons. Hess and Petrovich (1978) proposed that a relationship between eye color and sensitivity to pupillary cues are due to some evolutionary mechanism or indicate an acquired cultural effect. Possible influences of culture receive support from a study by Tarrahian and Hicks (1979). They showed that Iranian children are sensitive to pupillary cues at an earlier age than American children. This is interesting, in view of the fact that the Iranian culture may be considered to be "pupil intensive," in that veiled Iranian women can use only the eyes, and possibly the brows, as facial communication cues while in public. Tarrahian and Hicks noted that in America, where pupil-size cues may be less important, the meaning of pupil cues might be incidentally learned when the individual begins to experience sexual situations in which increases in pupil size are likely to occur in others. Although these results seem to suggest that cultural factors may play a role in sensitivity to pupil size, there is yet no reasonable explanation as to why lighter-eyed persons or women should have greater sensitivity. In this last set of studies, it should be pointed out that pupil sizes of subjects were not measured while they drew in pupils. Pupillary size measures could be an interesting addition to these kinds of studies to indicate something about the state of the individual participant while drawing in the pupils.

Pupil Size and Mental Activity

The amount of pupil response during mental activity has been shown to be a function of how hard an individual has to work. The first researchers to show this were Hess and Polt (1964), who asked people to do mental multiplication. Level of difficulty was gradually increased from 7×8 to 16×23, and pupil size increases reflected difficulty level. The increases ranged from 4% to 30% in diameter from prequestion to preanswer period, with pupil size decreasing immediately after the answer was given. Thus, the pupillary response appears to reflect the information-processing load placed on the nervous system by cognitive tasks. In another experiment (Polt, 1970), the threat of a mild electric shock for incorrect answers resulted in greater amounts of effort to solve problems, and this, in turn, produced greater pupil dilation. Beatty (1982) concluded that the amplitude of the task-evoked pupillary response (TEPR) is an index of a common factor related to the processing demands of memory, language processing, reasoning, and perception.

Short-Term Memory

Pupil size was observed as subjects listened to strings of three to seven digits presented at a rate of one per second (Kahneman and Beatty, 1966). After a 2-second pause, each string was repeated by subjects at the same rate. The researchers found progressive pupillary dilation with the presentation of each digit, with maximum dilation being reached after all digits were presented. Then, as each digit was repeated, pupillary constriction occurred and reached its baseline when the last digit was reported. Also, the amount of pupil dilation at the pause was a function of the number of items in the string, that is, it was greatest with seven digits (4.1 mm) and least with three digits (3.6mm). The interpretation was that pupil dilation varied directly with momentary cognitive load. In another study, Beatty and Kahneman (1966) found similar pupillary size variations when digits were retrieved from long-term memory, for example, with a familiar telephone number. Subjects were required to recall a telephone number when presented with a one-word cue, such as "home" or "office," and to present the digits at a 1-second rate. The magnitude of pupil dilation was larger with these familiar digits as compared to a string of seven unfamiliar digits presented for recall. As before, pupil diameter decreased with each digit reported, returning to baseline as the last digit was given. A number of studies by Kahneman and his associates have indicated that progressive pupil dilation occurred when lists of materials were presented for processing. Kahneman and Wright (1971) showed that pupillary response was greater when subjects were required to recall an entire series of items than when they recalled only part of the information. Stanners, Headley, and Clark (1972) reported greater pupil diameter for subjects asked to recall information from memory, as compared to a requirement to recognize items presented. They suggested that this could reflect different processing in recall and recognition, or more intense rehearsal produced by the requirement to recall information. In other words, the less the required effort, the less is pupil enlargement.

Language Processing

Differential changes in pupil size occurred when persons were asked to generate visual images to abstract and concrete words (Paivio & Simpson, 1966). It was found that engagement in imagery produced increases in pupil size, with greater amounts occurring to abstract words (e.g., liberty), compared to concrete words (e.g., house). Further, time to reach maximum dilation was greater with abstract words, perhaps because it was more difficult to generate images to abstract terms. Pupillary dilation did not occur during reading or listening to passages that varied in difficulty (Carver, 1971). This led Carver to conclude that pupil size cannot be used as an objective indicator of whether or not the person is processing language. However, this conclusion is at odds with the majority of evidence. For example, Stanners et al. (1972) observed larger increases in pupillary size when more complex sentences were presented via tape recorder. In addition, task-evoked pupillary responses have been studied as subjects processed meaningful sentences differing in complexity (Ahern & Beatty, 1981). Greater degrees of grammatical complexity were reported to produce the larger pupillary responses. An interesting example of how linguistic organization of sentences

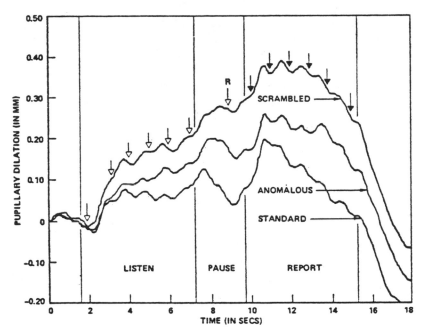

FIG. 10.2. Task-evoked pupillary responses for six-word sentences differing in linguistic organization. Standard sentences were meaningful English sentences. Anomalous sentences used the same syntactic frames but with words interchanged between sentences to render the strings nearly meaningless. Scrambled sentences had neither syntactic nor semantic organization. Both syntactic and semantic organization independently reduced the processing load imposed by the sentence repetition task. Open arrows indicate presentation of words and the response cue; filled arrows indicated timing clicks.

affects task-evoked responses was given by Beatty (1982). Sentences composed of six words each had three levels of organization, and subjects were asked to reproduce all three types. The more disorganized sentences were harder to reproduce. As a result, a sentence reading, "Many blind roses play heavy trouble" led to larger dilations than, "Should blind people lead quiet lives?" Eliminating syntactic organization completely by using random strings of words as in, "Rains children milk golden usually medals" led to the largest responses of all. Figure 10.2 depicts the task-evoked pupillary responses during the listen, pause, and report portions for the three kinds of sentences.

Perception

Pupillary dilation has been related to the difficulty encountered by subjects in a pitch discrimination task (Kahneman & Beatty, 1967). The subject's task was to judge whether the comparison tone was higher or lower than the standard tone.

When the difficulty in distinguishing between the two became greater, subjects showed increased dilation. Hakerem and Sutton (1966) measured pupillary response to threshold (barely perceptible) visual stimuli. No pupillary dilation occurred to stimuli that were not detected or when the subject was not asked to detect the weak light flashes. However, when subjects were required to detect whether a flash was present or absent, and they correctly discriminated a flash, pupillary dilation occurred. Beatty (1975) found similar results when subjects were required to detect a weak tone that was present during one half of the experimental trials. Pupil dilation occurred only when a presented signal was detected by the subjects. Beatty concluded that the pupillary dilations reflected changes in nervous system activation, which accompanied perceptual processing.

The probability that a stimulus will be presented has been found to affect pupil size (Friedman, Hakerem, Sutton, & Fleiss, 1973). For example, stimuli that have a lower probability of being presented result in larger pupil responses than higher probability stimuli. Qiyuan, Richer, Wagonner, and Beatty (1985) examined the effects of probability of auditory stimuli on pupillary response. They confirmed that probability affects pupil response, and also reported that omitting an expected stimulus results in dilation. The finding that stimulus omissions resulted in dilations indicates that a physical stimulus does not have to be presented to produce a response, but that some mental representation of an expected stimulus can be sufficient. In this respect, the pupillary response is similar to the P300 component of the event-related brain potential. In a study by Beatty (1982), pupillary changes were recorded as subjects detected random target tones over a 48-minute period. Signal detection performance deteriorated over time in the task, and this was accompanied by a decrease in the amplitude of the pupillary response over the course of the session. These results are very similar to changes reported for event-related brain potentials and visual signal detection. Beatty (1982) made the point that his pupillary results, along with the brain response data, argue for a decreased response to task-relevant stimuli, as a function of time, at both cortical and subcortical levels.

Pupillary responses to taboo, emotional, and neutral words were measured for groups of introverts, extroverts, and ambiverts as identified by the Eysenck Personality Inventory (Stelmack & Mandelzys, 1975). Subjects were presented with 12 taboo words (e.g., whore), 12 emotional words (e.g., vomit), and 24 neutral words (e.g., field). The introverts had the largest average pupil size under all conditions. This result supported Eysenck's hypothesis that introverts have generally higher levels of physiological arousal than other personality types.

Negative Affect

Hess (1972) noted in various studies that certain types of negative stimuli produce a constriction in pupil size, for example, pictures of crippled children. However, if the negative picture has "shock content" (e.g., a picture of a mutilated person), dilation may occur initially, followed by constriction after repeated presentations. Thus, the emotional reaction produces a sympathetic nervous system response (pupil dilation), and after it wears off, the constriction occurs and reflects aversion, or "perceptual avoidance". Hess (1972) contended that ". . . there is a continuum of pupil responses to stimuli, ranging from extreme dilation for interesting or pleasing stimuli to extreme constriction for material that is unpleasant or distasteful to the viewer" (p. 511). Other investigators have challenged this claim of bidirectionality of the pupil response. For example, Loewenfeld (1966) reviewed effects of various sensory and psychological stimuli and concluded that none, except increased light intensities, caused pupillary constriction. Woodmanscc (1967) reported an opposite result, that is, pupillary dilation in 13 of 14 female college students who viewed a picture of a murder scene. Libby, Lacey, and Lacey (1973) reported that unpleasant visual stimuli produced greater dilation than pleasant stimuli. Several of their 34 subjects, however, did show consistent pupillary constriction to a few stimuli. Janisse (1974) found a positive relationship between pupil size and affect intensity but no evidence of constriction to negative stimuli. In general, the results of other investigators cast doubt on Hess' hypothesis regarding pupillary constriction to unpleasant stimuli.

In summary, there appears to be substantial research support for the claim that pupillary diameter increases with stimuli that produce positive affect. Pupillary constriction with negative stimuli is still controversial, and may be a response limited to a few individuals and a small range of stimulus conditions.

Attitudes

It has been suggested that pupil size might be a more valid index of attitude toward persons or things than more traditional methods, for example, interviews or questionnaires (Hess, 1972). One example is a study of Barlow (1969), who showed slides of three political leaders (Lyndon Johnson, George Wallace, and Martin Luther King) and one unknown person to White subjects classified as "liberal" or "conservative." The liberals showed pupillary dilation to Johnson and King, and constrictions to Wallace. The conservatives showed an opposite response pattern. Thus, the pupils of subjects dilated to photographs of persons with whom they agreed, and were constricted to those of different political persuasion. A study by Clark and Ertas (1975) questioned the use of pupil size as an index of attitude. These investigators showed pictures of 1972 presidential candidates (Richard Nixon and George McGovern) and a picture of a stranger to supporters of either of these candidates. In another condition, the candidates' last names and the name Smith were spoken. All three pictures were associated with constriction, with names producing dilation. It is obvious from these conflicting kinds of results that the question of attitude and pupil size requires a great deal of additional work.

Information Processing, Learning, and Pupil Size

Poock (1973) found that pupil diameter was related to information-processing speed. He first determined maximum processing capacity (100%) by having subjects press buttons corresponding to displayed numerals as fast as possible. Then subjects alternately processed numerals at 50%, 75%, 100%, and 125% of maximum capacity. Significant increases in pupil diameter over baseline levels (viewing a blank slide) were found when subjects were required to process information at 75% and 100% of capacity. However, when the requirement was raised to 125% of capacity, pupillary constriction occurred.

Digit strings of 5, 9, and 13 were used with 14 female college students who were asked to reproduce them immediately after hearing the strings (Peavler, 1974). There was a trend toward increased pupil size with each successive digit in the 5- and 9-digit conditions. However, the 13-digit condition revealed that dilation leveled off immediately after presentation of the 10th digit. This suggested to Peavler that information-processing effort was momentarily suspended at this point. This point of no further dilation corresponded to the short-term memory capacity of the subjects, which was approximately nine digits in this experiment. Average pupillary diameter increased from about 5.0 mm with the first digit to 5.6 mm with the ninth.

Kahneman and Peavler (1969) measured pupil diameter in a verbal learning task. The learning trials were presented under conditions of either high incentive (5 cent reward for each item learned) or low incentive (1 cent reward). The high-incentive items were more efficiently learned than the low-incentive ones (55% vs. 18%), and they produced larger pupillary dilations (4.04 mm vs. 3.97 mm). In another learning study, Colman and Paivio (1970) measured pupillary activity during paired-associates learning. The abstractness of the words were varied, and subjects learned the pairs under standard memorizing conditions or using imagery as an aid. Pupillary dilation was greater under the standard, more difficult learning condition. The results also showed larger pupil size with the abstract word pairs that were more difficult to learn.

The studies reviewed in this section show clearly that pupillary diameter changes occur during information processing, and that the change is related to degree of mental effort required. The increases in pupillary dilation observed with heavy information-processing loads may be related to elevated CNS activity under higher load conditions. Beatty believes that the pupillary response provides a quantitative index of load on the nervous system.

It becomes clear as one considers research in pupillometry and behavior that variables such as information processing load and task difficulty (whether it be mental multiplication or developing images to abstract terms) will cause pupillary diameter to increase. This is true for a variety of different cognitive tasks, including short-term memory, language processing, reasoning, and perceptual discrimination and detection. Interest value and novelty of stimuli also play a role in pupillary changes. Janisse (1977) has cautioned that the light reflex (constriction from increased illumination) may contaminate results when visual displays are used. However, this possibility can be reduced through the use of fixation points, constant illumination of visual displays, and auditory stimuli.

The value of pupillometry in attitude measurement and in the study of nonverbal communication has not yet been convincingly demonstrated. It is also clear that although pupillary dilations are reliably observed as responses to interesting or pleasant stimuli, the claim that constriction occurs to unpleasant or negative stimuli has not been upheld. Reliable pupillary constrictions are observed as a function of increasing fatigue. It has generally been found that pupil size decreases slowly during the day from early morning to late at night due to fatigue. One possibility is that fatigue-related decreases in pupillary diameters are primarily due to parasympathetic nervous system activity.

The modern era of pupillometry was ushered in by the provocative work of Hess and his associates. It continues as a very interesting research area that has implications for the study of human behavior in a variety of situations.

EYE MOVEMENTS

The Control of Eye Movements

Eye movements are controlled by cerebral and subcortical systems in conjunction with cranial nerves and sets of eye muscles attached to the outside of the eyeball. The cerebral areas involved in eye fixations are the occipital and frontal cortices. Innervation of the eye muscles is by the third (oculomotor), fourth (trochlear), and sixth (abducens) cranial nerves. They influence movements of three separate pairs of eye muscles: the superior and inferior rectus, the lateral and medial rectus, and the superior and inferior obliques (see Fig. 10.3). The superior and inferior recti contract to move the eyes up or down. The lateral and medial recti allow movements from side to side, and the obliques control rotation of the eyeballs. The three sets of muscles are reciprocally innervated to allow one pair to relax while another pair contracts. The purpose of eye movements is to fixate objects so they stimulate the foveal region of the eye, that is, the area of best acuity.

Fixation movements of the eye are controlled by two different neural mechanisms (Guyton, 1977). Voluntary fixations of the eyes on some object of choice, for example, the quick movements made while reading, are controlled by a small area in the premotor cortex of the frontal lobes. The maintenance of involuntary fixation and slow following movements are controlled by areas in the occipital cortex. The operation of this intricate eye movement system can be disrupted by brain damage due to disease or stroke, and by common drugs, including alcohol

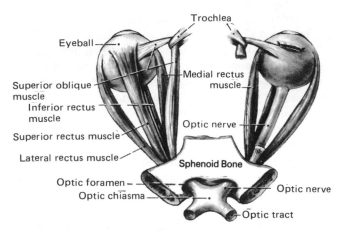

FIG. 10.3. Extrinsic muscles of the eye. (Inferior oblique muscle not shown.)

and barbiturates. Shackel (1967) identified three common types of eye movements:

1. Saccadic: This refers to movements of the eyes from one fixation point to the next. A fixation pause lasts for about $\frac{1}{4}$ to 1 second, and the saccade (movement) lasts for approximately $\frac{1}{50}$ to $\frac{1}{10}$ of a second, depending on how long it takes to make the next fixation. Saccadic movements occur so quickly that they only occupy 10% of the total time spent in eye movements, whereas fixation accounts for 90% of the time (Guyton, 1977). Visual processing of information generally takes place only during fixations.

2a. Smooth Pursuit: This is the eye movement that occurs when a moving object is fixated and followed by the eyes. The rate of movement can closely approximate that of the object, up to 60 degrees per second and beyond. (In this case, perception can occur while the eye is in motion.)

2b. Smooth Compensatory: This is a movement to correct for body or head tilt to maintain an upright view of the visual field. (It is an "automatic" or reflex activity.)

3. Nystagmoid: These are oscillations of the eyes, often consisting of slow horizontal sweeps and quick returns to the original eye position. There are three causes of nystagmoid movements: (a) where eye defects or the visual field prevent adequate fixation; (b) when the vestibular system is impaired; or (c) when there is impairment of visual or vestibular pathways in the CNS. It should be noted that small spontaneous saccadic drifts, and other movements, occur in the normal eye at rest. When these small movements are effectively eliminated, for example, by stabilizing an image on a certain portion of the retina through optical techniques, a fixated image gradually fades and disappears.

To these three basic varieties of eye movement we should add the rapid eye movements (REM) of sleep and eye blinks. The REMs of sleep occur sporadically, are variable in amplitude, and last from a few minutes to a half-hour or more. Blinking of the eyelids lasts about .2 to .4 second and, on the average, occur at 2- to 10-second intervals, with wide individual variability.

Recording Eye Movements

Four of the basic methods commonly used to measure eye movements are the contact-lens method, the corneal reflection method, television camera scanning, and a technique termed *electrooculography* (EOG). The EOG technique is briefly outlined here. The basis for the EOG is the steady (approximately .40 to 1 mV) potential difference that exists between the cornea and retina of the eye. The cornea is electrically positive, whereas the back of the eye at the retina is negative. When the eyes are fixed straight ahead, recording electrodes detect a steady baseline potential. When eye movements occur, the potential across the electrodes changes and a corresponding deflection is produced in the pen of a recorder. When the eyes move, the potential at the electrode becomes more positive or negative, depending on the direction of movement. The EOG can record eye movements up to 70 degrees to the left and right of central fixation, to an accuracy of about 1.5 to 2.0 degrees. Electrode pairs placed horizontally on the skin surface, at the corners of the eyes, detect horizontal movements. Electrodes placed above and below the eyes detect vertical movements. What is really being detected is a change in dc potential that is produced when the eyes move (see Fig. 10.4). The pen deflection in the ink-writing system will be either positive or negative, depending on the polarity of the connections, and the amplitude of the deflection is linearly related to the extent of movement, up to about 30 degrees from center. Horizontal movements may be recorded by measuring across one eye or across both eyes with electrodes placed near the external canthus (outside) of each eye (see Fig. 10.5). For monocular recording, one electrode must be at the side of the nose near the internal canthus, with the other at the external canthus. The EOG recorded from one eye is considered to reflect the position of the other eye unless stated differently. The binocular measure provides more reliable results (Shackel, 1967). For precise recordings, the electrodes must be placed adjacent to the horizontal plane passing through the cornea of the eye. Researchers commonly use a binocular placement for horizontal eye movement, and monocular for vertical movements.

Problems in EOG Recordings.   Shackel (1967) described three problems in the recording of EOG: (a) the small magnitude of the EOG signal, (b) the existence of skin potentials in the same frequency band as EOG signals, and (c) slow drift, often caused by unclean electrodes and poor contact. The first of these problems can be overcome through the use of a suitable, sensitive recorder. Most physio-

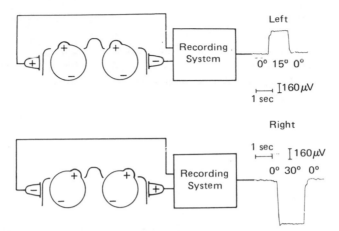

FIG. 10.4. Basis of electrooculography. The eyeball is like a small battery. As it rotates, the poles of the "battery" come nearer to the respective electrodes on the adjacent skin. The change in direct potential, and thus the angle of rotation, can be recorded.

logical recording devices are satisfactory, provided they have appropriate couplers for dc recordings. The skin potential response can be minimized by careful preparation of the skin underlying the electrode by rubbing the area with a wet cloth, a cotton ball, or with a slightly abrasive electrode paste. Another possible problem, that of slow drift, may be minimized by following the preparation routine outlined next.

Preparation of Electrodes and Subject. The electrodes used for EOG measurement are similar to the small disc or cup electrodes used in EEG recordings. They may be made of either silver or stainless steel. The electrodes should be nonpolarizing, small, and light enough to enable attachment with surgical tape or an adhesive collar. The dc drift caused by electrode polarization can be recognized as a steady deflection of the recording pen in one direction. Electrodes should be kept in an airtight container, washed in distilled water, and then placed in a saline solution with the leads shorted together before use. Paste is then applied to the electrodes before they are placed on the skin. When using adhesive collars, one side is attached to the electrode, and paste is applied to fill the electrode through the collar opening. Then the collar is attached to the skin surface and the leads are then connected to your recording device. After proper preparation, skin resistance between the electrodes should be less than 2000 Ohms. The subject's head must be held in one constant position with regard to the center of the visual field. Some researchers employ a chin rest to accomplish this, whereas others make an impression of the subjects's teeth in dental plastic and have the subject position his or her mouth on this "bite board" before each trial. While the head

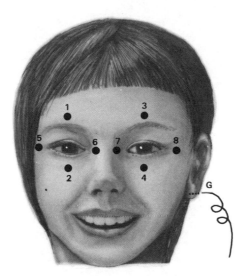

FIG. 10.5. Placement of electrodes for eye movement recordings.
Electrodes 1 and 2, and 3 and 4 are for vertical movement recordings.
Electrodes 5 and 6, and 7 and 8 are for horizontal recordings (monocu-
lar). The most common horizontal placements are 5 and 8 (binocular).
Vertical recordings are usually monocular. G, ground electrode is lo-
cated at left mastoid area, behind the ear.

is fixed in place, the system is calibrated directly in degrees of eye movement by
having the subject fixate a series of points at known angles of eye rotation. The
gain may be adjusted so that one division on the recording paper equals 1 degree
or 2 degrees of eye movement. Typical recordings of saccadic and pursuit movements are depicted in Fig. 10.6. The records shown in Fig. 10.6 are monocular
for the vertical movements and binocular for the horizontal ones. The careful
recording of EOG can result in a great deal of stability and repeatability of results
over a period of time.

EYE MOVEMENTS AND BEHAVIOR

In the next few sections, we discuss the measurement of eye movements during
mental activities, visual search, and perception. Included under mental activities
are learning, problem solving, reading, and the possible utility of a particular
type of EOG as a genetic marker in psychopathology.

Mental Activity and Eye Movements

The primary function of eye movements is to allow the eyes to alter their position
and focus on objects of interest. Saccadic movements bring objects into foveal

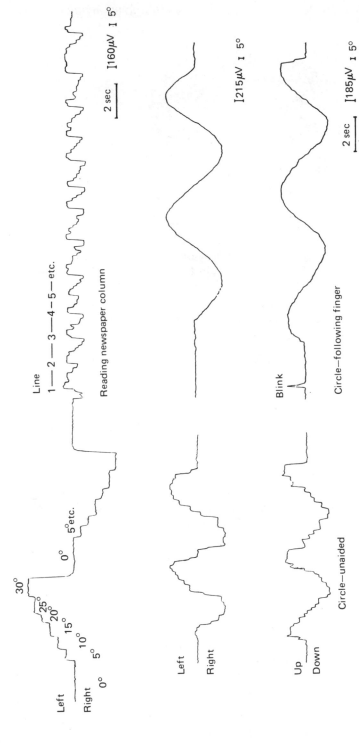

FIG. 10.6. Typical recordings of saccadic and pursuit movements. The subject fixates a series of points at 5 deg. intervals, reads a newspaper column, tries to scan smoothly around a circle by himself, and follows a fingertip drawn around the circle. Note also the typical wave form of a blink, on the vertical recording only, with sharp rise and fall and short duration.

vision through quick adjustments, whereas pursuit motions adjust eye movements to moving objects. However, eye movements have also been related to mental activities, such as learning and problem solving.

Eye Movements and Learning

A series of experiments by McCormack and colleagues have used eye movements in conjunction with paired-associate learning to support a two-stage conceptualization of verbal learning. It is hypothesized that subjects consolidate responses during an initial, or "response-learning," phase and then connect responses to stimuli in a second, or "hook-up," stage. These researchers have found, for example, that efficient performers spend more time fixating on the stimulus word from the outset in a learning task, as compared to inefficient learners of paired-associates (Haltrecht & McCormack, 1966). (In paired-associates learning, a set of stimulus words must elicit a specific set of response words for successful completion.) In another experiment, it was found that fixation of response words decreased as learning progressed, whereas time spent viewing the stimulus words increased (McCormack, Haltrecht, & Hannah, 1967). Furthermore, viewing time of response and stimulus words diverged more quickly when subjects learned an easy list (high response similarity) than when they performed with a difficult list (low response similarity; McCormack, Hannah, Bradley, & Moore, 1967). Thus, there is evidence here that is consistent with the notion that eye movement pattern varies with stage of learning, and it may differ for slow and fast learners.

Eye Movements, Problem Solving, and Cognitive Mode

Eye movements of subjects were measured as they were presented with two horizontal arrays of pictures under three conditions: (a) when no problem solving was required, (b) when the pictures were used in the solution of a problem, and (c) after problem solving (Nakano, 1971). The average number of eye fixations was greatest when the pictures were needed to solve the problems, and lowest after the problem solving was completed. Ehrlichman and Barrett (1983) studied saccadic eye movements made during two kinds of cognitive activity: verbal-linguistic and visual-imaginal, tasks that did not require viewing of stimuli. Previous research suggested that people make more eye movements to questions calling for verbal processes than to ones requiring visual imagery. A sample verbal question was "What does this proverb mean: One today is worth two tomorrows?"; and a sample imaginal question was "What does your stove look like?". Prior work was confirmed, because resting eye movement rates were close to rates associated with imagery questions, whereas rates for verbal questions were much higher. Ehrlichman and Barrett suggested that the differences in eye movement rate reflect differences in internal sampling rate or shifts in cognitive operations. According to this view, interpreting a proverb would require more cognitive operations than generating, inspecting, and describing an image.

An interesting observation by Teitlebaum (1954) concerned the movement of a person's eyes either to the left or right when reflecting on a question asked by another person. This observation was investigated in more detail by Day (1964), who confirmed that the eyes move leftward or rightward in a consistent manner after persons had been asked a question requiring some thought. For example, you might ask a person to spell "Mississippi." The individual is usually unaware of the lateral movement, which can easily be observed by another person sitting opposite to the subject. It has been hypothesized that those persons who move their eyes rightward are left hemisphere dominant, whereas those who move their eyes to the left are presumed to be right-hemisphere dominant (Bakan, 1969).

Some evidence to support this proposal was obtained by Kinsbourne (1972), who found that right-handed subjects had a tendency to move their eyes to the right for verbal problems and either up or to the left for spatial problems. Hence, the eyes moved in a direction opposite to the hemisphere involved in the solution of the problem. However, Kinsbourne did not find these differences for numerical problems. He also reported that in left-handed subjects, the direction of movement did not correspond to problem type. This may be related to the fact that about 60% of left-handers are left-hemisphere dominant in language functions, whereas 40% are right-hemisphere dominant. Kocel, Galin, Ornstein, and Merrin (1972) observed that verbal and arithmetic questions elicited more rightward movements of the eyes than did spatial and musical questions. This result was interpreted as further support for the hypothesis that direction of lateral eye movement indicates activation of the contralateral hemisphere of the brain.

Gur (1975) tested 32 right-handed male students on spatial and verbal problems when sitting behind the subjects and when facing them. The filmed eye movements showed that they moved leftward with spatial problems and rightward for verbal problems when the experimenter sat behind the subjects. This finding corroborated previous ones. However, when the experimenter faced the subjects, the eyes moved predominantly in one direction, either left or right, regardless of problem type. Thus, the influence of problem type appears to be maximized when the experimenter's presence is minimized. Gur, Gur, and Harris (1975) reported that the eye movements of 17 left-handed subjects were haphazard even when the experimenter sat behind them and, therefore, were uncorrelated with problem type. This result supports the view that right-handers show a higher degree of hemispheric lateralization for various functions than do left-handed persons. None of the preceding studies used a physiological measure of brain activation to support the concept of contralateral hemispheric activation with direction of gaze. To partially fill this empirical gap, Shevrin, Smokler, and Kooi (1980) asked whether a disposition to look either left or right to questions would be related to larger brain responses (event-related potentials) on the contralateral side. The subjects were 20 right-handed individuals, and results indicated that left-looking persons had larger right-hemisphere ERP amplitudes to visual stimuli. The opposite was true for right-looking subjects. What is now needed to confirm the relationship between direction of looking and hemispheric activation is a study that obtains brain response (either EEG or ERP) simultaneous with the cognitive task.

In summary, studies of eye movements during problem solving suggest that lateralization of brain function may be reflected by the direction of this movement. The eyes move rightward for verbal analytic problems and leftward for spatial problems, suggesting activation of the contralateral hemisphere. A greater degree of lateralization for right-handers is also indicated by the experimental results.

Eye Movements and Reading

The study of eye movements during reading has been an area of basic laboratory research since the early 1900s (Woodworth, 1938; Woodworth & Schlosberg, 1954). Comparisons of eye movement patterns of slow and fast readers have been conducted in applied contexts to determine whether this information could be used in the development of remedial reading programs. A study by Buswell (1920), cited by Woodworth and Schlosberg (1954), examined the eye movement reading patterns of students at 13 levels from first grade to college. The results indicated the following, regarding the development of reading skills: (a) There was a steady decrease in number of eye fixations per line of reading material with higher grade levels (18.6 in first grade and 5.9 in college); (b) the fixations became shorter in duration (660 msec in first grade and 252 msec at college level); and (c) the number of regressive movements decreased from an average of 5.1 per line for first graders to .5 for college students. (Regressive movement refers to returning the eyes to earlier portions of the material being read.) Studies of slow and fast readers at the same grade level indicated that more efficient readers made fewer and shorter duration eye fixations and did not regress to early material as did inefficient readers.

The study of eye movements and reading continued through the 1930s and 1940s (see a review by Venezky, 1977), but not much had been done in this area until relatively recently, when researchers became interested in studying the eye movements of dyslexics and other individuals with reading difficulties. For example, Lefton (1978) studied the eye movement patterns of fifth grade children with reading disabilities while they did a letter-matching task. For his experiment, Lefton defined reading-disabled children as those of normal intelligence and no sensory defects, whose reading scores were $1\frac{1}{2}$ grades below average. The results showed that the reading-disabled children needed an unusually large number of eye fixations to do the task, more than did normal-reading third graders. Lefton has argued that abnormal eye movement patterns are the result of poor reading, and training in systematic gathering of information would be of help to poor readers. In support of Lefton's position have been studies reporting no difference between the eye movements of dyslexics and normal controls in a tracking task (Olson, Kleigl, & Davidson, 1983; Stanley, Smith, & Howell et al., 1983) but abnormal eye movements for dyslexics while reading (Olson et al. 1983). However, Pavlidis (1981) reported differences between dyslexics and normal readers' eye movements in a tracking task. The chief characteristic of dyslexics was the excessive number of regressive eye movements made while fixating sequentially illuminated rows of lights. Pavlidis (1985) pointed out that although there is a research concensus about the erratic eye movements of dyslexics during reading, the hypotheses proposed to explain these differences vary among investigators. The three types of hypotheses are: (a) erratic eye movements reflect problems that dyslexics have with the reading material; (b) erratic eye movements cause dyslexia; (c) erratic eye movements and dyslexia are symptoms of independent but parallel central deficits. Much of the recent research suggests that defective oculomotor control is not a causal factor in dyslexia, but that the dyslexic's abnormal eye movements in reading are due to cognitive problems such as deficits in processing information. Therefore, remedial reading programs for dyslexics should emphasize the development of thinking and information-processing strategies, not the pacing of eye movements.

Eye Movements and Psychopathology

A great deal of interest has been generated over the past 10 to 15 years in the possible link between unusual eye movements during tracking and different kinds of mental illness. The possibility of using deviant pursuit tracking eye movements as genetic markers in schizophrenia has been proposed by Holzman and associates (e.g., see Holzman et al., 1977). Other investigators have also reported discrepancies in the smooth pursuit EOGs of psychiatric patients. This is a potentially important area of study, but there have been procedural problems, such as not using objective indicators of poor eye tracking, that could affect reliability of results. Iacono and Lykken (1979) used improved techniques for recording and quantifying eye movements in a study of normal identical twins during tracking. The subjects were required to track a spot of light across a screen and both smooth pursuit and saccadic eye movements were analyzed. There were large differences between twin pairs in tracking ability, but within twin pairs, eye movement patterns were very similar. Testing in two sessions one week apart showed high consistency in scores, suggesting the stability of these measures over time. Long-term stability was dramatized in a follow-up conducted with fifty-two of the original twins 2 years later (Iacono & Lykken, 1981). Smooth pursuit and saccadic eye tracking proficiency were consistent with performance measured 2 years earlier, indicating that the tasks used tap relatively stable individual differences in traits. Levin (1984) contends that the dominant pattern of eye movement deficit in schizophrenics is the disruption of smooth pursuit by saccadic eye movements. He has suggested that this disruption is due to dysfunction of frontal lobe mechanisms in schizophrenics. Levin further contends that disturbances in attention and information processing of schizophrenics is similar to that of persons with frontal lobe lesions. Other researchers have reported that male college students identified as having impaired smooth pursuit eye movements were more likely to be diagnosed as having a "schizotypal" personality disorder than students identified as high-accuracy trackers (Siever, Coursey, Alterman, Buchsbaum & Murphy, 1984). They suggested that the tracking deficit might reflect a vulnerability for this type of disorder. The significance of saccadic interruptions in smooth pursuit EOGs is still not certain, despite the claims of some that it might be a biological marker of schizophrenia. The interruptions are related to poorer tracking performance, but they are also related to a tendency to have a series of sharp peaks, or spikes, superimposed on the EOG record. Those persons who have this type of "spiky" EOG produced more saccadic interruptions than subjects with smooth EOGs. Further, it has been found that this spiky type of record represents brain wave (EEG) artifact superimposed on the EOG (Iacono & Lykken, 1981). One possibility mentioned by Iacono and Lykken is that the superimposed EEG is alpha activity, a notion that is supported by work of scientists who found that alpha was absent from EEG of normal subjects during successful smooth-pursuit, but was present when saccades began to appear in the record. Perhaps the saccades represent periods of increased alpha activity that appear in the records of poor trackers because of some attentional deficit. Lower degrees of task engagement would lead to increased alpha activity.

Eye Movements in Visual Search

Visual search refers to examining the visual field to locate a desired object, for example, looking for a familiar face in a crowd of people. Ford, White, and Lichtenstein (1959) studied eye movements during free search for targets in a circular field subtending 30 degrees of visual angle. By "free search" the authors meant the kind of visual task involved in monitoring an empty visual field in which objects could appear at any time and at any location as, for example, in the case of an airplane pilot watching the sky for significant objects. The researchers found that, in free search, subjects averaged three eye fixations per second. The mean duration was found to be 280 msec for each fixation, and the average eye sweep covered 8.60 degrees of visual angle. The eye fixations were not distributed evenly over the search area, and the investigators suggested that patterns of eye movement would be influenced by extent and shape of the field searched and the time available for search. Their last suggestion was confirmed in a study by White and Ford (1960), who investigated eye movements during radar search and found eye patterns to be very different from the "free search" situation. The presence of the rotating scan-line on the radar set resulted in much more predictable, circular, search patterns. (The scan-line represents the radar antenna sweeping the sky for targets.) The mean fixation time was 370 msec (vs. 280 msec in free search), and the authors suggested that this was due to the greater restraints on eye movements produced in the more restricted radar task; that is, more fixations were made in free search. The greatest number of fixations occurred at about 4 degrees to 7 degrees from the center of the circular radar display.

Mackworth, Kaplan, and Metlay (1964) studied eye movements during a vigilance task. The detection task involved noticing a .5 second pause in a revolving dial pointer. Under the four experimental conditions, subjects monitored either one or two dials, with frequent or infrequent signals. They found that (a) detection probability for two dials was one-half that for one dial, and (b) in the one-dial condition, every missed signal was fixated without being detected. This latter point is noteworthy, because it indicted that fixation of a signal or target does not necessarily mean that it will be detected or recognized as such by the visual system. Mackworth has referred to this phenomenon as "looking without seeing."

Based on studies of eye movements, Gould (1969) concluded that the location of eye fixations on a display depends on four general factors: (a) the search task itself, (b) prior information about the target, (c) the purpose (as contained in instructions) of the subject, and (d) previous experience. For example, Gould and Schaffer (1965) found that subjects practiced in tachistoscopic perception required fewer fixations to find targets than those without this experience. These investigators recorded eye movements while subjects scanned patterns to compare the sum of three digits in each of four peripheral cells with that of three digits in a central (target) cell. Both larger target sums and greater target–nontarget similarity caused longer fixations.

Gould and Peeples (1970) recorded eye movements during a search task in which subjects had to determine how many of eight comparison patterns matched a standard pattern. One finding was that standard patterns were fixated longer than target patterns, even though they were identical. In addition, target patterns were fixated longer than nontarget patterns, suggesting that with unlike patterns, fixation stopped as soon as a difference was noted, whereas identical patterns led to fixation that ended only when all identical elements had been verified.

It has been found that the presence of irrelevant (nontarget) stimuli can influence the extent of saccadic movements made to detect a target (Coren & Hoenig, 1972a). Irrelevant targets result in longer search times, because target and nontarget stimuli must be sorted out. The effects of different methods of coding a target on search time and number of eye fixations were studied by Luria and Strauss (1975). They reported that color coding alone led to the fewest number of eye fixations and shortest search time. A combination of color and shape coding was second best, and shape alone was next best. The intermediate performance with the color-shape code may indicate that the subjects used color primarily and were slightly distracted by shape. The least efficient detection, in terms of the number of eye fixations required, was for the uncoded targets.

In summary, studies of eye movements during visual search have produced some basic information about the number and duration of eye fixations in the first stages of visual information processing. Mackworth's data indicated that fixation of a target may not be sufficient for detection. The mean number of fixations tends to parallel detection time, and the presence of irrelevant (nontarget) stimuli influences the extent of saccadic sweeps made to detect targets. Irrelevent stimuli also result in longer eye fixations during visual search. Color coding of targets seems to improve search time.

Eye Movements and Perception

The measurement of eye movements has been utilized by several investigators interested in the problems of pattern recognition and discrimination. In a study by Gould and Schafer (1967), subjects were alternately instructed to find patterns that either matched or did not match a standard pattern. Eye movement recordings indicated that subjects spent more time fixating patterns that exactly matched a memorized standard than on those which differed, suggesting that detailed comparisons of features were being made.

Noton and Stark (1971a,b) analyzed eye movements of subjects while they viewed different patterns in a "learning" phase and during a "recognition phase". In the first, or learning phase, they merely viewed five different patterns for 20 seconds each. In a second, or recognition phase, these five patterns were again viewed, along with five new ones. Analyses of eye movements indicated that subjects followed similar paths for a given pattern, and the sequence of movements was usually the same in the recognition phase as it was in the learning phase. This led Noton and Stark to suggest that memory for features of a picture is established sequentially by the memory of eye movements required to look from one feature to the next. The characteristic pattern of eye movements for a subject viewing a given stimulus has been termed a "scan path" by Noton and Stark. Gould and Peeples (1970) also reported consistent scan paths for their subjects. However, Luria and Strauss (1975) did not find consistent scanning strategies among their subjects. This led the latter investigators to suggest that the use of a characteristic scanning technique may depend on the type of search task.

What have eye movement studies revealed about how people look at pictures? A study by Mackworth and Morandi (1967) indicated that portions of a picture rated as highly informative by one group of people were fixated more frequently by another group of individuals who examined the pictures while their eye

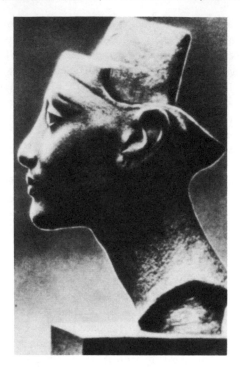

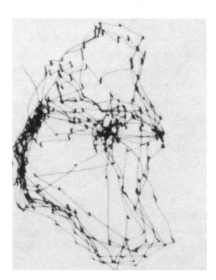

FIG. 10.7.   The bottom photograph is a record of eye movements made during free examination of the top photograph with both eyes for 3 minutes.

movements were measured. Yarbus (1967) found different patterns of eye movements while subjects viewed the same painting of a family scene under a variety of instructions. For example, when asked to estimate the wealth of the family, fixations centered on furniture and on clothing worn by women. When asked to estimate the ages of persons in the picture, eye fixations on faces became the most numerous. Thus, it seems that the information one wishes to derive from a visual scene will determine the pattern of eye movements used in examining the picture. In Fig. 10.7 eye movement patterns show the greatest number of fixations around the eyes, nose, and mouth of the sculpture.

Loftus (1972) found that durations of eye fixations did not affect recall of a picture, but that the number of fixations made during a fixed period of viewing did affect later recognition. That is, the greater the number, the more likely was the person to recognize the picture at another time. In another study, 20 subjects rated the informativeness of various regions in 10 pictures, and another 20 viewed each of the pictures for 20 seconds while their eye movements were measured (Antes, 1974). The findings were like those of Mackworth and Morandi, in that informative regions of pictures were fixated immediately. However, Antes also found that whereas initial fixations were on informative areas, the less informative detail received a greater proportion of the fixations later in the viewing sequence. Data from this and previous experiments also suggest that observers use information from peripheral vision to fixate immediately on informative areas. Gould (1974) pointed out that people tend to fixate on contours more frequently than on other areas of a picture. This is because contours carry critical information as to the shape, and therefore the identification of objects in the picture.

Research findings on visual search indicate that significant portions of visual stimuli attract eye fixations. Characteristic scan paths appear to exist, but their role in pattern recognition has not been determined. In looking at pictures, people tend to fixate those areas that contain the most information, especially in the early stages of viewing. The purpose of a viewer will also determine how he or she looks at a picture. A higher number of fixations during a viewing period seems related to superior recall of that picture.

Eye Movements and Illusions

In recent years, a good deal of attention has been given to the study of eye movements while persons experience various kinds of visual illusions. The familiar Muller-Lyer figure is one example. It will be recalled that the line with an attached arrow head pointed inward looks shorter than an identical line with the arrow head directed outward. It has been found that with prolonged inspection, the magnitude of the illusion decreases, although it does not disappear completely. One explanation for this concerns feedback provided by erroneous eye movements regarding the nature of the distortion. If eye movements are restricted to one portion of the figure, less information will be fed back, and the

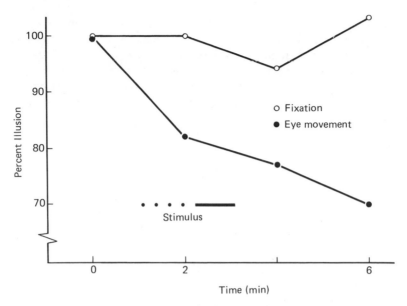

FIG. 10.8. Percentage of illusion is plotted against inspection time in minutes. The inset shows the Oppel-Kundt stimulus configuration used in the experiment.

illusion will persist to its full extent. An experiment that supports this eye movement hypothesis was conducted by Festinger, White, and Allyn (1968). They found that the Muller-Lyer illusion became less powerful when eye movements were made over the entire figure than when only one part of the figure was fixated. A similar result was found for the Oppel-Kundt figure, which also produces illusory differences in length of line (Coren & Hoenig, 1972b). In the Oppel-Kundt illusion, a divided horizontal space (e.g., four equally spaced dots) is seen as having greater linear extent than a solid horizontal line of identical length (see inset of Fig. 10.8). Two groups of 15 subjects each observed this illusion. One group made saccadic eye movements over the entire length of the illusion, whereas the other group fixated on the junction between the divided and undivided space. The illusion decreased over time for the eye movement group but not for the fixation group (see Fig. 10.8).

Eye movements were recorded while subjects experienced a "rebound illusion" (Mack, Fendrich, & Sirigatti 1973). The rebound illusion occurs when the eyes pursue a luminous object in the dark. When the object comes to an abrupt stop, it appears to rebound sharply backward. Experiments by Mack and colleagues indicated that the illusion is caused by an overshoot of the target by the eye, at the point at which the target stops. Thus, it appears that eye movement studies may provide valuable information regarding the bases for various kinds of visual illusion.

The Eyeblink in Fatigue and Perception

Stern (1980) has pointed out that the oculomotor control system is very sensitive to fatigue, boredom, and lapses in attention. Stern and his associates have found that long closure duration, the time the eyes remain closed during blinking, is related to reduced alertness. They have noted too that during reading there is an inhibition of blinking, which becomes more pronounced as a function of the reader's interest in the material. A flurry of blinks then occurs as the reader turns the page. In one experiment, blink rate was found to increase from an initial average rate of 15.7 blinks per minute to 26.2 per minute at the end of a 1-hour reaction time session (Stern, 1980). Blink closure duration followed a similar pattern, and was closely related to measures of reaction time performance. In a study out of Stern's laboratory (Goldstein, Walrath, Stern, & Strock, 1985), it was discovered that blink rate and duration were both less in a visual task than an auditory one. This result suggests that blink rate and duration lessen when the requirement is to process visual information. Bauer, Strock, Goldstein, Stern, and Walrath (1985) argued that blink suppression is due to increased cognitive demand that directs attention to task-relevant stimuli. Their study of blinking during an auditory discrimination task led them to conclude that blinks are delayed until decisions about external stimuli have been made and responses to those stimuli completed. Thus, such variables as blink rate and duration may be related to cognitive (decision making and discrimination) functions.

The next two chapters cover measures of cardiovascular activity and their relation to behavior. A representative summary of the voluminous research on the associations between heart activity and psychological functioning is presented in chapter 11. Discussions of blood pressure and blood volume are the topics of chapter 12.

REFERENCES

Ahern, S. K., & Beatty, J. (1981). Physiological evidence that demand for processing capacity varies with intelligence. In M. Friedman, J. P. Dos, & N. O'Connor (Eds.), *Intelligence and learning* (pp. 201–216). New York: Plenum Press.

Antes, J. R. (1974). The time course of picture viewing. *Journal of Experimental Psychology, 103*, 62–70.

Bakan, P. (1969). Hypnotizability, laterality of eye movement and functional brain asymmetry. *Perceptual & Motor Skills, 28*, 927–932.

Barlow, J. D. (1969). Pupillary size as an index of preference in political candidates. *Perceptual & Motor Skills, 28*, 587–590.

Bauer, L. O., Strock, B. D., Goldstein, R., Stern, J. A., & Walrath L. C. (1985). Auditory discrimination and the eyeblink. *Psychophysiology, 22*, 629–635.

Beatty, J. (1975). *Prediction of detection of weak acoustic signals from patterns of pupillary activity preceding behavioral response* (Tech. Rep. No. 140). Los Angeles: University of California, Department of Psychology.

Beatty, J. (1982). Task-evoked pupillary responses, processing load, and the structure of processing resources. *Psychological Bulletin, 91*, 276–292.

Beatty, J. (1986). The pupillary system. In M. G. H. Coles, E. Donchin, & S. W. Porges (Eds.), *Psychophysiology: Systems, processes and applications* (pp. 43–50). New York: Guilford Press.

Beatty, J., & Kahneman, D. (1966). Pupillary changes in two memory tasks. *Psychonomic Science, 5*, 371–372.

Bernick, N., Kling, A., & Borowitz, G. (1971). Physiologic differentiation of sexual arousal and anxiety. *Psychosomatic Medicine, 33*, 341–352.

Buswell, G. T. (1920). An experimental study of the eye-voice span in reading. *Supplemental Education Monograph, 17*, 507–510.

Carver, R. P. (1971). Pupil dilation and its relationship to information processing during reading and listening. *Journal of Applied Psychology, 55*, 126–134.

Chapman, L. J., Chapman, J. P., & Brelje, T. (1969). Influence of the experimenter on pupillary dilation to sexually provocative pictures. *Journal of Abnormal Psychology, 74*, 396–400.

Clark, W. R., & Ertas, M. A. (1975). A comparison of pupillary reactions to visual and auditory stimuli in a test of preferences for presidential candidates. *JSAS: Catalog of Selected Documents in Psychology.*

Coren, S., & Hoenig, P. (1972a). Effect of non-target stimuli upon length of voluntary saccades. *Perceptual & Motor Skills, 34*, 499–508.

Coren, S., & Hoenig, P. (1972b). Eye movements and decrement in the Oppel-Kundt illusion. *Perception & Psychophysics, 12*, 224–225.

Colman, F., & Paivio, A. (1970). Pupillary dilation and mediation processes during paired-associate learning. *Canadian Journal of Psychology, 24*, 261–270.

Darwin, C. (1872). *The expression of emotion in man and animals.* London: Murray.

Day, M. E. (1964). An eye-movement phenomenon relating to attention, thought and anxiety. *Perceptual & Motor Skills, 19*, 443–446.

Ehrlichmann, H., & Barrett, J. (1983), "Random" saccadic eye movements during verbal-linquistic and visual-imaginal tasks. *ACTA Psychologica, 53*, 9–26.

Festinger, L., White, C. W., & Allyn, M. R. (1968). Eye movements and decrement in the Muller-Lyer illusion. *Perception & Psychophysics, 3*, 376–382.

Ford, A., White, C. T., & Lichtenstein, M. (1959). Analysis of eye movements during free search. *Journal of the Optical Society of America, 49*, 287–292.

Friedman, D., Hakerem, G., Sutton, S., & Fleiss, J. L. (1973). Effect of stimulus uncertainty on the pupillary dilation response and the vertex evoked potential. *Electroencephalography & Clinical Neurophysiology, 74*, 272–283.

Geacintov, T., & Peavler, W. (1974). Pupillography in industrial fatigue assessment. *Journal of Applied Psychology, 59*, 213–216.

Goldstein, R., Walrath, L. C., Stern, J. A., & Strock, B. D. (1985). Blink activity in a discrimination task as a function of stimulus modality and schedule of presentation. *Psychophysiology, 22*, 629–635.

Gould, J. D. (1969). *Eye movements during visual search* (Research Rep. No. 2680). Yorktown Heights, NY: IBM.

Gould, J. D. (1974). *Looking at pictures* (Research Rep. No. RC 4991). Yorktown Heights, NY: IBM.

Gould, J. D., & Peeples, D. R. (1970). Eye movements during visual search and discrimination of meaningless, symbol and object patterns. *Journal of Experimental Psychology, 85*, 51–55.

Gould, J. D., & Schaffer, A. (1965). Eye Movement patterns during visual information processing. *Psychonomic Science, 3*, 317–318.

Gould, J. D., & Schaffer, A. (1967). Eye-movement parameters in pattern recognition. *Journal of Experimental Psychology, 74*, 225–229.

Gur, R. E. (1975). Conjugate lateral eye movements as an index of hemispheric activation. *Journal of Personality & Social Psychology, 31*, 751–757.

Gur, R. E., Gur, R. C., & Harris, L. J. (1975). Cerebral activation, as measured by subjects' lateral eye movements, is influenced by experimenter location. *Neuropsychologia, 13*, 35–44.

Guyton, A. C. (1977). *Basic human physiology: Normal function and mechanisms of disease.* Philadelphia: Saunders.

Hakerem, G. (1967). Pupillography. In P. H. Venables & I. Martin (Eds.), *Manual of psychophysiological methods* (pp. 335–349). Amsterdam: North-Holland.

Hakerem, G., & Sutton, S. (1966). Pupillary response at visual threshold. *Nature, 212,* 485–486.

Haltrecht, E. J., & McCormack, P. D. (1966). Monitoring eye movements of slow and fast learners. *Psychonomic Science, 6,* 461–462.

Hamel, R. F. (1974). Female subjective and pupillary reaction to nude male and female figures. *Journal of Psychology, 87,* 171–175.

Hess, E. H. (1972). Pupillometrics. In N. S. Greenfield & R. A. Sternbach (Eds.), *Handbook of psychophysiology* (pp. 491–531). New York: Holt, Rinehart & Winston.

Hess, E. H. (1975). *The tell-tale eye.* New York: Van Nostrand Reinhold.

Hess, E. H., & Petrovich, S. B. (1978). Pupillary behavior in communication. In A. W. Siegman, & S. Feldstein (Eds.), *Nonverbal behavior & communication* (pp. 159–179). Hillsdale, NJ: Lawrence Erlbaum Associates.

Hess, E. H., & Polt, J. M. (1960). Pupil size as related to interest value of visual stimuli. *Science, 132,* 349–350.

Hess, E. H., & Polt, J. M. (1964). Pupil size in relation to mental activity during simple problem solving. *Science, 143,* 1190–1192.

Hess, E. H., Seltzer, A. L. & Shlien, J. M. (1965). Pupil responses of hetero- and homosexual males to pictures of men and women: A pilot study. *Journal of Abnormal Psychology, 70,* 165–168.

Hicks, R. A., Williams, S. L., & Ferrante, F. (1979). Pupillary attributions of college students to happy and angry faces. *Perceptual & Motor Skills, 48,* 401–402.

Holzman, P. S., Kringlen, E., Levy, D. L., Proctor, L. R., Haberman, S. J., & Yasillo, N. (1977). Abnormal pursuit eye movements in schizophrenia: Evidence for a genetic indicator. *Archives of General Psychiatry, 34,* 802–805.

Iacono, W. G., & Lykken, D. T. (1979). Electro-oculographic recording and scoring of smooth pursuit and saccadic eye tracking: A parametric study using monozygotic twins. *Psychophysiology, 16,* 94–107.

Iacono, W. G., & Lykken, D. T. (1981). Two-year retest stability of eye tracking performance and a comparison of electro-oculographic and infrared recording techniques: Evidence of EEG in the Electro-oculogram. *Psychophysiology, 18,* 49–55.

Janisse, M. P. (1974). Pupil size, affect and exposure frequency. *Social Behavior & Personality, 2,* 125–146.

Janisse, M. P. (1977). *Pupillometry.* Washington, DC: Hemisphere Publishing.

Kahneman, D., & Beatty, J. (1966). Pupil diameter and load on memory. *Science, 154,* 1583–1585.

Kahneman, D., & Beatty, J. (1967). Pupillary responses in a pitch-discrimination task. *Perception & Psychophysics, 2,* 101–105.

Kahneman, D., & Peavler, W. S. (1969). Incentive effects and pupillary changes in association learning. *Journal of Experimental Psychology, 79,* 312–318.

Kahneman, D., & Wright, P. (1971). Changes of pupil size and rehearsal strategies in a short-term memory task. *Quarterly Journal of Experimental Psychology, 23,* 187–196.

Kinsbourne, M. (1972). Eye and headturning indicates cerebral lateralization. *Science, 176,* 539–541.

Kocel, K., Galin, D., Ornstein, R., & Merrin, E. L. (1972). Lateral eye movement and cognitive mode. *Psychonomic Science, 27,* 223–224.

Lefton, L. A. (1978). Eye movements in reading disabled children. In J. W. Senders, D. F. Fisher, & R. A. Monty (Eds.), *Eye movements and the higher psychological functions* (pp. 225–237). Hillsdale, NJ: Lawrence Erlbaum Associates.

Levin, S. (1984). Frontal lobe dysfunctions in schizophrenia: I: Eye movement impairments. *Journal of Psychiatric Research, 18,* 27–55.

Libby, W. L., Lacey, B. C., & Lacey, J. I. (1973). Pupillary and cardiac activity during visual attention. *Psychophysiology, 10,* 270–294.

Loftus, G. R. (1972). Eye fixations and recognition memory for pictures. *Cognitive Psychology, 3,* 525–551.

Loewenfeld, I. E. (1966). Pupil size. *Survey of Ophthalmology, 11,* 291–294.

Lowenstein, O., & Loewenfeld, I. E. (1962). The pupil. In H. Davson (Ed.), *The eye: Vol. 3, Muscular mechanisms* (pp. 301–340). New York: Academic Press.

Lowenstein, O., & Loewenfeld, I. E. (1964). The sleep–waking cycle and pupillary activity. *Annals of the New York Academy of Sciences, 117,* 142–156.

Luria, S. M., & Strauss, M. S. (1975). Eye movements during search for coded and uncoded targets. *Perception & Psychophysics, 17,* 303–308.

Mack, A., Fendrich, R., & Sirigatti, S. (1973). A rebound illusion in visual tracking. *American Journal of Psychology, 86,* 425–433.

Mackworth, N. H., Kaplan, I. T., & Metlay, W. (1964). Eye movements during vigilance. *Perceptual & Motor Skills, 18,* 397–402.

Mackworth, N. H., & Morandi, A. J. (1967). The gaze selects informative details within pictures. *Perception & Psychophysics, 2,* 547–552.

McCormack, P. D., Haltrecht, E. J., & Hannah, T. E. (1967). Monitoring eye movements during the learning of successive paired-associate lists. *Journal of Verbal Learning and Verbal Behavior, 6,* 950–953. (a)

McCormack, P. D., Hannah, T. E., Bradley, W. J., & Moore, T. E. (1967). Monitoring eye movements under conditions of high and low intralist response (meaningful) similarity. *Psychonomic Science, 8,* 517–518.

Nakano, A. (1971). Eye movements in relation to mental activity of problem-solving. *Psychologia: An International Journal of Psychology in the Orient, 14,* 200–207.

Noton, D., & Stark, L. (1971a). Scanpaths in saccadic eye movements while viewing and recognizing patterns. *Vision Research, 11,* 929–942.

Noton, D., & Stark, L. (1971b). Eye movements and visual perception. *Scientific American, 224,* 34–43.

Olson, R. R., Kleigl, R., & Davidson, B. J. (1983). Dyslexic and normal reader's eye movements. *Journal of Experimental Psychology: Human Perception and Performance, 9,* 816–825.

Paivio, A., & Simpson, H. M. (1966). The effect of word abstractness and pleasantness on pupil size during an imaginary task. *Psychonomic Science, 5,* 55–56.

Pavlidis, G. Th. (1981). Do eye movements hold the key to dyslexia? *Neuropsychologia, 19,* 57–64.

Pavlidis, G. Th. (1985). Eye movements in dyslexia: Their diagnostic significance. *Journal of Learning Disabilities, 18,* 42–50.

Peavler, W. S. (1974). Pupil size, information overload, and performance differences. *Psychophysiology, 11,* 559–566.

Peavler, W. S., & McLaughlin, J. P. (1967). The question of stimulus content and pupil size. *Psychonomic Science, 8,* 505–506.

Polt, J. M. (1970). Effect of threat of shock on pupillary response in a problem-solving situation. *Perceptual & Motor Skills, 31,* 587–593.

Poock, G. K. (1973). Information processing vs. pupil diameter. *Perceptual & Motor Skills, 37,* 1000–1002.

Qiyuan, J., Richer, F., Waggoner, B. L., & Beatty, J. (1985). The pupil and stimulus probability. *Psychophysiology, 22,* 530–534.

Shackel, B. (1967). Eye movement recordings by electroculography. In P. H. Venables & I. Martin (Eds.), *Manual of psycho-physiological methods* (pp. 299–334). Amsterdam: North-Holland.

Shevrin, H., Smokler, I., & Kooi, K. A. (1980). An empirical link between lateral eye movements and lateralized event-related brain potentials. *Biological Psychiatry, 15,* 691–697.

Siever, L. J., Coursey, R. D., Alterman, I. S., Buchsbaum, M. S., & Murphy, D. L. (1984). Impaired smooth pursuit eye movement: Vulnerability marker of schizotypal personality disorder in a normal volunteer population. *American Journal of Psychiatry, 141,* 1560–1566.

Simms, T. M. (1967). Pupillary response of male and female subjects to pupillary difference in male and female picture stimuli. *Perception & Psychophysics, 2,* 553–555.

Stanley, G., Smith, G. A., & Howell, E. A. (1983). Eye-movements and sequential tracking in dyslexic and control children. *British Journal of Psychology, 74,* 181–187.

Stanners, R. F., Headley, D. B., & Clark, W. R. (1972). The pupillary response to sentences: Influences of listening set and deep structure. *Journal of Verbal Learning and Verbal Behavior, 11,* 257–263.

Stelmack, R. M., & Mandelzys, N. (1975). Extraversion and pupillary response to affective and taboo words. *Psychophysiology, 12,* 536–540.

Stern, J. A. (1980). *Aspects of visual search activity related to attentional processes and skill development* (Final Report, Contract F49620-79-C0089). Washington, DC: Air Force Office of Scientific Research.

Tarrahian, G. A., & Hicks, R. A. (1979). Attribution of pupil size as a function of facial valence and age in American and Persian children. *Journal of Cross Cultural Psychology, 10,* 243–250.

Teitelbaum, H. A. (1954). Spontaneous rhythmic ocular movements: Their possible relationship to mental activity. *Neurology, 4,* 350–354.

Tryon, W. W. (1975). Pupillometry: A survey of sources of variation. *Psychophysiology, 12,* 90–93.

Venezky, R. L. (1977). Research on reading processes: A historical perspective. *American Psychologist, 32,* 339–345.

White, C. T., & Ford, A. (1960). Eye movements during simulated radar search. *Journal of the Optical Society of America, 50,* 909–913.

White, G. L., & Maltzman, I. (1977). Pupillary activity while listening to verbal passages. *Journal of Research in Personality, 12,* 361–369.

Williams, S. L., & Hicks, R. A. (1980). Sex, iride pigmentation, and the pupillary attribution of college students to happy and angry faces. *Bulletin of the Psychonomic Society, 10,* 67–68.

Woodmansee, J. J. (1967, August). *The pupil reaction as an index of positive and negative affect.* Paper presented at the convention of The American Psychological Association, Washington, DC.

Woodworth, R. S. (1938). *Experimental psychology.* New York: Holt.

Woodworth, R. S., & Schlosberg, H. (1954). *Experimental psychology.* New York: Holt.

Yarbus, A. L. (1967). Eye movements and vision. New York: Plenum Press.

11
Heart Activity
and Behavior

Why should the heart be of interest in psychophysiological research? After all, it is merely a muscular pump that pushes out blood to the rest of the body. True, but as we noted in chapter 1, there are written records to show that very early scientists observed that changes in cardiac activity were related to such psychological phenomena as "love sickness." In fact, it is more than likely that changes in heart activity that occurred in fear-producing situations were noticed by cave people, who lived many thousands of years ago. The association of the heart with love, cupid's bow, and Valentine's day also reflects individual perceptions of heartbeat changes that occur with emotional reactions. Today we use scientific methods to study changes in heart activity, not only during obviously emotional situations but also in the performance of more subtle tasks, such as signal detection and problem solving. We shall see that experimental evidence indicates significant interactions of heart activity with somatic (muscle) and central (brain) activity. These findings have been elaborated in the cardiac–somatic concept of Paul Obrist and the intake–rejection formulation of John and Beatrice Lacey, as discussed in chapter 15. In this chapter, the changes in heart activity that occur in various behavioral situations are considered. The behavioral effects that we examine include motor activities, mental tasks, perceptual and orienting reactions, emotional reactions, and conditioning. The section on conditioning briefly considers investigations of classical and instrumental conditioning of heart activity. But, first, we briefly review the anatomy and physiology of the heart and how its activity is measured.

ANATOMY AND PHYSIOLOGY OF THE HEART

The heart is a muscular, four-chambered organ whose main function is to supply blood, which contains nutriments and oxygen necessary for the functioning of

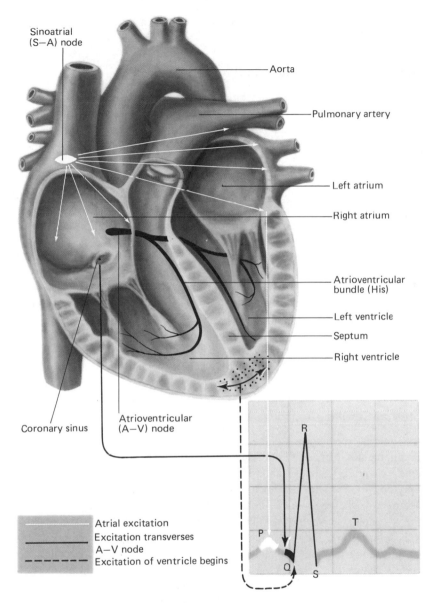

FIG. 11.1. Conducting system of the heart showing source of electrical impulses produced on electrocardiogram.

body cells, to the tissues of the body. The heart is about the size of a man's fist. It weighs approximately 300g in the male and 250g in the female. The four chambers are the right and left atria (on top) and the right and left ventricles (on the bottom). Figure 11.1 is a cutaway drawing that shows the various heart chambers. The atria are receiving chambers for blood that has been returned to the heart by the veins. The ventricles pump blood via arteries to the lungs and the rest of the body.

Heart Structures Involved in Blood Circulation

The right atrium receives blood from all body tissues except the lungs. The veins that bring blood to the right atrium are (a) the superior vena cava (blood from the upper body), (b) the inferior vena cava (blood from the lower body), and (c) the coronary sinus (blood from the heart itself). The blood flows from the right atrium to the right ventricle and from there to the lungs (via the pulmonary artery). In the lungs, carbon dioxide is removed from the blood and oxygen is added. The oxygenated blood is then returned to the left atrium by four pulmonary veins. From there, it goes to the left ventricle, which then pumps the oxygenated blood through the aorta to the rest of the body.

Control of the Heartbeat (Cardiac Cycle)

The heartbeat, which we can hear through a stethoscope and record with the electrocardiograph, represents the contracting that the heart does to pump blood to other body areas. The human heart normally contracts at a rate of about 72 beats per minute (bpm) at rest. This average rate translates to just over 100,000 times per day and between 2.5 and 3.0 billion times in a lifetime of 70 to 80 years. The control of this beating is by mechanisms both internal and external to the heart.

Internal Cardiac Control

The internal mechanism of the heartbeat consists of a system of specialized fibers, including: (a) the sinoatrial (S-A) node, (b) the atrioventricular (A-V) node, (c) the A-V bundle, and (d) the left and right bundles of conducting fibers (Guyton, 1977). The S-A node is located in the right atrium, and its regular electrical discharge produces the normal rhythmic contraction of the entire heart. The S-A node is also known as the pacemaker, with a rate of 120 bpm at normal body temperature. However, the vagus nerve inhibits the pacemaker and holds the rate down to approximately 70–80 bpm. The impulse for contraction is slightly delayed at the A-V node before passing into the ventricles. The A-V bundle then conducts the impulse into the ventricles, and Purkinje fibers conduct the impulse for contraction to all parts of the ventricles. The contraction phase of the heart is known as *systole,* whereas the relaxation phase is termed *diastole.*

External Cardiac Control

The normal regular rate of contraction may also be influenced by external factors, that is, by nerves from the autonomic (ANS) and central (CNS) nervous systems. The parasympathetic (PNS) system influences the S-A and A-V nodes via the vagus nerve. Its influence results in the slowing of the heartbeat. This influence is produced by the release of the neurotransmitter acetylcholine at the vagus nerve endings, which, in turn, results in the slowing of activity at the S-A node (cardiac pacemaker) and a slowing of the cardiac impulse passing into the ventricles (Guyton, 1977). The SNS has the opposite effect; that is, it produces an increase in heart rate. It exerts this effect through the release of norepinephrine at the sympathetic nerve endings. This results in (a) an increase in the rate of S-A node discharge, (b) increased excitability of heart tissue, and (c) an increase in force of contraction of both atrial and ventricular musculature. The SNS acts to increase cardiac output in certain emotional situations or at extreme levels of exercise. However, it should be noted that HR increases are often due to decreased vagus nerve inhibition (PNS). Thus, changes in heart rate depend on SNS and PNS activity, so an increase can be due to a decrease in PNS activity, an increase in SNS activity, or both. Cardiac output refers to the amount of blood pumped by the heart. At rest, this is approximately 5 to 6 liters per minute, but can increase to five times that amount with heavy exercise. Also changing during vigorous exercise is the distribution of blood in various body tissues. For example, whereas the muscles receive 15 to 20% of the cardiac output of blood at rest, the amount changes to 80 to 85% with strenuous exercise or work (Astrand & Rodahl, 1977).

At one time, it was thought that the medulla exerted the primary control over certain reflex actions concerned with influencing heart rate. However, it is now known that other CNS structures, including the hypothalamus, cerebellum, and amygdala, also contribute to these reflexes.

Carotid Sinus Reflex

Baroreceptors (pressure sensitive) are present in the carotid sinus, located in the neck at about the level of the chin. The carotid sinus is supplied by fibers from the glossopharyngeal (IXth) cranial nerve. When pressure on the walls of the carotid sinus is low, because of decreased blood pressure, this information is transmitted to a cardiac acceleration center in the medulla. At this point, sympathetic fibers are brought into action to increase heart rate and, in addition, to bring the pressure of the carotid sinus up to an acceptable level. The basic function of the baroreceptors is to ensure an adequate blood supply to the brain. Thus, we see the operation of a feedback mechanism that maintains heart rate and blood pressure within certain limits. The reader who is interested in more detail on this topic may want to consult a review of central mechanisms in the control of heart rate by Cohen and MacDonald (1974). There are other internal and external factors that can influence heart rate, including the metabolism of the heart itself, chemical factors, and hormonal influences.

MEASUREMENT OF HEART ACTIVITY

The study of electrical changes occurring during the heart's contractions was made possible by Willem Einthoven of Holland in 1904 (Pardee, 1933). He developed an instrument sensitive and quick enough to follow the small, rapidly varying currents produced by the heart. It had been known since 1856 that the heart's contraction was accompanied by the production of an electric current. In 1887, Waller showed that the current could be recorded from the surface of the body if proper contact was made between wires from a galvanometer and two body locations on either side of the heart. Einthoven's string galvanometer made the recording of heart activity practical in the early 1900s, and it was soon to become widely used in large European clinics at about that time. This early recording device and modern ones take advantage of the fact that a portion of the electrical impulse that passes through the heart during contraction spreads to the surface of the body. If electrodes are placed on the skin, the electrical potentials generated by the heart can be recorded. When these potentials are amplified and recorded on an ink writer, the resulting measurement is called the electrocardiogram (ECG). The normal ECG is composed of characteristic deflections referred to as P, Q, R, S, and T waves. These wave components of the ECG are depicted in Fig. 11.2. The relatively small P wave is produced by electrical currents generated just before contraction of the atria. The QRS complex is caused by currents generated in the ventricles during depolarization just prior to ventricular contraction. Note that the R wave is the most prominent component of the QRS component. The T wave is caused by repolarization of the ventricles. Atrial repolarization does not result in a separate ECG wave because it is masked by the more pronounced ventricular-related changes. The depolarization and repolarization that occurs in cardiac muscle fibers is similar in principle to the depolarization and repolarization that occurs in neurons. That is, depolarization occurs as the ionic activity inside of the fiber becomes positive with respect to the outside, and repolarization is a return to internal negativity and external positivity.

Wave Component Durations

The time between the start of the P wave and the beginning of the QRS complex (or P–Q interval) is about 160 msec (Guyton, 1977). The Q–T interval, or the time from the beginning of the Q wave to the end of the T wave, is about 300 msec. Because the cardiac cycle lasts about 830 msec (based on a rate of 72 bpm), there are approximately 370 msec between the end of the T wave and the beginning of the next atrial contraction. The heart actually spends less time contracting than relaxing; for example, with a cycle of 800 msec, it is in ventricular systole for 300 msec and in diastole for 500 msec.

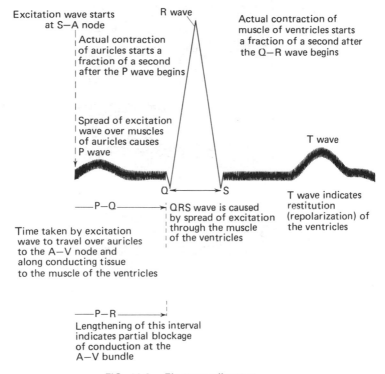

Excitation wave starts
at S—A node

| Actual contraction
| of auricles starts a
| fraction of a second
| after the P wave begins

R wave

Actual contraction of
muscle of ventricles starts
a fraction of a second after
the Q—R wave begins

| Spread of excitation
| wave over muscles
| of auricles causes
| P wave

T wave

Q ← → S

——P—Q——————→| QRS wave is caused
| by spread of excitation
Time taken by excitation | through the muscle
wave to travel over auricles | of the ventricles
to the A—V node and
along conducting tissue
to the muscle of the ventricles

T wave indicates
restitution
(repolarization) of
the ventricles

——P—R————→|
Lengthening of this interval
indicates partial blockage
of conduction at the
A—V bundle

FIG. 11.2.   Electrocardiogram.

Limb Leads for Recording the ECG

There are several standard limb leads for ECG recording. They are as follows:

Lead I: Electrodes are attached just above the wrists on the insides of the right
and left arms. The polarity is selected so that when the left arm lead is
positive, with respect to the right, there is an upward deflection of the P and R
segments of the ECG.

Lead II: Electrodes are attached above the right wrist and above the left ankle.
The polarity is chosen such that there is an upward deflection of the P and R
waves of the ECG when the ankle lead is positive relative to the arm placement.

Lead III: Electrodes are attached above the left wrist and above the left ankle.
Again, the polarity is selected so that there is an upward deflection of the P
and R waves when the ankle placement is positive relative to the arm lead.
Normal ECG records obtained through the use of these three lead placements
are shown in Fig. 11.3.

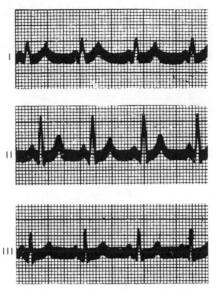

FIG. 11.3.   Normal electrocardiograms recorded from three standard electrocardiographic leads.

The leads just described are adequate in situations where subjects are lying down or sitting or standing in one place. However, for active subjects, sternal or axillary leads are preferred. Sternal leads are placed over bone (sternum), and are therefore relatively immune to movement artifacts (see Fig. 11.4). The placement of chest leads illustrated in Fig. 11.4 shows the upper electrode placed on the manubrium of the sternum and the lower lead on the xiphoid process of the sternum. An upward deflection on the ECG is obtained when the upper electrode is positive relative to the lower one. The axillary (underarm) leads are also depicted in Fig. 11.4 and show placements at the level of the heart. They are moderately free from movement artifacts, but because they are over muscle tissue, arm movements may produce EMG artifacts.

Amplitude and Recording Characteristics of the ECG

In the normal ECG, lead II produces an R wave that ranges in amplitude up to about 2 mV (Brener, 1967). This 2-mV peak is much larger than that encountered in either EEG or EMG recordings. The 2-mV peak amplitude must be amplified by a factor of about 2500 to bring it to a usable level. The procedure in clinical work is to use a gain setting that will allow a vertical deflection of 1 cm equal to 1 mV. A slightly higher gain would be used by researchers in psychophysiology. Paper speeds of 25 mm/sec enable good resolution of the various components of the ECG, and are necessary when investigators want information

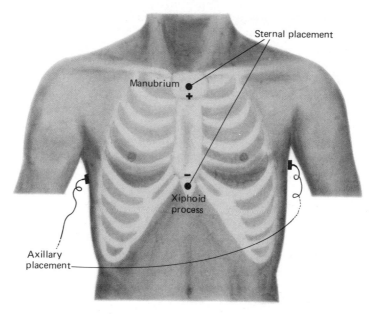

FIG. 11.4. Placement of electrodes at manubrium and xiphoid pro-cess of sternum enables recording of ECG with active subjects. The axillary placements are not as free from EMG artifact as are the sternal leads.

on interbeat intervals. When information on rate only is desired, speeds of 5 or 10 mm/sec are adequate.

Measures in Research

In studies of human performance, heart rate or heart period (HP) are commonly used as measures of heart activity. The HR is based on the number of beats per unit of time, for example, in beats per minute (BPM). It is based on the occur-rence of the most prominent component of the ECG, that is, the R wave. Thus, continuous recordings of HR may be taken and then BPM may be computed. Alternatively, 10 or 20 seconds of the activity in a given minute may be sampled and taken as the HR for that period. The HR may also be continuously monitored by electronic counters, which can automatically print out the rate for given time periods.

The HP measures the time between one R wave and the next. Another way of referring to HP is the interbeat interval (IBI). The HP, or IBI, is expressed in milliseconds, and may be automatically measured by an event per unit time (EPUT) meter (Brown, 1972). This device is commercially available, and can be connected to a printer to obtain a numeric readout of each heart period. Information regarding interbeat variability can be continuously provided through the use of commercially available cardiotachometers. These devices are available as modular units that can be plugged in for use with a particular physiological recorder. Researchers interested in changes in heart activity that can occur within a single cardiac cycle make use of the HP, or IBI, measure. Those interested in longer-term changes that occur over a period of 30 sec. or more may use BPM. Still another way of looking at cardiac changes is in terms of HR variability. This is a measure of the stability of HR during baseline or during the performance of a task. For example, it has been suggested that attention-demanding tasks that require information processing result in less variation of HR from reading to reading (Walter & Porges, 1976). Those interested in an alternate view of examining HR variability, other than using a variance statistic, may want to consult Heslegrave, Ogilvie, and Furedy (1979). They presented evidence to show that the combination of a successive difference mean square (SDMS) procedure as the variability statistic and IBI for the HR measure is best for assessing changes in HR variability under certain conditions. In addition, IBI may be preferable to BPM for showing average HR changes between conditions.

The ECG can be recorded on any physiological recorder that provides a pen deflection of 1–15 mm for each millivolt of signal and can process frequencies from 0.1 to 125 Hz (Brown, 1972). It is recorded with an A.C. amplifier. The ECG is not difficult to obtain, because it is a relatively large signal and does not require as much amplification as some other measures (e.g., EMG). With lower degrees of amplification, one is less likely to pick up unwanted electrical activity. Stern, Ray, and Davis (1980) pointed out that because HR has a frequency of about 1 Hz (one cycle per second), a filter can be set at 20 to 30 Hz, reducing the problem of 60 Hz noise and removing most muscle artifact. However, as with other physiological measures, the proper use and application of electrodes is critical in obtaining a good record.

Impedance Cardiography.   The impedance cardiograph (ZCG) technique can provide valuable information about physical function of the heart, as a supplement to electrical data provided by the ECG. The kinds of physical functions that may prove useful to psychophysiologists include cardiac output, stroke volume, ventricular ejection time, myocardial contractility, and total peripheral resistance.

The recording principle in impedance cardiography is that when a high frequency (e.g., 100 kHz) constant-current (4 mA) signal is passed across the thoracic cavity (chest), the impedance measured between two electrodes will vary with the volume of the cavity. The impedance decreases as volume increases. Double strips of electrode tape are placed around the neck and the chest at diaphragm level (see Miller & Horvath, 1978). The top and bottom electrode strips are connected to a high-frequency signal source, while the middle two record impedance changes (see Fig. 11.5 for a schematic diagram). Impedance cardiograph devices are available commercially, as are the strip chart recorders

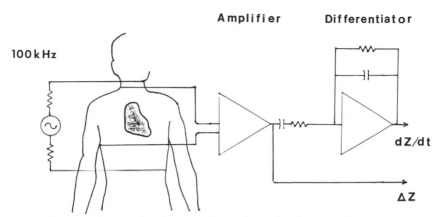

FIG. 11.5.   Schematic Diagram of Impedance Cardiograph. (Courtesy Dr. Glenn Albright, Baruch College, C.U.N.Y.)

to which they are attached. The records may be hand scored from the chart paper or, if recorded on FM tape, they may be processed off-line with a computer program.

As explained earlier, cardiac output is a measure of the amount of blood, in liters, that the heart pumps per minute. Other measures that may be estimated with impedance cardiography include stroke volume (the amount of blood pumped per beat), myocardial contractility (the degree to which the heart muscle contracts in pumping blood), ventricular ejection time (the time it takes for the left ventricle to eject blood), and total peripheral resistance (resistance to blood flow in the body). Figure 11.6 illustrates an impedance cardiograph record and how the various values are derived. The Z_0 value is total impedance between leads 2 and 3 (the two inner leads); dZ/dt is the first derivative of the change of impedance during a cardiac cycle; VET is ventricular ejection time; and R-Z is the time interval from the R wave of the ECG to maximum ejection as indicated by the peak of dZ/dt. Tursky and Jamner (1982) explained that psychophysiologists see promise for impedance cardiography as a method for measuring relative contributions of the PNS and SNS to cardiac functions and as a useful technique in studies of hypertension. The technique also has clinical applications in measuring cardiac function before and after heart surgery. Miller and Horvath (1978) concluded that impedance cardiography gives a reliable within-subject estimate of relative changes in measures such as stroke volume and cardiac output, but is not as useful for comparing measures between subjects. In making impedance cardiograph recordings, subjects must be carefully instructed to hold their breath while several cardiac cycles are obtained (about 10 seconds), otherwise breathing artifact may appear. Thus, the researcher must take certain precautions in using this technique. As is seen in later portions of this chapter, studies of cardiac activity using the impedance technique are increasing in number.

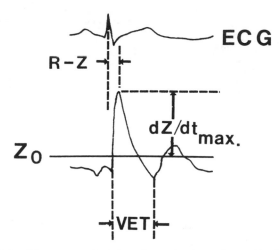

FIG. 11.6.   Measurements taken from the Impedance Cardiograph. (Courtesy Dr. Glenn Albright, Baruch College, C.U.N.Y.)

Electrodes in ECG Recordings

A number of good commercially available electrodes may be used for research purposes. Electrodes can be made of stainless steel or silver. They are usually in the shape of flat discs, or cups, measuring from $\frac{1}{2}$ in. to 2 in. across. They may be held in place by adjustable rubber straps, suction cups, surgical tape, or adhesive plastic strips. Some excellent electrodes have been developed in connection with the space program, and are especially suited for long-term recordings, that is, 24 hours or more. One example is a silver disc embedded in a rubber suction cup with a center-mounted sponge that contains the electrolyte.

Electrodes should be applied to hairless sites, if possible. The area of application may be briskly rubbed with a gauze pad until the skin is slightly pink. Then electrode jelly or paste is applied to the electrode before it is attached to the recording site. Electrodes should not be so tightly attached that they cause discomfort or muscle tremor. The latter can cause artifacts in the record. On the other hand, they must be prevented from moving, because this will also result in distorted recordings. As mentioned previously, the sternal lead is preferred for the moving subject. It also has the advantage of producing a large R wave. Leads II and III also produce large R waves. The large R wave is important in terms of ease of analyzing the data and providing a suitable signal for triggering automatic counters. Brown (1972) has recommended that the amplified R wave be used to activate a Schmitt trigger, a device that will enable signals to activate counters or cardiotachometers in a reliable manner.

For a freely ranging subject, telemetry or portable recorders may be used. Telemetry is far more comfortable for the subject. The subject wears electrodes and a small FM or AM transmitter (as light as 18 g), capable of sending heart signals to a recorder at another location, where the information may be recorded on FM tape. Miniature portable recorders enable ECGs to be obtained from subjects or patients as they do about their daily activities (e.g., see Gunn, Wolf, Block, & Person, 1972). Electrodes attached to the sternum and rib cage are fed into a small recorder that amplifies the signal and records it on a tape. Such recording units weigh about 2 to 3 lb. and are attached around the patient's or subject's waist with a belt. usually, the recordings are made for a 24-hour period. The large mass of data obtained can be analyzed by modern computer techniques in a matter of minutes.

HEART ACTIVITY AND BEHAVIOR

The number of studies devoted to heart activity and human behavior are considerable. The heart and the brain are favorite topic organs of the psychophysiologist. The studies described in this chapter are, by necessity, only representative of the large volume of research conducted over approximately the last 15 or 20 years. We consider relationships between heart activity and the following: motor performance, cognition, perception, attention, emotional reactions, motivation, personality factors, and conditioning.

Motor Performance and Heart Activity

It is well known that vigorous muscular activity produces a requirement for increased blood supply, and that heart activity speeds up under these conditions. Hence, under continued strenuous motor performance, higher HR would be expected. However, there are motor activities, for example, simple RT, that require only periodic and bricf movements, involving muscles to a minimal degree. In this section, we examine two categories of motor activities: (a) the type associated with quick, unstrenuous reactions, as in studies of RT, and (b) those in which continuous, complex, or strenuous motor performance is required.

Reaction Time. An interesting body of literature has grown concerning the relationship between cardiac activity and RT. A number of investigators have found that decreased HR occurs during the fixed foreperiod of simple RT experiments (e.g., Lacey, 1967; Obrist, Webb, & Sutterer, 1969; Webb & Obrist, 1970). There have been suggestions that greater magnitudes of HR slowing are related to faster RTs.

Although HR deceleration has sometimes been associated with faster RTs in situations where foreperiods are used, this does not appear to hold when the HR is controlled by external factors or when no warning signal is used. For example, Nowlin, Eisdorfer, Whalen, and Troyer (1970) manipulated the HR of 14 cardiac patients (with pacemakers) and found no relation between RT and different rates of cardiac pacing. In another study, Surwillo (1971) measured HR and RTs of 100 healthy males in three experimental sessions. Stimuli occurred at random (no warning or foreperiod), and RTs were collected in three experimental sessions as HR varied spontaneously. Cardiac deceleration to stimuli was not observed under these conditions. Thus, these last two studies indicate that HR slowing and RT were unrelated when an external cardiac pacemaker was used and when stimuli were presented without regular foreperiods.

Botwinick and Thompson (1971) measured RTs at different phases of the cardiac cycle of 13 elderly males. Stimuli were programmed to occur at the R wave, or at .2, .4, or .6 second after the R wave. The preparatory interval was kept constant among these four conditions of stimulation. The RT did not vary with the phase of the cardiac cycle of these 13 subjects or in another group of 31 younger male subjects.

Obrist, Howard, Sutterer, Hennis, and Murrell (1973) studied the relationship between RT, HR, and measures of task-irrelevant somatic activity (eye movements and blinks, chin EMG, general bodily activity, and respiration). The subjects were four groups of children (4-, 5-, 8-, and 10-year-olds) and an adult reference group. The purpose was to study the cardiac–somatic hypothesis that HR and ongoing somatic activities vary in a similar direction. The investigators expected that the younger children would show more somatic activity because of inability to inhibit restlessness. They reported that for all groups a decrease in HR and a drop in task-irrelevant somatic activities were coincident with making the relevant responses. However, they failed to find a lawful developmental trend (i.e., changes with age) of incremental HR deceleration, although RT was faster in older children. Klorman (1975) measured HR and RT in groups of preadolescent (10 years of age), adolescent (14 years), and young adult (19 years) males. The task was simple RT with a relatively long (5-second) foreperiod. His HR findings agreed with those of Obrist et al. (1973), in that there was no systematic age differences in cardiac deceleration, even though older subjects had quicker RTs.

Lacey and Lacey (1977) used a fixed-foreperiod RT paradigm and measured heart period (R–R interval) as a function of time at which an imperative stimulus was presented in the cardiac cycle. They found that magnitude of HR deceleration during the preparatory interval depended on where in the cardiac cycle the imperative (response) signal was presented. If it occurred early (4th decile) in the cardiac cycle, deceleration was much greater than if the imperative signal came late (10th decile) in the cycle. Earlier stimuli produce greater HR deceleration because they have more time to exert an influence (Velden, Barry, & Wolk, 1987). Lacey and Lacey attributed the speed of this deceleration to the rapid control exerted by the vagus nerve upon HR.

Phasic cardiac responses of eight subjects were studied during choice RT (Jennings & Wood, 1977). The cardiac cycle time was varied by presenting stimuli at either the R wave or 350 msec later. An interesting finding was that when responses occurred early in the cycle, anticipatory deceleration ended and shifted to acceleration within the same heartbeat. However, if responses occurred later than 300 msec after the R wave, the shift from slowing to speeding was delayed until the next heartbeat. To explain this, Jennings and Wood hypothesized that the vagal inhibitory activity responsible for slowing of HR ends when a task is completed, and therefore, the shift to speeding depends on the time course of vagal inhibition. The RT data showed that magnitudes of both HR deceleration and accelerative recovery were larger for faster responses. However, speed of RT was not related to time of stimulation in the cardiac cycle. Coles, Pellegrini, and Wilson (1982) found that both warning stimuli and stimuli to respond produced a decelerative effect on HR. An interesting aspect of this was that the deceleration was not found with slow HR subjects while they were breathing in. Thus, the influence of vagus nerve slowing was modified by level of HR and phase of the respiratory cycle. Coles and colleagues found no evidence for a cardiac cycle time effect on RT speed. Methodologically, their results suggest the importance of considering respiratory phase in evaluating cardiac cycle time effects.

In summary, it is well established that HR deceleration occurs during the fixed foreperiod of an RT task. The relationship between magnitude of HR slowing and speed of RT is still a point of controversy. It is clear that when an RT task is performed under conditions in which HR is externally manipulated, or without fixed foreperiods or warning signals, there is no HR decrease associated with the period just prior to the response or during the response itself. The general findings suggest that unmanipulated cardiac deceleration represents a preparation to respond when an individual expects a significant stimulus. Developmental changes in HR deceleration have not been found, although RT is faster in adolescents and young adults than in children. Recent findings indicate that magnitude of HR deceleration during the preparatory interval of an RT task depended on time of event occurrence within the cardiac cycle. In addition, it has been found that when RT responses occurred early enough in a cardiac cycle, deceleration terminated and shifted to acceleration within the same heartbeat. Speed of RT has not been found to be related to time of stimulation in the cardiac cycle. Vagal activity has been proposed as a mechanism in the HR slowing observed in these situations.

Complex Motor Performance and Heart Activity.   Ohkubo and Hamley (1972) obtained measures of HR during a 5-day period while individuals learned to drive a car. The subjects were 12 young males who were instructed in driving along an isolated course five times during each day of training. As proficiency increased, a marked decrease was observed in HR during both rest and driving periods. Studies of HR increases in novice sport parachutists indicate that maximal rates are reached when the plane reaches the jump altitude. A more convenient way of measuring HR responses in a stressful situation was used by Lewis, Ray, Wilkinson, and Ricketts (1984), when they introduced the "zipwire" slide. In this situation, a person slides down a 60-foot wire via a pulley from a 35-foot height. The task allows experimenters to repeat a number of trials over a relatively brief period. In their study, Lewis and collaborators had male and female subjects without previous risk sport experience (e.g., no skydiving) complete eight runs on the zipwire while HR and self-reports of anxiety level were obtained. Telemetered HR was obtained in seven stages, from climbing the ladder to reaching the ground. The HR peaked during the slide, and levels for males and females were similar. However, females reported more anxiety than males. An interesting sex difference emerged, in that females who had the greatest elevations in HR also reported the highest anxiety, but males with highest HR increases reported the lowest anxiety levels. One might speculate that the more anxious males could hide this fact in the self-report, but not in their HR measures.

An interesting observation is that HR often increases more during the performance of certain motor tasks than would be expected purely on the basis of increases of energy expenditure. This was first reported for a reaction time–avoidance task where subjects were required to react quickly to avoid an electric shock (Obrist et al, 1974). Increases in HR occurred after the response was made, and motor activity was not very great. Turner, Caroll, and Courtney (1983) examined HR and respiration changes while subjects played a computer game called "Space Invaders," and also when the game proceeded automatically with motor activities not effecting the outcome. It was clear that the HR increases during actual playing of the game were much greater than expected from the energy used. Also, some subjects showed larger-than-average HR reactivity to the Space Invader task, a mean of 15.7 bpm compared to 1.9 bpm for low reactors. The low and high reactors differed by only .7 bpm on the control condition. This study affirms previous findings that HR increases beyond metabolic requirements in challenging perceptual motor tasks, and that some individuals may be classified as high HR reactors.

Heart Activity and Mental Performance

In this section, we consider heart activity and mental performance in situations where the task or task situation was not intended to be stressful or provoke an emotional reaction. The latter type of relationship is examined in a subsequent section. This section focuses on the relationship between cardiac activity and verbal learning, problem solving, and cognitive activity (thoughts and imagery).

Verbal Learning.   In one study of verbal learning, Andreassi (1966) investigated the relationship between HR, SCL, SCRs, and difficulty of materials to be learned. (The SCL and SCR findings were discussed in chapter 9.) The mean HR was significantly higher when the subjects learned the easiest list than when they performed with lists of moderate or high difficulty. Thus, superior performance was related to elevated HR. The results suggested that during superior performance, the individuals became more involved in the learning task, and this effect was reflected in the increased HR. A similar finding was reported by Malmo (1965), who found that HR was consistently higher during tracking trials where performance was better, as compared to the poor-performance trials.

Andreassi and Whalen (1967) reported that the HR of college students was elevated during learning to criterion compared to resting. When the same list was presented for 20 additional trials after original learning, HR showed a significant decrease. Finally, the requirement to learn a new list of materials produced a significant increase in HR. In a second experiment, these researchers asked new subjects to learn a list of verbal materials to a criterion of perfect recitation. After this, the list was practiced for two sets of trials. The original learning was associated with an average increase in HR of from 79 to 87 bpm. The mean HR decreased to 83 bpm in the first overlearning session and to 81 bpm in the final set of 20 list repetitions. The decreased HR was interpreted in terms of an habituation of physiological responsivity when the individuals were no longer required to assimilate novel materials.

To briefly summarize, elevated HR occurs during the acquisition phase of verbal learning, especially if performance is successful. Continued repetition of familiar materials will produce a decrease in HR.

Problem Solving.   Lacey has presented a theoretical framework that relates HR to a subject's interaction with his or her environment (e.g., Lacey, Kagan, Lacey, & Moss 1963; Lacey, 1967). According to this theoretical orientation, decreased HR during performance of a task is associated with increased sensitivity to stimulation, and occurs when a situation requires mental intake of environmental stimuli. This theory further states that increased HR accompanies stimulus rejection or mental elaboration, as during the solution of a problem. Steele and Lewis (1968) found support for the second of these hypotheses. They measured HR of subjects in four age groups while the individuals solved problems involving mental arithmetic. The age groups were 6 to 8 years, 9 to 11, 12 to 15, and 16 to 27. They found an immediate acceleration in HR with each problem, which lasted for three cardiac cycles and then fell below resting levels. This was true for subjects in all age groups, because degree of cardiac acceleration did not vary as a function of age. Thus, the results support the hypothesis that cardiac acceleration accompanies the mental elaboration, or active processing of information necessary in problem solving and other cognitive tasks.

Goldstein, Harman, McGhee, and Karasik (1975) monitored HR and SCL continuously while 20 male undergraduates solved either seven riddles (humorous) or seven problems. One theory of humor (cognitive) suggests that humor is basically a problem-solving process, involving both a perception of, and a resolution of, certain features of the joke. Riddles were chosen for comparison with problems because they resemble them structurally; that is, they have a similar question (Q) and answer (A) format. The researchers tested the hypothesis that physiological arousal would occur during the Q portion of the riddle or problem, and drop to the prestimulus level shortly after the punch line or answer is provided. The riddles were unsolvable because the subjects never heard them before, and the problems were also insoluble because the 3 seconds between Q and A was not sufficient time to allow solutions. A sample riddle used was: Q: "How can you tell an honest politician?" A: "When he's bought, he stays bought." A sample problem used was: Q: "What is the least common multiple of 3, 8, 9, and 12?" A: "72." The results showed that cardiac activity did not differentiate between riddles and problems. Heart rate increased once a riddle or a problem was presented, and decelerated when the solution was given. Thus, heart rate did not differentiate between riddles and problems, but the basic results are similar to those of other experiments, in that HR increases occurred when the information of the riddle was being processed and then dropped as the answer was given and the person waited for the next item.

Imagery and Meditation.   The question here concerns the effects of thoughts and images on heart activity. Although common experience might tell us that thinking about certain activities can produce a physiological response, the verification of this intuitive notion is not simple. Suppose an experimenter asks a subject to imagine being fearful while HR is being measured? If a change is observed, the problem then arises concerning whether the physiological response results from the instruction to "image" or the imagery itself. Although there has not been much research in this area, the findings that have been obtained are suggestive. For example, Schwartz (1971) developed a procedure to obtain cardiac responses to specific internal (thought) stimuli in the absence of external stimuli. Upon the presentation of a tone, subjects were asked to think of a number sequence. The number sequence was followed by thoughts of letters (e.g., A, B, etc.) or of emotional words (e.g., rape, death). The subjects were asked to experience any thoughts that accompanied these letters or words. The results showed that subjects had significantly higher HRs when thinking about emotional words than when thinking about letters. The data clearly indicated that different thought sequences can produce different cardiac responses. A promising technique that uses imagery to evoke different emotional states has been described by Roberts and Weerts (1982). Subjects were carefully selected according to their ability to imagine arousing emotional scenes during a screening interview. There were significant HR increases for the high anger and fear imagery versus the low intensity conditions. It was also suggested that subjects showing the largest physiological changes focused on their responses in the emotional imagery, rather than the stimuli.

    A number of physiological responses were recorded while subjects practiced transcendental meditation, or TM, according to the method of the Marharishi Mahesh Yogi (Wallace & Benson, 1972). During meditation, HR slowed, SCL decreased, and EEG alpha activity increased, among other changes, and the subjects were described as being in a wakeful but very relaxed state. In fact, the investigators observed that the physiological changes during TM, a relatively easily learned technique, were very similar to those observed in highly trained yoga experts and in Zen monks, who have had 15 to 20 years of experience in meditation. These results led the authors to suggest that the possibilities for clinical application of this relaxing technique should be investigated. The effects of different imaginary scenes on persons classified as Type A or Type B personality was studied by Baker, Hastings, and Hart (1984). Scenes were either neutral or designed to provoke the Type As in accordance with the concept of Type A as being inpatient, competitive, and hard driving. A sample provocative scene was, "You are standing in a slowly moving line at the store. Although the sign says '10 items, cash only,' the person in front of you has 15 items and wants to write a check." Scenes such as these produced much higher increases in HR and neck EMG in Type A individuals, while neutral scenes did not differentiate the groups.

In summary, the studies reviewed indicate that HR can be influenced by images and thoughts. There is much need for further work in this area to indicate the cardiac effects of various qualities and intensities of mental and imaginal experience.

Heart Activity and Perception

This section examines cardiac correlates of perceptual thresholds and stimulus significance.

Perceptual Thresholds.   Auditory thresholds were measured under conditions designed to test Lacey et al.'s (1963) suggestion that lowered HR could lead to greater sensory sensitivity (Edwards & Alsip, 1969). Twenty-five tones (near threshold levels) were presented during high HR, and 25 during periods of low HR. They found no difference in the number of correct detections under high and low HR. Saxon and Dahle (1971) measured auditory thresholds during periods of induced low and high HRs. The subjects exercised for 2.5 minutes, and auditory thresholds were measured after 3 to 4 minutes of rest. These thresholds were compared with those obtained at resting HR levels. There was a mean increase of 18 bpm after exercise, compared to the resting level, and detection thresholds were lower, that is, sensitivity was greater, at resting levels than after higher HR was induced. The researchers interpreted their results in support of the Lacey et al. formulation.

Elliott and Graf (1972) tested the hypothesis that subjects would be most sensitive to visual stimuli during the P wave, and least during the QRS complex, of the cardiac cycle. They presented subjects with 96 stimuli at four phases of the cycle: P, QRS, T, and T-P. No detection differences were found at any of these four phases. Velden and Juris (1975) also failed to find variations in perceptual performance with phases of the cardiac cycle. Their subjects were required to detect a 1000-Hz tone from a white noise background while heart activity was measured.

Although a relationship between sensory sensitivity and cardiac cycle has not been established, Schell and Catania (1975) have presented some evidence that a general cardiac deceleration is related to increased sensory acuity. Their 24 subjects were tested under conditions in which a warning signal preceded the threshold stimulus by a time sufficient to allow a cardiac response. Greater HR deceleration occurred when the threshold visual stimulus was detected than when it was not. The authors concluded that degree of sensitivity to the environment may be predicted by observing cardiac activity. Carriero and Fite (1977) also found superior perceptual performance related to cardiac deceleration. In their experiment, individuals judged the relative positions of a black bar projected on a screen. They found that accurate judgments were accompanied by greater cardiac deceleration to stimulus onset than were inaccurate judgments. However, they noted that this relationship existed only during the first half of the experiment.

In summary, the suggested relationship between perceptual sensitivity and phase of the cardiac cycle has not been confirmed by research findings. However, there is some evidence that cardiac deceleration, in general, may be related to superior perceptual performance. These results are similar to those reported for RT and cardiac activity.

Stimulus Significance.   The effects of a 1000-Hz tone (about 70 db) on HR were studied by Keefe and Johnson (1970). They reported a complex HR response that consisted of an initial small deceleration followed by a more marked acceleration and then by another deceleration. A similar finding for a 1000-Hz tone (85 db) was reported by Graham and Slaby (1973), that is, a triphasic HR response of deceleration–acceleration–deceleration. However, for broad-band white noise (50–10,000 Hz at 85 db), a diphasic cardiac response was obtained, that is, acceleration followed by deceleration (see Fig. 11.7). The differential effects of these two types of auditory stimulation should be taken into account in studies of cardiac response to auditory stimulation.

Hatton, Berg, and Graham (1970) found that if sound intensity is high enough, rapid rise time produces HR acceleration that occurs within the first second of stimulus onset. However, if rise time is gradual, acceleration begins only after a 1- or 2-second delay, even with high intensities.

The heart responses of 38 female students to a high-speed dental drill were measured by Gang and Teft (1975). Sixteen of the persons tested were dental hygiene students, and 22 were liberal arts majors. The sound level of the dental drill ranged from 90 to 95 db. Cardiac accelerations were obtained to the sound of the dental drill, but they were most pronounced in those subjects who had unpleasant experiences in the dental office as patients and who were not familiar

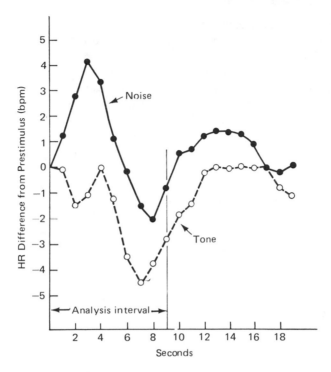

FIG. 11.7. HR change from a prestimulus period averaged over 10 presentations of 5-second 85-db white noise and a 1000 Hz tone.

with the high-speed drill. Those who had pleasant experiences in the dental office and were familiar with the drill had the smallest amount of HR acceleration. The authors concluded that the subjects were responding not only to the intensity of the stimulus but also to its meaning.

In summary, auditory stimuli will result in HR changes. The responses to pure tones versus white noise are different. The response to a meaningful stimulus (dental drill) tended to be greater than to nonmeaningful stimuli. In general, the initial HR response is a decrease with moderate intensities (less than 75–80 db) and an increase with higher intensities (Turpin, 1986).

Heart Activity, Attention, and the Orienting Response

Attention refers to the act of focusing on some aspect of a stimulus situation. Over the years, a great deal of evidence has accumulated to show that physiological changes accompany variations in attention. One common observation is that HR slows briefly either before an expected event or following a significant but unexpected occurrence. Jennings (1986) discussed some situational characteristics that influence HR deceleration. Included among these are: (a) the event must be a significant one to the person; (b) the estimate of event occurrence must be fairly precise; (c) when anticipation ends, the deceleration stops; and (d) detection difficulty enhances deceleration. Thus, a decrease in HR is an indicator of the initiation and termination of an attentional state. Current theorists have differing perspectives regarding the role of HR deceleration in attentional situations. In the view of Lacey and Lacey (1980), the decrease in HR enhances receptivity to new stimuli and improves response effectiveness. Graham (1979) interpreted cardiac deceleration mainly in terms of enhancing the input of stimuli. In contrast to the Laceys and to Graham, Obrist (1981) emphasized the decrease in motor activity that accompanies HR deceleration. To Obrist, the HR change is not a direct effect of attention, but an indirect one caused by a quieting of motor activity. These conceptual viewpoints are discussed further in chapter 15.

Graham and Clifton (1966) reviewed the hypotheses of Sokolov (1963) and Lacey, et al. (1963) regarding heart activity during the orienting response (OR). They noted that Sokolov proposed cardiac acceleration as the OR to novel stimuli, whereas Lacey et al. hypothesized HR deceleration as facilitating the reception of stimuli. Graham and Clifton reviewed a number of studies in which HR changes took place in response to weak and moderate stimuli and showed habituation over trials. They concluded that the OR was accompanied by HR deceleration and that HR acceleration most likely represented a "defense reaction" to stimuli of "prepain" intensity. Pursuing this question further, Raskin, Kotses, and Bever (1969) found that an 80-db stimulus resulted in a brief HR deceleration, whereas one of 120 db produced HR acceleration (see Fig. 11.8). Thirty males received 30 presentations of .5-second white noise at each level of stimulation. The brief HR deceleration to the 80-db stimulus was interpreted as representing the OR, whereas it was concluded that the acceleration to the 120-db stimulus reflected a defensive reaction (DR). Turpin and Siddle (1983) filled in the range of stimuli by using tones of 45, 60, 75, 90, and 105 db while recording HR. Stimuli up to 75 db produced cardiac deceleration, whereas the higher intensities elicited acceleration. These results supported the Graham-Clifton formulation of the OR and DR. Note that the HR analysis in Fig. 11.8 is based on beat-by-beat changes. The abbreviations PA and BC in Fig. 11.8 stand for forehead-skin pulse amplitude and forehead-skin blood content, respectively.

As discussed in chapter 4, REM sleep has been associated with dreaming. Periods of rapid nystagmoid eye movements, called "eye bursts," or EB, occur during REM sleep and have been related to orientation to dream content. Taylor, Moldofsky, and Furedy (1985) hypothesized that if EBs represent orientation to dream content, then HR deceleration should occur, just as it occurs in the waking OR. In support of their hypothesis, they found that HR decelerations preceded eye bursts in REM sleep. There is suggestive evidence that dream intensity is high during EB periods, but Taylor and colleagues failed to waken their subjects for dream reports during EB or more quiet periods. Nevertheless, their study suggests some interesting possibilities for further work.

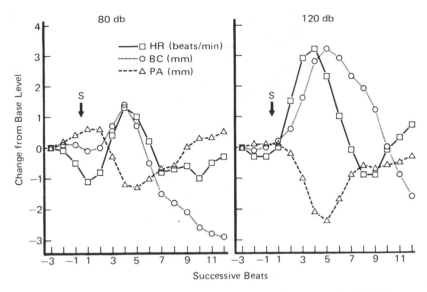

FIG. 11.8.   Beat-by-beat changes in mean PA (pulse amplitude), BC (blood content) and HR from prestimulus beat 3 produced by 30 presentations of two stimulus intensities.

In another approach to studying the OR, Hare (1972) used slides of homicide victims to study HR response to unpleasant stimulation. Forty-nine college students participated in this experiment, in which a beat-by-beat analysis of HR was performed. Hare reported three different groups of responders based on the HR data. One group of 9 subjects showed acceleration, 12 gave marked deceleration, and the remaining 28 persons produced moderate deceleration. The results support the contention that the OR consists of HR deceleration and that the DR consists of HR acceleration. However, the generalizability of the finding is somewhat limited as a result of the individual differences found. The result regarding individual differences was followed up by Hare (1973). In this study, he recorded HR of 10 females who feared spiders and compared them to 10 others who did not fear spiders. The 20 subjects viewed six spider slides and 24 slides of neutral objects, for example, landscapes. It was predicted that those persons who feared spiders would show a DR in the form of accelerated HR. The prediction was confirmed, as Hare observed that subjects with spider fears had HR acceleration and those without showed deceleration, especially when they found the slides interesting. The two groups showed no differences with respect to the neutral slides. Thus, the type and intensity of stimuli used and the possible role of individual differences should be considered in studies of the OR and DR. This latter point was made clear in a study by Eves and Gruzelier (1984). They found evidence for individual differences in response to very high intensity tones (112 to 127 db). Initial HR acceleration was followed by another large increase in one group of subjects ("accelerators"), but this secondary increase did not occur in another group ("decelerators"). Subjects apparently differed in their evaluation of the aversiveness of, and response to, identical stimuli, as also noted in the study using a dental drill. There is good support for the hypothesis that HR deceleration is associated with the OR and stimulus intake, whereas HR acceleration accompanies the DR and stimulus rejection.

In a study of persons listening to continuous verbal text, Spence, Lugo, and Youdin (1972) found a decrease in HR when they directed their attention to external stimuli. The individuals listened to a taped psychoanalytic interview while HR was measured. Cardiac deceleration was associated with the main theme of the therapeutic interview, that is, references to termination of the patient's treatment. Although this experiment did not investigate the OR in terms of a reaction to a discrete stimulus, the general result is congruent with the notion that attention to external stimuli results in cardiac deceleration.

Heart Rate and Affective Processes

Affective processes, as considered here, include HR changes that have been recorded in situations that are likely to produce "emotional" reactions in people. Some situations that qualify are those that involve stressors, fear, anger, frustration, competition, and motivation.

Stress. Research on cardiovascular responses to stressors is currently an active area. The approaches are interesting and consider factors such as whether an individual copes actively or passively with a stressor, the type of task, parental history of cardiovascular disease, and personality factors, such as the Type A/B dichotomy. Many of the studies examine systolic and diastolic blood pressure as well as HR changes, and for this reason they are discussed in chapter 12, under "Blood Pressure and Behavior."

There are a number of experiments that have used electric shock as a stressful stimulus and investigated cardiac activity in response to the shock itself or in anticipation of the shock. Elliott (1974) reviewed several studies that showed a decrease in HR just prior to the shock. However, he pointed out that this change was a phasic one; that is, it occurred in the few seconds before the stressful stimulus. Elliott observed that when one looks at the longer-term (tonic) effects, say over a period of minutes, HR increases occur under threat of an electric shock. An example of a short-term (phasic) decrease in HR is a result obtained by Obrist et al. (1969), in which deceleration took place in anticipation of a "very painful" electric shock. On the other hand, tonic acceleration was reported by Deane (1969), who told subjects that they would receive a shock at a specific point in a sequence of numbers. Interestingly, Deane's subjects showed increased HR at the beginning of the number series and a decrease just before and during the expected time of the shock.

Bankart and Elliott (1974) found that a large HR increase (about 20 bpm) occurs in a situation where a subject is waiting for the first shock to occur. This "first trial" effect habituates rapidly over subsequent trials. Elliott (1975) measured HR and eye blinks of 32 subjects who expected shocks at different probability levels. There was a 30-second countdown period in which the experimenter counted from 10 to 0. The shock probability varied among 0%, 50%, and 100%. Anticipation of a shock resulted in significantly higher HR than when no shock was expected. The cardiac response did not show evidence of habituation under the 50% and 100% probabilities, and there was no difference in HR under these two conditions. The "first trial" effect was again reported.

The effects of a real-life stress on HR of 12-year-old females was studied by Shapiro (1975). An interesting aspect of Shapiro's experiment is that he compared the responses of 17 girls raised in a kibbutz with those of 19 other Israeli girls raised in an urban environment. The measures were taken as the girls received immunization injections. In addition to HR, three behavioral measures were taken: (a) a self-rating about fear of needles, (b) a self-rating regarding expected intensity of pain, and (c) ratings of reactions by a nurse in the injection area. The measures of HR were taken one day before the injection, at the time of the injection, and 1 week after. The lower HR for the kibbutz girls (mean of 72 bpm) as compared to the urban girls (79 bpm) corresponded with their behavioral measures, indicating a more relaxed attitude to needle penetration. Shapiro postulated that educational policies in the kibbutz, which emphasize the helpfulness of medical personnel, may have been responsible for the physiological and behavioral differences observed.

Another technique that has been used to produce stress involved the introduction of a demanding task for subjects to perform. Frankenhaeuser and Johansson (1976) had people perform three tasks of varying difficulty while they measured HR and epinephrine excretion. They found, as have previous investigators, that performance did not deteriorate much when the task became more demanding. However, physiological arousal did increase as a function of task difficulty; that is, both HR and epinephrine excretion increased. In addition, subjective ratings of distress increased with demanding tasks. The authors interpreted the results as showing the high physiological cost of adapting to stressful situations. In other words, our performance may not drop under stressful conditions, but we pay for this with increased bodily energy expenditure.

In summary, both phasic decreases and tonic increases in HR have been obtained in studies where the anticipation of an electric shock is a prominent component. These results are not contradictory, but merely indicate momentary HR decreases just prior to the occurrence of the shock and a generally elevated HR over the extended course of an experimental session. Investigations into the effects of shock probability on cardiac response indicate a relation between no shock (low HR) and shock (higher HR), rather than a systematic function dependent on probability levels. The experiment by Shapiro regarding a real-life stressful situation, and its differential effects on two social groups, is provocative and, hopefully, this type of research will be repeated in a variety of situations. Other real-life evaluations have revealed higher HR in naval pilots during takeoff and landing on aircraft carriers than during bombing runs (Roman, Older, & Jones, 1967), and elevated HR in physicians during stressful periods of daily life (Ira, Whalen, & Bogdonoff, 1963).

Fear, Anger, and Frustration.   As discussed in the first chapter of this book, changes in physiological activity that occur in different emotional states are important considerations in theories set forth by Cannon and James-Lange. Coles (1983) pointed out that in Cannon's approach, physiological changes are only by-products of emotional states, whereas to James-Lange, the physiological responses constitute the main part of the emotional experience. He further pointed out that contemporary researchers have attempted to answer three questions that are generated by these theories: (a) Do different emotional states reveal themselves in specific patterns of physiological activity?, (b) Can individuals detect their own patterns of physiological activity?, and (c) How does perception of physiological activity influence the emotional reaction?

There is little doubt that HR will rise under the threat of shock or in an anger-producing situation (Elliott, 1974). Other studies of fear and frustration also indicate HR increases related to these feeling states. One of the difficult questions over the years, however, has been whether patterns of HR change will enable one to differentiate between emotional reactions, for example, fear and anger. In a classic experiment by Ax (1953), pulse rate and blood pressure showed greater increases in fear than in anger, among other differences. However, although this result suggested different patterns of physiological response in fear and anger, Elliott (1974) believes that the finding may be related to whether the subjects were more inclined to action by a fear of electrocution than they were by anger toward an insult. Elliott is of the opinion that the accumulated research has not shown HR to be useful in differentiating emotional states. However, Ekman, Levenson, and Friesen (1983) observed differential HR with posed facial expressions of various emotions. In addition, the subjects (actors and scientists) were asked to relive emotional experiences for 30 seconds. In the posed emotion task, subjects were told precisely which muscles to contract in producing expressions of fear, anger, disgust, sadness, happiness, and surprise. Heart rate changes associated with anger, fear, and sadness were all greater than for happiness, surprise, and disgust. The relived emotion task was not as effective in producing cardiac changes, but higher skin conductance was found for sadness, as compared to other negative emotions. Ekman and colleagues concluded that contracting facial muscles into universal expressions of emotion produced differential autonomic activity. This interesting approach requires further research and confirmation.

The second question regarding sensitivity to internal physiological changes has received some preliminary answers. Individual differences in sensitivity to

HR has been found to be influenced by providing knowledge of results (Ashton, White, & Hodgson 1979). Similar findings have been reported for the improvement of sensitivity to blood pressure changes through knowledge of results about such changes (Greenstadt, Shapiro & Whitehead 1986). Thus, with appropriate feedback, individuals can be trained to be sensitive to internal physiological changes. In a study by Ludwick-Rosenthal and Neufeld (1985), subjects were successful at "tracking" their own heart beat. The tracking consisted of tapping their index finger in synchrony with their ongoing HR. They further reported that subjects who performed better had higher HR and higher levels of current anxiety than those whose "interoceptive acuity" was not as high. Information regarding HR led to improved detection performance. The tendency was for individuals to greatly underestimate their HR prior to receiving HR information.

The question regarding effects of physiological changes on emotional reaction has produced some controversy. The results of a study by Schachter and Singer (1962) suggest that generalized physiological activation causes the subject to explain the perceived changes in terms of some emotion. College students were injected with adrenalin (which speeds up bodily activities) and put into situations designed to arouse either "euphoria" or "anger" through the use of stooges. The emotion was labeled according to the situation produced. Plutchik and Ax (1967) objected to the suggestion that all emotional states are physiologically identical and differentiated only by cognitive factors. They criticized many aspects of the Schachter and Singer study, but agreed with the basic idea that emotional states are due to interactions of physiological arousal and cognitive factors.

There are a number of studies that have examined physiological changes in situations designed to produce frustration and fear. The effects of frustration on cardiac response were studied by Rule and Hewitt (1971). Subjects were asked to learn lists of verbal materials. During the learning sessions, verbal reinforcement was provided by a peer. Three groups of 30 subjects each received either an easy list with neutral comments from their peers, a difficult list with neutral comments, or a difficult list with derogatory comments. This last condition was considered to be "highly thwarting," in that it involved both frustration and insult. The other two conditions were considered as being low or moderate in amount of "thwarting," and thus merely frustrating. The persons subjected to both frustration and insult did not differ in cardiac rate during the learning period, but when made aware of an opportunity to administer electric shock to their peers, in a role reversal, this "high-thwarted" group displayed elevated HR, compared to the low and moderate groups. Thus, the insulted subjects did not show greater HR increases than the other groups until given the opportunity to retaliate against their tormentors!

Klorman and his colleagues have conducted a series of studies in which HR measures were taken while subjects viewed fearful or neutral stimuli. In one study, Klorman (1974) identified 45 females who had a high fear of snakes.

Measures of cardiac activity were obtained as they watched films of seascapes or snakes. The main finding was that the cardiac response habituated with repeated presentation of the feared stimuli. Habituation was reduced when high fear stimuli were introduced earlier. A second study by Klorman, Wiesenfeld, & Austin (1975) categorized 32 female subjects as either high or low in fear of mutilation. The subjects viewed neutral (photographic poses), mutilation (burn and accident victims), and incongruous slides (e.g., a bald man with lemons attached to his ears) as HR was measured. The fearful subjects showed increased HR to mutilation slides, whereas the low-fear persons showed cardiac deceleration. Both groups responded to incongruous stimuli with HR deceleration. These results were interpreted as indicating defensive reactions in fearful individuals and orienting responses in the low-fear subjects.

The authors saw these results as extending Hare's (1973) results with spiderfearful persons to those with a fear of mutilation. Similar results were obtained by Klorman, Weissberg, and Wiesenfeld (1976), when mutilation slides produced cardiac acceleration in 13 fearful persons and lowered HR in 13 low-fear subjects. Neutral (standard photographs) and incongruous (e.g., a young woman with shaving cream on her face and an electric razor in her hand) resulted in HR decreases in additional samples of 13 high- and low-fear persons. The results support Hare's (1972) conclusion that individual differences in reaction to a supposed "fear" stimulus will determine whether HR acceleration or deceleration will occur.

In summary, there is suggestive evidence that pattern of physiological responding varies with different emotional states, that sensitivity to internal changes may be enhanced by training, and that physiological arousal interacts with cognitive factors in producing an emotional state. It has been observed that frustration plus insult will lead to an increase in HR when the victim has a chance to retaliate. A series of investigations of reactions to "fearful" stimuli support the notion that HR will accelerate in persons who actually fear the stimulus and will decelerate in those who do not fear the "unpleasant" stimulus but instead find it morbidly interesting.

Motivation

Elliott (1974), on the basis of his own prior research, concluded that the effects of increasing the amount of an incentive (e.g., money) usually produced an increase in tonic HR during the performance of the relevant task (Elliott, 1969; Elliott, Bankart, & Light, 1970). Evans (1971) reported that rivalry (a desire to win) caused significant increases in tonic HR, that is, HR measured over at least a 1-minute period. He interpreted this increase as indicating the incentive nature of competition. In a follow-up study, Evans (1972) measured HR of 64 men and 64 women while they participated in placing objects of different sizes and shapes into a form board. Half of the males and half of the females completed the task under competitive and noncompetitive conditions. The introduction of competition resulted in an average increase in HR of 10 bpm, regardless of resting HR level. Evans interpreted this result as supporting Elliott's work, indicating that incentive increases are accompanied by elevations in tonic HR.

Fowles (1983) made a strong case for the view that HR is closely linked to appetitive motivational states (positive incentives). In a test of this notion, Fowles, Fisher, and Tranel (1982) used money rewards and took HR measures during the performance of a continuous motor task. They found that HR was significantly higher when subjects were paid 2 cents for each success, compared to subjects given feedback only. A follow-up study by Tranel, Fisher, and Fowles (1982) showed that the increases in HR were related to the amount of the reward; more money led to higher HR. Also, when the money reward was discontinued, HR decreased. These and similar results by Fowles and his colleagues have led them to repeat pleas by other psychophysiologists (e.g., Stern, Farr, & Ray, 1975) to study physiological responses in situations that are pleasurable. Fowles et al. (1982) wrote that "To this end, we might modify the traditional view that cardiac acceleration occurs in anticipation of fight or flight to read 'fight, flight, or fun' . . ." (p. 512).

To summarize, it appears that increased incentive level can produce an elevation in cardiac rate. In addition, the introduction of competition may be inferred to have incentive or motivational effects, because it results in tonic HR acceleration. However, the possible roles of fear of failure or apprehension about comparisons, or individual reactions to rivalry, have not been delineated in HR studies that have used competition as an independent variable. Greater use of HR and other physiological measures is encouraged in studies of response to pleasure.

Influence of Personality and Social Factors on Heart Rate

The concept of a Type A behavior pattern characterized by impatience, competitiveness, and hostility and related to an increased risk for coronary heart disease (CHD) was advanced by Friedman & Rosenman (1974). The Type B pattern is relatively free of these behavioral traits and presents a picture of a generally more relaxed person who shows little aggressive drive and who is not always in a hurry. Coronary heart disease is the major cause of death in the United States and is thought to result from damage to the coronary arteries from atherosclerosis (a thickening of the arterial walls). The disease results in myocardial infarction (death of heart tissue), angina pectoris (a syndrome of chest pain caused by insufficient oxygen supply to heart muscle) and sudden death. Researchers have been attempting to relate Type A/B personality to patterns of physiological change, especially changes involving the cardiovascular system. Studies focusing on changes in diastolic and systolic blood pressure are covered in chapter 12. Investigations emphasizing HR are discussed here.

A number of studies indicate that individuals identified as Type A either through a structured interview or the Jenkins Activity Survey (JAS) show increased cardiovascular activity over baseline rates, compared to Type Bs, when engaged in a task. (Krantz, Glass, Shaeffer, & Davia, 1982). This has been shown in a variety of populations including college students, working-class adults and coronary patients. However, qualifications must be made because differences in A/B reactions seem to depend on the type of task or experimental environment. For example, Type A/B differences are observed in situations that involve challenge, competition, or harassment. Differences in A/B HR reactivity emerged in a task involving cognitive (short-term memory) activity, but not while performing an engaging video perceptual motor task (Juszczak & Andreassi, 1987). Type A/B differences did not emerge in response to the cold pressor test or balloons bursting; tasks that could be considered irrelevant to Type A characteristics (Goldband, 1980). In accord with this notion, Stern & Elder (1982) found that the effectiveness with which Type As reduced their own HR depended on the challenge produced in a biofeedback situation. For example, when told that HR reduction was a rare ability, Type As reduced HR more than did Type Bs. When told that HR reduction was a common ability, Type Bs achieved greater reduction. These results suggest interesting possibilities for exploiting Type A behavior in reducing Type A symptoms.

An emerging area of research is that of social psychophysiology (see Cacioppo & Petty, 1983). The approach taken is to measure physiological changes in the context of various social psychological variables such as attitude change, cognitive dissonance, or emotional communication. An example is the use of physiological measurements to confirm the existence of tensions and their subsequent release in cognitive dissonance. The concept of cognitive dissonance was introduced by Festinger to describe the state produced when there is a difference between a person's attitude and behavior. The conflict is resolved by a change in attitude to match the behavior, but in the meantime the person is said to experience a tension that he or she is motivated to relieve. Croyle and Cooper (1983) used HR and EDA as measures of arousal in a dissonance situation in which one half of the subjects were asked to write an essay supporting a campus ban on alcohol, even though an attitude survey had shown them opposed to the ban. The other subjects wrote an essay in agreement with their attitudes. Those in the dissonant condition were more aroused after writing the essay than other subjects. However, the arousal was observed as increased EDA, because HR showed no dissonance effect. In another study, a positive effect for HR was found because attitude toward a stimulus was influenced by the subject's perceived response. In this experiment, Valins (1966) asked men to examine pictures of Playboy centerfolds while they listened to what they believed was their own HR. False feedback was given, and HR did not vary while they viewed one half of the nude photos, and increased or decreased for the other half. The men later rated the photos accompanied by HR change (either up or down) as more attractive than the others. Therefore, subject's evaluations of stimuli were influenced by their perceived HR changes. Cross fertilization between the fields of psychophysiology and social psychology has yielded, and will continue to yield, some fascinating findings.

Interactions Between Heart and Brain Activity.   One of the main aspects of the intake–rejection hypothesis of the Laceys (see chapter 15) is that changes in cardiovascular activity influence brain activity. For example, the decreased HR that occurs under instructions to detect signals leads to a decrease in the inhibitory influence of baroreceptors on cortical function, resulting in enhanced brain activity and improved performance. We have discussed earlier the lack of evidence to support performance effects of HR acceleration–deceleration, but there is evidence that brain activity is influenced by cardiac events. Walker and Sandman (1979) measured evoked brain potentials to light flashes when subject's HR were low, high, or moderate. The P2 component of the visual ERP from over the right hemisphere was larger at low HR than for moderate or high rates, indicating greater cortical sensitivity at the low HR. However, left-hemisphere responses did not differ as a function of HR. Sandman, Walker, and Berka (1982) wrote that these findings are consistent with those suggesting that tasks requiring attention to the environment are associated with low HR and ERPs recorded from the right hemisphere. They suggested that the heart may influence perceptual/attentional functions by selectively influencing right-hemisphere activity.

Further evidence for cardiovascular–brain influences was reported by Walker and Walker (1983). The EEG recorded from over left and right hemispheres was comprised of slower frequencies during ventricular systole than EEG sampled during diastole. No hemispheric difference was observed. The results were extended to the enhancement of auditory ERPs observed when tones were presented during the diastolic phases of pulse pressure, a period of lowered cardiovascular activity (Sandman, 1984). The effect appeared most reliably in responses recorded from the right hemisphere. An experiment by Hantas, Katkin, and Reed (1984) provided some evidence that perception of cardiovascular activity may be processed more effectively in the right hemisphere. Subjects classified as "right hemisphere preferent" were better at detecting their own heartbeat than those classified "left hemisphere preferent." When knowledge of results was given, all subjects showed significant improvements in performance, but the right-hemisphere preferent individuals maintained their superiority. The studies reviewed here indicate interesting interactions between cardiovascular and brain activity, and demonstrate that the brain's influence on the heart is not a one-way street. The results thus far also suggest that cyclic physiological events, such as systole and diastole, may modulate the impact of external stimuli on the central nervous system. The questions of possible performance differences with changes in cardiac–cortical interaction, and the meaning of hemispheric effects require further investigation.

Conditioning of Heart Activity

A brief discussion of classical and operant conditioning procedures was present-ed in chapter 9. In this section, some representative investigations of classical and instrumental conditioning of cardiac activity are discussed.

Classical Conditioning.   It has long been known that ANS responses can be modified by classical conditioning. For example, Kimble (1961) mentioned changes in GSR and respiration that were produced by the CS in various experi-ments, in addition to the well-known salivary response (e.g., Pavlov's dog). Heart rate has also been classically conditioned, that is, a CS formerly paired with a pleasant (food) or unpleasant (electric shock) stimulus can produce a change in HR. For example, Notterman, Schoenfeld, and Bersh (1952) measured HR in a classical conditioning situation and reported cardiac deceleration just before the onset of the UCS (shock). Obrist et al. (1969) also observed a condi-tioned HR deceleration that took place in the CS (light)–UCS (shock) interval. Although these studies indicate conditioned deceleration of HR, Van Egeren, Headrick, and Hein (1972) obtained results that revealed individual HR dif-ferences in an aversive classical conditioning experiment. These investigators used two experimental paradigms in studying the cardiac responses of two groups of subjects during classical conditioning. The HR changes indicated three kinds of response during the CS–UCS interval: initial acceleration followed by deceleration, deceleration only, and initial deceleration followed by acceleration. The findings illustrate the importance of considering individual differences in experiments dealing with the conditioning of heart activity. Recall also that a previously mentioned study by Hare and Blevings (1975) showed HR accelera-tion in high-fear subjects prior to the UCS (spider slides).

The possible effects of respiration on concurrent HR changes during condi-tioning were examined by Headrick and Graham (1969). Three groups of 20 persons each were given conditioning trials as follows: respiration controlled at normal rates, controlled at fast rates, or uncontrolled. Significant HR responding occurred in all three groups during the CS (tone) UCS (electric shock) interval. There were three components to the HR response: deceleration immediately after the CS, followed by a brief acceleration, and a large deceleration just prior to the UCS. Thus, this study seems to rule out respiration effects in classical condition-ing of HR. Obrist (1976) has offered explanations of anticipatory HR decelera-tion during the CS–UCS interval in terms of both behavioral and biological strategies. The behavioral approach explains the HR changes in terms of physio-logical interactions. For example, Obrist's data have indicated that HR decelera-tion is due to a momentary increase in vagal (parasympathetic) excitation, which overrides sympathetic acceleratory effects.

Furedy and Poulos (1976) explored the possible use of body tilt as a UCS in conditioning a decrease of HR. In a first experiment, they established that tilting the body from a head-up to a head-down position produced a mean cardiac deceleration to less than 60 bpm by the ninth second after UCS onset. (The subjects were strapped to a "tilt-table," and the duration of the tilt was 9 seconds.) In a second experiment, Furedy and Poulos (1976) demonstrated that classical conditioning of HR deceleration could be accomplished by using a tone as the CS and body tilt as the UCS. This time, 32 tilts were each performed after a 1.7-second duration tone. However, the 12 subjects produced a mean conditioned deceleration of only 4 bpm. This was a small conditioned response relative to the large unconditioned response of over 30 bpm in the first experiment. An encouraging aspect of this study is that the classically conditioned cardiac deceleration was obtained with a stimulus other than the often-used electric shock. A test of the hypothesis that relevant imagery enhances classical conditioning of HR was conducted by Arabian (1982). Using head-tilt as the UCS, one group of subjects was instructed to imagine the tilt-UCS whenever the CS was presented, whereas the other group imagined a car ride (irrelevant imagery). The hypothesis was supported, because the relevant imagery group showed a much larger conditioned HR deceleration.

In summary, the classical conditioning of HR has been reported in a number of experiments. The most common UCS has been electric shock, which has usually produced cardiac deceleration. The role of individual differences may explain variations in cardiac patterning sometimes observed in the CS–UCS interval. The possible influence of respiratory variations on HR changes seems to have been ruled out. Investigators have implicated vagal (parasympathetic) excitation in producing HR deceleration in the CS–UCS interval.

Instrumental Conditioning. The term *instrumental conditioning* is used here to refer to changes in physiological activity that occur as a result of reinforcement. For example, an individual is provided with a continuous display of his or her heart activity and is reinforced when HR rises above a certain level. The rise in HR is thus instrumental in obtaining the reinforcement. The reinforcement may be the achievement of a desirable event (e.g., monetary reward) or the avoidance of something unpleasant (e.g., an electric shock). The terms *instrumental* and *operant* conditioning are used interchangeably, although some workers in the field (e.g., Kimmel, 1973) prefer to use the word "operant" to refer to unique instrumental conditioning procedures in which responses are "emitted" independently of identifiable external stimuli. Recall that in the classical conditioning situation, the reinforcement (UCS) is presented whether or not the subject makes a particular response.

For quite some time (from the late 1930s to the early 1960s), most investigators agreed that the modification of ANS responses by instrumental conditioning was not possible, but that these same visceral responses were amenable to classical conditioning. Kimble (1961) reflected the thought of the time when he stated that "autonomic responses apparently cannot be instrumentally conditioned at all'' (p. 108). However, some research findings have accumulated since then indicating that subjects can learn to modify their HR and other autonomic responses in an instrumental conditioning paradigm. An important aspect is the provision of feedback, or knowledge of results, to the individual so that he or she knows that the desired response is being achieved (e.g., see Bergman & Johnson, 1972). Early demonstrations of instrumental conditioning of HR were provided by Shearn (1962) and Hnatiow and Lang (1965). Shearn (1962) used a conditioning paradigm in which HR increases postponed the delivery of an electric shock. The experimental subjects produced more HR accelerations over the five sessions than the control subjects. Shearn reported changes in respiration, which, he suggested, could have mediated the HR change. However, after being alerted to this possible contaminating effect of respiration, experimenters have either monitored or controlled breathing in studies conducted since then. Hnatiow and Lang (1965) reported the successful stabilization of HR when subjects were instructed to keep their heart rates as steady as possible and were provided with a visual display of HR. Control subjects, who were provided with false feedback, did not show a reduction in HR variability. Lang (1974) pointed out that the magnitude of HR control achieved in various studies has been modest, especially HR deceleration, and he attributed this partially to the difficulties in providing all the environmental controls necessary to perform instrumental conditioning studies with humans (e.g., subject isolation, powerful reinforcers). He also suggested that HR control is a type of skill learning, and some individuals are better at it than others.

The importance of individual differences in learning control of HR was underscored by McCanne and Sandman (1976) in an extensive review of operant HR conditioning. They suggested that individual differences in physiological responding occur during instrumental HR conditioning and that a study of these differences might help to understand how voluntary control is achieved over HR. They had earlier ruled out changes in respiration, muscle activity, and cardiac–somatic interaction (with the CNS as the control mechanism) as possible bases for operant control over HR. However, this is controversial, because critics have emphasized the difficulty of demonstrating HR changes without concurrent somatic changes, for example, respiration (Blanchard & Young, 1973; Katkin & Murray, 1968). Thus, the student should be cautioned that this area is controversial and also rather unsettled in terms of comprehending the underlying mechanisms that allow instrumental control of HR. Examples of investigations into the possible instrumental control of HR, utilizing persons with normal cardiovascular function, are presented next.

The effects of varying incentive (monetary) on the voluntary control of HR speeding and slowing were investigated by Lang and Twentyman (1976). Fifty subjects received four HR control sessions over a 3- to 4-week period. The results showed that subjects can alter HR directionally, and that performance was improved with monetary incentives. Frequent reinforcement, additional incentives, and practice with feedback produced optimal HR change performance. The researchers postulated that the findings support an interpretation of HR feedback training as being similar to the learning of a psychomotor skill. This implication is stronger for HR speeding than for HR slowing, because only incentive altered slowing, whereas speeding was also influenced by other factors manipulated. Lang (1977) discussed the difficulty of demonstrating HR slowing, the small size of the effect, and its possible dependence on respiratory changes.

Fairly large increases in HR were instrumentally conditioned in an experiment by Hatch (1980). Further, intermittent delivery of the feedback was more effective than continuous feedback in producing the result. Slowing of HR was also brought under voluntary control, but the schedule of reinforcement did not affect the degree of deceleration. Hatch used a wide range of psychomotor tasks to test the hypothesis that voluntary HR control was related to motor skills. The results were contrary to the hypothesis that the same abilities underlie skeletal motor and visceral (HR) learning. In an interesting approach, McKinney, Gatchel, Brantley, and Harrington (1980) obtained fairly large HR reductions (9 bpm, on the average) in a training procedure that combined feedback with tangible rewards. During a generalization test (no feedback), the tangible reward group produced an average HR decrease of 13 bpm, compared to virtually no HR reduction in a continuous feedback only group. Thus, we see a sizable HR deceleration when subjects receive rewards in addition to information regarding changes in HR.

One possible application of instrumental control of HR might be the reduction of cardiovascular reactivity in a stressful situation. There is some experimental evidence that this may be possible. For example, McCanne (1983) found that practice at controlling HR led to reduced HR while viewing stressful scenes in a film. Self-reports of beliefs about ability to control HR were related to the reductions observed during film viewing. This suggests the possibility that expectancy effects may reduce autonomic responding during stress. Perski, Engel, and McCroskery (1982) reviewed several studies that showed that humans can be taught to control HR while anticipating or experiencing a variety of aversive stimuli. An example is the study of Victor, Mainardi, and Shapiro (1978), who demonstrated that HR acceleration produced by placing a hand in ice-water can be modified by training in HR slowing. Ratings of painfulness decreased during HR slowing. Perceptions of stimuli and reactions to them may be changed by the instrumental conditioning procedure.

In summary, research on the instrumental conditioning of HR indicates that cardiac activity may be brought under some degree of voluntary control. It appears that increases are more easily attained than decreases, although the role of tangible reward has not been fully explored. The exact mechanisms underlying this voluntary control are not known. Researchers have variously suggested that the HR changes are mediated by respiratory factors, by muscle activity, and by factors similar to those that influence the learning of a motor skill (e.g., practice with feedback, motivation, and frequent reinforcement). This area is still controversial, and, so far, the hypothesis proposing the similarity of visceral and motor learning has not been supported. The possibility of voluntary control over HR has important clinical implications, regardless of the source of this control. Some of the findings have indicated that HR control may lessen responsivity to stressful stimuli. Clinical applications of biofeedback are discussed in chapter 14.

Research on the relationship between cardiac activity and behavior continues to occupy the time of many researchers. Many empirical findings and some interesting concepts have stemmed from these studies, for example, those of the Laceys and Obrist and colleagues, which are discussed more fully in chapter 15. Chapter 12 discusses two physiological measures, blood pressure and blood volume, and their relation to behavior.

REFERENCES

Andreassi, J. L. (1966). Some physiological correlates of verbal learning task difficulty. *Psychonomic Science, 6,* 69–70.

Andreassi, J. L., & Whalen, P. M. (1967). Some physiological correlates of learning and overlearning. *Psychophysiology, 3,* 406–413.

Arabian, J. M. (1982). Imagery and Pavlovian heart rate decelerative conditioning. *Psychophysiology, 19,* 286–293.

Ashton, R., White, K. D., & Hodgson, G. (1979). Sensitivity to heart rate: A psychophysical study. *Psychophysiology, 16,* 403–406.

Astrand, P., & Rodahl, K. (1977). *Textbook of work physiology.* New York: McGraw-Hill.

Ax, A. R. (1953). The physiological differentiation between fear and anger in humans. *Psychosomatic Medicine, 15,* 147–150.

Baker, L. J., Hastings, J. E., & Hart, J. D. (1984). Enhanced psycho-physiological responses of Type A coronary patients during Type A-relevant imagery. *Journal of Behavioral Medicine, 7,* 287–306.

Bankart, C. P., & Elliott, R. (1974). Heart rate and skin conductance in anticipation of shocks with varying probability of occurrence. *Psychophysiology, 11,* 160–174.

Bergman, J. S., & Johnson, H. J. (1972). Sources of information which affect training and raising of heart rate. *Psychophysiology, 9,* 30–39.

Blanchard, E. B., & Young, L. D. (1973). Self-control and cardiac functioning: A promise yet unfulfilled. *Psychological Bulletin, 79,* 145–163.

Botwinick, J., & Thompson, L. W. (1971). Cardiac functioning and reaction time in relation to age. *Journal of Genetic Psychology, 119,* 127–132.

Brener, J. (1967). Heart rate. In P. H. Venables & I. Martin (Eds.), *Manual of psychophysiological methods* (pp. 103–131). Amsterdam: North-Holland.

Brown, C. S. (1972). Instruments in psychophysiology. In N. S. Greenfield & R. A. Sternbach (Eds.), *Handbook of psychophysiology* (pp. 159–195). New York: Holt.

Cacioppo, J. T., & Petty, R. E. (1983). *Social psychophysiology.* New York: Guilford.

Carriero, N. J., & Fite, J. (1977). Cardiac deceleration as an indicator of correct performance. *Perceptual & Motor Skills, 44,* 275–282.

Cohen, D. H., & MacDonald, R. L. (1974). A selective review of central neural pathways involved in cardiovascular control. In P. A. Obrist, A. H. Black, J. Brener, & L. V. DiCara (Eds.), *Cardiovascular psychophysiology* (pp. 33–59). Chicago: Aldine.

Coles, M. G. H. (1983). Situational determinants and psychological significance of heart rate change. In A. Gale & J. A. Edwards (Eds.), *Physiological correlates of human behavior* (pp. 171–186). New York: Academic Press.

Coles, M. G. H., Pellegrini, A. M., & Wilson, G. V. (1982). The cardiac cycle time effect: Influence of respiration phase and information processing requirements. *Psychophysiology, 19,* 648–657.

Croyle, R. T., & Cooper, J. (1983). Dissonance arousal: Physiological evidence. *Journal of Personality and Social Psychology, 45,* 782–791.

Deane, G. E. (1969). Cardiac activity during experimentally induced anxiety. *Psychophysiology, 6,* 17–30.

Edwards, D. C., & Alsip, J. E. (1969). Stimulus detection during periods of high and low heart rate. *Psychophysiology, 5,* 431–434.

Ekman, P., Levenson, R. W., & Friesen, W. V. (1983). Autonomic nervous system activity distinguishes among emotions. *Science, 22,* 1208–1210.

Elliott, R. (1969). Tonic heart rate: Experiments on the effects of collative variables lead to a hypothesis about its motivational significance. *Journal of Personality and Social Psychology, 12,* 211–288.

Elliott, R. (1974). The motivational significance of heart rate. In P. A. Obrist, A. H. Black, J. Brener, & L. V. DiCara (Eds.), *Cardiovascular psychophysiology* (pp. 505–537). Chicago: Aldine.

Elliott, R. (1975). Heart rate in anticipation of shocks which have different probabilities of occurrences. *Psychological Reports, 36,* 923–931.

Elliott, R., Bankart, B., & Light, T. (1970). Differences in the motivational significance of heart rate and palmar conductance: Two tests of a hypothesis. *Journal of Personality and Social Psychology, 14,* 166–172.

Elliott, R., & Graf, V. (1972). Visual sensitivity as a function of phase of cardiac cycle. *Psychophysiology, 9,* 357–361.

Evans, J. F. (1971). Social facilitation in a competitive situation. *Canadian Journal of Behavioral Science, 3,* 276–281.

Evans, J. F. (1972). Resting heart rate and the effects of an incentive. *Psychonomic Science, 26,* 99–100.

Eves, F. F., & Gruzelier, J. H. (1984). Individual differences in the cardiac response to high intensity auditory stimulation. *psychophysiology, 21,* 342–352.

Fowles, D. C. (1983). Motivational effects on heart rate and electro-dermal activity: Implications for research on personality and psychopathology. *Journal of Research in Personality, 17,* 48–71.

Fowles, D. C., Fisher, A. E., & Tranel, D. T. (1982). The heart beats to reward: The effects of monetary incentives on heart rate. *Psychophysiology, 19,* 506–513.

Frankenhaeuser, M., & Johansson, G. (1976). Task demand as reflected in catecholamine excretion and heart rate. *Journal of Human Stress, 2,* 15–23.

Friedman, M., & Rosenman, R. H. (1974). *Type A behavior and your heart.* New York: Knopf.

Furedy, J. J., & Poulos, C. X. (1976). Heart-rate decelerative Pavlovian conditioning with tilt as UCS: Towards behavioural control of cardiac dysfunction. *Biological Psychology, 4,* 93–106.

Gang, M. J., & Teft, L. (1975). Individual differences in heart rate responses to affective sound. *Psychophysiology, 12,* 423–426.

Goldband, S. (1980). Stimulus specificity of physiological response to stress and the Type A coronary-prone personality. *Journal of Personality & Social Psychology, 39,* 670–679.

Goldstein, J. H., Harman, J., McGhee, P. E., & Karasik, R. (1975). Test of an information-processing model of humor: Physiological response changes during problem and riddle-solving. *Journal of General Psychology, 92,* 59–68.

Graham, F. K. (1979). Distinguishing among orienting, defense and startle reflexes. In H. D. Kimmel, E. H. Van Olst, & J. F. Orlebeke (Eds.), *The orienting reflex in humans* (pp. 137–167). Hillsdale, NJ: Lawrence Erlbaum Associates.

Graham, F. K., & Clifton, R. K. (1966). Heart-rate change as a component of the orienting response. *Psychological Bulletin, 65,* 305–320.

Graham, F. K., Slaby, D. A. (1973). Differential heart rate changes to equally intense white noise and tone. *Psychophysiology, 10,* 347–362.

Greenstadt, L., Shapiro, D., & Whitehead, R. (1986). Blood pressure discrimination. *Psychophysiology, 23,* 500–509.

Gunn, C. G., Wolf, S., Block, R. T., & Person, R. J. (1972). Psychophysiology of the cardiovascular system. In N. S. Greenfield & R. A. Sternbach (Eds.), *Handbook of psychophysiology* (pp. 457–489). New York: Holt.

Guyton, A. C. (1977). Basic human physiology: Normal function and mechanisms of disease. *Philadelphia:* Saunders.

Hantas, M. N., Katkin, E. S., & Reed, S. D. (1984). Cerebral lateralization and heartbeat discrimination. *Psychophysiology, 21,* 274–278.

Hare, R. D. (1972). Cardiovascular components of orienting and defensive responses. *Psychophysiology, 9,* 606–614.

Hare, R. D. (1973). Orienting and defensive responses to visual stimuli. *Psychophysiology, 10,* 453–464.

Hare, R. D., & Blevings, G. (1975). Defensive responses to phobic stimuli. *Biological Psychology, 3,* 1–13.

Hatch, J. P. (1980). The effects of operant reinforcement schedules on the modification of human heart rate. *Psychophysiology, 17,* 559–567.

Hatton, H. M., Berg, W. K., & Graham, F. K. (1970). Effects of acoustic rise time on heart rate response. *Psychonomic Science, 19,* 101–103.

Headrick, M. W., & Graham, F. K. (1969). Multiple component heart rate responses conditioned under paced respiration. *Journal of Experimental Psychology, 79,* 486–494.

Heslegrave, R. J., Ogilvie, J. C., & Furedy, J. J. (1979). Measuring baseline-treatment differences in heart rate variability: Variance versus successive differences mean square and beats per minute versus interbeat interval. *Psychophysiology, 16,* 151–157.

Hnatiow, M., & Lang, P. J. (1965). Learned stabilization of cardiac rate. *Psychophysiology, 1,* 330–336.

Ira, G. H., Whalen, R. E., & Bogdonoff, M. D. (1963). Heart rate changes in physicians during daily "stressful" tasks. *Journal of Psychosomatic Research, 7,* 147–150.

Jennings, J. R. (1986). Bodily changes during attending. In M. G. H. Coles, E. Donchin, & S. W. Porges (Eds.), *Psychophysiology: Systems, processes & applications* (pp. 268–289). New York: Guilford.

Jennings, J. R., & Wood, C. C. (1977). Cardiac cycle time effects on performance, phasic cardiac responses and their intercorrelation in choice reaction time. *Psychophysiology, 14,* 297–307.

Juszczak, N. M. & Andreassi, J. L. (1987). Performance and physiological responses of Type A and Type B individuals during a cognitive and perceptual motor task. *International Journal of Psychophysiology, 5,* 81–90.

Katkin, E. S., & Murray, E. N. (1968). Instrumental conditioning of autonomically mediated behavior: Theoretical and methodological issues. *Psychological Bulletin, 70,* 52–68.

Keefe, F. B., & Johnson, L. C. (1970). Cardiovascular responses to auditory stimuli. *Psychonomic Science, 19,* 335–337.

Kimble, G. A. (1961). *Hilgard and Marquis' conditioning and learning.* New York: Appleton-Century-Crofts.

Kimmel, H. D. (1973). Instrumental conditioning. In W. F. Prokasy & D. C. Raskin (Eds.), *Electrodermal activity in psychological research* (pp. 255–282). New York: Academic Press.

Klorman, R. (1974). Habituation of fear: Effects of intensity and stimulus order. *Psychophysiology, 11,* 15–26.

Klorman, R. (1975). Contingent negative variation and cardiac deceleration in a long preparatory interval: A developmental study. *Psychophysiology, 12,* 609–617.

Klorman, R., Wiesenfeld, A. R., & Austin, M. L. (1975). Autonomic responses to affective visual stimuli. *Psychophysiology, 12,* 553–560.

Klorman, R., Weissberg, R. P., & Wiesenfeld, A. R. (1976, October). *Individual differences in fear and autonomic reactions to affective stimulation.* Paper presented at meeting of Society for Psychophysiological Research, San Diego, CA.

Krantz, D. S., Glass, D. C., Shaeffer, M. A., & Davia, J. E. (1982). Behavior patterns and coronary disease: A critical evaluation. In J. T. Cacioppo & R. E. Petty (Eds.), *Perspectives in cardiovascular psychophysiology* (pp. 315–346). New York: Guilford.

Lacey, B. C., & Lacey, J. I. (1977). Change in heart period: A function of sensorimotor event timing within the cardiac cycle. *Physiological Psychology, 5,* 383–393.

Lacey, B. C., & Lacey, J. I. (1980). Cognitive modulation of time-dependent primary bradycardia. *Psychophysiology, 17,* 209–221.

Lacey, J. I. (1967). Somatic response patterning and stress: Some revisions of activation theory. In M. H. Appley & R. Trumbull (Eds.), *Psychological stress: Issues in research* (pp. 14–42). New York: Appleton-Century-Crofts.

Lacey, J. I., Kagan, J., Lacey, B. C., & Moss, H. A. (1963). The visceral level: Situational determinants and behavioral correlates of autonomic patterns. In P. H. Knapp (Ed.), *Expression of emotions in man* (pp. 161–196). New York: International Universities Press.

Lang, P. J. (1974). Learned control of human heart rate in a computer directed environment. In P. A. Obrist, A. H. Black, J. Brener, & L. V. Dicara (Eds.), *Cardiovascular psychophysiology* (pp. 392–405). Chicago: Aldine.

Lang, P. J. (1977). *Presidential address.* Annual meeting of the Society for Psychophysiological Research, Philadelphia, PA.

Lang, P. J., & Twentyman, C. T. (1976). Learning to control heart rate: Effects of varying incentive and criterion of success on task performance. *Psychophysiology, 13,* 378–385.

Lewis, D., Ray, W. J., Wilkinson, M. O., & Ricketts, R. (1984). Self-report and heart rate responses to a stressful task. *International Journal of Psychophysiology, 2,* 33–37.

Ludwick-Rosenthal, R., & Neufeld, R. W. J. (1985). Heart beat interoception: A study of individual differences. *International Journal of Psychophysiology, 3,* 57–65.

Malmo, R. B. (1965). Physiological gradients and behavior. *Psychological Bulletin, 664,* 225–234.

McCanne, T. R. (1983). Changes in autonomic responding to stress after practice at controlling heart rate. *Biofeedback & Self-Regulation, 8,* 9–24.

McCanne, T. R., & Sandman, C. A. (1976). Human operant heart rate conditioning: The importance of individual differences. *Psychological Bulletin, 83,* 587–601.

McKinney, M., Gatchel, R., Brantley, D., & Harrington, R. (1980). The input of biofeedback manipulated physiological change on emotional state. *Basic & Applied Psychology, 1,* 15–21.

Miller, J. C., & Horvath, S. M. (1978). Impedance cardiography. *Psychophysiology, 15,* 80–91.

Notterman, J. M., Schoenfeld, W. N., & Bersh, P. J. (1952). A comparison of three extinction procedures following heart rate conditioning. *Journal of Abnormal and Social Psychology, 47,* 674–677.

Nowlin, J. B., Eisdorfer, C., Whalen, R., & Troyer, W. G. (1970). The effect of exogenous changes in heart rate and rhythm upon reaction time performance. *Psychophysiology, 7,* 186–193.

Obrist, P. A. (1976). The cardiovascular–behavioral interaction as it appears today. *Psychophysiology, 13,* 95–107.

Obrist, P. A. (1981). *Cardiovascular psychophysiology: A perspective.* New York: Plenum.

Obrist, P. A., Howard, J. L., Sutterer, J. R., Hennis, R. S., & Murrell, D. J. (1973). Cardiac-somatic changes during a simple reaction time task: A developmental study. *Journal of Experimental Child Psychology, 16,* 346–362.

Obrist, P. A., Lawler, J. E., Howard, J. L., Smithson, K. W., Martin, P. L., & Manning,

J. (1974). Sympathetic influences on the heart in humans: Effects on contractilitly and heart rate of acute stress. *Psychophysiology, 11,* 405–427.

Obrist, P. A., Webb, R. A., & Sutterer, J. R. (1969). Heart rate and somatic changes during aversive conditioning and a simple reaction time task. *Psychophysiology, 5,* 696–723.

Ohkubo, T., & Hamley, E. J. (1972). Assessment of human performance in learning a skill involved in driving. *Journal of Human Ergology, 1,* 95–110.

Pardee, H. B. (1933). *Clinical aspects of the electrocardiogram* (3rd ed.). New York: Harper.

Perski, A., Engel, B. T., & McCroskery, J. H. 1982. The modification of elicited cardiovascular responses by operant conditioning of heart rate. In J. T. Cacioppo & R. E. Petty (Eds.), *Perspectives in cardiovascular psychophysiology* (pp. 296–314). New York: Guilford.

Plutchik, R., & Ax, A. F. (1967). A critique of "Determinants of emotional state by Schachter, J., & Singer, J. E. (1962)." *Psychophysiology, 4,* 79–82.

Raskin, D. C., Kotses, H., & Bever, J. (1969). Cephalic vasomotor and heart rate measures of orienting and defensive reflexes. *Psychophysiology, 6,* 149–159.

Roberts, R. J., & Weerts, T. C. (1982). Cardiovascular responding during anger and fear imagery. *Psychological Reports, 50,* 219–230.

Roman, J., Older, H., & Jones, W. L. (1967). Flight research program: VII. Medical monitoring of Navy carrier pilots in combat. *Aerospace Medicine, 38,* 133–139.

Rule, B. G., & Hewitt, L. S. (1971). Effects of thwarting on cardiac response and physical aggression. *Journal of Personality and Social Psychology, 19,* 181–187.

Sandman, C. A. (1984). Augmentation of the auditory event related potentials of the brain during diastole. *International Journal of Psychophysiology, 2,* 111–119.

Sandman, C. A., Walker, B. B., & Berka, C. (1982). Influence of afferent cardiovascular feedback on behavior and the cortical evoked potential. In J. T. Cacioppo & R. E. Petty (Eds.), *Perspectives in cardiovascular psychophysiology* (pp. 189–222). New York: Guilford.

Saxon, S. A., & Dahle, A. J. (1971). Auditory threshold variations during periods of induced high and low heart rates. *Psychophysiology, 8,* 23–29.

Schacter, S., & Singer, J. E. (1962). Cognitive, social and physiological determinants of emotional state. *Psychological Review, 69,* 379–399.

Schell, A. M., & Catania, J. (1975). The relationship between cardiac activity and sensory acuity. *Psychophysiology, 12,* 147–151.

Schwartz, G. E. (1971). Cardiac responses to self-induced thoughts. *Psychophysiology, 8,* 462–467.

Shapiro, A. H. (1975). Behavior of Kibbutz and urban children receiving an injection. *Psychophysiology, 12,* 79–82.

Shearn, D. N. (1962). Operant conditioning of heart rate. *Science, 137,* 530–531.

Sokolov, E. (1963). *Perception and the conditioned reflex.* New York: MacMillan.

Spence, D. P., Lugo, M., & Youdin, R. (1972). Cardiac change as a function of attention to and awareness of continous verbal text. *Science, 176,* 1344–1346.

Steele, W. G., & Lewis, M. (1968). A longitudinal study of the cardiac response during a problem-solving task and its relationship to general cognitive function. *Psychonomic Science, 11,* 275–276.

Stern, G., & Elder, R. D. (1982). The role of challenging incentives in feedback-assisted heart rate reduction for coronary-prone adult males. *Biofeedback & Self Regulation, 7,* 53–69.

Stern, R. M., Farr, J. H., & Ray, W. J. (1975). Pleasure. In P. H. Venables & M. J. Christie (Eds.), *Research in psychophysiology* (pp. 208–233). New York: Wiley.

Stern, R. M., Ray, W. J., & Davis, C. M. (1980). *Psychophysiological recording.* New York: Oxford.

Surwillo, W. W. (1971). Human reaction time and endogneous heart rate changes in normal subjects. *Psychophysiology, 8,* 680–682.

Taylor, W. B., Moldofsky, H., & Furedy, J. J. (1985). Heart rate deceleration in REM sleep: An orienting reaction interpretation. *Psychophysiology, 22,* 342–352.

Tranel, D. T., Fisher, A. E., & Fowles, D. C. (1982). Magnitude of incentive effects on heart rate. *Psychophysiology, 19,* 514–519.

Turner, J. R., Caroll, D., & Courtney, H. (1983). Cardiac and metabolic responses to "space invaders": An instance of metabolically exaggerated cardiac adjustment? *Psychophysiology, 20,* 544–549.

Turpin, G. (1986). Effects of stimulus intensity on autonomic responding: The problem of differentiating orienting and defense reflexes. *Psychophysiology, 23,* 1–14.

Turpin, G., & Siddle, D. A. (1983). Effects of stimulus intensity on cardiovascular activity. *Psychophysiology, 20,* 611–624.

Tursky, B., & Jamner, L. D. (1982). Measurement of cardiovascular functioning. In J. T. Cacioppo & R. E. Petty (Eds.), *Perspectives in cardiovascular psychophysiology* (pp. 19–92). New York: Guilford.

Valins, S. (1966). Cognitive effects of false heart-rate feedback. *Journal of Personality and Social Psychology, 4,* 400–408.

Van Egeren, L. F., Hedrick, M. N., & Hein, P. L. (1972). Individual differences in autonomic responses: Illustration of a possible solution. *Psychophysiology, 9,* 626–633.

Velden, M., Barry, R. J., & Wolk, C. (1987). Time dependent bradycardia: A new effect. *International Journal of Psychophysiology, 4,* 299–306.

Velden, M., & Juris, M. (1975). Perceptual performance as a function of intracycle cardiac activity. *Psychophysiology, 12,* 685–692.

Victor, R., Mainardi, J. A., & Shapiro, D. (1978). Effects of biofeedback and voluntary control procedures on heart rate and perception of pain during the cold pressor test. *Psychosomatic Medicine,* 216–225.

Wallace, R. K., & Benson, H. (1972). The physiology of meditation. *Scientific American, 226,* 84–90.

Walker, B. B., & Sandman, C. A. (1979). Human visual evoked responses are related to heart rate. *Journal of Comparative & Physiological Psychology, 93,* 717–729.

Walker, B. B., & Walker, J. M. (1983). Phase relations between carotid pressure and ongoing electrocortical activity. *International Journal of Psychophysiology, 1,* 65–73.

Walter, G. F., & Porges, S. W. (1976). Heart rate and respiratory responses as a function of task difficulty: The use of discriminant analysis in the selection of psychologically sensitive physiological responses. *Psychophysiology, 13,* 563–571.

Webb, R. A., & Obrist, P. A. (1970). The physiological concomitants of reaction time performance as a function of preparatory interval and preparatory interval series. *Psychophysiology, 6,* 389–403.

12

Blood Pressure, Blood Volume, and Behavior

Blood pressure (BP) is one of the most frequently measured physiological variables. Its measurement in the physician's office and the hospital or clinic far exceeds its use as a variable in psychological research. This is because of its importance as a general index of cardiovascular function and the health of individuals. Research on the effects of psychological stimuli on blood pressure dates back to at least the 1920s, when Nissen, as one example, obtained blood pressure readings of patients in a dentist's chair. Pressures rose sharply as soon as the dentist entered the room! (Woodworth & Schlosberg, 1954).

Blood volume (BV) is a much less familiar term than blood pressure. It refers to the amount of blood that is present in a certain portion of body tissue at a given time. Blood volume changes occur as a function of local metabolic requirements, and an important factor affecting it is the behavior in which the individual is engaged. Early studies of blood volume include those of Shepard, who reported, in 1906, that the expectation of a stimulus led to decreased hand blood volume and an increase in brain volume (Woodworth & Schlosberg, 1954). This chapter examines BP and BV as physiological variables in psychological research. The blood pressure and blood volume responses, and their relation to behavior, are presented after a brief discussion of the anatomy and physiology of these measures.

ANATOMY AND PHYSIOLOGY OF THE BLOOD VESSELS

Blood vessels may be divided into several categories on the basis of their size, function, and microscopic characteristics. These categories include the large

TABLE 12.1
Structure of Blood Vessels

Vessel	Outer Layer: Tunica Adventitia	Middle Layer: Tunica Media	Inner Layer: Tunica Intima
Large arteries (elastic)	Thick layer, consisting of connective tissue	Layer consists largely of elastic fibers with some muscle	Thin endothelial cells resting on connective tissue
Muscular arteries (medium)	Thick layer, consisting of connective tissue	Fewer elastic fibers, more smooth muscle	Thin endothelial cells resting on connective tissue
Small arteries (arterioles)	Thin	Consists of muscular tissue	Layer composed almost entirely of endothelium
Capillaries	Absent	Absent	Endothelial layer, one cell thick
Veins	Thin layer	Thinner, little muscle or elastic tissue	Endothelial lining with scant connective tissue

Source: Taken from S. W. Jacob and C. A. Francone, *Structure and function in man* (2nd ed.). Philadelphia: W. B. Saunders, 1970.

elastic arteries, medium-sized muscular arteries, small arteries (arterioles), capillaries, and veins (Jacob & Francone, 1970). The blood vessels are composed of three layers: an inner tunica intima, a middle tunica media, and an outer tunica adventitia. (Note the direct use of the latin word for a layer of clothing or "tunica" in each of these terms.) Table 12.1 outlines the structures of these various kinds of blood vessels. Figure 12.1 illustrates the structural layers of arteries and veins.

Basically, the arteries are tubes with thick walls, branching out from the aorta to carry blood to all parts of the body. Arteries are made up of smooth muscle fibers and elastic membrane tissue. This gives them an elastic property, enabling them to stretch when pressure is applied and then readily return to normal when pressure is relaxed.

The arterioles are the smallest arteries in the body. They enable blood to enter capillary beds (Guyton, 1977). The capillaries are tiny vessels, one cell layer thick (about 10 microns), that allow the actual exchange of carbon dioxide and oxygen in the lungs and of nutrients and wastes in body tissues. The blood leaves the capillary beds by small venules, which form into small veins and eventually into larger veins, which carry blood back to the heart. Veins are not as muscular as arteries and have valves that prevent the backflow of blood.

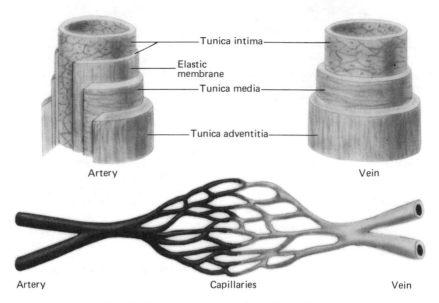

Tunica intima——

Elastic
membrane

——Tunica media——

——Tunica adventitia——

Artery   Vein

Artery   Capillaries   Vein

FIG. 12.1.   Component parts of arteries and veins.

Innervation of Blood Vessels

All of the blood vessels of the body, except the capillaries, are innervated by
nerve fibers from the SNS alone (Guyton, 1977).

The SNS produces varying degrees of constriction of the blood vessels. This
is controlled via the vasomotor center, which is located in the reticular substance
of the brain (lower pons and upper medulla). The hypothalamus of the brain can
exert powerful inhibitory or excitatory effects on the vasomotor center. Cortical
effects have not been as well defined.

The vasomotor center maintains what is called sympathetic vasoconstrictor
tone, which is essential in keeping arterial blood pressure at an appropriate
functioning level. Normal sympathetic tone keeps almost all of the blood vessels
of the body constricted to about half of maximum diameter. With increased SNS
activity, vessels can be further constricted. On the other hand, by inhibiting the
normal tone, blood vessels can be dilated. Thus, normal sympathetic tone allows
both vasoconstriction and vasodilation of blood vessels. The PNS exerts no
direct influence over the peripheral blood vessels (Gardner, 1975). The sympathetic vasoconstrictor substance is norepinephrine, which acts upon the smooth
muscle tissue of blood vessels.

Regulation of Blood Pressure

Jacob and Francone (1970) listed five factors that function to maintain arterial
blood pressure:

1. Cardiac factor: This refers to the volume of blood expelled each time the left ventricle contracts.

2. Peripheral resistance: This is produced primarily by the arterioles, which vary their diameter over a wide range.

3. Blood volume: Blood volume refers here to the relatively constant volume of blood cells and plasma within the whole circulatory system. If blood volume is low, then blood pressure is reduced.

4. Viscosity: Increased viscosity of blood causes a greater resistance to flow and, therefore, a higher arterial pressure. If blood hematocrit increases, so does the friction between successive layers of blood, and viscosity increases drastically. (The hematocrit refers to the percentage of blood that is composed of cells. Thus, if a person has a hematocrit reading of 42, it means that 42% of the blood volume is composed of cells and 58% is plasma). The hematocrit value of a normal man is about 42, whereas that of a normal woman is about 38 (Guyton, 1977).

5. Elasticity of arterial walls: When elasticity of the larger arteries decreases, systolic pressure rises. Systolic blood pressure refers to the pressure exerted on arterial walls during ventricular systole (contraction), whereas diastolic pressure is related to ventricular diastole.

Stretch receptors (baroreceptors) in the carotid sinuses and in the aorta transmit signals to the vasomotor system of the brain stem according to arterial pressure. These baroreceptors are ''spray'' type nerve endings, lying in the walls of the arteries, that are stimulated when stretched. The baroreceptors are not stimulated by pressures between 0 and 60 mm Hg, but above this level they progressively increase their firing rate until a maximum is reached at about 180 mm Hg. (Guyton, 1977). Heart rate and blood pressure are inversely related through the baroreceptor reflex, so that a drop in arterial pressure quickly leads to an increase in heart rate (Steptoe, 1980). However, under certain conditions, such as exercise or unpleasant stimulation, BP and HR may increase together. Usually, if blood pressure becomes elevated, reflex signals from the vasomotor center slow the heart and dilate the blood vessels. Thus, stimulation of baroreceptors by pressure in the arteries reflexly causes arterial pressure to decrease, whereas low pressure produces the opposite effect, that is, pressure is reflexly caused to rise back toward normal. Although the baroreceptor reflex is important in regulating moment-to-moment changes in arterial pressure, it is unimportant in the long-term control of blood pressure, because the baroreceptors adapt in 1 or 2 days to a given pressure level. The more long-term control of BP is determined by the balance between fluid intake and output, in which the kidneys play an important role. Blood pressure varies within the cardiac cycle, for example, it rises sharply with ventricular systole. Blood pressure level also changes from beat to beat, posing difficulties in measurement (e.g., see Tursky, Shapiro, & Schwartz, 1972).

Regulation of Blood Volume

The normal adult has a blood volume of approximately 5000 ml (5 liters). This figure varies with such factors as age, sex, build, race, environment, and disease (Grollman, 1964). In this chapter, we are interested in examining changes in blood volume that occur in the performance of various mental and physical tasks. That is, shifts in the blood volume of various body parts that occur in different kinds of activities. These shifts in blood volume are dependent on the arterial blood flow into an area and the venous outflow from an area. Therefore, those factors mentioned earlier with respect to vasoconstriction or vasodilation of blood vessels (e.g., SNS activity, baroreceptor reflex) are also of importance in regulating blood volume. There is also a reflex for the control of blood volume (Guyton, 1977). For example, if blood volume of the body increases, stretch receptors in the atria and large veins transmit signals to the vasomotor center. Reflex signals involving both the vasomotor center and the hypothalamus then cause the kidneys to increase their fluid output, thus reducing total body fluid and blood volume.

MEASUREMENT OF BLOOD PRESSURE

The methods we describe for the measurement of blood pressure are known as indirect techniques. The true measurement of blood pressure can only be achieved by penetrating an artery to insert a sensing device. This direct measurement of intra-arterial BP would be a problem in the psychophysiology laboratory using human subjects, because of discomfort for participants and possible medical complications.

The most familiar blood pressure measuring technique involves the use of a sphygmomanometer (from the Greek word sphygmos, meaning "pulse"). The method involves the use of a pressure cuff, a rubber bulb, a mercury (Hg) manometer, and a stethoscope. The pressure cuff is wrapped around the upper arm and inflated to a level well above the expected systolic pressure (say, 175 mm Hg). The stethoscope, which has been placed over the brachial artery, picks up no sound at this level, because the artery has been collapsed by the cuff pressure. The cuff pressure is then very gradually reduced, until sounds are heard. Gradual reductions of about 2 mm Hg per second on the mercury manometer allows fairly accurate measurements of BP. The sounds are produced by small amounts of blood passing through the cuff and are called Korotkoff sounds, after the man who first used this method in the early 1900s. The pressure on the manometer is noted when the first sound is heard with each pulsation. This is the systolic pressure and, for a normal adult, ranges between 95 and 140 millimeters (mm) Hg, with 120 mm Hg being average (Cromwell et al., 1976). The pressure in the cuff is then reduced further, until the sounds are no longer heard. When the sounds disappear, the manometer reading at that point indicates diastolic pressure. Normal diastolic pressure ranges between 60 and 89 mm Hg for the adult. The Korotkoff sounds are believed to be caused by blood jetting through the partly collapsed artery. The jet causes turbulence in the open artery beyond the cuff, and this sets up the vibrations heard in the stethoscope. This technique is termed the *auscultatory method* of obtaining blood pressure, and is adequate for the physician who is mainly concerned that his patients fall within a normal range. However, for psychophysiological research, it is necessary to have automated, accurate techniques that enable frequent measurements of blood pressure. It should be noted, too, that the systolic reading is obtained when the heart is contracting to push blood into the arteries, whereas the diastolic reading is obtained when the heart relaxes between beats. Tiny cuff systems for measuring systolic pressure from the finger have been developed, but BP values obtained in this way have not been found comparable to brachial values, making interpretation difficult. In addition, finger recording systems are very prone to contamination by movement.

Tursky (1974) has pointed out that the auscultatory method leads to an underestimate of systolic blood pressure. This is because the pressure in the cuff must be lower than that in the artery in order for the Korotkoff sound to be heard. A problem also exists in measuring diastolic pressure by this means, because it, too, depends on changes in sound. Tursky et al. (1972) developed an automated constant-cuff pressure system to overcome this error of measurement. This technique determines the relationship between a fixed-cuff pressure and arterial pressure at each heartbeat. The presence and absence of the Korotkoff sound is then used to establish a median pressure. The system was tested on a patient who had arterial pressure recorded directly from the brachial artery of the left arm while systolic pressures were obtained from the right arm with the constant-cuff procedure. Measures on five sets of 32 beats showed a close correspondence in systolic pressure obtained with each method (all comparisons were less than 2 mm Hg apart).

Pulse wave velocity (PWV) is the rate of travel of pressure pulse waves through the arterial system. This measure does not use a cuff, but obtains a reading of time for the pulse to occur at two points along an artery. Thus, for example, pressure transducers may be placed over the brachial and radial arteries of one arm. Steptoe, Smulyan, and Gribbon (1976) described an adaptation of a technique of measuring pulse wave velocity (PWV) in which the interval between the R wave of the ECG and radial (wrist) pulse pressure is obtained. The resulting transit time (TT) is used as an indirect measure of blood pressure change. Test trials indicated a high relation between TT and average blood pressure measured directly from an artery. However, other investigators have found TT related to systolic BP but not to diastolic (e.g., Lane, Greenstadt, Shapiro, & Rubenstein, 1983; Obrist, Light, McCubbin, Hutcheson, & Hoffer, 1979). Other problems, such as difficulty in calibration and sensitivity to movement artifacts, limit the usefulness of the TT technique (Larsen, Schneiderman, & Posin, 1986).

Another automated technique, which uses ultrasound to measure movements of the brachial artery, has been described by Cromwell et al. (1976). The principle used is similar to sonar, in that high-frequency sound is directed at the artery and reflected. Changes in the sound produced as the artery expands and contracts are detected as a "Doppler shift" and translated into blood pressure. Doppler shift refers to changes in the pitch of a sound as an object moves toward or away from a listener. The Doppler signals clearly identify the opening (diastole) and closing (systole) of the artery as the cuff pressure decreases. These sounds are analogous to the Korotkoff sounds, and allow continuous measures of systolic and diastolic pressures. Of the available automatic BP measuring devices, Larsen et al. (1986) considered the Doppler system of Aaslid and Brubaak (1981) to be the most promising. Using this method, a close relation was shown between the BP obtained by the Doppler system and intra-arterial BP obtained from the other arm. Recording is semi-continuous, because observation periods of 2 minutes are interspersed with 5 to 15 seconds of cuff deflation to permit venous blood flow to adjust. Pain occurs only when venous return is obstructed for long periods, and movement artifact is avoidable under most conditions.

Gunn, Wolf, Black, and Person (1972) briefly described a portable device for the automatic measurement of blood pressure. A cuff is inflated on a programmed schedule and records systolic and diastolic pressure on a miniature tape recorder. The instrument can be worn by a freely moving person, enabling the continuous recording of blood pressure (up to 10 hours) as he or she goes about his or her daily activities. The use of these portable devices has great potential for psychophysiologists who wish to study BP reactions to daily activities, and for physicians desiring to measure effects of antihypertensive treatments. So far, few investigators have taken advantage of this potential. A hospital nursery was the site where a new device was tested for the measurement of BP and heart rate in newborn infants (Hall, Thomas, Friedman, & Lynch, 1982). The device detects pressure pulsations in the cuff and records them automatically. The authors found the technique simple to use and more reliable than Doppler devices in this application. The lowest BP readings were obtained when the 77 infants were sleeping (78 systolic, 40 diastolic), and the highest (82 systolic, 45 diastolic) occurred while they were sucking. The HR was lowest while they slept (126 BPM), and it was highest when they cried (144 BPM).

MEASUREMENT OF BLOOD VOLUME

Brown (1967) pointed out that *plethysmography* is a term used to describe various techniques of measuring blood volume changes in a limb or segment of tissue. The term is derived from the Greek "plethysmos," which means "an enlargement''. Three basic types of devices for recording blood volume changes were described by Brown (1967):

1. Hydraulic or pneumatic systems, in which fluids or air detect a volume change in an observed part and transmit this to a recording device.

2. Electrical impedance, which reflects changes in impedance by tissue to the passage of high-frequency alternating current, as a function of volume change.

3. Photoelectric transducers, which measure changes in the intensity of a light passed through a tissue segment, for example, a fingertip or an earlobe. The intensity varies as a function of the amount of blood in the tissue from moment to moment. It should be noted that photoelectric techniques do not reflect absolute blood volume but only changes within a given person. Comparisons across subjects cannot be made.

Because blood volume measures are relative, most investigators examine changes within each subject from some baseline period and compare this to effects produced by the experimental conditions. Stern, Ray, and Davis (1980) pointed out that change between baseline and treatment is usually expressed as a percentage, and the magnitude of change is measured as the difference between the lowest point of a pulse and its peak. Photoelectric devices to measure blood volume changes have been described by Tursky and Greenblatt (1967) and Lee, Tahmoush, and Jennings (1975). The device described by Tursky and Greenblatt involves the use of a pair of fiberoptic light guides. One guide is connected to a regulated light source that transmits light to the skin, and a second, attached to a photocell, records changes in reflected light corresponding to volume changes. Lee et al. (1975) used a reflective transducer that combines an infrared light-emitting diode (LED) and a silicon phototransistor. This device can be applied to almost any area of the body to measure changes in vascular activity (see also Tahmoush, Jennings, Lee, Camp, & Weber, 1976).

Cook (1974) pointed out that there are two elements of plethysmographic change that can be measured. These are the relatively slow engorgement of an area, just described as blood volume, and a rapid component referred to as pulse volume or pulse amplitude. Pulse volume represents the pumping action of the heart as represented in local blood vessels. Blood volume and pulse volume can be measured with the same photoplethysmographic device, using different coupling and gain settings, on separate channels of a recorder. Blood volume measurements obtained with a photoplethysmograph require the use of a DC amplifier with a preamplifier and appropriate transducer (e.g., photoelectric cell placed on an earlobe). Pulse volume measures require AC coupling of the amplifier because the changes that occur are more rapid. Figure 12.2 shows sample traces of blood volume, pulse amplitude, and blood flow. The tracings show that all the measures are sensitive to an environmental stimulus; in this case, a 95-db tone presented simultaneously to the two ears.

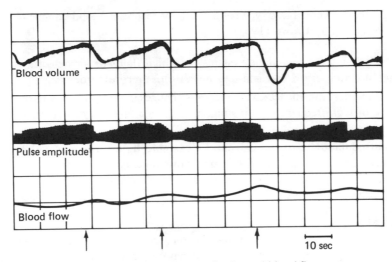

FIG. 12.2.   Blood volume, pulse amplitude, and blood flow responses from the finger to a 95-db, 1000-Hz tone. Arrows mark the onset of stimulus presentation.

A vaginal photoplethysmograph has been developed (see Geer, Morokoff, & Greenwood, 1974; Sintchak & Geer, 1975) for measuring changes in vaginal blood volume. This device, in addition to a penile strain gauge, was used by Heiman (1977) in a study on sexual arousal patterns in males and females. Briefly, the vaginal device is a hollow cylinder, $1\frac{3}{4}$ in. long and $\frac{1}{2}$ in. in diameter, and houses a small lamp and a photocell. It is inserted into the vagina, and the indirect light reflected back to the photocell from the vaginal wall is measured. The amount of reflected light varies with changes in vaginal vasoconstriction.

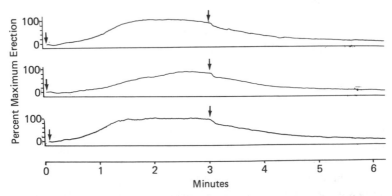

FIG. 12.3.   Sample polygraph tracings showing measurement characteristics of penile transducer. Arrows indicate onset and offset of 3-minute film segments.

The penile strain gauge fits around the shaft of the penis, near the coronal ridge, and measures changes that occur with erection or return to the flaccid state. Laws and Bow (1976) described a penile strain gauge of this type in detail. Figure 12.3 illustrates some data obtained by Laws and Bow from a single subject during the viewing of a 3-minute segment of pornographic film. Depicted is the course of penile erection from zero to maximum and the return to baseline.

BLOOD PRESSURE AND BEHAVIOR

In this segment, we examine a number of studies that have employed blood pressure as one of the physiological variables in studies relating to human behavior. There is no question that BP increases with most types of mental and physical activity. Questions that investigators are interested in concern the amount of change, moderating effects of various kinds of mental activities, emotional and stress effects, effects of the environment, and personality factors. Also discussed in this section are the conditioning of blood pressure and effects of motor activities and fitness on BP. We shall see that researchers have provided some answers to these questions, but that they have also uncovered new questions that require new answers.

Mental Activity and Blood Pressure

The relationship between a number of physiological variables and ''mental load'' was investigated by Ettema and Zielhuis (1971). The physiological measures included blood pressure, HR, and respiration rate. The researchers manipulated mental load by varying the amount of information processed by subjects in a given period of time. High and low tones were presented over earphones in a random sequence. The high tone required pressing a pedal with the left foot, whereas the low tone signaled the same action by the right foot. Each of 24 young adults had the various physiological measures recorded during rest and during processing of 20, 30, 40, or 50 signals per minute. Systolic and diastolic blood pressure showed systematic increases as information-processing load increased. The same was true for HR and respiration rate. The authors concluded that increased cardiovascular and respiratory functions are useful indices regarding mental load and may be important in assessing this aspect of industrial work.

The effects of solving difficult problems on BP and other cardiovascular measures was studied by McCubbin, Richardson, Langaer, Kizer, and Obrist (1983). The subjects were 24 male undergraduates who were promised bonus money if they completed a series of problems rapidly and accurately. Systolic pressures increased from 127 to 138 mm Hg from pretest to test periods, and an average increase from 70 to 79 mm Hg was observed for diastolic pressures. Heart rates for the same comparisons increased from 64 to 71 BPM. Cardiovascular measures were found to covary with levels of plasma epinephrine and norepinephrine, causing the investigators to conclude that sympatho-adrenomedullary responsivity may be an important mechanism of individual differences in response to the mental stress involved in solving difficult problems.

Cardiovascular responsivity of women classified as Type A and B personalities were studied by Lane, White, and Williams (1984) as they completed a challenging mental arithmetic test. The Type A concept was developed by two research cardiologists to describe individuals who are competitive, impatient, and hostile (Friedman & Rosenman, 1974). The relative absence of this pattern is called Type B. The Type A individual is considered to be two times as likely to develop coronary heart disease than Type B persons. Current theories suggest that Type A behaviors are accompanied by excess cardiovascular and neuroendocrine response, leading to disease of coronary arteries (atherosclerotic plaques). In the study by Lane and colleagues, females scoring high and low on the Type A scale had measures of BP, HR, and forearm blood flow taken during mental subtraction. Both groups showed equivalent, significant elevations of BP from resting to task conditions; approximately 10% for systolic pressure, 15% for diastolic pressure and 16% for HR. Another analysis, however, revealed that a subset of Type A females, who had a family history of hypertension, responded more than Type Bs. Thus, family history of hypertension and gender are additional factors to consider in studying the relations between Type A/B pattern and cardiovascular response. The Type A/B personality pattern and BP are considered further in a later section of this chapter. Drummond (1983) monitored BP and HR of 18 mild hypertensives and 18 normotensives during rest, mental arithmetic, and head-up tilt. The BP and HR of the hypertensives were higher than the normals when both were at rest. In addition, BP levels increased more in hypertensives while doing mental arithmetic and performing head-up tilt. The greater responsivity of hypertensives in this study supports the view that excess sympathetic nervous system activity contributes to the elevated BP levels observed in hypertension. Thus, as researchers learn more about the basic mechanisms of BP response in various kinds of tasks, they also contribute to knowledge about factors that may contribute to hypertension, such as heredity and personality.

There are some kinds of mental activity that can lead to a lowering of BP. For example, lower systolic pressures were observed in 112 persons practicing Transcendental Meditation (TM) when their values were compared to a matched control group (Wallace, Silver, Mills, Dillbeck, & Wagoner, 1983). The difference was also independent of diet and exercise. Those who had meditated for more than 5 years showed lower levels than meditators with less than 5 years' experience. In another study, the effects of TM was compared to progressive muscle relaxation (PMR) with respect to effects on BP and HR (Throll, 1982). Physiological variables were measured in a pre-experimental session and again at 5, 10, and 15 weeks after practicing each technique. The TM group had greater decreases during meditation and during activity than the PMR group. The groups had shown no pre-experimental differences. The more significant results for meditators were explained in terms of the greater amount of time the TM group spent on their technique, in addition to the difference between the two techniques themselves. This brief review has shown that mental activities, such as problem solving, can lead to BP increases, whereas some other activities, such as practicing transcendental meditation, result in decreases.

Emotional Reactions, Stress, and Blood Pressure

It has been reported that both frustration and attack produced increased levels of diastolic and systolic blood pressure (Gentry, 1970). In that study, 30 males and 30 females were subjected to frustration (interrupted and not allowed to complete an intelligence test), attack (personal insults by an experimenter), or control conditions. A gender difference was found, in that males generally had greater increases in systolic pressure than did females, with no differences noted for diastolic changes. Doob and Kirshenbaum (1973) measured blood pressure and digit-symbol performance in four groups of 10 persons each, after they were subjected to various combinations of frustration and aggression. The blood pressure and digit-symbol performance were recorded both before and after the following conditions: (a) not frustrated, viewed neutral film; (b) not frustrated, viewed aggressive film; (c) frustrated, viewed neutral film; and (d) frustrated, viewed aggressive film. Persons in Group (d) showed the greatest increase in systolic BP from the first to second reading. Those in Groups (b) and (c) showed a small increase, whereas individuals in Group (a) had slight decreases. The authors interpreted the results as contrary to the idea that movies depicting aggression are tension-reducing for either frustrated or nonfrustrated persons; rather, the effects of frustration and aggression seem to be additive in terms of cardiovascular response.

Along similar lines, Geen and Stonner (1974) found that subjects who were given electric shocks, and who then viewed an aggressive film about revenge, showed higher BP levels at the conclusion of the film than did persons who were not shocked and who were told that the theme of the film was either altruism or professionalism. Geen and Stonner suggested that the meaning attached to observed violence affects aggression by lowering inhibitions against aggressiveness and by raising arousal levels. Geen (1975) followed this study with another, in which the effects of being shocked and viewing "real" violence were compared with neutral treatment and observing a film of "fictional" violence. The combination of prior shock (attack) and observation of real violence produced the highest levels of BP. This and the prior study indicated to Geen that the observation of violence facilitated the expression of aggression by raising the viewer's level of emotional arousal. Effects of emotional expression on cardiovascular response played a role in results obtained by Harburg, Blakelock, and Roeper

(1979) who analyzed coping styles in a frustrating situation. They tested the hypothesis that certain coping reactions to an angry boss would be conducive to elevated BP. The subjects were 492 males and 252 females (ages 25–60) who completed a questionnaire measuring three types of coping: (a) suppressing anger by ignoring or walking away from the conflict situation; (b) venting anger; and (c) analyzing the problem and restoring a fair job situation. The individuals using the first two strategies had significantly higher BP levels than those using the third one. Thus, giving vent to anger or ignoring the situation completely seem to be maladaptive both from a behavioral and cardiovascular perspective.

The question of cardiovascular response differences with various emotional imagery was examined by Schwartz, Weinberger, & Singer (1981). College students were asked to produce imagined states of happiness, sadness, anger, fear, relaxation, and a control imagery state, while seated and when they exercised. Anger imagery produced the greatest overall increases in BP and HR and was distinctly opposite from relaxation. Sadness was unique, because systolic BP was very similar under seated and exercise conditions. Similar results were obtained by Roberts and Weerts (1982), who examined cardiovascular responding during fear and anger imagery. They, too, found greater BP increases for anger than fear imagery. Matthews, Manuck, and Saab (1986) used a naturalistic stressor (giving a 5-minute speech in class) to evaluate cardiovascular response in anxious and in angry high school students. Anxious students showed elevated systolic BP and HR while giving the speech, whereas adolescents who were frequently angry, and expressed their anger outwardly, had elevated diastolic BP. Adolescents who had exaggerated cardiovascular responses ("reactors") to mental subtraction and mirror-tracing in an additional laboratory test also showed elevated BP and/or HR in the field setting (class speech). This finding suggests that responses in laboratory settings may be good indicators of responding in every day life situations. This also fits in with findings of McKinney et al. (1985), who showed that laboratory measures of BP using standard stressors (e.g., cold pressor test) were related to ambulatory measures of BP taken at home and at work. In several of the studies reviewed here, anger played a prominent role in elevated BP whether it was naturally present or derived through imagery. This basic research could have important health implications. Redford Williams and his associates (Williams, Barefoot, & Shekelle, 1985) are involved in research investigating the role or anger and hostility in producing cardiovascular disease.

Cardiovascular responsivity to stress is currently receiving a great deal of research attention. Research designs are complex and consider such factors as type of task, whether an individual is able to actively cope with a stressor, history of parental hypertension, and personality factors (e.g., Type A/B). Stress can be defined as the bodies' response to some demanding psychological or physical stimulus. The stimulus itself is the "stressor." An example of a psychological stressor might be a mental multiplication task, whereas a physical stressor might be submerging a hand in a bucket of ice water (cold pressor). A number of studies support the conclusion that individuals with a family history of essential hypertension show greater cardiovascular reactivity to stress than those without a positive history. However, there is some recent evidence that differential responding may also be related to type of task. For example, Ditto (1986) compared reactivity of 24 males with positive family histories of hypertension to 24 without this hereditary factor while they performed three different tasks. Two of the tasks were considered to be active coping stressors because subjects could avoid poor performance by accurate responding (Stroop word-color interference and mental arithmetic). A third condition did not allow active coping (isometric hand-grip). As predicted, family-history subjects showed greater systolic BP increases than non-family-history persons to the two active coping stressors (Stroop and mental arithmetic). Light and Obrist (1983) have reported that persons high in cardiovascular reactivity show larger systolic BP and HR responses during tasks requiring active coping. In their study, 72 young men had measures taken while performing a reaction time task where winning money was easy, difficult, or impossible. The subjects termed "high reactors" were those who showed greater HR increases when the task started, and who maintained this higher level over lower HR reactors, regardless of task difficulty. Lovallo, Pincomb, and Wilson (1986) also studied high and low reactors in active and passive coping tasks and obtained similar results. Both BP and HR were more highly elevated during active coping for the high HR reactors. The passive condition involved exposure to noise and electric shock, and the active coping task permitted subjects to avoid the noise and shock. Allen, Sherwood & Obrist (1986) compared cardiovascular and respiratory responses to a cold pressor, three levels of exercise on a bicycle ergometer, and under instructions to react quickly to avoid an electric shock to the leg. The cold pressor and reaction time stress both produced an increase in systolic BP of about 17%. But the diastolic increase was much greater for the cold pressor stressor (25%) than for reaction time (7%). Also of interest was the finding that graded increases in the bicycle exercise resulted in steady increases in systolic BP, but no increase in diastolic BP. What might be considered as examples of physical stressors (cold pressor and bicycle pedaling) produced very different effects on diastolic BP.

To summarize, changes in blood pressure occur in laboratory situations where subjects are frustrated or threatened with electric shock. The combination of being attacked or frustrated and viewing an aggressive film seems to result in reliable increases in BP. The effects of anger on BP, whether naturally occuring or induced through imagery, has been noted. The effects of stress on BP have been shown in a variety of studies. The mechanisms are complex, however, as indicated by results showing higher BP in tasks that allow active coping, and the differential responding by those categorized as "high reactors" emphasizes the role of individual differences in physiological response in a given situation. The interaction effect between active coping and high reactivity is dramatic.

Conditioning of Blood Pressure

Much of the basic research on changing BP levels through instrumental conditioning has been motivated by the possible development of a technique for the treatment of patients who suffer from essential hypertension. This disorder is one of elevated blood pressure without a demonstrable cause and is implicated in heart disease and strokes. In this segment, we consider attempts to instrumentally condition blood pressure level in normal subjects, whereas in chapter 14, the use of this technique with hypertensive patients is considered.

The pioneering work of DiCara and Miller (1968), in which instrumental conditioning of blood pressure of rats was attempted, has prompted other researchers to try a similar approach with humans. For example, Shapiro, Tursky, Gershon, and Stern (1969) provided 20 normal male subjects with information (feedback) about their systolic pressure and reinforced half of them for decreasing it and the other half for increasing it. They developed an application of the auscultatory technique to provide automatic feedback of systolic pressure at each successive heartbeat, that is, feedback regarding upward or downward changes in pressure was given with each beat. Short duration lights and tones signaled blood pressure that was in the right direction. After every 20 signals of this type, the subjects received a reinforcement. The reinforcer was a nude centerfold from the pages of Playboy magazine, projected on a screen for 5 seconds. The results indicated that systolic blood pressure can be modified by external feedback and operant reinforcement. This occurred in a single session consisting of 25 trials.

In a follow-up study, Shapiro, Tursky, and Schwartz (1970) found that the changes in blood pressure levels were independent of HR. Shapiro, Schwartz, and Tursky (1972) extended their findings to diastolic pressure in another study of instrumental conditioning in 20 normal males. This time, the reinforcers consisted of slides of landscapes, slides of nude women, and money. Measures of HR and respiration were also obtained. The group reinforced for pressure increases had a mean diastolic pressure difference of 7.0 mm Hg (10% of baseline level) as compared to the decrease group (up increased 4 mm Hg, down decreased 3 mm Hg). The authors expressed optimism about the possible application of this technique to hypertensive patients, especially in view of the relatively brief (25 or 35 minutes) training periods used in the studies.

The work of Shapiro and colleagues has been criticized by Blanchard and Young (1973) for using different feedback modes (visual and auditory) and reinforcers (slides and monetary rewards). They also criticized the lack of a no-feedback control group. These criticisms were addressed in a study by Fey and Lindholm (1975), in which two groups of normal subjects received feedback contingent on either increases or decreases in systolic BP, and two other groups received either noncontingent feedback or no feedback. The subjects participated in three 1-hour experimental sessions over a 3-day period. Progressive and significant drops in systolic pressure were seen in the decrease group over the 3-day period. No systematic changes were observed in the other three groups. The authors pointed out that visual feedback alone seemed to be as effective as the feedback-reinforcer combination previously used in the instrumental conditioning of blood pressure. They concluded that contingent feedback is effective in lowering BP and that ability to do this is improved with practice over a few days.

In a related line of research, investigators have been studying ability to discriminate variations in one's own blood pressure. Shapiro, Redmond, McDonald, and Gaylor (1975) found that six hypertensive persons were able to detect up or down variations in BP when asked to report every 30 seconds whether pressure had changed. Discriminations were better with larger BP changes. In another study, Cinciripini, Epstein, and Martin (1979) recorded BP of moderately hypertensive individuals who had daily BP variations of at least 15 mm Hg. Significant improvements in estimation were observed when subjects were given immediate knowledge of results regarding BP levels. In a larger-scale study, Greenstadt, Shapiro, and Whitehead (1986) examined the benefits of discrimination training on the ability of 72 normotensive males to detect changes in their own BP. The subject's task was to decide whether his BP was higher during the first or second of two consecutive 5-sec. periods. Immediate feedback was provided regarding correctness of decisions, and accuracy was rewarded with money. The results showed that, when given feedback, subjects showed a significant improvement in ability to discriminate BP, in only two sessions. There was also evidence for the relative independence of systolic and diastolic BP. Still unresolved was the mechanism by which subjects learned to make the discrimination; that is, whether cues came from internal sources or were the result of variations in the pressure cuff itself.

This brief review has shown that modest, but consistent, decreases in BP have been instrumentally conditioned in a number of studies. In addition, there is some evidence that people can learn to discriminate changes in their own BP levels when given immediate feedback. This line of research has both academic interest in terms of physiological responses that can be instrumentally conditioned and is also potentially of clinical importance in the treatment of essential hypertension, because high blood pressure is not usually associated with body sensations, a fact that has led to its being called a "silent" disease.

Social-Environmental Factors and Blood Pressure

The effects on BP of verbally communicating with other individuals has been studied and reveals interesting findings. For example, elevations in BP were observed in both normotensive and hypertensive persons while talking to others (Lynch, Long, Thomas, Malinow, & Katcher, 1981). Subjects with higher resting BP showed greater increases while talking than people with lower pressures. In some hypertensive persons, increases in BP of 25 to 40% occurred within 30 sec. after the initiation of speech. In another study, increased BP was found for 40 college students when they engaged in a variety of verbal activities with either a high-status person or an equal-status person (Long, Lynch, Machiran, Thomas, & Malinow, 1982). However, the BP increases of the 20 subjects speaking to a high-status person were significantly greater than those who interacted with an equal-status individual. Thus, part of the BP increase was related to the process of verbally communicating and part to the social distance between individuals. The cardiovascular responses of a group of 30 nurses were measured before and after they spoke to an individual or a group of nurses (Thomas et al., 1984). Blood pressures and heart rates were higher when speaking than when at rest, and higher still when speaking in front of a group. It is clear that interacting socially through verbal communication will cause increases in BP. Other important factors include relative status of the two individuals, the number of people involved, and pre-experimental levels of BP.

Environmental psychologists and sociologists have been interested in the effects of crowding on human behavior and welfare. A study that relates to this question is one conducted by D'Atri, Fitzgerald, Kasl, and Malinow (1981), in which the effects of crowded housing on BP of 568 male inmates was investigated. The prisoners, whose average age was 25, showed significant increases in systolic BP when transferred from single-occupancy cells to multiple-occupancy dormitories. Those who remained in single cells showed no BP increase, and those who returned to cells after a short stay in dormitories had a drop in BP. Crowding is probably not the only factor in causing the increased BP noted in this study. Important factors are the threat to life and safety and the increased vigilance that must be exercised by prisoners in a dormitory situation. Effects on BP of city and country living were examined by Rao, Inbaraj, and Subramaniam (1984). They measured BPs of a random sample of 961 rural and 1073 urban women in southern India. For both the systolic and diastolic BPs, the urban values were significantly higher than the rural. Crowding may be a factor in this urban–rural comparison, but also to be considered are other differences in lifestyle between country and city. These include type of job, socioeconomic level, and availability of housing, as just some examples.

The presence of a dog has been found to lead to a lowering of blood pressure in humans. In one study, a group of 9–16-year-olds had BP and heart rate measured while resting or reading in the presence of a friendly animal (Friedmann, Katcher, Thomas, Lynch, & Messent, 1983). Having a dog present led to lowered BP and heart rate under all conditions. The effect was greater when the dog was present initially than when it was introduced in the second half of the experiment. Similar results were obtained by Baun, Langston, and Thoma (1984), who measured BP and heart rate while subjects (age 24–74) petted a known dog, an unknown dog, or read a book. The lowest cardiovascular response levels occurred while petting a familiar dog and when quietly reading. In experiments like these, the presence of a friendly animal may cause subjects to modify their perceptions of the experimenter and the experimental situation by making them appear more friendly and less threatening.

Motor Activities, Fitness, and Blood Pressure

Measurement of BP and heart rate of male college students were made while they participated in a competitive perceptual-motor task (TV tennis) (Dembroski, MacDougall, Eliot, & Buell). In an interesting approach, the health records of participants were examined to determine frequency of minor illnesses. Dembroski and colleagues reported that subjects who responded during the contest with extreme increases in diastolic BP and heart rate were more likely to have frequent minor illnesses than those responding with low or moderate increases. In a study by Ray, Brady, and Emurian (1984), subjects performed a synthetic work task (multiple task performance battery) over a period of 3 days while BP, heart rate, and pulse amplitude were recorded. Auditory stimulation, in the form of 93 decibel "pink noise," was presented for 10 minutes of each 30-minute task period. Performance of the task alone led to increases in BP and heart rate, and drops in pulse amplitude. The addition of noise stimulation produced further increases in BP and decreases in pulse amplitude, but no further changes in heart activity. No habituation was reported for either BP or vasomotor (pulse amplitude) responses to noise stimulation. This last finding is reminiscent of those that report increased blood pressures and cases of hypertension for workers in noisy factory environments than for those working in relatively quiet factories (e.g., Jonsson & Hansson, 1977).

It is well known that regular, vigorous exercise training decreases cardiovascular response to fixed amounts of exercise. The observed pattern of lower heart rate and increased stroke volume represents more efficient functioning of the heart. However, results concerning effects of training on BP during rest and exercise have not been consistent. Some have reported lower pressures at rest in trained normotensives, whereas others have not. Hull, Young, and Ziegler (1984) conducted a study to determine whether physical fitness is correlated with lower responsivity of BP and heart rate to various kinds of stressors. These responses were measured during four kinds of stress: (a) passive psychological stressor (film of industrial accidents); (b) Stroop word-color interference (active psychological stress); (c) cold pressor (passive physical stress); and (d) running to exhaustion on a treadmill (active physical stressor). The subjects were 35 men and 20 women, aged 21–64, who spent at least 30 min. per day in exercise or a hobby. They were divided into four groups varying in aerobic fitness. Fitness was defined in terms of length of time spent on a treadmill before feeling exhausted. Among persons 40 years of age or older, fitness was associated with lower resting systolic BP and lower diastolic BP to both types of psychological stress and to active physical stress. However, more and less fit persons under age 40 did not differ on any of the cardiovascular measures. As reported in previous studies of this type, heart rates were lower in fit persons at most times. Similar results were obtained by Light, Obrist, James, and Strogatz (1987). The subjects were 174 men, aged 18–22, divided into low, moderate, and high exercise groups based on self-reports about weekly aerobic exercise. Low-exercise individuals showed greater cardiovascular response to both a stressful reaction time task and exercise than those in the high-exercise group. This greater response was shown by group differences in systolic BP and heart rate, and is a relatively new finding regarding differences between more and less fit young adults to a stressful behavioral task. The topic area of aerobic fitness and cardiovascular response to stressors is one that certainly deserves more research attention. So far, the suggestive results seem to argue in favor of the cardiovascular benefits of being physically fit.

Personality Factors Affecting Blood Pressure

The research on personality factors has been dominated by comparisons of Type A and Type B behavior patterns with respect to their cardiovascular reactions. The behavior profile of the Type A person is that of a competitive, hostile, and impatient achiever. Individuals lacking these characteristics are labeled Type B. Clinical studies suggest that Type A individuals are more likely to suffer from a variety of cardiovascular disorders, such as coronary heart disease (CHD) and atherosclerosis (Jenkins, 1976). One view is that these disorders may be due in part to greater cardiovascular reactivity of Type As compared to Type B individuals (Matthews, 1982). In general, studies do indicate that Type A's cardiovascular response is greater than Type B's in a variety of situations. As cases in point, Type As have shown differential responding under a variety of different experimental situations that involved the manipulation of different stressors, such as uncontrollable noise, harassment, competition, presence of a hostile individual, task difficulty, challenge, and incentives. For example, Dembroski, MacDougall, Herd, and Shields (1979) randomly assigned 80 Type A and B males to conditions of high or low challenge while they engaged in RT and cold pressor tasks. Type A subjects had greater systolic BP and heart rate increases than Type Bs. This finding of elevated systolic BP is an especially consistent finding in a variety of situations. Harassment by a hostile individual during a competitive task led to increases in systolic BP and heart rate of Type As, but not Type Bs (Glass et al., 1980). Higher elevations of systolic BP was found for Type As compared to Type Bs even before the start of an arithmetic task in which money rewards were given (Contrada, Wright, & Glass, 1984). Holmes, McGilley, and Houston (1984) had 30 Type A and 30 Type B subjects work on a short-term memory task that was easy, moderate, or difficult. Again, systolic BP increased more for As than Bs, but only during the difficult task.

Research findings support the possible utility of the Type A concept with teen-age and younger children. In one study, 3–6-year-old boys who scored high on competitiveness, impatience/anger, and aggression (components of Type A behavior) responded to challenge with a greater increase in systolic BP than Type Bs (Lundberg, 1983). Systolic pressures of teens (13–18 years) was also found to be related to Type A behavior (Siegel, Matthews, & Leitch, 1983). An additional finding was that high variability in systolic BP was related to high levels of hostility and the rapid speech pattern characteristic of Type A persons. Research indicating that Type A persons have larger BP responses than Bs regardless of type of stressor suggests that Type A individuals are more reactive to stimuli. In a study by Blumenthal et al. (1983), Type A persons showed increased systolic BP in both monetary incentive and non-incentive conditions. In contrast, Type B individuals only showed increased systolic BP when trying to win money.

Many of the investigations into the relationship between Type A/B behavior and cardiovascular response have used males as subjects. Research with females has thus far indicated differences from findings with males. For example, Mac-Dougall, Dembroski, and Krantz (1981) reported that, unlike males studied earlier, female Type As and Bs did not differ in their systolic or diastolic BP to a RT or cold pressor task. However, they did show elevated systolic BP during a structured interview and an oral history quiz given by another woman. Thus, under a challenging interpersonal exchange, Type A women may show more cardiovascular response than Type Bs. In another study, Lane et al. (1984) reported that Type A and B women had similar blood pressure and heart rate increases to a mental arithmetic task. Thus, the Type A women were not hyper-responsive, compared with Type B. But the authors report that a subsample of Type A women, who also had a positive family history for hypertension, had larger cardiovascular responses under challenging conditions. Lawler, Schmeid, Mitchell, and Rixse (1984) also reported no difference in cardiovascular responding of college-age Type A and B women to cognitive tasks. To examine the possible relationship between family history of hypertension and Type A/B behavior more closely, Lawler and Schmied (1986) investigated cardiovascular responsiveness of a larger sample of Type A and B women subjected to interpersonal and competitive stressors (oral quiz and Stroop color-word interference). Women with positive family histories did have higher levels of systolic BP, but this was not related to Type A behavior. The authors concluded that Type A behavior is not related to cardiovascular responsivity in young adult women. Therefore, although fairly well established for males, the cardiovascular–A/B relationship still needs to be further investigated in women.

A personal characteristic suspected to be of importance in excessive cardiovascular response, in addition to Type A behavior, is heart rate reactivity. This characteristic shows itself as a tendency for an individual to show large BP or heart rate changes to various challenges and has been demonstrated in a number of psychophysiology laboratories. This type of reactivity was shown to be independent of Type A influences in a study conducted by Lovallo et al. (1986). The subjects were 44 young men classified as Type A or B. In addition, 16 of them were defined as high heart-rate reactors, because they had changes in heart rate of 20 beats per minute or more to a cold pressor test. The experimental task involved RT with monetary rewards for fast responses. Those persons who were high reactors had the greatest changes in systolic and diastolic BP, heart rate, and other measures of cardiovascular response. The high reactors were equally distributed among Type As and Bs. These researchers believe that heart rate reactivity is a relatively stable trait that generalizes from cold pressor to other tasks.

The Type A concept has been useful in stimulating research on cardiovascular response in a variety of situations. Thus far, one of the most consistent observations is the greater increase in systolic BP that occurs in Type As while engaged in challenging tasks. There is some evidence that the concept may predict cardiovascular response in young children and teenagers. On the other hand, results have been less positive for young adult women. Future research may see heart rate reactivity emerge as a more important predictor of cardiovascular responsivity than personality factors.

BLOOD VOLUME AND BEHAVIOR

The studies in this section fall into three main categories. These are (a) blood volume and sexual response; (b) orienting reflexes and blood volume; and (c) conditioning of blood volume responses.

Blood Volume and Sexual Response

Direct measures of genital changes have become increasingly important methods in the study of sexual behavior and preferences. The main genital change that occurs in sexual arousal and behavior is the vasocongestion of the vaginal, clitoral, and penile areas. The blood that flows to these areas remains and causes the tissue to become enlarged and warmer. Psychophysiologists have taken advantage of these facts in devising techniques to measures changes in genital temperature, blood volume, and blood flow in studying sexual arousal in a variety of situations. As Geer (1975) has observed, nongenital measures have not proven as useful in sex research as have genital ones.

Zuckerman (1972) examined the use of various physiological measures in studying human sexual response and noted that EDA, HR, respiration, and pupillary diameter did not appear to be sensitive to arousal produced by sexual stimuli or to accurately reflect sexual preferences. Blood pressure, however, did show a graded response to erotic stimuli. Zuckerman concluded that penile erection measures have proven to be the most sensitive indexes of sexual arousal in the male and have differentiated between preferred and nonpreferred sexual objects.

The work of researchers such as Geer and his associates has resulted in the development of more satisfactory devices for the measurement of genital blood volume in the female (Geer et al., 1974; Sintchak & Geer, 1975). Levine and Wagner (1978) developed a sophisticated device that measures blood flow in vaginal tissue. A device for measuring temperature from the labia majora of female genitalia has been described by Henson and Rubin (1978), and they reported that increases in labial temperature are related to erotic stimulation. Richards, Bridger, Wood, Kalucy, and Marshall (1985) described two penile strain gauges for measuring changes in penis circumference with sexual arousal. Additionally, groin skin temperature has been proposed by Rubinsky, Hoon, Eckerman, and Amberson (1985) as a measure of psychosexual arousal for both males and females. When compared to penile circumference and vaginal blood volume and pulse amplitude measures, during erotic film presentations, similar results were obtained with groin temperature for most of the subjects (10 males and 10 females). Let us now review some representative work in this field.

Geer, O'Donohue, and Schorman (1986) wrote that psychophysiology has contributed information on sex differences and practical problems in sexuality. For example, it has been assumed that women were not as responsive to explicit erotic stimuli as men. However, a study using physiological measures found that women are quite responsive to erotic stimuli even when there is no romantic context (Heiman, 1977). Geer and collaborators (1974) used a device to measure vaginal blood volume and pulse volume during the presentation of erotic and nonerotic films to 20 female college students. Two female experimenters described the research to subjects in detail during the first session. In the second session, the subjects inserted the vaginal probe, in privacy, and after a 3-minute rest period, viewed the two films. The erotic film was 8 minutes in duration and showed a young man and woman engaged in foreplay, oral–genital sex, and intercourse. The 8-minute nonerotic film depicted scenes of battles and court life during the time of the Crusades. Both blood volume and pulse volume were significantly higher during viewing of the erotic film than during the nonerotic film. In another study, Geer (1974) described a procedure used in his laboratory in which young men and women were asked to imagine an arousing sexual scene while they were alone in a private, comfortable room. Measures of penile volume and vaginal pulse volume were made in the room without observers and with no erotic stimuli present. After 2 to 3 minutes, increases in the size of the penis and elevated vaginal pulse volume were observed. A postrecording questionnaire indicated that the subjects were sexually aroused by their fantasies. Thus, Geer concluded, it is clear that cognitive factors influence sexual arousal.

Vaginal blood volume and pulse volume were obtained as adult women (aged 19 to 35) masturbated to orgasm (Geer & Quartararo, 1976). Pulse volume increased greatly during masturbation and postorgasm periods over baseline levels. However, although blood volume increased during masturbation and postorgasm, it decreased dramatically at the onset and during orgasm. The researchers postulated that the drop in blood volume during orgasm reflects SNS activity. This is consistent with the model of sexual activity that proposes that sexual arousal is controlled by the PNS, whereas orgasm is under SNS influence.

Heiman (1977) compared the sexual arousal of males and females, using a combination of genital and subjective measures. In Heiman's study, 59 female and 9 male undergraduates completed three sessions during which genital blood volume and pulse volume were measured. The subjects listened to various kinds of tapes which were: erotic, erotic-romantic, romantic, or control (contained neither erotic nor romantic materials). A 2-minute subject-generated fantasy preceded and followed each tape. The main findings were that (a) erotic and erotic-romantic contents resulted in similar increases in genital pulse amplitude and blood volume in both sexes, (b) there was high agreement between subjective ratings of sexual arousal and the genital measures, and (c) individuals became aroused during sexual fantasy.

The question of whether women show a change in sexual arousal at different states in the menstrual cycle was investigated by Hoon, Bruce, and Kinchloe (1982). The subjects were sexually experienced women ranging in age from 20 to 28. Vaginal blood volume, pulse amplitude, and labial temperature were measured while subjects listened to erotic tapes and when they engaged in erotic fantasies. Measures were taken at the premenstrual, menstrual, follicular, ovulatory, and luteal stages of the cycle. All three physiological measures and a rating scale of self-arousal indicated increases in sexual arousal with erotic stimulation. Most importantly, the researchers reported that arousability was the same at all stages of the menstrual cycle.

Cognitive factors have been found to play a role in male sexual arousal. For example, Geer and Fuhr (1976) found that distraction produced by engagement in a cognitive task resulted in lower arousal to erotic stimuli. A similar result was found for women subjects in an experiment by Adams, Haynes, and Brayer (1985). Vaginal blood volume and pulse amplitude were recorded while the 24 women listened to descriptions of explicit sexual activity. The cognitive distractor was a visually presented addition task. There was significant physiological and subjective arousal to erotic materials. However, when the distractor was added, physiological arousal decreased dramatically.

In summary, a number of recent studies that have used measures of genital blood volume or pulse amplitude indicate genital responses to sexual stimuli, sexual activity, subjective sexual arousal, and sexual fantasy. In addition, measures of genital response have provided evidence to dispel the idea that women are only sexually responsive during certain phases of the menstrual cycle. The detrimental effects of a distractor on sexual arousability has also been extended from males to females.

Blood Volume and the Orienting Reflex

Changes in blood volume form an important part of the orienting reflex as described by Sokolov (1963). Sokolov reported increases in forehead blood volume with novel or unexpected stimuli and decreases when stimuli were painful or threatening. According to Sokolov, increases in cephalic blood volume reflect the orienting reflex or response (OR), and the OR leads to improved perceptual ability. Conversely, decreases in blood volume reflect a defensive response (DR) that protects the organism by making it less sensitive to threatening or painful stimuli. The OR is said to habituate with continued stimulus presentation, and the DR is said to be immune to this effect. Although Sokolov's theory still remains to be established, it has been found that blood volume changes do occur in various parts of the body as a result of unexpected or novel stimuli.

The orienting response and its speed of habituation were investigated by Levander, Lidberg, and Schalling (1974). Young male subjects were presented with a series of 100-db tones (1-second duration) at intervals varying between 35 and 60 seconds. Decreases in finger blood volume and pulse volume were used as the physiological measures of the OR. Both responses were relatively large with the presentation of the first tone, and both habituated (i.e., decreased in response amplitude) as a function of additional tone presentations. The researchers noted that the pulse volume responses habituated faster than the blood volume responses, suggesting a degree of independence between these measures.

The effects of stimulus repetition on habituation of the OR was also studied by Ginsberg and Furedy (1974). They measured finger blood volume and pulse volume of 20 subjects who listened to a series of 80-db tones. They found that pulse volume responses habituated to the repetitive stimulation, but blood volume did not.

The effects of stimulus intensity and rise time on the OR were tested by Oster, Stern, and Figar (1975). They used tones of 70 and 90 db, with fast (10 μsec) and slow (100 msec) rise times. Sixty subjects had blood volume responses recorded from the head (temporal artery) and finger. As Sokolov predicted, head (cephalic) blood volume shifted from dilation to constriction with increased sound intensity. However, the constriction response habituated, thus not meeting one of Sokolov's criteria for a DR. Completely different types of stimuli and procedures were used by Hare (1973) in assessing blood volume as an indicator of the orienting and defensive responses. The subjects were 20 young females, 10 of whom feared spiders and 10 who did not. The fearful group responded with decreased forehead blood volume to pictures of spiders, whereas the nonfearful group had the opposite response. The vasoconstriction would indicate the DR, whereas the vasodilation would suggest the OR, thus providing results in line with Sokolov's theory.

In summary, blood volume and pulse volume appear to change with the introduction of new or unexpected stimuli. With regard to blood volume responses, some of the research findings partially support Sokolov's theory regarding the relation between cephalic vasoconstriction and vasodilation and the DR and OR, respectively. Differences between habituation rate of the blood volume and pulse volume responses may indicate a partial physiological independence of these two measures.

Conditioning of Blood Volume

Conditioning of the vasomotor response has been reported with both classical and instrumental approaches. For example, Shean (1968) produced a classically conditioned finger blood volume decrease in a situation where the CS was the word "boat" and the UCS was an electric shock. Acquisition and extinction of the vasoconstriction response was observed in those subjects who later indicated that they were aware of the relationship between the CS and UCS.

Blood volume changes have also been instrumentally conditioned. For example, Christie and Kotses (1973) found that cephalic (head) blood volume could be brought under stimulus control in eight subjects who participated in six separate sessions. A photoplethysmographic device was positioned over the temporal artery of the head to detect blood volume changes. Four of the subjects received feedback and reinforcement for vasodilation, whereas the other four were conditioned to produce vasoconstriction. The four persons reinforced for vasodilation showed this response in the period during which the reinforcement was available, whereas the other four reliably produced vasoconstriction. The authors suggested the further investigation of this technique for possible use in the treatment of migraine headache, because this disorder has been linked to vasodilation of cephalic arteries.

The next two chapters consider practical applications of physiological measures. Chapter 13 is concerned with a number of diverse applications ranging from lie detection to attempts at better understanding of behavior disorders. Chapter 14 presents applications of biofeedback in various clinical situations.

REFERENCES

Aaslid, R., & Brubaak, A. O. (1981). Accuracy of an ultrasound Doppler servo method for non-invasive determination of instantaneous and mean arterial blood pressure. *Circulation, 64,* 753–759.

Adams, E. A., III, Haynes, S. N., & Brayer, M. A. (1985). Cognitive distraction in female sexual arousal. *Psychophysiology, 22,* 689–696.

Allen, M. T., Sherwood, A., & Obrist, P. A. (1986). Interaction of respiratory and cardiovascular adjustments to behavioral stressors. *Psychophysiology, 23,* 532–541.

Baun, M., Langston, N. F., & Thoma, L. (1984). Physiological effects of human/companion animal bonding. *Nursing Research, 33,*126–129.

Blanchard, E. B., & Young, L. D. (1973). Self-control of cardiac functioning: A promise as yet unfulfilled. *Psychological Bulletin, 79*, 145–163.

Brown, C. C. (1967). The techniques of plethysmography. In C. C. Brown (Ed.), *Methods in psychophysiology* (pp. 54–74). Baltimore: Williams & Wilkins.

Blumenthal, J. A., Lane, J. D., Williams, R. B., McKee, D. C., Haney, T., & White, A. (1983). Effects of task incentive on cardiovascular response in Type A and Type B individuals. *Psychophysiology, 20*, 63–70.

Christie, D. J., & Kotses, H. (1973). Bidirectional operant conditioning of the cephalic vasomotor response. *Journal of Psychosomatic Research, 17*, 167–170.

Cinciripini, P. M., Epstein, L. H., & Martin, J. E. (1979). The effects of feedback on blood pressure discrimination. *Journal of Applied Behavioral Analysis, 12*, 345–353.

Contrada, R. J., Wright, R. A., & Glass, D. C. (1984). Task difficulty, Type A behavior pattern, and cardiovascular response. *Psychophysiology, 21*, 638–646.

Cook, M. R. (1974). Psychophysiology of peripheral vascular changes. In P. A. Obrist, A. H. Black, J. Brener, & L. V. Dicara (Eds.), *Cardiovascular psychophysiology* (pp. 60–84). Chicago: Aldine.

Cromwell, L., Arditti, M., Weibell, F. J., Pfeiffer, E. A., Steele, B., & Labbock, J. A. (1976). *Medical instrumentation for health care.* Englewood Cliffs, NJ: Prentice-Hall.

D'Atri, D. A., Fitzgerald, E. F., Kasl, S. V., & Malinow, K. L. (1981). Crowding in prison: The relationship between changes in housing mode and blood pressure. *Psychosomatic Medicine, 43*, 95–105.

Dembroski, T. M., MacDougall, J. M., Heard, J. A., & Shields, J. L. (1979). Effect of level of challenge on pressor and heart rate responses in Type A and B subjects. *Journal of Applied Social Psychology, 9*, 209–228.

Dembroski, T. M., MacDougall, J. M., Slaats, S., Eliot, R. S. & Buell, J. C. (1981). Challenge-induced cardiovascular response as a predictor of minor illnesses. *Journal of Human Stress, 7*, 2–5.

DiCara, L. V., & Miller, N. E. (1968). Instrumental learning of systolic blood pressure responses by curarized rats: Dissociation of cardiac and vascular changes. *Psychosomatic Medicine, 30*, 489–494.

Ditto, B. (1986). Parental history of hypertension, active coping, and cardiovascular reactivity. *Psychophysiology, 23*, 62–70.

Doob, A. N., & Kirshenbaum, H. M. (1973). The effects on arousal of frustration and aggressive films *Journal of Experimental Social Psychology, 9*, 57–64.

Drummond, P. D. (1983). Cardiovascular reactivity in mild hypertension. *Journal of Psychosomatic Research, 27*, 291–297.

Ettema, J. H., & Zielhuis, R. L. (1971). Physiological parameters of mental load. *Ergonomics, 14*, 137–144.

Fey, S. G., & Lindholm, E. (1975). Systolic blood pressure and heart rate changes during three sessions involving biofeedback or no feedback. *Psychophysiology, 12*, 513–519.

Friedman, E., Katcher, A. H., Thomas, S. A., Lynch, J. J., & Messent, P. R. (1983). Social interaction and blood pressure: Influence of animal companions. *Journal of Nervous & Mental Diseases, 17*, 461–465.

Friedman, M., & Rosenman, R. H. (1974). *Type A behavior and your heart.* New York: Knopf.

Gardner, E. (1975). *Fundamentals of neurology* (6th ed.). Philadelphia: Saunders.

Geen, R. G. (1975). The meaning of observed violence: Real vs. fictional violence and consequent effects on aggression and emotional arousal. *Journal of Research in Personality, 9*, 270–281.

Geen, R. G., & Stonner, D. (1974). The meaning of observed violence: Effects on arousal and aggressive behavior. *Journal of Research in Personality, 8*, 55–63.

Geer, J. H. (1974, August). *Cognitive factors in sexual arousal: Toward an amalgram of research strategies.* Paper presented at the annual convention of the American Psychological Association, New Orleans, LA.

Geer, J. H. (1975, October). *Sexual functioning—Some data and speculations on psychophysiological assessment.* Paper presented at the Behavior Assessment Conference, West Virginia University.

Geer, J. H., & Fuhr, R. (1976). Cognitive factors in sexual arousal: The role of distraction. *Journal of Consulting & Clinical Psychology, 44,* 238–243.

Geer, J. H., Morokoff, P., & Greenwood, P. (1974). Sexual arousal in women: The development of a measurement device for vaginal blood volume. *Archives of Sexual Behavior, 3,* 559–564.

Geer, J. H., O'Donohue, W. T., & Schorman, R. H. (1986). Sexuality. In M. G. H. Coles, E. Donchin, & S. W. Porges (Eds.), *Psychophysiology: Systems, processes and applications* (pp. 407–430). New York: Guilford.

Geer, J. H., & Quartararo, J. D. (1976). Vaginal blood volume responses during masturbation and resultant orgasm. *Archives of Sexual Behavior, 5,* 1–42.

Gentry, W. D. (1970). Sex differences in the effects of frustration and attack on emotion and vascular processes. *Psychological Reports, 27,* 383–390.

Ginsberg, S., & Furedy, J. J. (1974). Stimulus repetition, change, and assessments of sensitivities of and relationships among an electrodermal and two plethysmographic components of the orienting reaction. *Psychophysiology, 11,* 35–43.

Glass, D. C., Krakoff, L. R., Contrada, R., Hilton, W., Kehoe, K., Mannucci, E. G., Collins, C., Snow, B., & Elting, E. (1980). Effect of harassment and competition upon cardiovascular and plasma catecholamine responses in Type A and Type B individuals. *Psychophysiology, 17,* 453–463.

Greenstadt, L., Shapiro, D., & Whitehead, R. (1986). Blood pressure discrimination. *Psychophysiology, 23,* 500–509.

Grollman, S. (1964). *The human body.* New York: Macmillan.

Gunn, C. G., Wolf, S., Black, R. T., & Person, R. J. (1972). Psychophysiology of the cardiovascular system. In N. S. Greenfield & R. A. Sternbach (Eds.), *Handbook of psychophysiology* (pp. 457–489). New York: Holt, Rinehart, & Winston.

Guyton, A. C. (1977). *Basic human physiology.* Philadelphia: Saunders, Harburg, E., Blakelock, E. H., & Roeper, P. J. (1979). Resentful and reflective coping with arbitrary authority and blood pressure: Detroit. *Psychosomatic Medicine, 51,* 189–202.

Hall, P. J., Thomas, J. A., Friedman, E., & Lynch, J. J. (1982). Measurement of neonatal blood pressure: A new method. *Psychophysiology, 19,* 231–236.

Hare, R. D. (1973). Orienting and defensive responses to visual stimuli. *Psychophysiology, 10,* 453–464.

Heiman, J. R. (1977). A psychophysiological exploration of sexual arousal patterns in females and males. *Psychophysiology, 14,* 266–274.

Henson, D. E., & Rubin, H. B. (1978). A comparison of two objective measures of sexual arousal of women. *Behaviour Research & Therapy, 16,* 143–151.

Holmes, D. D., McGilley, B. M., & Houston, B. K. (1984). Task-related arousal of Type A and Type B persons: Level of challenge and response specificity. *Journal of Personality & Social Psychology, 46,* 1322–1327.

Hoon, P. W., Bruce, K., & Kinchloe, B. (1982). Does the menstrual cycle play a role in sexual arousal? *Psychophysiology, 19,* 21–27.

Hull, E., Young, S. H., & Ziegler, M. G. (1984). Aerobic fitness affects cardiovascular and catecholamine responses to stressors. *Psychophysiology, 21,* 353–360.

Jacob, S. W., & Francone, C. A. (1970). *Structure and function in man* (2nd ed.). Philadelphia: Saunders.

Jenkins, D. C. (1976). Recent evidence supporting psychologic and social risk factors for coronary disease. *New England Journal of Medicine, 294,* 1033–1038.

Jonsson, A., & Hansson, L. (1977). Prolonged study of a stressful stimulus (noise) as a cause of raised blood pressure in man. *Lancet, 1,* 86–87.

Lane, J. D., Greenstadt, L., Shapiro, D., & Rubinstein, E. (1983). Pulse transit time and blood pressure: An intensive analysis. *Psychophysiology, 20,* 45–49.

Lane, J. D., White, A. D., & Williams, R. B. (1984). Cardiovascular effects of mental arithmetic in Type A and Type B females. *Psychophysiology, 21,* 39–46.

Larsen, P. B., Schneiderman, N., & Pasin, R. D. (1986). Physiological bases of cardiovascular psychophysiology. In M. G. H. Coles, E. Donchin, & S. W. Porges (Eds.), *Psychophysiology: Systems, processes and applications* (pp. 122–165). New York: Guilford.

Lawler, K. A., & Schmied, L. A. (1986). Cardiovascular responsivity, Type A behavior and parental history of heart disease in young women. *Psychophysiology, 23,* 28–32.

Lawler, K. A., Schmied, L. A., Mitchell, V. P., & Rixse, A. (1984). Type A behavior and physiological responsivity in young women. *Journal of Psychosomatic Research, 28,* 197–204.

Laws, D. R., & Bow, R. A. (1976). An improved mechanic strain gauge for recording penile circumference change. *Psychophysiology, 13,* 596–599.

Lee, A. L., Tahmoush, A., J., & Jennings, J. R. (1975). An LED-transistor photoplethysmograph. *IEEE Transactions on Biomedical Engineering, 22,* 248–250.

Levander, S. E., Lidberg, L., & Schalling, D. (1974). Habituation of the digital vasoconstrictive orienting response. *Journal of Experimental Psychology, 102,* 700–705.

Levine, R. J., & Wagner, G. (1983). Haemodynamic changes of the human vagina during sexual arousal assessed by a heated oxygen electrode. *Journal of Physiology, 275,* 23–24.

Light, K. C., & Obrist, P. A. (1983). Task difficulty, heart rate reactivity, and cardiovascular responses to an appetitive reaction time task. *Psychophysiology, 20,* 301–312.

Light, K. C., Obrist, P. A., James, S. A., & Stogatz, D. S. (1987). Cardiovascular responses to stress: II. Relationships to aerobic exercise patterns. *Psychophysiology, 24,* 79–86.

Long, J. M., Lynch, J. J., Machiran, N. M., Thomas, S. A., & Malinow, K. L. (1982). The effect of status on blood pressure during verbal communication. *Journal of Behavioral Medicine, 5,* 165–172.

Lovallo, W. R., Pincomb, G. A., & Wilson, M. G. (1986). Heart rate reactivity and Type A behavior as modifiers of physiological response to active and passive coping. *Psychophysiology, 23,* 105–112.

Lundberg, U. (1983). Note on Type A behavior and cardiovascular responses to challenge in 3–6–yr old children. *Journal of Psychosomatic Research, 27,* 39–42.

Lynch, J. J., Long, J. M., Thomas, S. A., Malinow, K. L., & Katcher, A. H. (1981). The effects of talking on the blood pressure of hypertensive and normotensive individuals. *Psychosomatic Medicine, 43,* 25–33.

MacDougall, J. M., Dembroski, T. M., & Krantz, D. S. (1981). Effects of types of challenge on pressor and heart rate responses in Type A and Type B women. *Psychophysiology, 18,* 1–9.

Matthews, K. A. (1982). Psychological perspectives on the Type A behavior pattern. *Psychological Bulletin, 91,* 293–323.

Matthews, K. A., Manuck, S. B., & Saab, P. G. (1986). Cardiovascular responses of adolescents during a naturally occurring stressor and their behavioral and psychophysiological predictors. *Psychophysiology, 23,* 198–209.

McCubbin, J. A., Richardson, J. E., Langaer, A. W., Kizer, J. S., & Obrist, P. A. (1983). Sympathetic neuron function and left ventricular performance during behavioral stress in humans: The relationship between plasma catecholamines and systolic time intervals. *Psychophysiology, 20,* 102–110.

McKinney, M. E., Miner, M. H., Ruddel, H., McIlvain, H. E., Witte, H., Buell, J. C., Eliot, R. S., & Grant, L. B. (1985). The standardized mental stress test protocol: Test–retest reliability and comparison with ambulatory blood pressure monitoring. *Psychophysiology, 22,* 453–463.

Obrist, P. A., Light, K. C., McCubbin, J. A., Hutcheson, J. S., & Hoffer, J. L. (1979). Pulse transit time: Relationship to blood pressure and myocardial performance. *Psychophysiology, 16,* 292–301.

Oster, P. J., Stern, J. A., & Figar, S. (1975). Cephalic and digital vasomotor orienting responses: The effect of stimulus intensity and rise time. *Psychophysiology, 12,* 642–648.

Rao, P. S., Inbaraj, S. G., & Subramaniam, V. R. (1984). Blood pressure measures among women in south India. *Journal of Epidemiology & Community Health, 38,* 49–53.

Ray, R. L., Brady, J. V., & Emurian, H. H. (1984). Cardiovascular effects of noise during complex task performance. *International Journal of Psychophysiology, 1,* 335–340.

Richards, J. C., Bridger, B. A., Wood, M. M., Kalucy, R. S., & Marshall, V. R. (1985). A controlled investigation into the measurement properties of two circumferential penile strain gauges. *Psychophysiology, 22,* 568–571.

Roberts, R. J., & Weerts, T. C. (1982). Cardiovascular responding during anger and fear imagery. *Psychological Reports, 50,* 219–230.

Rubinsky, H. J., Hoon, P. W., Eckerman, D. A., & Amberson, J. I. (1985). Groin skin temperature: Testing the validity of a relatively unobtrusive physiological measure of psychosexual arousal. *Psychophysiology, 22,* 488–492.

Schwartz, G. E., Weinberger, D. A., & Singer, J. A. (1981). Cardiovascular differentiation of happiness, sadness, anger, and fear following imagery and exercise. *Psychosomatic Medicine, 43,* 343–364.

Shapiro, A., Redmond, D. P., McDonald, R. H., & Gaylor, M. (1975). Relationships of perception, cognition, suggestion and operant conditioning in essential hypertension. *Progress in Brain Research, 42,* 299–312.

Shapiro, D., Schwartz, G. E., & Tursky, B. (1972). Control of diastolic blood pressure in man by feedback and reinforcement. *Psychophysiology, 9,* 296–304.

Shapiro, D., Tursky, B., Gershon, E., & Stern, M. (1969). Effects of feedback and reinforcement on the control of human systolic blood pressure. *Science, 163,* 588–590.

Shapiro, D., Tursky, B., & Schwartz, G. E. (1970). Differentiation of heart rate and systolic blood pressure in man by conditioning. *Psychosomatic Medicine, 32,* 417–423.

Shean, G. D. (1968). Vasomotor conditioning and awareness. *Psychophysiology, 5,* 22–30.

Siegel, J. J., Matthews, K. A., & Leitch, C. J. (1983). Blood pressure variability and the Type A behavior pattern in adolescence. *Journal of Psychosomatic Research, 27,* 265–272.

Sintchak, G., & Geer, J. H. (1975). A vaginal plethysmograph system. *Psychophysiology, 12,* 113–145.

Sokolov, E. N. (1963). *Perception and the conditioned reflex.* New York: Macmillan.

Steptoe, A. (1980). Blood pressure. In I. Martin & P. Venables (Eds.), *Techniques in psychophysiology* (pp. 247–274). New York: Wiley.

Steptoe, A., Smulyan, H., & Gribbon, B. (1976). Pulse wave velocity and blood pressure change: Calibration and applications. *Psychophysiology, 13,* 489–493.

Stern, R. J., Ray, W. J., & Davis, C. M. (1980). *Psychophysiological recording.* New York: Oxford.

Tahmoush, A. J., Jennings, J. R., Lee, A. L., Camp, S., & Weber, F. (1976). Characteristics of a light emitting diode-transistor photo-plethysmograph. *Psychophysiology, 13,* 357–362.

Thomas, S. A., Friedman, E., Lottes, L. S., Gresty, S., Miller, C. & Lynch, J. J. (1984). Changes in nurses' blood pressure and heart rate while communicating. *Research in Nursing & Health, 7,* 119–126.

Throll, D. A. (1982). Transendental Meditation and progressive relaxation: Their physiological effects. *Journal of Clinical Psychology, 38,* 522–530.

Tursky, B. (1974). The indirect recording of human blood pressure. In P. A. Obrist, A. H. Black, J. Brener, & L. V. DiCara (Eds.), *Cardiovascular psychophysiology,* (pp. 93–105). Chicago: Aldine.

Turksy, B., & Greenblatt, D. J. (1967). Local vascular and thermal changes that accompany electric shock. *Psychophysiology, 3,* 371–362.

Tursky, B., Shapiro, D., & Schwartz, G. E. (1972). Automated constant cuff-pressure system to measure average systolic and diastolic blood pressure in man. *IEEE Transaction on Biomedical Engineering, 19,* 271–276.

Wallace, R. K., Silver, J., Mills, P. J., Dillbeck, M. C., & Wagoner, D. E. (1983). Systolic blood pressure and long term practice of the Transcendental Meditation and TM-Sidhi programs. Effects of TM on systolic blood pressure. *Psychosomatic Medicine, 45,* 41–46.

Williams, R. B., Barefoot, J. C., & Shekelle, R. B. (1985). The health consequences of hostility. In M. A. Chesney & R. H. Rosenman (Eds.), *Anger and hostility in cardiovascular and behavior disorders.* (pp. 173–186). Washington: Hemisphere.

Woodworth, R. S., & Schlosberg, H. (1954). *Experimental psychology.* New York: Holt.

Zuckerman, M. (1972). Physiological measures of sexual arousal in the human. In N. S. Greenfield & R. A. Sternbach (Eds.), *Handbook of psychophysiology* (pp. 709–740). New York: Holt, Rinehart & Winston.

13

Applications of Physiological Measures to Practical Problems

Over the years, psychophysiologists have developed, or stimulated the development of, increasingly sensitive and sophisticated instruments to measure the physiological variables in their psychological studies. The refined instruments and techniques have led to a precision that allows the measurement of physiological responses in many practical applications. The question addressed in this chapter is: "How can the measurement of physiological responses help in the solution of practical problems?" In order to answer this question, we examine a number of research studies in a variety of areas. The main difference between the studies described in this chapter and those in earlier ones is that applied research is generally performed in order to provide a solution to an immediate problem. This is not to say that basic research (that is, research accomplished with no particular application in mind) is not of practical value. It is often the case that basic research leads to applications of techniques and information that are very useful, and many times basic and applied studies support and complement each other.

The applications that we consider are concerned with detection of deception, sensory system testing, mental retardation, nervous system disorders, behavior disorders, and vigilance.

DETECTION OF DECEPTION

The use of physiological measures to determine when an individual is lying is controversial and has a long history. The controversy exists over the accuracy of the techniques and their use in personnel selection and in granting security clearances, as well as in criminal investigations. Woodworth and Schlosberg (1954) observed that the principle of SNS discharge (arousal) and its effects on inhibiting salivary secretion was used by the ancient Chinese in lie detection. The unfortunate suspect was given rice powder to chew on and then forced to spit it out. If the powder was still dry, the suspect was guilty! It was assumed that the guilty person would be fearful because of lies told during the interrogation process, and that this fright interfered with salivation. Obviously, a guilty person would not be able to moisten the dry rice! Furedy (1986) wrote that the earliest written account of psychophysiological observation in the detection of deception came from a Hindu medical source dating about 900 B.C. In this account, persons who lied about using poison on others showed such physiological changes as blushing, and behaviors such as rubbing their hair. Thus, vasodilation of facial blood vessels (blushing) was the physiological change taken to indicate deception.

About 80 years ago, Munsterberg (1908), in his book *On the Witness Stand,* suggested that measures of emotional reactions such as respiration, heart rate, blood volume, and changes in skin conductance should be investigated as possible aids in distinguishing between the innocent and the guilty suspect. He recommended caution in the use of this approach, because "the innocent man, especially the nervous man, may grow as much excited on the witness stand as the criminal when the victim and the means of the crime are mentioned; his fear that he may be condemned unjustly may influence his muscles, glands and blood vessels as strongly as if he were guilty" (1908, p. 132). Munsterberg suggested instead that the measures be used in situations where a certain item of information could only be known to a witness of the crime. Later, a student of Munsterberg by the name of Marston attracted the interest of two police officers in using physiological measures to detect lying (Kleinmuntz & Szucko, 1984). The forerunner of the modern polygraph was developed by one of these policemen (Larson) and perfected by the other (Keeler). This equipment became the mainstay of professional polygraphers, and is known as the Keeler polygraph. The laypublic has come to associate the word "polygraph" with lie detection. Any instrument that measures more than one physiological response simultaneously can be termed a "polygraph." The Keeler device measures respiration, skin resistance, and blood pressure.

The approach suggested many years ago by Munsterberg has more recently been described by Lykken (1959, 1974) as the guilty knowledge test (GKT). Lykken distinguished the GKT from the lie detection (LD) approach, because in LD the interrogator asks direct relevant questions such as, "Did you rob the bank?" mixed with irrelevant ones such as, "Are you sitting down?". In contrast, the GKT involves the preparation of questions so that a multiple-response situation is created. Thus, for example, in a situation where a robber pretended that he wanted to take out a loan for paying doctor bills, before showing his gun, the interrogator would tell the suspect that the guilty person will know the supposed purpose of the loan. Then the interrogator lists five possibilities (e.g., car, vacation, gift, doctor bills, new appliance) and the suspect repeats each of them while the various physiological measures (e.g., SCR, respiration, blood pressure) are recorded. Lykken found only one field study of the LD technique that he thought adequate in terms of the criteria against which LD validity could be measured. This real-life study by Bersh (1969) unfortunately did little to establish the validity of the physiological response portions of the test. Lykken (1974) deplored the increasing use of the LD test in industry and suggested that it is worthless in both screening employees and in detecting thieves. He estimated that there are 3,000 persons giving over several million polygraph tests in industry each year.

The GKT was classified as an information test by Podlesny and Raskin (1977), because its use presumes that a person's critical information can produce differential physiological responses to various items. Information tests are distinguished from deception tests, which are based on the assumption that differential physiological response occurs to certain questions when the person is deceptive. This presumed differential physiological responding is the basis for the control question test (CQT) (Podlesny & Raskin, 1977). Furedy, Davis, and Gurevich, (in press) criticized the CQT on the basis of differential significance between the relevant and control questions. As an example, they cited a case involving alleged child sexual abuse in which one relevant question was "Did you lick X's vagina?" The control question used as a comparison was "Did you ever do anything you were ashamed of?" On the basis of greater physiological response to the relevant question, the suspect, a 74-year-old crossing guard, was accused of the crime. Furedy and colleagues argued that, even for an innocent examinee, the impact of such a relevant question could far outweigh that of the so-called control question, in a test where both are supposed to have equal significance for an innocent person. Thus, in that kind of situation, the CQT is not measuring deception, but an emotional reaction to a highly charged question.

In comparing the two questioning techniques, the GKT is superior to the CQT. This is because the GKT can be standardized, as any psychological test should, whereas the CQT cannot, error rates can be specified with GKT, and it is less vulnerable to faking (see Furedy & Heslegrave, in press). The widespread adoption of the GKT by professional polygraphers (most of whom are not scientists) is unlikely, because the CQT is procedurally entrenched.

Two extensive reviews of lie detection have appeared as chapters in books (Barland & Raskin, 1973; Orne, Thackray, & Paskewitz, 1972). In addition to the criminal investigation and industrial applications of LD, Orne et al. (1972) have pointed out that it is commonly used for screening individuals for security purposes in certain government agencies. Orne and his colleagues detailed the procedures followed by interrogators in real-life situations. Apparently, professional polygraphers rarely vary their techniques in a systematic way, a practice that makes it difficult to establish the validity of the various aspects of the procedure. For example, Orne et al. asked whether the polygrapher makes his or her decision of "guilty" or "innocent" on the basis of a pretest interview, the person's dossier, the physiological responses, a post-test interrogation, or some other subtle behaviors that an experienced criminal investigator might notice. Orne et al. (1972) concluded, as did Woodworth and Schlosberg (1954), that LD in a real-life situation is an art rather than a science, and the same comment applies today. Scientific evaluation of the contribution of physiological responses to the LD situation is, therefore, very difficult, because it is only one part of a comprehensive procedure. An important question is whether the use of physiological measures helps in detecting deception. To test this adequately, all other potential influences on a decision about truthfulness must be controlled.

The fact that most professional polygraphers are not trained psychologists has contributed to the lack of scientific validation of the techniques. Kleinmuntz and Szucko (1984) accused psychologists of having neglected the study of polygraphic lie detection. They contended that this procedure is a psychometric instrument that, thus far, has not been demonstrated to possess sufficient reliability and validity. (In psychometric terms, reliability refers to consistency, and validity evaluates the degree to which a procedure actually measures what it claims to measure.) Further, Kleinmetz and Szucko cited studies in which as many as 37% to nearly 50% of innocent subjects were classified as guilty. This represents a high rate of "false positives" (i.e., in this instance, incorrectly identifying innocent persons as guilty). However, in an earlier study, Raskin, Barland, and Podlesny (1977) assessed the reliability and validity of polygraph techniques and presented a much more promising picture. They evaluated the results of eight experiments that included field studies of criminal suspects and laboratory "mock crime" experiments. They also evaluated the belief that psychopathic criminals can "beat the polygraph", a contention based on the belief that psychopaths are practiced and habitual liars and have little guilt about the consequences of their actions. The main conclusions were that polygraph examinations using the CQT or GKT were approximately 90% accurate when properly conducted and evaluated. They also reported that deception in diagnosed psychopaths was as easy to detect as in nonpsychopaths.

In a study of LD in psychopaths and nonpsychopaths, Raskin and Hare (1978) obtained additional results regarding the notion that psychopaths can beat the polygraph test. They used a sample of 48 prisoners, half of whom were diagnosed psychopaths. Half of each group were "guilty" of taking $20 in a mock crime, and the other half were "innocent." A polygraph examination was conducted after a field-type interview. The measures were respiration, electrodermal activity, and cardiovascular response. The test results yielded 88% correct decisions, 4% wrong, and 8% inconclusive. The psychopaths were as accurately detected as nonpsychopaths. In addition, psychopaths showed evidence of stronger electrodermal responses and HR decelerations in the CQT used. Lykken (1978) criticized this conclusion about psychopaths on the basis that the mock crime situation used had nothing to do with fear or guilt, and was probably viewed as an interesting game by the subjects. He also questioned Raskin's claim of 90% accuracy in detection and, based on his own analysis of past studies, Lykken concluded that the accuracy rate is more like 64% to 71%, against 50% chance expectancy. Coupled with Lykken's estimate of 49% to 55% of false positives, a serious indictment against polygraphic LD is delivered. The finding of no difference between detection rate for psychopaths and non-psychopaths also raises some concern. If the physiological measures do not differentiate between those who feel guilty about lying and those who don't, then what is being measured?

The debate about polygraph examinations has continued and, in his 1981 book entitled *A Tremor in the Blood,* Lykken affirmed his skepticism about the lie detection industry, while at the same time attempting to stimulate interest in the psychophysiological investigation of lie detection for the purpose of criminal investigation. One point made by Kleinmuntz and Szucko (1984) is that more psychophysiologists should do research in this area because of the important social and political implications of lie detection. At present, polygraph testing is not only done in criminal investigation but in pre-employment screening, periodic screening of employees, and in private investigations. Therefore, psychologists have an obligation to use their scientific skills to resolve some of the issues and prevent potential abuse through the use of inadequately validated techniques.

Laboratory Studies in the Detection of Deception

Several investigators have pointed out that there is no unique pattern of physiological response to deception (e.g., Lykken, 1981; Orne, 1975). However, laboratory studies are necessary in an attempt to establish which physiological measures offer the greatest promise for detecting deception. In their review, Podlesny and Raskin (1977) wrote that the main advantage of laboratory studies is that the truthfulness of the response can be controlled and compared with the physiological response given. This is in contrast to real-life situations, in which the decision about truthfulness or deception may never be verified in some cases. On the other hand, the laboratory subject may not be highly motivated to evade detection and may not be representative of a typical population of criminal suspects.

In a laboratory study (Thackray & Orne, 1968), 30 subjects were told that they would be interrogated as though they were suspected of being espionage agents. They were given a set of code words and were questioned by an experimenter who did not know the words but who had a list of questions that related to these words. The physiological measures obtained during interrogation were respiration amplitude, changes in skin conductance, skin potential, systolic blood pressure, and finger volume. They found that SCRs, SPR, and finger blood volume were effective in discriminating deception in this situation. They observed that several previous studies had indicated SCR as the best single index of deception. Systolic blood pressure and respiration amplitude gave inconsistent results. Orne et al. (1972) noted that most laboratory studies agree that SCR is superior to other physiological variables in the detection of deception. Similarly, Barland and Raskin (1973) concluded that the physiological response that has shown the greatest success in discriminating between truthfulness and deception in the laboratory has been electrodermal activity. The usefulness of SCR in field situations, however, has been disputed. Most field examiners claim that blood pressure and respiration are more useful in detecting deception than EDA measures. In their opinion, the SCR is too sensitive to be useful in differentiating between relevant and irrelevant questions in a highly emotional criminal interrogation (e.g., Arthur, 1971). The issue is still not resolved, and would seem to be one that could benefit from scientific cooperation between professional polygraphers and psychophysiologists.

Barland and Raskin (1975) used a mock crime situation in which the physiological variables included measures of cardiovascular activity (relative blood pressure, pulse amplitude), SCR, and respiration. Thirty-six subjects were "guilty" of taking $10, and 36 were "innocent". A pretest interview was conducted, during which control questions were formulated. One purpose of their experiment was to evaluate, in the laboratory, techniques commonly used in the field. They found that deceptive subjects showed larger increases in cardiovascular response to relevant questions, whereas truthful persons had larger responses to control items. The SCR measure successfully distinguished between truth and deception, and longer respiratory cycles were found during lying. Pulse amplitude did not differentiate between lying and telling the truth.

One of the assumptions in the use of the GKT is that suspects who are aware of crime-relevant information will show greater physiological responsivity to questions about relevant items than to irrelevant ones. To test this assumption, three groups of innocent subjects were given the same crime-relevant information as members of a group that were guilty of a mock crime (Bradley & Warfield, 1984). The physiological measure was EDA. The results showed that detection scores of guilty subjects were higher than those in any of the innocent groups. Thus, only those persons who were attempting to deceive were detected with a high rate of accuracy. From this study, it appears that innocent subjects, in a laboratory setting, may have guilty information, be examined with the GKT, and be judged innocent. In another interesting study, Bradley and Ainsworth (1984) examined the effects of alcohol on lie detection. The main finding was that alcohol intoxication during a mock crime reduced detectability with detection scores based on EDA (heart rate and respiration were not as useful).

Measures of EDA, respiration, blood pressure, pulse amplitude, and volume, and heart rate have been commonly used in studies of deception. Podlesny and Raskin (1977) suggested that several other measures may have potential value as correlates of deception and should be further investigated. These include muscle activity, ocular activity (including eye blinks and eye movements), pupillary diameter, EEG, micromomentary expressions, and voice analyses. Micromomentary expression refers to analyses of filmed sequences of facial changes in a deception situation. Voice analyses include the study of frequency and amplitude changes in the vocal pattern during deception. Kubis (1973) evaluated two voice analysis techniques in LD and compared the results with those yielded by a polygraph test in a mock crime situation. Accuracy obtained with both voice analysis techniques gave results that were no different from chance, whereas the traditional polygraph test produced significant numbers of correct detections. Horvath (1978) obtained essentially the same results as Kubis when he compared a voice analysis technique (Psychological Stress Evaluator, or PSE) with electrodermal activity. Accuracy with the PSE was at chance levels, whereas hit rates based on EDA were significantly higher.

The value of scientific controversy as to the validity of polygraphic lie detection is that it has led to open discussion of the issues and, hopefully, will lead to empirical studies to resolve some of the questions. Furedy (1986) argued that a "specific effects" approach must be used in evaluating polygraphy. This would require that improvements in detection of deception by an examiner using polygraphy be precisely defined. Another consideration is the issue of accuracy afforded by the polygraphic charts alone (i.e., scored "blind" or without the scorer's contact with the person being interrogated). According to Lykken this accuracy level is about 70%, versus a 50% chance level, compared to Raskin's estimate of 90% accuracy. It is clear that both of these estimates are above chance; the protagonists disagree about how much above chance. Furedy also has suggested that factors that affect accuracy should be subject to scientific scrutiny, especially in field studies. Another set of relevant issues can be studied in the more controlled laboratory setting and include obtaining information about psychological factors (e.g., memory, incentives, beliefs about effectiveness of detection apparatus), as well as physiological ones (e.g., most accurate measures, drug effects) that affect detection of deception.

The message of this section is that the validity and usefulness of polygraphic lie detection is controversial. Part of the problem is whether physiological responses vary with the act of lying or whether they reflect anxiety stemming from justified guilt or the possibility of being wrongly accused. It is unimportant whether the false positive (error) rate is 10% or 40%. In human terms, this means that between 10% and 40% of individuals examined may be falsely accused and their reputations destroyed. Another part of the problem concerns a lack of standardization of techniques and procedures of questioning. Psychophysiologists should take up the challenge of lie detection research instead of cringing when they hear about alleged abuses of the procedure in courts, governmental agencies, or industrial settings. They should cooperate to a greater extent with professional polygraphers to learn more about field procedures used in an attempt to identify factors that influence reliability and validity of the technique. Once sufficient information has been generated, we may either witness detection of deception procedures based on physiological measures and sound psychometric and theoretical foundations, or we may have evidence to argue for the banning of polygraphic lie detection in our society.

CLINICAL APPLICATIONS OF PHYSIOLOGICAL MEASURES

The utilization of physiological measures has been applied in a variety of clinical situations in the past few years. Some of the applications have included testing of vision, hearing (audiometry), brain responses in retarded individuals, and brain activity in neurological and behavioral disorders. Examples of how physiological responses have been used in these various clinical situations are briefly described in the sections that follow.

Auditory System Tests

The use of auditory ERPs to assess hearing deficits in retarded children, infants, and children with multiple handicaps (e.g., those with cerebral palsy) has been increasing in recent years. Because traditional auditory testing requires that the subject indicate verbally or by gesture that he or she has heard a sound, a technique that can evaluate the integrity of the auditory system without requiring such a response would be of value for testing certain individuals. Rapin (1974) has observed that the auditory ERP is a powerful physiologic test of hearing because it indicates that stimulation by sound has caused a response to occur in the auditory system and the brain. She has found that early diagnosis of hearing deficits with ERPs can allow early remediation, for example, several infants were fitted with hearing aids before they were 6 months of age because ERPs showed their hearing to be impaired. Rapin is of the opinion that evoked potential audiometry is too demanding a technique for routine use with cooperative patients but is justified for use with selected cases, similar to those just mentioned.

Rapin, Graziani, and Lyttle (1969) studied behavioral responses to sound and the AEPs of 51 children whose mothers had German measles during the first 3 months of pregnancy. Of the remaining 38, judged to be hearing-impaired through behavioral responses, 27 had AEPs that indicated moderate or severe hearing deficits. Only 13 of the children were classified as normal in response to sound.

Children who required intensive care as newborns, because of low birth weight or other medical complications, have a higher incidence of sensory deficits and speech and language disorders. In one study, 28% of infants with histories of low birth weight or neonatal asphyxia had auditory ERP abnor-

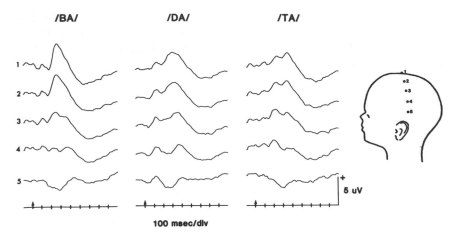

FIG. 13.1.   Mean cortical AEP recorded from a group of newborns to the speech sounds /ba/, /da/, and /ta/. Note the waveshape differences between responses recorded at the midline from those recorded overlying the lateral surface of the termporal lobe. These responses have a differential maturational course. The waveshape and amplitudes of the responses differ as a function of the auditory stimulus. Stimulus onset at arrow.

malities (Cone-Wesson, Kurtzberg, & Vaughan, 1983). These abnormalities represent dysfunction in the auditory system. Because auditory system integrity is essential in oral language development, hearing assessment in early infancy is very important and may dictate the use of intervention strategies such as hearing aids. Kurtzberg, Hilpert, and Kreuzer (1984) found that cortical auditory ERPs to speech sounds /da/ and /ta/ and to 800 Hz tones were less mature for low birth weight (less than 3.3 lb.) infants than full-term babies, even though they were tested at the same age. The differences lessened at subsequent age levels of two and three months, but Kurzberg and Vaughan (1985) speculated about the possible detrimental impact of these early abnormalities on later language development. Kurtzberg and colleagues (1984) recorded auditory ERPs of newborn infants in response to the speech sounds /ba/, /da/, and /ta/. The different waveforms obtained with three positive components that varied in latency according to the stimulus used indicates that the newborn auditory system discriminates between speech sounds (see Fig. 13.1). These researchers suggested that the ability of the newborn brain to discriminate among speech sounds may provide a useful tool for early diagnosis of auditory system processing.

In summary, the brief review presented here indicates that auditory ERPs can be especially useful in detecting auditory system deficits in cases where other testing is not feasible, for example, with infants or certain retarded individuals. The use of auditory ERPs in newborns will aid in early diagnosis of conditions that could lead to speech and language deficits in later life.

Visual System Tests

A number of studies have indicated that visual ERPs could be used to detect the presence of lesions at various levels of the visual system (Regan, 1972). In an early study, Vaughan, Katzman, and Taylor (1963) found that patients suffering from hemianopia produced VEPs that were 50% greater in amplitude from over the unaffected hemisphere. Hemianopia refers to defective vision in which there is blindness in half of the visual field. The patients studied by Vaughan et al. had homonymous hemianopia, which affected either the right or left halves of the visual fields of both eyes; thus, damage involved either the right or left occipital areas. The hemianopic patients could be differentiated from both normal and brain-damaged persons who did not have visual defects, with VEP measurements. The most striking difference was the depressed amplitude of an early positive wave peaking between 50 and 60 msec. A follow-up study by Vaughan and Katzman (1964) confirmed the usefulness of positive (latency 50–60 msec) components of the VEP in identifying patients with hemianopic defects involving the central 10 degrees of the visual field. In addition, they reported that visual disorders could be localized by recording both VEPs and electroretinogram (ERG). For example, retinal disease was found to be associated with changes in both VEP and ERG (electrical activity of the retina) with stimulation of the involved eye. Optic nerve disease was indicated by loss or suppression of the VEP with stimulation of the involved eye, accompanied by a normal ERG. Damage of areas before the optic chiasm (optic nerve) were associated with loss of the VEP. Damage in areas between the lateral geniculate bodies and visual cortex were associated with loss of the early VEP components and preservation of the late ones.

The results of a number of studies suggest that the VEP may be used as a test of visual acuity. For example, Harter and White (1968) found that when a checkerboard stimulus pattern was in sharp focus, there was a large negative VEP component at 100 msec and a positive wave at 180 msec. As the image was defocused (contours of the checkerboard pattern were degraded), there was a progressive decrease in amplitude of these two components. White and Bonelli (1970) found that VEP amplitude with binocular stimulation was greater with focused images than defocused ones. Further, the degree of binocular summation shown by the VEPs was also related to quality of the image, because summation was maximal with sharply focused patterns. In another study, White and Hansen (1975) tested the effects of presenting images, which differed in focus, to the two eyes. This technique produces image relationships that are similar to clinical cases of amblyopia, in which the image seen by one eye is extremely dim or defocused. In some cases, it was observed that one eye gave a stronger contour response than the other. The studies by White and his colleagues suggest very strongly that the VEP can be used to test visual acuity and may prove useful in the prescription of corrective lenses to a population that is difficult to test—for example, the very young or the retarded.

Visual ERPs were measured in 22 children suffering from amblyopia in response to unpatterned (light) versus patterned (checkerboard) stimulation (Lombroso, Duffy, & Robb, 1969). The VEP to patterned light was abnormally depressed when derived from the amblyopic eye, whereas unpatterned light produced no difference for amblyopic and normal eyes. The researchers concluded that the cortex is the major site of defect in this condition because it is here that cells responding to pattern or shape are found. A volume edited by Bodis-Wollner (1982) contains accounts of a number of studies that have used visual ERPs in neurology and diagnosing visual problems. The articles include studies of visual ERPs in glaucoma, retinal disease, and amblyopia and is recommended to those interested in a more detailed account of applications.

An interesting possible application of the visual ERP has been described by Kinney and McKay (1974), who have used it to distinguish between individuals with differing types of color vision defects. They tested 16 normals, 8 deuteranopes (red–green confusion), 8 protanopes (insensitivity to deep red), and 1 tritanope (red–blue–green confusion). The persons with normal color vision produced VEPs to patterns formed by color differences, whereas the color-defective individuals produced no VEPs to targets formed of colors they could not discriminate. Again, this type of approach could be used in testing color vision of persons incapable of giving accurate verbal responses.

The visual ERP to light flashes was obtained for 79 low-birth-weight infants and compared to a group of full-term infants at 40 weeks postconceptional age for both groups (Kurtzberg, 1982). Only 51% of the low-birth-weight infants had normal occipital visual ERPs at 40 weeks postconceptional age. Visual ERP abnormalities persisted in 75% of the low-weight babies at the age of 1 year. Another technique of stimulation to obtain visual ERPs is that of pattern stimulation, involving reversals of black and white checkerboards or gratings. The occipital pattern VEP from the full-term newborn consists of a small positive wave at about 175 msec, followed by a negative component at 250 msec, and a positive peak at about 350 msec after reversal (Kurtzberg & Vaughan, 1985). The pattern VEP recorded from various scalp areas at various ages from newborn to 6 months is shown in Fig. 13.2. Note the prominence of components at the occipital location and the increasing complexity of waveforms with age. The prominent occipital component indicates the importance of this area in pattern perception, and the increase in wave complexity reflects development of the infants' visual system.

By changing the size of elements within the pattern, (e.g., check sizes) it is possible to estimate visual acuity of the infant. If a visual ERP is not obtained with one check size, larger checks are used until a response is elicited. If no VEP is obtained, even with large check sizes, then visual system dysfunction may be present. The visual ERPs to varying check sizes are a function of maturation level of the infant and integrity of the visual system.

In summary, the visual ERP shows development of the infant visual system

PATTERN VEP

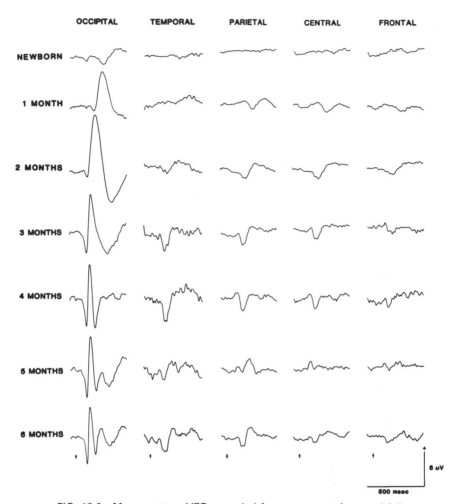

FIG. 13.2   Mean pattern VEP recorded from a group of normal full-term infants from birth through 6 months. The occipital response recorded in the newborn consists of a small positive-negative-positive complex with peak latencies of 175, 250, and 350 msec after pattern reversal. The latency of the major positive component progressively decreases throughout the first 6 months of life. Secondary components begin to develop at 1 month, but do not become prominent until 2 months. Pattern reversal occurs at arrow.

and can provide estimates of acuity. Normative developmental data could allow the use of corrective lenses in infants whose acuity is deviant.

ERPs in the Evaluation of Mental Retardation

The approach here has been to compare ERP waveforms produced by retardates and normals. For example, Rhodes, Dustman, and Beck (1969) compared the VEP of 20 bright and 20 dull children. The bright children had an average full-scale WISC score of 130, whereas the dull group averaged 79. Only children who had no record of brain damage or emotional disturbance were tested. The VEP components (latencies between 100–250 msec) were recorded from occipital and central areas were larger for the bright children. These same VEP components were consistently larger over the right hemisphere (C_4) than the left (C_3). This central hemispheric amplitude asymmetry was not observed for the dull group. No latency differences were noted between the two groups.

Bigum, Dustman, and Beck (1970) measured visual ERPs and somatosensory ERPs from normal children and a sample suffering from Down's syndrome (mongolism). Down's syndrome is characterized by consistent physical features (e.g., protruding tongue, flat nose), and mental retardation. The subjects were 24 retarded children ranging in age from 6 to 16 years, who were matched in age with 24 normal children. They found hemispheric VEP amplitude asymmetries for the normals but not the Down's syndrome subjects, a result similar to that of Rhodes et al. (1969). The SEP for Down's syndrome children was also different, that is, components beyond 150 msec were greater in amplitude than those of normals. Amplitude asymmetries in the VEP were also found in normal children, but not in retardees, by Richlin, Weisinger, Weinstein, Gianni, and Morganstern (1971). Again, the amplitudes were higher from right-hemisphere derivations.

The habituation of the auditory ERP to clicks in normal and Down's syndrome infants was studied by Barnet, Ohlrich, and Shanks (1971). They found that normal infants, aged between 5 and 13 months, showed progressive amplitude decreases in the auditory ERP with repetitive stimulation. However, Down's syndrome infants of similar age did not show such habituation. The researchers suggested that habituation may reflect development of normal sensory capabilities, because normal newborns also did not show it. In another study, the auditory ERPs of young adults with Down's syndrome were compared with those of normal young adults (Straumanis, Shagass, & Overton, 1973). The ERPs were larger in amplitude for the retardates than for the controls. These investigators proposed that the increased amplitude ERP reflects a defect in brain inhibitory mechanisms. The finding of larger ERPs for Down's syndrome adults may be related to a slow habituation similar to that reported for Down's syndrome infants by Barnet et al. (1971).

One finding that seems to be consistent in the studies reviewed here is the amplitude asymmetries found in the VEPs of normal children but not in retarded subjects. Dustman and Beck (1976) observed that this lack of asymmetry in VEPs has been found in Down's syndrome, in dull children, and following the ingestion of alcohol. They speculated that the reticular formation produces differential activation in the hemispheres of normal persons and that in the less efficient brain, this hemispheric differentiation is less developed, reduced, or completely missing.

It is apparent that additional research is needed before the mechanisms underlying ERP differences in normals and retardates are elucidated. A novel approach is that of John et al. (1977), who have used sophisticated computer analyses of ERP data in attempts to classify learning disabilities, mental retardation, and a variety of other disorders. The approach used by John and his colleagues is termed *neurometrics* and employs ERP and EEG analyses of responses to a variety of visual, auditory, and somatosensory stimuli. Multiple tasks and multiple measures are used, and comparisons are made across populations. John, Prichep, Fridman, and Easton (1988), in a review of neurometric applications, reported that learning-disabled and mentally retarded children have been distinguished neurometrically in a number of studies conducted in different countries. They wrote that "Healthy, normally functioning individuals with a wide diversity of cultural and ethnic backgrounds display brain electrical activity consonant with the same set of quantitative descriptors. This supports the proposition that the organ responsible for cognition is fundamentally similar for all healthy members of the human species" (1988, p. 168). The neurometric approach of John and his colleagues is ambitious and of potential importance. However, one weakness is that the approach relies on correlational statistics that tell little about function. An interesting summary and critique of neurometrics was presented by Gale and Edwards (1986), and the interested reader is referred to this work.

The EEG and ERP in the Evaluation of Nervous System Disorders

It was not long after Berger's publication about recording EEG from the intact human scalp that clinicians began to use the technique in diagnosing neurological problems. Among the disorders that produce abnormal EEG patterns are tumors, drug overdose, encephalitis, and meningitis. The most significant abnormalities in the waking adult are (a) delta waves, (b) spike activity (high voltage discharges of short duration), (c) theta waves of 4–7 Hz (not always abnormal), and (d) asymmetry of wave frequency in the two hemispheres. Brain lesions may suppress the alpha rhythm on the side of the damage. Delta waves are commonly associated with brain damage (from hemorrhage or tumor) and are often observed over the damaged area. Spike wave activity is often seen in convulsive disorders, such as epilepsy. In patients with petit mal epilepsy (less severe than grand mal), a three per-second spike wave is common. (See Fig. 13.3 for a

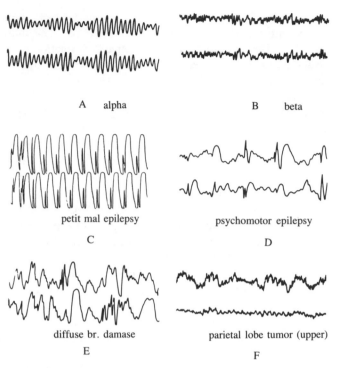

A   alpha   B   beta

petit mal epilepsy   psychomotor epilepsy
       C   D

diffuse br. damase   parietal lobe tumor (upper)
       E   F

FIG. 13.3. Electroencephalograms. (A) Normal alpha rhythm. (B) Beta
waves. (C) Three-per-second spike waves in petit mal epilepsy. (D)
Spikes and spike waves from temporal lobes in psychomotor epilepsy.
(E) Numerous abnormal wave forms in a child with diffuse brain
damage. ("hypsarrhythmia"). (F) Delta wave focus (upper portion) in
parietal lobe tumor.

sample of some normal and abnormal brain wave patterns.) Patients with temporal lobe or "psychomotor" epilepsy often show spike complexes that occur
over the affected lobe. The EEG is a safe, non-invasive procedure that is useful
in detecting abnormal brain activity. One drawback of the EEG is in the interpretation of "borderline" records, because these type of patterns show up in
about 20% of the normal population (Simpson & Magee, 1973).

The use of the EEG-derived ERP is more recent in neurological evaluations.
Beck, Dustman, and Lewis (1975) have found ERPs to be more useful in the
determination of "brain death" than the EEG. They cited a case of a 41-year-old
woman in a coma who produced a flat (isoelectric) EEG. However, stimulation
with flashes of light resulted in a VEP indicating that her brain, although severely
damaged, was still alive, because it responded to sensory stimulation. The finding by Jewett, Romano, and Williston (1970) that responses from the subcortical
brain stem of humans could be elicited by auditory stimuli and recorded at the

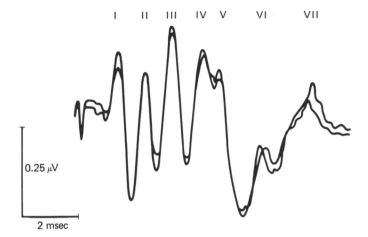

FIG. 13.4.   Auditory brain stem responses from normal subject in response monaural click signals, 65 db SL, presented at 10 per second.
Clicks were presented to right ear and recordings derived from vertex
and right earlobe electrodes (Cz-A$_2$). Total of 2048 click trials were
used to form each of two averages presented. Roman numerals I
through VII designate sequence of upward peaks comprising response. Note that amplitude calibration is in submicrovolt range and
sweep duration is 10 msec. In this figure, positively at vertex (Cz)
electrode is in upward direction.

vertex on the scalp has led to the use of this technique in evaluating subcortical
function. Because the cells generating the activity are a considerable distance
from the recording electrodes, these brain stem potentials have also been referred
to as "far-field potentials" (Jewett & Williston, 1971). Starr and Achor (1975)
reported that they have found auditory brain stem potentials to be useful in
evaluating the mechanisms of coma and in localizing midbrain and brain stem
tumors. They pointed out that the brain stem potential is independent of attention
level, that latencies and components vary systematically, and they are abolished
by damage to the auditory system. The response consists of a series of seven
components (labeled I through VII) that occur during the first 10 msec after
stimulation and are of very low amplitude (less than a microvolt). Responses to
binaural stimulation can be measured by placing an active electrode at Cz and the
reference electrode on the right earlobe. Stimulation may be provided by auditory clicks at a rate of 10 per second. Figure 13.4 shows an auditory brain stem
potential.
    Starr and Achor (1975) compared the brain stem responses of six normal
subjects with a variety of patients whose potentials were measured at bedside.
They concluded that the finding of normal brain stem potentials in a comatose
patient suggests that the coma is due to metabolic (e.g., uremia) or toxic (e.g.,

drug overdose) causes and that the brain stem has been spared. The absence of all components after wave III was associated with a tumor that damaged the midbrain. The absence of all waves after I was correlated in another case with damage to the cochlear nucleus (in the medulla). Wave I was related to activity of the auditory portion of the 8th cranial nerve.

In another set of clinical observations, Starr and Hamilton (1976) correlated abnormalities of the auditory brain stem potential with confirmed (at operation or autopsy) locations of brain damage. They reported that the midbrain must be intact for waves IV through VII to occur. Widespread brain stem lesions were correlated with the absence of all components after wave I. Extensive brain stem lesions followed anoxia in three patients who showed a wave I that was normal in amplitude but delayed in latency. Wave I represents the initial component of 8th (auditory) cranial nerve activity. The second wave includes secondary activity in the 8th nerve plus activity in the superior olive and trapezoid body. Wave III has been localized to the pons, whereas IV and V appear to be generated near the inferior colliculus. Waves VI and VII reflect activity in the neurons transmitting impulses from thalamus and to auditory cortex (Vaughan & Arezzo, 1988).

The use of pattern-evoked VEPs in clinical neurology gained impetus after the report of Halliday, McDonald, and Mushin (1973), in which delays in the VEP were recorded in patients suffering from multiple sclerosis (MS). A combined battery of VEP to different check sizes, brainstem-evoked potential, and somatosensory ERP was compared to magnetic resonance imaging (MRI) in the diagnosis of MS (Geisser et al., 1987). The VEP was considered abnormal if the P100 was greatly delayed or if the waveform was deviant or absent. The criteria for abnormal brainstem potentials were long central transmission (latency difference between waves I and V) and poorly defined or absent components of the waveform. The SEP was considered abnormal if central transmission was delayed (site of neck contralateral parietal cortex). The MRI was used to detect areas where neurons lost their myelin covering. The ERP battery had a sensitivity of 90.5%, compared with 71.4% for MRI in diagnosing 23 patients with possible MS. The authors pointed out that whereas ERPs may fail to show lesions well defined by MRI, they can detect degeneration too small to be detected by MRI. Thus, MRI and ERPs are complementary diagnostic techniques. A follow-up study by Novak, Wiznitzer, Kurtzberg, Geisser, & Vaughan (in press) evaluated 111 patients with suspected MS, and 16 with a definite diagnosis with pattern ERPs. They found that the use of several check sizes, along with half visual field stimulation, led to increased sensitivity of visual ERPs in diagnosing MS.

Cerebral and spinal somatosensory ERPs were recorded in children with CNS degenerative disease by Cracco, Bosch, and Cracco (1980). The ERPs were obtained at various spinal cord levels, and at Cz, to peroneal nerve stimulation (back of knee). The cerebral ERPs were absent in 14 of the 17 patients (compared to normals), and conduction velocity over spinal cord segments was delayed in 12 of the patients. Celesia (1982) reported that delayed or absent pattern

VEPs have been reported in optic neuritis, optic atrophy, and compression of the optic nerve. He stated that VEPs are useful in determining early lesions of the optic nerves and in monitoring early compression of the optic nerve by tumors. Further, the VEPs can be used to quantify the effects of surgery, because they show restoration with post-operative improvement in visual function. Huntington's Chorea (HC) is a severe degenerative disease of the CNS that is inherited. Persons who had one parent afflicted with HC are said to be at risk (AR) for developing this disease. At least two studies have found decreased visual ERPs in patients already suffering from HC. Lawson, Barrett, Kriss, and Halliday (1984) studied the visual ERPs of 9 HC patients, 18 at risk individuals, and 15 control subjects. The P100 responses for HC patients were reduced in amplitude, but the AR and controls did not differ.

Thus, there are a number of studies that indicate that EEG and ERPs are useful in the detection and diagnosis of some neurological disorders. Although only a few representative studies have been presented here, there are many investigations in progress at various hospitals and laboratories, indicating that ERP has become an important additional diagnostic tool for the neurologist.

Physiological Responses and Behavioral Disorders

Brain ERPs and Psychiatric Diagnosis.   Regan (1972) expressed the belief that the application of ERPs to the study of behavior disorders is a difficult task, both scientifically and conceptually. However, several investigators have developed approaches that result in differential results with psychiatric patients and normal subjects. For example, Callaway, Jones, and Layne (1965) recorded auditory ERPs to 1,000-Hz and 600-Hz tones from schizophrenic patients and normal control subjects. The tones were presented randomly and were equated for loudness at about 65 db. In normal subjects, the two tones produced very similar ERPs, whereas in schizophrenics, the ERPs were different. This difference was later attributed to greater variability in the responses of schizophrenics, that is, the ERPs of the patients were not as consistent as those of the normals (Callaway, Jones, & Donchin, 1970). Callaway (1975) suggested that the high degree of ERP variability in schizophrenics is partly related to the unstable and variable thought processes of these patients. However, he believes that ERP variability is of limited value in studying schizophrenia, because, among other reasons, patients differing in diagnostic category (e.g., depression) also produce highly variable ERPs.

Another approach has been that of Shagass and associates, who used the somatosensory ERP to study "recovery functions" in psychiatric and non-psychiatric patients (see Shagass, 1972). The technique involved the presentation of two electric shock stimuli, in close succession (intervals between stimuli may vary from 20 to 200 msec), and measuring the amplitude of the second ERP relative to the first. The amplitude ratio of the second ERP to the first is the

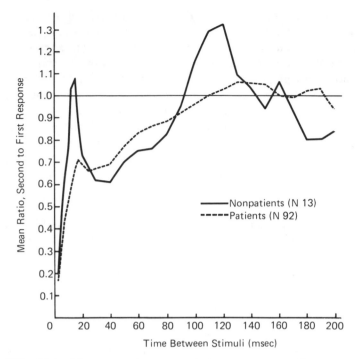

FIG. 13.5. Mean somatosensory (primary component) recovery curves for 13 nonpatients and a heterogeneous sample of 92 psychiatric patients. Note biphasic pattern of curve in nonpatients and greater recovery at 20 msec than by patients.

measure of recovery of cortical excitability after stimulation. The higher the ratio, the greater the recovery. Figure 13.5, from Shagass and Schwartz (1964), shows that somatosensory ERP recovery ratios during the first 20 msec were greater in nonpatients than in patients. That is, this initial phase of recovery was delayed or reduced in the patients with behavior disorders. The amount of recovery in the visual ERP was also found to be reduced in psychiatric patients in a number of studies cited by Shagass (1972).

The ERP approach of Callaway in studying psychiatric disorders tended to emphasize changes in the response that took place 100 msec or more after the stimulus, and that of Shagass focused on components that occurred within 100 msec after stimulus presentation, especially the first 20 msec. Another approach is to examine the relationship between psychiatric disorders and the CNV. For example, McCallum and Walter (1968) reported that persons suffering from severe anxiety neurosis had contingent negative variation (CNV) waves that were much lower in amplitude than those of normal controls, especially when a distracting stimulus was introduced. Other patient groups that have reportedly evidenced reduced CNVs, when compared to nonpatients, were schizophrenics (McCallum & Abraham, 1973) and psychopaths (McCallum, 1973). Although the CNV distinguished between patients and nonpatients, there seems to be little or no differentiation among patient categories. An interesting finding is that of increased frontal CNV in schizophrenics (Tecce & Cole, 1976). The observation that frontal CNV amplitude also increases in head injury suggests to Tecce and Cattanach (1987) that neural disinhibition might be a factor in producing this effect. The CNV and P300 were studied in a group of 16 chronic alcoholics and 16 matched controls (Skerchock & Cohen, 1984). The subjects were screened neurologically, and all alcoholics were without alcohol or psychotropic drugs for at least 3 weeks. The alcoholics showed significantly lower CNV amplitudes compared to normals. The authors suggested that this decrement may represent subtle frontal lobe dysfunction due to alcoholism. The P300 amplitudes did not differ, but P300 latencies were longer for the alcoholics, possibly indicating impaired stimulus evaluations. An international pilot study, which standardized procedures in the various laboratories, studied CNV in mental illness (Timsit-Berthier et al., 1984). Depressed patients displayed disruption in CNV development, and a portion of the CNV wave (designated M2) was selective for schizophrenia. The authors were encouraged about the further investigation of CNV in psychiatric patients.

Another ERP that has been studied in relation to behavior disorder is the P300. For example, Roth and Cannon (1972) compared this late positive wave in 21 schizophrenics and a group of controls matched for age and race. The late waves of the schizophrenics were significantly lower in amplitude than for nonpatients. Roth, Horvath, Pfefferbaum, and Kopell (1980) and Roth, Pfefferbaum, Kelly, Berger, and Kopell (1981) also found reduced P300 amplitudes and increased RTs to low probability targets, and decreased P180 latencies to high probability nontargets for schizophrenics. These findings would be expected for less motivated subjects who paid less attention to the experimental task, and points to one of the problems in using ERPs with the mentally ill. In a thoughtful paper, Roth, Tecce, Pfefferbaum, Rosenbloom, and Callaway (1984) discussed the problems and possible approaches in using ERPs in psychiatric diagnosis.

When studies of the relationship between ERPs and behavior disorders were first begun in the 1960s, researchers had high hopes for the use of the technique both for differential diagnosis and as a possible aid to understanding the neurological bases of these disorders. These early goals have not yet been realized, but work continues in this important area.

EEG and Schizophrenia.   In a review, Itil (1977) concluded that the most important finding in EEG research relating to schizophrenia is that patients have less well-organized alpha activity and more low-voltage fast activity (beta) than normals. He postulated that available data support the position that desynchronized high-frequency beta activity may be the physiological correlate of a genetic predisposition to schizophrenia. In a representative study, Itil, Hsu, Klingberg, Saletu, and Gannon (1972) found that a sample of 100 schizophrenics had significantly higher voltage beta activity (ranging from 24 to 33 Hz) than a sample of 100 normal subjects. Itil (1977) suggested that further work is needed to correlate quantitative EEG findings with possible biochemical factors in schizophrenia. One biochemical theory is that schizophrenics have an excess of dopamine, a neurotransmitter substance, in their brains. This notion would be tentatively supported by the high-frequency EEG usually reported for schizophrenics.

Buchsbaum (1977) summarized some EEG research comparing schizophrenics with normals and wrote that patients generally show diminished alpha, faster and more prolonged blocking of alpha by a stimulus, and greater effect of eye-opening or closing on alpha. The pattern of high beta and low alpha occurs in normals engaged in processing information. Buchsbaum suggested that these findings indicate that the resting schizophrenic is in a constant state of cortical processing, a state consistent with psychological models of deficient filtering of sensory input or sensory overload in schizophrenics. Venables (1983) noted that there are EEG data to indicate asymmetrical brain function in schizophrenics. Initial suggestions of disturbed asymmetry of function in schizophrenics came from studies of EDA (Gruzelier & Venables, 1974).

Electrodermal Activity and Behavioral Disorders.   In a study by Gruzelier and Venables (1973) larger electrodermal responses were recorded from the right hand than the left. These and other results supported the idea that schizophrenia is associated with dysfunction in the opposite hemisphere; in this sense the left, because a lack of inhibitory influence would be indicated by the excessive right-hand response. Depressed patients showed an opposite asymmetry, supporting a theory that these two psychoses are associated with dysfunction of opposite hemispheres. Later work has indicated differential EDA in two varieties of schizophrenia (Gruzelier, 1984). Patients with larger right-hand responses had blunted affect, emotional withdrawal, and reduced energy level, among other symptoms. Those with larger left-hand responses showed more "florid" features, including delusions, hallucinations, and flight of ideas. These results suggest that a control mechanism disruption occurs in the left hemisphere for those with low affect and in the right hemisphere for patients with florid features.

Lader and Noble (1975) noted that patients categorized as anxiety neurotics show elevated levels of skin conductance (SCL) and greater numbers of spontaneous fluctuations (SCRs) than do normal controls. Venables (1975) reviewed a number of studies that investigated the relationship between EDA and schizophrenia. The trend of results seem to indicate that (a) higher-than-normal levels of skin conductance occur in some schizophrenics; (b) chronic schizophrenics appear to show a faster recovery to baseline SCL than normals; (c) chronic schizophrenics show higher levels of spontaneous SCRs than normals; and (d) schizophrenics who give orienting responses do not habituate to the stimulus as quickly as normals. The general trend for EDA seems to support the contention of some investigators that chronic schizophrenics are overaroused, because high levels of EDA indicate elevated SNS activity.

In an application of EDA to learning disability, Mangina and Beuzeron-Mangina (1988) proposed that stimulation with a variety of stimuli while maintaining subjects within an "optimal" range of physiological activity leads to improved academic performance. The EDA measured bilaterally (both hands) is kept within a pre-established optimal range of 6.5 to 8.5 μmhos, primarily through auditory stimulation of left, right, or both ears, depending on which hand shows "underactivation" (5.0 μmhos or below) or "overactivation" (10.1 umhos or above). Contralateral cortical control over EDA has been indicated in human and animal studies. In the Manginas' technique, the beneficial effects of stimulation on the underdeveloped synaptic connections in the brains of the learning disabled is assumed. This approach is an interesting application of EDA and activation theory (see chapter 15).

Schalling, Lidberg, Levander, and Dahlin (1973) measured SCRs and finger-pulse volume of criminal subjects who scored either high or low on a scale of psychopathy. They found that the group scoring high in psychopathy had fewer spontaneous SCRs during a tone stimulation period and a post-stimulation rest period than the other group. The investigators suggested that the lower degree of responsivity to stimuli in the more psychopathic subjects might be related to the hypothesis that states of low cortical arousal are a main correlate of psychopathy (see Hare, 1975). No differences in finger-pulse volume were found.

Skin conductance responses, penile volume, and ratings of slides depicting sexual scenes were measured by Kercher and Walker (1973) in a group of 28 convicted rapists and 28 inmates convicted of crimes unrelated to sex. No significant differences were found between the groups on the penile volume measures. However, the rapists produced larger SCRs to the erotic material and gave more negative ratings to the sexual themes than the control inmates. These findings were interpreted as suggesting that the erotic stimuli were unpleasant for the rapists.

Cardiovascular Activity and Behavioral Disorders.   Venables (1975) indicated that there has been little research attempting to relate heart activity to schizophrenia. A sample study is that of Spohn, Thelford, and Cancro (1971), who reported HR deceleration to pictorial slides in both normal and schizophrenic subjects. These results agree with earlier ones indicating HR deceleration with attention to external stimuli by normal subjects. Patients suffering from panic disorder were monitored over a 24-hour period with ambulatory HR measurement (Taylor, Telch, & Havvik, 1983). When panic attacks occur, patients often experience a variety of unpleasant symptoms, including palpitations, shortness of breath, sweating, faintness, and others indicating exaggerated sympathetic nervous system response. The HR monitoring showed significantly elevated levels of HR during panic episodes and suggest the usefulness of this technique with individuals suffering frequent attacks with HR greater than 110 BPM. The monitoring would be of use in adjusting the level of medication required to bring the excessive physiological response under control.

The effects of a stimulant drug, methylphenidate (Ritalin), on autonomic responses (including HR and SC) of hyperactive children with attention deficit disorder was studied by Solanto and Conners (1982). Some workers in this field think that Ritalin is effective because hyperactive children are actually underaroused, and the excessive activity represents an attempt to compensate for the low arousal level. The researchers found that HR was significantly increased with Ritalin but EDA was not. Improvements in motor performance (RT) were attributed to the reduction of extraneous motor activity produced by the medication. Obviously, much remains to be done in this area, especially on the long-term effects of Ritalin on physiological response and associated health implications.

Pulse rate and forearm blood flow were measured in 31 cases of psychotic depression, before and after a series of electroshock treatments (Noble & Lader, 1971). Clinical improvement subsequent to shock treatments was accompanied by increased forearm blood flow. Pulse rate did not change. These investigators suggested that depressive illness is related to decreased blood flow, which may involve a disturbance of hypothalamic control.

In a review of physiological measures that have been studied in relation to psychopathy, Hare (1975) indicated that most of the cardiovascular research in this area is conceptually based on the orienting response and on Lacey's (1967) hypothesis that sensory intake is associated with HR deceleration and sensory rejection with HR acceleration. In a representative study, Hare (1968) found that the cardiovascular components of the OR (i.e., HR deceleration and finger vasoconstriction) were relatively slow to habituate in psychopaths.

In summary, the work briefly reviewed here only scratches the surface with respect to the number of studies that have attempted to relate physiological response to various behavior disorders. However, it is hoped that a feeling for the type of work in the area has been conveyed. Much more remains to be done and established in this potentially fruitful area.

Physiological Correlates of Vigilance Performance

The problem of vigilance decrement, enunciated so well by Mackworth (1950), is still with us. There has been increasing attention in recent years to the physiological changes that occur during the course of a vigil. A book on vigilance edited by Mackie (1977) reveals a variety of performance situations and measures that are being used. For example, prolonged night automobile driving and physiological changes were studied by O'Hanlon and Kelley (1977). In three separate experiments, the performance of 41 young males was monitored while measures of EEG and HR were taken. The main performance indicator was the frequency of drifting out of lane, that is, the number of times the white line or road shoulder were touched during the drive. All driving was done on actual roads in California. The time of driving ranged from 109 to 315 minutes and averaged 200 minutes. Each driver used the same vehicle and started the run at 10:00 P.M. An observer was present in the vehicle with the driver at all times. The subjects were divided into groups of 21 "better" and 20 "poorer" performers on the basis of the lane-drifting measure. The better drivers tended to have higher rates of heart activity and lower amounts of heart rate variability than the poorer drivers. The HR of both groups decreased progressively over the course of the drive. In three cases, the experimenter took control of the vehicle when the subject's performance became very erratic and they appeared more asleep than awake. The EEG records of these three subjects confirmed this, revealing bursts of delta or theta activity. The drivers were unaware that the experimenter took control, suggesting that persons who were at a dangerously low level of arousal while driving did not realize it. More studies of this type are needed, especially when the tremendous losses in traffic accidents and other kinds of accidents are considered. One might visualize night drivers, or radar operators, or pilots of the future wearing physiological monitors that sound an alerting bell or buzzer when the recorded activity signals a potentially dangerous low level of activity.

The recording of physiological measures of drivers operating vehicles in heavy traffic was accomplished by Zeier (1979). Drivers drove the same 14km course through the city of Munich on two different occasions; one time with manual transmission and once with automatic shift. The cars were BMWs that were identical in all other respects. When driving with manual transmission, HR, HR variability, and number of SCRs were significantly higher than when driving with automatic transmission or riding as a passenger. The results indicate that driving with manual transmission produces greater activation of the SNS. The authors concluded that under city traffic conditions, stress reduction due to using automatic shift may promote improved health and safety.

PERSONNEL APPLICATIONS OF PHYSIOLOGICAL MEASURES

The relationship among job satisfaction, perceived effort, and HR was measured in 40 female factory workers (Khaleque, 1981). The average HR of satisfied workers was significantly lower than that of dissatisfied ones. In addition, there was a significant correlation between job satisfaction and HR, that is, greater satisfaction was related to lower HR. There was no relation between perceived effort and HR. The results have interesting health implications with regard to the long-term cardiovascular effects of job dissatisfaction. A number of studies have shown that repetitive industrial tasks are associated in some workers with job dissatisfaction and in others with emotional stress. Assembly line inspection or production tasks are common examples of industrial jobs. Weber, Fussler, O'Hanlon, Gierer, and Grandjean (1980) measured the effects of four different repetitive tasks on several physiological measures. All of the repetitive tasks were associated with depressed EEG alpha, increased HR, and elevated adrenaline excretion. Two of the tasks required discrimination and were accompanied by higher neck EMG and less boredom and drowsiness. The results point up the possible stressful effects of repetition and the potential importance of job design in reducing these effects.

Donchin, Kramer, and Wickens (1986) made a case for the potential utility of ERPs in studying job workload and the design of tasks. They cited studies that indicate that P300 is sensitive to perceptual demands of a primary task, because the P300 amplitude to a secondary task probe decreases with increased difficulty of a primary task. Thus, it may serve as a good index of the relative demands of primary and secondary tasks on an operator. This is an important consideration in the design of jobs in modern complex man–machine systems where multiple tasks must be performed. Because ERPs have been found useful in studying cognitive activities, Donchin and his co-workers advocate their use as analytical tools in measuring and understanding mental workload.

Reports from the Navy Personnel Research and Development Center in San Diego, California suggest that ERPs are more accurate in predicting on-the-job performance of naval personnel than traditional psychological tests (Lewis, 1983a, 1983b). Research results suggest that ERPs are related to success or failure in a remedial reading program, that ERPs distinguished between prematurely discharged recruits and those of equal aptitude who successfully completed training, and in predicting performance of antisubmarine warfare sonar operators, among other findings. These promising results will have to be confirmed by researchers in other laboratories.

EYE MOVEMENTS AND NEUROLOGICAL DIAGNOSIS

Eye-tracking performance is impaired in Parkinson's disease, stroke victims, and in patients with dementia. Hutton, Nagel, and Loewenson (1984) tested Alzheimer, depressed, and elderly normal controls on their ability to track a spot of light across a screen. The smooth-pursuit tracking performance of Alzheimer patients was worse than in the other groups, and there was a correlation between tracking dysfunction and severity of the disease. Thus, both eye-tracking dysfunction and severity of Alzheimer's are probably related to the severity of brain deterioration. To maintain a clear image of a moving target, the oculomotor system uses both saccadic and smooth-pursuit eye movements. Saccades correct for errors of position between fovea and target, whereas pursuit tracking moves the eye at a speed that matches that of the target. Kenyon, Becker, Butters (1984) and Kenyon, Becker, Butters, and Hermann (1984) measured both saccadic and smooth-pursuit movements in Wernicke-Korsakoff's syndrome. Korsakoff syndrome is due to chronic alcoholism coupled with thiamine deficiency. In the acute Wernicke state, the patient is confused and suffers visual disorders. After treatment, the patient reverts to the chronic Korsakoff state characterized by inability to learn new information and impaired ability to recall events prior to onset of illness. Among the perceptual changes are chronic deficits in ability to process visual information. Kenyon, Becker, Butters, and Hermann (1984) found abnormal saccadic movements 2–7 years after the onset of Korsakoff's, a result consistent with cerebellar and frontal lobe dysfunction. Smooth-pursuit eye movements are also abnormal in these patients, indicating that eye movement disorders are a feature of Korsakoff's syndrome and reflect the diffuse damage that this condition produces in the nervous system.

This chapter has indicated the diversity in potential applications of physiological measures. Another area of application is that of biofeedback, in which the clinical goal is the learned self-regulation of physiological response to alleviate some disorder. Many published reports have appeared on this topic over the past two decades. As a result, the next chapter is devoted solely to a consideration of those biofeedback applications whose expressed purpose has been to treat various ailments, ranging from tension headache to high blood pressure.

REFERENCES

Arthur, R. O. (1971). The GSR Unit. *Journal of Polygraph Studies, 5*, 1–4.

Barland, G. H., & Raskin, D. C. (1973). Detection of deception. In W. F. Prokasy & D. C. Raskin (Eds.), *Electrodermal activity in psychological research* (pp. 417–477). New York: Academic Press.

Barland, G. H., & Raskin, D. C. (1975). An evaluation of field techniques in detection of deception. *Psychophysiology, 12*, 321–330.

Barnet, A. B., Ohlrich, E. S., & Shanks, B. L. (1971). EEG evoked responses to repetitive auditory stimulation in normal and Down's syndrome infants. *Developmental Medicine and Child Neurology, 13*, 321–329.

Beck, E. C., Dustman, R. E., & Lewis, E. G. (1975). The use of the Averaged Evoked Potential in the evaluation of central nervous system disorders. *International Journal of Neurology, 9*, 211–232.

Bersh, P. J. (1969). A validation of polygraph examiner judgments. *Journal of Applied Psychology, 53*, 399–403.

Bigum, H. B., Dustman, R. E., & Beck, E. C. (1970). Visual and somato-sensory evoked responses from Mongoloid and normal children. *Electroencephalography and Clinical Neurophysiology, 28*, 576–585.

Bodis-Wollner, I. (1982). *Evoked potentials.* Annals of the New York Academy of Sciences, Vol. 388. New York: N.Y. Academy of Sciences.

Bradley, M. T., & Ainsworth, D. (1984). Alcohol and the physiological detection of deception. *Psychophysiology, 21*, 63–71.

Bradley, M. T., & Warfield, J. F. (1984). Innocence, information, and the Guilty Knowledge Test in the detection of deception. *Psychophysiology, 21,* 683–689.

Buchsbaum, M. S. (1979). Neurophysiological aspects of the schizophrenic syndrome. In L. Bellak (Ed.), *The schizophrenia syndrome* (pp. 152–180). New York: Grune & Stratton.

Callaway, E. (1975). *Brain electrical potentials and individual psychological differences.* New York: Grune & Stratton.

Callaway, E., Jones, R. T., & Donchin, E. (1970). Auditory evoked potential variability in schizophrenia. *Electroencephalography & Neurophysiology, 29,* 421–428.

Callaway, E., Jones, R. T., & Layne, R. S. (1965). Evoked responses and segmental set of schizophrenia. *Archives of General Psychiatry, 12,* 83–89.

Celesia, G., (1982). Steady state and transient visual evoked potentials in clinical practice. In I. Bodis-Wollner (Ed.), *Evoked potentials* (pp. 290–305). New York: New York Academy of Sciences.

Cone-Wesson, B., Kurtzberg, D., & Vaughan, H. G. Jr. (1983, March). *Detection of auditory system dysfunction in very low birthweight infants.* Paper presented at the meeting of the Society for Ear, Nose, & Throat Advance in Children, San Diego, CA.

Cracco, J., Bosch, V. V., & Cracco, R. Q. (1980). Cerebral and spinal somatosensory evoked potentials in children with CNS degenerative disease. *Electroencephalography & Clinical Neurophysiology, 49,* 337–445.

Donchin, E., Kramer, A., & Wickens, C. (1986). Applications of brain event-related potentials to problems in engineering psychology. In M. G. H. Coles, E. Donchin, & S. W. Porges (Eds.), *Psychophysiology: Systems, processes & applications* (pp. 702–718). New York: Guilford.

Furedy, J. J. (1986). Lie detection as psychophysiological differentiation: Some fine lines. In M. G. H. Coles, E. Donchin, & S. W. Porges (Eds.), *Psychophysiology: Systems, processes, & applications* (pp. 683–701). New York: Guilford.

Furedy, J. J., Davis, C., & Gurevich, M. (in press). Differentiation of deception as a psychological process: A psychophysiological approach. *Psychophysiology.*

Furedy, J. J., & Heslegrave, R. J. (in press). The forensic use of the polygraph: A psychophysiological analysis of current trends and future prospects. In J. R. Jennings, P. K. Ackles, & M. G. H. Coles (Eds.), *Advances in psychophysiology* (Vol. 4). Greenwich, CT: JAI Press.

Gale, A., & Edwards, J. A. (1986). Individual differences. In M. G. H. Coles, E. Donchin, & S. W. Porges (Eds.), *Psychophysiology: Systems, processes & applications* (pp. 431–507). New York: Guilford.

Geisser, B. S., Kurtzberg, D., Vaughan, H. G., Jr., Arezzo, J. C., Aisen, M. L., Smith, C. R., LaRocca, N. G., & Scheinberg, L. C. (1987). Trimodal evoked potentials compared with magnetic resonance imaging in the diagnosis of multiple sclerosis. *Archives of Neurology, 44,* 281–284.

Gruzelier, J. H. (1984). Hemispheric imbalances in schizophrenia. *International Journal of Psychophysiology, 1,* 227–240.

Gruzelier, J. H., & Venables, P. H. (1973). Skin conductance responses to tones with and without attentional significance in schizophrenic and non-schizophrenic psychiatric patients. *Neuropsychologia, 11,* 221–230.

Halliday, A. M., McDonald, W. I., & Mushin, J. (1973). Visual evoked responses in the diagnosis of multiple sclerosis. *British Medical Journal, 4,* 661–664.

Hare, R. D. (1968). Psychopathy, autonomic functioning and the orienting response. *Journal of Abnormal Psychology Monographs, 73,* 1–24.

Hare, R. D. (1975). Psychopathy. In P. H. Venables & M. J. Christie (Eds.), *Research in psychophysiology* (pp. 325–348). New York: Wiley.

Harter, M. R., & White, C. T. (1968). Effects of contour sharpness and check-size on visually evoked cortical potentials. *Vision Research, 8,* 701–711.

Horvath, F. (1978). An experimental comparison of the psychological stress evaluator and the galvanic skin response in detection of deception. *Journal of Applied Psychology, 63,* 338–344.

Hutton, J. T., Nagel, J. A., & Loewenson, R. B. (1984). Eye tracking dysfunction in Alzheimer-type dementia. *Neurology, 34,* 99–102.

Itil, T. M. (1977). Qualitative and quantitative EEG findings in schizophrenia. In L. R. Mosher (Ed.), *Schizophrenia* (pp. 61–79). Rockville: National Institute of Mental Health.

Itil, T. M., Hsu, W., Klingberg, H., Saletu, B., & Gannon, P. (1972). Digital-computer-analyzed all-night sleep EEG patterns (sleep patterns) in schizophrenics. *Biological Psychiatry, 4,* 3–16.

Jewett, D. L., & Williston, J. S. (1971). Auditory evoked far-fields averaged from the scalp of humans. *Brain, 94,* 681–696.

Jewett, E. L., Romano, M. N., & Williston, J. S. (1970). Human auditory potentials: Possible brainstem components detected on the scalp. *Science, 167,* 1517–1518.

John, E. R., Karmel, B. Z., Corning, W. C., Easton, P., Brown, D., Ahn, H., John, M., Harmony, T., Prichep, L., Toro, A., Gerson, I., Bartlett, F., Thatcher, R., Kaye, H., Valdes, P., & Schwartz, E. (1977). Neurometrics, numerical taxonomy identifies different profiles of brain functions within groups of behaviorally similar people. *Science, 196,* 1393–1410.

John, E. R., Prichep, L. S., Fridman, J., & Easton, P. (1988). Neurometrics: Computer-assisted differential diagnosis of brain dysfunctions. *Science, 239,* 162–169.

Kenyon, R. V., Becker, J. T., & Butters, N. (1984). Oculomotor function in Wernicke-Korsakoff's syndrome: II. Smooth pursuit eye movements. *International Journal of Neuroscience, 25,* 53–65.

Kenyon, R. V., Becker, J. T., Butters, N., & Hermann, H. (1984). Oculomotor function in Wernicke-Korsakoff's syndrome: I. Saccadic eye movements. *International Journal of Neuroscience, 25,* 53–65.

Kercher, G. A., & Walker, C. E. (1973b). Reactions of convicted rapists to sexually explicit stimuli. *Journal of Abnormal Psychology, 81,* 46–50.

Khaleque, A. (1981). Job satisfaction, perceived effort and heart rate in light industrial work. *Ergonomics, 24,* 735–742.

Kinney, J. A. S., & McKay, C. (1974). Test of color-defective vision using the visual evoked response. *Journal of the Optical Society of America, 64,* 1244–1250.

Kleinmuntz, B., & Szucko, J. J. (1984). Lie detection in ancient and modern times. *American Psychologist, 39,* 766–776.

Kubis, J. F. (1973). *Comparison of voice analysis and polygraph as lie detection procedures* (Contract DAADO5-72-C-0217). U.S. Army Land Warfare Laboratory, Aberdeen Proving Ground, Aberdeen, MD.

Kurtzberg, D. (1982). Event-related potentials in the evaluation of high-risk infants. In I. Bodis-Wollner (Ed.), *Evoked potentials* (Vol. 388, pp. 557–571). New York: New York Academy of Sciences.

Kurtzberg, D., Hilpert, P., & Kreuzer, J. A. (1984). Differential maturation of cortical auditory evoked potentials to speech sounds in normal full term infants and very low birthweight infants. *Developmental Medicine & Childhood Neurology, 16,* 466–475.

Kurtzberg, D., & Vaughan, H. G., Jr. (1985). Electrophysiologic assessment of auditory and visual function in the newborn. *Clinics in Perinatology, 12,* 277–299.

Lacey, J. I. (1967). Somatic response patterning and stress: Some revisions of activation. In M. H. Appley & R. Trumbell (Eds.), *Psychological stress: Issues in research* (pp. 14–44). New York: Appleton-Century-Crofts.

Lader, M., & Noble, P. (1975). The affective disorders. In P. H. Venables & M. J. Christie (Eds.), *Research in psychophysiology* (pp. 259–281). New York: Wiley.

Lawson, E., Barrett, G., Kriss, A., & Halliday, A. M. (1984). P300 and VEPs in Huntington's Chorea. In R. Karrer, J. Cohen, & P. Teuting (Eds.), *Brain and information: Event-related potentials* (Vol. 425, pp. 592–597). New York: New York Academy of Sciences.

Lewis, G. W. (1983a). Event-related brain electrical and magnetic activity: Toward predicting on-job performance. *International Journal of Neuroscience, 18,* 159–182.

Lewis, G. W. (1983b). *Bioelectric predictors of personnel performance: A review of relevant research at the Navy Personnel Research and Development Center.* NPRDC TR 84-3, San Diego, CA: Navy Personnel Research and Development Center.

Lombroso, C. T., Duffy, F. H., & Robb, R. M. (1969). Selective suppression of cerebral evoked potentials to patterned light in amblyopia ex anopsia. *Electroencephalography & Clinical Neurophysiology, 27,* 238–247.

Lykken, D. T. (1959). The GSR in the detection of guilty. *Journal of Applied Psychology, 43,* 385–388.

Lykken, D. T. (1974). Psychology and the lie detector industry. *American Psychologist, 29,* 725–739.

Lykken, D. T. (1978). The psychopath and the lie detector. *Psychophysiology, 15,* 137–142.

Lykken, D. T. (1981). *A tremor in the blood.* New York: McGraw-Hill.

Mackie, R. R. (1977). *Vigilance: Theory, operational performance and physiological correlates.* New York: Plenum Press.

Mackworth, N. H. (1950). *Researches on the measurement of human performance.* (MRC Spec Rep. 268). London: H. M. Stationary Office, Medical Research Council.

Mangina, C. A., & Beuzeron-Mangina, J. H. (1988). Learning abilities and disabilities: Effective diagnosis and treatment. *International Journal of Psychophysiology, 6,* 79–90.

McCallum, W. C. (1973). The CNV and conditionability in psychopaths. *Electroencephalography & Clinical Neurophysiology, 33,* 337–343.

McCallum, W. C., & Abraham, P. (1973). The contingent negative variation in psychosis. *Electroencephalography & Clinical Neurophysiology, 33,* 329–335.

McCallum, W. C., & Walter, W. G. (1968). The effects of attention and distraction on the contingent negative variation in normal and neurotic subjects. *Electroencephalography & Clinical Neurophysiology, 25,* 319–329.

Munsterberg, H. (1908). *On the witness stand.* New York: Doubleday, Page and Co.

Noble, P., & Lader, M. (1971). Depressive illness, pulse rate and forearm blood flow. *The British Journal of Psychiatry, 119,* 261–266.

Novak, G. P., Wiznitzer, M., Kurtberg, D. Geisser, B. S., & Vaughan, H. G., Jr. (in press). The utility of visual evoked potentials using hemifield stimulation and several check sizes in the evaluation of suspected multiple sclerosis. *Electroencephalography and Clinical Neurophysiology.*

O'Hanlon, J. F., & Kelly, G. R. (1977). Comparison of performance and physiological changes between drivers who perform well and poorly during prolonged vehicular operation. In R. R. Mackie (Ed.), *Vigilance: Theory, operational performance and physiological correlates* (pp. 87–109). New York: Plenum Press.

Orne, M. T. (1975). Implications of laboratory research for the detection of deception. In N. Ainsley (Ed.), *Legal admissability of the polygraph* (pp. 94–119). Springfield, IL: C. C. Thomas.

Orne, M. T., Thackray, R. I., & Paskewitz, D. A. (1972). On the detection of deception. In N. S. Greenfield & R. A. Sternabach (Eds.), *Handbook of psychohysiology* (pp. 743–785). New York: Holt, Rinehart & Winston.

Podlesny, J. A., & Raskin, D. C. (1977). Physiological measures and the detection of deception. *Psychological Bulletin, 84,* 782–799.

Rapin, I. (1974). Testing for hearing loss with auditory evoked responses—successes and failures. *Journal of Communication Disorders, 7,* 3–10.

Rapin, I., Graziani, L. J., & Lyttle, M. (1969). Summated auditory evoked responses for audiometry: Experience in 51 children with congenital rubella. *International Journal of Audiology, 8,* 371–376.

Raskin, D. C., Barland, G. H., & Podlesny, J. A. (1977). Validity and reliability of detection of deception. *Polygraph, 6,* 1–39.

Raskin, D. C., & Hare, R. D. (1978). Psychopathy and detection of deception in a prison population. Psychophysiology, 15, 126–136.

Regan, D. (1972). *Evoked potentials in psychology, sensory physiology and clinical medicine.* London: Chapman and Hall.

Rhodes, L. E., Dustman, R. E., & Beck, E. C. (1969). The visual evoked response: A comparison of bright and dull children. *Electroencephalography & Clinical Neurophysiology, 27,* 364–372.

Richlin, M., Weisinger, M., Weinstein, S., Giannini, M., & Morganstern, M. (1971). Interhemispheric asymmetries of evoked cortical responses in retarded and normal children. *Cortex, 1,* 98–105.

Roth, W. T., & Cannon, E. H. (1972). Some features of the auditory evoked response in schizophrenics. *Archives of General Psychiatry, 27,* 466–471.

Roth, W. T., Horvath, T. B., Pfefferbaum, A., & Kopell, B. S. (1980). Event-related potentials in schizophrenics. *Electroencephalography & Clinical Neurophysiology, 48,* 127–139.

Roth, W. T., Pfefferbaum, A., Kelly, A. F., Berger, P. A., & Kopell, B. S. (1981). Auditory event-related potentials in schizophrenia and depression. *Psychiatry Research, 4,* 199–212.

Roth, W. T., Tecce, J. J., Pfefferbaum, A., Rosenbloom, M., & Callaway, E. (1984). ERPs and psychopathology: I. Behavioral process issues. In R. Karrer, J. Cohen, & P. Teuting (Eds.), *Brain and information: Event-related potentials* (Vol. 425, pp. 496–522). New York: New York Academy of Sciences.

Schalling, D., Lidberg, L., Levander, S. E., & Dahlin, Y. (1973). Spontaneous autonomic activity as related to psychopathy. *Biological Psychology, 1,* 83–97.

Shagass, C. (1972). *Evoked potentials in psychiatry.* New York: Plenum Press.

Shagass, C., & Schwartz, M. (1964). Evoked potential studies in psychiatric patients. *Annals of New York Academy of Science, 112,* 526–542.

Simpson, J. F., & Magee, K. R. (1973). *Clinical evaluation of the nervous system.* Boston: Little, Brown.

Skerchock, J. A., & Cohen, J. (1984). Alcoholism, organicity and event-related potentials. In R. Karrer, J. Cohen & P. Teuting (Eds.), *Brain and information: Event-related potentials* (Vol. 425, pp. 623–628). New York: New York Academy of Sciences.

Solanto, M. V. & Conners, C. K. (1982). A dose-response and time action analysis of autonomic and behavioral effects of methylphenidate in attention deficit disorder with hyperactivity. *Psychophysiology, 19,* 658–667.

Spohn, H. E., Thetford, P. E., & Cancro, R. (1971). The effects of phenothiazine medication on skin conductance and heart rate in schizophrenic patients. *Journal of Nervous and Mental Disease, 152,* 129–139.

Starr, A., & Achor, L. J. (1975). Auditory brainstem responses in neurological disease. *Archives of Neurology, 32,* 761–768.

Starr, A., & Hamilton, A. E. (1976). Correlation between confirmed sites of neurological lesions and abnormalities of far-field brainstem responses. *Electroencephalography & Clinical Neurophysiology, 41,* 595–608.

Straumanis, J. J., Jr., Shagass, C., & Overton, D. A. (1973). Auditory evoked responses in young adults with Down's syndrome and idiopathic mental retardation. *Biological Psychiatry, 6,* 75–79.

Taylor, C. B., Telch, M. J., & Havvik, D. (1983). Ambulatory heart rate changes during panic attacks. *Journal of Psychiatric Research, 17,* 261–266.

Tecce, J. J., & Cattanach, L. (1987). Contingent negative variation. In E. Niedermeyer & F. Lopes da Silva (Eds.), *Electroencephalography: Basic principles, clinical applications and related fields* (pp. 657–679) Baltimore: Urban & Schwarzenberg.

Tecce, J. J. & Cole, J. O. (1976). The distraction-arousal hypothesis, CNV, and schizophrenia. In D. I. Mostofsky (Eds.), *Behavior control and modification of physiological activity* (pp. 162–219). Englewood Cliffs, NJ: Prentice-Hall.

Thackray, R. I., & Orne, M. T. (1968). A comparison of physiological indices in detection of deception. *Psychophysiology, 4,* 329–339.

Timsit-Berthier, M., Gerono, A., Rousseau, J. C., Mantanus, H., Abraham, P., Verhey, F. H. M.,

Lamers, T., & Emonds, P. (1984). An international pilot study of CNV in mental illness: Second report. In R. Karrer, J. Cohen, & P. Teuting (Eds.), *Brain and information: Event-related potentials* (Vol. 425, pp. 629–637). New York: New York Academy of Sciences.

Vaughan, H. G., Jr., & Arezzo, J. C. (1988). The neural basis of event related potentials. In T. W. Picton (Ed.), *Human event-related potentials* (Vol. III, pp. 45–96). Amsterdam: Elsevier.

Vaughan, H. G., & Katzman, R. (1964). Evoked response in visual disorders. *Annals of The New York Academy of Sciences, 112*, 305–319.

Vaughan, H. G., Katzman, R., & Taylor, J. (1963). Alterations of visual evoked response in the presence of homonymous visual defects. *Electroencephalography & Clinical Neurophysiology, 15*, 737–746.

Venables, P. H. (1975). Psychophysiological studies of schizophrenic pathology. In P. H. Venables & M. J. Christie (Eds.), *Research in psychophysiology* (pp. 282–324). New York: Wiley.

Venables, P. H. (1983). Some problems and controversies in the psychophysiological investigation of schizophrenia. In A. Gale & J. A. Edwards (Eds.), *Physiological correlates of human behavior* (Vol. 3, pp. 207–232). New York: Academic Press.

Weber, A., Fussler, C., O'Hanlon, J. F., Gierer, R., & Grandjean, E. (1980). Effects of repetitive work on physiological response. *Ergonomics, 23*, 1033–1046.

White, C. T., & Bonelli, L. (1970). Binocular ummation in the evoked potential as a function of image quality. *American Journal of Optometry and Archives of the American Academy of Optometry, 47*, 304–309.

White, C. T., & Hansen, D. (1975). Complex binocular interation and other effects in the visual evoked response. *American Journal of Optometry and Physiological Optics, 52*, 674–678.

Woodworth, R. S., & Schlosberg, H. (1954). *Experimental psychology*. New York: Holt.

Zeier, H. (1979). Concurrent physiological activity of driver and passenger when driving with and without automatic transmission in heavy city traffic. *Ergonomics, 22*, 799–810.

14

Clinical Applications
of Biofeedback

Biofeedback means providing immediate and continuous information regarding certain physiological processes about which the individual would normally be unaware. Thus, a person might be provided with data regarding muscle potentials in the left forearm, level of blood pressure, heart rate, or perhaps the type of brain wave being produced at the moment. A basic premise in biofeedback applications is that if an individual is given information about biological processes, and changes in their level, the person can learn to regulate this activity. Therefore, with appropriate conditioning and training techniques, an individual can presumably learn to control body processes that were long considered to be automatic and not subject to voluntary control, as well as to improve control of voluntary skeletal muscle. As is noted in this chapter, there is some evidence to support the basic premise that the provision of feedback has specific effects, for instance, that information about muscle tension and skin temperature can lead to self-altered levels of each.

The basic premise regarding learned control over physiological responses has theoretical and practical implications. On the theoretical side, it means that certain physiological processes controlled by the autonomic nervous system (e.g., blood pressure, heart rate, skin temperature) must be reexamined to determine the extent to which they are subject to voluntary self-regulation. On the practical side, it offers the possibility that physical maladies, such as hypertension (high blood pressure) or cardiac arrhythmias (irregular heartbeats), may be alleviated by self-regulation.

The studies reviewed in this chapter represent only a small portion of the large volume of clinically oriented biofeedback research that has been generated in the past two decades, and, hence, they can only be considered as a representative summary of the work performed. The attempt is to describe what clinical researchers have been doing and concluding about their applications of biofeedback to specific human disorders. The potential benefits of this research are great. However, overenthusiastic or premature claims about therapeutic effectiveness could harm the field by reducing its credibility. It bears repeating that biofeedback researchers and therapists would do well to heed the advice of Neal Miller (1974), who said, "This is a new area in which investigators should be bold in what they try but cautious in what they claim" (p. xviii).

There are a number of questions regarding biofeedback training (BFT) that require answers. For example:

1. What is actually learned as a consequence of BFT? Is it an awareness of some internal response, or is it an awareness of associations between stimuli and responses?,

2. What are the variables that influence learning, and how do they exert their effect? For example, what are the effects of the quality and quantity of reinforcements used to promote learning?

3. Which physiological responses are best to modify with respect to a specific disorder? For example, is lowering of blood pressure best achieved through feedback of BP, or is feedback of hand skin temperature more effective?

4. To what extent does transfer of training take place from the clinic or laboratory to real life? That is, can the individual self-regulate a physiological response at home as well as in the clinic?

5. How are the factors of motivation and expectancies to be handled in BFT? Are persons with greater motivation and expectations of success better able to learn physiological self-regulation?

6. To what degree does the BFT situation operate as a placebo effect? Are there nonspecific influences created by the equipment and related procedures because the patient believes in their effectiveness?

7. How does BFT compare with other possible approaches to altering physiological response, such as relaxation, meditation, suggestion, or hypnosis?

At the conclusion of this chapter, the reader should have some preliminary notions about the extent to which these questions have been answered by the representative summary of BFT research presented. Problems of a theoretical and empirical nature that confront biofeedback researchers are discussed in a thoughtful paper by Black and Cott (1977). The question of whether BFT has a specific effect on a target physiological function has sparked a lively debate among psychologists. Comments by Furedy (1987) regarding placebo versus specific effects hold that specific effects of biofeedback still need to be demonstrated. Shellenberger and Green (1987) have countered that biofeedback has no specific effects, because it is not the treatment. They contended that studies demonstrate the value of self-regulation (the treatment) for symptom alleviation. These opposing positions require resolution through research showing that BFT leads to self-regulation and that this produces specific effects that are clinically beneficial. Prior to examining clinical studies, a typical biofeedback situation, aimed at training a person to increase production of alpha EEG, is described.

AN EXAMPLE OF A BFT SITUATION

The production of alpha waves may be achieved by almost any person who relaxes with eyes closed in a quiet room. We define alpha activity here as a regular EEG signal, occurring between 8 and 13 cycles per second, at an amplitude of approximately 20 to 60 μV. It is more difficult to produce alpha activity with the eyes opened (e.g., see Brown, 1974).

Let us suppose that our objective is to attempt to train increases in the production of alpha activity under eyes-opened conditions and compare this with alpha training under an eyes-closed condition. The EEG may be recorded by some standard bipolar or monopolar electrode placement from over the occipital or parietal areas. Some commercially available equipment only permits the use of the bipolar technique. In this case an O_2-P_2, or an O_1-P_1 derivation may be used. The EEG activity is filtered and amplified by equipment that is set to produce a signal whenever the activity meets the criteria set up for alpha; in this instance, waves that occur at a frequency of 8 to 13 Hz and at an amplitude between 20 and 60 μV (see Fig. 14.1). Assume that the equipment provides the subject with a tone over headphones every time activity in the alpha range is detected. (An evaluation of various commercially available alpha feedback devices was compiled by Schwitzgebel & Rugh, 1975; and Rugh, 1979, provided a critical review of BFT devices in general.) The tone that occurs with alpha is the feedback that tells the person that he or she is achieving the desired response. The output of our alpha detecting equipment will also go to another device that records the amount of alpha activity produced during a given time period, for example, during a 1-minute or a 10-minute interval. Hence, a tone results when a person is producing alpha waves, and no tone occurs in the absence of alpha. The subject might simply be asked to keep the tone on as long as possible. At the end of each training segment (say, 1 minute), the person is informed about the actual amount of alpha produced or is simply told, "Very good, keep up the good work," and to try to keep the tone on for a longer period of time during the next training interval. Monetary rewards or other incentives can also be provided for good performance. The experimenter keeps a record of the amount of alpha activity produced over a number of training trials.

The BFT may continue for a number of days of weeks, and a record of performance plotted as a "learning curve" over the period of the experiment can be kept. The procedure should include the alternation of "alpha on" trials with

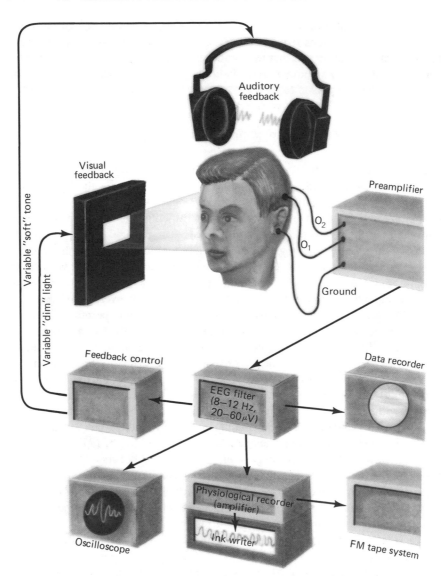

FIG. 14.1. Schematic drawing of alpha wave feedback instrumentation similar to that which might be used in a research setting. The physiological recorder and oscilloscope enable monitoring of the accuracy of EEG biofeedback. The amount of alpha activity is accumulated on the data recorder, which can provide digital readout or print. Information about amount of alpha production is fed back to the subject via headphones (tone) or visual display (light). This basic equipment array can be used to feed back information of a variety of physiological responses, according to a researchers needs. Sophisticated computer graphics may be displayed to subjects to provide more accurate feedback than simple lights or tones.

"no alpha" trials. In the latter case, the person is asked to prevent the tone from sounding. The object of this procedure is to allow the subject to clearly differentiate between the alpha and nonalpha situation, and it also ensures that increased alpha production is not merely due to unlearned baseline changes. The training in alpha on and alpha off (or bidirectionality) helps to clarify for the person what is being done and the sensory consequences involved. It is important, too, because it demonstrates the learned control of being able to turn a physiological response on or off as desired. An eventual goal of BFT is to have the person produce the desired physiological response without the benefit of the electronic equipment providing the feedback. Ways to achieve this include having subjects practice the production of alpha without the provision of feedback during regular training sessions, between sessions at home, and after training has been completed. Performance with and without feedback can be determined, that is, in terms of the percentage of alpha activity, under the two conditions. Alternatively, the feedback signal can be gradually removed so that it is less and less frequently presented over sessions, until it is completely absent. During the gradual removal of the feedback signal, the subject is informed about his or her level of alpha production after each trial. Subjects may return several months after the completion of training to test their retention of alpha-producing skills and for possible retraining sessions. This same basic procedure can be used in attempts to train regulation of other physiological responses such as blood pressure, heart rate, EMG, EDA, and skin temperature. A simple equipment configuration for providing EMG feedback is shown in Fig. 14.2. Many persons practicing BFT use this simpler form of instrumentation.

In the next section, we consider physiological measures that have been used in a BFT context in attempts to alleviate specific disorders.

THE ELECTROMYOGRAM (EMG) IN BIOFEEDBACK APPLICATIONS

The EMG has been used extensively in biofeedback applications ranging from the treatment of tension headache to attempts at the alleviation of stuttering.

EMG and Tension Headache

Tension headache usually results from sustained contraction of skeletal muscles of the forehead, scalp, and neck (Friedman & Merritt, 1959). Budzynski, Stoyva, and Adler (1970) have reported alleviation of tension headache by having patients reduce EMG levels in frontalis (forehead) and splenius (neck) muscles through BFT. In another report, Budzynski, Stoyva, Adler, and Mullaney (1973) demonstrated that a combined program of frontalis EMG feedback and relaxation practiced at the patient's home was effective in treating tension headaches.

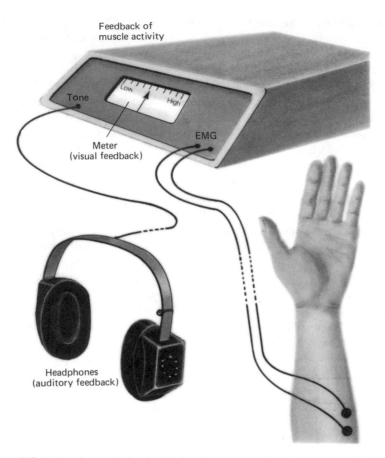

FIG. 14.2. A much simpler biofeedback system than that depicted in FIG. 14.1 may be used in clinical applications. The EMG system shown above illustrates the provision of information regarding changes in forearm EMG level. Decreased or increased EMG may be indicated by changes in tone, or lights and amount of change read off a visual scale.

The effectiveness of frontalis EMG biofeedback and passive relaxation instructions in treating tension headache was studied by Haynes, Griffin, Mooney, and Parise (1975). The college-student subjects were assigned to either a BFT group, a relaxation group, or a control group (no treatment). Both of the treatment procedures were more effective than no treatment in reducing the frequency of headaches. Essentially the same results were obtained by Cox, Freundlich, and Meyer (1975), who compared the efficacy of frontalis EMG/BFT, relaxation instructions, and a medication placebo on the frequency, duration, and intensity of tension headaches. The 27 subjects, who were equally divided among the three conditions, ranged in age from 16 to 64 years and had a history of chronic headache ranging from 1 to 39 years. The EMG feedback and relaxation instructions were found to be equally superior treatments to the glucose placebo in reducing headache activity and frontalis EMG. The feedback and relaxation effects were similar.

Hutchings and Reinking (1976) compared the effectiveness of three forms of muscle relaxation training in tension headache control. The group that had EMG biofeedback-assisted relaxation showed larger gains than the relaxation alone groups. A follow-up study of these patients (Reinking & Hutchings, 1981) indicated that at 6 and 9 months after sessions ended, the most important variable in continued success was whether patients still practiced relaxation exercises. Thus, although EMG-assisted relaxation led to faster acquisition of lower muscle activity, other variables were important in determining whether patients continued to use what was learned. Among these were belief in the treatment process and reported changes in personality variables following treatment. The importance of continued practice of relaxation techniques and transfer of the relaxation response to everyday situations were emphasized as important for continuance of the improvement initially attained. Thus, EMG/BFT, relaxation techniques, and combinations of the two help to alleviate tension headaches. More information is needed about the duration of the beneficial effects and the relative effectiveness of the various techniques in treating tension headache.

In several of the studies cited, relaxation techniques were as effective as EMG feedback in alleviating tension headache. A valid question for clinical researchers to provide an answer to is "why use the EMG devices if relaxation alone can benefit the patient?" A number of good relaxation techniques do exist, and these include progressive muscle relaxation, autogenic phrases, breathing exercises, visual imagery techniques, meditation, and others. Thus, the clinician has a large number of techniques that could be used alone or in combination with physiological feedback. Whenever relaxation techniques are combined with BFT, it will be difficult to separate out the effects of each in the clinical or research situation. However, most clinicians feel comfortable using this combination because they maintain that it is important in achieving criterion levels of physiological activity and in selecting the most effective relaxation techniques. Many of them argue that the biofeedback equipment provides objective indications of physiological change, and the amount of change, as treatment progresses, and it helps to convince patients that they can learn to self-regulate certain physiological responses, such as skin temperature, muscle tension, and heart rate. The relaxation techniques are seen as vehicles to lower autonomic, skeletal, and CNS activity to produce physiological levels that are then reinforced by feedback from the equipment. There is at least one study indicating that frontalis EMG biofeedback led to improvements in tension headache sufferers when relaxation techniques alone failed (Blanchard et al., 1982). The possibility still exists that the equipment produces at least some beneficial results through a placebo effect, that is, a nonspecific influence that the equipment has because the patient believes in its effectiveness. As stated previously, this is an issue that biofeedback researchers need to address in order to separate out specific and placebo effects. With regard to equipment placebo effects, researchers could compare the effectiveness of BFT provided by equipment versus feedback provided verbally, with no equipment visible, in promoting physiological change.

EMG Feedback and Stuttering

It has been established that between 40 and 50 million children in the Western world stutter badly (Coleman, 1976). This speech disorder is characterized by blocking of speech or the repetition of initial sounds of words, especially in a socially stressful situation. In an application of EMG feedback to stuttering, Guitar (1975) trained three adult male stutterers to reduce facial and neck EMG prior to speaking selected sentences. Decreases in stuttering were associated with decreased lip EMG in one patient, lower EMG at a laryngeal site in another, and a combination of lip and laryngeal EMG decrease in the third. A systematic program was then instituted with a 32-year-old male stutterer, in which feedback training to reduce EMG during speech resulted in the elimination of stuttering during both face to face conversations and telephone calls. A follow-up showed that stuttering was still substantially improved 9 months after laboratory had training ended.

Lanyon, Barrington, and Newman (1976) found that feedback of masseter (jaw) muscle activity led to a reduction of muscle tension. The reduction in tension was associated with a major reduction in stuttering in the six persons studied. In a follow-up investigation, Lanyon (1977) taught 19 stutterers to relax their masseter muscles under conditions of EMG feedback. In a series of three studies, it was found that reduced muscle tension was followed by reduced stuttering. Lanyon also reported that relaxation was generalized to periods of no EMG feedback after explicit instructions and constant reminders to do so were given.

A hypothesis made by Craig and Cleary (1982) was that EMG of the speech musculature is higher for stuttered than for non-stuttered words. They confirmed this hypothesis in a clinical study with three young males (aged 10, 13, and 14). The patients were trained to reduce speech muscle tension (levator and superior orbiculoris oris muscles) with EMG feedback. Stuttering was reduced in the clinic, and then was reduced 60–80% in the home environment. A 9-month follow-up showed continued improvement. The case studies reported on here are uncontrolled; that is, there is no comparison of results for individuals who did not receive the treatment over the study period. However, the use of EMG biofeedback may offer a viable treatment for stuttering. As with any application, further clinical trials and controlled investigations are required to separate biofeedback effects from other treatment variables such as therapist attention, verbal exchanges, suggestions for managing stress, the clinical atmosphere, or simply participating in a self-help program.

EMG Feedback in Neuromuscular Disorder

The amplification and feedback of EMG signals has been found to be helpful in neuromuscular re-education. Basmajian, Kukulka, Narayan, and Takebe (1975) have used EMG feedback to assist patients in improving the strength and voluntary control of muscles that are weak, unreliable, and poorly controlled as a result of a stroke. One condition that may occur after a stroke is "foot drop." Paralytic foot drop is characterized by an inability to contract the muscles that bend the ankle to raise the foot. The patient often wears a brace to assist in walking. Basmajian and colleagues divided 20 patients with foot drop into two therapeutic groups: (a) 40 minutes of exercise, three times a week for 5 weeks, and (b) 20 minutes of exercise and 20 minutes of EMG/BFT over the same period. The tibialis anterior muscle (lower leg) was selected for training, because it is the main muscle involved in lifting the ankle. The group receiving BFT showed an improvement in both strength of flexion and range of movement that was approximately twice as great as the other group. In addition, three patients in the BFT group were able to discard their braces. In another clinical study, Takebe and Basmajian (1976) found that patients treated with a peroneal nerve (leg) stimulator for 5 weeks and those treated with BFT for 5 weeks showed and maintained improvement of their walking pattern as compared to patients who received physical therapy only. These investigators believe that the feedback indicating residual muscle activity can play an important role in muscular re-education in stroke patients. In an update, Basmajian, Regenos, and Baker (1977) reported that, of 25 patients treated for foot drop, 16 were able to discard their leg braces entirely after 3 to 25 sessions. In addition, age of the patient and duration of the foot-drop condition did not affect the treatment outcome. Failures were related to poor motivation, discontinuance of treatment, spasticity, or concurrent illnesses.

Middaugh (1977) reported on the use of EMG/BFT with 12 patients suffering from neuromuscular dysfunction because of nervous system damage. The subjects were asked to produce 30-second contractions in a muscle that was below functional strength. The EMG feedback, in each of the two sessions, was a continuous tone that varied in pitch proportional to the amount of activity. A comparison of results for feedback versus no-feedback trials revealed that EMG activity was an average of 16% higher on feedback trials (a significant difference). Time since injury was not a factor, and all patients showed a positive effect. Thus, Middaugh concluded that EMG feedback had a substantial effect on motor unit recruitment that was independent of locus of nervous system damage or time since occurrence of the injury.

A variety of clinical studies in which EMG feedback was used in attempts to treat the muscular symptoms of a wide variety of disorders including cerebral palsy, poliomyelitis, hemiplegia, torticollis, and rectosphincter incontinence were discussed by Engel-Sittenfeld (1977). Fairly successful results were achieved with torticollis and rectosphincter responses. Torticollis is a movement disorder in which spasms in the neck muscles cause the head to be twisted back and disrupt normal head control. Alleviation of torticollis through the reduction of muscle tension via EMG feedback has been reported by several investigators (e.g., Cleeland, 1973). Control of the rectal sphincter muscle was achieved by six incontinent patients, aged 6 to 54, with BFT (Engle, Nikoomanesh, & Schuster, 1974). Follow-ups at periods ranging from 6 months to 5 years found four patients completely continent and the other two improved.

The use of monetary incentives to enhance EMG feedback was studied in five stroke patients with paralysis on one side of the body (Santee, Keister & Kleinman, 1980). Integrated EMG from tibialis and gastrocnemius muscles during flexion of the affected foot was recorded. The EMG feedback training produced greater range of motion than unassisted practice, and the addition of monetary incentives improved the effects.

The promising results obtained thus far argue for the further clinical evaluation of BFT in treating neuromuscular disorders. Basmajian and Hatch (1979) concluded that EMG biofeedback is a significant tool in the re-education of weak muscles and the relaxation of hyperactive ones.

EMG Feedback and Anxiety

It is estimated that 5% of persons in the United States suffer from chronic anxiety: "a persistent or recurrent state of dread or apprehension accompanied by signs of physiological arousal" (Raskin, Johnson, & Rondestvedt, 1973, p. 263). The effects of deep muscle relaxation, achieved through frontalis muscle BFT, on 10 chronically anxious patients was investigated by Raskin et al., (1973). (Middaugh has pointed out, in a personal communication, that frontalis feedback primarily involves facial muscles, and simultaneous relaxation of muscles throughout the body does not necessarily occur. The term "deep muscle relaxation" implies generalized effects that are not yet established.) The patients in the Raskin study had not been helped by psychotherapy or medication for the 2-year period before the investigation. All 10 patients reached the criterion of 2.5 μV/min of EMG activity or less, averaged over a 25-minute period. The training time of the daily sessions varied from 2 to 12 weeks. Four of the 10 persons improved in self-ratings of anxiety level. The relaxation training had impressive effects on the insomnia of five of the six patients with sleep disturbances. In addition, the four patients with headaches experienced a reduction in the frequency and intensity of their headaches.

The effectiveness of frontalis EMG/BFT and muscle relaxation training were compared for 28 anxiety neurotics (Canter, Kondo, & Knott 1975). One half of

them reported panic episodes (e.g., tachycardia, difficulty breathing, etc.) associated with the anxiety. The EMG/BFT resulted in lower levels of muscle activity and greater relief of anxiety than progressive muscle relaxation alone for
the majority of patients. Gatchel, Korman, Weis, Smith, and Clarke (1978)
showed BFT more effective in EMG reduction than false feedback, but there was
no differential effect on anxiety reduction. A positive result was obtained by
Weinman, Semchuk, Gaebe, and Mathew (1983), who hypothesized that BFT
along with relaxation training would be more effective for anxious patients with
high amounts of recent life stress than those with low amounts. The results
supported the hypothesis, as the high-stress group showed changes on anxiety
measures, depression, and EMG, whereas the low-stress individuals showed no
change after 10 sessions of biofeedback-assisted relaxation. The high-stress
group attributed improvement to the belief that they were in control of their
minds and bodies.

The evaluation of these anxiety studies is made difficult because most of them
were uncontrolled. However, the results of several clinical studies and the one
controlled investigation suggest that EMG/BFT is useful with certain types of
anxiety.

EMG Feedback and Asthma

Frontalis EMG relaxation has been used in a BFT situation with asthmatic
patients (Fried, 1974). Asthma is characterized by episodes of bronchospasm,
during which the person has great difficulty in breathing. The episode or bronchospasm may be initiated by allergens in the environment, by emotional reactions, or both (Bates, Macklem, & Christie 1971). One aspect of the EMG
feedback strategy is that it might enhance the effects of more general relaxation
training procedures. In Fried's study, the feedback of auditory clicks provided
information about rising EMG in the forehead muscles. The patients were trained
to keep the EMG at a low level during the presentation of slides depicting
flowers, trees, dust, or whatever was usually effective in the induction of an
asthmatic attack. This procedure seemed to reduce the number and severity of
attacks and enabled the person to feel that he had more control over the situation.

In another study, Kotses, Glaus, Crawford, Edwards, and Scherr (1976)
investigated the effects of operantly produced frontalis muscle relaxation on peak
expiratory flow rates (PEFR) scores in asthmatic children. The PEFR is a measure of efficiency in expelling air from the lungs. The subjects were 36 asthmatic
summer campers ranging in age from 8 to 16 years. They were divided into a
contingent feedback group, a noncontingent feedback group, and a no-treatment
group. The contingent feedback group received a tone for changes in EMG,
whereas the noncontingent received tones that were not related to EMG in any
systematic fashion. These two groups participated in nine sessions spread over 3
weeks. PEFR was obtained daily from all 36 subjects by persons who were

unaware that it would be used in a study. The EMG training group showed an increase in PEFR over the pretraining level, whereas the noncontingent and no-treatment groups did not evidence a change. The researchers concluded that the reduction of frontalis EMG through BFT was associated with the alleviation of some symptoms of bronchial asthma. Kotses and his associates repeated these results in a follow-up study (Kotses, Glaus, Bricel, Edwards, & Crawford, 1978). Other studies indicated that PEFR was influenced by changes in facial EMG and not in limb muscles, an effect seen in both asthmatics and normals (Kotses & Glaus, 1981). These workers indicated that the underlying mechanisms for this relationship between facial muscle tension changes and PEFR is not understood clearly at this time, and that work is needed to determine whether the EMG changes initiate reflex activities that affect breathing. According to Kotses and Glaus (1981), only facial muscle feedback and airways resistance feedback (information about resistance in breathing structures and lung airways) have produced short-term breathing improvements in asthmatics. Long-term effects of these treatments are unknown. Thus, a great deal of research effort is required before techniques such as these can be used alone or as a supplement to current treatment of asthmatics. A promising approach involves training asthmatics to respond to provoking stimuli with slow diaphragmatic breathing and relaxation (reported by Tibbetts & Peper in the 1988 Proceedings of the Biofeedback Society of America). The technique includes the use of an inexpensive spirometer to provide feedback about inhalation volume, and encouraging results were reported.

Feedback and Hyperactivity

The term *hyperactivity* is used to describe a group of symptoms that include overactivity, short attention span, impulsivity, low frustration tolerance, and in some cases, aggressive behavior. Hyperactivity is often associated with "attention deficit disorder." A widely used drug to control hyperactivity is methylphenidate (Ritalin), a stimulant that paradoxically acts a tranquilizer on children. According to a 1987 estimate by the drug's manufacturer, it is prescribed for 500,000 patients annually. Possible side effects are nausea and stunted growth with long-term use.

Frontalis EMG was recorded and fed back to a hyperactive 6-year-old boy during 11 sessions over an 8-week period (Braud, Lupin, & Braud, 1975). The boy was asked to turn off a tone that signaled the presence of muscular tension. EMG level decreased within and across training sessions. Improvement was observed in school and at home as long as the boy continued to practice and use the techniques of relaxation learned in the laboratory. This suggestive study was followed up by a larger-scale one (Braud, 1978). The effects of frontalis EMG/BFT and progressive relaxation was examined with 15 hyperactive children (6 to 13 years) and 15 nonhyperactives (6 to 15 years). Both EMG and progressive relaxation exercises resulted in muscular tension reductions in all subjects over 12 sessions. In the hyperactives, improvements in behavioral ratings (especially aggression) and test scores (digit span, coding) were observed. The improvements occurred in both medicated and unmedicated hyperactives, but were more pronounced in the nonmedicated individuals. One possibility is that the nonmedicated children were more motivated to learn the self-control techniques because they could not depend on medication.

A study using EMG-assisted relaxation training with hyperactives was reported by Denkowski, Denkowski, and Omizo (1983). Forty-eight hyperactive males, aged 11–14 were assigned to treatment and control groups. The treatment consisted of frontalis EMG feedback combined with imagery relaxation techniques once every 2 weeks over a period of 12 weeks. The controls attended sessions without feedback or relaxation being introduced. Pre- and post-session measures showed EMG reduction and improved reading and language scores for the treatment group, but not for controls. In addition, locus of control changed from external to internal for the biofeedback group, suggesting a greater feeling of self-control. A follow-up study by Denkowski, Denkowski, and Omizo (1984) implicated locus of control as a predictor of success in EMG treatment of hyperactivity. This suggests that internally oriented individuals are better at gaining control over their own physiological processes. A variety of results with hyperactives indicate improved academic performance, increased self-control, and a decrease in disruptive behavior as a function of EMG-assisted relaxation. Hence, this approach certainly merits further consideration as a primary or adjunct treatment for hyperactivity.

THE EEG IN BIOFEEDBACK APPLICATIONS

EEG Biofeedback and Epilepsy

Three delineated forms of epilepsy—grand mal, petit mal, and psychomotor—produce seizures or attacks that are accompanied by disturbances in the EEG pattern. There are many neurological conditions that lead to epileptic seizures, and, therefore, the cause of seizures may differ from one patient to another. The Epilepsy Foundation estimates that there are 4 million epileptics in the United States. About 20% to 25% of epileptics have poorly controlled seizures, even with medication.

Attempts to treat epilepsy have focused on influencing the EEG pattern through BFT. The use of EEG/BFT to reduce incidence of seizures stems from the work of Sterman and colleagues, who noted an increase in 12–16 Hz EEG in cats given reinforcement for suppressing a bar-pressing response. This 12–16 Hz activity was termed the *sensorimotor rhythm* (SMR), because it was most prominent over sensorimotor cortex. The finding that cats previously trained to enhance SMR activity were able to delay the onset of seizures induced by a convulsant drug led Sterman and associates to try SMR training in epileptic patients. For example, Sterman and Friar (1972) reported the suppression of seizures in an epileptic patient who had been conditioned to produce 11 to 14 Hz EEG through BFT. Sterman (1973) has suggested that the SMR may be an EEG phenomenon related to brain mechanisms that mediate motor suppression. The reduction of seizures in severe epileptics using SMR training has been reported subsequently by a number of investigators.

Sterman, MacDonald, and Stone (1974) reported that four epileptics had a reduction in seizure frequency when biofeedback was used to train the production of 12 to 14 Hz EEG from over the Rolandic (central) cortex. Seifert and Lubar (1975) worked with three male and three female adolescent epileptics whose seizures were not well controlled by drugs. The patients were provided with feedback whenever they produced a half-second of 12 to 14 Hz activity of a specified magnitude. They observed a significant reduction in the number of seizures during the first 3 to 4 months of treatment in five of the six epileptics. The BFT sessions were 40 minutes long and scheduled three times a week.

Sensory motor rhythm training was used with eight epileptics whose seizures were frequent, severe, and not controlled by anticonvulsant drugs (Lubar & Bahler, 1976). Six of the eight patients were studied in an extension of SMR training initiated by Seifert and Lubar (1975). In addition to 12 to 14 Hz activity, patients were provided feedback of 4 to 7 Hz activity that indicated epileptiform spike activity. They were to suppress their epileptiform activity. The patients continued to show improvement in the form of decreased seizure frequency. The addition of feedback regarding epileptiform activity enabled some patients to develop the ability to block many of their seizures. The more successful patients demonstrated an increase in the amount and amplitude of SMR during the training period.

A lack of relation between the SMR and seizure reduction was reported by Kuhlman and Allison (1977). These investigators used both contingent and non-contingent feedback to train 9 to 14 Hz Rolandic EEG activity. Although seizure reduction occurred in three of the five patients, it was associated with increases in the amount and frequency of alpha, and not with enhancement of the SMR. Johnson and Meyer (1974) used a sequence of relaxation training, EMG feedback, and feedback of alpha and theta EEG frequencies with an 18-year-old epileptic who had suffered severe grand mal seizures since the age of 8. After the relaxation and EMG feedback phases, EEG training was administered in 36 sessions over a 1-year period. Seizure frequency dropped by 46% during the 12-month period. A 3-month follow-up subsequent to the end of training indicated that seizure rate remained at the lower level. Kuhlman (1978) suggested that the human analog of the 12–16 Hz SMR in cats is an EEG of 8–13 Hz, and he called this rhythm *Mu*. The features of Mu that distinguish it from alpha are that it is localized to the sensorimotor area, it occurs in the absence of movement, and it is not attenuated by visual stimulation. The contention that the SMR in cats does not have a human analog in the same frequency range is controversial, and has not yet been resolved. Kuhlman (1978) trained an increase in 9–14 Hz EEG from sensorimotor area of five patients. He controlled for placebo effects by giving 12 initial sessions during which feedback was noncontingent to the EEG. After 50 training sessions, seizure reductions occurred in 3 of 5 patients (average of 60% decrease). The EEG changes were mixed: one successful patient showed increased alpha, one shifted to higher frequencies, and the third had a decrease in slow-wave activity. Kuhlman suggested that a "normalization" of EEG occurred for these three patients.

A study was conducted by Whitsett, Lubar, Holder, Pamplin, and Shabsin (1982) to examine EEG/BFT with 8 severely epileptic patients. All experienced multiple seizures each month, and were not helped by drugs. The study was conducted double-blind so that neither patients nor technicians knew the feedback contingencies. The patients were reinforced initially for (a) suppression of 3–7 Hz activity, (b) enhancement of 12 to 15 Hz, or (c) simultaneous suppression of 3–7 enhancement of 12–15 Hz activity. Sleep recordings of EEG provided support for the hypothesis that EEG/BFT led to changes in epileptic EEG that were reflected in sleep recordings. Thus, they concluded that EEG/BFT can produce changes in epileptic patients that result in an alteration of both seizure pattern and the sleep EEG. A novel approach was used by Sterman (1984), who reported on the use of a computer soccer game to provide feedback of SMR. In the game, a ball moves into the goal area when 12–15 Hz activity occurs, and the goal defense is eliminated when 4–7 Hz activity is suppressed. Training sessions were carried out for 6 weeks, with three per week. Sterman reported a reduction of seizure rates by more than 50% with contingent BFT. Comparison of pre- and post-BFT sleep EEG showed that normalization of abnormal EEG with contingent SMR enhancement and 4–7 Hz suppression was related to greater amounts of seizure reduction (60%). Sterman believes that the changes seen with SMR training are due to decreases in abnormal thalamocortical excitability that occur with training.

In summary, suggestive findings indicate a relation between EEG/BFT and seizure reduction in epilepsy. Training in a specific EEG frequency does not seem necessary for achieving "normalization" of brain wave pattern. The best approach for training seems to involve suppressing epileptiform activity and enhancing normal EEG patterns, regardless of the particular frequency. The combined procedure of enhancing 12–15 Hz activity while reducing 4–7 Hz activity, used by Sterman as one example, seems to have promise. The disabling nature of epileptic seizures for so many individuals and the detrimental side effects of medications used are strong arguments for continued funding of this type of research by governmental agencies. Research on EEG/BFT with epileptics is time-consuming and costly; however, the potential benefits are great.

EEG/BFT: Drug Use and Chronic Pain

The effects of EEG alpha and EMG feedback on anxiety, marijuana use, and sleep were studied by Lamontagne, Hand, Annable, and Gagnon (1975). Three groups of eight persons each were assigned to either EEG, EMG, or control conditions and did not know which treatment they were receiving. Training was limited to 40-minute sessions on four consecutive days. The EMG group maintained an improved level of muscular relaxation during training, whereas the EEG group failed to retain gains in alpha from one session to the next. A slight reduction in drug use was observed during training and at follow-up periods of 3 and 6 months. Improvements in duration and quality of sleep were observed in all groups (including control subjects), suggesting a possible placebo effect associated with participating in the study.

Melzack and Perry (1975) worked with 24 patients suffering from chronic pain of pathological origin, including cancer. A combination of alpha feedback training, hypnotic training, and placebo effects reduced pain in a significant number of patients. Although the majority of patients learned to increase alpha activity during training sessions, the investigators concluded that pain relief results not from the increase in this EEG activity, but from suggestion, relaxation, and the feeling of being able to control pain that resulted from participation in the study.

In a review of clinical applications, Kuhlman and Kaplan (1979) found little evidence to support the use of EEG/BFT with drug abusers or with various types of pain (e.g., migraine or tension headache). A major part of any improvements observed could be accounted for by placebo and other nonspecific factors.

Biofeedback of Heart Activity

Operant conditioning of HR was used with eight patients who suffered from premature ventricular contractions (PVCs), by Weiss and Engel (1971). The PVC is a dangerous irregularity in the heartbeat. The training included approximately 30 sessions, 10 of which involved learning to increase HR, 10 in which HR decrease was taught, and 10 in which HR decreases and increase were alternated throughout the session. Decreases in the number of PVCs were associated with the slowing of HR. Five of the eight patients were able to control their PVCs in the laboratory and to transfer the learned effect outside the laboratory. Training with the other three patients was not successful. In two of these cases, the hearts may have been too diseased to beat regularly for prolonged periods of time.

A 29-year-old woman with sinus tachycardia (periodic occurrence of occasional very fast HR, in this case from 200 to 240 bpm) was taught to regulate her HR with BFT (Bleecker & Engel, 1973). The patient was alternately trained to increase and decrease her HR. The presence of a green light indicated that HR was to be quickened, whereas a red light meant that she was to slow her HR. A yellow light indicated the desired state. The patient was ultimately able to control her HR away from the laboratory without feedback. However, Weiss and Engel (1975) were unable to consistently increase ventricular heart rate (VHR) in three patients with complete heart block. The three patients suffered from a condition in which the atria and ventricles beat with independent rhythms. The atrial rhythm was normal, but the ventricular rhythm was abnormally slow (e.g., 30 to 45 bpm). The inability to alter VHR with BFT was attributed to the interruption of impulse conduction between the atria and ventricles of the heart in these patients.

Patients with ischemic heart disease (inadequate blood supply to the heart) were not as capable as an age-matched sample of healthy males or a group of college students in learning to modify their HR via BFT (Lang, Troyer, Twentyman, & Gatchel, 1975). The college students had the best performance in terms of ability to learn to increase and decrease HR. The authors interpreted the results as supporting the hypothesis that age and disease interfere with ability to profit from feedback training in the control of HR.

This brief presentation suggests that heartbeat irregularities may be amenable to biofeedback training. As Engel (1977) has indicated, there is insufficient data to allow a definitive evaluation of BFT as a primary therapy or as an adjunct therapy in these cardiac disorders. However, sufficient evidence exists to encourage the clinical testing of BFT alone and in conjunction with other therapy in the treatment of various heart irregularities.

BLOOD PRESSURE AND BFT APPLICATIONS

The cardiovascular abnormality known as high blood pressure, or hypertension, is estimated to occur in 5% to 10% of the general population in the United States (Shapiro, Mainardi, & Surwit, 1977). One of the first studies to use BFT in an attempt to regulate hypertension via BFT was that of Benson, Shapiro, Tursky, and Schwartz (1971). They used BFT with seven patients suffering from high blood pressure. Decreases in systolic blood pressure, ranging from 16 to 34 mm Hg, were obtained in five of the individuals. The effectiveness of the training in terms of transfer outside of the laboratory situation is not known, because no follow-up data were obtained.

Schwartz and Shapiro (1973) discussed general procedures, findings, and theoretical issues in the biofeedback training of blood pressure regulation. They noted that a common training procedure is to provide "binary" feedback, that is, the subject knows with each heartbeat whether blood pressure has gone up or down. In the binary feedback–reward situation, the subject is provided with information regarding momentary fluctuations in blood pressure, and a reward is presented for a sustained (tonic) change in some direction (e.g., when systolic pressure has decreased by at least 5 mm Hg). They also pointed out that "baseline" blood pressure values may change either up or down over a session, independent of learning. For example, increases may occur if the stimuli used for feedback or reward are arousing, and decreases will be observed as subjects adapt to the experimental situation. Thus, researchers must be careful to control for these in order not to misinterpret changes from baseline as indicating a therapeutic effect. Schwartz and Shapiro mentioned that the novelty of the experimental situation plus expectancy may operate as a placebo effect, thus making it difficult to assess the effects of BFT alone. However, the placebo effect should not be regarded in a negative light. Stroebel and Glueck (1973) pointed out that the novelty of a BFT situation with its equipment, feedback displays, and the possibility for self-regulation of certain processes may produce a placebo effect that has good results, especially, for example, if it can produce a reduction in the blood pressure of hypertensives. There are difficulties associated with depending on placebo effects, because not enough is known about the conditions and types of persons in which they are operative. Hence, the utility of a placebo as a method of treatment is limited, because these unknowns make the control of this effect very difficult.

Motivation looms as an important factor in any learning situation, and is crucial in BFT. The problem of motivating hypertensive patients has been discussed by Schwartz and Shapiro (1973), who noted that, unlike the tension headache patient, individuals with high blood pressure typically have little or no discomfort from this condition. The rewarding effects of blood pressure reduction, therefore, are not readily recognized by the patient, and it is important to ensure that these patients are properly motivated in the BFT situation.

Elder, Ruiz, Deabler, and Dillendoffer (1973) studied a group of 18 hypertensive patients in an experimental design that assigned 6 patients to a nonfeedback (control) group, 6 to a group who were given feedback (light) for reductions in diastolic pressure, and 6 who were given verbal praise as well as the feedback. The combination of feedback plus praise produced decreases in diastolic pressure up to 25% of baseline over a period of 4 days. Both feedback groups showed decreases compared to the control group, which essentially stayed at the same level throughout the pretraining and training sessions. An interesting aspect was the decrease in systolic pressure that occurred even though feedback was provided only for decreases in diastolic pressure. A follow-up 1 week after the final session showed blood pressure at levels similar to those recorded in the last training session.

A simple feedback system for teaching hypertensive patients to lower their pressure was described by Blanchard, Young, and Haynes (1975). The patient received feedback of systolic pressure each minute via a closed-circuit television display. The technique was found effective in reducing the pressure of four hypertensive patients. Seven hypertensive patients participated in 2-hour BFT sessions over a 9-week period in a study conducted by Goldman, Kleinman,

Snow, Bidus, and Korol (1975). Feedback, contingent upon beat-by-beat decreases in systolic pressure, was provided by an automated blood pressure monitoring system. Four control subjects had three weekly sessions in which blood pressure was monitored without feedback. Significant decreases in both systolic and diastolic pressure were reported for the patients but not for the control group.

A number of hypertensive patients were taught to control and reduce their level of systolic BP in a study conducted by Kristt and Engel (1975). Pre-BFT BP readings were first compiled at home over a 7-week period. Then the patients were trained to raise, to lower, and to alternately raise and lower systolic BP. Finally, BP readings were taken at home during a 3-month follow-up period. Reductions in BP between 10% to 15% occurred between the pretraining period and the follow-up. Changes in diastolic and systolic BP were observed. The lowered pressures occurred in patients suffering from a variety of ailments, including heart arhythmias and cardiomegaly (enlarged heart).

This brief review of BP biofeedback in treating hypertension indicates that it may have clinical value. However, feedback of other physiological measures, such as skin conductance level (SCL) and EMG, combined with relaxation techniques, have proven effective in lowering the BP of hypertensives. Several well-conducted studies of Patel and associates have illustrated the benefits of a treatment program in which biofeedback is only one element. Yoga exercises for complete mental and physical relaxation, combined with BFT of SCL, led to improved blood pressure levels in 16 of 20 hypertensive patients (Patel, 1973). Patel used SCL, instead of continuous blood pressure feedback, because she wanted to avoid entering an artery to obtain direct readings. (Other investigators mentioned in this section obtained indirect BP readings, i.e., without entering an artery.) Patel attributed the beneficial effects to the control of SNS activity through yogic relaxation and through BFT influence over SCL (a response controlled by the SNS). The patients participated in $\frac{1}{2}$-hour sessions, three times a week, over a period of 3 months and showed average decreases of 25mm Hg for systolic BP and 14mm for diastolic. In a second study, Patel (1975) found average decreases in systolic BP of 26 to 28mm Hg and 15 to 16mm Hg for diastolic. These improvements were maintained at follow-up 12 months later. In a well-controlled study, Patel and North (1975) shortened the procedure to 12 sessions over 6 weeks and again achieved lowered BP in hypertensives. This time, the experimental subjects were treated first and evidenced improvements. Later, the controls were treated and showed similar gains. Follow-ups at 4 and 7 months showed that improvements were still in evidence. Patel seems to have developed an effective combination of feedback and relaxation training to achieve reduction of BP in hypertensives. An important aspect of her program is the practice of relaxation exercises at home. The continuance of relaxation exercises on a regular basis after the formal program has ended is essential if the gains realized are to continue. Although this puts demands on the person, a positive aspect of this is that the relaxation techniques do not have side effects and are not as costly as medications that might otherwise have to be used. The next section discusses applications of skin temperature measurements in BFT, and includes studies using ST with hypertensives.

APPLICATIONS OF SKIN TEMPERATURE BFT

Skin Temperature BFT and Raynaud's Disease

Skin temperature (ST) has been found to be related to blood flow in skin tissue as measured by plethysmography (Sargent et al., 1972). Thus, increases or decreases in ST would be related to vasodilation and vasoconstriction of blood vessels. Because degree of vasoconstriction is under sympathetic control, ST is an indirect measure of SNS activity. The continuous measurement of ST involves low cost and portable instrumentation with sensors that can be conveniently applied to numerous body areas. This makes ST especially attractive as a measure in ailments that involve changes in ST or SNS activity.

The BFT of ST has been described in the treatment of patients suffering from Raynaud's disease by Surwit, Pilon, and Fenton (1977) and Taub (1977). The symptoms of Raynaud's disease include intermittent constriction of arteries or arterioles of the hands and feet (vasopastic attacks). During an episode, the affected extremities (fingers or toes) undergo sequential color changes; from white to deep blue to bright red. The fingers become cold and numb, and pain can be severe and debilitating. The symptoms are elicited by cold and/or emotional stress and may be temporarily alleviated by heat. One postulated mechanism for Raynaud's is a hyperactive SNS, and a common treatment has been sympathectomy, a procedure in which SNS innervation of the blood vessels is surgically interrupted. According to Sedlacek (1979), many patients remain untreated because they have been told there is little that can be done about the disorder. The disease affects four times as many women as men.

Surwit et al. (1977) trained 30 female patients with Raynaud's disease to control finger ST with either autogenic training or a combination of autogenic training and feedback of skin temperature. Autogenic relaxation requires that the patient repeat certain phrases presented on a tape or in writing. The phrases involve suggestions of "heaviness and warmth" in various body areas, for example, "my hands feel heavy and warm." In the study by Surwit and colleagues, patients were trained either at home or in the laboratory. All were able to maintain finger skin temperature in a cold environment (exposure to temperatures down to 63 degrees F for a period of 1 hour). In addition, the patients reported significant reductions in both frequency and intensity of attacks. There was no difference between the autogenic training alone, as compared to autogenic training plus skin temperature feedback. These researchers suggested that other forms of relaxation, including meditation, progressive relaxation, or various forms of yoga, be investigated as possible aids in the treatment of Raynaud's disease.

The training of three Raynaud's disease patients to self-regulate increases in hand temperature was reported by Taub (1977). At times, patients began sessions with hand temperatures at or only slightly above room temperature. For example, at a room temperature of 70 degrees F, a patient might have a hand ST of only 70 to 72 degrees. At the same room temperature, a normal person would have a ST of about 85 to 90 degrees F. With training, the patients were able to increase hand temperature into the normal range. After 20 training sessions, 2 patients reported decreases in the number and severity of attacks and the ability to prevent them by using, without feedback, techniques learned in the laboratory. The third patient, also trained in the winter, avoided the cold, and training effects could not be evaluated. Sedlacek (1979) reported that 80% of 20 Raynaud's patients in his private practice successfully learned self-regulation of symptoms caused by vascular spasms. Patients practiced home exercises for 15 minutes two times a day. If patients stop home practice or are over-stressed, symptoms often return. Follow-ups at 12 to 36 months showed all but two of the successful patients in control of the symptoms. Freedman, Lynn, Ianni, and Hale (1981) used ST feedback in the treatment of 6 patients with Raynaud's disease and 4 with Raynaud's phenomenon. The distinction is that whereas Raynaud's disease cannot be explained by a known pathology, Raynaud's phenomenon is due to some physical disorder, for example, rheumatoid arthritis. Twelve sessions of ST feedback alone allowed all 10 patients to decrease their symptoms to 7.5% of the original frequencies, and to maintain improvement throughout a full year of climatic changes. The results cited so far, although clinically impressive, were obtained in the absence of an untreated control group.

A controlled study of ST biofeedback in Raynaud's disease was conducted by Guglielmi, Roberts, and Patterson (1982). Thirty-six patients were assigned to a ST increase group (12), an EMG relaxation group (12), and a no-treatment control group (12). Patients in the training groups had 20 sessions, and all 36 kept records of their symptoms throughout the study. Although all patients reported a marked improvement in symptoms, there were no statistically significant differences among the 3 groups in number and duration of vasospastic attacks. The authors attributed the improvements to nonspecific factors, such as keeping records of symptoms and warming weather over the course of the study (January to June). However, examination of the results show that the duration and frequency of attacks was lower for the two training groups, and raise the possibility that the lack of statistical significance was due to the small number of persons in each group.

Preliminary results are encouraging, but the data available are still insufficient to firmly establish the efficacy of BFT in treating Raynaud's disease. The promising clinical results certainly warrant continued use of BFT with Raynaud's, especially because a surgical alternative is drastic and not always effective.

Skin Temperature BFT and Hypertension

Previously, we discussed the regulation of BP using feedback of systolic and diastolic pressure, mostly in operant conditioning paradigms. The question of whether feedback of other physiological responses can assist in lowering BP may be answered affirmatively. Datey (1976) appears to have been the first to report on the use of skin temperature, or thermal, feedback with hypertensives, showing substantial BP reductions in the majority of cases. Another report, by Green, Green, and Norris (1979), showed reductions of BP in hypertensives using ST to train foot warming. Six of 7 patients originally on medication were able to remain unmedicated while maintaining BP below 140/90mm Hg. Since then, the use of a program that combines feedback of ST, relaxation techniques, home monitoring of BP, and home practice of relaxation has been found effective in lowering BP of hypertensives by researchers at the Menninger Foundation (Fahrion, Norris, Green, Green, & Snarr, 1986) and at the State University of New York at Albany (Blanchard et al., 1987). For example, Fahrion and associates (1986) found significant reductions in systolic and diastolic BP and medication use in 77 patients with essential hypertension. A multimodal procedure was used, which included biofeedback-assisted training aimed at self-regulation of hand and foot ST. Most patients were able to discontinue medication while reducing BP by 15mm Hg for systolic and 10mm Hg for diastolic readings. Follow-up data on 61 patients over an average of 33 months indicated continuance of good control in 51% of patients and partial control in 41%. The remaining 8% were unsuccessful in lowering BP or medications to a clinically significant extent.

Blanchard and McCoy (1984) have noted the effectiveness of thermal feedback in lowering BP. Thermal BFT was used in 16 sessions for 20 patients, and progressive relaxation alone was used for 22 matched hypertensives. The patients were classified as mildly to moderately hypertensive and were taking two medications for BP control at the beginning of the program. Biofeedback of finger ST was superior to relaxation training in reducing BP and maintaining it at the lower level after 3 months with only one of the original drugs. This represented a significant savings in money and also reduced the risks of side effects by taking one medication instead of two.

The importance of continued home practice of relaxation techniques in the maintenance of lowered BP was underscored in a study by Hoelscher (1987). Planned withdrawals of practice for periods of 3 and 10 weeks led to increased levels of BP, followed by decreases with resumption of practice. In addition to home practice, Stroebel (1982) has advocated the use of a 6-second quieting response (QR) to generalize the effects of relaxation procedures to everyday situations. Patients are encouraged to practice this brief relaxation exercise whenever they encounter stressful situations and whenever some meaningful environmental cue occurs, for example, a telephone ring. The purpose of the QR is to attain a degree of automaticity to relaxation in the presence of stressful and nonstressful events in everyday life.

Cohen and Sedlacek (1983) divided 30 hypertensives into 3 groups: a waiting list control (no treatment), a relaxation only group, and a relaxation plus thermal and EMG feedback group. The only significant reduction was for the relaxation plus feedback group at the end of the 20 sessions. This group showed average decreases of 13mm Hg for systolic and 12mm Hg for diastolic pressure.

In an earlier section of this chapter, the effectiveness of skin conductance biofeedback in treating hypertension was noted in the work of Patel. The work with ST feedback suggests that a similar mechanism might be at work with both physiological measures. Because SCL and ST are ultimately reflections of sympathetic nervous system activity, it is probable that the regulation of SNS activity is the important factor in lowering BP, and this regulation is influenced by relaxation techniques, therapist contact, and other nonspecific factors as well. Continued research on, and clinical use of, a multimodal technique (including hand and foot ST feedback) as advocated by the Menninger group is encouraged by the results observed to date.

Skin Temperature BFT and Migraine

Sargent, Green, and Walters (1972) and Sargent, Walters, and Green (1973) have used a combination of skin temperature BFT and autogenic training to treat migraine headaches. Migraine is a severe form of headache often accompanied by nausea and blurring of vision. It is believed to be due to dilation in superficial cranial arteries (Dalessio, 1972), and during the headache phase the pain is one-sided and throbbing, often resulting in a constant ache spreading over the scalp and head. Sargent et al. (1972) treated 62 migraine patients with skin temperature BFT (handwarming) and autogenic procedures. Clinical ratings indicated that 74% of the migraine sufferers were improved. Sargent and colleagues (1973) reported that the combined handwarming training and autogenic procedures produced improvement in 81% of 42 migraine patients who were followed for more than 150 days. These investigators believe that one mechanism operative in their approach is the voluntary relaxation of the portion of the SNS serving the hand, resulting in the increased flow of blood to that area. Presumably, the effects of SNS relaxation spread to other body areas, including superficial (head) arteries. However, the researchers did not investigate this possible spread of relaxing effects to other body parts, thus leaving the reasons for the effect rather uncertain. The lack of control groups and little attempt to identify nonspecific and placebo effects serve to weaken this early work. Nevertheless, it has led to a great deal of clinical work and research on the use of ST feedback with migraine.

A controlled investigation of ST feedback with migraine patients was conducted by Blanchard, Theobald, Williamson, Silver, and Brown (1978). Thirty patients were divided into three groups: (a) finger ST feedback with autogenic relaxation; (b) relaxation alone, or (c) no treatment. The treatment sessions were 2 times a week over a 6-week period. Both treatment groups were improved at the end of training, whereas the control patients were not. These gains were still in effect at the end of a 3-month follow-up. Gauthier Lacroix, Cote, Doton, Drolet (1985) assigned 22 female migraine patients to finger ST feedback, blood volume pulse feedback (BVP), and control group. Both finger ST training and temporal artery BVP feedback were effective in treating migraine. The researchers did not find a relationship between therapeutic expectancy and migraine relief. These last two studies used control groups and demonstrated beneficial effects of biofeedback alone and in combination with relaxation. In order to establish the use of thermal feedback with migraine patients, more controlled and longer-term follow-up studies are required. However, the findings so far are encouraging.

BLOOD VOLUME BFT AND MIGRAINE

Feedback of a direct cephalic vasomotor response (CVMR) was used by Feuerstein, Adams, and Beiman (1976) and Friar and Beatty (1976) with migraine patients. Both sets of investigators used BFT to train self-regulation of vasoconstriction in superficial temporal arteries, that is, those located in the temporal area above the ears. They reported success in treating migraine with BFT employing the CVMR.

Price and Tursky (1976) measured changes in temporal artery blood volume and finger blood volume in 40 migraine sufferers and 40 matched controls. The objective was to train vasodilation by providing feedback about increases in hand temperature. Ten subjects from each group were assigned to one of four treatments: (a) feedback, (b) false feedback, (c) relaxation induced by taped instructions, and (d) a neutral-type control. Responses of migraine sufferers were very different from those of the controls. Normal subjects produced vasodilation in accordance with experimental demands, but the migraine patients tended to show constriction, or no change, of blood vessels. There were no significant differences in vasodilation between the BFT and relaxation conditions. Both of these latter procedures were better than the irrelevant listening task in producing vasodilation. Price and Tursky suggested that migraine sufferers be studied to determine whether stressful stimuli produce temporal artery vasoconstriction, which in turn results in headaches. A further suggestion was that if this is the case, then migraine patients might be trained not to respond to such stimuli with vasoconstriction. Feuerstein and Adams (1977) investigated the use of CVMR and EMG (frontalis) BFT in two migraine and two tension-headache patients. Training consisted of six sessions of CVMR and six EMG biofeedback sessions for all patients. The CVMR training helped migraine patients, and EMG training helped tension headache patients to reduce the frequency and duration of headaches.

The hypothesis that BFT to produce temporal artery constriction would be superior to dilation feedback in alleviating migraine was proposed by Gauthier et al. (1985). Training patients to voluntarily constrict the temporal artery mimics the action of ergotamine used as medication for migraine headaches. Three groups of migraine patients were given feedback for temporal artery constriction, dilation, or served as wait-list controls. The BFT consisted of 15 sessions over 8 weeks. All patients completed 5 weeks of self-monitoring of headaches and medication use before and after the BFT period. To the surprise of these workers, and contrary to their hypothesis, both the vasoconstrict and vasodilate groups showed improvements in frequency, intensity, and duration of migraine attacks. The waiting list controls showed no change. The researchers found evidence that reductions in migraine were associated with decreased variability in blood vessel constriction and dilation. This led them to suggest an alternate hypothesis that voluntary vasoconstriction and vasodilation were effective because they allowed greater regulation of vasomotor activity. Research to test this hypothesis would be designed to show that reductions in migraine headaches are caused by decreases in vasomotor variability.

In summary, recent results with blood volume feedback for migraine sufferers seem promising with respect to alleviating symptoms and understanding more about the origins of migraine. However, as with the other measures, blood volume BFT requires further testing as a treatment for migraine headache.

In conclusion, there is suggestive evidence that BFT can improve the symptoms of certain disorders. The EMG applications are numerous. Positive results obtained with EMG feedback for tension headache seem as much due to nonspecific factors as the feedback itself. The nonspecific factors include the learning of relaxation techniques, therapist attention, home practice, monitoring of symptoms, changes in lifestyle, and other factors that have been mentioned in this chapter. The use of EMG with stuttering is only suggestive, whereas its application to neuromuscular disorders is very promising. The lack of controlled studies of EMG feedback with anxiety patients makes this application preliminary at best. Biofeedback with asthmatics is still in an exploratory stage. Initial encouraging results with hyperactivity should set the stage for larger-scale studies with good control procedures. The continued use of EEG feedback with epileptics should be encouraged to follow up promising possibilities. Self-regulation of cardiac activity in clinical situations has not developed beyond the exploratory level, perhaps because the ready availability of medications reduces both clinician and patient motivation to explore this area in depth. The use of skin temperature feedback with hypertensives has provided good results. The same can be said for skin temperature feedback with migraine and Raynaud's patients. The use of blood volume feedback with migraine patients is still at an early stage of development.

What is needed is more good clinical research on all of these applications of biofeedback to clinical disorders. Controlled studies that isolate the specific effects of biofeedback are also desirable. The adequate control procedure would be to expose both treatment and control groups to the same procedures, except for the physiological feedback provided for feedback groups.

If a multimodal treatment package including self-regulation, relaxation techniques, stress management, and counseling can be shown to be effective in alleviating certain physical disorders such as hypertension, the biofeedback practitioner would get little argument from the patient or insurance carriers who benefit from reduced medical costs and medication side effects. From a scientific standpoint, however, it is essential to know the contribution of each element in the treatment package to the improvement.

The questions raised at the beginning of this chapter have not been adequately answered to date, and the process of investigating these and other questions related to BFT will keep applied and basic researchers busy for years to come.

We have seen by now that a tremendous amount of information has been gathered by psychophysiologists. What has been presented thus far represents only a small portion of the basic and applied research accomplished to date. The next chapter considers some of the major conceptual formulations that have been developed and used in attempts to integrate and explain some of the diverse findings in psychophysiology.

REFERENCES

Basmajian, J. V., & Hatch, J. P. (1979). Biofeedback and the modification of skeletal muscular dysfunctions. In R. J. Gatchel & K. P. Price (Eds.), *Clinical applications of biofeedback: Appraisal & status* (pp. 97–111). New York: Pergamon Press.

Basmajian, J. V., Kukulka, C. G., Narayan, M. G., & Takebe, K. (1975). Biofeedback treatment of foot-drop after stroke compared with standard rehabilitation technique: Effects on voluntary control and strength. *Archives of Physical Medicine and Rehabilitation, 56,* 231–236.

Basmajian, J. V., Regenos, E. M., & Baker, M. P. (1977, March). Rehabilitation biofeedback for stroke patients. Second Joint Conference on Stroke, American Heart Association, Miami, Florida.

Bates, D. B., Macklem, P. T., & Christie, R. V. (1971). *Respiratory function in diseases.* Philadelphia: Saunders.

Benson, H., Shapiro, D., Tursky, B., & Schwartz, G. E. (1971). Decreased systolic blood pressure through operant conditioning techniques in patients with essential hypertension. *Science, 173,* 740–741.

Black, A. H., & Cott, A. (1977). A perspective on biofeedback. In J. Beatty & H. Legewie, (Eds.), *Biofeedback and behavior* (pp. 7–19). New York: Plenum Press.

Blanchard, E. B., Andrasik, F., Neff, D., Teders, S., Pallmeyer, T., Arena, J., Jurish, S., Saunders, N., & Ahles, T. (1982). Sequential comparisons of relaxation training and biofeedback in the treatment of three kinds of chronic headache or, the machines may be necessary some of the time. *Behavior Research & Therapy, 20,* 469–481.

Blanchard, E. B., & McCoy, G. C. (1984). Preliminary results from a controlled evaluation of thermal biofeedback as a treatment for essential hypertension. *Biofeedback & Self-Regulation, 9,* 471–495.

Blanchard, E. B., McCoy, G. C., McCaffery, R. J., Berger, M. Musso, A. J., Wittrock, D. A., Gerardi, M. A., Halpern, M., & Pangburn, L. (1987). Evaluation of a minimal-therapist-contact thermal biofeedback treatment program for essential hypertension. *Biofeedback and Self-Regulation, 12,* 93–104.

Blanchard, E. B., Theobald, D. E., Williamson, D. A., Silver, B. V., & Brown, D. A. (1978). A controlled evaluation of temperature biofeedback in the treatment of migraine headaches. *Archives of General Psychiatry, 41,* 121–127.

Blanchard, E. B., Young, L. D., & Haynes, M. R. (1975). A simple feedback system for the treatment of elevated blood pressure. *Behavior Therapy, 6,* 241–245.

Bleecker, E. R., & Engel, B. T. (1973). Learned control of cardiac rate and cardiac conduction in the Wolff-Parkinson-White syndrome. *New England Journal of Medicine, 288,* 560–562.

Braud, L. W. (1978). The effects of frontal EMG biofeedback and progressive relaxation upon hyperactivity and its behavioral concomitants. *Biofeedback & Self-Regulation, 3,* 69–89.

Braud, L. W., Lupin, M. N., & Braud, W. G. (1975). The use of electromyographic biofeedback in the control of hyperactivity. *Journal of Learning Disabilities, 8,* 420–425.

Brown, B. B. (1974). *New mind new body.* New York: Harper & Row.

Budzynski, T., Stoyva, J., & Adler, C. (1970). Feed-back-induced muscle relaxation: Application to tension headache. *Journal of Behavior Therapy & Experimental Psychiatry, 1,* 205–211.

Budzynski, T., Stoyva, J., Adler, C. S., & Mullaney, D. J. (1973). EMG biofeedback and tension headache: A controlled outcome study. *Psychosomatic Medicine, 35,* 484–496.

Canter, A., Kondo, C. Y., & Knott, J. R. (1975). A comparison of EMG feedback and progressive muscle relaxation training in anxiety neurosis. *British Journal of Psychiatry, 127,* 470–477.

Cleeland, C. S. (1973). Behavioral techniques in the modification of spasmodic torticollis. *Neurology, 23,* 1241–1247.

Cohen, J., & Sedlacek, K. (1983). Attention and autonomic self-regulation. *Psychosomatic Medicine, 45,* 243–257.

Coleman, J. C. (1976). *Abnormal psychology and modern life.* Dallas: Scott, Foresman.

Cox, D. J., Freundlich, A., & Meyer, R. G. (1975). Differential effectiveness of electromyograph feedback, verbal relaxation instructions, and medication placebo with tension headaches. *Journal of Consulting & Clinical Psychology, 43,* 892–898.

Craig, A. R., & Cleary, P. J. (1982). Reduction of stuttering by young male stutterers using EMG feedback. *Biofeedback & Self-Regulation, 7,* 241–255.

Dalessio, D. (1972). *Wolff's headache and other head pain* (3rd. ed.). New York: Oxford University Press.

Datey, K. K. (1976, March). *Temperature regulation in the management of hypertension.* Paper presented at the meeting of the Biofeedback Research Society, Colorado Springs, CO. (Abstract).

Denkowski, K. M., Denkowski, G. C., & Omizo, M. M. (1983). The effects of EMG-assisted relaxation training on the academic performance, locus of control, and self-esteem of hyperactive boys. *Biofeedback & Self-Regulation, 8,* 363–375.

Denkowski, K. M., Denkowski, G. C., & Omizo, M. M. (1984). Predictors of success in the EMG biofeedback training of hyperactive male children. *Biofeedback & Self-Regulation, 9,* 253–264.

Elder, S. T., Ruiz, Z. R., Deabler, H. L., & Dillendoffer, R. L. (1973). Instrumental conditioning of diastolic blood pressure in essential hypertensive patients. *Journal of Applied Behavior Analysis, 6,* 377–382.

Engel, B. T. (1977). Biofeedback as treatment for cardiovascular disorders: A critical review. In J. Beatty & H. Legewie (Eds.), *Biofeedback and behavior* (pp. 395–401). New York: Plenum Press.

Engel, B. T., Nikoomanesh, P., & Schuster, M. M. (1974). Operant conditioning of rectosphincteric responses in the treatment of fecal incontinence. *The New England Journal of Medicine, 290,* 646–649.

Engel-Sittenfeld, P. (1977). Biofeedback in the treatment of neuromuscular disorders. In J. Beatty & H. Legewie (Eds.), *Biofeedback and behavior* (pp. 427–438). New York: Plenum Press.

Fahrion, S., Norris, P., Green, A., Green, E., & Snarr, C. (1986). Biobehavioral treatment of essential hypertension: A group outcome study. *Biofeedback & Self-Regulation, 11,* 257–277.

Feuerstein, M., & Adams, H. E. (1977). Cephalic vasomotor feedback in the modification of migraine headache. *Biofeedback & Self-Regulation, 2,* 241–254.

Feuerstein, M., Adams, H. E., & Beiman, I. (1976). Cephalic vasomotor and electromyographic feedback in the treatment of combined muscle contraction and migraine headaches in a geriatric case. *Headache, 16,* 232–237.

Freedman, R. R., Lynn, S. J., Ianni, P., & Hale, P. A. (1981). Biofeedback treatment of Raynaud's disease and phenomenon. *Biofeedback & Self-Regulation, 6,* 355–365.

Frair, R., & Beatty, J. (1976). Migraine: Management by trainer control of vasoconstriction. *Journal of Consulting & Clinical Psychology, 44,* 46–53.

Fried, J. J. (1974). Biofeedback: Teaching your body to heal itself. *Family Health, 6,* 18–21.

Friedman, A. P., & Merritt, H. H. (1959). *Headache: Diagnosis and treatment.* Philadelphia: Davis.

Furedy, J. J. (1987). Specific versus placebo effects in biofeedback training: A critical lay perspective. *Biofeedback & Self-Regulation, 12,* 169–184.

Gatchel, R. J., Korman, M., Weis, C. B., Smith, D., & Clarke, L. (1978). A multiple response evaluation of EMG biofeedback performance during training and stress-induction conditions. *Psychophysiology, 15,* 253–258.

Gauthier, J. Doyon, J., Lacroix, R., & Drolet, M. (1983). Blood volume pulse biofeedback in the treatment of migraine headache: A controlled evaluation. *Biofeedback & Self-Regulation, 8,* 427–442.

Gauthier, J., Lacroix, R., Cote, A., Doyon, J., & Drolet, M. (1985). Biofeedback control of migraine headaches: A comparison of two approaches. *Biofeedback & Self-Regulation, 10,* 139–159.

Goldman, H., Kleinman, K. M., Snow, M. Y., Bidus, D. R., & Korol, B. (1975). Relationship between essential hypertension and cognitive functioning: Effects of biofeedback. *Psychophysiology, 12,* 569–573.

Green, E., Green, A., & Norris, P. (1979). Preliminary report on a new non-drug method for the control of hypertension. *Journal of the South Carolina Medical Association, 75,* 575–582.

Guglielmi, R. S., Roberts, A. H., & Patterson, R. (1982). Skin temperature biofeedback for Raynaud's disease: A double-blind study. *Biofeedback & Self-Regulation, 7,* 99–120.

Guitar, B. (1975). Reduction of stuttering frequency using analog electromyographic feedback. *Journal of Speech & Hearing Research, 18,* 672–685.

Haynes, S. N., Griffin, P., Mooney, D., & Parise, M. (1975). Electromyographic biofeedback and relaxation instructions in the treatment of muscle contraction headaches. *Behavior Therapy, 6,* 672–678.

Hoelscher, T. J. (1987). Maintenance of relaxation-induced blood pressure reductions: The importance of continued relaxation practice. Biofeedback & Self-Regulation, 12, 2–12.

Hutchings, D., & Reinking, R. H. (1976). Tension headaches: "What form of therapy is most effective?" *Biofeedback & Self-Regulation, 1,* 169–183.

Johnson, R. K., & Meyer, R. G. (1974). Phased biofeedback approach for epileptic seizure control. *Journal of Behavior Therapy & Experimental Psychiatry, 5,* 185–187.

Kotses, H., & Glaus, K. D. (1981). Applications of biofeedback to the treatment of asthma: A critical review. *Biofeedback & Self-Regulation, 6,* 573–593.

Kotses, H., Glaus, K. D., Bricel, S. K., Edwards, J. E., & Crawford, P. L. (1978). Operant muscular reduction and peak expiratory flow rate in asthmatic children. *Journal of Psychosomatic Research, 22,* 17–23.

Kotses, H., Glaus, K. D., Crawford, P. L., Edwards, J. E., & Scherr, M. S. (1976). Operant reduction of frontalis EMG activity in the treatment of asthma in children. *Journal of Psychosomatic Research, 20,* 453–459.

Kristt, D. A., & Engel, B. T. (1975). Learned control of blood pressure in patients with high blood pressure. *Circulation, 51,* 370–378.

Kuhlman, W. N. (1978). Functional topography of the human mu rhythm. *Electroencephalography and Clinical Neurophysiology, 45,* 290–294.

Kuhlman, W. N., & Allison, T. (1977). EEG feedback training in the treatment of epilepsy: Some questions and some answers. *Pavlovian Journal of Biological Science, 12,* 112–122.

Kuhlman, W. N., & Kaplan, B. J. (1979). Clinical applications of EEG feedback training. In R. J. Gatchel & K. P. Price (Eds.), *Clinical applications of biofeedback: Appraisal and status* (pp. 65–96). New York: Pergamon.

Lamontagne, Y., Hand, I., Annable, L., & Gagnon, M. (1975). Physiological and psychological effects of alpha and EMG feedback training with college drug users. *Canadian Psychiatric Association Journal, 20,* 337–349.

Lanyon, R. I. (1977). Effect of biofeedback-based relaxation on stuttering during reading and spontaneous speech. *Journal of Consulting and Clinical Psychology, 45,* 860–866.

Lanyon, R. I., Barrington, C. C., & Newman, A. C. (1976). Modification of stuttering through EMG biofeedback: A preliminary study. *Behavior Therapy, 7,* 96–103.

Lubar, J. F., & Bahler, W. W. (1976). Behavioral management of epileptic seizures following EEG biofeedback training of the sensorimotor rhythm. *Biofeedback & Self-Regulation, 1,* 77–104.

Melzack, R., & Perry, C. (1975). Self-regulation of pain: The use of alpha feedback and hypnotic training for the control of chronic pain. *Experimental Neurology, 46,* 452–469.

Middaugh, S. (1977). Comparison of voluntary muscle contractions with and without EMG feedback in persons with neuromuscular dysfunction. Paper presented at the 17th annual meeting of the Society for Psychophysiological Research.

Miller, N. E. (1974). Introduction. In N. E. Miller, T. X. Barber, L. V. DiCara, J. Kamiya, D. Shapiro, & J. Stoyva (Eds.), *Biofeedback and self-control 1973: An Aldine annual on the regulation of bodily processes and consciousness* (pp. 11–20). Chicago: Aldine.

Patel, C. H. (1973). Yoga and biofeedback in the management of hypertension. *Lancet, 2,* 1053–1055.

Patel, C. H. (1975). Twelve-month follow-up of yoga and biofeedback in the management of hypertension. *Lancet, 1,* 62–67.

Patel, C. H., & North, W. R. S. (1975). Randomized controlled trial of yoga and biofeedback in management of hypertension. *Lancet, 2,* 93–99.

Price, K. P., & Tursky, B. (1976). Vascular reactivity of migraineurs and non-migraineurs: A comparison of responses to self-control procedures. *Headache, 16,* 210–217.

Raskin, M., Johnson, G., & Rondestvedt, J. W. (1973). Chronic anxiety treated by feedback-induced muscle relaxation. *Archives of General Psychiatry, 28,* 263–267.

Reinking, R. H., & Hutchings, D. (1981). Follow-up to: "Tension headaches: What form of therapy is most effective?" *Biofeedback & Self-Regulation, 6,* 57–62.

Rugh, J. D. (1979). Instrumentation in biofeedback. In R. J. Gatchel & K. P. Price (Eds.), *Clinical applications of biofeedback: Appraisal & Status* (pp. 187–203). New York: Pergamon.

Santee, J. L., Keister, M. E., & Kleinman, K. M. (1980). Incentives to enhance the effects of electromyographic feedback training in stroke patients. *Biofeedback & Self-Regulation, 5,* 51–56.

Sargent, J. D., Green, E. E., & Walters, E. D. (1972). The use of autogenic feedback training in a pilot study of migraine and tension headaches. *Headache, 12,* 120–124.

Sargent, J. D., Walters, E. D., & Green, E. E. (1973). Psychosomatic self-regulation of migraine headaches. *Seminars in Psychiatry, 5,* 415–428.

Schwartz, G. E., & Shapiro, D. (1973). Biofeedback and essential hypertension: Current findings and theoretical concerns. *Seminars in Psychiatry, 5,* 493–503.

Schwitzgebel, R. L., & Rugh, J. D. (1975). Of bread, circuses, and alpha machines. *American Psychologist, 30,* 363–370.

Sedlacek, K. (1979). Biofeedback for Raynaud's disease. *Psychosomatics, 20,* No. 8, 21–25.

Seifert, A. R., & Lubar, J. F. (1975). Reduction of epileptic seizures through EEG biofeedback training. *Biological Psychology, 3,* 157–184.

Shapiro, D., Mainardi, J. A., & Surwit, R. S. (1977). Biofeedback and self-regulation in essential hypertension. In G. E. Schwartz & J. Beatty (Eds.), *Biofeedback: Theory and research* (pp. 313–347). New York: Academic Press.

Schellenberger, R., & Green, J. (1987). Specific effects and biofeedback versus biofeedback-assisted self-regulation training. *Biofeedback & Self-Regulation, 12,* 185–210.

Sterman, M. B. (1973). Neurophysiologic and clinical studies of sensorimotor EEG biofeedback training: Some effects on epilepsy. *Seminars in Psychiatry, 5,* 507–524.

Sterman, M. B. (1984). The role of sensorimotor rhythmic EEG activity in the etiology and treatment of generalized motor seizures. In T. Elbert, B. Rockstroh, W. Luutzenberger, & N. Birbaumer (Eds.), *Self-regulation of the brain and behavior* (pp. 42–54). Heidleberg: Springer.

Sterman, M. B., & Friar, L. (1972). Suppression of seizures in an epileptic following EEG feedback training. *Electroencephalography & Clinical Neurophysiology, 33,* 89–95.

Sterman, M. B., MacDonald, L. R., & Stone, R. K. (1974). Biofeedback training of the sensorimotor EEG rhythm in man: Effects on epilepsy. *Epilepsia, 15,* 395–416.

Stroebel, C. F. (1982). *QR, the quieting reflex: A six-second technique for coping with stress, anytime, anywhere.* New York: Putnam.

Stroebel, C. F., & Glueck, B. C. (1973). Biofeedback treatment in medicine and psychiatry: An ultimate placebo? *Seminars in Psychiatry, 5,* 379–393.

Surwit, R. S., Pilon, R. N., & Fenton, C. H. (1977, October). *Behavioral treatment of Raynaud's Disease.* Paper presented at the 17th Annual Meeting of the Society for Psychophysiological Research, Philadelphia, PA.

Takebe, K., & Basmajian, J. V. (1976). Gait analysis in stroke patients to assess treatment of footdrop. *Archives of Physical Medicine and Rehabilitation, 57,* 305–310.

Taub, E. (1977). Self-regulation of human tissue temperature. In G. E. Schwartz & J. Beatty (Eds.), *Biofeedback: Theory and research* (pp. 265–300). New York: Academic Press.

Weinman, M. L., Semchuk, K. M., Gaebe, G., & Mathew, R. J. (1983). The effect of stressful life events on EMG biofeedback and relaxation training in the treatment of anxiety. *Biofeedback & Self-Regulation, 8,* 191–205.

Weiss, T., & Engel, B. T. (1971). Operant conditioning of heart rate in patients with premature ventricular contractions. *Psychosomatic Medicine, 33,* 301–322.

Weiss, T., & Engel, B. T. (1975). Evaluation of an intra-cardiac limit of learned heart rate control. *Psychophysiology, 12,* 310–312.

Whitsett, S. F., Lubar, J. F., Holder, G. S., Pamplin W. E., & Shabsin, H. S. (1982). A double-blind investigation of the relationship between seizure activity and the sleep EEG following EEG biofeedback training. *Biofeedback & Self-Regulation, 7,* 193–209.

15

Concepts in Psychophysiology

Explanatory concepts enable scientists to categorize and understand large amounts of data. They also suggest hypotheses to be tested and questions to be asked by investigators of various phenomena and, thus, help to guide the researcher. The answers obtained through experimental study may suggest modifications or elaboration of existing concepts, or a relationship with other formulations. Within the field of psychophysiology, the most elaborate of the concepts deal with cardiovascular or autonomic reactivity in one form or another. Concepts concerning brain responses are as numerous but not as well developed. Thus, the field of psychophysiology does not have an all-inclusive conceptual framework within which most of the collected data may be tested, integrated, and interpreted. Instead, there are a number of concepts that have relevance for the interpretation of experimental findings. Some of these concepts, at least in part, contradict one another. Perhaps one day the various concepts may be reconciled and subsumed within one or a few theoretical frameworks that will account for most of the existing data. This is probably an overly optimistic goal, but one for which scientists in diverse areas, including psychophysiology, constantly strive.

Scientific concepts and theories enable isolated findings and information to be bound together in a meaningful pattern. They provide a basis for the interpretation of past and present information and act as stimulators for future investigations. The very experiments that are suggested by a given scientific concept may be responsible for the modification or elimination of the concept. The development of concepts includes the sharpening of predictive value and modifications to accommodate an increasing number of new facts. The development of these kinds of concepts is one sign of a maturing science. The concepts that are discussed in this chapter are the law of initial values, autonomic balance, activation, stimulus response specificity, individual response specificity, cardiac–somatic coupling, adaptation and rebound, and orienting and defensive responses. In addition, conceptual approaches in the areas of social psychophysiology and event-related brain potentials are briefly considered.

THE LAW OF INITIAL VALUES

The law of initial values (LIV) states that a particular physiological response to a given stimulus or situation depends on the prestimulus level of the system being measured (e.g., see Wilder, 1957, 1967, 1976). More specifically, the law says that the higher the level, the smaller will be the increase in physiological responding to a given stimulus. On the other hand, the higher the level, the larger will be the decrease in response produced by stimuli normally capable of producing decreases. How might the LIV predict a change in HR in a given situation? It has been found that subjects who are fearful of mutilation show an acceleration in HR to slides of accident victims (Klorman, Weisenfeld, & Austin, 1975). The LIV would predict that if HR is higher than usual for these persons, HR acceleration would not be as pronounced as it would be for a lower prestimulus rate. Thus, a "ceiling effect" of sorts would operate for HR increases. Suppose, further, that the prestimulus rate was also higher than usual for individuals who customarily show HR deceleration to mutilation slides. In effect, these subjects would now have more room for a downward shift in HR. Although this test has not actually been carried out, it is an example of a procedure that could be used to test the predictive power of the LIV.

Wilder (1967) considered the LIV to apply to all responses under the control of the autonomic nervous system. However, experimental results indicate that not all physiological responses are subject to effects of prestimulus level. For example, Hord, Johnson, and Lubin (1964) found that the LIV operated as predicted for HR and respiration rate responses, but not for skin conductance or skin temperature. The experimental paradigm they used tested the LIV with respect to the part that predicts smaller upward changes in a given function with higher prestimulus levels of that activity. The physiological responses of 105 persons were measured to experimental stimuli that included sounds, lights, and mental arithmetic. When the prestimulus level of each physiological function was compared with poststimulus levels, the results led Hord et al. to conclude that the LIV does not hold for skin conductance or skin temperature.

Libby, Lacey, and Lacey (1973) predicted that pupil dilation and HR deceleration would occur as a characteristic response of subjects to interesting pictorial stimuli. Their predictions were confirmed based on the analyses of responses of 34 male subjects. Incidental to their main analysis was the observation that the magnitude of change in the two physiological variables was related to prestimulus level in both, thus supporting the LIV. They cautioned, however, that their repeated experience revealed wide variations in the relationship between prestimulus levels and responsivity, depending on the experimental conditions, the stimulus situation, and even the subjects used. Thus, further restrictions are imposed on the applicability of the LIV, and a need to delineate the extent of its limitations is emphasized.

Results for finger blood volume that were consistent with the LIV were obtained by Lovallo and Zeiner (1975). The cold pressor (CP) test was used as the stimulus. The CP is a procedure that involves the immersion of an extremity, in this case the left foot, in a bucket of ice water. It is often used to test degree of vasoconstriction upon stimulation, because blood vessels of the skin become narrowed when exposed to cold temperatures. The reseachers predicted that when vasoconstriction was maximal, the CP (severe cold) would produce vasodilation, and when vasodilation was high, vasoconstriction would result. Room temperature was used to manipulate the prestimulus state of the peripheral vasculature, that is, a room temperature of 12 degrees C (54 degrees F) produced prestimulus vasoconstriction, and a temperature of 32 degrees C (90 degrees F) resulted in vasodilation. The subjects were also tested at a room temperature of 22 degrees C (72 degrees F). The results of the CP were in line with their predictions because the response magnitude was not only dependent on the stimulus, but was related to the initial level of vascular tonus (i.e., vasoconstriction or vasodilation). Figure 15.1 depicts a portion of the results from the study of Lovallo and Zeiner.

White (1977) reviewed a number of studies, using salivation as a measure, to determine whether response magnitude was related to prestimulus level. The studies used different methods, subjects, and stimuli. White concluded that, in general, the LIV did not hold for salivation. In addition, Scher, Furedy, and Heslegrave (1985) found that LIV was not confirmed for two cardiovascular variables (HR and T-wave amplitude) when a between-subjects design was used. However, the LIV did hold for these same variables when a within-subjects design was used, that is, a procedure where each subject serves as his or her own control.

Peripheral blood flow underlies finger skin temperature, and it has been noted that right-handed persons frequently have higher skin temperature in their right hands than in their left hands (Jamieson, 1987). The LIV was shown to operate for finger skin temperature as subjects responded to cognitive stressors, for example, counting backwards by 17s. Jamieson (1987) reported that, in keeping with LIV, persons whose rights hands were initially warmer responded with a greater temperature decrease of the right hand.

In summary, the LIV is a concept that focuses on the level of prestimulus activity for a physiological measure in determining magnitude of response. Experimental investigations suggest that certain physiological variables change in a way predicted by the law (e.g., respiration, and vascular tonus). Other measures, for example, skin conductance and salivation, show changes that do not appear

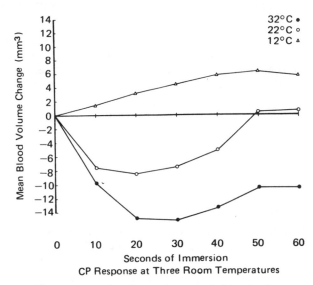

FIG. 15.1.   Three curves showing an increase in blood volume to cold pressor for subjects tested under 12 deg. C room temperature and increasingly large decreases in blood volume for those tested at 22 deg. C and 32 deg. C.

to be consistent with the LIV. Libby et al. (1973) urged further investigations to establish the conditions under which the concept holds true. Furedy and Scher (in press) argued that the LIV should be considered as an empirical generalization that requires further testing to specify its boundaries, and that it should not yet be "enshrined" as a methodological rule. Although these caveats are important, it is also true that the LIV has alerted investigators to the possible influence of prestimulus physiological activity on reactions to stimuli.

AUTONOMIC BALANCE

The concept of autonomic balance examines human performance and behavior in the context of autonomic nervous system imbalance, that is, the extent to which sympathetic nervous system or parasympathetic nervous system is dominant in an individual. The name most prominently associated with this concept is that of Wenger and his associates (Wenger, 1941, 1948, 1966; Wenger & Cullen, 1972). Wenger and co-workers have proposed that, in a given individual, either the SNS or the PNS may be dominant. The degree to which one or the other is dominant may be estimated by an empirically determined weighted score called $\bar{A}$ (autonomic balance). The person's $\bar{A}$ is derived from a number of autonomically innervated functions, which include palmar skin conductance, respiration

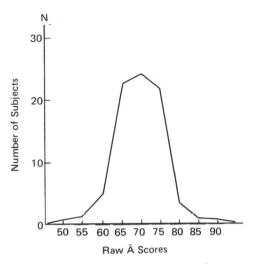

FIG. 15.2.   The frequency distribution of the mean Ā scores (estimates of autonomic balance) for 87 children, ages 6 to 12.

rate, heart period, salivation, forearm skin conductance, pulse pressure, and red dermographia (persistence of red skin after stroking with a stimulator). High Ā scores indicate PNS dominance, whereas low A scores reflect relative SNS dominance. The predominance of this autonomic factor for an individual remains constant from year to year but may show phasic changes to external or internal stimuli. The central tendency of these estimates of the autonomic factor are what Wenger means by autonomic balance (Wenger & Cullen, 1972).

Wenger (1941) has proposed that the distribution of Ā scores should be approximately normal (i.e., bell shaped, see Fig. 15.2) for a large random sample of individuals. In fact, Wenger has found such a distribution for samples of children (1941) and adults (1948). The curve plotted in Fig. 15.2 depicts an average Ā of 70. Thus, individuals who score below this value would be SNS dominant and those above reflect PNS dominance, in relation to other persons in the sample. The amount by which the A score differs from the central value would indicate increasing degrees of imbalance. The procedure to obtain Ā scores is described by Wenger and Cullen (1972).

Wenger and his associates have conducted many large-scale studies to determine the nature of the Ā scores in different samples of individuals. For example, Wenger (1948) studied autonomic balance in 225 military persons hospitalized for "operational fatigue" and 98 Air Force personnel diagnosed as "psychoneurosis-anxiety state." An example of their findings was that neurotic individuals had faster respiration, higher blood pressure, and lower finger temperature than persons suffering from fatigue. This trend would indicate greater SNS activity for anxiety neurotics. A sample of 488 Air Force cadets produced a normal distribution of Ā scores with an average at 69, very similar to that of the sample of children tested in 1941. Wenger, Engel, and Clemens (1957) concluded that autonomic factor scores are related to certain personality patterns and diagnostic categories such as anxiety psychoneurosis, battle fatigue, and asthma. They also hypothesized in 1957 that differences in autonomic response patterns, supplemented by differences in autonomic balance could be used to predict which persons will not react favorably to physical or psychological stress and those who might develop psychosomatic disorders. In a study designed to test the hypothesis that patients with different psychosomatic disorders would show different response patterns for variables under ANS control, Wenger, Clemens, and Cullen (1962) tested the responses of 100 hospitalized males under controlled resting states and with the CP test. The patients included 31 with stomach ulcers, 36 with gastritis, and 33 with skin disorders (including 17 with neurodermatitis). The variables measured included HR, respiration rate, skin conductance, finger pulse volume, blood pressure, and skin temperature. One finding was that the resting Ā score of each patient group indicated greater SNS activity than a group of 93 normal subjects. There was no significant difference in reactivity to CP among the patient groups. Patients with gastritis, however, seemed more different from normals than other patient groups. In general, the results did not support the hypothesis but did show differences in Ā score for patients and nonpatients.

Smith and Wenger (1965) estimated Ā for 11 graduate students under phasic anxiety (immediately before taking an oral examination for the Ph.D. degree) and under relatively relaxed conditions, either 1 month later (eight persons) or 1 month earlier. The hypothesis that A would significantly decrease during anxiety, thus indicating SNS dominance, was confirmed. For example, on the day of the examination the subjects had less salivary output, higher blood pressure, shorter heart period, and higher sublingual (under tongue) temperature. In another study, Wineman (1971) investigated changes in Ā during the menstrual cycle of five young women. The autonomic variables studied were sublingual temperature, heart period, diastolic blood pressure, salivary output, and skin conductance. During menses, the follicular and ovulatory phases, Ā scores were higher, indicating PNS dominance. However, during the luteal phase (which is accompanied by decreased estrogen and increased progesterone levels), the Ā scores were lowest. Thus, Wineman concluded that the decreased estrogen levels were accompanied by a relative increase in SNS dominance.

Lovallo and Zeiner (1975) reviewed a number of studies in which the CP test was used to determine patterns of physiological responsivity. They viewed the results of these studies as useful in understanding homeostatic mechanisms, especially in relation to the concepts of LIV and autonomic balance. (Homeostasis is the term coined by W. B. Cannon to describe the tendency of the body to maintain a state of equilibrium in the face of external and internal changes.) Lovallo and Zeiner provided support for the use of LIV in understanding the magnitude and direction of responses to stimuli, as well as interactions between base levels of activity and task performance under stress. They also emphasized the interaction between initial values and autonomic balance in determining an individual's response to a given stimulus. Thus, we see a possible complementarity between LIV and autonomic balance in understanding physiological responsivity.

In summary, the concept of autonomic balance, and the $\bar{A}$ score, appears to provide a useful mechanism through which the relative dominance of the PNS or SNS of an individual may be established. However, relatively few studies to test and expand this concept have been performed, despite the fact that it has existed for some time. Most of the studies conducted to date have been performed by Wennger and his associates. Its value as a conceptual model would be enhanced if further studies testing its applicability, for example, in understanding psychosomatic disorders, were performed by a larger number of investigators.

ACTIVATION

The concept of activation attempts to explain the relationship between variations in level of physiological activity and changes in behavior. According to Duffy (1972), the description of behavior at any particular instant requires consideration of the goal toward which it is directed and the intensity of the behavior. The intensity of behavior is most commonly called "activation" (sometimes arousal) and can be reflected in the level of responsivity in a number of physiological variables. For example, increasing levels of HR, blood pressure, muscle potentials, skin conductance, and EEG desynchronization are related to increased activation, whereas decreased levels of these same variables would indicate lowered activity. Various formulations of this concept are found in the writings of Duffy (1934, 1957, 1962, 1972), Hebb (1955), Lindsley (1951), and Malmo (1959, 1962). A consistent idea in the writings of those who supported the activation concept is that level of performance rises with increases in physiological activity of an organism up to a point that is optimal for a given task, and beyond this point, further increases cause a drop in performance. Thus, one basic proposition of this concept is that performance is optimal at some intermediate level of physiological activation, and the relation between the two can be described by an inverted-U-shaped curve (see Fig. 15.3). The function plotted in Fig. 15.3 is based on a discussion by Malmo (1962). An important role is given to the ascending reticular activating system (ARAS) by Malmo in regulating level of cortical excitability and, hence, performance.

Let us examine how "activation" might operate in an everyday situation. Suppose that a person is very sleepy or drowsy early in the morning. The level of activation as reflected in various physiological measures would be low, and performance, for example, in a RT task, would be poor. Later on in the day, when the physiological variables register at some intermediate level for this individual, performance would be best. If, then, the individual's performance

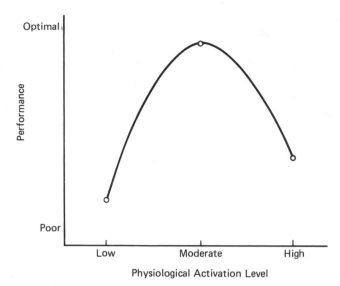

FIG. 15.3.   The hypothetical inverted-U relationship indicates that performance is best at some moderate level of physiological activation. Malmo (1962) ascribes the upturn in the curve to effects of nonspecific stimuli that influence the cortex through the ARAS. Activity in a circulating chain of neurons is said to be facilitated by impulses arriving at the cortex. Overstimulation, on the other hand, causes neurons in the chain to be less excitable and produces the downturn in the curve observed at high activation levels.

and physiological responses are measured when he or she is in a state of panic, or very high excitement, efficiency would be low while activation would be extremely high. This last situation would produce the downturn in the curve, thus producing the inverted-U-shaped function.

Empirical support for the activation concept is derived mainly from studies in which level of physiological activity is manipulated and performance measures are taken, and from neurophysiological findings regarding the arousal functions of the reticular formation of the brain. In the first category of studies, which offer empirical support for an inverted-U-shaped relation between activation and performance, are the many studies of induced muscle tension (IMT) effects on task efficiency. An early example is a study by Courts (1939), who investigated the effects of six IMT levels on verbal learning. He found that an IMT level of one fourth of maximum was optimal for learning. Higher degrees of tension were also superior to the no-tension condition. However, at a level of three-fourths maximum IMT, learning efficiency fell below the no-tension condition, thus yielding an inverted-U-shaped relationship between level of muscle tension and performance. In a review by Courts (1942), it was noted that performance in a wide variety of tasks has been improved with IMT. Tasks for which detrimental effects were noted involved motor adjustments, for example, tossing balls at a target. Moderate levels of IMT have been found to facilitate perception of strings of numbers (Shaw, 1956) and recognition of forms (Smock & Small, 1962). Malmo (1959) contended that muscle tension induction is one way to systematically increase activation. This contention is supported by studies of Freeman and Simpson (1938), who found that skin conductance increased with increased IMT, and those of Malmo and Davis (1956), who found high relationships between skeletal muscle activity and two autonomic measures. (heart rate and blood pressure). In addition, Pinneo (1961) measured forearm EMG, SCL, EEG, HR, and respiration while six levels of IMT were produced by a dynamometer in the right hand. Pinneo reported that all of these physiological responses showed regular and continuous rises as a function of IMT level. Thus, there is good evidence that IMT is related to changes in activation.

One study frequently cited in support of the activation concept is that of Freeman (1940). This investigator measured skin conductance and RT of a single subject over a series of 100 experimental sessions. The observations were made at various times of day, over a number of days, when the subject varied widely in levels of alertness. Freeman found a curvilinear, inverted-U-shaped relation between skin conductance and RT, in which RTs were slower at high and low conductance levels and fastest at the middle levels. Stennett (1957) manipulated activation level through the use of incentive and found an inverted-U-relation between tracking performance and two measures of physiological arousal (skin conductance and EMG). However, an inverted-U was not found by Schlosberg and Kling (1959), who attempted to repeat the Freeman (1940) study with a larger number of subjects. Nor was it indicated in a study by Kennedy and Travis (1948), who investigated the relationship between frontalis muscular tension, reaction time, and level of performance in a continuous tracking task. Kennedy and Travis found a linear relationship between EMG level and performance, that is, tracking and RT were poor at low EMG levels and better at the higher levels of muscle tension. A similar finding was reported by Andreassi (1966) for the relationship between skin conductance and RT in a continuous monitoring task in which subjects had to respond to infrequent and random auditory signals. Andreassi found that RT was fast when SCL was high and slow when SCL was low. Intermediate SCL was not associated with best RT performance. It was suggested that perhaps an inverted-U-shaped function will be observed only when levels of activation are purposely manipulated to produce very high and low levels of physiological activity.

Purposeful manipulation of SCL to between 6.5 to 8.5 μmhos, on both hands was related to optimal performance of children in processing visual and auditory stimuli (Mangina & Beuzeron-Mangina, 1988). Physiological underactivation was defined as bilateral SCLs lower than 5.01 μmhos, and overactivation was indicated by an SCL of 10.1 μmho or more, both when processing cognitive information. When SCL fell below 6.49 μmho, an alerting tone was presented automatically to increase SCL. If the SCL continued to drop, light flashes and postural manipulations (stand up–sit down) were used. Relaxation techniques were used when SCL was considered to be too high. According to these investigators, these "optimal" activation strategies have implications for helping the learning disabled to improve school performance. In another study, relaxation exercises were used to decrease level of physiological activity just before teacher candidates were about to be tested on their teaching ability by a panel of judges (Helin & Hanninen, 1987). Compared to controls, the individuals who listened to an 18-minute relaxation cassette just prior to the test had better scores and lower systolic BP during the examination. In addition, males showed decreased trapezius EMG during the test, whereas females had reduced heart rates. Complex interactions among gender, personality, and physiological response make it difficult to interpret the Helin and Hanninen results simply in terms of the activation concept.

The neurophysiological bases for the activation concept are found in studies of the reticular formation. Moruzzi and Magoun (1949) discovered that electrical stimulation of the brain stem reticular formation (BSRF) of anesthetized cats shifted the EEG recorded at the cortex from high-voltage slow waves to low-voltage fast waves. The cat's EEG showed the signs of a normal arousal from sleep. The excitable area included the central core of the brain stem extending from the medulla up to the hypothalamus (see Fig. 15.4). Moruzzi and Magoun concluded that the reticular formation acted as a general alarm mechanism that aroused the cortex, and they referred to it as the reticular activating system (RAS). Further work by these investigators and others who studied the behavioral and physiological effects of stimulation and lesions in the RAS led to the recognition of this system's importance in maintaining wakefulness and producing arousal of cortical areas under appropriate stimulus conditions. Lindsley (1951) reviewed evidence that lesions in the ARAS (ascending reticular activating system) abolished the activation pattern of the EEG and produced a behavioral picture of apathy and somnolence. Lindsley (1956) noted that the ARAS projects fibers to, and receives projections from, the cerebral cortex, indicating mechanisms for interaction between these two areas of the brain. Thus, the central location and connections to and from the ARAS point to its potential as a mechanism for regulating and integrating input to other levels of the CNS. Fuster (1958) has provided evidence that moderate electrical stimulation of the ARAS can facilitate visual perception and RT in monkeys. High-intensity stimulation of the ARAS led to a decrement in performance, as would be predicted by proponents of the activation concept.

Duffy (1972) reviewed many studies that lend support to the activation concept. One criticism of the concept (Lacey, 1967) is that autonomic, central (electrocortical), and behavioral activation are different forms of arousal, each with its own complexities. Thus, for example, increased cardiac activity is not necessarily related to elevated cortical activity, and, in fact, is accompanied by

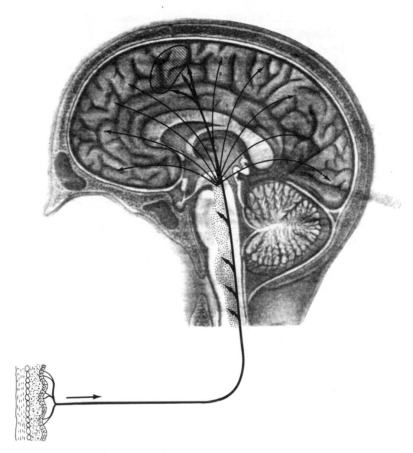

FIG. 15.4. The reticular formation is the area stippled in this cross section of the brain. A sense organ (lower left) is connected to a sensory area in the brain by a pathway extending up the spinal cord. This pathway branches into the reticular formation. When a stimulus travels along the pathway, the reticular formation may "awaken" the entire brain (arrows).

decreased brain activation. The Laceys' concepts are discussed more fully later in this chapter. However, Eason and Dudley (1971) provided an example of a situation where various physiological responses do vary simultaneously in the same direction. Three levels of activation were produced by manipulating experimental conditions as follows: (a) subjects were told that they would be shocked if they did not respond quickly to light flashes ("high activation"), or (b) they were merely instructed to react as quickly as possible to the flashes ("moderate activation"), or (c) they were told to observe the light flashes without responding ("low activation"). All of the physiological variables measured (HR, SCL,

EMG, and visual-cortical-evoked potentials) increased with higher levels of activation. Although HR deceleration was observed just prior to the response signal at all levels of activation, the major trend showed a generalized activation that was similar for cortical, somatic, and autonomic variables.

Sjoberg (1975) manipulated level of physiological activation in 25 subjects by having them work at five different loads on a bicycle ergometer. The relation between the index of activation (HR) and RT was described as an inverted-U, that is, performance was better at a medium activation level than at high and low levels. Maclean, Ohman, and Lader (1975) stressed quick responses and provided feedback of performance under a ''high activation'' condition, and instructed subjects to merely count stimuli in a ''low activation'' condition. Measures of auditory ERPs and SCL were affected by the activation manipulations in a consistent way, that is, high activation led to higher-amplitude evoked potentials and SCL. They concluded that different physiological measures co-vary when level of activation is manipulated.

In summary, it may be said that there is a good deal of empirical support for an activation concept that relates level of physiological activity to behavioral intensity. The support stems mainly from studies in which the level of physiological activity is experimentally manipulated and from neurophysiological evidence regarding the importance of the reticular formation in regulating levels of alertness. One weakness of the concept has been its lack of precision in specifying an a priori optimal physiological level for a given group of individuals performing a task under conditions in which level of activation has not been purposely manipulated. This may be difficult because of large individual differences in any index of physiological activation that may be used. Another weakness has been the failure of its proponents to consider different patterning of physiological responses in different experimental situations. Thus, there are instances when one physiological measure increases while another decreases simultaneously. Nevertheless, the concept has stimulated a great deal of research and can predict changes in physiological activity and performance under straightforward conditions of physical manipulation (e.g., IMT) and some psychological manipulations (e.g., Eason & Dudley, 1970).

STIMULUS RESPONSE (SR) SPECIFICITY

The concept of stimulus response specificity refers to a patterning of physiological responses according to the particular stimulus situation. It has been discussed in the writings of Ax (1953), Lacey, Bateman, and VanLehn (1953), Lacey, Kagan, Lacey, and Moss (1963), and Engel (1972), among others. The concept states that an individual's pattern of physiological activity (e.g., HR, EMG, SCL, respiration, and blood pressure) will be similar in a given situation, and that the pattern may vary when the situation is different. One basic question here is whether the pattern of physiological response will indicate the kind of emotion being experienced. Or, to put it another way, what is the pattern of response in happiness versus sadness, or in anger versus fear, or in disgust versus surprise? One of the first investigators to study this experimentally was Ax (1953), who induced fear in his 43 subjects who received "accidental" shocks because of a bumbling experimenter. Anger was produce in the same persons through insults and criticism delivered by an "arrogant" and "incompetent" assistant. Ax found greater increases in respiration rate and SCL in fear than in anger. However, greater increases in EMG, diastolic blood pressure, and greater decreases in HR were observed in anger as compared to fear. There were higher intercorrelations among the physiological reactions for anger than fear, indicating to Ax that there was greater coordination of responses during anger. Additional evidence that patterning of physiological response can differentiate emotional states comes from a study by Ekman, Levenson, and Friesen (1983). These researchers studied 6 emotions (surprise, disgust, sadness, anger, fear, and happiness) produced through two tasks: (a) directed facial action and (b) relived emotion. In the directed action condition, subjects produced different facial muscle patterns, whereas the other condition required them to re-experience particular emotional events. Heart rate increased more in anger and fear than in happiness, and skin temperature increased more in anger than happiness. Sadness produced larger skin conductance responses than fear, anger, and disgust. These intriguing findings require additional follow up and confirmation.

Engel (1959) compared physiological responses when subjects were hungry and when a limb was submerged in ice water (CP test). A different pattern of responding was noted under these two conditions. Responses to the CP test included increases in HR and blood pressure and a decrease in finger pulse volume. On the other hand, hunger produced decreases in blood pressure and respiration rate and an increase in skin temperature.

Variations in the stimulus situation produced different patterns in physiological respondings, as reported by Lacey (1959). He gave examples of situations in which HR showed a decrease while SCL increased, and instances in which they changed in the same direction (see Fig. 15.5). The divergent response of these two measures was referred to by Lacey as "directional fractionation of response." This term describes stimulus situations in which direction of change in physiological activity is contrary to the view that ANS responses must co-vary simultaneously, up or down, in a given situation.

Lacey (1959) also presented evidence that tasks involving cognitive functioning (e.g., mental arithmetic) are accompanied by increases in HR, whereas those emphasizing perceptual activities (e.g., attention to visual stimuli) led to HR deceleration. He suggested that cardiac deceleration facilitated "intake" of environmental stimuli, whereas acceleration was associated with attempts to exclude or "reject" those stimuli that would be disruptive to the performance of some cognitive function. Lacey et al. (1963) observed that cognitive activities

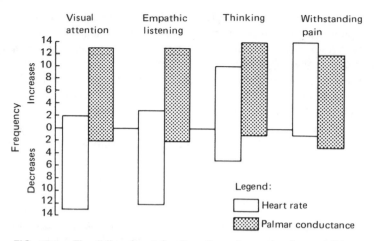

FIG. 15.5.   The "directional fractionation of response" according to
the nature of subjects' tasks. For the 15 subjects whose responses are
shown here, all four stimulus conditions produced increases in palmar
conductance, but visual and auditory attending resulted in heart rate
decreases, whereas the other tasks involving "rejection" of input resulted in heart rate increases.

were accompanied by HR increases, whereas primarily perceptual functions led
to cardiac deceleration.

Directional fractionation of response has also been reported by Andreassi,
Rapisardi, and Whalen (1969) and Hare (1972). Andreassi and colleagues found
HR to be significantly higher when subjects were required to respond to an
irregular pattern of signals than with a fixed interval. In contrast, SCL and SCRs
were elevated for the fixed intervals, as compared to the variable presentations.
The variable pattern was likened to a cognitive task, because it required more
mental effort to anticipate signals when they occurred at irregular intervals.
Thus, HR acceleration occurred, as would be predicted by Lacey et al. (1963) for
cognitive tasks. On the other hand, relatively lower HR levels were observed
with regular signals, presumably because simple attention was involved in performing the task. Hare (1972) measured HR, SCL, and vasomotor activity (finger and cephalic vasoconstriction) while subjects viewed slides of homicide
victims. One group was instructed to rate the slides on a 7-point scale of unpleas-
antness (raters), whereas the other group merely viewed the slides (nonraters).
The nonraters showed directional fractionation, which included cardiac deceleration, increased SCL, digital vasoconstriction, and cephalic vasodilation. However, the raters did not display fractionation, because they showed HR acceleration, an increase in SCL, and both digital and cephalic vasoconstriction. The
results for raters were interpreted as being consistent with the hypothesis that HR
increases are associated with cognitive activity. The rise in SCL was attributed to

the fact that increased requirements for evaluation caused the subjects to notice more disturbing aspects of the slides.

Libby et al. (1973) found that pupil dilation was greater to unpleasant stimuli, and cardiac slowing was related to pleasantness. Pictures rated as pleasant produced greater HR deceleration than those rated unpleasant. These results are a further example of directional fractionation and stimulus response specificity. A different method was used to obtain directional fractionation in an experiment by Gatchel (1976). He trained a group of subjects to produce HR deceleration while SCL was simultaneously measured, and found that slowing of HR was accompanied by increases in SCL.

Cardiac deceleration has been assigned an important role in the regulation of brain function and performance in later refinements of the "intake–rejection" hypothesis. For example, Lacey (1967) argued that changes in HR and blood pressure can influence cortical activity and thereby affect sensitivity to stimuli. A decrease in HR would be sensed by baroreceptors in the carotid and aortic arteries, resulting in decreased visceral feedback to cortical areas, thus causing increased cortical activity. This is partially based on neurophysiological evidence from animal studies that have shown that level of cardiovascular activity can affect EEG frequency (Bonvallet, Dell, & Hiebel, 1954). Cardiovascular feedback has been shown to inhibit rage response in cats (Bartorelli, Bizzi, Libretti, & Zanchetta, 1960; Baccelli, Guazzi, Libretti, & Zanchetta, 1965). In addition, Galin and Lacey (1972) recorded HR, respiration, EEG, and RT in cats under conditions in which the midbrain reticular formation was either stimulated or not stimulated. They reported that HR deceleration sometimes accompanied reticular stimulation, indicating that HR slowing and CNS arousal could occur simultaneously.

Lacey and Lacey (1978) discussed some neurophysiological findings that strongly support the notion that sensory and motor functions can be inhibited by increases in baroreceptor activity (Coleridge, Coleridge, & Rosenthal, 1976; Gahery & Vigier, 1974). For example, Coleridge et al. (1976) found that stimulation of carotid baroreceptors inhibited the activity of single neurons in the motor cortex. Lacey and Lacey pointed out that, by inference, sensory and motor functions may be facilitated by decreased baroreceptor afferent activity. A relation between a measure of brain activity (CNV), HR deceleration, and RT efficiency has been reported by Lacey and Lacey (1970). They found that the greater the HR deceleration during the foreperiod of a RT task, the greater was the CNV, and both of these were related to efficient RT, for example, higher CNV amplitudes and greater HR decelerations were accompanied by fast RTs. In a later study, Lacey and Lacey (1977) reported that magnitude of HR deceleration was differentially affected during a single cardiac cycle, depending on when a signal to respond occurred within that cycle. This latter study was more fully discussed in chapter 11. The Laceys' hypothesis concerning cardiovascular feedback effects on attention has been criticized by Elliott (1972) and Hahn (1973).

The criticisms generally called for clarification of terms such as "attention," and less reliance on HR alone as a dependent measure of cortical effects.

In summary, the studies of the Laceys and others have indicated support for stimulus or situational response specificity. That is, a consistent pattern of physiological responses will occur in a given situation. In addition, "directional fractionation," in which different physiological variables show different directions of response, has been reported in a number of investigations, particularly those that require subjects to note and detect environmental events. The "intake–rejection" hypothesis has developed into a concept concerning interactions between cardiovascular activity and the brain and its effects on behavior, especially sensorimotor performance. Available neurophysiological and psychophysiological data have prompted the Laceys to propose that decreases in cardiovascular activity facilitate sensorimotor performance and attentional processes by increasing brain activity. According to their formulation, the increased brain activity is produced by afferent feedback from baroreceptors. Conversely, increased cardiovascular activity (e.g., HR and blood pressure) decreases efficiency in the same types of activities, because increased afferent feedback from the same baroreceptors inhibits cortical and subcortical activity. There is some evidence for improvement in behavioral efficiency during periods of lowered HR (Sandman, McCanne, Kaiser, & Diamond, 1977), and for the influence of the cardiovascular system on brain activity (Sandman, 1984; Walker & Walker, 1983). Criticisms of the Lacey's concepts regarding the significance of heart rate changes for behavior were made by Carroll and Anastasiades (1978). This thoughtful critique focuses on the nature of the intake–rejection environment in cardiac dynamics and the role of cardiovascular changes in regulating brain-attentional activities. Regardless of criticisms made, it is obvious that concepts advanced by the Laceys have stimulated research on brain-autonomic interactions in behavior, and on the significance of cardiac dynamics for behavior.

INDIVIDUAL RESPONSE (IR) SPECIFICITY

In the previous section, we saw that the concept of stimulus response specificity referred to the characteristics of the stimulus situation that produced a typical response from most subjects. In contrast, the concept of individual response specificity says that a particular subject has characteristic responses to most stimuli. These two concepts may seem to be contradictory at first glance, but they are not (Engel, 1972; Sternbach, 1966). The concept of stimulus response (SR) specificity refers to similar pattern of physiological response of most persons to a given stimulus situation, while individual response (IR) specificity involves consistency of an individual's response hierarchy in a variety of stimulus situations.

The concept of IR specificity has had an interesting historical development (see Sternbach, 1966). Briefly, it had been reported by Malmo and Shagass (1949) that psychiatric patients with a history of cardiovascular problems and those with headaches and neck pains had higher EMG in response to pain. Malmo and associates proposed the principle of "symptom specificity" to describe situations in which psychiatric patients respond to stressful stimuli according to the physiological mechanism underlying the symptom. This principle was applied to normals by Lacey and associates (1953) and formulated as "autonomic response specificity," or what is now called "individual response specificity". The notion that individuals would respond maximally with a certain physiological response was confirmed in the 1953 study (Lacey et al.). They measured SCL, HR, and HR variability under four "stressful" conditions: cold pressor, mental arithmetic, letter association, and hyperventilation. Evidence was found for maximal response in the same physiological variable under different stress conditions. Further, they concluded that some people responded to different stimuli with a fixed pattern, for example, the greatest response change might be HR, followed by SCL and then HR variability. An example of this response, patterning to various stimulating conditions was provided by Lacey (1959). He obtained results that indicated similar response patterns to the CP test, mental arithmetic, and word fluency within a given subject. For example, diastolic blood pressure decreased for one subject, whereas it consistently increased for a different subject under the conditions just mentioned. Engel (1960) measured a number of physiological variables in a group of young women while they were presented with a variety of stimulus conditions. The data indicated the simultaneous occurrence of IR specificity and SR specificity for these subjects. Moos and Engel (1962) reported that hypertensive subjects showed more blood pressure changes in reacting to stressors than did arthritic patients. However, those with arthritis showed more EMG increases in muscles overlying the arthritic joints than did hypertensives. Hodapp, Weyer, and Becker, (1975) reported that 20 hypertensives responded to landscape slides with a greater rise in systolic blood pressure than did a group of 31 matched normal control subjects. Thus, the concept of IR specificity may have implications for studying certain psychosomatic reactions, as initially suggested by the work of Malmo and Shagass (1949).

Findings having relevance to the concepts of IR specificity and activation were obtained by Schnore (1959). A group of male subjects had a number of physiological measures taken (including forearm EMG, HR, systolic blood pressure, and respiration rate) while they performed tracking or arithmetic tasks under conditions designed to produce low or high arousal. For example, under high-arousal conditions for tracking, subjects performed under the threat of an electric shock, whereas in the low-arousal condition, tracking trials were presented as though they were not part of the experiment proper. The results indicated that during the different stimulus situations, subjects showed highly individual response patterns (both somatic and autonomic), even when variations produced increases in the overall level of activation. These findings were interpreted in support of Lacey et al. (1953) and Lacey and Lacey (1958) with regard to IR specificity for autonomic variables. Further, Schnore reported that four of the measures (HR, blood pressure, respiration rate, and right forearm EMG) consistently differentiated between high- and low-arousal conditions. Schnore observed that, despite individual patterns of response, persons placed in an arousing situation showed an increase in most physiological functions. The increases were relative, as, for example, although an individual might have shown increases in HR and EMG under arousal, the level of HR may have been high and EMG low in comparison with others.

There are limitations to the IR specificity concept. Lacey and Lacey (1958) pointed out that although most persons may have some tendency for IR specificity, quantitative differences exist. This point is illustrated in a study of Wenger, Clemens, Coleman, Cullen, and Engel (1961), who found that only 8 of 30 male subjects (27%) showed complete IR specificity. A tendency toward a stable hierarchy in autonomic response pattern to different stimuli was found in 22 of the subjects (73%). Sternbach (1966) presented several studies that indicate that IR specificity is unstable over time, especially as the number of stimulus and physiological response variables are increased. The possible role of explicit (e.g., instructions) and implicit (e.g., preconceived ideas) sets of subjects as possible factors affecting IR specificity have also been discussed by Sternbach (1966).

CARDIAC–SOMATIC CONCEPT

According to the cardiac–somatic concept, cardiac response changes are seen as facilitating the preparation for, and performance of, a behavioral response. For example, there is an association between cardiac response (e.g., HR deceleration) and the inhibition of ongoing somatic activity not relevant to performance of the task (Obrist, Webb, Sutterer, & Howard, 1970). Reductions in somatic and cardiac activity are viewed as biological manifestations of changes in attention (Obrist et al., 1974). Further, HR deceleration is considered to reflect a central (brain) mechanism that adjusts cardiac activity to metabolic requirements. The major proponents of this view have been Obrist and his associates, who have emphasized that the "coupling" between cardiac–somatic responses occurs because both are reflections of brain processes concerned with preparatory activities.

Support for the concept is derived from a variety of studies by Obrist and colleagues (Obrist, Webb, & Sutterer, 1969; Obrist et al., 1970; Webb & Obrist, 1970). For example, Obrist et al. (1970) measured somatic activity (chin EMG and eye blinks) and HR while subjects performed a simple RT task in which various foreperiods were used. In one group of 31 subjects, HR decelerations were blocked by intravenous administrations of atropine, which inhibits the vagus nerve. Another 31 persons performed without the drug. When cardiac deceleration was not blocked, faster reaction times were associated with greater decreases in both heart and muscle activity. The cessation of eye movements and blinks was the most pronounced effect. Blocking cardiac deceleration, however, did not influence performance. The HR deceleration observed in the RT task was explained in terms of processes initiated in the brain that had effects on both heart and muscle responses. In another study, Obrist (1968) found that increases in somatic activity paralleled increases in HR. A classical aversive conditioning situation was employed in which EMG increases from the chin and jaw were accompanied by cardiac acceleration. This was interpreted as evidence for cardiac–somatic linkage.

The relationship among RT, HR, and measures of task-irrelevant somatic activity (e.g., eye movements and blinks) were studied by Obrist, Howard, Sutterer, Hennis, and Murrell (1973). The subjects were four groups of children (4, 5, 8, and 10 years old) and an adult reference population. It was reported, for all groups, that a decrease in HR and a drop in task-irrelevant somatic activities were coincident with making the relevant response.

It was suggested by Obrist and his colleagues (1974) that HR may be uncoupled for somatic activity under conditions of intense stress brought about by a subject's uncertainties and that involve sympathetic nervous system influences. Thus, they proposed that HR is coupled to somatic activity in behavioral situations that involve minimal sympathetic influences on the heart, that is, are not stressful. To test this proposal, Lawler, Obrist, and Lawler (1976) measured HR and somatic activity of 25 male college students and 25 fifth-grade boys while they performed a choice RT task. Attention was manipulated by varying uncertainty (probability of a warning signal occurring) and motivation (money and feedback vs. no money and no feedback). With respect to the cardiac–somatic relationship, variations in uncertainty produced systematic effects only on HR during the foreperiod, that is, HR accelerations increased as uncertainty increased. Variations in motivation were differentiated only by forearm EMG during the foreperiod; it increased with increases in motivation. However, increases in motivation increased the average level of both HR and forearm EMG. Thus, the variable of stimulus uncertainty seemed to result in cardiac–somatic uncoupling. Further, forearm EMG increases during the foreperiod were considered as relevant somatic activity and were contrasted to decreases in chin EMG.

Obrist (1976) argued that situations in which the individual is minimally involved, or relatively passive (e.g., simple RT), are those in which cardiac–somatic coupling is evident. That is, the emotional involvement is such that the cardiovascular system is mobilized for a metabolic state that is not demanding. However, emotional states that evoke active coping mechanisms mobilize the cardiovascular system for dealing with high metabolic requirements. Lacey and Lacey (1974) did not agree that the metabolic relationship between HR and somatic activity explains decreased HR during the preparatory interval of a RT trial. They believed that the somatic changes reported by Obrist and associates for the RT paradigm are small and not metabolically significant. Haagh and Brunia (1984) examined cardiac–somatic coupling during the foreperiod of a simple RT task and found only partial support for the concept. In agreement with the hypothesis, they found HR, eye movements, and jaw EMG to be decreased at the end of the foreperiod and just prior to the response. However, contrary to the concept, there was no EMG decrease in a number of response-irrelevant muscles (e.g., soleus and tibialis). Haagh and Brunia believed that the EMG changes observed facilitate response execution.

Some support for the idea that emotional involvement may mobilize the cardiovascular system comes from a study by Obrist et al. (1978). They studied the effects of varying the subject's opportunity to cope with stressors on tonic levels of HR, carotid pulse wave, and BP (diastolic and systolic). In a first experiment, persons who believed that they could control an aversive stimulus (shock) maintained elevated levels of HR, carotid pulse wave, and systolic BP, as compared to those who believed that they could not control the shock. In a second experiment, three stressors were used. The subjects had no control over two of these (CP and a sexually arousing pornographic movie), but did have control over a third one (electric shock) that could be avoided by good performance. The subjects had significantly elevated levels of HR, carotid pulse, and systolic BP during the portion of the experiment where they could control the stressor. The effects of sympathetic innervation on responsivity during coping and no-coping conditions was examined in a third experiment. Sympathetic innervations were blocked with a beta-adrenergic blocking agent (propranolol, 4 mg intravenously). The results showed that when SNS influence on the heart and vasculature were blocked, the physiological response differences between coping and no-coping situations were abolished. The authors interpreted the results as evidence that providing a subject with an opportunity to cope with stressful events produces more appreciable sympathetic influences on the cardiovascular system than conditions where control is minimal (viewing an erotic movie) or not possible (inescapable shock).

Obrist and colleagues noted in later work that the effects of coping and no-coping situations differ for individuals, with greater effects seen in what they termed "reactive subjects." These reactive persons show greater cardiovascular response to any novel or challenging event, a tendency that reflects differences in adrenergic excitation. The Obrist team has noted that although reactive and non-reactive persons show little differnce in HR during baseline conditions, the reactives show much larger increases in HR to the cold pressor or shock avoidance tasks (e.g., as much as 48 bpm in shock avoidance). These reactivity differences in HR have led Obrist (1981) to include blood pressure in his studies, and he found that systolic BP also showed appreciable changes in the high "myocardial reactors." These observations about individual differences in HR and SBP reactivity in young adults raised the question as to whether the reactive persons are more likely to develop hypertension later in life. This intriguing question, with its important health implications, can only be answered by longitudinal studies. In the meantime, Obrist and his colleagues have provided evidence that young adults with hypertensive parents showed greater HR reactivity during shock avoidance than those with normotensive parents (Hastrup, Light, & Obrist, 1982). Similar, but less dramatic, findings were reported for SBP. This suggests a common factor that may relate to a predisposition to high cardiovascular reactivity and parental hypertension. Obrist and his colleagues continue to explore the influences of stressors on cardiovascular reactivity, as evidenced in Obrist, Light, James, and Strogatz (1987) and Light, Obrist, James, and Strogatz (1987).

The cardiac–somatic concept has been fruitful with regard to suggesting experiments. Obrist and his colleagues have expanded a great deal on the original approach, as evidenced by the coping–no coping paradigms and recent studies concerning the psychophysiology of hypertension. Current and future research will determine the eventual form of the cardiac–somatic concept and hypotheses generated in explorations of the psychophysiology of stress. In this context, it should be noted that none of the concepts presented in this chapter are completely fixed, and their forms may change as additional research findings foster new interpretations.

CONCEPTS AND SOCIAL PSYCHOPHYSIOLOGY

Social psychophysiology represents a relatively new area of research rather than a psychophysiological concept. However, I include it here because it is an area that is a potentially rich source of concepts that can be studied within the context of traditional psychophysiology. To paraphrase Cacioppo and Petty (1983), social psychology studies the behavioral effects of human interactions, whereas psychophysiology investigates relations between physiological events and behavior. Theories in social psychology abound, and the objective techniques of psychophysiology can provide a means to validate some of these theories as well as to elucidate important aspects of human interaction. The social psychophysiological approach has been used in the study of attitudes, persuasion, sexual arousal, social facilitation, and dissonance. For example, in a dissonance study, heart rate and electrodermal activity were used to confirm the existence of tensions and their subsequent release in cognitive dissonance (Croyle & Cooper, 1983). The concept of dissonance was introduced by Festinger to describe the state produced when there is a discrepancy between a person's attitude and behavior. In the Croyle and Cooper study, subjects were required to write essays in agreement or disagreement with pre-existing attitudes. Those in the dissonant condition showed greater arousal in the form of increased electrodermal activity than the other subjects. Thus, the state of dissonance was reflected in a physiological response, and the construct received some independent support.

An important role is attached to communication in social psychophysiology. An area of interest in this connection has been the communication of emotions through facial expressions. In chapter 8, studies of facial EMG in emotional expression were discussed. Researchers such as Paul Ekman and Gary Schwartz have found different patterning of facial EMG in the enacting of various emotions. Ekman (1984) has presented evidence for biologically based and evolved facial expressions of emotion from his studies of subjects from various cultures, including primitive New Guinean natives. Sackheim and Gur (1983) made a case for facial asymmetry in the communication of emotion based on findings that the left side of the face displays emotions more intensely. This is presumably due to the contralateral influence of the right hemisphere in both the control of emotional responses and muscles on the left side of the face. It is obvious that social psychophysiology is a welcome addition to traditional psychophysiological approaches. It is hoped that this area will see further development in the future.

HABITUATION AND REBOUND

Habituation describes the decrease in physiological responsivity that occurs with repeated presentation of the same stimulus. For example, a change in skin conductance may be produced when a person's name is called out, but as the name is repeated over and over again, the novelty or unexpectedness wears off and the SCR may diminish until it is nonexistent. The psychological effect may be likened to boredom produced by the repetition of the same stimulus. Sternbach (1966) observed that although we do not know why habituation (another term is adaptation) occurs, it might be considered in terms of survival value for the species. For example, it would be a waste of energy if a number of similar stimuli, occurring in rapid succession, produced the same magnitude of response as the initial one, especially if they were non-threatening. On the other hand, it would be maladaptive if we quickly habituated to a potentially dangerous stimulus, like a truck approaching us as we started to cross a street.

The phenomenon of rebound may be observed when physiological variables return to values below those of prestimulus levels. If the SNS response to an intense stimulus, such as an electric shock or a pistol shot, is large in magnitude, then we may observe a poststimulus return of physiological variables to values below the level seen before the startling event. This overshooting of prestimulus levels in a direction opposite to that produced by an intense stimulus is called "rebound." Lang, Rice, Greenfield, and Sternbach (1972) pointed out that rebound is not due exclusively to antagonistic functions of the SNS and PNS, because it is observed to occur in responses mediated solely by the SNS (e.g., SCL). Sternbach (1966) noted that although we do not know why rebound occurs, it must be taken into account in the conduct of experimental investigations.

ORIENTING AND DEFENSIVE RESPONSES

Pavlov (1927) described a reflex that apparently enables animals to attend to novel and possibly biologically important stimuli. He noticed that a conditioned response failed to occur in a dog if an unusual stimulus was attended to by the dog who had previously evidenced conditioning. The response was termed the "orienting", or "what is it?" reflex. Lynn (1966) described some of the physiological changes observed to occur when a novel stimulus is presented to humans. They include increased SCL, EMG, and pupil dilation; activation of the EEG pattern; a decrease in HR; vasoconstriction in the limbs; and vasodilation in the blood vessels of the head. These physiological changes are said to be directed at facilitating the perception of, and a possible response to, the new stimulus.

Sokolov (1963) distinguished between the orienting response and the defensive response. Whereas the OR occurred to novel stimuli, the DR was indicated as an accompaniment of intense, potentially painful, stimuli. In addition, the OR habituates rapidly and the DR very slowly. The OR enhances perceptibility of stimuli, and the DR protects against the possible bad effects of intense stimulation. Graham and Clifton (1966) suggested that the OR would be accompanied by HR deceleration, whereas HR acceleration would most likely represent a DR to stimuli of prepain intensity. This suggestion was confirmed in a study by Raskin, Kotses, and Bever (1969), in which HR deceleration (OR) was observed to occur with an 80-db (moderate) sound, whereas an increase in HR (DR) was produced by a 120-db (intense) sound. However, the dominant cephalic response was vasoconstriction. Hence, the cephalic vasomotor responses did not differentiate between ORs and DRs.

Hare (1973) reported HR of 10 persons who feared spiders and compared them to 10 others who were not fearful. The 20 subjects viewed six spider slides and 24 slides of neutral objects (e.g., landscapes). The individuals who feared spiders showed a DR in the form of accelerated HR, whereas the persons who were not afraid evidenced HR deceleration (OR), especially when they found the slides to be interesting. There seems to be a correspondence with the Laceys' "intake–rejection" hypothesis here. Namely, it appears that HR deceleration is associated with stimulus intake and the OR, whereas HR acceleration accompanies stimulus rejection and the DR. The OR–DR concept has obvious implications for psychophysiological research. However, Lang et al. (1972) have noted several difficulties with Sokolov's conceptualization. For example, it does not explain selective attention or emotional specificity very well, and in addition, it has proven difficult to obtain measures of the DR.

A. S. Bernstein and I. Maltzman have sought to expand OR theory as advanced by Sokolov to include cognitive activity of the individual. Recall that Sokolov stressed the match–mismatch of stimuli to neuronal models as the critical factor in producing the OR (see chapter 9). Both Bernstein and Maltzman have argued that stimulus significance as well as novelty, is important in the OR. Bernstein emphasized that interactions between stimulus significance and uncertainty trigger the OR. Also, Maltzman believed that a "cortical set", present prior to the stimuli, influences the OR. Other researchers have contributed ideas regarding the nature of the OR, and these were presented in chapter 9, because they were in the context of electrodermal research. It is clear that Sokolov's OR theory has been heuristic and that additional research may lead to revisions to accommodate findings regarding influences of pre-existing sets and cognitive activity on the OR.

CONCEPTUALIZATIONS CONCERNING EVENT-RELATED POTENTIALS

Researchers studying ERPs have borrowed concepts from other areas to help explain their findings. An example is the notion of "resource allocation" taken from theories of information processing to describe the effects of varying difficulty of a primary task on brain response to a secondary task stimulus. Models of excitation–inhibition in the visual system have been used to explain relationships between visual masking and ERPs. The OR has also been used to explain results of certain ERP studies, as have attentional mechanisms and concepts regarding the asymmetrical functions of the left and right hemispheres of the brain. Some of the theories have been simplistic and inadequate, such as the "neural efficiency hypothesis," which attempted to provide a rationale for a relation between intelligence and brain responses (see chapter 6). A search through chapters 6 and 7 of this book will reveal that a number of other concepts have been invoked to explain ERP results. Among these are the explanation of N400 as an attempt to reinterpret information, the recognition of the Nd wave as an early endogenous component related to attention and its distinction from the exogenous N1, and the "mismatch negativity" attributed to the N2 component. This processing negativity has been related to a mismatch between a current stimulus and a "neuronal model" established by a previous stimulus, a notion reminiscent of the neuronal model of stimuli proposed in Sokolov's concept of the OR. A theory of processing negativity has been proposed by Naatanen (see chapter 6). Additionally, an NA component occurring prior to N2 has been said to reflect an earlier stage of stimulus processing than N2 (see chapter 6).

Intentions to move and expectancies have been related to such slowly developing brain potentials as the readiness potential (RP) and contingent negative variation (CNV). The relative contributions of the psychological processes called distraction and attention were proposed as critical in CNV development (see chapter 7). The inverse relation that has been found between stimulus probability and P300 amplitude emphasizes the endogenous-cognitive nature of this component. Additionally, P300 amplitude has been related to decision confidence and its latency to stimulus evaluation time. Researchers also proposed that P300 represents neural activity that occurs whenever a neuronal model of a stimulus must be updated. Further, whether the model will be updated depends on the surprise value and relevance of the stimuli (see chapter 7). Johnson suggested that P300 can be accounted for by three dimensions of behavior; (a) subjective probability, (b) stimulus meaning, and (c) information transmission (see chapter 7). The classic P300 response has also been separated into P3a and P3b components based on behavioral and physiological data. In addition, the picture is made more complex by the identification of slow wave components that overlap in time the appearance of P300, and outlast its disappearance by hundreds of milliseconds. Thus, we have a situation in ERP research where there are many hypotheses and concepts to explain empirical findings, but they tend to be fragmentary. An integrating effort is needed that would help to unify the various ERP constructs under several major concepts rather than having dozens of different explanatory devices. Integrating attempts such as those of Johnson (1986) for P300, Nataanen, and Picton (1987) for the N1 wave, and Rebert, Tecce, Marczynski, Pirch, and Thompson (1986) for relations among ERPs, neural anatomy and brain chemistry are the kinds of efforts that will help to consolidate masses of ERP data under fewer explanatory concepts.

The concepts that we have discussed in this chapter were advanced by a relatively small number of workers in the field of psychophysiology. Still required are theories that help to integrate the various conceptual approaches. The concepts presented here have had the effect of stimulating much research. Data collection in the field is currently proceeding at a rapid pace, and we may look forward to the confirmation and refinement of present concepts and the development of new ones.

REFERENCES

Andreassi, J. L. (1966). Skin-conductance and reaction-time in a continuous auditory monitoring task. *The American Journal of Psychology, 79,* 470–474.

Andreassi, J. L., Rapisardi, S. C., & Whalen, P. M. (1969). Autonomic responsivity and reaction time under fixed and variable signal schedules. *Psychophysiology, 6,* 58–69.

Ax, A. (1953). The physiological differentiation between fear and anger in humans. *Psychosomatic Medicine, 15,* 433–422.

Baccelli, G., Guazzi, M., Libretti, A., & Zanchetta, A. (1965). Pressoceptive and chemoceptive aortic reflexes in decorticate and decerebrate cats. *American Journal of Physiology, 208,* 708–714.

Bartorelli, C., Bizzi, E., Libretti, A., & Zanchetta, A. (1960). Inhibitory control of sinocarotid pressoceptive afferents on hypothalamic autonomic activity and sham rage behavior. *Archives Italiennes de Biologie, 98,* 309–326.

Bonvallet, M., Dell, P., & Hiebel, G. (1954). Tonus sympathique et activite electriqu corticale. *Electroencephalography & Clinical Neurophysiology, 6,* 119–144.

Cacioppo, J. T., Petty, R. E. (1983).*Social psychophysiology.* New York: Guilford.

Carroll, D., & Anastasiades, P. (1978). The behavioral significance of heart rate: The Laceys' hypothesis. *Biological Psychology, 7,* 249–275.

Coleridge, H. M., Coleridge, J. C. G., & Rosenthal, R. (1976). Prolonged inactivation of cortical pyramidal tract neurons in cats by distension of the carotid sinus. *Journal of Physiology, 256,* 635–649.

Courts, F. A. (1942). Relation between muscular tension and performance. *Psychological Bulletin, 39,* 347–367.

Courts, F. A. (1939). Relation between experimentally induced muscle tension and memorization. *Journal of Experimental Psychology, 25,* 235–256.

Croyle, R. T., & Cooper, J. (1983). Dissonance arousal: Physiological evidence. *Journal of Personality and Social Psychology, 45,* 782–791.

Duffy, E. (1934). Emotion: An example of the need for reorientation in psychology. *Psychological Review, 41,* 184–198.

Duffy, E. (1957). The psychological significance of the concept of "arousal" or "activation." *Psychological Review, 64,* 265–275.

Duffy, E. (1962). *Activation and behavior.* New York: Wiley.

Duffy, E. (1972). Activation. In N. S. Greenfield & R. A. Sternbach (Eds.), *Handbook of psychophysiology* (pp. 577–622). New York: Holt, Rinehart, & Winston.

Eason, R. G., & Dudley, L. M. (1971). Physiological and behavioral indicants of activation. *Psychophysiology, 7,* 223–232.

Ekman, P. (1984). Expression and the nature of emotion. In K. Scherer & P. Ekman (Eds.), *Approaches to emotion* (pp. 319–343). Hillsdale, NJ: Lawrence Erlbaum Associates.

Ekman, P., Levenson, R. W., & Friesen, M. V. (1983). Autonomic nervous system activity distinguishes among emotions. *Science, 221,* 1208–1210.

Elliott, R. (1972). The significance of heart rate for behavior: A critique of Lacey's hypothesis. *Journal of Personality & Social Psychology, 22,* 398–409.

Engel, B. T. (1959). Some physiological correlates of hunger and pain. *Journal of Experimental Psychology, 57,* 389–396.

Engel, B. T. (1960). Stimulus–response and individual-response specificity. *Archives of General Psychiatry, 2,* 305–313.

Engel, B. T. (1972). Response specificity. In N. S. Greenfield & R. A. Sternbach (Eds.), *Handbook of psychophysiology* (pp. 571–576). New York: Holt, Rinehart, & Winston.

Freeman, G. L. (1940). The relationship between performance level and bodily activity level. *Journal of Experimental Psychology, 26,* 602–608.

Freeman, G. L., & Simpson, R. M. (1938). The effect of experimentally induced muscular tension upon palmar skin resistance. *Journal of General Psychology, 18,* 319–326.

Furedy, J. J., & Scher, H. (in press). The Law of Initial Values: Differential testing as an empirical generalization versus enshrinement as a methodological rule. *Psychophysiology.*

Fuster, J. M. (1958). Effects of stimulation of brain stem on tachistoscopic perception. *Science, 127,* 150.

Gahery, Y., & Vigier, D. (1974). Inhibitory effects in the cuneatenucleus produced by vago-aortic afferent fibers. *Brain Research, 75,* 241–246.

Galin, D., & Lacey, J. I. (1972). Reaction time and heart rate response pattern: Effects of mesencephalic reticular formation stimulation in cats. *Physiology & Behavior, 8,* 729–739.

Gatchel, R. J. (1976). The effect of voluntary control of heart rate deceleration on skin conductance level: An example of response fractionation. *Biological Psychology, 4,* 241–248.

Graham, F. K. & Clifton, R. K. (1966). Heart-rate change as a component of the orienting response. *Psychological Bulletin, 65,* 305–320.

Haagh, S. A. V. M., & Brunia, C. H. M. (1984). Cardiac–somatic coupling during the foreperiod in a simple reaction-time task. *Psychological Research, 46,* 3–13.

Hahn, W. W. (1973). Attention and heart rate: A critical appraisal of the hypothesis of Lacey and Lacey. *Psychological Bulletin, 79,* 59–70.

Hare, R. D. (1972). Response requirements and directional fractionation of autonomic response. *Psychophysiology, 9,* 419–427.

Hare, R. D. (1973). Orienting and defensive responses to visual stimuli. *Psychophysiology, 10,* 453–464.

Hastrup, J. L., Light, K. C., & Obrist, P. A. (1982). Parental hypertension and cardiovascular response to stress in healthy young adults. *Psychophysiology, 19,* 615–622.

Hebb, D. O. (1955). Drives and the C.N.S. (conceptual nervous system). *Psychological Review, 62,* 243–254.

Helin, P., & Hanninen, O. (1987). Relaxation training affects success and activation on a teaching test. *International Journal of Psychophysiology, 5,* 275–287.

Hodapp, V., Weyer, G., & Becker, J. (1975). Situational stereotype in essential hypertension patients. *Journal of Psychosomatic Research, 19,* 113–121.

Hord, D. J., Johnson, L. C., & Lubin, A. (1964). Differential effect of the law of initial value (LIV) on autonomic variables *Psychophysiology, 1,* 79–87.

Jamieson, J. (1987). Bilateral finger temperature and the law of initial values. *Psychophysiology, 24,* 666–669.

Johnson, R. (1986). A triarchic model of P300 amplitude. *Psychophysiology, 23,* 367–384.

Kennedy, J. L., & Travis, R. C. (1948). Prediction and control of alertness. II: Continuous tracking. *Journal of Comparative & Physiological Psychology, 41,* 203–210.

Klorman, R., Weisenfeld, A. R., & Austin, M. L. (1975). Autonomic responses to affective visual stimuli. *Psychophysiology, 12,* 553–560.

Lacey, B. C., & Lacey, J. I. (1974). Studies of heart rate and other bodily processes in sensorimotor behavior. In P. A. Obrist, A. H. Black, J. Brener, & L. V. DiCara (Eds.), *Cardiovascular psychophysiology* (pp. 538–564). Chicago: Aldine.

Lacey, B. C., & Lacey J. I. (1977). Change in heart period: A function of sensorimotor event timing within the cardiac cycle. *Physiological Psychology, 5,* 383–393.

Lacey, B. C., & Lacey, J. I. (1978). Two-way communication between the heart and the brain: Significance of time within the cardiac cycle. *American Psychologist, 33,* 99–113.

Lacey, J. I. (1959). Psychophysiological approaches to the evaluation of psychotherapeutic process and outcome. In E. A. Rubinstein & M. B. Parloff (Eds.), *Research in psychotherapy* (pp. 173–192). Washington, DC: American Psychological Association.

Lacey, J. I. (1967). Somatic response patterning and stress: Some revisions of activation theory. In M. H. Appley & R. Trumbull (Eds.), *Psychological stress: Issues in research* (pp. 14–42). New York: Appleton-Century-Crofts.

Lacey, J. I., Bateman, D. E., & Van Lehn, R. (1953). Autonomic response specificity: An experimental study. *Psychosomatic Medicine, 15,* 8–21.

Lacey, J. I., Kagan, J., Lacey, B. C., & Moss, H. A. (1963). The visceral level: Situational determinants and behavioral correlates of autonomic response patterns. In P. H. Knapp (Eds.), *Expression of the emotions in man* (pp. 122–155). New York: International Universities Press.

Lacey, J. I., & Lacey, B. C. (1958). Verification and extension of the principle of autonomic response stereotypy. *American Journal of Psychology, 71,* 50–73.

Lacey, J. I., & Lacey, B. C. (1970). Some autonomic-central nervous system interrelationships. In P. Black (Ed.), *Physiological correlates of emotion* (pp. 214–236). New York: Academic Press.

Lang, P. J., Rice, D. G., Greenfield, N. S., & Sternbach, R. A. (1972). The psychophysiology of emotion. In N. S. Greenfield & R. A. Sternbach (Eds.), *Handbook of psychophysiology* (pp. 623–643). New York: Holt, Rinehart, & Winston.

Lawler, K. A., Obrist, P. A., & Lawler, J. E. (1976). Cardiac and somatic response patterns during reaction time task in children and adults. *Psychophysiology, 13*, 448–455.

Libby, W. L., Lacey, B. C., & Lacey, J. I. (1973). Pupillary and cardiac activity during visual attention. *Psychophysiology, 10*, 270–294.

Light, K. C., Obrist, P. A., James, S. A., & Strogatz, D. S. (1987). Cardiovascular responses to stress: II. Relationships to aerobic exercise patterns. *Psychophysiology, 24*, 79–86.

Lindsley, D. B. (1951). Emotion. In S. S. Stevens (Ed.), *Handbook of experimental psychology* (pp. 473–516). New York: Wiley.

Lindsley, D. B. (1956). Physiological psychology. *Annual Review of Psychology, 7*, 323–348.

Lovallo, W., & Zeiner, A. R. (1975). Some factors influencing the vasomotor response to cold pressor stimulation. *Psychophysiology, 12*, 499–505.

Lynn, R. (1966). *Attention, arousal and the orientation reaction.* Oxford: Pergammon Press.

Maclean, V., Ohman, A., & Lader, M. (1975). Effects of attention, activation and stimulus regularity on short-term "habituation" of the averaged evoked response. *Biological Psychology, 3*, 57–69.

Malmo, R. B. (1959). Activation: A neurophysiological dimension. *Psychological Review, 66*, 367–386.

Malmo, R. B. (1962). Activation. In A. J. Bachrach (Ed.), *Experimental foundations of clinical psychology* (pp. 386–422). New York: Basic Books.

Malmo, R. B., & Davis, J. F. (1956). Physiological gradients as indicants of "arousal" in mirror tracing. *Canadian Journal of Psychology, 10*, 231–238.

Malmo, R. B., & Shagass, C. (1949). Physiologic study of symptom mechanisms in psychiatric patients under stress. *Psychosomatic Medicine, 11*, 25–29.

Mangina, C. A., & Beuzeron-Mangina, J. H. (1988). Learning abilities and disabilities: Effective diagnosis and treatment. *International Journal of Psychophysiology, 6*, 79–90.

Moos, R. H., & Engel, B. T. (1962). Psychophysiological reactions in hypertensive and arthritic patients. *Journal of Psychosomatic Research, 6*, 227–241.

Moruzzi, G., & Magoun, H. W. (1949). Brain stem reticular formation and activation of the EEG. *Electroencephalography & Clinical Neurophysiology, 1*, 455–473.

Naatanen, R., & Picton, T. W. (1987). The Ni wave of the human electric and magnetic response to sound: A review and an analysis of component structure. *Psychophysiology, 24*, 375–425.

Obrist, P. A. (1968). Heart rate and somatic-motor coupling during classical aversive conditioning in humans. *Journal of Experimental Psychology, 77*, 180–193.

Obrist, P. A. (1976). The cardiovascular–behavioral interaction as it appears today. *Psychophysiology, 13*, 95–107.

Obrist, P. A. (1981). Cardiovascular psychophysiology: A perspective. New York: Plenum.

Obrist, P. A., Gaebelein, C. J., Teller, E. S., Langer, A. W., Gringnolo, A., Light, K. C., & McCubbin, J. A. (1978). The relationship among heart rate, carotid dP/dt and blood pressure in humans as a function of the type of stress. *Psychophysiology, 15*, 102–115.

Obrist, P. A., Howard, J. L., Lawler, J. E., Galosy, R. A., Meyers, K. A., & Gaebelein, C. J. (1974). The cardiac somatic interaction. In P. A. Obrist, A. H. Black, J. Brener, & L. V. DiCara (Eds.), *Cardiovascular psychophysiology* (pp. 136–162). Chicago: Aldine.

Obrist, P. A., Howard, J. L., Sutterer, J. R., Hennis, R. S., & Murrell, D. J. (1973). Cardiac-somatic changes during a simple reaction time task: A developmental study. *Journal of Experimental Child Psychology, 16*, 346–362.

Obrist, P. A., Light, K. C., James, S. A., & Strogatz, D. S. (1987). Cardiovascular responses to stress: I. Measures of myocardial response and relationship to high resting systolic pressure and parental hypertension. *Psychophysiology, 24*, 65–78.

Obrist, P. A., Webb, R. A., & Sutterer, J. R. (1969). Heart rate and somatic changes during aversive conditioning and a simple reaction time task. *Psychophysiology, 5*, 696–723.

Obrist, P. A., Webb, R. A., Sutterer, J. R., & Howard, J. L. (1970). Cardiac deceleration and reaction time: An evaluation of two hypotheses. *Psychophysiology, 6*, 695–706.

Pavlov, I. P. (1927). *Conditioned reflexes: An investigation of the physiological activity of the cerebral cortex*. London: Oxford University Press.

Pinneo, L. R. (1961). The effects of induced muscle tension during tracking on level of activation and on performance. *Journal of Experimental Psychology, 62*, 523–531.

Raskin, D. C., Kotses, H., & Bever, J. (1969). Cephalic vasomotor and heart rate measures of orienting and defensive reflexes. *Psychophysiology, 6*, 149–159.

Rebert, C. S., Tecce, J. J., Marczynski, T. J., Pirch, J. H., & Thompson, J. W. (1986). Neural anatomy, chemistry and event-related brain potentials: An approach to understanding the substrates of mind. In W. C. McCallum, R. Zappoli, & F. DeNoth (Eds.), *Cerebral psychophysiology: Studies in event-related potentials* (pp. 343–392). Amsterdam: Elsevier.

Sackheim, H. A., & Gur, R. C. (1983). Facial asymmetry and the communication of emotion. In J. T. Cacioppo & R. E. Petty (Eds.), *Social psychophysiology* (pp. 307–352). New York: Guilford Press.

Sandman, C. A. (1984). Augmentation of the auditory event-related potentials of the brain during diastole. *International Journal of Psychophysiology, 2*, 111–120.

Sandman, C. A., McCanne, T. R., Kaiser, D. N., & Diamond, B. (1977). Heart rate and cardiac phase influences on visual perception. *Journal of Comparative & Physiological Psychology, 91*, 189–202.

Scher, H., Furedy, J. J., & Heslegrave, R. J. (1985). Individual differences in phasic cardiac reactivity to psychological stress and the law of initial value. *Psychophysiology, 22*, 345–348.

Schlosberg, H., & Kling, J. W. (1959). The relationship between "tension" and efficiency. *Perceptual & Motor Skills, 9*, 395–397.

Schnore, M. M. (1959). Individual patterns of physiological activity as a function of task differences and degree of arousal. *Journal of Experimental Psychology, 58*, 117–128.

Shaw, W. A. (1956). Facilitating effects of induced tension upon the perception span for digits. *Journal of Experimental Psychology, 51*, 113–117.

Sjoberg, H. (1975). Relations between heart rate, reaction speed, and subjective effort at different work loads on a bicycle ergometer. *Journal of Human Stress, 1*, 21–27.

Smith, D. B., & Wenger, M. A. (1965). Changes in autonomic balance during phasic anxiety. *Psychophysiology, 1*, 267–271.

Smock, C. D., & Small, V. H. (1962). Efficiency of utilization of visual information as a function of induced muscular tension. *Perceptual & Motor Skills, 14*, 39–44.

Sokolov, E. N. (1963). Perception and the conditioned reflex. New York: MacMillan.

Stennett, R. G. (1957). The relationship of performance level to level of arousal. *Journal of Experimental Psychology, 54*, 54–61.

Sternbach, R. A. (1966). *Principles of psychophysiology*. New York: Academic Press.

Walker, B. B., & Walker, J. M. (1983). Phase relations between carotid pressure and ongoing electrocortical activity. *International Journal of Psychophysiology, 1*, 65–74.

Webb, R. A., & Obrist, P. A. (1970). The physiological concomitants of reaction time performance as a function of preparatory interval and preparatory interval series. *Psychophysiology, 6*, 389–403.

Wenger, M. A. (1941). The measurement of individual differences in autonomic balance. *Psychosomatic Medicine, 3*, 427–434.

Wenger, M.A. (1948). Studies of autonomic balance in Army Air Force personnel. *Comparative Psychology Monographs, 19*.

Wenger, M. A. (1966). Studies of autonomic balance: A summary. *Psychophysiology, 2*, 173–186.

Wenger, M. A., Clemens, T. L., Coleman, D. R., Cullen, T. D., & Engel, B. T. (1961). Autonomic response specificity. *Psychosomatic Medicine, 23*, 185–193.

Wenger, M. A., Clemens, T. L., & Cullen, T. D. (1962). Autonomic functions in patients with gastrointestinal and dermatological disorders. *Psychosomatic Medicine, 24*, 268–273.

Wenger, M. A., & Cullen, T. D. (1972). Studies of autonomic balance in children and adults. In N.

S. Greenfield & R. A. Sternbach (Eds.), *Handbook of psychophysiology* (pp. 535–569). New York: Holt, Rinehart, & Winston.

Wenger, M. A., Engel, B. T., & Clemens, T. L. (1957). Studies of autonomic response patterns: Rationale and methods. *Behavioral Science, 2,* 216–221.

White, K. D. (1977). Salivation and the law of initial value. *Psychophysiology, 14,* 560–562.

Wilder, J. (1957). The law of initial values in neurology and psychiatry. *Journal of Nervous & Mental Disease, 125,* 73–86.

Wilder, J. (1967). *Stimulus and response: The law of initial value.* Bristol: J. Wright.

Wilder, J. (1976). The "law of initial values," a neglected biological law and its significance for research and practice (1931). In S. W. Porges & M. G. H. Coles (Eds.), *Psychophysiology* (pp. 38–46). Stroudsberg: Dowden, Hutchinson & Row.

Wineman, E. W. (1971). Autonomic balance changes during the human menstrual cycle. *Psychophysiology, 8,* 1–6.

Appendix I
Environmental Influences
on Physiological Responses

Physical environmental factors can have dramatic effects on physiological activity. These environmental factors may be either internal (e.g., chemical substance) or external (e.g., air temperature). It is important to know about these effects not only for human welfare, but in the context of psychophysiological research. Certain commonly used substances, such as coffee, tea, soft drinks, alcohol, nicotine, and medications can influence physiological responses. Thus, investigators must be aware of these possible effects when carrying out psychophysiological studies. They can control for possible unwanted influences by asking subjects to abstain from using certain substances for a suitable length of time before participating in an experiment.

Some of the studies presented here may not be strictly psychophysiological, in that they fail to use a behavioral measure. However, the influence of environmental factors must be considered because of the effects they may produce on both behavioral and physiological responses. Our discussion of environmental effects starts with the EEG and continues in the same order in which the various physiological measures are presented in the main body of this book. The material presented in the EEG section covers, for the most part, research performed subsequent to a review by Shagass (1972). In another comprehensive review, Stroebel (1972) discussed the behavioral and physiological effects of drugs and included sections on EEG and autonomic response patterns.

INTERNAL AND EXTERNAL ENVIRONMENTAL
FACTORS AND THE ELECTROENCEPHALOGRAM

Drugs

The EEG is a valuable tool for objective assessments of psychoactive drugs, or those that have either a psychologically depressing or stimulating effect. This

TABLE A.1
Drugs Commonly Employed for Mind Alteration

	Type	Examples
Experience expanding	Hallucinogens	LSD
		Mescaline
		Marijuana
	Stimulants	Amphetamines
		Cocaine
		Caffeine
Experience restricting	Opiates (narcotics)	Heroin
		Morphine
		Methadone
	Depressants	Barbiturates
		Alcohol
		Nicotine
		Tranquilizers
		Solvents
		Methaqualone

Source: From H. Brown, Brain and Behavior, Oxford University Press, 1976, p. 296.

usefulness is further enhanced when behavioral or performance tests, as well as blood samples to determine the amount of the drug in the bloodstream, are conducted. In addition, the use of drugs in EEG studies may help to understand some of the biochemical factors in the brain that are involved in the production of the EEG.

Table A.1 is taken from Brown (1976) and provides a useful classification of some familiar drugs and their psychological effects. We examine effects on EEG of psychoactive drugs in the hallucinogen, opiate, and depressant categories.

The effects of drugs on behavior are by no means always clear-cut and understandable. There are many factors operating, including the "placebo effect." The placebo effect refers to the fact that the mere taking of a pill may have powerful suggestive effects so as to influence either some physiological response or behavior. A placebo is an inert substance, such as lactose, which can be made into pill form and may be administered in experiments to separate real effects of an active drug from suggestion effects of pill taking. Brown (1976) advised that correlations between drug actions and their consequences must be treated with caution. For example, alcohol may alter emotionality by depressing cortical inhibitory systems, whereas amphetamines produce a similar effect by stimulating subcortical facilitory areas. Let us now examine some studies of drugs and their effects on the EEG.

LSD.   Lysergic acid diethylamide (LSD) is a known "psychotomimetic" drug that produces some symptoms of mental illness, such as hallucination and changes in mood and behavior. Investigators who have measured brain activity after administration of LSD generally agree that EEG amplitude decreases, alpha rhythms disappear, and the tracings become low in voltage and high in frequency (Rodin & Luby, 1966). The LSD effects increase progressively over a period of 1 to 2 hours following intravenous administration. Thus, the psychological effects may be related to faster brain activity, indicating a more aroused nervous system. The effects of LSD and several other psychoactive agents were studied by Fink, Itil, and Clyde (1966). Their computer analyses of the EEG spectrum indicated that beta activity was enhanced by LSD.

Marijuana.   The effects of marijuana on EEG and psychological test performance were studied by Dornbush, Fink, and Freedman (1971). The subjects were 10 male medical students who smoked cigarettes containing a high amount of marijuana (22.5 mg), a low amount (7.5 mg), or a placebo (the placebo was oregano, a spice that supposedly looks, smells, and tastes like "pot"). Measures of EEG, reaction time, short-term memory, and time estimation were taken under the different conditions. An increase in the percentage of time spent in alpha (8 to 13.5 Hz) activity and decreases in beta (18.5 and 24.5 Hz) and theta (4 to 7.5 Hz) activity occurred with the high dose but not with the low dose or the placebo. In addition, RT was reliably slowed, and performance on a short-term memory task was inhibited by the high dose. Accuracy of time estimation was not affected at any of the dose levels used. A similar result was obtained by Roth, Galanter, Weingartner, Vaughan, and Wyatt (1973), who tested the effects of smoking cigarettes containing marijuana or synthetic trans-tetrahydrocannabinol (THC) on EEGs of 12 young chronic users. The amount of EEG alpha activity increased with the marijuana but not with the placebo. The THC showed EEG effects that were in between the marijuana and the placebo, although both the THC and the marijuana cigarettes contained 10 mg of the drugs. Thus, the amount of alpha activity, the brain wave associated with a relaxed waking state, increased with marijuana use in these two experiments.

Heroin and Methadone.   The short-term effects of heroin on the EEG and other physiological measures was investigated by Volavka, Levine, Feldstein, and Fink (1974). Nineteen detoxified male postaddicts received 25 mg of heroin intravenously, on two occasions, and a placebo, also intravenously, on two other occasions. Heroin produced a significant decrease in EEG frequency within the first 5 minutes after injection. The decrease peaked at 15 minutes postinjection and remained at peak level when the 30-minute observation period ended. Respiration rate decreased from a mean of 18.5 cycles per minute before the injection to 7.6 cycles within 5 minutes after the administration of heroin. The authors suggested the possibility that some portion of the EEG decrease may have been caused by changes of blood chemistry resulting from decreased ventilation. An RT test indicated that reactions of the 19 subjects were significantly slower within 15 to 20 minutes after heroin injection than after the placebo.

The drug methadone is an analgesic that has widespread use as a detoxifying agent for narcotic addicts. Kay (1975) described the effects of methadone administration and withdrawal on the EEG of six volunteer prisoners. The procedure involved the oral administration of 100 mg of methadone daily during a stabilization phase lasting 51 to 56 days. Then an abstinence phase was instituted, which entailed a complete, abrupt withdrawal of methadone for a 5-month period. During the stabilization phase, significantly increased amounts of delta and theta activity and a slowing of alpha activity in the EEGs of the waking subjects were observed. The EEG activity returned to the normal control level after 10 weeks of the withdrawal period. The author pointed out that chronic administration of narcotic analgesics, such as methadone, may produce persistent functional changes in the nervous system. The appearance of delta waves in the EEG records of awake subjects is considered to be abnormal. The alpha changes (slowing) produced by the administration of methadone over a long period of time were similar to those obtained by Volavka et al. (1974) with the administration of a single dose of heroin. Both drugs had obvious CNS effects, as indicated by the records of brain activity.

Hypnotics and Tranquilizers.   Single doses of hypnotic drugs (nitrazepam and amylobarbitone) produced EEG changes in 10 normal subjects that were still observable 18 hours after administration (Malpas, Rowan, Joyce, Scott, 1970). In a follow-up study (Malpas, Legg & Scott 1974) with 10 anxious patients, the EEG showed changes with administration of hypnotic drugs (slow waves indicative of drowsiness and sleep), but the changes were not so pronounced as those noted in the earlier study with normal subjects. The authors suggested that the minor EEG changes in the 1974 study might have been due, in part, to the development of drug tolerance, because the hypnotics were taken for seven consecutive nights rather than in a single dose as in the 1970 study. West and Driver (1974) concluded that the EEG can be of value in diagnosing barbiturate intoxication in heroin-methadone addicts who deny taking barbiturates. They reported an investigation of 15 young addicts in which a greater amount of rhythmic fast components of the EEG was found in the records of those patients who admitted taking barbiturates than in those who denied it and had negative urines to back up their claims.

Nakra, Bond, and Lader (1975) examined the tranquilizing effects of metoclopramide (Maxolon) and prochlorperazine on EEGs and motor performance of 10 volunteers. The EEG was recorded from the left temporal area and from the vertex. The two drugs were given at .15 mg/kg of body weight, over a period of weeks. Both drugs increased the amount of slow-wave activity (2 to 4 Hz) and feelings of lethargy and sedation. However, neither had significant effects on the measure of motor performance used (e.g., RT and key tapping rate).

Alcohol.   Murphree (1973) noted that 1 minute after injection of a barbiturate (thiopental), fast-frequency activity of 21 to 25 cps appeared in the EEG record.

This curious phenomenon, in which activation of the EEG is produced by a substance that is supposed to be a depressant, is known as the "barbiturate buzz" and appears after relatively small doses of intravenously injected barbiturates (e.g., 1.5 mg/kg of thiopental). The question that Murphree asked was whether such effects could be found after drinking an alcoholic beverage. The EEG of a male subject was recorded for 10 minutes after drinking borboun whiskey (1.00 ml/kg pure alcohol). This is the equivalent to about 6 oz. of 80-proof whiskey for a 150-lb person. The EEG record showed a mixture of high-amplitude alpha with a "buzz" in the beta range. The subject acted giddy and "high" before and after the recording. Results from this and other subjects led Murphree to conclude that alcohol can produce stimulant effects as well as being a depressant in other instances. He suggested that the fast EEG activity observed after ingestion of alcohol may be due in part to disinhibition in the CNS and in part to catecholamine release. Catecholamines have a sympathomimetic action; that is, they mimic the stimulating effects of the SNS.

Although the short-term effect of alcohol may be to produce EEG activation, the longer-term effects of alcohol are to slow brain activity. This is illustrated in a study of "experimental hangover" performed by Sainio, Leino, Huttunen, and Ylikahri (1976). The EEGs of 27 healthy male volunteers were recorded 14 to 16 hours after they drank an amount of pure alcohol equivalent to drinking about 11 oz. of 80-proof whiskey, for a 150-lb individual. (Individuals who weighed more or less were given proportionate amounts, based on body weight.) At the 14- to 16-hour interval, when hangover is supposed to peak, 5 of the subjects reported severe hangover, 21 mild hangover, and 1 reported no hangover at all. Analyses of the EEG at this time showed a decrease and slowing of alpha activity and an increase in theta activity (4 to 7 Hz). A significant increase in the amount of 7 to 8 Hz activity was noted, as compared to the control condition in which subjects drank water. The researchers ruled out blood alcohol level, acidoses, hypoglycemia, or fatigue as a cause of the EEG change and concluded that the slowing of EEG during hangover was caused by the depressant action of alcohol, or its metabolites, on cortical function. Thus, the long-term effects of alcohol seem to be different in terms of EEG activity than short-term effects. No "barbituate buzz" was reported by Sainio et al., but it must be noted that they recorded 14 to 16 hours after alcohol ingestion, whereas Murphree recorded EEG immediately afterward.

A number of investigations have indicated that fast EEG activity is a distinctive characteristic of alcoholics, and that it may be genetically transmitted. Gabrielli et al. (1982) tested the hypothesis that 11–13-year-old sons of alcoholic fathers would show an excess of fast EEG activity. The EEGs of a sample of 27 children of alcoholics and 258 children of non-alcoholic parents were compared. The hypothesis was confirmed because male children at high risk for alcoholism themselves (25–30%) showed faster EEG activity than male children at low risk. The authors speculated that drinking alcohol may be reinforced by the slower brain waves, and more relaxed state, produced in those with a tendency towards fast brain activity. If such a relationship could be established, then perhaps a more acceptable way of slowing brain activity could be encouraged in persons at risk for becoming alcoholic.

Nicotine (Smoking).   Ulett and Itil (1969) tested the effects of cessation and resumption of cigarette smoking (nicotine) on the EEGs of eight males who were heavy smokers (more than one pack of cigarettes a day). The individuals tested were deprived of cigarettes for 24 hours, during which time the EEG showed a slowing of activity. This slowing was reversed when two cigarettes were smoked after the deprivation period. A similar result was obtained by Philips (1971). Six moderate smokers were tested after smoking for 5 minutes or engaging in conversation for 5 minutes. After smoking, the EEG showed an "activation pattern" in the form of decreased amplitude and a desynchronized EEG record. Thus, nicotine seems to speed EEG activity of smokers. Knott and Venables (1977) measured EEG alpha of 10 nonsmokers, 17 deprived smokers, and 13 nondeprived smokers before and after they smoked two cigarettes. The deprived smokers had a slower dominant alpha frequency than nonsmokers before the two groups smoked. The two cigarettes brought their EEG frequency up to the level of nonsmokers. Knott and Venables discussed the possibility that smoking is an attempt by smokers to achieve the psychological state associated with higher alpha frequencies, that is, one of increased efficiency and attention. They indicated that their results support the hypothesis that deprived smokers, as compared to nonsmokers, are characterized by a state of cortical underactivity, and smoking increases their activity to a level comparable to that which nonsmokers are at naturally. In a study of Herning, Jones, and Bachman (1983), the EEG patterns of heavy smokers (2 packs a day) was slowed when they were deprived of nicotine cigarettes. The EEG changes were in the form of greater amounts of theta activity and a decrease in the dominant alpha frequency. Smoking a nicotine cigarette led to faster EEG patterns that lasted from 30 to 90 minutes.

In summary, the studies reviewed in this section indicate that marijuana and heroin both have depressant effects on brain activity and performance (methadone has effects similar to heroin). Two tranquilizers (Nakra et al., 1975) increased EEG slow-wave activity but had no performance effects. Hypnotic drugs produced slowing of EEG, whereas LSD resulted in low-amplitude, high-frequency brain waves. Alcohol was seen to have short-term activating effects, but produced depressant effects after a longer period of time. Fast EEG activity (excess of beta, and deficient alpha, theta, and delta activity) characteristic of alcoholics has also been found in sons of alcoholics, suggesting a biological characteristic that may be inherited. Nicotine (cigarette smoking) appears to speed the EEG frequency of smokers and bring it up to the level of nonsmokers.

Hormones

The endocrine system consists of ductless glands that secrete their chemicals (called hormones) directly into the bloodstream. These hormones have profound influences over many body functions, and, in addition, their undersecretion or oversecretion may have behavioral effects. The endocrine system is regulated by the nervous system (primarily through connections between the hypothalamus and pituitary gland) and, therefore, the EEG may be able to reflect interactions between these systems. EEG activity has been found to be increased in cases of hyperthyroidism (excessive secretion of the hormone thyroxin) and decreased in hypothyroidism (Hermann & Quarton, 1964; Thiebaut, Rohmer, & Wackenheim, 1958). A lack of adrenal cortical hormones has been related to slow brain activity, which can be speeded up through administration of the hormone cortisone (Engel & Margolin, 1942).

Vogel, Broverman, and Klaiber (1971) conducted two studies to examine the effects of gonadal (sex) hormones on EEG responses. The EEG response measured was the "driving" response, defined as the production of EEG waves at the same frequency as a flashing light for two consecutive seconds. Thus, for example, if a flashing light was presented to a subject 15 times a second, the driving response would be evidenced if EEG waves occurred at a rate of 15 cycles per second for at least a 2-second period. Vogel et al. found that EEG driving was significantly less when blood estrogen levels were high. The first study was done with 14 normally menstruating women and significantly less EEG driving was observed during the preovulatory phase of the menstrual cycle, when blood estrogen levels are rising, than in the postovulatory phase, when both estrogen and progesterone levels are high. In a second study, the EEG driving response was manipulated by administering estrogen and progesterone to six women who required hormone therapy for secondary amenorrhea; that is, their menstrual cycle had stopped completely some time after it had started in puberty. For these women, EEG driving was decreased significantly after administration of estrogen, compared to the EEG response that occurred after combined administration of estrogen and progesterone. It was hypothesized that estrogen inhibited the EEG driving response through the steroid's known ability to inhibit monoamine (oxidase) MAO. The MAO reduces supplies of monoamines in the brain, such as norepinephrine, which facilitate neural transmission. Thus, if MAO activity in the brain is depressed, EEG driving should be diminished, because substances that enhance transmission block the driving response to light. Because progesterone is an antagonist to estrogen, their combined administration should allow EEG driving to occur, as was found in the Vogel et al. study.

A later experiment by Vogel, Broverman, Klaiber, and Kobayasri (1974) provided further support for the hypothesis regarding the relationship between MAO activity and the EEG driving response. This time, 10 male subjects were given the drug isocarboxazid (Marplan), which is known to inhibit MAO. A reduced level of MAO in blood samples, several days after the administration of Marplan, was significantly related to decreases in the EEG driving response. They interpreted these results as reflecting the disruptive effect of central adrenergic processes on EEG driving response to photic stimulation.

In a related study, Creutzfeldt et al. (1976) studied EEG changes during the menstrual cycle of 32 normal women, aged 20 to 28. The EEGs, blood hormone levels, and psychological test performances were measured for 16 spontaneously menstruating women and 16 women taking oral contraceptives. A significant increase in dominant alpha frequency occurred in the spontaneous group during the luteal phase of the cycle, and this increase in alpha was significantly correlated with an improvement in RT, simple arithmetic, and spatial orientation. (The luteal phase is one in which the hormone progesterone reaches a peak level, and it occurs shortly after ovulation.) No such acceleration of alpha frequency nor performance improvement was observed in the oral contraceptive group. As a possible physiological mechanism for the increase in alpha frequency, the authors postulated a shortening of inhibitory postsynaptic potentials (IPSPs) in the thalamus during the luteal phase. They speculated that this decreased inhibition might also cause the improvement in RT and other tests. Another interesting suggestion by these authors is that the increased alpha frequency might be the physiological basis of premenstrual tension, that is, the increased CNS activation may be the basis for the increased feelings of irritability noticed by women at the end of the luteal phase, just prior to menstruation. The several studies reviewed indicate that hormones can affect EEG activity. However, these internal events may be difficult to control in the usual experimental situation.

Oxygen

The CNS is critically dependent on oxygen supply for its functioning. Hence, it would be logical to expect changes in the oxygen supply, or factors that influence it, to be reflected in brain activity. Past studies have indicated that a lack of oxygen caused a slower frequency and higher amplitude EEG, whereas oxygen excess increased EEG frequency (Engel, 1945; Gibbs, Williams, & Gibbs, 1940). Several recent investigations have examined oxygen effects somewhat indirectly, that is, through studies of elderly persons, whose cerebral blood flow and oxygen are usually reduced, and through alterations in the usual breathing mixture as encountered in deep sea diving habitats and at high altitudes.

The relationship between cerebral blood flow and EEG frequency has been clearly demonstrated by Ingvar, Sjolund, and Ardo (1976). They found a high positive correlation between EEG frequency and a measure of cerebral blood flow and oxygen consumption; that is, EEG frequency decreased with decreased blood flow and oxygen consumption.

A number of studies cited by Cole, Branconnier, and Martin (1975) indicate that EEG activity in elderly persons sometimes shows a slowing, for example, a decrease in alpha frequency. Papaverine HCL (Pavabid) is a vasodilator (a drug that dilates blood vessels and increases blood flow). Cole et al. administered Papaverine (300 mg) to 10 healthy elderly persons (mean age of 68) over a 2-week period. They reported that Papaverine altered EEG activity by increasing the percentage of time spent in alpha, without affecting mood or psychological test performance. The psychological tests included one of short-term memory (digit span), problem solving (Block Design), attention (continuous performance test), and self- and machine-paced digit symbol substitutions. The authors suggested that the lack of effect on psychological test performance may have been due to the fact that the subjects were already functioning at high levels.

The EEGs of 10 centenarians (persons 100 years of age or older) were examined by Hubbard, Sunde, and Goldensohn (1976). Seven of the 10 subjects were considered "healthy," because they were living in a community and had been examined for evidence of CNS or psychiatric disorder. The EEGs of the three persons with CNS disease were abnormal. The average EEG frequency of the seven healthy subjects was 8.62 Hz, or 1 to 2 Hz slower than the alpha rhythm reported for normal middle-aged and young adults, respectively. Three of these seven subjects showed one EEG abnormality, a presence of slow waves in the delta range. The authors noted that, from these results, it would appear that the fall in alpha frequency becomes negligible after 80 to 90 years of age. Hubbard et al. (1976) concluded that results for centenarians are compatible with the notion of a causal relationship between artherosclerosis, a drop in cerebral blood flow, increased incidence of slow waves, and a decrease in alpha frequency.

Rostain and Charpy (1976) investigated the effects on EEG of two simulated deep dives, in which subjects breathed a helium-oxygen mixture. Previous research had established that deep diving to a simulated depth of 300 m (about 990 ft) produced increased theta rhythm, a decrease of alpha and beta, and a lowering of the level of vigilance. The Rostain and Charpy (1976) experiment took place in two stages: In the first part, two subjects stayed at 500 m (about 1,650 ft) for 100 hours, and in the second, two subjects stayed at 610 m (about 2,000 ft) for 80 minutes. EEG changes, relative to "surface" recordings, were similar to the previous study in that theta activity increased, fast activity was depressed, and an EEG resembling Stage 1 sleep appeared. The authors concluded that the EEG changes could result from deficits in cerebral oxygenation, decreased blood flow, or to alterations in metabolic processes caused by hyperbaric (high air pressure) conditions.

The effects of sleep at high altitudes on the EEG as compared to sea-level sleep was investigated by Reite, Jackson, Cahoon, and Weil (1975). All-night sleep EEG was recorded from six male army recruits, first during two nights at sea level (160 ft) and then during four nights while sleeping at the Pikes Peak research station (14,110 ft). Sleep at high altitude was initially characterized by decreases in Stage 3 and 4 sleep (see Table 4.1) and an increase in number of awakenings. This was accompanied by subjective complaints of sleeplessness. The authors were unsure whether the results were due to less oxygen intake (hypoxemia) at the high altitude or to alkalosis (increase in blood pH levels) often present after arrival at high altitude. Both hypoxia and alkalosis decreased during continuous exposure to altitude, and the authors related this to improvements in the objective and subjective quality of sleep as the experiment progressed in time.

In summary, studies in which oxygen deficit is indicated provide evidence for a slowing of EEG activity associated with such decreased supply.

Body Temperature

An early study of body temperature effects on the EEG indicated that alpha wave frequency increased with temperature increases (Hoagland, 1936). Essentially the same conclusion was reached by O'Hanlon, McGrath, and McCauley (1974), who increased body core temperature (to 102.2 degrees F) by diathermy while EEG and perceptual acuity was measured. In this study, "body core" referred to temperature measured at the subject's tympanic membrane (eardrum) by a thermistor. Previous experimentation had shown that tympanic temperature approximates brain temperature. The results of the O'Hanlon study revealed that mean alpha frequency increased with increase in body core temperature. The reason for this increase in synchronous brain activity with increase in body temperature and increases in the amount of unsynchronized (beta) activity with decreases in body temperature still remains unknown, but may be related to the role of metabolic factors in the production of EEG activity.

EFFECTS OF ENVIRONMENTAL FACTORS ON EVENT-RELATED BRAIN POTENTIALS (ERPs)

This section examines some studies dealing with the effects of drugs, hormones, and oxygen level on ERPs.

Drugs

There are numerous studies of the effects of pharmacologic agents on ERPs. Many of these were reviewed by Shagass (1972), who noted that various changes in ERPs occur as the result of drug action. For example, diazepam has been found to reduce the amplitude of the visual ERP (VEP) and somatosensory ERP (SEP). This would imply that beneficial effects with a psychiatric population are related to decreased cortical responsivity to sensory stimuli, and Shagass suggested that it may improve the functioning of central mechanisms by improving the balance between excitatory and inhibitory processes. Lithium has been frequently used in the treatment of manic-depressive patients in recent years. Manic-depressives show tremendously exaggerated mood swings, ranging from extreme excitement to immobilizing depression.

Tranquilizers and Barbiturates.   The commonly used tranquilizer Valium (diazepam) has been found to decrease the amplitude of human VEPs (Bergamasco,

1966). The effects of 7.5 to 10 mg of intravenously administered Valium on the VEPs and SEPs of nine normal persons was investigated by Ebe, Meier-Ewert, and Broughton (1969). The amplitudes of both VEPs and SEPs was reduced.

Saletu, Saletu, and Itil (1972) investigated the effects of chlorpromazine and diazepam on the SEPs of healthy male subjects. Chlorpromazine is a widely used antipsychotic drug. Whereas the placebo did not affect the SEP, 50 mg of chlorpromazine prolonged latencies of all components 2 hours after administration. In addition, chlorpromazine resulted in decreased amplitudes of the late components of the SEP (those occurring at 150 msec or later). Diazepam (5 mg) resulted in a decrease in SEP amplitude. Thus, it appears that both drugs suppressed brain activity, with the chlorpromazine having more potent effects because it prolonged both latency and amplitude changes.

Tecce, Cole, and Savignano-Bowman (1975) measured CNV and RT of 28 normal women after they were given 50 mg of chlorpromazine or a placebo. The experimental paradigm was that of a constant foreperiod RT situation in which S1 was a light flash and S2 was a tone that occurred 1.5 seconds after the light and was terminated by a key press. They found that this relatively small dose of chlorpromazine significantly reduced electrical brain activity (CNV) and lowered alertness (slower RTs) in the third hour after administration of the drug. Tecce et al. concluded that CNV amplitude appears to be an accurate indicator of drug-produced changes in alertness. In summary, the general pattern of results for diazepam and chlorpromazine is one in which brain activity is suppressed.

The effects of a barbiturate on the VEP were illustrated by Bergamini and Bergamasco (1967). Thiopental was administered intravenously and was found to modify the VEP by decreasing its amplitude during initial stages of anesthesia. When barbiturate anesthesia was deeper (and delta waves were present in the EEG), the early components of the VEP completely disappeared, that is, those that normally occurred before 60 msec.

The effects of two barbiturates on CNV and attention performance was tested by Tecce, Cole, Mayer, and Lewis (1977). Thirty male subjects were randomly assigned to either pentobarbital (100 mg), phenobarbital (100 mg), or placebo groups (10 subjects per group). Pentobarbitol has short duration effects, whereas those of phenobarbital are relatively long-lasting. The CNV was recorded from frontal (Fz), central (Cz), and parietal (Pz) scalp areas. The measure of attention was time to respond to a target letter in a series of letters. The only significant drug effect was a decrease in CNV amplitude recorded from Pz 2 hours after administration of phenobarbital. This was accomplished by a decrement in attention performance.

Amphetamine is a CNS stimulant and has been used as an antidepressant in psychiatric patients. Amphetamine had an unexpected effect on the CNV in the first hour after administration in a number of normal individuals (Tecce & Cole, 1974). Thirteen of 20 adults who were given 10 mg of dextroamphetamine evidenced lower CNV amplitudes and drowsiness during the first hour following administration of the drug. The other seven showed alertness and increased CNV amplitude. All subjects showed increased alertness and CNV amplitudes 2 and 3 hours following administration of the drug. Tecce and Cole concluded that amphetamine is not a simple CNS stimulant but can produce an early transient depression in brain activity, accompanied by feelings of lethargy in some persons. Methylphenidate (brand name Ritalin) is a stimulant drug that, paradoxically, calms down hyperactive children with attention deficit disorder. This drug was used with normal young adults (Brumaghim, Klorman, Strauss, Levine & Goldstein, 1987) performing the Sternberg task, which involves short-term memory and RT. These researchers found that P300 latency was shorter and RT was faster under the drug versus placebo condition. Hence, methylphenidate shortened the timing of motor processes and the duration of stimulus evaluation time (P300 latency). Thus, results with barbiturates indicate suppression of brain activity, and one suggestive study with amphetamine indicated that early effects may be stimulating or depressing, depending on the individual, and methylphenidate appears to shorten RT and speed up evaluation time in normal young adults.

Effects of Marijuana on the ERP. Lewis, Dustman, Peters, Straight, and Beck (1973) tested the effects of known oral doses of tetrahydrocannabinol (THC), the active ingredient in marijuana, on the VEPs and SEPs of 10 male and 10 female subjects. The subjects were equally divided into two groups: frequent smokers (three times a week) and infrequent smokers (two times a month). Three dosage levels (.2, .4, and .6 mg/kg of body weight) were administered to each subject on flavored sugar cubes. (These dosage levels are equivalent to about 10 mg, 20 mg, and 40 mg of THC for a 150-lb subject.) The highest dose (.6 mg/kg) produced delays in the appearance of the various wave components of the VEP. There was little effect on amplitude. All dose levels produced subjective ''highs.'' The finding was interpreted in terms of decreased sensitivity of cortical and subcortical neurons due to the ingestion of THC, because visual responses were delayed after its administration.

Roth et al. (1973) studied the effects of smoking a marijuana cigarette (10 mg endogenous THC) on the auditory ERPs (AEPs) of 12 chronic users. A placebo cigarette (containing .5 mg of THC) and another cigarette containing synthetic THC (10 mg) were also smoked. Roth and colleagues found no latency effects, but decreased AEP amplitudes were noted with the real marijuana cigarette. The reduced effect of synthetic THC may be related to the fact that purified THC undergoes greater destruction during smoking than THC contained endogenously in the marijuana leaf.

Low, Klonoff, and Marcus (1973) measured visual and auditory ERPs and the CNV 45 minutes before and 45 minutes after smoking a marijuana cigarette containing high (9.1), low (4.8), or less than .01 mg of THC. Performance in a complex auditory discrimination task was simultaneously measured. High doses of marijuana resulted in longer auditory ERP latencies, and interfered with the discrimination task. The CNV increased in amplitude was a consequence of marijuana smoking. Kopell, Tinklenberg, and Hollister (1972) also found enhancement of CNV with THC. Thus, marijuana appears to slow, and in one instance to reduce the amplitude of sensory ERPs. However, the evidence suggests an enhancement of CNV with marijuana. The enhancement has been interpreted by Kopell et al. as indicating that subjects who are intoxicated can better attend to relevant, simple stimuli as required in the CNV paradigm. These interesting marijuana effects on ERPs require further investigation.

Alcohol. The effects of alcohol on ERPs have been studied by a number of investigators. For example, Gross, Begleiter, Tobin, and Kissin (1966) measured auditory ERPs of 10 persons after they drank either 100 cc of water with ice or 100 cc of 90 proof whiskey (about 3 oz) with ice. All components of the AEP were reduced after ingestion of alcohol, with maximal effect noted 15 to 30 minutes after consumption. Similar results were found by Lewis, Dustman, and Beck (1970), who administered alcohol doses equivalent to about 1 and 3 oz for a 150-lb subject. Somatosensory and visual ERPs were measured after administration of either alcohol condition or water placebo. The higher alcohol dose reduced amplitudes of VEP and SEP late components. The smaller dose and placebo had no effect. Rhodes, Obitz, and Creel (1975) reported that alcohol reduced the amplitude of VEPs recorded from the central scalp. Similar to earlier studies, it was the later components (60 to 200 msec) that were affected most by the alcohol. Salamy and Williams (1973) demonstrated that as the blood alcohol concentration (BAC) level of subjects increased, amplitude of the SEP decreased. Again, the major effects were on later components of ERPs. Salamy (1973) also found the SEP amplitude to decrease with BAC. An illustration from Salamy (1973) is reproduced in Fig. A.1 and shows a clear decrease in the SEP for one subject from Condition A (placebo) to B (low dose) to C (high dose). Thus, it is clear that alcohol has an effect on the neural processes reflected by ERPs. The results of Lewis et al. (1970) led them to conclude that alcohol exerts a depressant effect on subcortical areas first (e.g., the reticular formation) and later on the cortex. It had previously been hypothesized that cortical effects appeared before subcortical ones.

Nicotine. Hall, Rappaport, Hopkins, and Griffin (1973) investigated the effects of smoking withdrawal and resumption on the VEP. They measured VEPs of nine smokers (three-quarters to three packs per day) to four intensities of light. The VEPs were taken during different baseline periods: before abstinence from smoking, after 12 and 36 hours of abstinence, and finally after resumption of smoking (one cigarette). The results showed a decrease in VEP amplitude during the no-smoking period and an increase in VEP amplitude when smoking was resumed. Hall and his associates suggested that the increased VEP amplitude indicated that the processing of sensory stimuli by the brain is changed when smokers use tobacco. Perhaps the withdrawal of nicotine for smokers is distract-

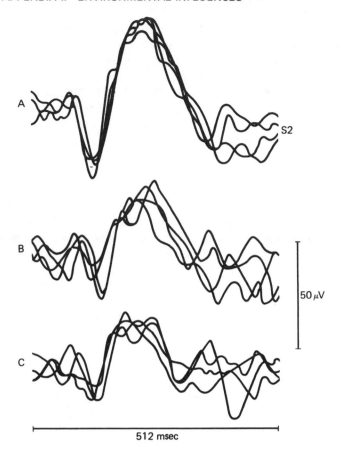

FIG. A-1.   Dose-response relationship between somatosensory evoked potential amplitude and blood alcohol concentration (BAC). Four super-imposed single EPs recorded from one subject under three alcohol treatments: A, placebo (BAC of 0 mg %); B, low dose (BAC of 50–65 mg %); high dose (BAC of 95-110 mg %).

ing, in which case it might result in lower VEPs. Distracting stimuli have been shown to reduce CNV amplitude (e.g., see Tecce, 1972).

In summary, the drug studies reviewed here indicate that tranquilizers have depressant effects on ERPs. Alcohol, marijuana, and barbiturates also have depressant effects, but the effects of marijuana are different from the other two, in that they are sometimes manifested as delays in ERP components, rather than as decreases in amplitude. There is nothing in the results of ERP studies to contradict the generally accepted notion that the effects of depressant drugs are mainly on the ARAS. Abstinence from cigarette smoking seems to depress the VEPs to original levels. This finding could be important in terms of the possible physiological mechanisms that cause certain individuals to become heavy smokers (i.e., does it activate their physiology to more effective levels?), or it may only reflect a distracting effect of nicotine withdrawal for these periods. More work is needed to settle this question.

Oxygen and Breathing Mixture Effects

When divers breathe compressed air at a depth of 100 feet or more, they may suffer from compressed air intoxication, sometimes referred to as *nitrogen narcosis*. Approximately 80% of the air we breathe at sea level is nitrogen. At sea level pressure, the nitrogen has no effects, but at high pressures, it can cause varying degrees of narcosis. (Oxygen is also toxic at high pressures and can cause convulsions and coma if breathed at high pressures for a prolonged period of time.) After an hour or more of breathing air at high pressures, some of the symptoms of alcohol intoxication are observed, including giddiness and drowsiness. Nitrogen narcosis has been referred to as "raptures of the depths" because it sometimes occurred in deep sea divers.

Bennett, Ackless, and Cripps (1969) showed that hyperbaric nitrogen and oxygen both depressed the amplitude of the auditory ERP. They concluded that these results supported the hypothesis that breathing these gases at high pressures affected such subcortical systems as the ARAS of the brain stem. The effects of inhaling 10%, 20%, and 30% nitrous oxide in oxygen were compared with those of pure oxygen in 12 normal individuals (Jarvis & Lader, 1971). Reaction time was also measured under each of these drug conditions. All components of the AEP were recorded according to dose level of nitrous oxide, with higher doses causing greater decreases in amplitude. RT was also prolonged in a dose-related manner.

Bevan (1971) recorded the AEP and CNV from 13 experienced divers before, during, and following an exposure to an increased air pressure simulating a depth of 300 ft in sea water. The AEP was significantly reduced, but the CNV was not. These results were interpreted as indicating different CNS generators for the AEP and CNV. It was also suggested that the AEP was attenuated because of inhibition effects on the ARAS, whereas the CNV was considered to be a self-propagating phenomenon, initiated by the interaction between specific and nonspecific and associational thalamic nuclei. However, Bevan's conclusion that the CNV and AEP are generated by independent mechanisms was questioned by Smith & Strawbridge (1974). They pointed out that the AEP is more complex (has more components) than the CNV, and a reduction in amplitude could reflect an actual change in amplitude of individual potentials, latency variations, or changes in cortical area acting in synchrony. In their own study, Smith and Strawbridge measured AEP, VEP, and CNV. They suggested that further studies be done on the effects of breathing pure oxygen at pressures greater than one atmosphere.

Aliphatic hydrocarbons, such as n-hexane, have the potential to be neurotoxic if fumes are breathed in for prolonged periods. To investigate the effects of n-Hexane exposure, Seppalainen, Raitta, and Huuskanen (1979) studied VEPs to light flashes of 15 workers occupationally exposed to n-hexane for 5–21 years and compared their responses to 10 healthy control persons. The amplitude of the VEP components was clearly smaller for n-Hexane exposed subjects. The changes were interpreted to indicate brain dysfunction, probably due to conduction blockage in axons. n-Hexane has been shown to cause axon damage in both experimental animals and humans, and the VEP results indicate that the visual systems of industrial workers are susceptible to its toxic effects.

In summary, hyperbaric conditions seem to have depressant effects on sensory ERPs but not on the CNV. Preliminary interpretations suggest a different generating mechanism for sensory ERPs and CNVs, an implication contained in the classifactory system of Vaughan (1969), in which sensory ERPs and CNVs were separately categorized. Important information about potential neurotoxins can be obtained through ERP investigations.

Effects of Hormones on the ERP

The undersecretion of the hormone thyroxin by the thyroid gland can have serious psychological effects in both infants and adults. A condition known as *myxedema* develops in adults with thyroxin deficiency (hypothyroidism) and is characterized by apathy and mental sluggishness, among other effects. The ERPs of patients with hypothyroidism were studied before and after administration of thyroid hormone (Nishitani & Kooi, 1968). The hormone resulted in decreased latencies and increased amplitudes of the ERP, indicating greater sensitivity of the nervous system to stimuli.

An excess of thyroxin, or hyperthyroidism, results in extreme nervousness, insomnia, and tremor owing to stimulating effects of this hormone on the nervous system. Hyperthyroidism was produced experimentally by administering 300 mg of the thyroid hormone triiodothyronine (T3) to normal persons (Kopell, Wittner, Lunde, Warrick, & Edwards 1970). The T3 was found to increase the amplitude of VEPs when subjects were not selectively attending to visual stimuli but had no effect when they were selectively attending. The researchers interpreted this as a reduction in selective attention, as measured by VEP amplitude, caused by T3; that is, the hormone appeared to increase cortical response to nonsignificant information, while not affecting response to significant stimuli.

The somatosensory and visual ERPs of 14 persons suffering from hyperthyroidism were compared with the ERPs of 45 normal control individuals in an experiment conducted by Takahashi and Fujitani (1970). They found that amplitudes of each component of the SEP and VEP were greater in hyperthyroid than in normal persons. No significant latency differences were noted between the patient and normal groups. Straumanis and Shagass (1976) administered T3 to 12 normal subjects and found increased SEP amplitudes during the first 100 msec following the stimulus. Thus, the general results for the thyroid hormone seem to correlate an excess with greater ERP amplitudes and deficiencies with lower amplitudes, possibly reflecting differential sensitivity of the CNS to stimuli when levels of this hormone are either high or low.

A number of investigators have reported that women have larger amplitude ERPs than men (e.g., see Shagass, 1972). Buchsbaum, Henkin, and Christiansen (1974) conducted an experiment to determine possible reasons for the noted sex differences. Visual and auditory ERPs of 166 normal males and females, aged 6 to 60, and 10 females with gonadal dysgenesis (lacking in estrogen or progesterone production) were measured. The 10 female patients were compared with normal women. The role of gonadal hormones in producing the sex differences in amplitude seemed to be ruled out on two counts: (a) females had larger ERPs than males at all ages (prepuberty and postmenopause), and (b) ERPs of female patients did not differ from those of normals. Greater auditory ERP amplitudes to 1000 Hz tones were obtained for women and girls as compared to men and boys in a study by Martineau, Tanguay, Garreau, Roux, and Lelord (1984). These differences were obtained at both Cz and Oz recording sites. One possible explanation for the difference was mentioned by Martineau and colleagues in their introduction, and this was that male–female differences may be related to shorter anatomical distances in the sensory pathways and between generators and scalp surface in females because of smaller average head and brain size. This is a possibility, but the issue remains unresolved.

ENVIRONMENTAL FACTORS AND THE ELECTROMYOGRAM (EMG)

Drugs

Girke, Krebs, and Muller-Oerlinghausen (1975) noted complaints of muscular weakness in manic-depressive patients undergoing long-term lithium treatment. To test the hypothesis that this was due to a disturbance in peripheral neuromuscular function, they measured EMGs of seven healthy volunteers before, during, and after lithium administration. The EMG was recorded from the extensor digitorum brevis muscle of the right foot. They found that the duration of potentials was increased and nerve conduction velocity was decreased after 1 week of lithium intake. Both muscle potential duration and nerve conduction returned to near prelithium levels 1 week after the administration of lithium sulfate was discontinued. The authors hypothesized that lithium may exert its effects by influencing magnesium metabolism, which in turn may affect the regulation of enzymes such as ATP.

Caffeine is one of the most widely used psychoactive substances, because it is present in common beverages such as coffee, tea, and soft drinks. Those who habitually consume large amounts of caffeine each day (equivalent to 5 cups or more of coffee) suffer from withdrawal symptoms, including increased muscle tension, headache, muscle aches, anxiety, irritability, and drowsiness (Rizzo, Stamps, & Fehr, 1988; White, Lincoln, Pearce, Reeb, & Vaida, 1980). In a study by White et al. (1980), high consumers of caffeine had elevated forearm EMG after 3 hours of abstinence, whereas low users stayed at the same level. Administration of caffeine speeded reaction times of both high and low user groups. Withdrawal of caffeine led to elevated scores on measures of anxiety (State-Trait Anxiety Inventory) for the heavy users.

Exercise

Milner-Brown, Stein, and Lee (1975) reported that the degree to which firing of motor units in one muscle are synchronized is affected by the use of the muscle in physical exercise. That is, the impulses from two or more motor units coincide in time more frequently than would be expected for unrelated firings. Recordings from the first dorsal interosseus muscle of the hand in seven weightlifters showed significantly more synchronization than in seven control subjects. Further, records from four additional subjects before and after 6 weeks of exercise involving the same hand muscle showed a significant increase in the level of motor unit synchronization The authors suggested that the different firing patterns of exercised versus nonexercised muscles may be due to enhancement of connections from motor cortex to spinal motoneurons to produce synchronization of motor units during steady, voluntary contractions. One may wonder whether this type of synchronization of motor units occurs in the development of a skilled motor performance.

ENVIRONMENTAL FACTORS AND ELECTRODERMAL ACTIVITY (EDA)

Hormones and Drugs

Venables and Christie (1973) discussed the possibility of hormonal influences on EDA. For example, they pointed out that progesterone has been found to decrease ecrrine gland sweat output and that ACTH has similar effects Presumably, then, these hormones have the potential to affect EDA. In fact, a decrease in resting SCL was found during the luteal phase in the menstrual cycle of 12 female subjects (Little & Zahn, 1974). Progesterone level reaches its peak during the luteal phase. Further, Little and Zahn found significant increases in SCR during the ovulatory portion of the menstrual cycle, the time when estrogen reaches peak levels in the body.

The effects of preanesthetic doses of diazepam on SCRs obtained under thiopental sodium induction was investigated by Williams, Jones, and Williams (1975). The subjects were physiologically normal young female patients about to undergo operations. One half received 10 mg of diazepam or 10 mg of a placebo intravenously. The diazepam subject required significantly less thiopental sodium (44%) to reach the point at which spontaneous SCRs abruptly ceased than did the placebo group. Corsico, Moiziszowica, Bursuck, and Rovaro (1976) compared the effects of two psychoactive drugs, etifoxine (300 mg) and dextroamphetamine (5 mg) on SCRs and pursuit-rotor performance of six undergraduates. All persons received a placebo and the two drugs in a double-blind procedure over a 3-week period. The subjects were tested before, 2 hours after, and 6 hours after drug administration. At the 2-hour period, both drugs led to significant reductions in SCR magnitude and improved pursuit-rotor performance as compared to the placebo condition. These differences disappeared 6 hours after the administration of the three treatments.

In summary, although the amount of data is scanty, it would appear that both hormones and drugs can affect EDA. Thus, investigators of electrodermal phenomena should be aware of these possible influences and gather appropriate information from subjects so that these factors may be accounted for in the design of their experiments.

Racial and Experimenter Effects

Johnson and Corah (1963) found that Black subjects had lower SCL than Whites. A number of other researchers have obtained similar findings (e.g., Bernstein, 1965; Johnson & Landon, 1965; Malmo, 1965). Johnson and Corah (1963) hypothesized that the difference might be due to either a thicker stratum corneum in Blacks or a difference in the number of active eccrine sweat glands. This latter hypothesis was tested in a study by Johnson and Landon (1965), in which they used 30 Black and 29 White subjects. No difference in the number of active sweat glands was found. However, Malmo (1965) found lower SCL for Blacks as compared to Whites and also reported a significant examiner effect. That is, subjects tested by one experimenter showed higher SCL than those seen by a second experimenter. However, the White and Black subjects did not respond differentially to the two experimenters. Juniper and Dykman (1967) reported that 29 White males had a higher sweat gland count than did 13 Blacks in a similar age range (20 to 60 years). In addition, SCL of Blacks was lower. The effects of race and experimenter's race were studied by Fisher and Kotses (1973). The SCL and SCR frequency and magnitude of 12 White and 12 Black subjects were measured under two conditions. Two Black and two White experimental assistants (naive as to the purpose of the study) obtained the measurements. Blacks had lower SCLs, as previously reported. The race of the experimenter did have an effect on SCR amplitude and frequency. For example, the size of the SCR was greater in magnitude and took longer to habituate for White subjects who were tested by Black experimenters. Fisher and Kotses concluded that novelty was a factor in the result, because the presence of Black experimenters was a relatively infrequent occurrence.

One common denominator in these studies seems to be skin color, that is, darker skin being related to lower SCLs. A device to objectively measure intensity of skin color (in reflectance units) was developed by Korol, Bergfeld, and McLaughlin (1975). These investigators measured skin color of 25 Whites and 25 Blacks with their "pigmentometer" and correlated these with SCL. They reported that degree of skin pigmentation was related to SCL, that is, the darker the skin color, the lower the SCL. It is still not clear whether the racial differences found are due to genetic elements other than skin color, for example, number of sweat glands, or some other factor. Perhaps studies comparing other racial groups would be of value in answering this basic question. In the meantime, skin color is a possible variable that investigators must be aware of in conducting studies.

Another variable is that of the experimenter's sex. As an example, Fisher and Kotses (1974) found that male subjects had higher SCL and a greater number of SCRs when a female served as experimenter than when the experimenter was a male. These experimenters also suggest a stimulus novelty explanation. That is, the female experimenter is a relatively novel situation in the psychological laboratory, and stimulus novelty has been related to EDA in past experimentation. However, arousal is also a possibility, especially when there is mutual attraction between female experimenters and male subjects.

Experimental Situation and EDA

When a subject enters a novel experimental situation, SCL is likely to be elevated. When he or she settles down and relaxes, SCL will drop, and when the actual experiment is about to start, it will again show an increase. This appears to reflect activity of the SNS in a new situation where the individual observes a large amount of electronic equipment in a strange laboratory and does not know what to expect. As has been pointed out by Woodworth and Schlosberg (1954), the changes in SCL and number of SCRs during the performance of an experimental task are affected by apprehension, relief, the work itself, and habituation. Because EDA is so sensitive to a variety of stimulus variables, it may be best to test subjects in more than one experimental session to enable situational effects to dissipate. Similarly, it may be desirable to use persons who have served in previous experiments, as long as this does not interfere with the nature of the study, to reduce these extraneous effects. These same observations would hold true in the use of other physiological measures, but are perhaps most critical in the measurement of the very sensitive EDA. Relatively long-term monitoring of EDA was accomplished for 12 persons during a normal working day (Turpin, Shine, & Lader, 1983). The subjects wore a portable recorder to record skin conductance, ambient temperature, and arm movements. They found that as temperature increased, the frequency of SCRs increased. It was also reported that long-term measurement results in lower SCLs, thus ambulatory monitoring provides a relative, rather than an absolute, measure of SCL.

ENVIRONMENTAL FACTORS AND PUPIL SIZE

Drugs

The narcotic analgesic, morphine, produces pupillary constriction through its CNS effects (Goth, 1964). Pupillometry was used by Robinson, Howe, Varni, Ream, and Hegge (1974) to study pupil size of 10 heroin users during the first 6 days of withdrawal. Five control subjects were used for comparison purposes. In the acute heroin intoxication state, the pupils of patients were significantly constricted relative to controls, with average diameters of 3.5 mm and 5.0 mm, respectively. Ten hours after the last dose of heroin, there was no difference between patients and controls. As withdrawal progressed, the pupils of patients continued to dilate until, at the end of the 6-day period, the patients had significantly larger pupils than controls. The authors concluded that pupil diameter is a good differential indicator of heroin intoxication and withdrawal.

Another drug that produces pupillary constriction is pilocarpine. It can produce this action if applied to the surface of the eye in a 1% solution. Pupillary dilation is produced by the drug atropine. In ophthalmologic and research settings, it is applied to the eye as a 0.5% to 1.5% solution. Homatropine is preferable to atropine because it is much shorter in duration of action (Goth, 1964). Pupillary dilation can also be caused by neosynephrine (Hansmann, Semmlow & Stark, 1974).

Ambient Illumination

Ambient illumination has an effect on pupil diameter such that intensity increases result in pupillary constriction, and decreases produce dilation. Woodhouse and Campbell (1975) examined the interesting hypothesis that the pupil constricts in bright light in order to lower retinal illumination and prepare the eye, in advance, for the return to dimmer illumination. To test this suggestion, they measured sensitivity of the eye when the pupil was dilated with a 2% homatropine solution and under natural (mobile) conditions. The eye was considerably more sensitive to stimuli with a mobile pupil than with a continually dilated pupil. Thus, they proposed that the natural pupil reduces the level of light adaptation by lowering retinal illumination, and this ensures more rapid dark adaptation upon the return to low light levels.

Effects of Drugs on Eye Movements

Holzman (1975) measured the effects of three different drugs on the pursuit eye movements of five normal adult males. The subjects were asked to follow a moving pendulum with their eyes for a 30-second period while horizontal eye movements were measured binocularly. Deviations from smooth-pursuit movements were quantified as velocity arrests (the number of times pursuit was interrupted when the eyes should have been tracking). The drugs diazepam (Valium) and chlorpromazine had no significant effects on pursuit movements. However, sodium secobarbital (Seconal, 100 mg) affected the ability to follow the moving target with smooth-pursuit eye movements. Prolonged testing of Seconal effects (130 mg) with one subject showed that this barbiturate produced eye-tracking and eye-movement disruptions that persisted for 24 hours.

The effects of Valium on the reading eye movements of 18 male college students was studied by Stern, Bremer, and McClure (1974). The administration of Valium, as compared to a placebo, produced an increased frequency of long fixation pauses, and increased duration of fixations, and a decreased velocity of saccadic eye movements during line shifts. These changes were correlated with a decrease in the amount of material read.

ENVIRONMENTAL FACTORS AND HEART ACTIVITY

Drugs

A number of drugs are known to affect heart activity. Among them are ones used for therapeutic purposes. For instance, the drug digitalis increases the contractility of cardiac muscle, or its capacity to do work. Nitroglycerin acts to increase blood flow to the heart by producing vasodilation (Goth, 1964).

Nicotine.   The effects of cigarette smoking on heart rate were studied by Elliott and Thysell (1968). The HR of 18 habitual smokers (one to two packs per day) were measured under three conditions:

1. Dragging on an unlit cigarette every 30 seconds for 5 minutes (sham smoking)
2. Deep breathing every 30 seconds for 5 minutes
3. Inhaling cigarette smoke every 30 seconds for 5 minutes

The investigators found that neither sham smoking (unlit cigarette) nor deep breathing influenced HR. However, actual smoking raised HR 20 bpm, on the average, over resting levels. Fifteen minutes after actual smoking ceased, the HR was still 11 bpm over resting levels. The authors interpreted the increased HR in terms of the increased heart activity required to overcome the vasoconstrictive effects of smoking, that is, HR speeded up to compensate for reduced blood flow.

The effects of rapid and normal cigarette smoking on HR, as compared to sham smoking, were investigated by Danaher, Lichtenstein, and Sullivan (1976). The rapid smoking condition consisted of inhaling every 6 seconds on a cigarette, whereas regular smoking involved inhaling a cigarette at a normal rate. The sham smoking condition was accomplished by inhaling on an unlit cigarette every 6 seconds. Rapid smoking of cigarettes produced significantly higher HR than regular smoking, and regular smoking resulted in HR that was significantly elevated over the sham smoking condition.

MacDougall (1983) found that cigarette smoking plus stress effects produced greater cardiovascular changes than either one alone. The stressor involved playing difficult video games under challenging conditions. Subjects who smoked under no stress averaged a 15 bpm increase in HR, a 12 mm Hg increase in systolic BP and a 9 mm Hg increase in diastolic BP. The individuals who smoked while engaged in the stressful task showed increases that approximately doubled these cardiovascular changes. The authors suggested that stress and smoking might combine to increase the risk for coronary heart disease.

The effects of smoking nicotine cigarettes on HR seem to be rather consistent, that is, a significant elevation occurs. Also, smoking while engaged in stressful tasks potentiates the effect.

Marijuana.   Clark, Greene, Karr, MacCannell, and Milstein (1974) tested the effects of marijuana on heart activity of 28 subjects, half of whom were experienced users. The drug was inhaled through a filtered breathing apparatus. The most consistent effect was an increase in HR. Clark (1975) reviewed a number of studies of marijuana effects on heart rate. Increases in HR from 18% to 51% over control levels have been reported with administration of synthetic ($\triangle$9 THC) or real marijuana. Some researchers suggest that marijuana produces its effects on heart activity through increased SNS activity mediated by epinephrine release. Others propose that marijuana may have its effects on HR by inhibiting vagus nerve activity, thus allowing HR to increase. The exact mechanisms of the effect still remain to be elucidated.

Cocaine.   Cocaine was administered intravenously, in doses ranging from 4 to 32 mg, to nine adult males (Fischman et al., 1976). Mean HR was 74 bpm predrug, 100 bpm after 16 mg of cocaine, and 112 bpm after 32 mg. In general,

HR peaked at 10 minutes, regardless of dose level, and returned to predrug baseline after 46 minutes. Control injections of saline solution had no effects on HR.

In summary, both marijuana and cocaine act to accelerate HR. The mechanism by which this increase is produced remains obscure.

Caffeine.   Caffeine at high doses resulted in an overall increase in ANS activity, as reported by Zahn and Rapoport (1987). The investigators used a range of caffeine levels, including a placebo, with both users and nonusers. Regardless of prior caffeine use, administration of caffeine produced increased HR, EDA, and systolic BP. Decreases in skin temperatures also occurred and were attributed to peripheral vasoconstriction. They found that caffeine did not improve RT or increase ANS activity during the RT task, as they had found in another study with children. Ceiling effects might have been operative because ANS arousal levels were already high and less likely to influence psychomotor performance. Rizzo et al. (1988) examined effects of caffeine withdrawal on HR deceleration during a variable foreperiod RT task. Their data indicated that nonusers improved their RTs in a second session 1 week later. These faster RTs were related to an increase in the degree of HR deceleration during the foreperiod. On the other hand, the users showed neither an improvement in RT nor a change in HR deceleration from the first to the second session. The user group was required to abstain from caffeine for 2 days prior to session two. The authors suggested that the effects of caffeine withdrawal may have negated RT practice effects and resulted in a lowered level of attention in the user group.

Water Submersion

Psychologists and physiologists have used soundproof chambers and water immersion to study the effects of reduced sensory input (isolation) on humans. The water immersion technique has been infrequently used, because subjects generally seemed to spend less time (voluntarily) in water immersion than in quiet room situations. Forgays and McClure (1974) conducted a study to compare tolerance to these two environments. The main dependent variables were time voluntarily spent in the two environments, subjective time estimates, and HR. The subjects were 10 healthy individuals (5 male and 5 female). The investigators reported that 7 of the 10 subjects tolerated the maximum time (6 hours) in the soundproofed cubicle, whereas only 2 remained submerged in a 7-ft tank of water for 6 hours. The water in the tank was at a very comfortable temperature (94 deg F), and subjects breathed through a face mask while suspended vertically by a harness. The average time spent in the room was $5\frac{1}{4}$ hours, compared to $4\frac{1}{2}$ hours in the water tank. The subjects underestimated the time they spent in the room by 1 hour, but they overestimated tank time by $\frac{1}{4}$ hour. The average HR was 67 bpm in the room and 81 bpm while submerged in a virtually weightless condition. The authors concluded that water immersion is a more stressful isolation condition, with subjects being more aroused than in the quiet room condition.

Gooden, Feinstein, and Skutt (1975) measured the HR of freely swimming scuba divers using ultrasonic telemetry. The HR data were obtained from six divers (three professional and three amateur) during a mission designed to perform a biological survey of a coral reef. The dives did not require strenuous physical effort, according to the researchers, and ranged in depth from 21 to 23 m. All of the divers showed elevated HR on the reef (106 bpm) as compared to measures taken just before entering the water (95 bpm). The highest HR on the reef was recorded from an amateur diver (153 bpm) and the lowest from an experienced diver (87 bpm). The individual differences in HR were quite large among the six divers, with the professional divers showing lower rates during dives than the amateurs. The results of the two experiments just described indicate that HR is higher during water submersion than under dry conditions.

ENVIRONMENTAL FACTORS AND BLOOD PRESSURE

Drugs

A number of drugs are known to affect blood pressure levels. For example, reserpine and pentobarbital sodium are known to lower blood pressure, whereas epinephrine increases it (Goth, 1964). The blood pressure of 79 healthy male students was measured 2 months before and on the day before final examinations (Ruttkay-Nedecky & Cagan, 1969). Subjects were administered either a barbiturate (10 mg of phenobarbital) or a placebo (double blind) on both occasions. Both the placebo and the barbiturate produced significant decreases in systolic and diastolic blood pressure measures.

The effects of two drugs (imipramine and methylphenidate) and a placebo on the blood pressure and pulse rate of 47 hyperactive children was studied by Greenberg and Yellin (1975). The children ranged in age from 6 to 13 years and completed an 8-week double-blind study in which half of the patients received one of the drugs followed by a placebo, whereas the other half received the placebo first. Imipramine was found to produce significant increases in blood pressure (both systolic and diastolic) and pulse rate. Methylphenidate did not affect either of these variables. The authors recommended caution in using imipramine to treat hyperactive children.

Exercise and Blood Pressure

Buccola and Stone (1974) studied a number of physiological variables of 36 elderly men before and after they participated in a 14-week exercise program.

The men ranged in age from 60 to 79 and participated in either a cycling program (20 subjects) or in a walk-jog program (16 subjects). The two groups trained for 25 to 50 minutes a day, 3 days a week. Both groups showed significant reductions in blood pressure and weight. Systolic pressure dropped from an average of 147 mm Hg to 141 mm Hg (4.1%), and diastolic decreased from 79 mm Hg to 72 mm Hg (8.9). Thus, elderly persons appear to benefit physiologically from regular light exercise.

To summarize, various drugs can result in the lowering or raising of blood pressure. Regulated physical exercise appears to have beneficial effects on BP measures in elderly persons.

REFERENCES

Bennett, P. B., Ackles, K. N., & Cripps, V. J. (1969). Effects of hyperbaric nitrogen and oxygen on auditory evoked responses in man. *Aerospace Medicine, 40,* 521–525.

Bergamasco, B. (1966). Studio delle modificazioni della responsivita corticale nell' uomo indotte de farmaci ad azione sul SNC. *Sistema Nervoso, 18,* 155–164.

Bergamini, L., Bergamasco, B. (1967). *Cortical evoked potentials in man.* Springfield: C. C. Thomas.

Bernstein, A. S. (1965). Race and examiner as significant influence on basal skin impedance. *Journal of Personality and Social Psychology, 1,* 346–349.

Bevan, J. (1971). The human auditory evoked response and CNV in hyperbaric air. *Electroencephalography & Clinical Neurophysiology, 30,* 198–204.

Brown, H. (1976). *Brain and behavior.* New York: Oxford.

Brumaghim, J. T., Klorman, R., Strauss, J., Levine, J. D., & Goldstein, M. G. (1987). Does methylphenidate affect information processing? Findings from two studies on performance and P3b latency. *Psychophysiology, 24,* 361–372.

Buccola, V. A., & Stone, W. J. (1974). Effects of jogging and cycling programs on physiological and personality variables in aged men. *The Research Quarterly, 46,* 134–139.

Buchsbaum, M. S., Henkin, R. I., & Christiansen, R. L. (1974). Age and sex differences in averaged evoked responses in a normal population, with observations on patients with gonadal sysgenesis. *Electroencephalography & Clinical Neurophysiology, 37,* 137–144.

Clark, S. C. (1975). Marijuana and the cardiovascular system. *Pharmacology, Biochemistry & Behavior, 3,* 299–306.

Clark, S. C., Greene, C., Karr, G. W., MacCannell, K. L., & Milstein, S. L. (1974). Cardiovascular effects of marijuana in man. *Canadian Journal of Physiology, and Pharmacology, 52,* 706–719.

Cole, J. O., Branconnier, R. J., & Martin, G. F. (1975). Electroencephalographic and behavioral changes associated with papaverine administration in healthy geriatric subjects. *Journal of the American Geriatrics Society, 23,* 295–300.

Corsico, R., Moiziszowica, J., Bursuck, L., & Rovaro, E. (1976). Evaluation of the psychotropic effect of etifoxine through pursuit rotor performance and GSR. *Psychopharmacologia, 45,* 301–303.

Creutzfeldt, O. D., Arnold, P. M., Becker, D., Langenstein, S., Tirsch, W., Wilhelm, H., & Wuttke, W. (1976). EEG changes during spontaneous and controlled menstrual cycles and their correlation with psychological performance. *Electroencephalography & Clinical Neurophysiology, 40,* 113–131.

Danaher, B. G., Lichtenstein, E., & Sullivan, J. M. (1976). Comparative effects of rapid and normal smoking on heart rate and carboxyhemoglobin. *Journal of Consulting & Clinical Psychology, 44,* 556–563.

Dornbush, R. L., Fink, M., & Freedman, A. M. (1971). Marijuana, memory and perception. *American Journal of Psychiatry, 128,* 194–197.

Ebe, M., Meier-Ewert, K., & Broughton, R. (1969). Effects of intravenous diazepam (valium) upon evoked potentials of photosensitive epileptic and normal subjects. *Electroencephalography & Clinical Neurophysiology, 27,* 429–435.

Elliott, R., & Thysell, R. (1968). A note on smoking and heart rate. *Psychophysiology, 5,* 280–283.

Engel, G. L. (1945). Mechanisms of fainting. *Journal of Mt. Sinai Hospital, New York, 12,* 170–190.

Engel, G. L., & Margolin, S. G. (1942). Neuropsychiatric disturbances in internal disease: Metabolic factors and electroencephalographic correlations. *Archives of Internal Medicine, 70,* 236–259.

Fink, M., Itil, T., & Clyde, D. (1966). The classification of psychoses by quantitative EEG measures. *Recent Advances in Biological Psychiatry, 8,* 305–312.

Fischman, M. W., Schuster, C. R., Resnekov, L., Shick, J. F. E., Krasnesor, N. A., Fennell, W., & Freedman, D. X. (1976). Cardiovascular and subjective effects of intravenous cocaine administration in humans. *Archives of General Psychiatry, 33,* 938–989.

Fisher, L. E., & Kotses, H. (1973). Race difference and experimenter race effect in galvanic skin response. *Psychophysiology, 10,* 578–582.

Fisher, L. E., & Kotses, H. (1974). Experimenter and subject sex effects in the skin conductance response. *Psychophysiology, 11,* 191–196.

Forgays, D. G., & McClure, G. N. (1974). A direct comparison of the effects of the quiet room and water immersion isolation techniques. *Psychophysiology, 11,* 346–349.

Gabrielli, W. F., Mednick, S. A., Volavka, J., Pollock, V. E., Schulsinger, F., & Itil, T. M. (1982). Electroencephalograms in children of alcoholic fathers. *Psychophysiology, 19,* 404–407.

Gibbs, F. A., Williams, D., & Gibbs, E. L. (1940). Modification of the cortical frequency spectrum by changes in CO_2, blood sugar and O_2. *Journal of Neurophysiology, 3,* 49–58.

Girke, W., Krebs, F. A., & Muller-Oerlinghausen, B. (1975). Effects of lithium on electromyographic recordings in man. *International Pharmacopsychiatry, 10,* 24–36.

Gooden, B. A., Feinstein, R., & Skutt, H. R. (1975). Heart rate responses of scuba divers via ultrasonic telemetry. *Undersea Biomedical Research, 2,* 11–19.

Goth, A. (1964). *Medical pharmacology.* St. Louis: C. V. Mosby.

Greenberg, L. M., & Yellin, A. M. (1975). Blood pressure and pulse changes in hyperactive children treated with imipramine and methylphenidate. *American Journal of Psychiatry, 132,* 1325–1326.

Gross, M. M., Begleiter, H., Tobin, M., & Kissin, B. (1966). Changes in auditory evoked response induced by alcohol. *The Journal of Nervous and Mental Disease, 143,* 152–156.

Hall, R. A., Rappaport, M., Hopkins, H. K., & Griffin, R. (1973). Tobacco and evoked potential. *Science, 180,* 212–214.

Hansmann, D., Semmlow, J., & Stark, L. (1974). A physiological basis for pupillary dynamics. In M. P. Janisse (Ed.), *Pupillary dynamics and behavior* (pp. 53–74). New York: Plenum.

Hermann, H. T., & Quarton, C. G. (1964). Changes in alpha frequency with change in thyroid hormone level. *Electroencephalography & Clinical Neurophysiology, 16,* 515–518.

Herning, R. I., Jones, R. T., & Bachman, J. (1983). EEG changes during tobacco withdrawal. *Psychophysiology, 20,* 507–512.

Hoagland, H. (1936). Electrical brain waves and temperature. *Science, 84,* 139–140.

Holzman, P. S. (1975). Smooth-pursuit eye movements, and diazepam, LPZ, and secobarbital. *Psychopharmacologia, 44,* 11–115.

Hubbard, O., Sunde, D., & Goldensohn, E. S. (1976). The EEG in centenarians. *Electroencephalography & Clinical Neurophysiology, 40,* 407–417.

Ingvar, D. H., Sjolund, B., & Ardo, A. (1976). Correlation between dominant EEG frequency cerebral oxygen uptake and blood flow. *Electroencephalography & Clinical Neurophysiology, 41,* 268–276.

Jarvis, M. J., & Lader, M. H. (1971). The effects of nitrous oxide on the auditory evoked response in a reaction time task. *Psychopharmacologia, 20,* 201–212.

Johnson, L. C., & Corah, N. L. (1963). Racial differences in skin resistance. *Science, 139,* 766–767.

Johnson, L. C., & Landon, M. M. (1965). Eccrine sweat gland activity and racial differences in resting skin conductance. *Psychophysiology, 1,* 322–329.

Kay, D. C. (1975). Human sleep and EEG through a cycle of methadone dependence. *Electroencephalography & Clinical Neurophysiology, 38,* 35–44.

Knott, V. J., & Venables, P. H. (1971). EEG alpha correlates of non-smokers, smokers, smoking, and smoking deprivation. *Psychophysiology, 14,* 150–156.

Koppell, B. S., Tinklenberg, J. R., & Hollister, L. E. (1972). Contingent Negative Variation amplitudes, marijuana and ethanol. *Archives of General Psychiatry, 27,* 809–811.

Koppell, B. S., Wittmer, W. K., Lunde, D., Warrick, G., & Edwards, D. (1970). Influence of triiodothyronine on selective attention in man as measured by the visual averaged evoked potential. *Psychosomatic Medicine, 32,* 495–502.

Korol, B., Bergfeld, G. R., & McLaughlin, L. J. (1975). Skin color and autonomic nervous system measures. *Physiology and Behavior, 14,* 575–578.

Lewis, E. G., Dustman, R. E., & Beck, E. C. (1970). The effects of alcohol on visual and somatosensory evoked responses. *Electroencephalography and Clinical Neurophysiology, 28,* 202–205.

Lewis, E. G., Dustman, R. E., Peters, B. A., Straight, R. C., & Beck, E. C. (1973). The effects of varying doses of 9-Tetrahydrocannabinol on the human visual and somatosensory evoked response. *Electroencephalography and Clinical Neurophysiology, 35,* 347–354.

Little, B. C., & Zahn, T. P. (1974). Changes in mood and autonomic functioning during the menstrual cycle. *Psychophysiology, 11,* 579–590.

Low, M. D., Klonoff, H., & Marcus, A. (1973). The neurophysiological basis of the marijuana experience. *Canadian Medical Association Journal, 108,* 157–164.

MacDougall, J. M. (1983). Selective cardiovascular effects of stress and cigarette smoking. *Journal of Human Stress, 9,* 13–21.

Malmo, R. B. (1965). Finger-sweat prints in the differentiation of low and high incentive. *Psychophysiology, 1,* 231–240.

Malpas, A., Legg, N. J., & Scott, D. F. (1974). Effects of hypnotics on anxious patients. *British Journal of Psychiatry, 124,* 482–484.

Malpas, A., Rowan, A. J., Joyce, C. R. B., & Scott, D. F. (1970). Persistent behavioral and electroencephalographic changes after single doses of nitrazepam and amylobarbitone sodium. *British Medical Journal, 2,* 762–765.

Martineau, J., Tanguay, P., Garreau, B., Roux, s., & Lelord, G. (1984). Are there sex differences in averaged evoked responses produced by coupling sound and light in children and adults? *International Journal of Psychophysiology, 2,* 177–184.

Milner-Brown, H. S., Stein, R. B., & Lee, R. G. (1975). Synchronization of human motor units: Possible roles of exercise and supraspinal reflexes. *Electroencephaography & Clinical Neurophysiology, 38,* 245–254.

Murphree, H. B. (1973). EEG and other evidence for mixed depressant and stimulant actions of alcoholic beverages. *Annals of the New York Academy of Sciences, 215,* 325–331.

Nakra, B. R. S., and Bond, A. J., & Lader, M. H. (1975). Comparative psychotropic effects of metoclopramide and prochlorperazine in normal subjects. *Journal of Clinical Pharmacology, 15,* 449–454.

Nishitani, H., & Kooi, K. A. (1968). Cerebral evoked responses in hypothyroidism. *Electroencephalography & Clinical Neurophysiology, 24,* 554–560.

O'Hanlon, J. F., McGrath, J. J., & McCauley, M. E. (1974). Body temperature and temporal acuity. *Journal of Experimental Psychology, 102,* 788–794.

Philips, C. (1971). The EEG changes associated with smoking. *Psychophysiology, 8,* 64–74.

Reite, M., Jackson, D., Cahoon, R. L., & Weil, J. V. (1974). Sleep physiology at high altitude. *Electroencephalography & Clinical Neurophysiology, 38,* 463–471.

Rhodes, L. E., Obitz, F. W., & Creel, D. (1975). Effect of alcohol and task on hemispheric asymmetry of visually evoked potentials in man. *Electroencephalogy & Clinical Neurophysiology, 38,* 561–568.

Rizzo, A. A., Stamps, L. E., & Fehr, L. A. (1988). Effects of caffeine withdrawal on motor performance and heart rate changes. *International Journal of Psychophysiology, 6,* 9–14.

Robinson, M. G., Howe, R. C., Varni, J. G., Ream, N. W., & Hegge, F. W. (1974). Assessment of pupil size during acute heroin withdrawal in Viet Nam. *Neurology, 24,* 729–732.

Rodin, E., & Luby, E. (1966). Effects of LSD-25 on the EEG and photic evoked responses. *Archives of General Psychiatry, 14,* 435–441.

Rostain, J. C., & Charpy, J. P. (1976). Effects upon the EEG of psychometric performance during deep dives in helium-oxygen atmosphere. *Electroencephalography & Clinical Neurophysiology, 40,* 571–584.

Roth, W. T., Galanter, M., Weingartner, H., Vaughan, T. B., & Wyatt, R. J. (1973). Marijuana and synthetic-trans-tetrahydrocannobinol: Some effects on the auditory evoked response and background EEG in humans. *Biological Psychiatry, 6,* 221–233.

Ruttkay-Nedecky, I., & Lagan, S. (1969). Blood pressure of students the day before examination: A double-blind study of the effects of barbiturate and placebo. *Psychotherapy and Psychosomatics, 17,* 196–200.

Sainino, K., Leino, T., Huttunen, M. O., & Ylikahri, R. H. (1976). EEG changes during experimental hangover. *Electroencephalography & Clinical Neurophysiology, 40,* 535–538.

Salamy, A. (1973). The effects of alcohol on the variability of the human evoked potential. *Neuropharmacology, 12,* 1103–1107.

Salamy, A., & Williams, H. (1973). The effects of alcohol on sensory evoked and spontaneous cerebral potentials in man. *Electroencephalography & Clinical Neurophysiology, 35,* 3–11.

Saletu, B., Saletu, M, & Itil, T. (1972). Effect of minor and major tranquilizers on somatosensory evoked potentials. *Psychopharmacologia, 24,* 347–358.

Seppalainen, A., Raitta, C., & Huuskonen, M. S. (1979). n-Hexane-induced changes in visual evoked potentials and electroretinograms of industrial workers. *Electroencephalography & Clinical Neurophysiology, 47,* 492–498.

Shagass, C. (1972). Electrical activity of the brain. In N. S. Greenfield & R. A. Sternbach (Eds.) *Handbook of Psychophysiology* (pp. 263–328). New York: Holt, Rinehart & Winston.

Smith, C. B., & Strawbridge, P. J. (1974). Auditory and visual evoked potentials during hyperoxia. *Electroencephalography & Clinical Neurophysiology, 37,* 393–398.

Stern, J. A., Bremer, D. A., & McClure, J. (1974). Analysis of eye movements and blinks during reading: Effects of Valium. *Psychopharmacologia, 40*(2), 171–175.

Straumanis, J. J., & Shagass, C. (1976). Electrophysiological effects of triiodothyroidism and propranolol. *Psychopharmacologia, 46,* 283–288.

Stroebel, C. F. (1972). Psychophysiological pharmacology. In N. S. Greenfield & R. A. Sternbach (Eds.), *Handbook of psychophysiology* (pp. 787–838). New York: Holt, Rinehart, & Winston.

Takahashi, K., Fujitani, Y. (1970). Somatosensory and visual evoked potentials in hypothyroidism. *Electroencephalography & Clinical Neurophysiology, 29,* 551–556.

Tecce, J. J. (1972). Contingent negative variation (CNV) and psychological processes in man. *Psychological Bulletin, 77,* 73–108.

Tecce, J. J., & Cole, J. O. (1974). Amphetamine effects in man: Paradoxical drowsiness and lowered electrical brain activity (CNV). *Science, 185,* 451–453.

Tecce, J. J., Cole, J. O., Mayer, J., & Lewis, D. C. (1977). Barbiturate effects on brain functioning (CNV) and attention performance in normal men. *Psychopharmacology Bulletin, 13,* 64–66.

Tecce, J. J., Cole, J. O., & Savignano-Bowman, J. (1975). Chlorpromazine effects on brain activity (contingent negative variation) and reaction time in normal women. *Psychopharmacologia, 43,* 293–295.

Thiebaut, F., Rohmer, F., & Wackenheim, A. (1958). Contribution a l'etude electroencephalographique des syndromes endocriniens. *Electroencephalography & Clinical Neurophysiology, 10,* 1–30.

Turpin, G., Shine, P., & Lader, M. (1983). Ambulatory electrodermal monitoring: Effects of ambient temperature, general activity, electrolyte media and length of recording. *Psychophysiology, 20,* 219–224.

Ulett, J. A., & Itil, T. M. (1969). Quantitative EEG in smoking and smoking deprivation. *Science, 164,* 969–970.

Vaughan, H. G. (1969). The relationship of brain activity to scalp recordings of event-related potentials. In E. Donchin & D. B. Lindsley (Eds.), *Averaged evoked potentials* (pp. 45–94). Washington, D.C.: NASA.

Venables, P. H., & Christie, M. J. (1973). Mechanisms, instrumentation, recording techniques and quantifications of responses. In W. F. Prokasy & D. C. Raskin (Eds.), *Electrodermal activity in psychological research* (pp. 41–73). New York: Academic Press.

Vogel, W., Broverman, D. M., & Klaiber, L. (1971). EEG responses in regularly menstruating women and in amenorrheic women treated with ovarian hormones. *Science, 172,* 388–391.

Vogel, W., Broverman, D. M., Klaiber, E. L., & Kobayasri, Y. (1974). EEG driving responses as a function of monamine oxidase. *Electroencephalography & Clinical Neurophysiology, 36,* 205–207.

Volavka, J., Levine, R., Feldstein, S., & Fink, M. (1974). Short term effects of heroin in man: Is EEG related to behavior? *Archives of General Psychiatry, 30,* 677–681.

West, L., & Driver, M. V. (1974). Antisocial behavior, barbiturate addiction and associated EEG changes. *British Journal of Psychiatry, 125,* 470–471.

White, B. C., Lincoln, C. A., Pearce, N. W., Reeb, R., & Vaida, C. (1980). Anxiety and muscle tension as consequences of caffeine withdrawal. *Science, 209,* 1547–1548.

Williams, J. G., Jones, J. R., & Williams, B. (1975). The chemical control of preoperative anxiety. *Psychophysiology, 12,* 46–49.

Woodhouse, J. M., & Campbell, F. W. (1975). The role of the pupil light reflex in aiding adaption to the dark. *Vision Research, 15*(6), 649–653.

Woodworth, R. S., & Schlosberg, H. (1954). *Experimental psychology.* New York: Holt.

Zahn, T. P., & Rapoport, J. L. (1987). Autonomic nervous system effects of acute doses of caffeine in caffeine users and abstainers. *International Journal of Psychophysiology, 5,* 33–41.

Appendix II
EEG Recording System

For EEG research, a good recorder should have the following specifications. The first stage of amplification (or gain) should allow for multiplication of the signal by a factor of at least 1,000. Additional amplification by a factor of 1,000 will raise it to a level suitable for data transmission or recording, an amplification of 1,000,000. The amplifier should be able to amplify frequencies of one cycle per second (almost down to direct current or DC) to 100 cycles. The recorder should be capable of rejecting 60-cycle interference from the electrical outlets in the room. Variable filtering should be provided to eliminate unwanted signals from the record. The main purpose of a filter is to prevent undesired frequency components from being recorded. Thus, if you are not interested in frequencies above 100 Hz, you would set your filter to screen these out. Variable filtering enables you to eliminate more than one frequency band.

A high-input impedance of 1 to 10 million Ohms is desirable, because it can reduce error caused by changes in electrode–scalp resistance. Impedance refers to opposition to current flow in a circuit. The sensitivity of the recorder should allow readings of 1, 2, 5, 10, 50, and 100 μV per each millimeter (mm) of pen deflection. The ink-writing system should be flexible enough to follow a signals over a wide range of possible interest, say, from 0 to 100 cycles per second. Connecting the output of the recorder to an oscilloscope enables viewing even higher frequencies (greater than 100 cycles or more) if desired.

Variable paper speeds should be available. A desirable paper speed for EEG recording is about 50 mm per second. Slower or faster speeds may be used, depending on the application. A calibrating device should enable the determination of signal amplitude on the ink-writer, whether the signal be externally or internally supplied. Calibrations should be done frequently, using the same filtering and amplifier settings as when actually collecting data.

An impedance meter built into the physiological recorder measures resistance of the skin (in thousands of Ohms) to a small electric current. If skin resistance is too high (greater than 5–10K Ohms) the recordings will not be clear. The equipment should be adequately grounded to prevent accidental electric shock. Grounding also eliminates unwanted electrical signals from the recording by sending them off to some neutral location. The third, or ground, lead of the plug is generally connected to a water pipe, and from there it reaches the earth surrounding the building.

When the EEG is recorded for clinical purposes, the patient may lie on his or her back, and the leads are attached to a terminal that then leads, by way of a large shielded cable, to the EEG recorder. In most research situations, except perhaps those studying EEG during sleep, the subject sits upright, because the investigator usually requires the person to engage in some type of activity, whether it be learning, problem solving, or signal detection. The laboratory should be quiet and free from auditory of visual distractions. A well-lit, air conditioned environment helps to make the subject comfortable in performing his or her task. Many EEG researchers use sound-attenuated, electrically shielded chambers for the conduct of their experiments. The subject is usually provided with a comfortable chair or bed in the experimental chamber. These chambers are commonly equipped with one-way viewing windows so that the subject can be observed from the outside or visual stimulus materials can be conveniently presented. A well-equipped laboratory also contains a multichannel FM tape system for permanent recordings of EEG or other physiological measures. These data can later be played back for additional or off-line analyses. The use of computers in the control of experiments and analyses of physiological data is very common among investigators in the area of psychophysiology. The use of Fast Fourier Transforms with EEG data enables spectral analyses of frequencies at any particular moment of the experiment. The interested reader is referred to informative chapters on setting up a psychophysiological laboratory (Gale & Smith, 1980) and on the use of computers in psychophysiological research (Rugg, Fletcher, & Lykken, 1980). Both chapters are contained in *Techniques in Psychophysiology,* edited by Martin and Venables (1980).

REFERENCES

Gale, A., & Smith, D. (1980). On setting up a psychophysiological laboratory. In I. Martin & P. H. Venables (Eds.), *Techniques in psychophysiology* (pp. 565–582). New York: Wiley.

Martin, I., & Venables, P. H. (Eds.). (1980). *Techniques in psychophysiology.* New York: Wiley.

Rugg, M. D., Fletcher, R. P., & Lykken, D. T. (1980). Computers in psychophysiological research. In I. Martin & P. H. Venables (Eds.), *Techniques in psychophysiology* (pp. 583–596). New York: Wiley.

Appendix III
Laboratory Safety

Laboratories that use physiological recorders should take proper precautions to protect human subjects or patients from possible electric shocks or burns. If an accidentally high electric current passes through the skin, it can produce pain or tissue damage. If it is very high and flows across the body, it could interfere with heart activity. Ventricular fibrillation of the heart is the most frequent cause of death in fatal electrical accidents.

PROTECTION AGAINST ELECTRIC SHOCK

Modern physiological recorders use various techniques to protect subjects from shock. For example, many of them use transistor circuits (in the first stage amplifiers connected to the electrodes) to isolate subjects from high-voltage circuits. However, even though the probability of shock is very low, additional precautions must be taken. One approach is to fuse each electrode lead to prevent shocks through inadvertent shorts between the electrodes and associated circuitry. A 5-mA fuse would limit electric current flow to a safe level in the event of a malfunction. This would be especially important when making recordings that require the placement of electrodes on either side of the body, as is commonly done in measuring heart activity, for example, electrodes placed on the right and left arms. Another approach would be to connect each electrode to ground through voltage-limiting diodes. (A diode is a device that limits current flow to one direction.)

Because electric current passed across the body is more dangerous than current limited to one side, the use of one-sided measurement is preferred where feasible. For example, skin conductance measures should be made from the same hand, rather than using two hands. Similarly, ground electrodes should be placed on the same side of the body as active electrodes whenever possible.

METHODS OF ACCIDENT PREVENTION

A number of techniques to prevent or minimize the probability of occurrence of an electrical shock have been outlined by Cromwell et al. (1976).

Grounding

Grounding may be achieved by connecting the metal case of a piece of equipment to ground by a wire or by using three-pronged plugs in which the ground connection is established by the round contact in the plug. In the event of an electrical short, the current will flow through the case and be shunted off to ground.

Use of Low Voltage

The use of low voltage calls for operating equipment at lower voltages than that provided by electrical outlets (they commonly provide 115 V). One way of doing this is to operate equipment from batteries. Another method is to use a small transformer that reduces the power requirement for operating the equipment (e.g., from 115 to 6 V).

Isolation of Subject-Connected Parts

Isolation requires the use of amplifiers that are completely isolated from ground.

Ground-Fault Interrupter

Interrupters involve the use of a circuit that is designed to automatically interrupt power, like a circuit breaker, when a person touches a defective piece of equipment and current returns to ground through his or her body.

DO'S AND DON'TS

In their book, Cromwell et al. (1976) have provided a list of "do's and don'ts" with respect to making the operation of electrical equipment as safe as possible. These lists are summarized here:

Do's

1. Familiarize yourself with the equipment by studying its proper usage as explained in the operating manuals.

2. Always follow correct operating procedures.

3. Report any irregularities of equipment function to appropriate personnel. For example, intermittent operation, slight electric shocks, or loose controls should be brought to the attention of an electronics technician or engineer or maintenance personnel employed by the equipment manufacturer.

Don'ts

1. Don't remove plugs from outlets by pulling the line cord. This can break or loosen the ground wire.

2. Don't use "adapter" plugs, that is, two-pronged plugs that enable you to plug a three-pronged equipment plug into an ungrounded outlet. The wiring should be redone to accommodate three-pronged plugs; otherwise, grounding is not possible.

3. Don't use extension cords. If absolutely necessary, use heavy-duty, three-wire cords that provide for ground connections.

4. Don't run carts over, or step on electrical cables or connectors. This can cause breaks in the ground wire.

5. Don't operate any piece of electrical equipment without being thoroughly familiar with its operation and possible shock hazards.

ADDITIONAL SAFETY

In a section on laboratory safety, Stern, Ray, and Davis (1980) suggested that plans for a medical emergency be made whenever a subject is under your supervision in a psychophysiology laboratory. There should be a prepared course of action for contacting appropriate emergency medical personnel or an ambulance, as needed. It is also suggested that the psychophysiological researcher, whether it be student or professional, does not unnecessarily alarm a subject whose physiological responses appear abnormal. For instance, if a subject's EKG appears to have abnormal characteristics, this should be confirmed on another occasion before suggesting to the subject that perhaps an EKG be done by a cardiologist.

Stern et al. (1980) also pointed out the importance of adhering to ethical standards in carrying out any type of experimentation with human subjects.

Some considerations include whether the procedure involves physical stress or anxiety, shame, or embarrassment to the subject. Provisions for supplying information about the study and answering questions before and after data collection should be made. Assurances about confidentiality of personal data and task performance should be given. Coercion should never be used, either prior to or after experimentation, and subjects should be allowed to terminate their participation in the study at any time they wish. Detailed guidelines for conducting experimentation with human subjects is contained in a manual entitled "Ethical Principles in the Conduct of Research with Human Participants" and can be obtained from the American Psychological Association, 1200 Seventeenth Street, N.W., Washington, DC. 20036.

REFERENCES

Cromwell, L., Arditti, M., Weibell, F. J., Pfeiffer, E. A., Steele, B., & Labok, J. A. (1976). *Medical instrumentation for health care*. Englewood Cliffs, NJ: Prentice-Hall.

Stern, R. M., Ray, W. J., & Davis, C. M. (1980). *Psychophysiological recording*. New York: Oxford University Press.

Subject Index

Copyrights and Acknowledgments

Fig. 1.1. Copyright © 1978 by Gahan Wilson. Reprinted by permission.

Fig. 2.1. From C. R. Noback and R. J. Demarest. *The Human Nervous System.* Copyright © 1975, McGraw Hill Publishing Company. Reprinted by permission.

Fig. 2.2. From C. R. Noback and R. J. Demarest. *The Human Nervous System.* Copyright © 1975, McGraw Hill Publishing Company. Reprinted by permission.

Fig. 2.3. From C. R. Noback and R. J. Demarest. *The Human Nervous System.* Copyright © 1975, McGraw Hill Publishing Company. Reprinted by permission.

Fig. 2.5. Modified from C. R. Noback and R. J. Demarest. *The Human Nervous System.* Copyright © 1975, McGraw Hill Publishing Company. Reprinted by permission.

Fig. 2.6. Modified from C. R. Noback and R. J. Demarest. *The Human Nervous System.* Copyright © 1975, McGraw Hill Publishing Company. Reprinted by permission.

Fig. 2.7. From S. P. Grossman. *Essentials of physiological psychology.* New York: Wiley, 1973, as taken from H. H. Jasper, "Electroencephalography" in W. Penfield & T. C. Erickson, Epilepsy and Cerebral Localization. Springfield: C. C. Thomas, 1941.

Fig. 2.9. Adapted from E. Callaway. *Brain Electrical Potentials and Individual Psychological Differences.* New York: Grune & Stratton, 1975. Reprinted by permission.

Fig. 2.10 Photo by courtesy of Drs. Williamson and Kaufman of New York University, 1989.

Fig. 2.11 From Carlson, N. R. *Physiology of Behavior* (2nd edition). Copyright © 1980, Allyn & Bacon, Inc., Redrawn with permission.

Fig. 2.12 From Carlson, N. R. *Physiology of Behavior* (2nd edition). Copyright © 1980, Allyn & Bacon, Inc., Redrawn by permission.

Fig. 4.1 Beatty, J. "Operant control of posterior theta rhythm and vigilance performance; Repeated treatments and transfer of training." In N. Birbaumer & H. D. Kimmel (Eds.), *Biofeedback and self-regulation*. Copyright © 1980, Lawrence Erlbaum Associates, Inc. Reprinted by permission.

Fig. 4.2 From F. Snyder and J. Scott. "The psychophysiology of sleep" in N. S. Greenfield and R. A. Sternbach (Eds.), *Handbook of psychophysiology*. Copyright © 1972 by Holt, Rinehart & Winston. Reprinted by permission of Holt, Rinehart & Winston.

Fig. 4.3 From F. E. Bloom and A. Lazerson. *Brain, Mind, and Behavior* (2nd edition). Copyright © 1985, 1988, Educational Broadcasting Company. Reprinted by permission of W. H. Freeman & Company.

Fig. 5.1 From H. G. Vaughan, Jr. "The relationship of brain activity to scalp recordings of event-related potentials" in E. Donchin & D. B. Lindsley (Eds.), *Average Evoked Potentials*. Washington, DC: NASA, 1969. Reprinted by permission.

Fig. 5.2 Left side of figure is from J. J. Tecce. "Contingent negative variation (CNV) and psychological processes in man," Psychological Bulletin, 1972, *77*, 73–108. Reprinted by permission. Right side of figure is adapted from H. G. Vaughan, Jr., et al. "Topography of the human motor potential," *Electroencephalography and Clinical Neurophysiology*. *25*, 1968, Fig. 2. Reprinted by Permission of the author and Elsevier Publishing.

Fig. 6.1 From W. S. Brown et al. "Contextual meaning effects on speech evoked potentials," *Behavioral Biology*, 1973, *9*, 755–761. Reprinted by permission.

Fig. 6.2 From Hillyard, S. A., & Hansen, J. C. "Attention: Electrophysiological Approaches." In M. G. H. Coles, S. W. Porges, & E. Donchin (Eds.), *Psychophysiology: Systems, Processes, Applications*. Copyright © 1986, The Guilford Press. Reprinted by permission.

Fig. 6.3 From A. F. Moskowitz et al. "Corners, receptive fields, and visually evoked cortical potentials," *Perception and Psychophysics*, 1974, *15*, 325–330. Reprinted by permission.

Fig. 6.4 From J. L. Andreassi et al. "Amplitude changes in the visual evoked cortical potential with backward masking," *Electroencephalography and Clinical Neurophysiology*, 1976, *41*, 384–398. Reprinted by permission.

Fig. 7.1 From J. J. Tecce. "Contingent negative variation and individual differences," *Archives of General Psychiatry,* 1971, *24,* 1–16. Copyright © 1971, American Medical Association. Reprinted by permission.

Fig. 7.2 From W. Becker et al. "Bereitschaftspotential preceding voluntary show and rapid hand movements" in W. C. McCallum and J. R. Knott (Eds.), *The Responsive Brain.* Copyright © 1976, John Wright & Sons, Ltd. Reprinted by permission.

Fig. 7.3 From S. Sutton, M. Braren, and J. Zubin. "Evoked potential correlates of stimulus uncertainty," *Science,* 1965, *150,* 1187–1188. Reprinted by permission.

Fig. 7.4 From N. K. Squires et al. "Two varieties of long latency positive waves evoked by unpredictable stimuli in man," *Electroencephalography and Clinical Neurophysiology,* 1975, *38,* 387–401. Reprinted by permission.

Fig. 8.1 From S. W. Jacob and C. A. Francone. *Structure and Function in Man.* Copyright © 1970, W. B. Saunders Co. Reprinted by permission.

Fig. 8.2 From S. W. Jacob and C. A. Francone. *Structure and Function in Man.* Copyright © 1970, W. B. Saunders Co. Reprinted by permission.

Fig. 8.3 Reprinted by permission of author and publisher from R. C. Wilcott and H. G. Beenken. "Relation of integrated surface electromyography and muscle tension," *Perceptual and Motor Skills,* 1957, *7,* 295–298.

Fig. 8.5 Adapted from J. F. Davis. *Manual of Surface Electromyography.* WADC Technical Report, 59–184, 1959. Used by permission.

Fig. 8.6 Copyright © 1974, The Society for Psychophysiological Research. Reprinted by permission of the publisher and the author from "Facial muscle tonus during REM and NREM sleep," by D. Bliwise, R. Coleman, B. Bergmann, M. Z. Wincor, R. T. Pivik, and A. Rechtschaffen, *Psychophysiology,* 1974, *11,* 497–508.

Fig. 8.7 Copyright © 1986, The Society for Psychophysiological Research. Reprinted by permission of the publisher and the author from "Guidelines for human electromyographic research," by A. J. Fridlund and J. T. Cacioppo, *Psychophysiology,* 1986, *23,* 567–589. (Updated diagram courtesy of Drs. Fridlund, Cacioppo and Tassinary.)

Fig. 9.1 From P. H. Venables and I. Martin (Eds.). *Manual of Psychophysiological Methods.* Copyright © 1967, North-Holland Publishing Co. Reprinted by permission.

Fig. 9.2 From *Essentials of Human Anatomy,* Sixth Edition, by Russell T. Woodburne. Copyright © 1978 by Oxford University Press, Inc. Reprinted by permission.

Fig. 9.3 Copyright © 1967, The Society for Psychophysiology Research. Re-

"Cephalic vasomotor and heart rate measures of orienting and defensive reflexes," by D. C. Raskin, H. Kotses, and J. Bever, *Psychophysiology*, 1969, *6*, 149–159.

Fig. 12.1 From S. W. Jacob and C. A. Francone. *Structure and Function in Man*. Copyright © 1970, W. B. Saunders Co. Reprinted by permission.

Fig. 12.2 From Cook, M. R. "Psychophysiology of Peripheral Vascular Changes." In P. A. Obrist, A. H. Black, J. Brener, & L. V. Dicara (Eds.), *Cardiovascular Psychophysiology*. Copyright © 1974, Aldine Press. Reprinted by permission.

Fig. 12.3 Copyright © 1976, The Society for Psychophysiological Research. Reprinted by permission of the publisher and the author from "An improved mechanical strain gauge for recording penile circumference change," by D. R. Lewis and R. A. Bow, *Psychophysiology*, 1976, 13, 596–599.

Fig. 13.1 From D. Kurtzberg and H. G. Vaughan, Jr. "Electrophysiologic assessment of auditory and visual function in the newborn" *Clinics in Perinatology*, Vol. 12, p. 283, Philadelphia: W. B. Saunders. Reprinted by permission of the authors and publisher.

Fig. 13.2 From D. Kurtzberg and H. G. Vaughan, Jr. "Electrophysiologic assessment of auditory and visual function in the newborn" *Clinics in Perinatology*, Vol. 12, p. 288, Philadelphia: W. B. Saunders. Reprinted by permission of the authors and publisher.

Fig. 13.3 From J. F. Simpson and K. R. Magee. *Clinical evaluation of the nervous system*. Copyright © 1973, Little-Brown Co. Reprinted by permission.

Fig. 13.4 From A. Starr and L. J. Achor. "Auditory brainstem responses in neurological disease," *Archives of Neurology*, 1975, *32*, 761–768. Copyright © 1975, American Medical Association. Reprinted by permission.

Fig. 13.5 From C. Shagass and M. Schwartz, "Evoked potential studies in psychiatric patients," *Annals of the New York Academy of Sciences*, 1964, *112*, 526–542. Reprinted by permission of the New York Academy of Sciences.

Fig. 15.1 Copyright © 1975, The Society for Psychophysiological Research. Reprinted by permission of the publisher and the author from "Some factors influencing the vasomotor response to cold pressor stimulation," by W. Lovallo and A. R. Zeiner, *Psychophysiology*, 1975, *12*, 499–505.

Fig. 15.2 Reprinted from M. A. Wenger and M. Ellington. "The measurement of autonomic balance in children: Method and normative data," *Psychosomatic Medicine*, 1943, *5*, 241–253. Used by permission.